Personality Theory, Moral Development, and Criminal Behavior

Personality Theory, Moral Development, and Criminal Behavior

Edited by

William S. Laufer
Northeastern University
School of Law

James M. Day
University of Pennsylvania

LexingtonBooks
D.C. Heath and Company
Lexington, Massachusetts
Toronto

208011

Library of Congress Cataloging in Publication Data

Main entry under title:

Personality theory, moral development, and criminal
behavior.

Bibliography: p.
Includes indexes.
1. Crime and criminals—Addresses, essays, lectures.
2. Personality—Addresses, essays, lectures.
3. Moral development—Addresses, essays, lectures.
4. Criminal psychology—Addresses, essays, lectures.
5. Interdisciplinary approach to knowledge—Addresses, essays, lectures.
I. Laufer, William S. II. Day, James M.
HV6211.P47   1983   364.3   82-47684
ISBN 0-669-05556-5

Copyright © 1983 by D.C. Heath and Company

Published simultaneously in Canada

Printed in the United States of America

International Standard Book Number: 0-669-05556-5

Library of Congress Catalog Card Number: 82-47684

To Our Parents and Families

Contents

Foreword

I have rarely seen such a complete grouping of papers, covering such a wide range of perspectives on a topic, as appear in this book. Chapters discuss theory, application, empirical analysis, and policy-relevant views of moral development and criminal behavior. Research is presented and discussed, and hypotheses to govern future research are suggested. The entire range of contemporary reasoning about moral development, personality formation, and the potential for criminal behavior is here in this exceptional book.

Moral development has been a subject of concern in our civilization at least since Plato and Aristotle. Attempts to measure moral development have been fraught with expected measurement and methodological problems, as has been the case with personality psychology. Personalities are formed; superegos are developed; moral norms are inculcated. Psychological forces interact with our larger environment and contribute to criminality. But how and when these processes occur has been the subject of considerable debate.

This book, perhaps more than any before it, explores these problems in detail, blending empirically derived data with theory and analysis. Researchers will benefit from the summary of current data and the directions suggested here for future research. U.S. criminologists, who are trained in sociology and social-systems analysis, will gain a broader perspective from the exposure to the psychological theory. Readers will obtain a greater understanding of criminal behavior.

I have some criticism of the methodological and theoretical perspectives of a few chapters; I think some of the contributors make inferences beyond their evidentiary material. But that is minor compared to my appreciation of the scope of this work. Carefully compiled and edited, it is certainly one of the best collections on personality theory and criminal behavior available in any language.

Marvin E. Wolfgang

Acknowledgments

The editors would like to acknowledge the immeasurable assistance of Robert Hogan, who found the time during his move from Baltimore to Tulsa to lend guidance and impart wisdom. We would also like to express our appreciation to Joseph Adelson, Michael Meltsner, and Nancy Herndon, for their active support of this project.

Introduction

William S. Laufer* and
James M. Day

This book is published at an important time in the history of criminology. Although it is virtually impossible to characterize the progress of an entire field—especially one as interdisciplinary as criminology—several broad themes are identifiable. First, in the presence of many conflicting theoretical perspectives, the development of etiological theory is often regarded with caution or disdain. Second, interdisciplinary study is in vogue; yet the challenge of integrative research has been discussed more often than conducted. Finally, positivist criminologists have responded defensively to neoclassicist writings and the emergence of Marxist or critical criminology. In part because of these developments, it is also a time of considerable unrest and dissatisfaction in the field. Such scholars as Radzinowicz and King (1977), Jeffery (1979), and Dinitz (1979) disparage criminology's success over the past several decades. They emphasize perhaps the only unifying theme in criminology today—a consensus that "the field stands in need of theoretical assessment, integration, and innovation" (Short 1979, p. 28).

One way to approach the goals of assessment, integration, and innovation is to evaluate the celebrated sociological theories of delinquent or criminal behavior—strain, differential association, and control theories—in terms of the theoretical orientations of allied disciplines. Insights from an allied field such as psychology have been and continue to be invaluable to criminology. Unfortunately, disciplinary partisanship in both fields has prevented a full acceptance of psychological principles and practices in mainstream criminology. Such partisanship has also cast psychologists in an uncertain role in the criminal-justice system (Brodsky 1977; Fowler and Brodsky 1978). Psychological theory and data are often incorporated in what has become known as *sociological criminology*; nonetheless, the two disciplines are estranged partners, each routinely operating with little acknowledgment of the other.

Although interdisciplinary fertilization has been hindered by a combination of partisanship and the ill-defined role of psychologists in the criminal-justice system, there are several exceptions (Megargee 1982; Monahan 1981; Gottfredson 1977). Most significant is the increased acceptance of U.S. forensic and correctional psychology (see Megargee and Bohn 1979). Numerous prominent theoretical exceptions also exist. For example, Wolfgang and Ferracuti's (1967) subculture-of-violence approach has produced a true integration of scholarly research in allied disciplines, including psychology. Eysenck's (1977) integrative model of antisocial behavior draws on various disciplines other than psychology. Jeffery's (1979) biosocial-theory approach to crime causation rests on psychological foundations, as do containment theory, introduced by Reckless (1961), and interpersonal-maturity-level (I-level) theory, developed by Sullivan, Grant, and Grant (1957).

That these are exceptions, however, is clear from the lack of scientific communication within criminology and psychology. Evidence of this poor communication is found in the content of criminal-justice texts which traditionally portray psychological theories that attempt to explain delinquent or criminal behavior only briefly and sometimes confuse them with psychiatric or psychoanalytic approaches. There are several reasons for this beyond those mentioned previously and beyond the fact that the historical roots of U.S. criminology are in sociology.

First, psychologists and psychiatrists are often blamed for naivete when they offer global theories, derived from small samples of incarcerated offenders, that attempt to explain all criminal behavior. These efforts typically fail to recognize the complex historical debate in criminology over multifactor and single-factor etiological theories, or to recognize some criminologists' annoyance at scientific "explanations" that try to account for all antisocial or asocial acts.

Second, the application of psychological models of criminal conduct is most visible in clinical settings where successful treatment outcome often is claimed but remains the exception. For example, innovative treatment practices have led some psychologists and psychotherapists to believe that a cure is available or imminent. The breakdown of many psychotherapeutic, behavioral, and psychopharmacological models when applied to antisocial populations, however, has overshadowed such successful programs as that of the California Youth Authority and is often cited as an example of psychology's weak contribution to criminology (see Koran and Brown 1977; Jeffery 1979).

Third, for years criminologists have been skeptical about the strength of the personality-criminality relationship (see Gibbons 1976). The early work of Metfessel and Lovell (1942) dismissed personality as an important causal or descriptive factor in criminal behavior. Schuessler and Cressey (1950) presented the first comprehensive review of research on the personality of criminals, which was updated seventeen years later by Waldo and Dinitz (1967). These studies were as pessimistic as the most recent review by Tennenbaum (1977), who observed that "the data do not reveal any significant differences between criminal and noncriminal psychology because most results are based on tautological argument. The conclusion remains that cursory personality testing has not differentiated criminals from noncriminals" (p. 228) (see Gearing 1979; Laufer, Johnson, and Hogan 1981; Laufer, Skoog, and Day 1982; Martin and Fischer 1978).

Fourth, the strained criminology-psychology relationship may be symptomatic of a problem of modern psychology itself—the problem of specialization on the one hand and methodology on the other, resulting in deficits in theory. As Robert Hogan suggests in chapter 20 of this book, while psychologists debate methodological purity, technical efficiency, and modal efficacy—from laboratory experimentation to deliberate psychological education—long-standing theories of human behavior, personality, and the goals of psychological intervention have neither been validated nor proved false, and little in the way of new theory has been generated.

These four criticisms of the application of psychology to criminology have some merit. It would be wrong, however, to accept this criticism without recognizing the sophisticated and interrelated research in both psychology and sociology. This book reaffirms the belief that personality and moral psychology can play an important role in describing or explaining criminal behavior. It is also founded on a belief that previous research in this area is still in its infancy in many respects and can only benefit from serious theoretical deliberation.

This book introduces a collection of original writings on criminal behavior by contributors spanning the major theoretical orientations in the psychology of personality and moral development. These include cognitive-developmental, biosocial, social-learning, social-psychological, and psychodynamic perspectives. The primary goal is to encourage the dissemination of innovative psychological theory into the criminological and psychological communities, where previous work has been dominated by decontextualized empirical studies with limited generalizability.

Personality

During the past decade, research relating personality and criminality has largely concerned itself with validating narrow hypothetical constructs, increasing the strength of institutional classificatory measures (such as the Minnesota Multiphasic Personality Inventory (MMPI)), and developing predictors of antisocial behavior. Most researchers have proceeded with little concern for a unified or deliberate theory. The lack of theory-based research, as previously stated, is symptomatic of a larger problem in psychology. Yet it is also surprising, given the vision of such pioneers in criminal psychology and psychiatry as Healy, Gross, Bjerre, Hollander, Karpman, Alexander, Münsterberg, and the Gluecks. It is even more surprising in view of the legal community's reliance on personality psychology at many procedural levels in the practice of criminal law—from competency hearings to the extensive use of personality evaluations in presentence investigation reports and the routine administration of personality tests by parole authorities and correctional institutions. Given the role that personality psychology plays in the criminal justice system, one might expect that sophisticated theory-based research in personality is prevalent and recognized as important in the law-psychology interface. Unfortunately, this is not the case.

Despite an increase in methodological sophistication, recent studies avoid important theoretical questions posed decades ago—questions dealing with the existence of a distinct personality associated with antisocial behavior, the relationship between personality and moral development in delinquent behavior, and the degree to which personality shapes antisocial (compared with prosocial) behavior. Part I discusses these questions and other significant issues in the personality-criminality relationship, from varied theoretical perspectives.

Moral Development

Part II focuses on issues of moral development and criminal behavior. This section is principally concerned with the implications of cognitive-developmental theory for understanding criminal behavior from both theoretical and practical perspectives.

In recent decades moral-development theory has evolved into a distinct academic enterprise within psychology and education—reinterpreting psychoanalytic formulations of moral functions, Piagetian conceptions of a universal sequence of stages of reasoning, and historical understandings of moral insanity and moral deficiency as bases for explaining criminal behavior and treating delinquency. The best-known theory, pioneered by Lawrence Kohlberg, views moral development as proceeding according to an invariant sequence of stages. Movement within these stages depends on cognitive maturation and personal social experience. Its foundations rest on several intellectual traditions in psychology, philosophy, and education.

Discussions of moral psychology and criminal behavior have appeared only briefly and infrequently in the psychological and criminological literature. Thus, unfortunately, little research extends moral-development theories to understanding immoral behavior or relates theoretical knowledge to correctional practice. The chapters in part II significantly close this gap.

Several chapters in this section discuss cognitive-developmental theory as applied to offender populations. One chapter deals with potential uses of the theory for designing and administering restitution programs. Another presents a critical analysis of moral-development theory that draws some alternatives to the views of Kohlberg. Other chapters explore the relations among personality, moral development, and psychopathy; adolescent reasoning; and techniques of neutralization.

Part III concludes with three critical statements of the future direction of personality and moral-development research. These chapters make apparent how much more sophisticated work is needed if we are to understand the psychological development of criminal behavior.

References

Brodsky, S.L., ed. *Psychologists in the criminal justice system.* Urbana: University of Illinois, 1977.

Dinitz, S. Nothing fails like a little success. In E. Sagarin, ed., *Criminology: New concerns.* Beverly Hills, Calif.: Sage, 1979.

Eysenck, H.J. *Crime and personality.* London: Routledge and Kegan Paul, 1977.

Fowler, R.D., and Brodsky, S.L. Development of correctional-clinical psychology program. *Professional Psychology,* 1978, *9*, 440-447.

Gearing, M.L. The MMPI as a primary differentiator and predictor of behavior in prison: A methodological critique and review of the literature. *Psychological Bulletin,* 1979, *86*, 929-963.

Gibbons, D.C. *Delinquent behavior.* Englewood Cliffs, New Jersey: Prentice-Hall, 1976.

Gottfredson, D.M. Five challenges. In S. Brodsky, ed., *Psycholgists in the criminal justice system.* Urbana: University of Illinois, 1977.

Jeffery, C.R. Criminology as an interdisciplinary behavioral science. In E. Sagarin, ed., *Criminology: New concerns.* Beverly Hills, Calif.: Sage, 1979.

Koran, L.M., and Brown, B.S. Psychologists in corrections and justice: Another view. In S. Brodsky, ed., *Psychologists in the criminal justice system.* Urbana: University of Illinois, 1977.

Laufer, W.S.; Johnson, J.; and Hogan, R. Ego control and criminal behavior. *Journal of Personality and Social Psychology,* 1981, *41*, 179-184.

Laufer, W.S.; Skoog, D.K.; and Day, J.M. Personality and criminality: A review of the California Psychological Inventory. *Journal of Clinical Psychology,* 1982, *38*, 562-573.

Martin, R.D., and Fischer, D.G. Personality factors in juvenile delinquency, A review of the literature. *Catalog of Selected Documents in Psychology,* 1978, *8*, Ms. 1759.

Megargee, E.I. Psychological determinants and correlates of criminal violence. In M.E. Wolfgang and N.A. Weiner, eds., *Criminal violence.* Beverly Hills, Calif.: Sage, 1982.

Megargee, E.I., and Bohn, M.J. *Classifying criminal offenders: A new system based on the MMPI.* Beverly Hills, Calif.: Sage, 1979.

Metfessel, M., and Lovell, C. Recent literature on individual correlates of crime. *Psychological Bulletin*, 1942, *39*, 133-164.

Monahan, J. Predicting violent behavior: An assessment of techniques. Beverly Hills, Calif.: Sage, 1981.

Radzinowicz, L., and King, J. *The growth of crime: The international experience.* New York: Basic Books, 1977.

Reckless, W.C. A new theory of delinquency and crime. *Federal Probation,* 1961, *25*, 42-46.

Schuessler, K.E., and Cressey, D.R. Personality characteristics of criminals. *American Journal of Sociology*, 1950, *55*, 476-484.

Short, J.F. On the etiology of delinquent behavior. *Journal of Research in Crime and Delinquency*, 1979, *16*, 28-33.

Sullivan, C.E.; Grant, M.Q.; and Grant, J.D. The development of interpersonal maturity: Applications to delinquency. *Psychiatry*, 1957, *20*, 272-283.

Tennenbaum, D.J. Personality and criminality: A summary and implications of the literature. *Journal of Criminal Justice*, 1977, *5*, 225-235.

Waldo, G.P., and Dinitz, S. Personality attributes of the criminal; An analysis of research studies, 1950-1965. *Journal of Research in Crime and Delinquency,* 1967, *4*, 185-202.

Wolfgang, M.E., and Ferracuti, F. *The subculture of violence: Towards an integrated theory in criminology.* London: Tavistock, 1967.

Part I
Personality Theory

1

A Role-Theoretical Model of Criminal Conduct

Robert Hogan and
Warren H. Jones

Introduction

This chapter presents a perspective on criminal conduct; it also presents some data that illustrate this perspective. Although the argument may be a bit complex in places, our general point is that being a criminal is one kind of social identity available to a large segment of modern society; its use, therefore, has a strategic aspect. Our perspective, a role-theoretical model called Socioanalytic Theory, draws on the major earlier efforts to conceptualize criminal conduct. This chapter reviews these perspectives and describes what we see as their distinctive strengths and weaknesses. We then present our own perspective, followed by our data and some final observations.

Sociological Theory

The topic of deviancy has been a central concern of sociological theory from its beginning as an empirical discipline. Sociological analyses differ from psychological analyses in a very interesting way: most sociologists regard people as innately conforming and believe deviancy must be explained; most psychologists, however, regard people as innately asocial and believe that conformity must be explained (see Hogan 1976). The fact that the two disciplines take such radically different perspectives on this topic may explain why there has been so little cross-fertilization between the disciplines.

In mainstream structural sociology, society is seen as an integrated set of social structures. From this perspective, criminality is regarded as a function of societal organization. The traditional argument, as set out by Merton (1949), for example, is that society prescribes certain goals (such as status) for everyone and also prescribes the permissible means to achieve these goals (such as quality education or membership in the appropriate social group). Finally, however, society rigorously restricts access to these means: very few working-class children are able to complete Harvard Medical School. Coveting the good life but denied access to the legitimate means of pursuing it, some people—criminals—choose illegitimate means to attain their goals. This kind of analysis confuses prediction with explanation and ignores individual differences, but it contains one very important insight. Structural sociology suggests that there is a strategic or deliberate element in working-class criminal careers. Becoming a criminal is in some sense a rational response to the problem of earning a living, particularly for those whose aspirations exceed the socially regulated opportunities available to them.

In the tradition of symbolic interactionism that extends from Cooley and Mead to Goffman, personality and social identity emerge from social interaction. Consequently, the key element in the socialization process is the development of role-taking ability. Through games and ritualized social interaction, children become able to think about their own conduct from the perspective of those others with whom they interact. The process of becoming sensitive to social expectations makes children self-conscious. In this way they develop self-images or social identities. The point here is that the development of role-taking ability or social sensitivity is seen as the crucial step in the socialization process, and there is considerable evidence to support the view that working-class criminals are pathologically deficient in role-taking ability (Gough 1948; Gough and Peterson 1952; Hogan 1973; Hogan and Kurtines 1972). A person with inadequate role-taking ability has a reduced capacity to see him- or herself as a social object, and this self-consciousness is the mechanism by which society ordinarily ensures adherence to its rules of conduct. Also, the self-images or social identities of such persons are likely to be characteristically deviant because of their reduced social sensitivity. The principal weakness of the symbolic-interactionist account of criminal behavior is that its analysis of social development remains largely untouched since its initial interesting but very sketchy formulation by Mead. Writers in this tradition have been slow to extend the analysis to childhood. At this point we will pass over, with no comment, control theory and differential association theory. To deal with these sociological pillars would take us too far afield.

Psychoanalytic Theory

After sociological theory, psychoanalysis provides perhaps the most popular single account of the origins of criminal behavior. As is well known, the crucial variable in psychoanalytic theory is the emotional relationship between the child and the same-sexed parent. In the traditional view, with the emergence of the Oedipus complex around age five, children develop intense feelings of rivalry with the same-sexed parent in competition for the favors of the opposite-sexed parent. If parents handle this conflict decisively, children (especially little boys) will repress their longings for the opposite-sexed parent and internalize the image of the same-sexed parent. This internalized image is the key to the socialization process—it is the source of both a child's conscience and his or her sex-role identity. The crucial element in superego formation is, therefore, the development of a strong emotional bond to a nurturant but authoritative (even punitive) same-sexed parent.

According to psychoanalytic formulations, the normal parent-child relationship failed to materialize in the case of male criminals: a father figure was either missing or inadequate, providing no affection, no discipline, or neither. In such cases, young boys would internalize neither a set of moral prohibitions nor a clear sex-role identity. Such boys have an impoverished conscience and, at the same time, are defensive about their masculinity. Consequently, their delinquent behavior reflects both their need to prove their manliness and the lack of a set of internal moral standards to regulate conduct.

There are, of course, substantial logical and conceptual problems with the psychoanalytic account of socialization. First, the final resolution of the Oedipus complex depends on a piece of theoretical nonsense (which is also empirically nonverifiable) known as castration anxiety. Moreover, the theory suggests that criminals have no capacity for guilt and argues incorrectly that the principal motives in human affairs are sex and aggression. Nonetheless, traditional psychoanalysis contains a set of vital, and in our judgment true insights about criminal development: (1) that moral conduct (or criminality) is organically related to the structure of an individual's personality; (2) that a person's moral posture is largely unconscious; (3) that a person's moral posture is closely linked to the kinds of relationships that existed between that person and his or her parents; and (4) that adult personality is shaped to some degree by childhood experiences (that is, that development matters). Unfortunately, contemporary psychologists, perhaps put off by the intemperate theorizing of the psychoanalytic tradition, have largely ignored or rejected these insights.

Social-Learning Theory

Social-learning theory is in some ways the wild child in the theoretical playground, spending large portions of its time beating up on other theoretical perspectives. Despite these anarchistic tendencies, the advocates of social-learning theory have made some very useful contributions to our understanding of delinquent conduct. The general argument is that children are somehow (in ways that are inexplicable from the empiricist perspective of learning theory) predisposed to model their behavior after that of powerful adult models. Without direct reinforcement they will incorporate and reproduce the behaviors of successful models. For children these models are usually their parents. Social-learning theorists have provided an invaluable service in unpacking the various parameters of the modeling process. At the same time, Bandura (1971) and Mischel (1974) have also devoted a good bit of attention to analyzing the problem of self-control. This complex literature, however, is far beyond the purview of this chapter.

In our judgment, perhaps the most important contribution of social-learning theory to the study of criminal conduct is *Adolescent Aggression* (Bandura and Walters 1959). In an interesting, carefully controlled, naturalistic study, Bandura and Walters show that delinquent adolescent boys, whose aggressiveness is part of their delinquency, are subtly but steadily reinforced for their aggression by their fathers. The fathers were themselves tough characters, who conveyed their pride in their offspring's toughness in a variety of ways. Here modeling comes together with traditional learning theory to explain anti-social behavior. Bandura and Walters, however, overlook the fact that along many parameters—independence, self-assurance, self-reliance—their delinquent boys were significantly advanced over—that is, more mature than—their carefully matched, nondelinquent controls.

We object to several aspects of social-learning theory: the ecological invalidity of much of the research, its general silence on the subject of individual differences, its avoidance of the topic of human emotion, its overemphasis on situational factors as the determinants of social conduct, and its mischaracterization of traditional personality psychology (see Hogan 1982a). Nonetheless, we heartily agree with the view that modeling and reinforcement are major factors in the development of criminal conduct.

Biosocial Theory

Over the past twenty years a substantial literature has developed which argues that some criminals may be born that way (Yochelson and Samenow 1976). Hutchings and Mednick (1974), for example, provide evidence that there is a heritable component to the scores on some personality measures that assess criminal tendencies.

The view that people can inherit genes for criminal conduct is simplistic. Specific dispositions that might predispose a person toward delinquency may be heritable, however. These might include an impoverished capacity to experience anxiety (Lykken 1957), which would make a person somewhat untrainable. Buss and Plomin (1975) posit four biologically based temperaments (emotionality, activity, sociability, and impulsivity) as being at the roots of personality. It is easy to imagine that a child who is very emotional, active, unsociable, and impulsive might be constantly in trouble with his or her adult caretakers and perhaps predisposed to delinquency. This biological model is interactional in the best sense of the word; it does not maintain that certain temperaments cause delinquency, but rather that the concurrence of these temperaments *and* certain kinds of family environments may lead to delinquent outcomes. On the other hand, the biosocial perspective has empirical problems; that is, research to test and fine-tune both the connections between heritable components of personality and criminal conduct, as well as mechanisms that underlie such connections, are beset with thorny methodological and ultimately ethical problems.

Summary

Each theoretical approach presented here provides important insights into the origins of criminal conduct. Structural sociology points out that there is an element of rationality in the choice of a criminal career. Social-learning theory suggests that the hostility and aggressiveness that precede and incubate a criminal life-style may be acquired by mimicking adult models and maintained through social reinforcement. Psychoanalysis tells us that the parent-child relationship is crucial in this process, that criminals are largely unaware of how deviant their values actually are, that the criminal life-style is an organic part of their personality, and consequently that criminals have deviant personalities, i.e., they are hostile toward authority and society in general. Symbolic interactionism points out that criminals are deficient in role-taking ability, and various biosocial theories suggest that there are organic factors that predispose certain people to criminality.

We agree with all these points. We think, however, that they can be incorporated in a single conceptual paradigm, the ingredients of which are presented in the next section.

Socioanalytic Theory

The first author worked for a while as a probation officer. The job consisted of investigating the family backgrounds of delinquent boys and making recommendations about ways to rehabilitate them. The work provided a. rich source of anecdotal material for subsequent theorizing about personality development. One particular incident, at the home of the mother of an entire family of delinquent boys, sparked the line of inquiry that follows. Two boys, both under five, were in the house during the interview with their mother. The woman seemed genuinely concerned about the welfare of her children and quite unhappy about how her older boys had turned out. About twenty minutes into the interview, one of the small boys interrupted to announce that the other boy was playing in his mother's closet. The woman rushed into the next room and, judging by the subsequent wails, administered a sound thrashing to the little malefactor. She returned and the sobbing shortly subsided. Then the second boy came to report that the first was playing in his mother's bureau. Again the woman went to the next room and gave the boy an industrious whacking. Over the period of ninety minutes this scenario was repeated several times; it was interesting because the children's behavior seemed neither to maximize pleasure nor minimize pain. However, if one assumed that the children wanted and needed their mother's attention, and that negative attention was preferable to none at all, then the entire sequence was interpretable. The sequence also holds the key to our view of the origins of criminal conduct.

Assumptions

We have presented our theoretical perspective at length elsewhere (Hogan 1982; Cheek and Hogan 1982). Consequently, we will simply list our principal assumptions here without providing supporting arguments. The first assumption is that *Homo sapiens* evolved as a group-living and culture-bearing animal, and that human capacity for social organization and the transmission of culture was the key to evolutionary success. Moreover, every human (and primate) group has a well-defined social structure, organized according to status. Accordingly, we assume that three primary needs underlie social conduct: for attention and approval, for status, and for predictability and order. Each is biologically mandated because it contributes to both individual and group survival.

These needs can often conflict, as when an individual's drive for status upsets the social order, or less dramatically, when an individual's striving for status brings jealousy and social disapprobation in its wake. Taken together, these needs also insure that all social interaction, from the most trivial to the most formal, is quite regular in its structure.

In a perceptive essay, Athay and Darley (1981) point out that, if the concept of personality is to have any meaning, then it must lie in its ability to explain social action; moreover, much personality research overlooks the fundamental fact that the subjects in psychological investigations are actors in social contexts trying to get others to do what they want. We would add that the public impression that arises from our social performances, whenever they occur, is the major social consequence of personality. Moreover, by virtue of our status as social animals, personality must be defined from two perspectives—that of the observer and that of the actor. From the observer's perspective personality refers to the distinctive social impression that an actor has created; more broadly, personality in this first sense refers to an actor's reputation in his or her social group.

From the actor's side, personality includes those structures within the person that regulate his or her behavior so as to generate his or her reputation. Four structures are particularly important for understanding personality in this second sense. First is the actor's self-image, self-concept, or personal identity. This is the view that a person holds about him or herself; it includes both content and evaluative characteristics but is also the view that the person would like others to believe. Second is the self-presentational tactics and role-playing behaviors an actor uses in order to project his or her desired self-image. Self-images, therefore, guide role performances in relation to others. The third structure is the actor's reference group, an internalized and personal view of the expectations of the significant others about whose approval or disapproval the actor cares. The fourth structure is the actor's skill at reading the expectations of his or her audiences, tailoring his or her self-presentations to those expectations, and accurately conveying his or her self-image through these role performances. These skills can be labeled *interpersonal sensitivity* and *interpersonal competence*.

Several points about this perspective should be emphasized:

1. Self-presentations are motivated by attempts to achieve attention and approval while avoiding negative sanctions and disapproval from reference groups and significant others. This is so for everyone; the issue is not whether one does self-presentation but whither the sources of approval/disapproval.
2. The self-presentational process is structured by self-images. Consequently, social interactions symbolically reflect the view of oneself to which one wishes others will subscribe.
3. Some people choose or are forced to adopt self-images that are less than ideal and even defensive.
4. There are individual differences in the degree to which people attend to internal (conscience) versus external (peer) reference groups. Maturity is typically associated with a balance between the two.
5. There are differences in the ability of individuals to project their self-images successfully, and these differences are strongly related to success and popularity within specific groups.
6. Over time, the aforementioned personality structures become automatic and unconscious; social conduct from the actor's point of view is typically experienced as natural and authentic (Hogan 1982b).

Personality Development

It follows from the preceding discussion that some major ways in which people differ are in terms of their self-images, self-presentational tactics, reference groups, interpersonal sensitivity, and interpersonal competence. We contend that these are the principal ways in which criminals differ from their law-observant conspecifics. These differences emerge from or are the end products of personality development, to which subject we now turn. This discussion will be brief; for a more elaborate treatment see Hogan (1982b).

We think of personality development in terms of three broad phases, each denoted by its own particular problems. The first phase concerns coming to terms with authority and results in the formation of character structure. The second phase involves adjusting to peer-group expectations and results in the formation of role structure. The third phase entails forming occupational and career plans and results in the development of a life-style.

Character Structure. The major developmental problem during the first phase revolves around making an accommodation to adult authority while at the same time learning the basic rules of the social game. This first period of development is largely authoritarian, as Piaget (1964) noted; parental rules and values are literally imposed on children. In contrast with Piaget, however, we believe this to be quite a pleasant time for many children. Some adults long for a return to the security and reassurance of this period. We also believe that children are born preprogrammed to accept adult authority—how else would they learn language? Given a reasonably normal relationship with their parents, their accommodation to authority is relatively effortless. The major parameters affecting this accommodation are parental warmth and restrictiveness. Warm, restrictive parents produce the most mature children. Cold, rejecting parents produce children at risk for becoming delinquent.

Parental rules, values, and expectations are transmitted during social interaction with children. Competent parents structure these interactions in terms of simple games. Through games like peek-a-boo or "What's that?"—typified forms of parent-child interaction (see Hogan 1982a)—parents teach their children, among other things, the basic rules that govern social interaction: older people are usually in charge, one must take turns, don't hit mother. In this way children also learn that social interaction is a kind of a game: it has an assumed purpose and it proceeds in terms of complementary roles (such as mother-baby). Children also learn that interaction take place *only* in terms of these games and their associated roles: outside of these primitive rituals there is no interaction. And from these games and the roles they play in relation to their parents, children internalize rather complex images of themselves (such as daddy's girl or mommy's boy); these are core self-images, central sources of personal identity. At the same time, children are taught, and consequently internalize, their parents' evaluation of them—someone worth paying attention to, someone who should be ignored; these core self-evaluations are fundamentally related to self-esteem. Moreover, the core self-images and self-evaluations that derive from this first developmental phase are surprisingly stable and enduring (see Block 1981). Finally, children who have been loved and competently played with during the first phase have a decisive advantage over their peers when they enter the second phase (Lieberman 1977).

Role Structure. About age five most children leave the exclusive care of their parents and begin to make their way in the extended family and the peer group, as encountered in their neighborhoods and/or nursery schools. Consequently, the major developmental problem during this second phase involves learning to interact socially with peers. As Piaget (1964) noted, peer interaction proceeds in terms of its own rules. Despite this egalitarian contrast with the authoritarian first phase of development, the second phase is not a romantic and democratic interlude sandwiched between infancy and adulthood. The peer group is often critical, capricious, and cruel; this can be a difficult time for some children, especially those who were poorly treated in the first phase.

Equipped with their core self-images and levels of self-esteem, children between the ages of five and eighteen are largely involved in peer interaction; during early adolescence they often seem obsessed by it. During peer interaction children must negotiate the roles they will play in relation to other children. Specifically, in an effort to maximize the approval and minimize the criticism of their peers, children try out various roles (athlete, tough kid, clown) to see what will work. The fortunate children are able to play the roles they want. More typically, however, compromises—some quite painful—are necessary. It follows that the roles children play in the peer group are often defensive, designed to disguise fears and inadequacies and to avoid social censure.

During peer interaction, as we have noted, children develop ways of reacting, typified ways of responding to the expectations of their peers. These self-presentational behaviors are designed to tell the other children how they want—or don't want—to be regarded. Over time these initially self-conscious ways of responding become habitual, then unself-conscious, and finally unconscious. This sequence is important because social performances must seem spontaneous if they are to be convincing.

From our perspective, self-images cause or guide role performances. This is the reverse of the model espoused by symbolic interactionism and contemporary social psychology, which claim that playing roles produces characteristic self-images (see Brown 1965, pp. 153-154). We believe that what we do during social interaction reflects our underlying self-images in a symbolic fashion—our actions are designed to tell others about our self-images, the views of ourselves that we would like others to believe. As noted, these self-images and their associated role performances are chosen so as to maximize peer approval and minimize peer disapproval. Parents equip their children with initial self-images. The peer group, however, will sanction only certain role performances. Hence the underlying self-image may have to be adjusted; in this sense one's identity is both bestowed and negotiated. Children who enter the peer group with low self-esteem and inappropriate self-images are at risk for social failure because social feedback from the peer group strengthens tendencies already in place.

Life-Style. The problem during the third period of development is to choose a mate and a vocation, to establish a family and a career. The self-images and self-presentational strategies developed in childhood and adolescence shape vocational choice in adulthood; there is a clear self-presentational component to a person's vocational choice and associated life-style. In announcing to others, for example, that one is a university professor, one immediately tells others how one is to be regarded, what others can expect of one during interactions, and some potential themes around which interaction can be organized. Vocational identity is one aspect of social identity more broadly conceived; one begins negotiating one's social identity in childhood and continues to do so throughout adult life. Changes in jobs and careers (for example, when an academic goes into business) reflect not so much a fundamental reorientation in one's self-image, such changes may reflect instead the fact that one has adopted a different, perhaps more congenial way of expressing the same image.

Conclusions. From the foregoing discussion we draw four general conclusions about criminal conduct.

1. We suspect that working-class criminals typically experience less than optimal conditions during the first two periods of development, which increases the probability of their choosing a criminal career in adulthood. During the first period (0-5 years), adult caretakers were rejecting and/or permissive, and/or themselves provided somewhat antisocial models. These children enter the second period of development (6-18) with poor interpersonal competencies and hostility to adult authority. This quickly leads to problems in adjusting to school (fighting with both teachers and peers) and to an uncooperative and rebellious interpersonal style.

2. A tough, defiant, rebellious interpersonal style, combined with a poor or nonexistent education in urban America, substantially facilitates the transition to a criminal career. Not every tough, undereducated, rebellious person is a criminal, nor are all criminals menacing or dumb. Our second point is that for many criminals being a criminal is part of their social identities; this is how they perceive themselves, how they present themselves, and the role they have chosen (or been pushed into) to play, for lack of a

better one. It is important to reemphasize that incipient criminals do not differ from their law-abiding counterparts in terms of their needs for approval, status, or predictability and control; the difference is initially in parental satisfaction of these needs in a manner conducive to conventional socialization, and subsequently in the relative incongruence (deriving from a deviant identity) between their self-presentations and the expectations of others.

3. Within the population of persons who have opted for a criminal identity, there is the same status hierarchy found in any human group: some will be better at it than others. Those who are good at it (high-status criminals) are indistinguishable from nondelinquents along many dimensions, such as intelligence, self-confidence, and self-control. Incompetent criminals will differ from competent ones along these same dimensions; thus low-status criminals will be less intelligent, anxious, and impulsive.

4. Given that some criminal careers are more successful than others, it is hard to specify precisely how criminals will differ from noncriminals in their self-presentational styles. Indeed, one review of the research on personality and criminality (Tennenbaum 1977) concluded that more differences have been found within samples of criminals and noncriminals than between them. The next section deals with this problem more extensively.

Criminal Self-Presentations

Several years ago an Oklahoma newspaper recounted the following story: a convicted felon who had been released on parole from prison broke into a service station; he then used the station's telephone to call the police and turn himself in. The ex-convict explained to police that before he was paroled, he was taking an art class in prison; he wanted to return to complete the course. Though clearly unusual, this episode emphasized the utility of examining criminal conduct in light of the specific self-images reflected in criminal behavior and the reference group to which the criminal is attending.

This section presents data from a variety of personality tests that we use to evaluate our conjectures about criminals' self-presentational style. First, however, we need to ask what scores on the various personality measures actually mean. What do the scales really assess? We do *not* believe that personality measures are a second-best way to observe behavior—that is, self-reports of necesssarily real conduct. Nor do we regard these scales as measuring *traits* as that term is normally defined (as enduring neuropsychic structures). Rather, we regard test taking as a form of self-presentation formally identical to the self-presentational processes underlying all other forms of social interaction. Personality test questions systematically sample self-presentational behaviors across varying ranges of topics or situations. Some inventories (such as the MMPI) sample exhaustively from a single domain of interpersonal conduct; others (such as the CPI) sample more broadly.

The claim that responses to personality-test items are self-presentations illuminates rather than obscures the concept of test validity, because it explains the mechanism involved. Scale validity is normally estimated in terms of correlations between scale scores and peer ratings, which of course are normally less than perfect. This correlation occurs because people do pretty much the same thing when they interact with a set of test items as when they interact with their peers—namely, they attempt to create a view of themselves that they expect the audience to believe. As we have suggested, some people will be more effective (and more consistent) in projecting their self-images than others; this produces the discrepancies that lower validity coefficients. At the same time, however, recent evidence suggest that even brief snippets of videotaped behavior are sufficient to allow naive judges to place stimulus persons into high and low Machiavellian groups with a significant degree of accuracy (Cherulnik et al. 1981). Thus interactional and test-taking self-presentations are quite comparable.

With these observations in mind, we turn to our data. As part of a larger study, we tested fifty-seven convicted felons who were on probation or parole. Subjects anonymously completed a questionnaire consisting, among other things, of eight four-item personality measures. These included anxiety (Taylor 1953), assertiveness (Rathus 1973), dogmatism (Rokeach 1960), externality (Rotter 1966), purpose-in-life (Crumbaugh 1968), self-esteem (Coopersmith 1967), shyness (Jones and Russell 1982), and social desirability (Crowne and Marlowe 1964). These abbreviated item clusters were used to encourage maximum participation and to sample broadly across personality domains. The clusters appeared to be reliable for four-item scales: alpha coefficients varied from .39 to .64, with a mean of .53, for the eight scales.

The felons, all male and convicted of a variety of offenses, were divided into two groups: those convicted of violent crimes or crimes with considerable potential for violence (assault, murder, armed robbery, rape, and so on), and those convicted of nonviolent crimes or crimes with less potential for violence (burglary, exhibitionism, embezzlement, and the like). Individuals convicted for drug- or alcohol-related offenses were specifically excluded from this analysis. The two groups were comparable in terms of marital status (50 percent of the nonviolent and 46.7 percent of the violent offenders were married) and previous criminal involvement (40.9 percent of the nonviolent and 38.3 percent of the violent offenders had previous felony convictions). The two groups did differ significantly in terms of age (nonviolent X = 28.91, violent X = 35.71, t (54) = 2.58, $p <$ .02). Not surprisingly, the nonviolent and violent groups also differed with respect to the proportion who had actually served prison sentences (9.1 percent and 58.1 percent, respectively, X (1) = 11.13, $p <$ .001). In our view, members of the violent group are more involved with their identities as criminals than members of the nonviolent group.

The two groups were compared in terms of their scores on the eight scales listed here. As the results in table 1-1 indicate, the more violent criminals obtained higher scores for self-esteem, assertiveness, dogmatism, purpose-in-life, and social desirability. At the same time, they received lower scores for anxiety and externality. The groups did not differ in terms of shyness. From a self-presentational perspective these results suggest that violent criminals, relative to nonviolent ones, project the image of persons who are composed, self-confident, assertive, opinionated, and self-reliant. As in the case of Bandura and Walters's (1959) aggressive boys, these violent felons show some surprising strengths and in fact appear more mature than nonviolent offenders on some common dimensions of psychiatric evaluation. The social stereotype of the thug appears to have some rough validity: he is tough and resourceful rather than neurotic and sniveling.

The inventory requested biographical information about the crime of which each subject was convicted; these results provided further confirmation for these conclusions. For example, the nonviolent offenders were more likely to claim that they were functioning under great stress in the period during which the criminal act took place (nonviolent = 61.9 percent, violent = 31.0 percent, X = 3.54, $p <$ .05) and more likely to indicate that they experienced a sense of guilt and shame as a consequence of their crime (nonviolent = 81.8 percent, violent = 46.4 percent, X (1) =

Table 1-1
A Personality Comparison of Violent and Nonviolent Criminals

	Means		
Variable	Nonviolent	Violent	t
Anxiety	10.92	9.33	1.82*
Assertiveness	11.42	9.88	2.02**
Dogmatism	14.88	16.15	2.48**
Externality	9.75	8.27	2.03**
Purpose-in-life	11.21	13.24	2.51**
Self-esteem	9.46	7.24	2.64**
Shyness	8.95	8.06	1.26
Social desirability	12.04	13.24	1.70*

*$p <$ .10.
**$p <$ .05.

Notes: n = 57. The assertiveness and self-esteem scales are reversed such that higher means indicated lower assertiveness and self-esteem. Two-tailed tests.

5.13, $p < .02$). Moreover, nonviolent offenders were more likely to admit that they actually committed or were guilty of a crime than were violent offenders (nonviolent = 77.3 percent, violent = 48.4 percent, $X(1) = 3.36$, $p < .06$). Although not significant, nonviolent offenders were more likely to claim that their criminal conduct was due to either an impulse or a compulsion (76.2 percent and 36.8 percent, respectively) than were violent offenders (60.7 percent and 20.7 percent).

These biographical data are consistent with the personality data presented earlier. More interesting is the manner in which the nonviolent criminals admitted their culpability but appealed to extenuating circumstances in order to reduce their responsibility; in contrast, the violent criminals displayed a sort of contemptuous denial of the crime, felt a corresponding lack of guilt, and attributed less blame to the environment.

The seeming discrepancy in the nonviolent group between admitting guilt while blaming environmental forces and uncontrollable internal urges (and the opposite pattern in the violent group) is interpretable from a self-presentational perspective. Two issues are involved—individual differences in social competence and reference groups. As suggested earlier, some people (in this case the violent criminals) are simply better at presenting themselves in a manner that confirms their self-image and social identity; this skill is associated with greater consistency of interpersonal performances. The violent and nonviolent criminals also seem to have different reference groups. Thus the hardcore, self-assured, dogmatic, inner-directed criminal stance of the violent group is perhaps directed toward the criminal subculture, whereas the nonviolent group seemed to have adopted a nervous, compliant, and contrite image for the benefit of the criminal-justice system and of straight society.

In a second study, 40 adjudicated delinquents from Arizona, arrested for drug-related offenses, were compared with 38 police cadets and 103 nursing aides from an inner-city Baltimore hospital. In this comparison, social class and education were perhaps more comparable than in many such delinquent-nondelinquent comparisons. There may be a sex-difference confound, although other data suggest this is not the case. The two groups were tested with the Hopkins Personality Inventory (HPI) (Hogan 1982b). The HPI is a recently developed personality inventory designed to assess six factors representing a systematic sampling from the entire domain of trait terms relevant to everyday performance, status, and popularity. Each scale consists of a set of homogeneous item composites (HICs; see Zonderman 1981) that reflect aspects or facets of the six larger dimensions: (1) intellectance, (2) adjustment, (3) ascendance, (4) likeability, (5) self-control, and (6) sociability. Analyses can be run either at the scale-score or the HIC level; here they were at the HIC level.

Table 1-2 presents correlations between various HICs and the delinquency-nondelinquency criterion. This array of results can be described

Table 1-2
Correlations between the Delinquency-Nondelinquency Criterion and the Variables Listed

Variable	Correlation
Alienation	
School success	−.20
Not anxious	−.13
No somatic complaint	−.14
No depression	−.43
No guilt	−.54
No social anxiety	−.12
Self-esteem	−.32
Respects parents	−.36
Vocational identity	−.40
Recklessness	
Calmness	−.28
Is cautious	−.31
Avoids trouble	−.73
Is playful	−.30
Not experience seeking	−.33
Not thrill seeking	−.38
Has high standards	−.36
Toughness	
Attentive to others	−.28
Dependability	−.34
Tolerance	−.43
Flattering	−.29
Caring	−.15
Being even tempered	−.39
Being cheerful	−.12
Being cooperative	−.35
Being trusting	−.39
Exhibitionism	
Enjoys crowds	.44
Exhibitionistic	.37

Notes: $n = 171$. $r = .12$. $p < .05$. A negative correlation means delinquents receive lower scores.

in terms of four themes: alienation (HICs 2, 13, 14, 18, and 20); recklessness (HICs 21, 22, 24, 25, and 26); interpersonal toughness (HICs 33, 34, 35, 40, and 41); and exhibitionism (HICs 38, 43, and 44). Alienated, reckless, tough, and exhibitionistic; this set of terms sounds like a job description for a Mafia hit-man, a Hemingway protagonist, a soldier of fortune, or a garden-variety mugger. Missing from this list, however, are the traditional stigmata of neurosis—anxiety and somatic complaint. We regard depression and guilt more as signs of alienation than psychopathology; the themes of depression and guilt are as present in the writings of Albert Camus and Saint John of the Cross as they are in these protocols, and they reflect world weariness and alienation rather than neurotic affliction. Reck-lessness, exhibitionism, and toughness seem to be core elements of the criminal identity.

Conclusion

The foregoing discussion leads to six points about the relationship between personality and criminal conduct. First, criminal conduct is organically re-lated to the structure of the criminal's personality. This conclusion may seem too simple; but it is surprisingly controversial in the context of current U.S. psychology today, where various writers seriously argue that there is no stable core to personality (Mischel 1968; Jones et al., 1971); that there are no links between personality and conduct; or that criminality exists prin-cipally in the eye of the beholder (Jones et al., 1971; Scheff 1966). Needless to say, we disagree with these conclusions.

Second, we suggest in the tradition of depth psychology that the choice of a criminal career is overdetermined, a joint function of childhood experi-ence, modeling, temperament, and the social opportunities available to de-veloping children. Further, the choice of a criminal career may be in some sense rational—but not necessarily conscious. Carl Jung repeatedly observed that important decisions in life are never made consciously; this must also be true in choosing a criminal life-style.

Third, the personality structure of our criminal samples is characterized by a relative absence of psychopathology, especially for those with well-integrated criminal identities. They may feel depression, alienation, and resentment of parents (see table 1-2). Nonetheless, one can feel one's life is going nowhere, that one has betrayed one's friends, and that one's parents were incompetent, and be right rather than neurotic (see Alloy and Abram-son 1979).

Fourth, we have described the personality structures of the "typical criminal" in terms of a particular kind of self-presentation (alienated, tough, reckless, and exhibitionistic) reflecting a particular underlying self-image. Nonetheless, in contrast with many social psychologists (Gergen 1981; Snyder 1974), we believe that these self-images and associated role perfor-mances are stable over remarkably long periods of time (see Block 1981). There is no contradiction between the views that personality is temporally stable and that it consists of typified self-presentations. In the case of criminals, this means that their toughness is real; they are truly unpleasant and undependable people whose ruthlessness cannot be wished away.

Fifth, for many working-class men, being a criminal is their social iden-tity. They want to be regarded as tough, reckless, and alienated; they manifest this through their exhibitionism. Consequently, rehabilitative efforts will have to take into account that: (1) people need to interact; (2) outside of our roles we have no way to interact; and (3) criminals are in a real sense doing the best they can to get by in the world. For rehabilitation to succeed, new identities must be constructed. The problem is not to overcome a neurosis but to acquire a new self-image, new self-presentational tactics, and new reference groups—in short, to negotiate a new social identity.

Our final point concerns the possibility that the reader will think a self-presentational analysis is uniquely applicable to criminal conduct. Because criminal careers involve, in varying degrees, subterfuge, lying, cheating, and worse, the self-presentational approach may superficially seem particularly appropriate as an analytical model. It is useful, however, for understanding moral postures of all kinds. We have argued that social identity and self-presentation are largely unconscious. Also as noted, even among criminals there are significant and meaningful differences in self-presentational strategies and reference groups, as well as the skill and success with which social identities are presented. Therefore, many criminals are functionally oblivious to the world entailed by a role-theoretical metatheory—unaware of the self-presentational aspect of their criminal identities. More important, we believe that this analysis holds for personalities that are not deviant. It explains social identities that are conventionally approved, even exalted (such as Albert Schweitzer or Mother Theresa). Malcolm X saw right to the heart of the issue when he remarked, "Doing good is a hustle too."

References

Alloy, C.B., and Abramson, L.Y. Judgments of contingency in depressed and nondepressed students: Sadder but wiser? *Journal of Experimental Psychology: General*, 1979, *108*, 441-485.

Athay, M., and Darley, J.M. Toward an interaction-centered theory of personality. In N. Cantor and J.F. Kihlstrom, eds., *Personality, cognition, and social interaction*. Hillsdale, N.J.: Erlbaum, 1981, 281-308.

Bandura, A. *Social learning theory*. Morristown, N.J.: General Learning Press, 1971.

Bandura, A., and Walters, R.H. *Adolescent aggression*. New York: Ronald Press, 1959.

Block, J. Some enduring and consequential structures of personality. In A.I. Rabin et al., eds., *Further explorations in personality*. New York: Wiley, 1981.

Brown, R. *Social psychology*. New York: Free Press, 1965.

Buss, A.H., and Plomin, R. *A temperamental theory of personality development*. New York: Wiley, 1975.

Cheek, J., and Hogan, R. Self-concept, self-presentation, and moral judgment. In J. Suls and A. Greenwald, eds., *Psychological perspectives on the self*, vol. II. Hillsdale, N.J.: Erlbaum, 1982.

Cherulnik, P.; Way, J.; Ames, S.; and Hutto, D. Impressions of high and low Machiavellian men. *Journal of Personality*, 1981, *49*(4), 388-400.

Coopersmith, S. *The antecedents of self-esteem*. San Francisco: Freeman, 1967.

Crowne, D., and Marlowe, D. *The approval motive*. New York: Wiley, 1964.

Crumbaugh, J. Cross-validation of purpose-in-life test based on Frankl's concepts. *Journal of Individual Psychology*, 1968, *24*, 74-81.

Gergen, K.J. The functions and foibles of negotiating self-conception. In M.D. Lynch, A.A. Norem-Hebeisen, and K.J. Gergen, eds., *Self-concept: Advances in theory and research*. Cambridge, Mass.: Ballinger, 1981.

Gough, H.G. A sociological theory of psychopathy. *American Journal of Sociology*, 1948, *53*, 359-366.

Gough, H.G., and Peterson, D.R. The identification and measurement of predispositional factors in crime and delinquency. *Journal of Consulting Psychology*, 1952, *16*, 202-212.

Hogan, R. Moral conduct and moral character. *Psychological Bulletin*, 1973, *79*, 217-232.

————. *Personality theory*. Englewood Cliffs, N.J.: Prentice-Hall, 1976.

————. Apples and oranges. *Contemporary Psychology*, 1982a.

————. A socioanalytic theory of personality. In M. Page and R. Dienstbier, eds., *Nebraska Symposium on motivation*. Lincoln: University of Nebraska Press, 1982b.

Hogan, R., and Busch, C. Moral action as auto-interpretation. Unpublished manuscript, Johns Hopkins University, 1982.

Hogan, R., and Cheek, J. Identity, authenticity, and maturity. In T.R. Sarbin and K.E. Scheibe, eds., *Studies in social identity*. New York: Praeger, 1982.

Hogan, R., and Kurtines, W. Sources of conformity in unsocialized college students. *Journal of Abnormal Psychology*, 1972, *80*, 49-51.

Hutchings, B., and Mednick, S. Registered criminality in the adoptive and biological parents of registered male adoptees. In J. Higgins and B. Bell, eds., *Genetics, environment, and psychopathology*. New York: Elsevier, 1974, 215-227.

Jones, E.E.; Kanouse, D.E.; Kelly, H.H.; Nisbett, R.G.; Walins, S.; and Weiner, B. *Attribution: Perceiving the causes of behavior*. Morristown, N.J.: General Learning Press, 1971.

Jones, W.H., and Russell, D. The social reticence scale: An objective instrument to measure shyness. *Journal of Personality Assessment*, 1982.

Lieberman, A.F. Preschoolers competence with a peer: Relations of attachment and peer experience. *Child Development*, 1977, *48*, 1277-1287.

Lykken, D.T. A study of anxiety in the sociopathic personality. *Journal of Abnormal and Social Psychology*, 1957, *59*, 6-10.

Merton, R.K. Social structure and anomie. In R.K. Merton, *Social theory and social structure*. Glencoe, Ill.: Free Press, 1949, 125-133.

Mischel, W. *Personality and assessment*. New York: Wiley, 1968.

_____. Processes in delay of gratification. In L. Berkowitz, ed., *Advances in experimental social psychology*, vol. VII. New York: Academic Press, 1974.

Piaget, J. *The moral judgment of the child*. New York: Free Press, 1964.

Rathus, S. A thirty-item schedule for assessing assertive behavior. *Behavior Therapy*, 1973, *4*, 398-406.

Rokeach, M. *The open and closed mind*. New York: Basic Books, 1960.

Rotter, J. Generalized expectancies for internal vs. external control of reinforcement. *Psychological Monographs*, 1966, *80* (Whole no. 609).

Scheff, T. *Being mentally ill*. Chicago: Aldine, 1966.

Snyder, M. Self-monitoring of expressive behavior. *Journal of Personality and Social Psychology*, 1974, *30*, 526-537.

Taylor, J. A personality scale for manifest anxiety. *Journal of Abnormal and Social Psychology*, 1953, *48*, 285-290.

Tennenbaum, D. Personality and criminality: A summary and implications of the literature. *Journal of Criminal Justice*, 1977, *5*, 225-235.

Yochelson, S., and Samenow, S.E. *The criminal personality*, vols. I, II. New York: Aronson, 1976.

Zonderman, A.B. Inventory scale construction by the method of homogenous item composites. Unpublished manuscript, Johns Hopkins University, 1981.

2

Applications of Interpersonal-Maturity Theory to Offender Populations

Marguerite Q. Warren

Interpersonal-maturity theory was created in the 1950s by a group of psychologists struggling to understand the personalities of offenders. Since then the theory has been expanded and revised, and its relevance for research and implications for intervention programs with offenders have been tested. This chapter presents an overview of the theory and its applications.

The first statement of the theory by Sullivan, Grant, and Grant appeared in *Psychiatry* in 1957. I-level theory is best described as an ego-development theory, comparable to what has been described elsewhere as moral development (Kohlberg 1969);[1] character development (Peck and Havighurst 1960); conceptual development (Harvey, Hunt, and Schroder 1961); and ego development (Loevinger 1966). I-level theory had its antecedents in child development, psychoanalytic theory, Lewinian theory, phenomenological psychology, and social perception. The most influential psychoanalytic approach was that of Harry Stack Sullivan, with its emphasis on interpersonal interactions.

I-level theory is not a theory of delinquency, but a general theory of personality development. It describes psychological developmental in all individuals in seven successive levels of interpersonal maturity, ranging from the least mature (which resembles the interpersonal interactions of a newborn infant) to an ideal of social maturity that is rarely, if ever, reached.

Each stage is defined by a crucial interpersonal problem that must be solved before further progress can occur. Not all individuals work their way through each stage; some may become fixed at a particular level. The successive levels are seen as definable points along a continuum of interpersonal development. It is assumed that individual delinquents will be found at various points along the continuum, like the individuals of any other population. The point is not that individuals are delinquent because they are immature,[2] but that the meaning of an individual's delinquency and the nature of the intervention strategies required will be clearer if his or her maturity level is identified.

During the late 1950s and early 1960s the theory served as a basis for a number of intervention studies with adult offenders. The first of these was conducted with Naval and Marine Corp court-martialed prisoners in a Navy Retraining Command (Grant and Grant 1959). Closed-living-unit groups of high- (I_4 and I_5), low- (I_2 and I_3), and mixed- (I_2-I_5) maturity-level subjects were randomly allocated to three types of training regimes, each run by a three-person treatment team. Team A used intensive group counseling, team C a strict-but-fair disciplinary regime. Team B used a mixture of the two approaches.

High-maturity subjects generally did significantly better than low-maturity ones on return to military duty. Teams A and B were significantly more successful with high- than with low-maturity subjects. Although the success rate for low-maturity subjects was highest with team C, this difference was not statistically significant. This study was a forerunner of studies of homogeneous programming for offenders and of the matching of treatment style to offender needs.

From 1961 through 1975 a series of experimental studies collectively known as the *differential-treatment studies* (Warren 1976) were conducted with juvenile offenders in the California Youth Authority. All these studies used a form of classification by I-level resulting from theoretical and empirical expansions during 1960 and 1961 (Grant 1961). Until then little systematic effort had been made to define subtypes within the I-level groups. Thus little attention had been given to the implications of differences within levels for treatment planning. The major impetus to this elaboration of the maturity-level classification was the need to develop rational treatment-control strategies for different types of delinquents in an experimental program called the Community Treatment Project (CTP).

The elaboration occurred in two areas—the definition of the subtypes within I-levels and preliminary descriptions of the differential treatment strategies. The assessment of I-level is based on individuals' ways of perceiving the world—for example, the complexity and differentiation with which they see themselves and others. The assessment of subtype within I-level represents an attempt to characterize individuals' typical modes of response to their view of the world. Although the maturity-level classification was theoretically derived, the subtype categories were empirically derived, based on observations of response patterns among delinquents within each I-level group. As a result, nine delinquent subtypes were identified (Warren et al. 1966).

Concepts of I-Level

According to I-level theory, all individuals have at any time a relatively consistent way of looking at the world and at themselves. Whatever individuals' experience is interpreted through their own social-perceptual frame of reference, which changes over time in ways that have a pattern that can be described. The social-perceptual frame of reference arises from an interaction between what they were born with and what they experience, out of which develops a relatively consistent set of expectations—a working philosophy of life. This nexus of expanding experience, expectations, and perceptions makes up the core of the personality. Social interaction is crucial in the development of this core, helping to elaborate the basic potential with which a person is born. The core of personality is not stable in content but is a framework around which various contents can be organized. In this sense, consistency and stability of the organization of the personality can be hypothesized.

The normal pattern of psychological development follows a trend of increasing involvement with people, objects, and social institutions. These involvements generate new situations containing inherent problems of perceptual discrimination about relationships between the self and the external environment. These discriminations lead to a cognitive restructuring of experience and expectancy. A new reference scheme is developed and a new level of integration achieved. Each new level of integration is the psychological counterpart of an increasingly efficient optical lens in the physical world. The more advanced the sequence of integration, the less the likelihood of perceptual distortion. With growth, persons can see themselves and the world more completely and operate more effectively.

The developmental sequence along the continuum of interpersonal maturity is not age specific. Because of differences in growth patterns, four-year-olds will not all have reached the same level of interpersonal maturity. As with physical growth, spurts occur at different times. The *order* of the steps, however, can be theoretically defined. Individuals reach a given stage of development by passing through each preceding step, not by skipping steps. In this way the theory resembles other ego-development theories.

The dimensions of the levels of interpersonal maturity include the way individuals perceive the world, the way they perceive themselves and others, and the relationships among these. The following discussion describes the characteristics of individuals at each level—what they have in common and how it differs from the characteristics of individuals at earlier and later points on the continuum. The focus is on the whole individual, not on isolated traits, behavior or feelings.

One major dimension concerns perceptual differentiation: how many and what kinds of distinctions the person tends to make in describing aspects of the world. The continuum represents an increasing capacity to look at the world in a complex and abstract way. In many ways individuals who are higher on this continuum are better off than those who are lower in their ability to function in a complex society. If people assume that everyone sees life just as they do, they may not comprehend what is going on in their interactions with others. Children who are significantly retarded in this socialization process are vulnerable because they cannot anticipate the impact of their behavior on others or of other's behavior on them. In this sense it is advantageous to progress as far as possible along the developmental continuum.

As previously stated, some persons become fixed at a particular level. Such persons maintain their position protectively, because there is something they cannot perceive or integrate. It may be too painful to grow, or there may be a lack of stimulation for growth.

The theory does not allow for regression in the usual sense. For example, a person does not retreat from I_4 to I_2 when sick and wanting to be babied. Once having seen that people are complex and that they play roles, the individual does not lose this perception even when feeling bad. *Behavioral* regression may occur, but *social-perceptual* regression does not.

Behavior is not an index of I-level. Any behavior may have several meanings; it is the meaning, not the behavior, that is relevant to identifying I-level. It is not that behavior is irrelevant, but it is not a referent for I-level. Behavior is, however, a major referent for identifying subtypes within I-level categories.

Integration Levels in Normal Development

The world of the newborn infant consists primarily of physiological tensions and satisfactions. Physiological needs being met or not met constitute the only distinction the newborn makes. Infants have not yet identified where they end and the rest of the world begins. Children's early exploratory movements begin to establish that distinction. They learn that interacting with different parts of themselves is different from interacting with the furniture. Biting the side of the crib is different from biting their own toes. We call these kinds of distinctions the *self/nonself separation*. Some childhood schizophrenics do not make this distinction. Theoretically, the integration of separateness from the world occurs at the first step on the continuum of development of interpersonal maturity: I_1.

The next developmental stage, I_2, has to do with early distinctions between persons and objects. Once aware of the distinction between self and nonself, developing personalities gradually perceive barriers to satisfaction and become concerned in a primitive way with how to control the rest of the world. Time and space are felt as delays to immediate gratification, and infants become vaguely aware that elements in the world also may act as barriers to gratification. Meeting such resistance, babies discover differences in the ways nonself elements interact with them. While continuing to deal with objects as if they were animate, children find that interactions with objects are relatively predictable, whereas interactions with persons are more variable. The child is not yet aware of feelings in others. At this stage of development, reality is still totally related to the child's own needs. The child is no longer the whole world, but he or she is still the hub of it. If needs are not being met, the child is aware that something is wrong. Through trial and error, children begin to solve this problem by attempting to find particular people who can play the role of giver. Children who are continually deprived become baffled, helpless, and fearful. Children whose needs are fairly regularly met feel secure enough to begin making further differentiations.

Children whose needs are met at the I_2 stage begin to observe that they themselves can play a part in getting their needs met. Fairly young children who are starting to talk begin to see that if they ask for things nicely, they are more apt to get them than if they yell or stamp their feet. They may also learn that if they stamp their feet a lot, they will get what they want. In either case they are learning that their behavior has something to do with whether they get what they want.

The assumption that a few rules or formulas are appropriate in all situations and with all individuals is an I_3 characteristic. At this stage children, to some extent, see other people as objects from which to get what they want, and rules as magic talismans of control. They try to use formulas to obtain giving behavior from the external world. They may test the limits of the rules, seeking to discover the unchanging formulas that will help them handle all problems that arise.

Normally developing children, growing up in an atmosphere of love and support, begin fairly early, probably by four or five years of age, to learn that dealing with the world is more complicated than applying simple formulas. The formulas do not work equally well with all people or in all situations. One formula says that when you behave in a disapproved way but say you are sorry, everything will be all right. If a child injures his or her baby brother and makes him cry, however, "I'm sorry" may not dissipate all of the mother's anger.

Assuming a general security for children in their families, such incidents can lead to growth-producing anxiety that can promote further distinctions about what is going on inside the individuals with whom the child interacts and can teach something about the differential appropriateness of the formulas. Children's behavior is still primarily influenced by their own needs; but as they move into the I_4 stage, they become aware of others' expectations also. A child, by introjecting into his own reaction system the responses of others to his behavior, begins to develop an internalized value system. This stage of beginning identification with adult models is sometimes called *superego development*. Children at the I_4 stage discover through play activities and fantasy conversations that they can resemble the powerful figures in their life. Such role playing leads to greater differentiation and capacity for social integration. We call this stage *global identification*—an identification with an oversimplified model with no weaknesses or inadequacies. Small children may admire courageous astronauts, want to be equally brave, and judge themselves harshly because they are scared of the dark. They accept the global image as representing the whole person. I_4 children evaluate themselves and others as *good* or *bad*. No ambiguities are tolerated. Because of this rigidity, children at this stage may feel self-critical when they fail to live up to their new standards.

Although, as indicated earlier, signs of beginning movement from I_3 to I_4 may be seen in children as young as four or five, many children do not make this step until early adolescence. The next step, from I_4 to I_5, does not appear to take place before middle or late adolescence. At the I_5 level, young persons begin to see that people are more complex than represented by the earlier frame of reference. They can handle ambiguities in people and situations without the harsh judgments of the I_4. They can respond to others as whole personalities—composites of needs, feelings, and behavior. They become aware of continuity in their own lives and the lives of others. Instead of the earlier indiscriminant use of roles, they begin to differentiate roles for themselves and others that are appropriate for different situations. They come to comprehend what others are feeling, and this frees them from some of the problems of overly intense identifications. Empathy with a variety of other kinds of persons becomes possible. I_5-level persons may tolerate and even enjoy the complexity and ambiguity in others, but role ambiguities in themselves may still arouse anxieties. They may be bothered by the incompatibility of the roles they play; they may feel diffuse, wondering which of their roles is basic—the "real me."

At the I_6 level one perceives differences between oneself and one's social roles. Individuals see that they need not become the role but may carry the role as a mode of response. This frame of reference allows individuals to see people, including themselves, as relatively enduring, stable organisms; they know that people are more than their various roles and shifting behavior.

At the I_7 level, perception of integrating processes in self and others occurs. The person is not only aware of self and roles but also begins to comprehend focusing or integrating processes. Along with increasing awareness of the process of integration in themselves, individuals begin to get some perspective on previous modes of experiencing. They no longer seek absolute realities but see a variety of ways of perceiving and integrating, some of which lead to more adequate expectations and hypotheses than others. This development greatly increases their capacity to understand and deal with people who are functioning at integration levels other than their own.

Developmental Stages and Delinquent Subtypes among Adolescents

As is seen from descriptions of the normal developmental stages, an individual moving toward physiological maturity while remaining at lower stages perceptually may appear increasingly deviant to society. Social institutions assume that individuals have reached an I_4 stage—feeling personally accountable for their behavior, having an internal evaluator that tells them what is right and what is wrong, understanding that people differ from each other in their needs and behavior, and so forth. Those individuals for whom these assumptions do not hold are at considerable disadvantage in understanding what is happening around them. The life of an I_2 at age nineteen still focuses on trying to maintain a position of comfort, on getting needs met in an unpredictable and arbitrary world. During adolescence I_3s are still searching for structure in novel situations so that stereotyped rules for behaving can be applied. They continue trying to control their worlds with overly simple formulas and are not attuned to the things going on inside others.

As indicated earlier, once a classification by social-perceptual dimensions (I-level) has been determined, a further distinction can be made according to persons' typical ways of responding to and dealing with their view of the world (delinquent subtype). Although the maturity-level classification system was theoretically derived, the subtype categories were empirically derived; they were based on observations of patterns of response that occurred frequently within each I-level group in a delinquent population. Thus, while the assumption is made that growth as described by I-levels will characterize the development of all individuals, subtypes identified are assumed to be specific to a delinquent population. Research comparing delinquent and nondelinquent adolescents confirms a nonsignificant difference between the two groups with respect to maturity level. The research also confirms the second assumption: most delinquents fall within the subtype descriptions and most nondelinquents do not (Harris 1978; see also chapter 7).

Because almost all juvenile delinquents can be classified at three of the seven maturity levels—I_2, I_3, and I_4—those levels have been further subdivided into subtypes. Delinquents classified at I_2 deal with their perception of the world in two major ways. Similarly, there are three typical response styles among delinquents classified at I_3 and four typical styles among those classified at I_4. A brief description follows:

Maturity Level 2 (I_2)

Individuals whose interpersonal understanding and behavior are integrated at this level primarily demand that the world take care of them. They see others primarily as givers or withholders and have no conceptions of interpersonal refinement beyond this. They have poor capacity to explain, understand, or predict the behavior or reactions of others. They are not interested in things outside themselves except as a source of supply. They

behave impulsively, unaware of anything except the grossest effects of their behavior on others.
Subtypes include:

1. *Asocial, aggressive* (Aa) responds with active demands and open hostility when frustrated.
2. *Asocial, passive* (Ap) responds with whining, complaining, and withdrawal when frustrated.

Maturity Level 3 (I_3)

Individuals who are functioning at this level, though somewhat more differentiated than the I_2, still have social-perceptual deficiencies that lead to an underestimation of differences among others and between themselves and others. More than the I_2, they understand that their own behavior has something to do with whether or not they get what they want. They make an effort to manipulate their environment to bring about giving rather than denying responses. They do not operate from an internalized value system but rather seek external structure in terms of rules and formulas for operation. Their understanding of formulas is indiscriminate and oversimplified. They perceive the world and their part in it on a power dimension. Although they can learn to play a few stereotyped roles, they cannot understand the needs, feelings, and motives of another person who is different from themselves. They are unmotivated to achieve in a long-range sense or to plan for the future. Many of these features contribute to their inability to predict accurately the response of others to them.
Subtypes include:

3. *Passive conformist* (Cfm) responds with immediate compliance to whoever seems to have the power at the moment.
4. *Cultural conformist* (Cfc) responds with conformity to specific reference group, delinquent peers.
5. *Antisocial manipulator* (Mp) operates by attempting to undermine the power of authority figures and/or usurp the power for him- or herself.

Maturity Level 4 (I_4)

Individuals whose understanding and behavior are integrated at this level have internalized a set of standards by which they judge their own and others' behavior. They can perceive a level of interpersonal interaction in which individuals have expectations of each other and can influence each other. They show some ability to understand reasons for behavior and to relate to people emotionally and on a long-term basis. They are concerned about status and respect and are strongly influenced by people they admire. Identification at this stage is with an oversimplified model based on dichotomous definitions of good and bad. No ambiguities are tolerated. Because of the rigidity of these standards, the person at this stage often feels self-critical and guilty.

Subtypes include:

6. *Neurotic, acting out* (Na) responds to underlying guilt with attempts to avoid conscious anxiety and condemnation of self.
7. *Neurotic anxious* (Nx) responds with symptoms of emotional disturbance to conflict produced by feelings of inadequacy and guilt.
8. *Situational emotional reaction* (Se) responds to immediate family or personal crisis by acting out.
9. *Cultural identifier* (Ci) responds to identification with a deviant value system by living out delinquent beliefs.

The maturity-level 5 category is used for less than 1 percent of the juvenile-delinquent population, and Harris found only 2 percent in a non-delinquent adolescent population (1978). Adult offender populations have been shown to have a higher percentage classified at this level, especially among drug offenders. Individuals at this stage can perceive and handle more ambiguities in people and situations. They are increasingly aware of complexity in self and others, aware of continuity in lives, more able to play roles appropriately. Empathy with various kinds of persons is possible.

Classification Methods and Occurrence of I-Level Groups

Before reporting the proportion of the juvenile-offender population that is classified in each subgroup, a brief description of the classification procedures is needed. The procedures used in the Community Treatment Project involved a semistructured interview that focused on the interviewee's perception of the world and response to it. The interviews were tape recorded so that two raters could independently identify the individual's I-level and subtype. An Interview Rating Questionnaire (Tolhurst et al. 1970) consisting of 193 rating items can be used by the interviewer as an aid in the rating process. Some clinical skill is required to make reliable ratings.

Attempts have been made to develop more structured methods for obtaining the classifications. Much of this work has been done by Carl Jesness of the California Youth Authority, who uses a complex computer scoring procedure based on data from the Jesness Inventory (155 true/false items) and the Jesness Behavior Checklist (80 items to be rated by the youth and correctional staff) (Jesness 1974). An additional method involves a highly structured interview, developed by Marcelle Frechette of the University of Montreal, which has been used with French-speaking delinquents in Quebec. The more highly structured assessment procedures appear to produce slightly lower average maturity-level ratings than does the semistructured interview. Provided trained raters are available, the open interview seems preferable for obtaining perceptual material.

Most of the information on proportions of offenders falling in the various classification categories comes from populations of juvenile delinquents (Warren 1978). Differences depend on the age range represented in the population and on whether structured or semistructured classification methods are used. With a population of more than 1,000 delinquents ranging in age from 11 to 19, and using the semistructured-interview classification method, the CTP found 4 percent classified at I_2, 31 percent at I_3, 64 percent at I_4, and less than 1 percent at I_5. Similar proportions were identified among English-speaking delinquent youths in Quebec. Samples of adult offenders have been shown to have a higher percentage of I_5s (Heide 1982). The largest I_3 subgroup was passive conformist for most of the samples, and uniformly the largest I_4 categories were neurotic anxious and neurotic acting out.

Implications of the Theory for Intervention with Offenders

One way to test a personality theory is by applying it in a field setting. The following sections illustrate the use of the theory as a conceptual frame for studying the treatment of delinquents.[3] A major source of information about the use of I-level classification in intervention programs comes from the group of studies referred to earlier as the differential-treatment programs operated within the California Youth Authority from 1961 to 1975 (Warren 1976). These programs attempt to identify the kinds of treatment settings, treater styles, and treatment modalities that were most successful with the various I-level subtypes of delinquent youths.

As indicated earlier, a major part of the definition of each subtype identifies the specific paths into delinquency for youths classified in that category. Once these paths are identified, goals of intervention can be established. For example, I_3 passive conformists see the world on a power dimension; on that totem pole, they are low men. They do not operate from internalized value systems but rather seek external structure in terms of rules and formulas for operation. Youths in this category usually fear and respond with strong compliance to peers and adults who seem to have the upper hand at the moment or seem more adequate than themselves. They consider themselves to be lacking in social knowhow and usually expect to be rejected by others. Delinquency usually results from a desperate need to obtain the social approval of peers by behaving in whatever way is prescribed, or from the fear of rejection by significant adults.

Treatment goals for the passive conformist include growth along the maturity continuum (at least to the point at which an internalized value system operates, or I_3 to I_4); and a change in self-definition toward security in decision making, ability to meet others' demands, assertiveness, and personal worth (Warren et al. 1966).

The goals of treatment, then, grow out of the nature of the problem for each of the subtypes, and the differential treatment strategies derive from the goals. Treatment strategies include at a minimum prescriptions for the characteristics of the setting in which the youth will be treated, the characteristics of the treater, and the specific treatment methods to be used.

Treatment Settings

Six of the California Youth Authority differential-treatment programs attempted to study the impact of different treatment settings on the various I-level subtypes. Three of these programs focused on the important correctional question of whether treatment in an institutional setting is preferable to treatment in a community-based program. The Community Treatment Project, phase I (CTP I), was a study of the differential impact of intensive community treatment versus incarceration on the various subtypes of the delinquent population (Palmer 1971). Including all classification categories, random assignment was made to (1) an intensive treatment program located in the youth's home community or (2) the regular Youth Authority Program (ten to twelve months in a training school followed by a period of parole). In the experimental community-based program, a differential-treatment plan (based on the youth's I-level subtype) was developed. Many of the delinquents could return to their own families if a treater helped the family provide the kind of home atmosphere the youth needed to continue growing and to stop delinquent behavior. If the youth could not return to his or her own home, every effort was made to place the youth in placement matching his or her specific needs.

The question asked in CTP I was which of the I-level subtypes do better in a community-based program, which types do better following an institutional stay, and which types do equally well (or poorly) in both settings. Outcome criteria included arrests, recidivism rates, favorable and unfavorable discharges from the Youth Authority, and postdischarge convictions. The benefits of treatment in the community setting were greatest for youths identified as neurotic. The antisocial-manipulator and the cultural-conformist (together called *power-oriented*) youths did better following an institutional stay. The passive-conformist group performed somewhat better in the community program than in the traditional program, although the outcome criteria were not consistent.

The Community Treatment Project, phase II (Palmer 1974) compared three programs, two in a community setting and one involving the traditional Youth Authority program of incarceration followed by parole. The first community program was built around a differential model (different and appropriate intervention for each delinquent subtype), a replication of the experimental program of phase I but conducted in another city. The second community program used a different treatment model, guided group interaction. Again one research question asked the comparative benefits of community and institution programs for each of the I-level subtypes. Findings were similar to those of phase I.

The Community Treatment Project, phase III (Palmer 1976), was also a study of treatment setting, comparing differential treatment begun in a residential setting (with later assignment to the community program) with differential treatment begun directly in the community setting, on various subgroups of offenders. The study focused particularly on those types of offenders who had been unsuccessful in either the community or institutional programs of CTP I and II—the hard-to-reach youths. Those classified as the more seriously disturbed neurotics benefited most from the residence-first approach; the power-oriented group benefited little from the residence-first program; and the passive-conformist group did not benefit at all from the residence-first program and did somewhat better with direct community release.

Combining these findings from CTP Phases I, II and III, it appears that the neurotic group (acting out and anxious) responded very well to a differential-treatment approach. This group can be divided on the basis of extent-of-disturbance criteria (defined by Palmer 1974), in order to recommend either the direct community release or the residence-first program. The traditional training-school program still represented the best alternative for the power-oriented group (cultural conformist and antisocial manipulator). The direct release into the differential-treatment-oriented community program seemed the most satisfactory alternative for the passive-conformist group.

In addition to these groups, the rest of the CTP population was classified in four rarely occurring groups, two I_2 subtypes and two I_4 subtypes. Too few cases were available in these groups to allow for definitive conclusions about preferred treatment setting.[4]

Three further studies assessed or compared various intervention atmospheres among community programs or among institutional programs. One of these, Differential Treatment Environments for Delinquents (Palmer 1972), was a study of five types of group homes, each representing a treatment environment specifically related to the growth and development needs of particular types of delinquent youths. In this program, the home atmosphere established by various group-home parents was determined and matched to the living-environment needs of I-level subtypes. Three long-term placement homes were established: (1) a *protective* home for the most immature and dependent subtypes (I_2 and I_3 passive conformist); (2) a *containment* home for middle-maturity youths needing very high structure (I_3 cultural conformist and antisocial manipulator); and (3) a *boarding* home for higher-maturity youths who needed an atmosphere of relative freedom (I_4 neurotic). Two additional homes were developed for short-term placements. One of these was a very highly structured home for use as a detention setting, the second a temporary-care home for youths not needing high structure.

All the homes except the short-term high-structure home were easy to establish using nonprofessionally trained group-home parents. CTP boys in long-term homes performed somewhat better than those not placed. The boarding home for high-maturity youths and the temporary-care home were particularly successful. High-maturity youths profited more from long-term placement than antisocial-manipulator and cultural-conformist youths.

An additional study of treatment environments was conducted in an institutional setting, the Preston Typology Study (Jesness 1971). Youths of six I-level subtypes were assigned to homogeneous or heterogeneous living units. In the homogeneous units, only youths of one I-level subtype lived together in a fifty-boy lodge. Homogeneity in the living units consistently decreased unit-management problems. Significantly fewer rule infractions, peer problems, or disciplinary transfers out of the units for closer confinement were found, primarily for three of the six subtypes: antisocial manipulator, cultural conformist, and acting-out neurotic. Other subtypes did equally well, in management terms, in homogeneous and heterogeneous living environments.

The final study of intervention setting was the Differential Education Project (Andre and Mahan 1972), conducted at two Youth Authority institutions. It involved determining the differential impact of homogeneous (by delinquent subtype) classrooms with matched teachers versus regular heterogeneous school assignments. For five subtypes of delinquents, characteristics of preferred teaching plans (atmosphere, methods, motivation procedures, control strategies, curriculum) were defined. The teachers in the homogeneous classrooms were enthusiastic. Observed teaching styles varied from highly unstructured to highly structured, from group focused to individual focused, and from very high student-teacher contact to low contact. Students in all the homogeneous classrooms did as well as or better than those in the regular classrooms. Of the five subtypes, the passive conformist benefited most from the homogenous classroom, showing both superior academic achievement and improvement in self-concept and attitudes toward school.

In summary, the data suggest that it does not matter which types of youth are placed in which types of settings. Delinquent behavior can probably be reduced in both community and residential programs by classifying youth and carefully matching youth and setting characteristics.

Treater Style

A number of the differential-treatment programs matched treater style to the characteristics and needs of particular subtypes of youths. This program element began in CTP I and continued in the differential-treatment program of CTP II. CTP III compared the impact of specialist (matched) treaters and generalist treaters. Worker matching was also a treatment component of the group-home project, the Preston Typology Study, and the Differential Education Project.

The rationale for matching treaters and types of youth is based on two assumptions. First, few treaters work equally well with all types of youths or with all types of treatment approaches. Although most clinical training programs aim to produce treaters with the capacity to deal effectively with the full range of clients, the typical correctional worker cannot work equally well with the entire range of delinquent subtypes.[5] The matching procedure attempts to capitalize on the special talents and concerns of specific workers and to minimize the possible effects of their areas of lesser talent or interest in certain kinds of problem individuals.

Second, treater matching operates at two levels, conceptual and emotional. Conceptually, workers understand some problems better than others. Some treaters have difficulty comprehending neurosis or understanding deviant values. Emotionally, not all treaters get the same payoff from certain kinds of client progress. Some may feel a great sense of accomplishment when a delinquent finally finishes a whole semester of school or holds a job for a month. Others only feel they have done a good day's work when clients show insight into the dynamics of their problems. Since the subtypes of youths vary considerably on dimensions reflecting improvement, the morale of treaters can be considerably affected by the cases assigned to them (Warren 1977b).

Palmer identified five treater styles corresponding to the five most frequently occurring I-level subtypes (1967, 1973). The major matching procedure involves a long taped interview with subsequent rating on 105 rating items to identify excellent matches, satisfactory matches, nonmatches, and negative matches for each subtype group. Other treater classification procedures include preference questionnaires and supervisor-peer ratings.

Research focused primarily on comparing youths who were well matched with treaters to those who were not well matched, all other conditions held constant. In a study comparing delinquents in CTP I, both the well-matched and unmatched youths were in the differential-treatment-oriented community-based program, on comparable-sized case loads with the same treaters and with comparable resources. Using a variety of outcome criteria (parole suspensions, revocations of parole and recommitments by the courts, postdischarge convictions, and the like), matching made a significant difference for the total group of youths,[6] for I_3 youths separately, for I_4 youths separately, and for a number of the individual subtypes. Matching of youths and treater style made the greatest difference in the case of subtype I_4 acting-out neurotic, with matched subjects having a revocation rate of 25 percent and unmatched 61 percent by the end of a two-year parole period. Not only did matching make a difference during the period of actual contact between the treater and the youth, but the data showed a carry-over of this impact four years beyond discharge from the correctional agency. Data for subtype I_4 anxious neurotic, for example, showed convictions for 60 percent of the unmatched group and only 33 percent of the matched group at this postdischarge point. It is clear that matching is more than a theoretical exercise.

Treatment Modalities

Two of the Youth Authority differential-treatment projects compared the impact of different treatment methods on various I-level subtypes. CTP II randomly assigned youths in the various I-level categories to community-based programs using (1) the differential-treatment model (DTM) (Warren et al. 1966) developed in CTP I, or (2) guided group interaction (GGI), a treatment method growing out of differential association theory (Empey and Lubeck 1971). Guided group interaction appeared to have the greatest positive impact on those offenders who were comfortable with confrontational interactions (such as acting-out neurotic or antisocial manipulator), whereas subtypes representing more dependent patterns (anxious neurotic, passive conformist) more quickly dropped out of the program. Overall, the differential-treatment model appeared to be more successful than the guided-group-interaction model, as reflected in recidivism rates (Palmer 1976). The outcome may relate to the fact that, whereas the GGI program worked only with the youths themselves, the DTM program worked also with their families and schools.

The Northern California Youth Center program was also a study of treatment methods (Jesness et al. 1972). It compared the impact of a behavior-modification program or a transactional-analysis program on the various I-level subtypes. Each of two Youth Authority training schools built its entire program around one of the two theoretical frameworks, and youths of each subtype were randomly assigned to the two programs. The behavior-modification program appeared to be particularly appropriate for delinquents identified as I_2 and I_3 cultural conformist. The transactional-analysis program, on the other hand, was most appropriate for those categorized as I_3 antisocial manipulator. For the I_4 delinquents the recidivism data did not indicate an advantage for either treatment modality, although both programs produced lower recidivism rates than the more traditional training-school programs.

Beyond the two differential-treatment programs aimed specifically at assessing treatment methods, CTP I and II obtained further information about the usefulness of certain treatment modalities. Family-group therapy was tried in these programs with the families of a variety of I-level subtypes. With few exceptions, this family approach, which requires the willingness of all family members to consider the family's problem, was successful only with the families of I_4 delinquents. With families of I_2 and I_3 youths, family education was more appropriate. Psychodrama techniques were effective in increasing the social-perceptual skills of I_2 youths, and role training was effective with I_3 youths. Psychotherapy, individually or in peer groups, was clearly inappropriate with I_2 and I_3 delinquents but had some success with I_4 neurotic youths.

Treatment with Specific Offender Subtypes

This section presents treatment rationales and strategies used in the community-based programs for the three most frequently occurring subtypes. It concludes with an assessment of our current state of knowledge about the treatment of the various I-level subtypes.

Neurotic Youths

Individuals classified in the neurotic category have reached the I_4 stage of ego development. In addition, as the label *neurotic* suggests, such individuals have a good deal of internal anxiety, guilt, and dysfunctional behavior. Delinquency thus has some private meaning and does not represent simply a material gain or a response to cultural pressure. It may involve the acting out of a family problem, an identity crisis, or a long-standing internal conflict.

The anxious subtype of the neurotic category shows various symptoms of emotional disturbance, such as depression or psychosomatic complaints. Tensions and fears usually result from conflict produced by feelings of failure, inadequacy, or underlying guilt. The acting-out subtype has little toler-

for conscious anxiety and often attempts to deny feelings of inadequacy, rejection, or self-condemnation by verbally attacking others, using boisterous distractions, or playing a variety of games.

Neurotic youths are typically prosocial. In behaving delinquently youths often violate their own beliefs, thus perpetuating their guilt. Self-concepts of neurotic youths have two major parts. They typically do not define themselves as delinquent, but self-definitions as crippled, hurt, inferior, or inadequate are common. On the other hand, they also present a compensatory image of actual or potential worthiness or accomplishment. The combination does not provide any stable inner buffer against deviance.

Neurotic youths are typically from neurotic families in which at least one parent also carries a great deal of guilt and a poor self-image. Family life is characterized by poor communication and a feeling on everyone's part that other family members are not meeting unspoken expectations. Often the delinquent youth seems to be bearing the family burden or making a rescue attempt. The primary feeling that permeates the family is one of ambivalence: members care about each other but also feel that they are not cherished and have somehow been hurt. Thus the bonds to society that grow out of attachments to parents are weakened or intermittent.

In treating neurotic youths, there is always the problem of simply substituting the neurotic nondelinquent for the neurotic delinquent. The Community Treatment Project was certainly committed to reducing or eliminating delinquency among the individuals assigned to it. In the case of the neurotic offender, however, it was held that the neurosis was the heart of the behavior problem. Treatment goals listed for the neurotic subtypes included: "reduction or resolution of internal conflicts; reduction of fear of own needs and impulses, and of use of defense mechanisms in harmful ways (to self or others); changed self-image in the direction of capacity for enjoyment and happiness . . . , sense of personal worth and of potential worth (as a mature person) to others. . . " (Warren et al. 1966). For the neurotic youth who did well in and following the CTP program, important factors seemed to be a disengagement from family problems, the availability of a strong and caring identification figure (the treater), and improved self-esteem.

The neurotic group is often dismissed casually because they seem to represent a less serious threat than do asocial or antisocial youths, in part because they are more understandable, and second, because our clinical training prepares us to treat the neurotic patient. Although the California research supports the supposition that we were more successful in treating this group than other subtypes, a number of factors show the importance of expending considerable treatment energy on this group. First, when the neurotic group proceeded through the usual correctional program without receiving the differential treatment conducted in the CTP, the failure rate was high, especially for the neurotic acting-out cases. These cases do not cure themselves; they do need treatment. Second, the neurotic group represents such a large proportion of the serious delinquent population that improving the chances of success of this group leads to a large overall success-rate increase for a correctional agency. Third, although the success rate for the neurotic group was higher when relevant treatment was conducted, the failure rate was far from zero. Further, conducting the treatment was a challenge. The neurotic delinquent rarely sat regularly in the therapist's office ready to unravel his or her difficulties. Instead, treatment was often conducted on the run, while acting-out (often delinquent) behavior continued.

In every area of criminal-justice outcome measurement, neurotic youths did better under the experimental treatment conditions than under comparison conditions (Warren 1976), in the following areas:

1. Comparison youths had more than twice as many arrests as experimental youths for each month in the community.
2. Comparison cases had twice the rate of convictions.
3. On twenty-four-month parole follow-up, 45 percent of the experimentals and 66 percent of the comparison cases had failed on parole.
4. Within five years of first parole release, 77 percent of the experimentals and only 40 percent of the comparison cases were given a favorable discharge by the parole board.
5. On a four-year postdischarge follow-up, comparison cases were arrested 81 percent more often and convicted 63 percent more often than experimentals.

CTP findings have been criticized as reflecting change in processing, not change in offender behavior (Lerman 1975). Although for the first four findings it is difficult to separate out youth behavior and decision making within the Youth Authority that might have favored experimentals, the last finding cannot be explained by discretionary staff decisions since the subjects had not been under agency jurisdiction for four years.

On other outcome measures the differences between the experimental and comparison neurotic cases were small. The experimentals did slightly better in school adjustment. No differences in the area of paid employment appeared during the first year on parole; experimentals did slightly better during the second year. With respect to social adjustment as measured by the California Psychological Inventory, the neurotic acting-out experimentals and the neurotic anxious comparison cases showed more positive change. As mentioned earlier, neurotic youth who were well matched with treaters were significantly more successful than those who were not well matched.

Power-Oriented Youth

This group includes many of those described as antisocial-character-disorder children (Friedlander 1949). They have also been called *psychopathic* and *sociopathic*. Individuals in this category have reached the I_3 stage of ego development.

One of the subtypes in the power-oriented group, the antisocial manipulator, is aggressively counteractive to power, attempting to undermine or circumvent the intent of authority figures. These youths do not wish to conform to standards set by anyone else and often attempt to take on a power role for themselves. The second subtype, the cultural conformist, comprises individuals who think of themselves as delinquent and tough, often earning status from gang membership. Neither subtype has close or trusting relationships with others; both attempt to create an image of emotional indifference and invulnerability. Antisocial behavior is not ego-alien for either of the subtypes.

The antisocial-manipulator subtype sometimes, especially under stress, appears openly angry and threatening. These youths are often described by correctional staff who try to control them as resentful, persistently trying to be the center of attention, verbally and/or physically explosive, suspicious, and/or grandiose in their thinking. They seem to pride themselves on their ability to successfully manipulate or outsmart others.

These individuals typically come from homes with a cold, brutal, and rejecting parent (usually the opposite-sexed parent) and a weak, helpless, and superficial same-sexed parent. The facade of invincibility used by this type of youth is often an unconscious cover-up for long-standing, intense fears of and primitive dependence on the abusive parent. Protective attachments to family are missing; the youth is contemptuous of the same-sexed parent and hates and fears the opposite-sex parent. The extent of this distrust of others precludes good peer relationships. The manipulativeness and unwillingness to conform leads to rejection in school and in youth agencies. There is no belief system that disallows deviance. Antisocial-manipulator youths define themselves as cynical, cool, smooth, delinquent, powerful—a definition in no way at odds with committing offenses.

Although the cultural-conformist subtype shows a higher rate of violent offenses than any other, the presenting picture to the authority system includes withdrawn affect, although barely concealed anger may be visible. These youths typically come from one-parent homes, usually mother only. The parent may be overwhelmed with financial and emotional problems. The youth may be treasured as an infant but ignored when the next child arrives. Such youths become street children, getting needs met by older siblings and peers and learning that adults are not need meeters. For this subtype, as for the antisocial-manipulator subtype, the parent(s) usually seem to have stopped developing at I_3. The children, at least during adolescence, do not seem to develop beyond the level of the parents.

For both power-oriented subtypes, treatment goals in CTP included growth toward I_4 and an increase in social perceptiveness and predictive ability; reduced fear of close relationships with others; a more direct expression of dependency needs; and changed self-definition in the direction of nondelinquency, personal worth, real adequacy, and maturity.

The CTP findings (Palmer 1976) indicate how little we know about treating this kind of offender.

1. The experimental subjects in this category were arrested 20 percent less often than comparison cases, but there was no difference on conviction rates.
2. Parole failure at twenty-four months was 40 percent for experimentals and 66 percent for comparison cases.
3. Favorable discharges were fewer for the experimentals; 43 percent compared with 53 percent of the comparison cases, and 23 percent of the experimentals compared with 15 percent of the comparison cases received unfavorable discharges.
4. Postdischarge arrests were 58 percent higher and convictions 30 percent higher for experimentals.

The power-oriented experimentals showed more positive change than the comparison cases on both social and personal adjustment, as measured by the pre/post California Psychological Inventory.

Thus, although the picture is mixed, CTP could certainly not claim to have discovered an effective treatment for power-oriented youth. The matched worker did not increase success for this group compared with the other categories. The differential-treatment-oriented residential program did not benefit this type of youth. There is some evidence that CTP treatment worked better with younger youths (those who entered the program at age 15 or less) than with older youths.

Passive-Conformist Youths

Individuals in this category have reached the same stage of social maturity as that described for the power-oriented group (I_3). They differ in their orientation toward the power dimension, however. These indivduals view others as powerful and themselves as weak. They are dominated by the need for social approval, complying almost automatically with whoever they think has the power at the moment. They usually expect to be rejected by others no matter how hard they try to please them. Although such persons long to be accepted by their peer group, they usually achieve no more than fringe membership. Offense behavior most often results from an attempt to gain peer approval.

The family situation for passive-conformist youths is characterized by instability and inconsistency. There appears to be some concern for the youth by a parent who, however, cannot provide a stable structure for growth. In many cases there is also a rejecting parent, whose approval the youth cannot win. Thus the youth has not seen love and strength combined in either parent. As with the power-oriented youth, the parents of the passive conformist provide neither a satisfactory identification model nor an atmosphere in which growth beyond I_3 can occur.

Passive-conformist youths present themselves as sincere, cooperative, and well intentioned but admit that they cannot control themselves or their environment. They feel dependent on others' rules for keeping out of trouble. The passive conformist wants to be good and hopes that others will be helpful and understanding. With this self-definition, it is a matter of chance whether others will encourage delinquency or law-abiding behavior. Treatment goals especially include a change in the youths' self-definition in the direction of security in decision making, ability to meet the demands of others, ability to assert themselves with others, capacity for growth, and feelings of personal worth. An additional goal involves maturing to the point at which an internal evaluator guides the youth's behavior from I_3 to I_4.

The outcome measures for this type of offender in CTP showed a mixed picture (Palmer 1976). Experimental subjects did well during the period of matched worker contact with them. They were arrested half as often and convicted four times less often than the comparison cases. On twenty-four-month parole follow-up, 51 percent were revoked, compared with 59 percent of the comparison cases. Within five years of first parole release, 78 percent (compared with 54 percent of comparison cases) received a favorable discharge; during the same period, 6 percent (compared with 14 percent of the comparison cases) received an unfavorable discharge. One-quarter of the cases moved from I_3 to I_4. Postdischarge convictions showed the success rate for experimentals not to hold up beyond agency contact, however, with comparison cases outperforming experimentals four years beyond discharge. Further, the experimentals did not perform as well as the comparison cases in the areas of school and paid employment. No difference was shown between the two groups on pre/post social adjustment; both groups showed positive change.

It is difficult to interpret these findings. Other studies have shown a similar reversal effect in which treated subjects show success during the treatment period but later fail (Jesness 1965; Cohen and Filipczak 1971).

One possibility is that during the treatment period but not later, discretionary staff decisions gave some advantage to the experimentals. Alternatively, one can blame social conditions, suggesting that even though the treated individuals improved, the environment to which the person returned made continuing success impossible. The problem is that CTP wishes to take credit for the long-term continuing success of the neurotic youth. If social conditions can make failures out of the passive-conformist youths, social conditions must then be given credit for the success of the neurotic group. Perhaps we can justify a difference, however. The neurotic youths are at a higher ego stage than the passive-conformist youths and thus less dependent on their external world. Seventy-five percent of the passive-conformist group ended treatment still focused primarily on the external world for clues as to how to behave. Under these conditions, chance plays an important role in subsequent law violation.

Other Subtypes

The remaining I-level subtypes were used to classify only 12 percent of the serious delinquent population. The two I_2 subtypes include children who were very primitive and damaged by brutal life experiences. The I_2 asocial, passive group was quite successful in CTP, showing lower recidivism than the comparison group and also showing growth to I_3 for 50 percent of the subtype group (Palmer 1970).[7] For both I_2 and I_3 youth there appeared to be an advantage to beginning treatment before age 15.

The two rarely occurring I_4 subtypes include youths who are developing in relatively normal ways. The cultural-identifier subtype—the youth who has identified with a deviant subculture—was more successful following a period of incarceration than in the community program. The situational/emotional-disorder group includes individuals whose delinquency arises from a crisis occurring in adolescence. Such youths have high success rates following both the experimental and the traditional Youth Authority programs.

The following summary of intervention with the various delinquent subtypes can be offered.

1. For the most immature or unsocialized youths (I_2), both growth along the maturity continuum and reduced recidivism have been shown for a differential-treatment program in the community. For the more passive I_2 youths, a protective foster or group home is appropriate. Beyond the formal treatment period, a special protective environment is often called for, especially for those showing minimum growth. For the more aggressive I_2 youths, an institutional program may be required. In such a setting, behavior modification has been shown to be more successful than a psychodynamic program (transactional analysis).

2. For the I_3 passive-conformist youth, a community-based program appears to have advantages over an institutional program; but reduced delinquency rates are maintained only during the period of matched treater contact. Those passive conformists who do not move to an I_4 level during intensive treatment (about three-quarters of them) may require a continuing highly structured living situation to prevent further offense behavior.

3. Less is known about how to bring about positive change in the I_3 antisocial-manipulator group than in any other I-level subtype. Youths of this type did no better in a differential-treatment program than following traditional training-school incarceration. In an institutional setting a transactional-analysis program proved more successful than a behavior-modification program.

4. The evidence is persuasive that, for those youths classified as I_4 neurotic, a differential-treatment program can be developed that will decrease their chances of committing further offenses. A matched worker is crucial with this group, and the extent-of-emotional-disturbance ratings are important in deciding between a direct community program and a residence-first program.

It would be premature to suggest that any of these studies has contributed the final word on the relationships between types of youths and types of settings, treaters, or treatment modalities. In toto, however, the studies represent evidence of the need for adequately complex research before we make global statements about the ways to intervene with delinquents.

The series of studies in differential treatment elicited some of the complexities that interact in the correctional treatment process and began to sort out the contributions to success or failure of offender characteristics, treater characteristics, treatment settings, and treatment methods. Because a unifying theoretical orientation (I-level) guided the experimentation, each successive program grew logically out of the previous ones.

The Relevance of I-level Theory to Criminal-Justice Processes and to Delinquency-Causation Theories

Although the studies described herein have ended for now, numerous juvenile correctional agencies continue to operate differential-treatment programs, to refine their treatment strategies, and to add to our knowledge of what works for various types of youths. While little of our resources go into treatment research, research using classification of offenders to better understand offending populations and to improve criminal-justice processing continues.

Two examples of such research, using I-level as the theoretical frame of reference, are found in chapter 7 by Philip Harris and chapter 11 by Kathleen

Heide. Harris asked the question: Is there a personality difference between delinquents and nondelinquents? By using the I-level classification system, he was able to show in a conceptually satisfying way where differences did and did not exist. He found little difference between the two groups in terms of progress along the ego-development scale (I-level)—that is, in terms of social-perceptual complexity. He found, however, that major differences do exist in the ways delinquents and nondelinquents *respond* to their social-perceputal view (subtype).

Heide investigated the possibility that differences exist among offenders in their understanding of—and thus their ability to succeed in—the criminal-justice process, restitution. She hypothesized that because offenders classified as I_4 and higher on the I-level scale would understand and accept the idea of accountability for their own behavior, they would be more successful in a restitution program than individuals classified as I_3 and lower. This hypothesis received some support.

An additional study by Warren (1982) serves as an example of the use of I-level classification to make sense of the various theories purporting to explain delinquency causation. In this research, the assumptions of four frequently used crime causal perspectives were assessed for their usefulness in explaining the delinquency of five I-level subtypes. The four delinquency-causation theories used were social-control theory (Hirschi 1969); cultural-deviance theory (Miller 1958; Sutherland 1947); psychodynamic theory (Konopka 1966; Toch and Redl 1978); and strain theory (Merton 1938). Female delinquents from the following five I-level categories were used in the study: I_4 anxious neurotic, I_4 acting-out neurotic, I_3 antisocial manipulator, I_3 cultural conformist, and I_3 passive conformist.

After the causal assumptions were listed for each delinquency theory, case records of delinquents representing each subtype were searched for evidence supporting (or not supporting) the assumptions of each of the four theories. High interrater agreement was shown for this task, using one rater who was and one who was not familiar with I-level theory. As might be expected, the assumptions of psychodynamic theory were met very well by the anxious-neurotic cases. The assumptions of cultural-deviance theory were well met by the cultural-conformist cases. The assumptions of strain theory were not met by any of the five subtypes. Had there been enough I_4 cultural-identifier cases to study among the female samples, however, strain assumptions might have fit very well. Social-control-theory assumptions held best for the passive-conformist and antisocial-manipulator subgroups. The acting-out-neurotic cases showed a mixed picture, with some showing best fit for psychodynamic theory and others showing best fit for social-control theory.

This research suggests the relevance of personality of classification in explanations of delinquency. The traditional crime causal theories are clearly differentially applicable to various subgroups of offenders. Rather than attempting to locate one correct theory to explain delinquency, future research might better aim to determine which theoretical perspective is best suited to explain which types of offenders (Warren and Hindelang 1976).

This chapter has attempted to show the relevance of an ego-development theory, interpersonal-maturity-level theory, for treatment and research with offender populations. It has argued that classification by stage of ego development produces relatively homogeneous groups for which rational treatment interventions can occur. Further, it has suggested that such a theoretical frame can give us a conceptual base for answering such questions as what causes delinquency and how delinquents differ from nondelinquents. The same process of using the theory to predict the outcome of research or to build rational and successful intervention programs serves simultaneously to offer a measure of construct validation for interpersonal-maturity theory.

Notes

1. See chapter 16 for a distinction between I-level theory and moral-development theory.

2. In this respect I-level theory differs from moral-development theory.

3. Other methods of testing I-level theory are shown in chapter 7 by Harris and chapter 11 by Heide.

4. For more detail on treatment outcome for the rarely occurring subtypes, see Warren (1976).

5. In this respect correctional workers are probably no different from teachers, social workers, and so on.

6. In a fifteen-month parole period, youths who were well matched with treaters had a failure rate (revocation of parole or recommitment by the court) of 23 percent, compared with a rate of 49 percent for those who were not closely matched. For a twenty-four month period the differences were 34 percent and 57 percent, respectively.

7. The I_2 asocial, aggressive youth was rarely declared eligible for CTP.

References

Andre, Carl R., and Mahan, JoAnn A. *Final report on the differential education project.* Educational Research Series, no. 11. Sacramento: California Youth Authority, 1972.

Cohen, H.L., and Filipczak, J. *A new learning environment: A case for learning.* San Francisco: Jossey-Bass, 1971.

Empey, L.T., and Lubeck, S. *The Silverlake experiment: Testing delinquency theory and community intervention.* Chicago: Aldine, 1971.

Friedlander, K. *The psychoanalytic approach to juvenile delinquency.* New York: International Universities Press, 1949.

Grant, M.Q. *Interpersonal maturity level classification: Juvenile.* Sacramento: California Youth Authority, 1961.

Grant, J.D., and Grant, M.Q. A group dynamics approach to the treatment of nonconformists in the Navy. *Annals of the American Academy of Political and Social Science,* 1959, 126-135.

Harris, P.W. The interpersonal maturity of delinquents and nondelinquents. Ph.D. diss., State University of New York at Albany, 1978.

Harvey, O.J.; Hunt, D.E., and Schroder, H.M. *Conceptual systems and personality organization.* New York: Wiley, 1961.

Heide, K.M. Classification of offenders ordered to make restitution by interpersonal maturity level and by specific personality dimensions. Ph.D. diss., State University of New York at Albany, 1982.

Hirschi, T. *Causes of delinquency.* Berkeley: University of California Press, 1969.

Jesness, C. *The Fricot Ranch study: Outcomes with small versus large living groups in the rehabilitation of delinquents.* Research report no. 47. Sacramento: California Youth Authority, 1965.

———. The Preston typology study: An experiment with differential treatment in an institution. *Journal of Research in Crime and Delinquency,* 1971, *8,* 38-52.

———. *Sequential I-level classification manual.* Sacramento: American Justice Institute, 1974.

Jesness, C.; DeRisi, W.; McCormick, P.; and Wedge, R. *The Youth Center Research Project: Final report.* Sacramento: California Youth Authority and American Justice Institute, 1972.

Kohlberg, L. Stage and sequence: The cognitive-developmental approach to socialization. In D. Goslin, ed., *Handbook of Socialization: Theory and Research.* Chicago: Rand McNally, 1969.

Konopka, G. *The adolescent girl in conflict.* Englewood Cliffs, N.J.: Prentice-Hall, 1966.

Lerman, P. *Community treatment and social control: A critical analysis of juvenile correctional policy.* Chicago: University of Chicago Press, 1975.

Loevinger, J. The meaning and measurement of ego development. *American Psychologist,* 1966, *21,* 195-206.

Merton, R. Social structure and anomie. *American Sociological Review,* 1938, *3,* 672-682.

Miller, W. Lower class culture as a generating milieu of gang delinquency. *Journal of Social Issues,* 1958, *14,* 5-19.

Palmer, T. *Personality characteristics and professional orientations of five groups of community treatment project workers.* A preliminary report on differences among treaters. Community Treatment Project Report Series, 1967, no. 1.

_____ . *California's Community Treatment Project, the phase I, II, and III experiments: Developments and progress.* Research Report no. 10, 1970.

_____ . California's community treatment project for delinquent adolescents. *Journal of Research on Crime and Delinquency,* 1971, *8,* 74-92.

_____ . *Differential placement of delinquents in group homes: Final report.* Sacramento: California Youth Authority and National Institute of Mental Health, 1972.

_____ . Matching worker and client in corrections. *Social Work,* 1973, *18,* 95-103.

_____ . The Youth Authority Community Treatment Project. *Federal Probation,* 1974, *38,* 3-14.

_____ . *Final report of the Community Treatment Project, phases 1, 2, and 3.* Sacramento: California Youth Authority and National Institute of Mental Health, 1976.

_____ . *Correctional intervention and research.* Lexington, Mass.: Lexington Books, D.C. Heath and Company, 1978.

Peck, R.F., and Havighurst, R.J. *The psychology of character development.* New York: Wiley, 1960.

Sullivan, C.E.; Grant, M.Q.; and Grant, J.D. The development of interpersonal maturity: Applications to delinquency. *Psychiatry,* 1957, *20,* 272-283.

Sutherland, E. *Principles of criminology.* Philadelphia: Lippincott, 1947.

Toch, H., and Redl, F. Psychoanalytic perspective. In H. Toch, ed., *Psychology of crime and criminal justice.* New York: Holt, Rinehart and Winston, 1978.

Tolhurst, G.E.; Dixon, D.E.; Howard, G.F.; Litke, M.; and Warren, M.Q. *Center for Training in Differential Treatment: Final report of phase I,* part 2, 1970, 134-145.

Warren, M.Q. Intervention with juvenile delinquents. In M. Rosenheim, ed., *Pursuing justice for the child.* Chicago: University of Chicago Press, 1976.

_____ . Correctional treatment and coercion: The differential treatment perspective. *Criminal Justice and Behavior,* 1977, *4,* 355-376.

_____ . Measuring the impact of specific therapist-patient matches in work with juvenile delinquents. Paper presented to the Society for Psychotherapy Research, Madison, Wisconsin, 1977b.

_____ . The impossible child, the difficult child, and other assorted delinquents: Etiology, characteristics and incidence. *Canadian Psychiatric Association Journal,* 1978, *23,* 41-61.

_____ . Delinquency causation in female offenders. In N.H. Rafter and E.A. Stanko, eds., *Judge, lawyer, victim, thief: Women, sex roles and the criminal justice system.* Boston: Northeastern University Press, 1982.

Warren, M.Q., and the Community Treatment Staff. *Interpersonal maturity level classification: Juvenile: Diagnosis of low, middle, and high maturity delinquents.* Sacramento: Califronia Youth Authority, 1966.

Warren, M.Q., and Hindelang, M. Differential explanation of offender behavior. In H. Toch, ed., *Psychology of crime and criminal justice.* New York: Holt, Rinehart and Winston, 1978.

3 Personality, Conditioning, and Antisocial Behavior

H.J. Eysenck

Crime has always been with us, as have theories of criminal conduct. Yet the serious scientific treatment of criminality is of very recent origin and has not yet outgrown its ideological and political roots. The extreme claims of Lombroso and others implicating biological and genetic factors can be balanced against those of Marxist scholars for the influence of modes of production and the distribution of material wealth. Both approaches are too one-sided to be taken seriously, but much empirical work is still interpreted as supporting either a biological or an environmental-social approach. Little improvement is likely until it is realized that humans are biosocial animals, linked with the animal kingdom through millions of years of evolution, but also influenced in their behavior by social factors deriving from culture, education, and other features of the society in which they live (Eysenck 1980a,b).

The postulate that both biological and social factors, and their interaction, are important in determining our conduct may not be a revolutionary proposal; but it is largely disregarded by many writers. In modern days, particularly, the very mention of biological factors is likely to damn those who have the temerity to disregard current shibboleths. The theory to be developed in this chapter is based largely on a combination of biological and social factors. Its development may be prefaced by a few words about the evolutionary development of the human brain.

McLean (1969) has given much support to the notion that the human brain is not a unified, single whole, but rather a combination of three-in-one brain, or *triune* brain, as he calls it. The three brains are morphologically and functionally distinct, and they derive from different stages in human evolution. At the bottom is the oldest or "reptile" brain; this is responsible for some of the more primitive and instinctive functions of human behavior. Superimposed on this is the so-called *paleocortex* or limbic system—later in development but still relatively primitive—which is concerned with emotions. Third and most distinctive of the human species is the neocortex, that giant growth of gray matter that envelops the rest of the brain and is concerned mainly with thinking, problem solving, and cognition in general.

Communication among these three brains, though of course not entirely absent, is much less effective than one might suppose. Particularly impressive are the facts associated with the development of neurotic disorders. Here we have conditioned fear responses and anxieties, acquired through a process of Pavlovian conditioning, that govern the behavior of the neurotic but are quite outside the control of his neocortex (Eysenck and Rachman 1965). A person with a cat phobia knows that his fears of cats are unreasonable and absurd, but this knowledge in no way helps him to overcome his fears. Only a process of Pavlovian extinction can do so, and no amount of ratiocination will help (Eysenck 1977a). Lest it be thought that neurotics are so scarce that they constitute a separate problem, we might recall that over 33 percent of the population have serious neurotic problems of one kind or another, and that at least half of this group will consult a professional psychiatrist at some point. Furthermore, most people have occasional difficulties with conditioned emotional responses of one kind or another, not serious enough to require professional help but nevertheless annoying and possibly harmful.

Pavlovian conditioning is relevant here because conditioning is the language of the limbic system, just as ordinary language is the way we communicate with the neocortex. Conditioning is thus a more primitive form of mediation, developed for the purpose of giving advanced warning of dangers. Though less effective than language and reasoning, it is nevertheless of considerable help to mammals and other animals that have developed this mode of communication. If the burnt child shuns the fire, this is more likely due to conditioning experiences than to reasoning. Many human behaviors, particularly those associated with emotion, are determined by conditioning experiences rather than by ratiocination.

Most people are familiar with Pavlov's original defining experiments of the conditioning paradigm, in which, by pairing the sound of a bell with the giving of food to a dog, Pavlov succeeded in making the dog salivate to the bell alone. Such experiments would not be relevant to our discussion except that conditioning is an effective way of associating emotions with previously neutral stimuli and thereby greatly enlarging the range of stimuli producing fear, anxiety, and other potent emotions (Martin and Levey 1978). Pavlov's great service to psychology was to work out the rules according to which conditioning proceeds and the laws governing the extinction of conditioned responses. We now have a much more sophisticated view of conditioning than did Pavlov, who never worked with humans. The old-fashioned idea of stimuli as simple sounds or flashes of light, and responses as simple muscle twitches or salivary responses, dies hard but is quite unrealistic. We now realize that stimuli, particularly for human beings, can be very complex and involve cognition quite extensively, as do responses that must be organized into meaningful wholes (Martin and Levey 1981). In what follows we will take for granted the knowledge of this more complicated system that has emerged from large-scale studies of conditioning in human beings. We will try to explicate in detail the way in which the acquisition of socialized behavior is mediated by the conditioning paradigm, how differences in ease of conditioning are related to personality, and how genetic factors interact with social ones in determining the way in which socialized behavior is acquired.

Before turning to the theory itself, it may be worthwhile to say a few words about the concept of crime. Many people have argued that this is a subjective concept, depending crucially on the particular mores of a given society at a particular time and thus lacking the objective definition needed for a scientific concept. Many examples are given of behaviors that were considered crimes in one place but not in another, or at one time but not at another: cigarette smoking, indulgence in alcoholic drink, homosexuality and lesbianism, adultery, prostitution, and other such so-called victimless crimes. Efforts to make people good by elevating venial sins into crimes have existed in practically all societies. Crimes against property or the person—burglary, theft, murder, rape, assault, and so on—constitute by far the largest part of the burden of crime that society must bear, however. This chapter deals with this more restrictive type of crime, leaving aside activities regarded as sinful by some but not by others, and prohibited by law in some societies but not in others.

We are concerned also with antisocial activity, which is not necessarily subject to the laws of a given country. Antisocial activity is a larger concept than criminal activity: although criminal activity, according to our definition, is always antisocial, antisocial activity is not always criminal. Thus an insolent or disruptive student is acting in an antisocial manner, but not a criminal one. Likewise, a person who quarrels with his neighbor incessantly is behaving in an antisocial manner, but not a criminal one. Our reasons for making this distinction will become obvious later.

The theoretical problems presented by the occurrence of criminal activity in a given society are actually twofold. Although it is possible that both problems may be answered in terms of a single theory, it is also possible that different theories are needed. The first problem lies in the existence of *individual differences*. People differ in the degree to which they indulge in antisocial conduct, along a continuum ranging from the saint, who never does, to the habitual criminal, psychopath, or sociopath, who continually and frequently indulges in such conduct. Most people lie somewhere between these extremes, with the majority occasionally indulging in such activities, but usually only to a minor degree and when assured of going undetected.

Differences in individuals along this continuum may have many causes, some social, others economic, others psychological. The focus in this chapter on psychological causes is not intended to minimize the importance of other types of factors. Even if social and economic factors are important, however, they can only act through the agency of the individual organism.

Poverty itself, for instance, cannot produce antisocial behavior; it is the individual who is not prevented from taking an action, such as theft, to alleviate this poverty, who in fact indulges in the activity in question. Objective facts about poverty, inequality of wealth, poor housing, and the like have no psychological effect in themselves; it is the individual's perception of these factors, and his or her reactions dictated by past experience, training, and personality, that mediate action. The classical error in sociological and economic theories is to disregard individual differences and to assume that nonpsychological causes act directly to produce behavior. There is a good deal of experimental literature to indicate that identical conditions are perceived differently by different persons and give rise to different behaviors.

The second problem is to account for a change in the rate of criminal activity occurring in a given population at a given time. It has been observed that during the period 1970-1980 in England there was a tremendous increase in violence against the person and in robbery. Such figures may not be too reliable because they can be influenced by the likelihood of a person reporting a crime to the police, the action taken by the police, the way statisticians deal with the reported incidents, and so forth. Crimes of the kind considered here, however, are nearly always reported and are clearly designated in criminal statistics. These well-documented figures all point to a great increase in criminality in most if not all of the countries of the Western world. Statistics for communist and Third World countries are not sufficiently trustworthy to permit any conclusion about what is happening there.

Our second question, therefore, is why such an increase has occurred at this time. Clearly the answer is not that there are now more people predisposed in terms of personality and genetics to act in an antisocial manner; the time has been much too short to produce any such changes, which according to biological reasoning would take thousands of years, not dozens. The question, therefore, is quite different from one relating to individual differences. Nevertheless, the two problems may have a common answer.

The question of genetic determinance of antisocial conduct is perhaps the most controversial—and almost the most fundamental—in the proposed theory. Two major lines of evidence suggest strongly that such determinants exist, although the interpretation of evidence is not as clear-cut as it may appear to some commentators. There is considerable evidence for a greater concordance in criminal activity for monozygotic (MZ) than for dizygotic (DZ) twins. Table 3-1 lists nine studies done in this field in several different countries, all with results in the same direction. When averaged, they suggest that MZ twins are over four times as likely to be concordant for criminal activity as are DZ twins; this enormous difference very strongly suggests the importance of genetic factors.

Table 3-1
Concordance Rates for Criminality in Nine Twin Studies

	MZ			DZ		
	Concordant	Nonconcordant	Concordance Rate (%)	Concordant	Nonconcordant	Concordance Rate (%)
Lange (1931)	10	3	77	2	15	12
Legra (1933)	4	0	100	0	5	0
Rosanoff et al. (1934)	25	12	68	6	54	10
Kranz (1936)	20	11	65	23	20	53
Stumpfl (1936)	11	7	61	7	12	37
Borgstrom (1939)	3	1	75	2	3	40
Yoshimasu (1965)	17	11	61	2	16	11
Hayashi (1967)	11	4	73	3	2	60
Christiansen (1968)	27	54	33	23	340	6
Total	128	103	55	68	467	13

Figure 3-1. Increase in Crime for 1970-1980 in England

There are, of course, errors involved in research of this type. Not all crimes are traced to their perpetrators. Some twins may be considered nonconcordant, although in fact they too are criminals. Errors of this kind would be likely to go in the direction of the null hypothesis, however—that is, counter to the genetic theory, since the theory proposes a marked difference between two groups and the function of most of the likely errors would be to erode that difference. Thus the observed difference would seem to be a very conservative estimate of the true difference, which is probably much stronger.

A word must be said about the view, often held by critics of the genetic approach, that because MZ twins are treated more similarly by their parents, teachers, and others, they are more likely to be similar in intelligence, personality, and so on, than are DZ twins. This would suggest an environmental rather than a genetic cause of the difference between MZ and DZ twins in degree of similarity. Loehlin and Nichols (1976) have looked at this suggestion in great detail and have found no relationship between degree of similarity in I.Q., personality, and behavior, on the one hand, and degree of similarity of paternal treatment on the other. Most of the instances of similar treatment reported for MZ twins are trivial and obviously irrelevant, such as dressing twins alike. Anyone wishing to take this objection to twin research seriously would have to provide direct evidence that the similarity in parental treatment of MZ twins was really relevant to the type of behavior under investigation.

Equally important are adoption studies, which compare the environmental connection between children and adoptive parents to the genetic connection between children and their natural parents. In the first of the three adoption studies to be mentioned, Schulsinger (1972) in Denmark compared fifty-seven psychopathic adoptees with fifty-seven non-psychopathic controls, equated for sex, age, social class, and in many cases neighborhood of rearing and age of transfer to the adopting family. Carefully defined criteria for psychopathic behavior were used in this study. Next, the investigator examined the case records of the biological and adoptive relatives of both psychopathic and control subjects. Despite the fact that adoption took place at an early age, there were no differences whatsoever between the adoptive families of the psychopathic under the control group. As for the biological family members of these groups, however, relatives of the psychopathic boys showed an incidence of psychopathy two and a half times as great, and an incidence of mildly psychopathic behavior also two and a half times as great, as was found in relatives of the control boys. In other words, the psychopathic boys took after their biological parents, not their adoptive parents.

In a similar study, Hutchings and Mednick (1974) studied a total sample of 745 adoptees. This large sample permitted them to examine the cross-fostering situation in some detail. Fifty-two adoptees were born to biological fathers who were not known to the police but had criminal adoptive fathers. The larger groups of 219 adoptees had criminal biological fathers but were adopted by fathers who were not known to the police. This can be taken as a direct test of whether having a criminal biological father is more important than having a criminal adoptive father with respect to predicting criminality in the adoptee.

When neither the biological father nor the adoptive father was known to the police, 10.4 percent of the adoptees were criminals. When both fathers were criminals, 36.2 percent of the adoptees were criminals. For the two cross-fostered groups the percentages are 11.2 percent (adoptive father criminal, biological father not) and 21.0 percent (natural father criminal, adoptive father not.) As the authors conclude, "Within the limits of the adoption methodology there appears to be a correlation between criminality in adoptees and criminality in their biological parents" (p. 226).

The third study to be discussed was carried out by Crowe (1972) in the United States. The investigators began by locating forty-one female offenders who were inmates of a women's prison reformatory and had given up their babies for adoption. At the time of the study, they had produced fifty-two offspring, ranging in age from 15 to 45 years. A properly matched control group of fifty-two offspring from noncriminal mothers who had been given up for adoption was also studied. The offspring of the criminal mothers had had more criminal arrests and had received a much greater number of convictions; these differences were fully significant statistically. They also had more moving traffic violations recorded against them; this is important because of the known link between criminality and traffic offenses. Here too we find a much greater resemblance between criminal and biological parents than between criminal and adoptive parents. It is difficult to explain these facts environmentally. Taken together with the concordance studies, they seem to prove the involvement of genetic mechanisms.

A few words of caution are in order before we try to interpret the social implications of these data. First, modern genetic theory does not claim that criminals are born and not made, a deduction often made by some people from data such as these. Criminal conduct is clearly a kind of human behavior, circumscribed and defined by social rules, and as such not directly inheritable. We can inherit only morphological, physiological, and biochemical characteristics of the nervous system that, when acted on by some kind of environment, result in conduct of a certain kind. Although genetic factors play a part in antisocial and criminal conduct, it is still necessary to investigate precisely what it is that is inherited and how inherited factors alter probabilities of indulging in antisocial behavior. In other words, the genetic hypothesis can never be considered sufficient by itself; it merely points to a direction in which research may go to complement the direct finding of heritability with the more detailed analysis of the morphological, physiological, and biochemical properties that have been inherited and that mediate the conduct in question.

Another important point is that estimates of heritability are always related to population parameters; that is, they refer to given populations at a given time and cannot be extrapolated to other populations or other periods even within the same country. Neither can heritability estimates be used to decide the relative importance of heredity and environment in individual cases; a general tendency for antisocial conduct to show a genetic determination tells us nothing about any particular individual. As much as we may like to point to heredity or environment as causal factors in a particular case, science gives no license for doing so.

The implication of genetic factors in any type of behavior is often regarded as conducive to therapeutic nihilism; it is believed that because heredity has certain effects, it is impossible to do anything about them. This is untrue, however, and denotes only an ignorance of genetic principles. Through our investigations of heredity we may learn much that enables us to control phenomena with which we are dealing. One example will suffice to establish this point.

Consider phenylketonuria, a disorder causing mental defect that affects about one child in 40,000. This disorder is known to be inherited through a single recessive gene, and the great majority of children suffering from it have a level of mental performance that is usually found in children half their age. These children can be distinguished from other mentally handicapped or from normal children by testing their urine, which yields a green-colored reaction with a solution of ferric chloride, due to the presence of derivatives of phenylalanine. Here we have a perfect example of a disorder produced entirely by hereditary causes, where the cause is simple and well understood, and where the presence of the disorder can be determined with accuracy.

Investigators have gone on to determine how the gene actually produces the mental defect. They found that children affected by phenylketonuria are unable to convert phenylalanine into tyrosine; they can break it down only to a limited extent. It seems that the incomplete breakdown of phenylalanine produces toxic substances that are poisonous to the nervous system. Fortunately, phenylalanine is not an essential part of the diet, provided that tyrosine is present in the diet. Consequently, it is possible to maintain these children on a diet that is almost free of phenylalanine, thus eliminating the danger of poisoning their nervous system. When this method of treatment is begun in the first few months of life, there is a very good chance that the child will grow up without the mental handicap he or she would otherwise have encountered. In other words, by understanding the precise way in which heredity works and by understanding precisely what it does to the organism, we can arrange a rational method of therapy that will make use of the forces of nature rather than trying to counteract them. Similarly, we should look at the effects of genetic implications in antisocial conduct and try to work out a theory of the physiological and psychological mediators that link the genetic causes with the observed behavior.

One likely candidate for this role is the mechanism of Pavlovian conditioning, mentioned at the beginning of this chapter. There is fairly wide agreement among students of criminal behavior that what calls for an explanation is not so much antisocial behavior—which, being egocentric and selfish, is in some ways more natural and characteristic of animals, young children, and so on. It is, rather, socialized behavior that must be learned. This learning process, which would thus enable the individual to acquire a conscience (not in the religious but in the scientific sense) is unlikely to be one of cognitive and rational learning; many studies have shown that criminals are as able as noncriminals to tell right from wrong. It is not ignorance of the law that prevents them from behaving in a socialized manner; it must be something entirely different.

I have suggested (Eysenck 1977b) that in our society youth is a period during which the individual is subjected to a large number of conditioning sequences, of a kind that eventually produce a conscience. In the typical Pavlovian situation a bell or some other neutral stimulus is the conditioned stimulus (CS), food is the unconditioned stimulus (UCS), and salivating and eating is the unconditioned response. By pairing the conditioned and the unconditioned stimuli a number of times, finally the conditioned stimulus—the bell—begins to evoke the conditioned response—salivation—by itself, without any presentation of food. In the social situation relevant to this hypothesis, antisocial behavior is the conditioned stimulus, punishment of some kind is the unconditioned stimulus, and pain/fear/anxiety is the unconditioned response.

By punishing antisocial behavior numerous times, parents, teachers, and others concerned with the upbringing of the child, including his or her peers, perform the role of the Pavlovian experimenter. Gradually the child's nervous system acquires a conditioned response of pain/fear/anxiety to the conditioned stimulus of evildoing, or even the contemplation of evildoing. This conditioned response acts as a conscience and prevents him or her from indulging in activities that, though self-serving, would have the very undesirable effect of drastically increasing the individual's anxiety level.

There is a body of experimental evidence, both from studies of young children and from studies of animals, supporting this general view and indicating the strength of the conditioned responses thus acquired, even with very mild punishments (Eysenck 1977b). Thus puppies who have been slapped over the rump with a folded piece of newspaper as a punishment for approaching food arbitrarily forbidden to them very soon acquire so strong a conditioned response of avoidance that they would have died of starvation when only this forbidden food was available, had the experimenter not terminated the experiment. Note that the punishment is extremely mild and does not hurt the dog in any way; nevertheless, the effect was extremely strong and persistent.

Three further points should be noted about experiments of this kind. Conscience may have two effects: it may prevent us from indulging in forbidden activities, or it may make us feel guilty about having taken part in them. Both effects can be reproduced experimentally in both young children and puppies. Again, when the dog is smacked on the rump with a folded newspaper *before* actually eating the forbidden food, he becomes conditioned to avoid the food. If, however, he is slapped *after* he has begun eating, he will go on eating the forbidden food on later occasions, but with all evidence of guilt—looking around carefully, hanging his head, slinking away from the food afterward, and so on. Thus different reactions can be induced through a process of conditioning depending on the precise timing of the unconditioned stimulus.

Another important point is that different dogs, depending on the ease with which they could be conditioned, showed greater or lesser socialization. As other experiments have shown, German shepherds are very law abiding; they are easily conditioned and are well known to animal fanciers and shepherds for this property. Basenjis, however, are natural psychopaths, difficult or almost impossible to condition, disobedient and antisocial (Scott and Fulker 1965). Thus conditioning theory may give us a clue to individual differences; perhaps those individuals who are genetically predisposed to form conditioned responses quickly, easily, and strongly are more likely to become law-abiding citizens, whereas those who form conditioned responses slowly, weakly, and only with difficulty are liable to lack the conscience that might prevent them from indulging in antisocial conduct.

The last point that emerges from these animal studies is that dogs who have been fed by the experimenter before the beginning of the experiment on conditioning acquired the conditioned response much more readily than did those who had been fed by other people in the laboratory. In other words, even in dogs one finds important social factors, suggesting that the nature of the agent performing the conditioning experiment may be crucial. In human terms, parents and others who have been instrumental in feeding and looking after the infant are probably the best agents to carry out the conditioning process. This conclusion will be no surprise to scientists who have approached the problem from many different disciplines such as sociology or psychoanalysis. The paramount role of the family in teaching children moral behavior has been emphasized by numerous workers; here is experimental support for this view, linking it with the actual conditioning process.

So far, it might be said, our theory is exclusively biological. How then does this agree with the statement that humans are biosocial animals and with the insistence that social as well as biological factors are crucial in the development of socialized or antisocial tendencies? As an answer, let me point to two considerations that crucially involve social factors. If we regard the acquisition of a conscience as resulting from a conditioning process, then we must add that this process depends not only on the conditionability of the individual, but also on the number of occasions when the CS-UCS combination is presented to the individual. Conditioned responses are acquired gradually over time, and many repetitions of these CS-UCS contingencies are required before strong conditioned responses are formed. The arrangement of such contingencies, however, and the number of contingencies presented to the child, are governed by external social factors—the mores of the society, the degree of permissiveness of the times in which the child is growing up, the attitudes of parents and teachers. A child who is easily conditionable requires fewer repetitions of the CS-UCS contingency than does one who is difficult to condition; but given enough repetition, the latter child too can be conditioned. Thus we have an equation with two terms, in which the final socialization is a product of the individual's conditionability and of the socially provided number of CS-UCS contingencies. This model is not purely biological but truly biosocial.

An equally important point is the content of the CS. Children from working-class backgrounds are often encouraged to be aggressive, whereas in middle-class settings such behavior is often punished. Thus we would expect children who were easily conditioned to grow up as rather peaceful adolescents in a middle-class setting but as particularly aggressive adolescents in a working-class environment. In other words, what is conditioned is a function of the social milieu in which the child grows up, which will determine precisely just what is incorporated in his or her conscience. There is direct evidence for this hypothesis in an experiment reported by Raine and Venables (1981). These investigators tested children coming from high and low social backgrounds, respectively, for conditionability, by pairing conditioned stimuli with electric shocks and measuring the amount of psychophysiological reaction acquired by the CS after a number of pairings. They also ascertained the children's degree of prosocial and antisocial behavior, predicting that those who conditioned well would appear prosocial when brought up by high-social-class parents, and antisocial when brought up by low-social-class parents. Conversely, children who condition poorly were predicted to turn out antisocial when coming from a high-social-class environment, and prosocial when coming from a low-social-class environment. Figure 3-2 shows the outcome of the experiment; it will be seen that the predictive crossover effect was actually observed by the investigators.

Thus we have another important interaction between conditioning as a biological variable, and social factors. What is being conditioned is clearly a vital aspect of the total problem, and much research work could positively be devoted to an extension of the Raine and Venables experiment, which appears to be of considerable theoretical and practical importance.

Even given the recognition of social factors in the conditioning theory, many people still doubt whether human beings, endowed as they are with the ability to formulate thoughts in some language or other, can really be said to be determined in their conduct by such primitive mechanisms as Pavlovian conditioning. We have already mentioned the strong evidence that conditioning is fundamental for the acquisition of neurotic disorders, and it is difficult to see why the absence of acquisition of conditioned responses should not be responsible for the failure of some individuals to acquire a conscience. There are indeed several lines of evidence pointing

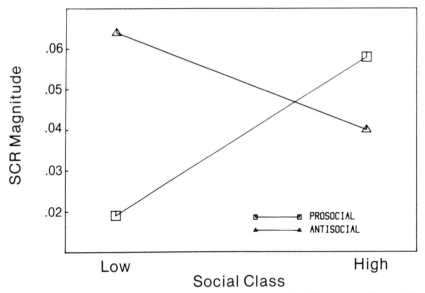

Source: A. Raine and P. Venables, "Classic Conditioning and Socialization—a Biosocial Interaction," *Personality and Individual Differences,* 1981, *2*, 273-283. Quoted with permission.

Figure 3-2. Conditioned Responses as a Function of Social Class and Antisocial Conduct in School

in that direction, which will be discussed presently. Let me here mention merely that Pavlov already recognized the importance of the development of language ability in humans and added a second signaling system to that provided by the conditioning paradigm. He pointed out that in humans words can act as conditioned and unconditioned stimuli, thus extending the field of conditioning to language behavior; and many other aspects of human behavior, such as evaluation behavior (Martin and Levey 1978) have since added to the rather rudimentary class of acts studied by Pavlov and his followers. Theories that neglect conditioning processes and rely on purely cognitive factors seldom take into account the many facts that support the conditioning hypothesis, and develop ad hoc theories rather than derive deductions about human conduct from well-established principles developed in the laboratory. For instance, to explain human conduct in terms of "expectancies" is a purely semantic device; expectancies themselves can be regarded as conditioned responses, which obey all the rules of conditioning laid down by Pavlov and his successors. We will not discuss the arguments between conditioning theories and social-learning theories; it is merely suggested that much of what passes as social learning is really a conditioning phenomenon in which certain cognitive consequences of the conditioning process are taken out of context and given a responsibility for mediating behavior which in the nature of things they cannot bear (Rachman 1978). If it be argued that explanations in terms of conditioning are dehumanizing and mechanistic, then the answer surely must be that certain aspects of our behavior always have derived from our evolution from more primitive ancestors, and that some of our behavior is thus caused; this does not detract from the equally important fact that other types of behavior are often more cognitive and recognizably human. It is not suggested that *all* our behavior is caused or determined by conditioning, the limbic system, and other primitive parts of the cortex; it is merely suggested that *some* of our behaviors are so determined.

Differences in conditionability are clearly dependent on various physiological factors, one of the most important of which appears to be *cortical arousal*. High cortical arousal or activation is connected with better conditioning, and poor cortical arousal with poor conditioning, in a fairly clear-cut manner. It might be worthwhile to investigate the relationship between various psychophysiological variables and antisocial behavior. This has been done particularly in relation to psychopathy (Hare 1970, 1975, 1978; Hare and Schalling 1978; Eysenck 1980c).

It is unfortunate that this research has been done on psychopaths because the concept of *psychopathy* and that of *criminality*, though covering similar ground, are not identical. Not all criminals are psychopaths, and not all psychopaths are criminals. All psychopaths behave in an antisocial manner, as do all criminals; but their psychopathic and antisocial behavior shown is of a particular kind that may not lead to criminal prosecution and prison sentences. *Psychopathy* was defined by Cleckley (1976) as being characterized by unreliability, untruthfulness and insincerity, lack of remorse or shame, inadequately motivated antisocial behavior, poor judgment and failure to learn from experience, pathologic egocentricity and an incapacity for love, general poverty in major affective reactions, specific loss of insight, unresponsiveness in general interpersonal relations, fantastic and uninviting behavior with drink and sometimes without, an impersonal sex life, the failure to follow any life plan, and trivial and poorly integrated life aims. On the favorable side there is a superficial charm, an absence of delusions and other signs of irrational thinking, and absence of nervousness or psychoneurotic manifestations. The concept of psychopathy so described clearly comes somewhat close to the personality dimensions of psychoticism, to be discussed later; here we merely note that although many criminals show psychopathic tendencies, by no means all of them do. Similarly, the behavior described by Cleckley does not necessarily lead to criminal activity, but may be merely antisocial in a manner that does not necessarily contravene the laws of the country. Nevertheless, psychopaths certainly behave in an antisocial and often in a criminal manner; hence evidence regarding their behavior is of considerable interest. Hare (1970) in his book on psychopathy makes it clear that many different types of investigation suggest that psychopathy is connected with cortical underarousal. He goes on to say that because of this, psychopaths develop conditioned anxiety reactions only with difficulty. There is a vast literature on the psychophysiological analysis of psychopaths as compared to controls, reviewed by Eysenck (1980c). It would be inappropriate here to go into detail regarding all these studies. There are many difficulties in interpretation, partly because different investigators have used different definitions of psychopathy. Nevertheless, there is general agreement that the data demonstrate a weakness in the conditioning of anxiety reaction on the part of psychopaths, thus confirming the major postulates in the theory developed.

We may summarize the work on conditioning and psychophysiological differences between individuals by saying that differences in conditionability—associated with differential content of the conditioning process and differential frequency of conditioning contingencies—adequately explain the observed differences in individual antisocial behavior. The same factors appear sufficient to explain the recent increments in antisocial behavior and criminal activity. The general growth in permissiveness in homes, schools, and courts has led to a significant reduction in the number of conditioning contingencies to which children are exposed. It would follow as a direct consequence that they would grow up with a much weaker conscience, and consequently that many more children would be led to engage in criminal and antisocial activities. Obviously the theory is not yet well enough established empirically to act as a paradigm, and other theories may also contain elements of truth. Our major claim is that the theory is firmly established enough to be taken seriously, that it explains and predicts numerous observable and observed phenomena, and that it acts as a guide to future research—for example, the collection of data on the actual way children are being conditioned, and the correlation of this with their future conduct in society.

Differences in conditionability are associated with differences in cortical arousal, which raises the question of the degree to which personality as a whole is connected with such physiological factors, thus also suggesting the possibility that personality itself may be directly connected with antisocial conduct. Three major factors in personality research have come up again and again in factor-analytic and correlational studies in many different countries (Royce 1973); these factors are extraversion as opposed to introversion; emotional instability or neuroticism as opposed to emotional stability; and psychoticism as opposed to superego functioning (Eysenck and Eysenck 1969, 1976). I have suggested that all three are involved in antisocial conduct, so that typically the person indulging in such conduct would be extraverted rather than introverted, emotionally unstable rather than stable, and high on psychoticism rather than on superego functioning (Eysenck 1977b). The evidence from many different sources, including many studies of adult incarcerated criminals; adolescent criminals, both incarcerated and not; and children are fairly conclusive in supporting this hypothesis (Eysenck 1977b).

Extraversion-introversion in particular is connected with differences in conditionability because the theory of extraversion links it with low cortical arousal (Eysenck 1967, 1981). There is a great deal of evidence—both direct (psychophysiological) and indirect (experimentally controlled laboratory testing)—that indicates that this theory is well supported by numerous studies along these two lines. There is also direct evidence that introverts condition better than extraverts; figure 3-3 shows the results of one such study. Bearing in mind the qualifications suggested in the Raine and Venables study discussed earlier—that the content of the conditioning process is crucial in determining *what* shall be learned—this result nevertheless suggests that by and large extraverted children would find greater difficulties in developing a proper conscience than introverted children, and that consequently they are more likely to grow up into adolescents and adults indulging in antisocial activities.

Another qualification necessary in interpreting existing data is Pavlov's law of protective or *transmarginal inhibition*. The data in figure 3-3 give results under conditions in which the UCS was relatively weak; where the UCS was relatively strong, we would expect the law of transmarginal inhibition to reverse the relationship between introversion and conditioning. As figure 3-4 indicates, this is indeed so. Introversion-extraversion thus appears to be a personality variable that is highly relevant to antisocial conduct. Many more experiments are available to indicate and explicate this relationship (Eysenck and Levey 1972; Jones et al. 1981; Martin and Levey 1969). Extraversion-introversion seems to be particularly important in dealing with children at the stage at which socialized conduct either is or is not acquired through the proper development of conscience. It is slightly less important in adolescence and apparently even less so in the case of criminal adults. The term *apparently* is used to indicate that the true relations may be somewhat different from those observed in questionnaire studies; since adult criminals are always incarcerated, often for long periods of time, the usual questions in a personality inventory may be irrelevant to the situation in which they find themselves. More direct studies of conditioning might provide much greater support for the theory (Eysenck 1977b).

Neuroticism or emotional instability act as a drive, according to the Hullian principles. This drive multiplies with whatever habits the individual

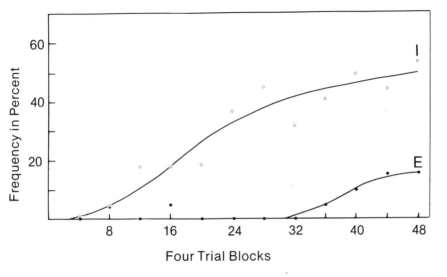

Source: H.J. Eysenck, Crime and Personality (London: Routledge and Kegan Paul, 1977).
Quoted with permission.

Figure 3-3. Frequency of Conditioned Eyeblinks for Introverts and Extraverts, Respectively

has acquired. In a person who as a child failed to acquire socialized
habits—and consequently habitually acts in an antisocial manner—a high
degree of neuroticism would multiply with this set of habits and produce an
even stronger degree of antisocial behavior. In accordance with this model,
we would expect neuroticism to be most important with adult criminals, less
so with adolescents, and least so with children. This is roughly what has
been found (Eysenck 1977b).

Psychoticism as a personality dimension is of particular interest in connection with antisocial and criminal behavior because it is strongly sex
related, men having much higher scores than women (Eysenck and Eysenck
1976). This is not surprising, as the personality traits included under this
term (aggressiveness, egocentricity, impulsiveness, and the like) are more
characteristic of males than of females. As one might imagine, psychoticism
is particularly linked with crimes of violence, and appears to be equally important at all stages of development, from childhood through adolescence
to adulthood (Powell 1978; Eysenck 1977b).

The evidence for the validity of these hypotheses is too various to
discuss (Eysenck 1977b). However, figure 3-4 may be used to illustrate
typical results. We are dealing here with schoolchildren who were ad-

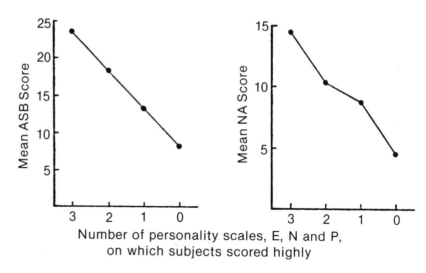

Source: H.J. Eysenck, *Crime and Personality* (London: Routledge and Kegan Paul, 1977).
Quoted with permission.

Figure 3-4. Antisocial Behavior in Children, as Related to Personality
Traits P, E, and N

ministered the Eysenck Personality Questionnaire, which gives measures of
P, E, and N. Two criteria of antisocial conduct were used, one provided by
ratings made by the teachers, the other the Antisocial Behavior Questionnaire (ASB), filled in by the children themselves and known to have a high
degree of reliability and validity. On the abscissa are graphed the number of
personality scales on which the children were above average, in the direction
of high antisocial conduct (that is, above average on P, above average on N,
and above average on E). In other words, zero refers to children who are
below average on P, E, and N; 3 refers to children who are above average
on all three scales. Thus the greater the number of scales on which a child is
above the average, the greater the number of antisocial activities indulged in
by him on both criteria. All the regressions are linear and very clear in their
indications; other similar studies have given similar results.

Two further points are worthy of mention. The first relates to the possible objection that these relationships between personality and criminality
may be observable only in Western cultures and may be an artifact of the
particular social systems obtaining there. This is not true, as indicated by
the fact that similar studies carried out in Third World and communist
countries have yielded similar results. It would appear that high scorers on

P, E, and N are more likely to transgress the laws of Western countries, communist countries, and Third World countries equally (Eysenck 1977b).

A last point is that all three personality dimensions have been shown to be strongly dependent on genetic determinants, to the extent of about two-thirds of the total variance (Fulker 1981). Here again, biological as well as social factors play a part in determining a person's behavior. Thus this finding is linked closely to the previous one that both antisocial and criminal conduct are dependent in part on genetic and in part on environmental and social factors.

One weakness of the theory so far developed is that it treats *criminality* or antisocial conduct as a unitary concept, whereas most experts would agree on the necessity to distinguish clearly between different types of criminality. This need is particularly apparent in relating criminality to personality, and figure 3-5 shows the results of a study in which an attempt was made to investigate five groups of criminals showing different types of criminal activity, namely confidence tricksters (con men), offenders against property laws, violent offenders, inadequate offenders, and a residual group taking part in many different types of crime. The figure shows the different combinations of personality variables characterizing each of these groups. Figure 3-6 shows similarly the results of a discriminant function analysis of the group, using both questionnaire data on the Eysenck Personality Questionnaire, and data obtained from the GSR (galvanic skin response) in an experimental investigation. At least *two* variates are needed to encompass all the relations between the different criminality groups and the experimental variables, demonstrating very clearly the need for a more detailed analysis of the type of antisocial activity indulged in.

One important criterion for a theory of antisocial and criminal conduct is whether it leads to methods of reducing such types of behavior. This argument is in line with the experimental and empirical philosophy of science, which requires us to manipulate the independent variable in order to observe changes in the dependent variable—here, the antisocial, criminal, or psychopathic behavior of given individuals. Conditioning theories have indeed been used to try to rehabilitate criminals (usually adolescents rather than adults). Although such attempts have usually been based on the concepts of operant conditioning rather than on Pavlovian conditioning, it might be suggested that these two types of conditioning, particularly in social situations, are so closely integrated that it would be very difficult to separate them. It would not be appropriate here to argue that the methods to be described have a large element of classical conditioning in them; but it may be suggested that it is this element that makes it possible to generalize the effects of treatment from the treatment situation to social situations encountered after release.

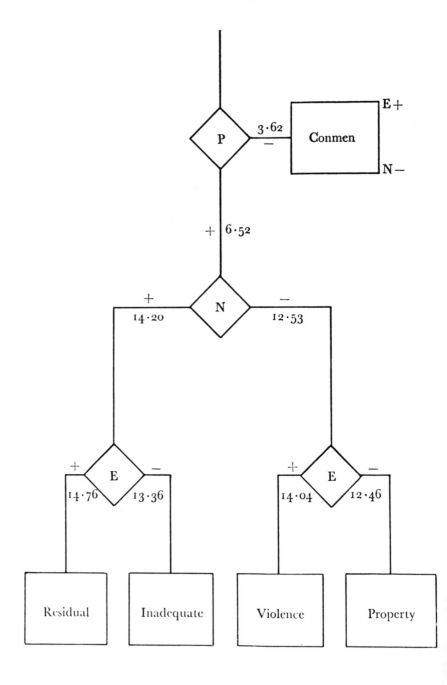

Source: H.J. Eysenck, *Crime and Personality* (London: Routledge and Kegan Paul, 1977). Quoted with permission.

Figure 3-5. Relationship between Type of Criminality and Personality

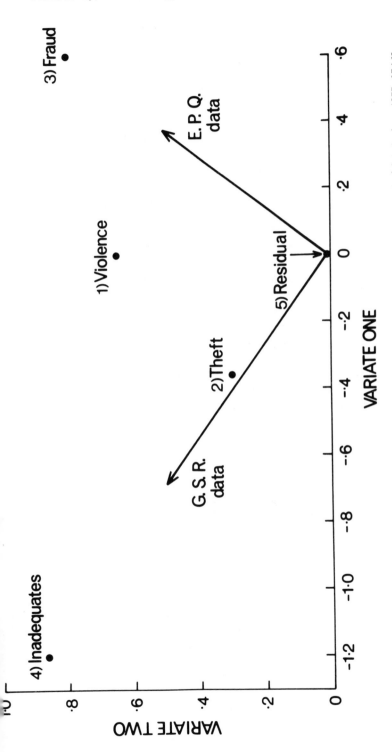

Source: S.B.G. Eysenck, J. Rust, and H.J. Eysenck. Personality and the classification of adult offenders. *British Journal of Criminology*, 1977, *17* 169-181. Quoted with permission.

Figure 3-6. Discriminate Function Analysis of Different Types of Criminality

However that may be, behavior therapists have derived their methods of treatment for criminals on the basis of conditioning theories (Stumphauser 1973, 1979; Feldman 1977). The major principles of behavior therapy for antisocial behavior (or any other undesirable behavior) are as follows:

1. Those behavioral manifestations that are deemed undesirable are clearly specified and a means of quantifying them established.
2. Attempts are made to reduce or eliminate those behaviors by controlling their environmental consequences—that is, using carefully structured reward and punishment contingencies that have been shown experimentally to be effective in modifying behavior.
3. Success of treatment is monitored throughout the procedure and at various follow-up points by comparison with appropriate control measures.

The term *punishment* is ambiguous, since it can refer either to retribution or to rehabilitation. These two aims have often been confused within the European penal system, although it is increasingly clear that traditional prison sentences have more to do with the former than the latter. There is no reason in learning theory to suppose that prison constitutes a form of punishment that reduces the likelihood of recurrence of antisocial behavior. The high rates of observed recidivism suggest that prison may even be a training ground for criminal attitudes and skills. Punishment as used by behavior therapists is applied carefully and systematically so as to diminish the frequency of the undesired behavior. In other words, rehabilitation, not retribution, is taken as the aim of treatment. Even then, punishment is recognized as being much less predictable in its effect on behavior than is positive reinforcement. Thus contingent rewards are generally preferred by behavior therapists.

Perhaps the most successful application of learning theory to the management and rehabilitation of criminals is seen in the *token economy*. Although today this is associated with B.F. Skinner's principle of operant conditioning, the method is by no means new. In 1840, when the British penologist Alexander Maconochie was appointed superintendent of Norfolk Island, a convict settlement off Australia, he found the conditions there grim and soul-destroying. Apparently, the colony had been run on the principle that prison life should be as painful and unpleasant as possible so that anyone released from it would resolve never to return and others hearing about it might be deterred from criminal acts. Maconochie's idea was quite revolutionary:

> I think that time sentences are the root of very nearly all the demoralisation which exists in prison. A man under a time sentence thinks only how he is

to cheat that time, and while it away; he hates labour, because he has no interest in it whatever, and he has no desire to please the officers under who he is placed because they cannot serve him essentially; they cannot in any way promote his liberation. . . . Now these evils would be remedied by introducing the system of task sentences. [Barry 1958]

Maconochie, then, proposed substituting for the old-fashioned sentence a *task sentence,* whereby the offender would stay in prison until he had earned a set number of marks of commendation. These marks would be awarded for specified amounts of labor and other forms of conduct. The details of his plan were as follows: on first entering the prison, the offender suffered a short period of restraint and deprivation, followed shortly by a second stage during which he could gain privilege, as well as shelter and food, by the earnings from his labor and good conduct. Purchases could be made by computing the value of the goods in marks, then setting them off against the marks earned by the prisoner. His tally of marks could be increased by frugal living, hard work, and exemplary conduct. Disciplinary offenses were not punished by the customary methods of inflicting pain, solitary confinement, or enforced labor, but by fines expressed in marks. As a third stage, prisoners were permitted to join with others in joint work projects in which the misconduct of one member might be punished by a loss of marks for the whole group. As the prisoner progressed through the system, the restraints on him were progressively lessened until the final period of detention resembled as far as possible the conditions he would encounter on release. All degrading practices such as leg irons and lashings were abolished so that the prisoner was never totally deprived of his humanity.

Despite official opposition, Maconochie managed to put these ideas in effect. The experiment seems to have been successful, and it is surprising that this system did not catch on widely and that only in recent years has there been much renewal of interest (Eysenck 1972).

A good modern example of the application of a token economy to antisocial behavior is the Achievement Place program run by E.L. Phillips (1968) and colleagues at the University of Kansas. Achievement Place is a home-style, community-based treatment facility that caters to about six to eight delinquent youths in their early teens at one time. Treatment is administered by a well-trained couple who are referred to as teaching parents. The aim is to provide the youths with academic, occupational, and social skills that might enable them to be more successful in obtaining legitimate rewards in the community and thus keep them out of trouble. A prime element of the program is a token economy in which the youths earn points for learning and engaging in socially appropriate behavior, and lose points for disruptive behavior such as aggressive statements. Points are later exchanged for privileges such as an allowance or permission to go home for the weekend. In addition, the youths themselves help to determine the motivational system by a degree of self-government; and attempts are made to build up reciprocally reinforcing relationships between inmates and teaching parents, such that the more artificial token reinforcement system can be faded out.

Kirigin et al. (1979) report results based on twenty-six youths who went through the Achievement Place program and a comparable group of thirty-seven youths who were either treated within a conventional institution or in danger of such institutionalization. Members of the latter subgroup were considered eligible for admission to Achievement Place; but there were insufficient places for all candidates, and they missed out on the basis of a random selection. Findings were for the most part very favorable to the new program. Youths who had been to Achievement Place were about half as likely to be institutionalized within two years after treatment as were similar youths originally treated in the institutional program. During treatment in Achievement Place there was a marked reduction in police and court contacts faced by the youths. In the second year after treatment, Achievement Place youths had fewer police and court contacts than before treatment, although equivalent-aged youths treated in an institution showed a similar reduction in skirmishes with the law (which raises a question about the long-term advantages of the new program). Achievement Place youths were, however, more likely to continue their education after treatment than were institutional youths. Finally, all consumers (youths; parents; and school, court, and welfare personnel) expressed satisfaction with the Achievement Place program, and the cost of treatment was calculated to be about one-third that of standard institutionalization. Therefore, although its impact on criminal propensities is yet to be proved, Achievement Place has shown itself to be cost-effective and superior in many respects to previous treatment approaches.

Since the token economy was only one component of the Achievement Place treatment (albeit a major one), it is reasonable to ask how much of the success of the overall program could be attributed to it. A clue to the probable importance of its contribution is seen in some data of Phillips (1968), who presents case studies showing how particular aspects of behavior responded to token reinforcements. For example, many of the boys were described by teachers as overly aggressive, on the evidence that they often made aggressive statements such as "I'll smash his car up if he does that again," or "I'll kill you." The frequency of such comments under various conditions of reinforcement in boys for whom aggression was deemed particularly problematic was greatly reduced. The use of such correction comments as "That's not the way to talk" was not successful by itself; but the imposition of fines expressed as a deduction of points was highly effective in eliminating aggressive statements during the three-hour daily observation periods. We do not know to what extent this verbal control generalized to other contexts where the threat of punishment did not apply, but we might expect that it would eventually become habitual. Similar analyses were reported showing the modification of other aspects of behavior such as punctuality, tidiness, and homework. Indications are, then, that the token economy has some efficacy in the management of antisocial behavior.

A more controversial behavioristic approach to treatment is *aversion therapy,* which involves the attempt to associate directly unpleasant experiences such as pain and nausea with tempting stimuli that it is felt would be better avoided. This approach has been used particularly with alcoholics and sexual deviates (Rachman and Teasdale 1969), but there are also occasional reports of its application to criminality. For example, Kellam (1969) reports treatment of a 48-year-old housewife with ten convinctions for stealing. A film was made of her stealing from a shop, and this was inserted into a sequence of disapproving faces. When this film was shown back to the woman, she received electric shocks to coincide with the disapproving faces. In this way it was hoped to associate shock-generating anxiety with disapproving faces and to connect both with the act of stealing. According to the patient's report, this treatment did generalize to the real world: three months later the urge to steal was effectively overridden by anxiety.

Unfortunately, there are no properly controlled studies of this approach with criminal behavior. Some therapists also have ethical misgivings about it. There is concern that such methods could be used against people's will to induce conformity to some arbitrary social standard; the case of homosexuality, which was once classified as a crime and treated in this manner, is often cited. This ethical objection can be best answered by noting that it would apply in principle to any intervention that was successful in reducing criminal behavior. If we want to rehabilitate criminals rather than just exact retribution or incarcerate them, then we must look for effective technologies that help us to do this. Aversion therapy shows some promise in this respect and therefore might have a place in the therapist's armamentarium. Nevertheless, many people do find the cruder forms of aversion therapy unpleasant; and social acceptability is one of the criteria that must be considered in choosing a treatment. Increasingly, it is felt that aversion therapy should not be used without the full consent and cooperation of the offender, that where possible the aversive experiences should be imaginary rather than physical, and that more appropriate substitute responses should be simultaneously strengthened by positive reinforcement so that the individual is offered some alternative behavior that is socially acceptable. In the Kellam shoplifting case, for example, it might have been wise to give the offender rewarded practice in making legitimate purchases.

The kind of experiences that turn out to be aversive are often surprising. Levinson, Ingram, and Azcarate (1968) used attendance at group-therapy sessions as an aversive stimulus to control rule breaking in an institution for juvenile delinquents. The boys could avoid group therapy by completing three successive months without serious misbehavior. This contingency led to a 43-percent reduction in misconduct reports. Clearly, what the staff may see as beneficial, and therefore desirable, may be perceived quite differently by the inmates.

Another event that seems to operate as a punishment is simple appearance in court. In a study by Berg, Hullin, and McGuire (1979), juvenile-court magistrates in the Yorkshire city of Leeds assisted with evaluation of two court procedures for the control of truancy by randomly allocating treatments to young offenders appearing before them. One procedure—the more commonly used in Britain in such circumstances—was that of making a *supervision order.* A social worker or probation officer was given supervision of the child, who only returned to court if the appointed welfare officer wanted further action from the magistrates. In the other procedure, referred to as *adjournment,* the court repeatedly adjourned the case and the child came back at varying time intervals at the discretion of the magistrates, depending on progress in school attendance since his last appearance. As a backup to either procedure, an interim-care order could be made, under which the child went into a residential assessment center for about three weeks. If all else failed, a *full-care order* would be applied. The social-services department would then decide whether the child should be placed in a community home or allowed to remain a while longer at home on trial. Since both these procedures had been used for some time with no agreement about their relative effectiveness, the magistrates were persuaded that a controlled trial with random allocation would be the only way to settle the question.

The results were clear-cut. Before appearing in court, both groups had been off school for an average of 75 percent ot the time. In the first six months afterward, the mean absence of the adjourned cases had fallen to 35 percent, whereas the supervising children were still away 50 percent of the time. When the next six-month period was looked at in the same way, the superiority of the adjournment procedure was maintained. It did not make any difference whether the child was a boy or a girl. When convictions for criminal offenses were considered as a measure of outcome, the results again favored the adjournment procedure. Before coming to court for truancy, the two groups did not differ significantly in the average number of offenses. After the court appearance, the number of criminal convictions dropped markedly in the adjourned group but was hardly reduced at all in the supervised group. The superiority of the adjourned group can also be seen in the percentage of cases with at least one criminal conviction before and after their court appearance for truancy.

Since adjournment appears to be a nontreatment and supervision approximates to counseling, it might seem surprising that the former is more effective in getting truants back to school and keeping them out of trouble with the law. Berg, Hullin, and McGuire suggest that the adjournment procedure may be superior because it involves the child's family to a greater extent. The parents have to accompany the child at each court appearance, which might mean taking time off work. They are thus actively engaged in treatment rather than being allowed to pass responsibility for the problem along to a welfare officer. Another possibility is that attendance at court, with the explicit danger of removal from home, is a more anxiety-provoking and motivating force than are pleasant chats with a sympathetic social worker. If this were true, we would account for its success in terms of the operant conditioning principle.

This has been a brief and consequently rather dogmatic statement of the theories involved, and a rather hasty survey of some of the numerous studies relevant to a proper evaluation of the theories. By no means have all these studies been positive in their findings. Usually, however, it is possible to detect certain weaknesses in the studies that fail to support the hypotheses—weaknesses that suggest that their negative outcomes may not be fatal to the theories in question. Obviously, many more studies directly relevant to the theory should be carried out before we can reach any definitive conclusions. Psychological theories tend to be embraced with ardor, defended in the absence of proper research, and finally found wanting and abandoned. For this reason alone, we make no far-reaching claims for the theory outlined, other than that it does serve to answer the two major questions raised—that of individual differences in criminality, and that of secular increase in criminality—in a manner that is congruent with a great deal of laboratory research into psychophysiology, personality, and conditioning. Furthermore, the theory does generate predictions and expectations in the field of treatment and rehabilitation, some of which have been of sufficient interest to make it likely that they may have considerable value in this field. The possibility exists that the successes of these rehabilitation methods lie in some feature other than that postulated. Again, we suggest that only further research can answer this question. As a minimum, however, it may be said that the conditioning and personality theory here outlined is a promising contender among the other theories in the field, one that may perhaps claim to have more factual evidence in its favor than any other. Possibly divergent theories are complementary rather than antagonistic; it is by no means clear why a single theory should be capable of explaining all the diverse facts of the complex type of behavior we call criminal. If a combination of theories is found to be necessary in order to encompass the whole field, it might be suggested that the conditioning and personality theory has singled out a particularly fundamental aspect of criminal behavior, and that whatever the final shape of such combined theory might be, it must encompass the established facts discussed in this chapter.

References

Barry, J.V., Alexander Maconochie. Melbourne: Oxford University Press, 1958.

Berg, I.; Hullin, R.; and McGuire, R. A randomly controlled trial of two court procedures in truancy. In D.P. Farrington, K. Hawkins, and S.M. Lloyd-Bostock, eds., *Psychology, law and legal processing.* London: Macmillan, 1979.

Borgstrom, C.A. Eine serie von kriminoliem zwillingen. *Archive für Rassenund Gesellschaftbiologie,* 1939, *33,* 334-343.

Christiansen, K.O. Threshold of tolerance in various population groups illustrated by results from the Danish Criminologie twin study. In A.V.S. de Reuck and R. Porter, eds., *The mentally abnormal offender.* Boston: Little, Brown, 1968.

Cleckley, H. *The mask of sanity.* St. Louis: Mosby, 1976.

Crowe, R. The adopted offspring of women criminal offenders. *Archives of General Psychiatry,* 1972, *27,* 600-603.

Eysenck, H.J. *The biological basis of personality.* Springfield: C.C. Thomas, 1967.

_____ . *Psychology is about people.* London: Allen Lane, 1972.

_____ . *You and neurosis.* London: Temple Smith, 1977a.

_____ . *Crime and personality.* London: Routledge and Kegan Paul, 1977b.

_____ . The bio-social model of man and the unification of psychology. In A.J. Chapman and D.M. Jones, eds., *Models of man.* Leicester: British Psychological Society, 1980a.

_____ . The bio-social nature of man. *Journal of Social and Biological Structures,* 1980b, *3,* 125-134.

_____ . Psychopathie. In U. Baumann, H. Berbalk, and G. Seidenstücker, eds., *Klinische Psychologie—Trends in Forschung und Praxis,* vol. 3. Vienna: Hans Huber, 1980c.

_____ . *A model for personality.* New York: Springer, 1981.

Eysenck, H.J., and Eysenck, S.B.G. *Personality structure and measurement.* London: Routledge and Kegan Paul, 1969.

_____ . *Psychoticism as a dimension of personality.* London: Hodder and Stoughton, 1976.

Eysenck, H.J., and Levey, A. Conditioning, introversion-extraversion and the strength of the nervous system. In V.D. Nebylitsyn and J.A. Gray, eds., *Biological bases of individual behavior.* London: Academic Press, 1972.

Eysenck, H.J., and Rachman, S. *The causes and cures of neurosis.* London: Routledge and Kegan Paul, 1965.

Feldman, M.P. *Criminal behaviour: A psychological analysis.* London: Wiley, 1977.

Fulker, D.W. The genetics and environmental architecture of psychoticism, extraversion and neuroticism. In H.J. Eysenck, ed., *A model for personality.* New York: Springer, 1981.

Hare, R.D. *Psychopathy.* London: Wiley, 1970.

_____. Psychophysiological studies of psychopathy. In D.C. Fowles, ed., *Clinical applications of psychophysiology.* New York: Columbia University Press, 1975.

_____. Electrodermal and cardiovascular correlates of psychopathy. In R.D. Hare and D. Schalling, eds., *Psychopathic behavior.* New York: Wiley, 1978.

Hare, R.D., and Schalling, D., eds. *Psychopathic behavior.* New York: Wiley, 1978.

Hayashi, G. A study of juvenile delinquency in twins. In H. Misuda, ed., *Clinical genetics in psychiatry.* Tokyo: Ogaku Shain, 1967.

Hutchings, B., and Mednick, S.A. Registered criminality in the adoptive and biological parents of registered male adoptees. In S.A. Mednick, F. Schulsinger, J. Higgins, and B. Bell, eds., *Genetics, environment and psychopathology.* Amsterdam: American Elsevier, 1974.

Jones, J.; Eysenck, H.J.; Martin, I; and Levey, A.B. Personality and the topography of the conditioned eyelid response. *Personality and Individual Differences,* 1981, *2,* 61-83.

Kellam, A.M. Shoplifting treated by aversion to a film. *Behaviour Research and Therapy,* 1969, *7,* 125-127.

Kirigin, K.A.; Wolf, M.M.; Braukmann, C.J.; Fixson, D.L.; and Phillips, E.L. Achievement place: a preliminary outcome evaluation. In J.S. Strumphauzer, ed., *Progress in behavior therapy with delinquents.* Springfield, Ill.: C.C. Thomas, 1979.

Kranz, H. *Lebensschicksale Criminelle Zwillinge.* Berlin: Springer, 1936.

Lange, J. *Crime as destiny.* London: Allen and Unwin, 1931.

Legra, A.M. Psychose und kriminalität bei zwillingen. *Zeitschrift für die Gesamte Neurologie und Psychiatrie,* 1933, *144,* 198-222.

Levinson, R.B.; Ingram, G.L.; and Azcarate, E. Aversive group therapy: Sometimes good medicine tastes bad. *Crime and Delinquency,* 1968, *14,* 336-339.

Loehlin, J.C., and Nichols, R.C. *Heredity, environment, and personality.* London: University of Texas Press, 1976.

Martin, I., and Levey, A.B. *The genesis of the classical conditioned re-*

sponse. London: Pergamon Press, 1969.

————. Evaluative conditioning. *Advances in Behaviour Research and Therapy,* 1978, *1,* 57-102.

————. Classical conditioning. In M. Christie and P. Mellett, eds., *Psychosomatic approaches in medicine.* London: Wiley, 1981.

McLean, P.D. A triune concept of the brain and behavior. Hinks Memorial Lecture, University of Toronto, 1969.

Phillips, E.L. Achievement Place: Token reinforcement procedures in a home-style rehabilitation setting for pre-delinquent boys. *Journal of Applied Behaviour Analysis,* 1968, *1,* 213-223.

Powell, G.E. Psychoticism and social deviancy in children. *Advances in Behaviour Research and Therapy,* 1978, *1,* 27-56.

Rachman, S., ed. Perceived self-efficacy: Analysis of Bandura's theory of behavioural change. *Advances in Behaviour Research and Therapy,* 1978, *1,* 137-269.

Rachman, S.J., and Teasdale, J. *Aversion therapy and the behaviour disorders.* London: Routledge and Kegan Paul, 1969.

Raine, A., and Venables, P. Classic conditioning and socialization—a biosocial interaction. *Personality and Individual Differences,* 1981, *2,* 273-283.

Rosanoff, A.J.; Handy, L.M.: and Rosanoff, I. Criminality and delinquency in twins. *Journal of Criminal Law and Criminality,* 1934, *24,* 923-934.

Royce, J.R. The conceptual framework for a multi-factor theory of individuality. In J.R. Royce, ed., *Multivariate analysis and psychological theory.* London: Academic Press, 1973.

Schulsinger, F. Psychopathy, heredity and environment. *International Journal of Mental Health,* 1972, *1,* 190-206.

Scott, J.P., and Fulker, J.L. *Genetics and the social behavior of the dog.* Chicago: University of Chicago Press, 1965.

Stumpfl, F. *Die Ursprünge des Verbrecheng.* Leipzig: Thieme, 1936.

Stumphauzer, J.S. *Behavior therapy with delinquents.* Springfield, Ill.: C.C. Thomas, 1973.

————. *Progress in behavior therapy with delinquents.* Springfield, Ill.: C.C. Thomas, 1979.

Yoshimasu, J. Criminal life curves of monozygotic twin pairs. *Acta Crimologica* (Japan), 1965, *31,* 5-6.

4

Criminality, Creativity, and Craziness: Structural Similarities in Three Types of Nonconformity

John A. Johnson

Robert R. Holt has suggested that there are three principal types of nonconformity: criminal, psychotic, and creative (Janis et al. 1969). Each type of nonconformity can be distinguished by its social consequences; yet in some cases the three types of nonconformity can be interrelated. Holt cites, for example, Raskolnikov, the protagonist of Dostoevsky's *Crime and Punishment*—a psychotic who committed a crime that he thought was an act of creative nonconformity.

Holt's observation raises an interesting question: Are the three types of nonconformity only superficially similar, or are the underlying personality dynamics for each the same? Is there a common deep structure for deviance, a *g* factor for nonconformity?

Although I had heard arguments about the parallels between creativity and psychoticism and between creativity and delinquency, I had never taken these arguments seriously. First of all, each of these phenomena—criminality, creativity, and craziness—constitutes a broad behavioral category that can be further divided into distinguishable subcategories. Second, each subcategory undoubtedly can be shaped by any of a number of predisposing influences. Despite this complexity, a general deviance factor may still influence all these types of nonconformity. This chapter describes my search for this general deviance factor.

The chapter is divided into two major sections. The first reviews the literature linking the three types of deviance. The second discusses deviance within a sociobiological framework and then describes my own theoretical and psychometric studies of nonconformity.

I would like to acknowledge the help of several colleagues who were involved in the construction of the original socioanalytic personality scales: Catherine M. Busch, Jonathan M. Cheek, Robert Hogan, David H. Schroeder, Robert Smither, and Alan B. Zonderman. My wife, Carolyn, helped prepare the illustration of the socioanalytic model. None of these people are responsible for errors of any form in this chapter.

Definitions

Norms and Normality

A nonconformist—whether criminal, crazy, or creative—deviates from some norm; hence *norm* needs to be defined. *Norm* has two distinct yet interrelated meanings. First, a norm describes a range of psychological functioning that is typical for a population. By this definition, any mental processes or behaviors that are common or frequent are normal; rare or unusual mental processes and behaviors are abnormal. A certain ambiguity exists in this definition because of the fuzziness of terms like *range, typical, frequent,* and *rare.* Consequently, some examples of normality are clear-cut (dreaming is normal; hallucinating is not); others, such as superstitious thinking, are more difficult to classify. Nonetheless, serious criminality, high-level creativity, and pronounced psychoticism are all abnormal by this definition.

According to this definition, norms are descriptive. They simply tell us which psychological processes are common or usual. A second definition of *norm* is prescriptive. A norm may tell us how we *ought* to think or behave. By this definition, criminality, craziness, and creativity differ in their normality. Criminality is clearly immoral and therefore abnormal; craziness is not usually considered immoral, only undesirable; creativity is often considered desirable but rarely labeled moral. Sometimes moral norms run counter to descriptive norms—for example, resisting group pressure to do what is right. Many psychologists regard conformity to descriptive norms as immoral and pathological; see Hogan and Emler (1978). More often, moral norms reflect descriptive norms because typical behavior usually promotes the welfare of a culture (Hogan, Johnson, and Emler 1978). Not discounting the importance or moral norms, this chapter will use the first (descriptive) definition of norms and normality. By this definition criminality, creativity, and craziness all clearly represent deviance from norms.

Creativity

Barron and Harrington (1981) have reviewed several common definitions of creativity. Some definitions require tangible, socially valuable products if a person is to be called creative. Others describe creativity as an ability, or what Schubert and Biondi (1977) call *problem-solving* creativity. A third kind of creativity refers to a general cognitive style and personality syndrome, often seen in artists, involving ideational fluency; conceptual overinclusion; preference for ambiguity, complexity, and asymmetric patterns; a tendency to form many and unusual associations; idiosyncratic thinking;

odd sensory and perceptual experiences; feelings of restlessness and the inclination toward impulsive outbursts; preference for solitude; rejection of common social values; broad interests; autonomy and independence of judgment; and attraction to artistic and aesthetic experiences. This third definition seems most fundamental in a psychological sense to the essence of creativity; hence the chapter uses that definition.

Criminality

A simple legal definition of criminality—that an individual is a criminal if found guilty of breaking a law—misses entirely the psychology of criminal behavior. For our purposes, *criminality* will be defined as a resemblance to what Pavlov called a choleric response to frustration. Choleric types are anxious and emotional and express their emotionality with aggressive outbursts, lawbreaking, and other antisocial behavior.

Craziness

Craziness is a folk concept that describes bizarre, unintelligible thinking and/or behavior. Craziness is unintelligible because it is typically self-defeating and foreign to normal (common) ways of thinking and behaving. Because the context of this chapter is deviance from social norms, the folk concept *craziness* is more appropriate than medical definitions. Technically, the focus here will be on the schizophrenias, or, more generally, *psychoticism*—a loss of contact with socially defined reality. To a lesser extent, the chapter looks at *anxiety neurosis*—a prevailing sense of fear without sufficient reason for being afraid—and at impulse disorders.

Criminality, Creativity, and Craziness

Creativity and Craziness

The idea that creativity is akin to so-called divine madness has a long history, going back at least as far as Plato. Even today schizophrenics in some cultures enjoy privileged social status as shamans or prophets with alleged precognitive powers and creative insight (see Erlenmeyer-Kimling and Parandowski 1966). Galton (1869) and Lombroso (1891) were among the first scientific researchers to conclude that mental illness often accompanies creative genius. Their books generated so many studies confirming the link between creativity and craziness that some investigators (see Claridge 1972) argue that further documentation is unnecessary. This short review of this literature cannot possibly cover all the relevant work in the area. The purpose of the present section is, first, to counter arguments *against* the link between creativity and craziness, and second, to describe some representative recent findings in the area.

People who deny the connection between creativity and craziness often argue that the pain, confusion, poor reality testing, and general maladjustment of someone in the throes of schizophrenia obviously differ from the inventiveness, resourcefulness, ingenuity, originality, and productivity of creative persons. The counterargument is that this claim focuses on outcomes or products (adaptation, productivity) rather than psychological dynamics. Barron and Harrington (1981) carefully distinguish three types of schizophrenia and creativity: (1) schizotaxia and originotaxia (inherited neurological anomalies responsible for ideational fluency, overinclusion, and cognitive complexity); (2) schizotypia and originotypia (personality organizations resulting from both the aforementioned neurological anomalies coupled with certain social learning experiences); and (3) schizophrenia and creativity (the social outcomes of the two types of personalities). Although the social outcomes of creativity and schizophrenia may indeed be very different, the two may be similar at the level of neurology and personality. Differences in outcomes may be due either to quantitative differences in the neurological anomaly or to the presence of a moderating variable (such as intelligence or ego strength) that shapes unusual thought processes into socially useful products.

Another kind of argument denying a commonality between creativity and craziness comes from humanistic psychologists who claim that creativity is essential to overall psychological health (for example, Maslow 1968). In this vein, Schubert and Biondi (1975) suggest that the apparent similarities between creativity and mental illness are superficial and unfounded—that to label originality as illness is to accept Freudian and puritan biases about conformity. Schubert and Biondi (1977) cite studies linking creativity to self-esteem, dominance, confidence, self-assertion, persistence, and self-discipline.

Several responses can be made to Schubert and Biondi's comments. First, the primary reason for their position appears to be philosophical rather than empirical. As humanists they are prone to *assume* that creativity is linked to mental health. Furthermore, their critique of Freud, puritanism, and the Protestant work ethic lies within the moral level of discourse (that is, norms as moral prescriptions rather than empirical descriptions). Second, they are more concerned with a problem-solving type of creativity than an artistic type of creativity; they state that it is the former that "seems to be associated less with reports of maladjustment by psychiatric pathology" (1977, p. 193). This chapter is concerned with artistic, not problem-solving creativity. Finally, in Schubert and Biondi's own literature review, there is as much evidence against their own thesis as for it.

Three types of research support the link between creativity and craziness. The first shows that persons diagnosed with mental disorder score higher than normals on creativity tests. The second shows a correlation between measures of psychopathology and creativity in relatively normal individuals. A third type of research demonstrates that highly creative persons score high on measures of psychopathology. Examples of each type of research follow.

Hasenfus and Magaro (1976) review studies describing the performance of schizophrenics on three kinds of creativity measures: (1) *ideational fluency* (naming as many ways as possible in which two objects are similar), (2) *preference for complex and asymmetrical designs*, and (3) the *tendency to see unusual associations*. Hasenfus and Magaro suggest that schizophrenics' well-documented tendency toward overinclusion on object classification tasks (their finding many ways to group objects in a single category; see Payne and Friedlander 1962) is conceptually equivalent to ideational fluency. Schizophrenics' preference for complexity is supported by two studies. Lewis (1971) found that certain types of schizophrenics score well above the mean on the Revised Art Scale, a well-known measure of creativity and preference for complexity. Davids (1964) showed that chronic schizophrenics liked ambiguity in auditory communications significantly more than two groups of normal subjects. Finally, the proposition that schizophrenics are prone to give more unusual associations than normals is strongly supported by the literature (Buss 1966; Higgins, Mednick, and Philip 1965; Higgins, Mednick, and Thompson 1966).

The next body of research concerns the correlation between psychopathological and creative tendencies in the normal population. Farmer (1974) found that the psychoticism score on the Eysenck Personality Questionnaire (EPQ) correlated highly with the originality score on Guilford's consequences test. Woody and Claridge (1977) compared all the scales of the EPQ (Extraversion, Neuroticism, Psychoticism, and Lie) to the total number of responses and the number of unique responses to the five sections of Wallach and Wing's creativity test. The correlations between Extraversion, Neuroticism, and the ten creativity scores were essentially zero. Psychoticism correlated .32 to .45 with the five total number scores and .61 to .68 with the five uniqueness scores. The Lie scale had a steady, significant, but small (about $-.2$) correlation across the creativity measures. (More will be said about the significance of this finding in the section on creativity and criminality.) Turning to a slightly different methodology, Claridge (1973) found that a number of psychophysiological measures that had been found previously to discriminate psychotics from controls were significantly related to scores on the Guilford divergent-thinking tests.

By far the greatest number of studies on the similarity between psychopathology and creativity deal with pathological personality traits and psychotic thinking in highly creative individuals. As noted earlier, this research was inspired primarily by Galton's (1869) *Hereditary Genius* and Lombroso's (1891) *The Man of Genius*. A rash of similar pathographies of genius followed (Barron 1965), supporting Dryden's famous remark, "Great wits are sure to madness near allied." Havelock Ellis's (1904) careful study of over nine hundred eminent persons listed in the *Dictionary of National Biography* failed to support Dryden's claim, however. Ellis showed that the incidence of full-blown psychosis in his select group was no greater than in the population at large. A similar, more recent study (Goertzel and Goertzel 1962) confirms Ellis's findings about psychosis in eminent persons.

Although Goertzel and Goertzel did not find a higher psychosis rate in their eminent group, they did find a number of other behavioral eccentricities and pathologies to be common. Furthermore, eminence or genius is not precisely creativity. White (1930), reanalyzing Ellis's data, found that people involved in creative work (artists, poets) showed more abnormal traits than noncreatives (soldiers, sailors).

Through the years, others have noted again that creative persons tend to have certain psychopathological traits (Juda 1949; Walder 1965). Drevdahl and Cattell (1958) found their creative artists and writers to be generally emotionally unstable. Creatives tend to use alcohol more than noncreatives (Barron and Harrington 1981; Goodwin 1973; Karlsson 1978; Martindale 1972). Andreason and Canter (1974) found that 73 percent of their creative writers suffered some psychiatric disorder, compared with 20 percent of their controls. Andreason and Powers (1975) demonstrated that creative writers show certain similarities to manic patients and that, consistent with Hasenfus and Magaro's reasoning, creatives score highly on the Goldstein-Scheere Object Sorting Test for schizophrenia. In fact, the writers scored higher on this test of overinclusion than did the schizophrenics in the study. In a similar study, using the Lovibond version of the Goldstein-Scheerer test, Dykes and McGhie (1976) found that both schizophrenics and creatives received high overinclusion scores. Götz and Götz (1979a) found that artists score higher than nonartists on Eysenck's Psychoticism scale; furthermore, successful artists score even higher on the scale than do less successful artists (Götz and Götz 1979b).

No literature review on creativity would be complete without mentioning the most extensive study of creativity yet undertaken. Between 1957 and 1962, living-in assessment studies of highly creative writers, architects, and mathematicians were conducted at the Institute of Personality Assessment and Research (IPAR) at Berkeley, California. These studies have produced a number of lasting contributions to our understanding of creativity, but the most important finding for the purposes of this chapter is that the creative writers scored in the upper 15 percent of the general population on *all* measures of psychopathology on the MMPI. The creative architects were less deviant but still higher than the general population on the MMPI indexes of psychopathology (Barron 1965). In particular, highly creative persons tend to obtain high scores on the MMPI scales *Sc* (schizophrenic) and *Pd* (psychopathic deviate) (Barron 1972b; MacKinnon 1962). What is unusual about these creative persons' scores is that they are accompanied by high scores on the ego-strength scale of the MMPI and by high scores for social effectiveness on the California Psychological Inventory (CPI). This led Barron (1965) to remark that creatives are both sicker and healthier psychologically than normals; in other words, they are much more troubled psychologically but have far greater resources to deal with their troubles.

The high scores obtained by creatives on *Sc* link creativity to schizophrenic thought disorder; the high scores on *Pd* link creativity to criminality (the original criterion for construction of the *Pd* scale). This leads us to the next section on creativity and criminality.

Creativity and Criminality

The relationship between creativity and criminality can be examined in three ways: (1) the creative potential of incarcerated criminals or identified delinquents, (2) the correlation between criminal and creative tendencies in normals, and (3) criminal or psychopathic behavior in creative persons.

To find creativity in criminals appears prima facie unlikely, yet several studies address the issue. In a noteworthy study, Panton (1958) administered the MMPI to 1,313 inmates at a North Carolina prison and found that the group peaked on the *Pd* and *Sc* scales—precisely the scales on which the creative individuals studied at IPAR peaked. A second kind of evidence comes from criminals' scores on infrequency or validity scales of various inventories. Producing rare responses on such scales may simply reflect carelessness but can also indicate creative thinking (see Gough 1968 for a description of low CPI Communality scores; Laufer, Skoog, and Day, 1982; and Weiss 1981). Laufer (1980) found that 201 inmates at the Maryland State Penitentiary scored high on the Infrequency scale of Holland's Vocational Preference Inventory; and Laufer, Johnson, and Hogan (1981) found low scores on the CPI Communality scale for a group of convicted murderers and a group convicted of drug-related crimes. These findings are consistent with Woody and Claridge's (1977) research showing a correlation between the EPQ Lie scale and creativity.

For a direct test of creativity in a criminal population, I applied Weiss's (1981) CPI regression equation for predicting creativity to CPI scores from a group of seventy convicted murderers. The equation (Creativity = 65.96

+ .63 Capacity for Status − .34 Sociability − .37 Good Impression − 1.15 Communality + .61 Empathy) was designed to predict creativity across different samples, and in fact predicted creativity in the architects, research scientists, and mathematicians studied at IPAR. The murderers scored appropriately low on Communality and Good Impression, but were about average on the other three scales. As a result, their creativity score turned out to be 49.6—almost exactly on the mean for Weiss's standardization group. This finding suggests that murderers are no more—but also no less-creative than architects, research scientists, and mathematicians in the general population.

Lynn's (1971) work supports the idea that there are individual differences in creativity in a criminal population. He suggests that there are three types of psychopaths: *aggressive*, who cannot control their impulses and are eventually caught and incarcerated; *inadequate*, who just drift along playing petty confidence tricks; and *creative*, many of whom manage to avoid being caught in their lawbreaking.

Several studies have assessed creativity in delinquents. Finch (1977) compared delinquent, emotionally disturbed, accelerated, and normal children on the Torrance test of verbal creativity, and concluded that socially and emotionally maladjusted children often have higher creative potential than adjusted children. Anderson and Stoffer (1977) found that nondelinquents outperform delinquents on several verbal portions of the Torrance tests, but delinquents score higher on the figural-elaboration portion of the tests. Rosenthal and Conway (1980) found no significant differences between nondelinquents and delinquents on the Torrance tests of unusual uses and nonverbal circles. However, Kaltsounis and Higdon (1977) found that verbal flexibility and originality scores from the Torrance tests were related to records of school offenses. It appears then that the evidence for the proposition that criminals and delinquents have creative potential is mixed and only partially supportive.

The second kind of research looks at associations between criminal tendencies and creativity in normal populations. First, Eysenck and Eysenck (1976) state that their Psychoticism scale is related to both psychosis *and* criminality. Thus the studies previously cited finding a correlation between the Psychoticism scale and creativity (Farmer 1974; Götz and Götz 1979a,b; Woody and Claridge 1977) link criminality to creativity. Doherty and Corsini (1976) found Kohlberg moral-maturity scores to correlate with creativity, fluency, and uniqueness scores on the Wallach-Wing test in a group of college women. This appears to contradict the relationship between criminal (nonmoral) behavior and creativity until one realizes that higher scorers on the Kohlberg index are *postconventional*. This means that high scorers in the Kohlbergian order are rebellious, smug, uninhibited, cynical, and vindictive; that is, they are—not unlike criminals—self-centered rather than group oriented. See Hogan (1970) and Johnson and Hogan (1981) for this often overlooked point about Kohlberg's system.

Finally, we come to studies indicating that creative persons have antisocial or criminal traits. Furcon, Baehr, and Zolik (1966) and Cashdon and Welsh (1966) found that creative individuals are nonconformists. Hammer (1966) described the artists in his study as rebellious; Bachtold (1980) found that the creative women in her study had a tendency to be troublesome and unconventional. Drevdahl (1956) found creative students to score high on the radicalism scale for the 16PF, and Drevdahl and Cattell (1958) found that creative writers and artists scored high on the 16PF radicalism and bohemianism scales. Barron (1965) reports that creative architects, writers, and mathematicians score lower than noncreatives on the CPI Socialization scale (originally constructed to assess a delinquent disposition) and on the MMPI *Pd* scale. Finally, Lynn (1971) notes that many creative people, especially in the arts, have led psychopathic sexual lives.

These studies show that what originally looked like a major conceptual leap between criminality and creativity may actually be smaller than was thought. Next, let us consider the link between criminality and craziness.

Criminality and Craziness

Eysenck and Eysenck (1976) have suggested that criminals and psychotics are similar along their psychoticism and neuroticism dimensions, and that the major difference between the two groups is that criminals are more extraverted. Lynn (1971) also draws this comparison between the two groups. Panton's (1958) large-scale MMPI study of prison inmates indicated marked psychopathology, especially in the schizophrenia dimension. Laufer's (1980) study of vocational interests in prison inmates showed low Masculinity and Status scores, suggesting that his population was depressed and troubled. His findings replicate previous personality and clinical studies of incarcerated felons (Toch 1979; Yochelson and Samenow 1976).

To close this brief section, I might note that *criminality* is not a category of the *Diagnostic and Statistical Manual (DSM* III*)*. Nonethless, many criminals would be classified as having personality disorders. The most recent version of the *DSM* has emphasized the uniqueness of the personality disorders by placing them on a separate axis; still, it is clear that psychopathic, sociopathic, and borderline personalities can easily be both psychopathological and criminal. Also, a number of disorders listed on Axis I are likely to bring an individual into trouble with the law. These include the substance-abuse disorders; paraphilias; and disorders of impulse control (pathological gambling, kleptomania, pyromania).

The foregoing literature review describes a number of studies indicating an empirical relationship among criminal, creative, and crazy forms of deviance. The next section provides a possible explanation for this empirical relationship.

A Sociobiological View of Nonconformity

Sociobiology is the study of the hereditary basis of social behavior. This section discusses evidence for a common genetic basis for criminality, creativity, and craziness; and the role of nonconformity in evolutionary adaptation.

Genetic Basis

This section first reviews the evidence for the genetic basis of the three types of nonconformity separately, and then the evidence linking the types together.

Crowe (1974) reports that at the time of his study, eight studies of criminal twins had been conducted. All the studies implicated hereditary liability for criminality, yet also suggested that life experiences play a role in the development of criminal behavior. Crowe's own study shows that heredity plays a role in the development of the antisocial personality. In another study, Hutchings and Mednick (1975) find a clear association for criminality between biological fathers and their sons who had been adopted by a normal family. Bohman (1978) investigated the genetic influence on alcoholism and criminality and concluded that hereditary factors strongly determine susceptibility to alcoholism and also predispose an individual toward criminality.

Barron and Harrington (1981) review the literature on the inheritance of divergent thinking. The consensus of these studies (Barron 1972a; Barron and Parisi 1977; Domino, Walsh, and Reznikoff 1976; Pezzullo, Thorsen, and Madaus 1972) is that twin resemblances in verbal divergent thinking do not show zygosity effects, but that there is a distinction between verbal and figural creativity, the basis of which is genetic.

That schizophrenia has a genetic basis is now beyond a reasonable doubt. Supporting evidence includes both pedigree studies showing how schizophrenia runs in families and identification of biochemical abnormalities in schizophrenics. A review of this literature can be found in Heston (1970), Shields (1968), Slater (1968), and Zerbin-Rüdin (1967).

The connection between creativity and craziness at the genetic level has been impressively documented by Karlsson (1968, 1970). After studying seven generations of Icelandic pedigrees, he found a high incidence of great creative achievement in many relatives of schizophrenics. In a study of foster children whose biological mothers were schizophrenic, Heston (1966) found that half the children were schizophrenic and half were highly artistic and imaginative. McNeil (1971) also found that mental illness and creativity in a group of adoptees was associated with mental illness of their biological parents.

The genetic link between psychopathology and criminality can be found in Eysenck and Eysenck's study of the psychoticism dimension. They found that high scorers on this dimension have both psychotic and criminal traits and that genetic factors are responsible for 81 percent of all differences between subjects. The other type of evidence connecting psychopathology and criminality at the genetic level comes from the well-known studies of patients with the chromosome constitution XYY. Patients with the XYY syndrome have a pronounced disposition toward personality deviation and criminality (Nielson and Tsuboi 1969).

To my knowledge, research that directly examines the genetic association between criminality and creativity has not been conducted, although Eysenck and Eysenck's high scorers on Psychoticism show unusual association of ideas, indicating creative tendencies.

Evolutionary Adaptation

If schizophrenia is genetically determined and the thought disorder associated with it is maladaptive, why does schizophrenia resist selective pressures and persist in the population? One simple answer is the Hardy-Weinberg law of population genetics, which states that even the most lethal gene will persist in the population at a fixed frequency if there is no selection against the heterozygous form. Most behavioral geneticists have not been content with this purely statistical explanation, however, and speculate that the genes involved in the expression of schizophrenia cannot be exclusively maladaptive.

Huxley et al. (1964) initially suggested that the schizophrenic gene was linked to adaptive genes such that schizophrenics had a higher resistance to wound shock, visceral perforation, and infections. Jarvik and Chadwick (1973), however, state that evidence for physiological advantages associated with schizophrenia is lacking. A more plausible explanation for the persistence of schizophrenia is that the disorder, like height and hair color, is polygenic, allowing for different *degrees* of expression (see Dobzhansky 1964). Partial expression of the syndrome leads to originality and creativity, which is adaptive; the genes for schizophrenia are transmitted by this successful group.

Evidence for the polygenic position comes from several sources. Mc-Conaghy and Clancy (1968) found that allusive thinking (overinclusion) is common in normals, more pronounced in schizophrenics, and genetically transmitted in both groups. Heston (1970) found that one-third of first-degree relatives of schizophrenics are schizoid, suggesting a continuum of the disorder. Gottesman and Shields (1968) found that the concordance rates of schizophrenia in monozygotic twins varied as a function of the severity of psychotic reaction, and that the MMPI profiles of non-ill persons and their schizophrenic co-twins were similar, with both groups peaking on the *Sc* scale. Finally, Claridge (1972), using evidence from many sources including his own psychophysiological data, argues that schizophrenia is a polygenetically determined continuum, its high and low ends leading to maladaptive behavior and the middle to creative, adaptive behavior.

Jarvik and Chadwick (1973) take a slightly different view of the adaptive features of schizophrenia. They argue that it is the schizoid-paranoid personality features of schizophrenia that are adaptive, particularly the paranoid features. Seclusive, suspicious, nonpsychotic carriers of the schizophrenic genes have a psychological advantage for survival in the threatening and competitive world our species inhabits. Jarvik and Chadwick note that the Greek hero, Odysseus, is a prototype of the successful schizoid-paranoid (see Stanford, 1968).

In a partially expressed form, then, schizophrenia can lead to creativity (Claridge 1972) or wariness and prudence (Jarvik and Chadwick 1973). In both cases a nonpsychotic carrier possesses a trait that is personally adaptive, and this increases the probability that the genes will be passed on.

One can also look at deviance and nonconformity within an ecological, cultural context. Because we are a social species and have depended on each other for our very survival, we are compelled to seek help and support from the other members of our group as well as to compete with them in a Darwinian sense (see Hogan, Johnson, and Emler 1978). We cannot survive without the support of our groups; therefore, if we fail to contribute to the welfare of the group, the group will not function viably, and we in turn will perish. Thus we can ask: How do deviance and nonconformity contribute to the welfare of the group?

Tiger and Fox (1971, pp. 52-54) provide an insightful answer to this question. They assume, first, that the capacity to obey the rules of culture is biologically determined and is distributed on a normal curve. Most people will be predisposed to learn quickly and conform to cultural rules; but there will always be a few rebels, so constituted that no amount of socialization will make them conform. Most people will be conformists because nature is essentially conservative: most mutations—whether genetic or cultural—are deleterious. Of the uneducable persons who resist socialization, most fall by the wayside. Occasionally, however, if conditions are right, they stumble on an innovation that, ironically, more efficiently preserves the status quo. Only occasionally do innovations lead to a truly different, new way of life. More often, an innovation is simply an improved way of accomplishing an old aim.

Tiger and Fox suggest that a culture will tolerate its "radical politicians, bloody-minded intellectuals, criminals, religious maniacs, unconventional artists, military geniuses, visionary poets, reformist priests, and revolutionary philosophers" because sometimes "their innovative behavior pays off." They argue that "a principle that runs throughout the evolution of organic life" is "that a species is essentially conservative but that it must allow for innovation. To strike a balance between these two forces is the quintessential evolutionary challenge" (p. 53; see also Hammer and Zubin 1968, for a similar view).

Tiger and Fox also argue that the disposition to conform or deviate is ultimately located in the central nervous system. Acknowledging that training has a great deal to do with the development of a conforming or rebellious personality, they emphasize that people's dispositions to learn or not to learn are present at birth. They cite as supporting evidence Pavlov's experiments with dogs: some dogs were easy to condition, but others resisted all attempts at conditioning. They also note that strains of easily trainable or recalcitrant animals can be bred.

Paul MacLean has also toyed with a model of social deviance based on neurology; he suspects that nonconformity is caused by a defect in the central core of the brain (Holden 1979). Normally the central core controls imitative (MacLean uses the term *isopraxic*) behavior. Examples of isopraxic behavior include the spread of gobbling in a turkey pen and the contagious applause and hooting at political rallies. MacLean notes that damage to the central core of a turkey's brain not only inhibits the isopraxic gobble response but also interferes with the turkey's ability to stick with the group. He speculates that a defect in brain development in some people may contribute to high-level creativity. He cites as a possible example Einstein, who in addition to being a creative genius was also an eccentric nonconformist and a loner. Thus "some individuals may become creative because of a constitutional incapacity for imitation . . . a defect of the nervous sytem that might interfere with the intercommunicative isopraxic process" (quoted in Holden 1979, p. 1067).

Whatever the specific hereditary and neurological mechanisms, deviance plays a functional role in society. A certain amount of nonconformity actually helps the human species to perpetuate itself. A psychometric model describing the place of personality deviance within the context of social roles and normal personality is described next.

Socioanalytic Theory

Socioanalytic theory (Hogan, Johnson, and Emler 1978; Hogan and Johnson 1981; Hogan 1982; Johnson, in preparation) is a comprehensive personality theory designed to explain the role of personality in human evolution. The theory assumes that the three most important problems affecting fitness in our species are (1) achieving status, (2) maintaining social support, and (3) successfully specializing in a role required by the culture. The theory relies heavily on the definitive work of Norman (1963), whose often replicated peer-rating study shows that five dimensions adequately describe the universe of personality traits: Extroversion/Surgency, Emotional Stability, Conscientiousness, Agreeableness, and Culture. The theory also builds on the work of Holland (1973), who describes the world of vocational-role specialization in six categories: Realistic, Investigative, Artistic, Social, Enterprising, and Conventional.

Within the socioanalytic theory, Norman's dimensions were reconceptualized and renamed as follows:

Ascendance (formerly Norman's Extraversion/Surgency) refers to ambition, energy, initiative, and leader-like qualities.

Adjustment (Emotional Stability) refers to absence of anxiety, depression, and guilt.

Rule attunement (Conscientiousness) refers to respect for authority, social rules, and contracts.

Likeability (Agreeableness) refers to tolerance, cooperativeness, warmth.

Intellectence (Culture) refers to how bright and clever one appears.

These personality dimensions are assumed to underlie biological success. That is, persons who are ambitious, well adjusted, attuned to the rules, pleasant, and smart will achieve status and popularity; and this in turn increases their biological fitness.

Two additional components were added to the model to account for differences in vocational-role specialization. *Sociability* is a part of the Ascendance-Extraversion-Surgency complex, and refers simply to whether one prefers working alone or with other people. Holland's Social and Enterprising vocational types represent high Sociability; Realistic and Investigative types represent low Sociability. *Ego Control* (see Block and Block 1979) refers to one's disposition to control one's ideational and behavioral impulses; see also McCrae and Costa's (1980) concept of openness to experience. Persons with high ego control are self-controlled, orderly, conventional, traditional, conservative, and predictable. High ego control defines Holland's Conventional type. Persons with low ego control are impulsive, disorganized, unconventional, experimenting, innovating, and unpredictable. Low ego control defines Holland's Artistic type.

Although Holland's model was designed to describe modern occupations, it can also describe social roles probably present near the beginning of our species' evolutionary history: hunters (Realistic), shamans (Investigative), artisans (Artistic), healers (Social), leaders (Enterprising), and lore-keepers (Conventional). Socioanalytic theory assumes that stabilizing selection has been operating on the genes predisposing people toward either end of the Sociability and Ego-Control dimensions such that all degrees of expression on both dimensions are found; this distributes people into the six role categories required by a culture. Because cultures are essentially conservative (Tiger and Fox 1971), we would expect to find more Conventional than Artistic occupations in society; this is precisely what Gottfredson, Holland, and Gottfredson (1975) found. If evolutionary selective pressures are shaping the joint distribution of Sociability and Ego Control such that people's personalities lead them into roles required by the culture, we should find that the distribution of personality characteristics in a population should match roughly the corresponding distribution of vocational-role requirements. Again, this is what Gottfredson, Holland, and Gottfredson found. (See Buss and Plomin (1975) for evidence on the heritability of sociability and ego control.)

Turning now to the measurement of the seven personality dimensions in socioanalytic theory, three different measures have been constructed: (1) a set of scales using items from the CPI; (2) an adjective-rating form with 49 Likert scales, each anchored by a pair of adjectives; and (3) an objective self-report form using 425 original items. The details of scale construction and validation are presented in Hogan and Johnson (1981), Hogan (1982), and Johnson (in preparation). Our principal concern here is a finding that appeared over and over during the validation of the scales: Rule Attunement (the opposite of criminality) and Ego Control (the opposite of creativity) are intimately related.

First, the two scales correlate highly and significantly across the three measures, despite no overlap in item content (.36 for the CPI version, .62 for the adjective-rating form, and .59 for the socioanalytic self-report scales). Second, the scores tend to covary across naturally existing groups. Table 4-1 shows that murderers and heavy marijuana users score relatively low on the CPI scales for both rule attunement *and* ego control; policemen tend to score relatively high on both dimensions. Rule Attunement and Ego Control also tend to show similar correlations with external criteria (see table 4-2).

Finally, two separate factor analyses failed to separate Rule Attunement from Ego Control. A factor analysis of the CPI scales yielded three inter-

Table 4-1

Comparison of Groups on the CPI Socioanalytic Scales

Group	N	Mean Scale Scores						
		ASC	ADJ	LIK	INT	SOC	RULE	EGO
Baltimore policemen	49	52.6	48.9	48.8	44.1	52.1	53.5	52.3
Oakland policemen	99	52.2	55.1	54.8	46.7	50.2	53.2	53.8
Murderers	70	46.7	44.4	44.2	44.7	47.4	44.4	49.2
Marijuana smokers	49	45.6	46.4	47.9	55.4	53.3	40.1	34.0
Principled nonsmokers	50	48.2	46.4	47.6	48.1	47.2	48.0	53.5
Phi Beta Kappas	57	47.1	46.6	49.5	54.7	48.3	55.0	50.0
Research scientists	45	47.3	54.3	54.5	59.4	47.4	51.6	48.3
Salesmen	44	60.7	57.0	51.0	52.7	55.8	51.9	55.8

Note: Means are reported as standard scores based on the total sample ($N = 463$) with a mean of 50 and standard deviation of 10. Scale abbreviations are: ASC = Ascendance; ADJ = Adjustment; LIK = Likeability; INT = Intellectence; SOC = Sociability; RULE = Rule Attunement; and EGO = Ego Control.

pretable factors, and loadings from Rule Attunement and Ego Control alone defined the second factor. The 425 items on the socioanalytic self-report inventory are grouped a priori into clusters that define facets within the seven dimensions. Rule Attunement contains facets called Caution, Dependability, and Trouble-Avoiding; Ego Control contains facets called Convergent Thinking, Predictability, Planful, Experience-Avoiding, and Thrill-Avoiding. Examples of items for these facets are given in table 4-3, along with facet intercorrelations. A factor analysis of all facets scores from all seven dimensions yielded six interpretable factors. Five of the factors were defined cleanly and precisely by loadings from the facets assigned a priori to the other five dimensions; the third factor in the analysis was clearly defined by loadings from the three Rule-Attunement facets and five Ego-Control facets.

The repeated failure to separate Rule Attunement and Ego Control was frustrating, for I considered the two dimensions conceptually unique. Divergent thinking, enjoyment of novelty, spontaneity, a changeable temperament, and enjoyment of sensory stimulation appeared to me to have nothing to do with rule flaunting, irresponsibility, and lawbreaking. Through the pursuit of novel experiences, the individual low on ego control may occasionally fail to meet social expectations about morality and proper behavior; but this is not necessarily the case. The empirical data disconfirmed my assumptions, however, and suggested that criminality and creativity are linked by a common personality dimension.

Ego control—a psychoanalytic expression coined by Block and Block (1979)—was a term originally adopted for convenience, without endorsing Freudian theory (see Laufer, Johnson, and Hogan 1981, p. 181). Experience indicates that Ego Control may be the best term for this dimension

Table 4-2
Correlates of Rule Attunement and Ego Control

Measure[a]	Rule Attunement	Ego Control
CPI version		
Judging-Perceiving	.35	.71
Survey of Ethical Attitudes	.35	.39
SAT—Quantitative	− .50	− .37
Marijuana use	− .34	− .53
Difficulty of college major	.20	.21
Police Academy grades	.16	.11
Ratings of sales effectiveness	− .01	− .02
Adjective Rating Form		
Survey of Ethical Attitudes	.42	.47
Agreeableness	.25	.29
Empathy	− .20	− .37
Independence of Judgment	− .37	− .55
CPI Rule Attunement	.58	.39
CPI Ego Control	.53	.44
Socioanalytic Self-Report Scales		
Socialization	.40	.26
Self-Control	.58	.44
Communality	.36	.25
Achievement via Conformance	.41	.31
Flexibility	− .34	− .44
CPI Rule Attunement	.59	.50
CPI Ego Control	.47	.64

Note: The samples here range in size from about 30 to 100 and are drawn from various student populations and adults employed in different occupations. All correlations are significant at at least the .05 level except the Police Academy grades and ratings of sales effectiveness.

[a]Clarification and references for the measures are as follows: Judging-Perceiving is from the Myers-Briggs Type Indicator (Myers 1962), scored in the direction of Judging; the Survey of Ethical Attitudes (Hogan 1970) measures two political-moral dimensions: social responsibility and conservatism (high end) and personal conscience and liberalism (low end); difficulty of college major was coded 1 = humanities, 2 = social sciences, 3 = biology or chemistry, 4 = engineering, physics, or mathematics; Agreeableness is from the Guilford-Zimmerman Temperament Survey (Guilford, Zimmerman, and Guilford 1976); Empathy (Hogan 1969) is scored from the CPI; Independence of Judgments was constructed by Barron (1953); and Socialization, Self-Control, Communality, Achievement via Conformance, and Flexibility are all standard scales from the CPI.

and that Freud was essentially correct about the common origin of creativity and antisocial behavior. Relaxation of control on the id leads to the primary-process mentation (that is, mental imagery, unusual associations, lack of linear time constraints) responsible for creativity and also to release of the two major antisocial drives—lust and aggression.

The literature review in the first section of this chapter, together with the data presented in this section, strongly suggests a general factor for devi-

Table 4-3

Intercorrelations among Rule-Attunement and Ego-Control Facets

Dimension/Facet	Sample Item
Rule Attunement	
1 Caution	I would do almost anything on a dare. (R)
2 Dependability	I rarely make a promise I don't keep.
3 Trouble-Avoiding	I have never been in trouble with the law.
Ego Control	
4 Convergent Thinking	I have a good imagination. (R)
5 Predictability	I don't like surprises.
6 Planful	I like to have a schedule and stick to it.
7 Experience-Avoiding	I like a lot of variety in my life. (R)
8 Thrill-Avoiding	I would enjoy sky diving. (R)

Intercorrelations

	1	2	3	4	5	6	7
2	.27						
3	.47	.35					
4	.17	.01	.20				
5	.11	.02	.10	.17			
6	.40	.41	.39	.18	.32		
7	.26	− .03	.35	.40	.35	.25	
8	.32	.15	.40	.14	.29	.29	.45

Note: Sample consists of diverse student and adult groups. Total $N = 268$. (R) indicates item scoring is reversed.

ance or nonconformity. The influence of this factor in human affairs, which I call *Ego Control*, is represented schematically in figure 4-1. Figure 4-1 is a composite picture of Eysenck's depiction of criminality and psychosis within Galen's type theory (Lynn 1971) and my own depiction of Holland's types within Galen's type theory (Hogan and Johnson 1981).

Placement of *criminality, creativity,* and *craziness* in their respective places near the low end of the ego-control dimension in figure 4-1 is based on the following observations. White (1930) found that artists, poets, and men of letters (Artistic and Investigative types) showed more abnormal personality traits than soldiers and sailors (Realistic types). Andreason and Canter's (1974) research supports Aristotle's dictum that artists have a tendency toward melancholia. Barron (1965) reports that creative persons tend to be Jungian perceptive types, and my CPI Ego-Control scale correlated .73 with this Judging-Perceiving dimension. Eysenck finds that psychiatric disorders fall into the melancholic quadrant, whereas criminality and psychopathy fall into the choleric quadrant (Lynn 1971). Finally, the disposition toward alcohol use, which may share a common genetic basis with criminality (Bohman 1978) and creativity (Karlsson 1978) could be a means of dampening the "aggressive cortical fires" that Pavlov claimed rage in the choleric type (Barron and Harrington 1981).

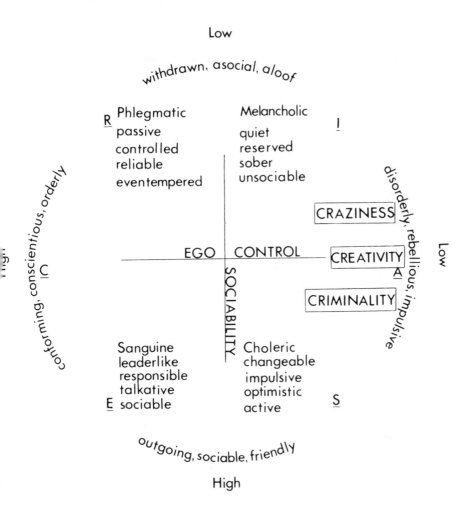

Adjectives around perimeter are from circumplex models of personality and adjectives under Galen types
are Eysenck's. See Hogan and Johnson (1981); underlined letters are Holland's types: R = Realistic, I =
Investigative, A = Artistic, S = Social, E = Enterprising, and C = Conventional.

Figure 4-1. Criminality, Creativity, and Craziness within the Socioanalytic Model

Galen types; Holland types; Ego Control; and criminality, creativity and craziness—to associate all these concepts may be a case of creative insight or crazy overinclusion. Only future research—probably in behavior genetics—will tell. Perhaps now that the commonality among the three types has been described, future research should examine the ways a general personality disposition toward nonconformity differentiates into these three very different phenomena.

References

Anderson, C.M., and Stoffer, G.R. Creative thinking and juvenile delinquency: A study of delinquent and non-delinquent youth on the Torrance Tests of Creative Thinking. *Journal of Creative Behavior*, 1977, *11*, 207.

Andreason, N.J.C., and Canter, A. The creative writer: Psychiatric symptoms and family history. *Comprehensive Psychiatry*, 1974, *15*, 123-131.

Andreason, N.J.C., and Powers, P.S. Creativity and psychosis: An examination of conceptual style. *Archives of General Psychiatry*, 1975, *32*, 70-73.

Bachtold, L.M. Psychoticism and creativity. *Journal of Creative Behavior*, 1980, *14*, 242-248.

Barron, F. Some personality correlates of independence of judgment. *Journal of Personality*, 1953, *21*, 287-297.

_____ . The psychology of creativity. In F. Barron, W.C. Dement, W. Edwards, H. Lindman, L.D. Phillips, J. Olds, and M. Olds, eds., *New directions in psychology II*. New York: Holt, Rinehart, and Winston, 1965.

_____ . *Artists in the making*. New York: Seminar, 1972a.

_____ . The creative personality: Akin to madness. *Psychology Today*, 1972b, *6*, 42-44, 84-85.

Barron, F., and Harrington, D.M. Creativity, intelligence, and personality. *Annual Review of Psychology*, 1981, *32*, 439-476.

Barron, R., and Parisi, P. Twin resemblances in expressive behavior. *Acta Geneticae Medicae et Gemellologiae*, 1977, Spring.

Block, J.H., and Block, J. The role of ego-control and ego-resiliency in the organization of behavior. In W.A. Collins, ed., *Minnesota symposia on child psychology*, vol. 13. New York: Erlbaum, 1979.

Bohman, M. Some genetic aspects of alcoholism and criminality—population of adoptees. *Archives of General Psychiatry*, 1978, *35*, 269-276.

Buss, A.H. *Psychopathology*. New York: Wiley, 1966.

Buss, A.H., and Plomin, R.A. *A temperament theory of personality*. New York: Wiley, 1975.

Cashdon, S., and Welsh, G.S. Personality correlates of creative potential in talented high school students. *Journal of Personality*, 1966, *34*, 445-455.

Claridge, G. The schizophenias as nervous types. *British Journal of Psychiatry*, 1972, *121*, 1-17.

_____ . A nervous typological analysis of personality variation in normal twins. In G. Claridge, S. Canter, and W.I. Humes, eds., *Personality differences and biological variations: A study of twins*. Oxford: Pergamon Press, 1973.

Crowe, R.R. An adoption study of antisocial personality. *Archives of General Psychiatry*, 1974, *31*, 785-791.

Davids, A. Psychodynamic and sociocultural factors related to intolerance of ambiguity. In R. White, ed., *The study of lives*. New York: Atherton Press, 1964.

Dobzhansky, T. *Mankind evolving*. New Haven: Yale University Press, 1964.

Doherty, W.J., and Corsini, D.A. Creativity, intelligence, and moral development in college women. *Journal of Creative Behavior*, 1976, *10*, 276-284.

Domino, G.; Walsh, J.; and Reznikoff, M. A factor analysis of creativity in fraternal and identical twins. *Journal of General Psychology*, 1976, *97*, 211-221.

Drevdahl, J.E., Factors of importance in creativity. *Journal of Clinical Psychology*, 1956, *12*, 21-26.

Drevdahl, J.E., and Cattell, R.B. Personality and creativity in artists and writers. *Journal of Clinical Psychology*, 1958, *14*, 107-111.

Dykes, M., and McGhie, A. A comparative study of attentional strategies of schizophrenic and highly creative normal subjects. *British Journal of Psychiatry*, 1976, *128*, 50-56.

Ellis, H. *A study of British genius*. London: Hurst and Blacket, 1904.

Erlenmeyer-Kimling, L., and Paradowski, W. Selection and schizophrenia. *American Naturalist*, 1966, *100*, 651-665.

Eysenck, H.J., and Eysenck, S.B.G. *Psychoticism as a dimension of personality*. Springfield: Thomas, 1976.

Farmer, E.W. Psychoticism and person-orientation as general personality characteristics of importance for different aspects of creative thinking. BSc thesis, University of Glasgow, 1974.

Finch, J. Comparison of creativity in disturbed, delinquent, accelerated, and normal children. *Journal of Creative Behavior*, 1977, *11*, 211.

Furcon, J.E.; Baehr, M.E.; and Zolik, E.S. Creative personality: A factor analytic study. Paper presented at the Midwestern Psychological Association Conference, Chicago, 6 May 1966.

Galton, F. *Hereditary genius: An inquiry into its laws and consequences*. New York: Appleton, 1869.

Goertzel, V., and Goertzel, M.G. *Cradles of eminence*. Boston: Little, Brown, 1962.

Goodwin, D.W. The muse and the martini. *Journal of the American Medical Association*, 1973, *224*, 35-38.

Gottesman, I.I., and Shields, J. In pursuit of the schizophrenic genotype. In S.G. Vandenberg, ed., *Progress in human behavior genetics*. Baltimore: Johns Hopkins University Press, 1968.

Gottfredson, G.D.; Holland, J.L.; and Gottfredson, L.S. The relation of vocational aspirations and assessments to employment reality. *Journal of Vocational Behavior*, 1975, *7*, 135-148.

Götz, K.O., and Götz, K. Personality characteristics of professional artists. *Perceptual and Motor Skills*, 1979a, *49*, 327-334.

_____. Personality characteristics of successful artists. *Perceptual and Motor Skills*, 1979b, *49*, 919-924.

Gough, H.G. *An interpreter's syllabus for the California Psychological Inventory*. Palo Alto, Calif.: Consulting Psychologists Press, 1968.

Guilford, J.S.; Zimmerman, W.S.; and Guilford, J.P. *The Guilford-Zimmerman Temperament Survey handbook*. San Diego: Educational and Industrial Testing Service, 1976.

Hammer, E.F. Personality patterns in young creative artists, *Adolescence*, 1966, *1*, 327-350.

Hammer, M., and Zubin, J. Evolution, culture, and psychopathology. *Journal of General Psychology*, 1968, *78*, 151-164.

Hasenfus, N., and Magaro, P. Creativity and schizophrenia: An equality of empirical constructs. *British Journal of Psychiatry*, 1976, *129*, 346-349.

Heston, L.L. Psychiatric disorders in foster home reared children. *British Journal of Psychiatry*, 1966, *112*, 819-825.

_____. The genetics of schizophrenic and schizoid disease. *Science*, 1970, *167*, 249-256.

Higgins, J.; Mednick, S.A.; and Philip, F.J. Associative disturbances as a function of chronicity in schizophrenia. *Journal of Abnormal Psychology*, 1965, *70*, 451-452.

Higgins, J.; Mednick, S.A.; and Thompson, R.E. Acquisition and retention of remote associates in process-reactive schizophrenia. *Journal of Nervous and Mental Diseases*, 1966, *142*, 418-423.

Hogan, R. Development of an empathy scale. *Journal of Consulting and Clinical Psychology*, 1969, *33*, 307-316.

_____. A dimension of moral judgment. *Journal of Consulting and Clinical Psychology*, 1970, *35*, 205-212.

_____. A socioanalytic theory of personality. In D.J. Bernstein, ed., *Nebraska Symposium on Motivation 1981: Response structure and organization*. Lincoln: University of Nebraska Press, 1982.

Hogan, R., and Emler, N.P. The biases in contemporary social psychology. *Social Research*, 1978, *45*, 479-534.

Hogan, R., and Johnson, J.A. The structure of personality. Paper presented at the 89th Annual Convention of the American Psychological Association, Los Angeles, September 1981.

Hogan, R.; Johnson, J.A.; and Emler, N.P. A socioanalytic theory of moral development. In W. Damon, ed., *New directions for child development*, vol. 2. San Francisco: Jossey-Bass, 1978.

Holland, J.L. *Making vocational choices: A theory of careers.* Englewood Cliffs, N.J.: Prentice-Hall, 1973.

Holden, C. Paul MacLean and the triune brain. *Science*, 1979, *204*, 1066-1068.

Hutchings, B., and Mednick, S. Registered criminality in the adoptive and biological parents of registered male criminal adoptees. In R.R. Fieve, H. Brill, and D. Rosenthal, eds., *Genetic research in psychiatry.* Baltimore: Johns Hopkins University Press, 1975.

Huxley, J.; Mayr, E.; Osmond, H.; and Hoffer, A. Schizophrenia as a genetic morphism. *Nature*, 1964, *204*, 220-221.

Janis, I.L.; Mahl, G.F.; Kagan, J.; and Holt, R.R. *Personality: Dynamics, development, and assessment.* New York: Harcourt, Brace, and World, 1969.

Jarvik, L.F., and Chadwick, S.B. Schizophrenia and survival. In M. Hammer, K. Salzinger, and S. Sutton, eds., *Psychopathology: Contributions from the social, behavioral, and biological sciences.* New York: Wiley, 1973.

Johnson, J.A. Personality from an ethological and evolutionary perspective. In preparation.

Johnson, J.A., and Hogan, R. Moral judgments and self-presentations. *Journal of Research in Personality*, 1981, *15*, 57-63.

Juda, A. The relationship between highest mental capacity and psychic abnormalities. *American Journal of Psychiatry*, 1949, *106*, 296-307.

Kaltsounis, B., and Higdon, G. School conformity and its relationship to creativity. *Psychological Reports*, 1977, *40*, 715-718.

Karlsson, J.L. Genealogic studies of schizophrenia. In D. Rosenthal and S.S. Kety, eds., *The transmission of schizophrenia.* Oxford: Pergamon, 1968.

_____ . Genetic association of giftedness and creativity with schizophrenia. *Hereditas*, 1970, *66*, 177-182.

_____ . *Inheritance of creative intelligence: A study of genetics in relation to giftedness and its implications for future generations.* Chicago: Nelson-Hall, 1978.

Laufer, W.S. Vocational interests of criminal offenders: A typological and demographic investigation. *Psychological Reports*, 1980, *46*, 315-324.

Laufer, W.S.; Johnson, J.A.; and Hogan, R. Ego control and criminal behavior. *Journal of Personality and Social Psychology*, 1981, *41*, 179-184.

Laufer, W.S.; Skoog, D.K.; and Day, J.M. Personality and criminality: A review of the California Psychological Inventory. *Journal of Clinical Psychology*, 1982, *38*, 562-573.

Lewis, N.P. Cognitive style, cognitive complexity, and behavior prediction in process and reactive schizophrenia. Ph.D. diss. Fordham University, 1971.

Lombroso, C. *The man of genius*. London: Walter Scott, 1891.

Lynn, R. *An introduction to the study of personality*. London: MacMillan Educational Limited, 1971.

MacKinnon, D.W. The personality correlates of creativity: A study of American architects. In P.E. Vernon, ed., *Creativity*. Hammondsworth: Penguin, 1962.

Martindale, C. Anxiety, intelligence, and access to primitive modes of thought in high and low scorers on remote associates test. *Perceptual and Motor Skills*, 1972, *35*, 375-381.

Maslow, A.H. *Toward a psychology of being*. New York: Van Nostrand, 1968.

McConaghy, N., and Clancy, M. Familial relationships of allusive thinking in university students and their parents. *British Journal of Psychiatry*, 1968, *114*, 1079-1087.

McCrae, R.R., and Costa, P.T., Jr. Openness to experience and ego level in Loevinger's sentence completion test: Dispositional contributions to developmental models of personality. *Journal of Personality and Social Psychology*, 1980, *39*, 1179-1190.

McNeil, T.F. Prebirth and postbirth influence on the relationship between creative ability and recorded mental illness. *Journal of Personality*, 1971, *39*, 391-406.

Myers, I.B. *Manual for the Myers-Briggs Type Indicator*. Princeton, N.J.: Educational Testing Service, 1962.

Nielsen, J., and Tsuboi, T. Intelligence, EEG, personality deviation, and criminality in patients with the XYY syndrome. *British Journal of Psychiatry*, 1969, *115*, 965.

Norman, W.T. Toward an adequate taxonomy of personality attributes: Replicated factor structure in peer nomination personality ratings. *Journal of Abnormal and Social Psychology*, 1963, *66*, 574-583.

Panton, J.H. MMPI profile configurations among crime classification groups. *Journal of Clinical Psychology*, 1958, *14*, 305-308.

Payne, R.W., and Friedlander, D. A short battery of simple tests for measuring overinclusive thinking. *Journal of Mental Science*, 1962, *108*, 362-367.

Pezzullo, T.R.; Thorsen, E.E.; and Madaus, G.F. The heritability of Jensen's level I and level II and divergent thinking. *American Educational Research*, 1972, *4*, 539-546.

Rosenthal, D.A., and Conway, M. Adolescents' creativity and non-conformity in school. *Psychological Reports*, 1980, *47*, 668.

Schubert, D.S.P., and Biondi, A.M. Creativity and mental health: Part I. The image of the creative person as mentally ill. *Journal of Creative Behavior*, 1975, *9*, 223-227.

———. Creativity and mental health: Part II. Creativity and adjustment. *Journal of Creative Behavior*, 1977, *11*, 186-197.

Shields, J. Summary of the genetic evidence. In D. Rosenthal and S.S. Kety, eds., *The transmission of schizophrenia*. London: Pergamon Press, 1968.

Slater, E. A review of earlier evidence on genetic factors in schizophrenia. In D. Rosenthal and S.S. Kety, eds., *The transmission of schizophrenia*. London: Pergamon Press, 1968.

Stanford, W.B. *The Ulysses theme: A study in the adaptability of a traditional hero*, 2nd ed. Ann Arbor: University of Michigan Press, 1968.

Tiger, L., and Fox, R. *The imperial animal*. New York: Holt, Rinehart and Winston, 1971.

Toch, H., ed., *Psychology of crime and criminal justice*. New York: Holt, Rinehart and Winston, 1979.

Walder, R. Schizophrenic and creative thinking. In H.M. Ruitenbeek, ed., *The creative imagination*. Chicago: Quadrangle Books, 1965.

Weiss, D.S. A multigroup study of personality patterns in creativity. *Perceptual and Motor Skills*, 1981, *52*, 735-746.

White, R.K. Note on the psychopathology of genius. *Journal of Social Psychology*, 1930, *1*, 311-315.

Woody, E., and Claridge, G. Psychoticism and thinking. *British Journal of Social and Clinical Psychology*, 1977, *16*, 241-248.

Yochelson, S., and Samenow, S.E. *The criminal personality*, vols. 1 and 2. New York: Aronson, 1976.

Zerbin-Rübin, E. Endogene Psychosen. In P.E. Becker, ed., *Humangenetik*. vol. 5, p. 2. Stuttgart: Thieme, 1967.

5

The Good, the Bad, and the Lawful: An Essay on Psychological Injustice

Craig W. Haney

U.S. criminal law is supremely individualistic. Premised on centuries-old notions of free will and personal causation, it holds only the individual lawbreakers personally responsible for presumably free but morally blameworthy choices. With rare exceptions, evil deeds are presumed to be the product of evil, defective persons. Since the criminal law holds only individuals responsible for crime, it is on individuals alone that the institutions of criminal justice—police, courts, prisons—are designed to act.

For nearly a hundred years now, professional psychology has helped buttress this perspective. In the nineteenth century, phrenology, Williams James' concept of *will,* the eugenics movement, and psychological-instinct theory were all used to add scientific legitimacy of sorts to the notion that criminality was a personal trait. In contemporary times, forensic and correctional psychologists provide elaborate individual-centered explanations for crime that, in one way or another, locate the source of criminality within individual lawbreakers. Discussions of the so-called criminal personality, levels of arrested moral development that supposedly distinguish criminals from law-abiding persons, and seemingly endless claims for the existence of a genetic basis to criminality give an academic, scientific gloss to a nineteenth-century view of human behavior that still dominates the criminal law.

Legal Decision Makers as Naive Personality Theorists

Our criminal-justice system is obsessed with a kind of moral character analysis in which decision makers attempt to account for *all* criminal behavior in terms of the personal characteristics of those who perform it. Of course, individual responsibility is the basic operating assumption of this system. Moreover, at numerous crucial stages, legal decisions are made by persons functioning essentially as intuitive psychologists who are highly vulnerable to what has been called fundamental attribution error—the tendency to discount situation and to explain behavior in terms of the personality or disposition of the actor (see Ross 1977). Indeed, legal decision makers make their moral and psychological assessments under conditions that virtually require simplistic, stereotypic thinking. In many instances these judgments are made quickly, are based on limited and superficial information, and are directed at persons whose life circumstances and situations are utterly unfamiliar to the decision makers themselves.

Intuitive or naive personality theorizing operates at all stages of the criminal-justice process. For example, Piliavin and Briar (1964) observe that the majority of police dispositions of juveniles are determined by "a youth's demeanor" (p. 210, emphasis in original). The police wield a tremendous amount of discretion in the field, and they exercise it largely as character analysts who decide on a suspect's intrinsic blameworthiness and criminality on the basis of superficial information. "Despite this dependence of disposition decisions on the personal characteristics of the youths," write Piliavin and Briar, "police officers actually had only very limited information about boys at the time they had to decide what to do with them" (p. 209).

At an entirely different level in the criminal-justice process, Sudnow (1965) has suggested that criminal attorneys make crucial decisions about their case referrals based on a very limited number of case and client characteristics. That is, they stereotype so-called normal crimes and criminals in the fashion of intuitive psychologists who invoke their own untested ideas about the kind of people who supposedly commit certain crimes and the manner in which they commit them. As a final example, the U.S. Supreme Court has countenanced a questionable form of judicial character analysis, approving the decision of a trial judge who purported to determine a defendant's veracity merely from personal observations from the bench. The Court not only acknowledged but legitimized this kind of naive psychologizing by trial judges, and explicitly endorsed the discounting of situational pressures in attempts to judge the moral worth of a defendant. See *United States* v. *Grayson,* 98 S.Ct. 2510 (1978).

These kinds of psychological or personality assessments are at the heart of the criminal-justice process. Not only do police, lawyers, and judges engage in them; probation officers, parole boards, and prison guards are also the captives of a dispositional world view in which snap judgments about character and morality are used to explain crime and guide decisions about punishment.

Criminal-justice officials have been aided and abetted in the commission of fundamental attribution error by professional forensic and correctional psychologists. Strictly speaking, of course, psychological theories of crime and deviance become *legally* operational only at the margins. The use of quasi-scientific discourse and authority in marginal cases, however, serves to legitimate the working assumptions of the system in more typical cases. In the courtroom, for example, forensic psychologists are called on to decide statistically infrequent questions like sanity and diminished capacity. Despite their statistical infrequency, however, the enormous publicity they receive invests these forensic battles over mental states with tremendous symbolic significance. Implicitly, these trials serve to define all other defendants—the enormous number over whom such battles are never waged—as psychologically responsible, not just legally, but scientifically as well. Heated debates over certain mental diseases and defects imply that the scientific community recognizes no other forms of exculpation.

Ironically, many defendants who are found psychologically adequate at trial—relatively free of mental disease or defect—are sentenced to some form of treatment upon conviction. For example, those who are incarcerated are strongly encouraged to obtain some form of psychological help; many jurisdictions make psychotherapy a functional prerequisite for release. Every convict knows that a positive psychological evaluation, even when it is not mandatory, improves his chances for parole. These practices further reinforce the popular belief that the proper target of criminal justice processing is the individual offender and his dysfunctional characteristics. Both the explanatory and the moral discourse of criminal law and criminal justice are limited by the straitjacket of individualistic psychologizing.

In particular, the work of forensic and correctional psychologists contributes directly to the prevailing fiction that personal shortcomings rather than accidents of birth distinguish criminals from the law-abiding. Since failures of will, defects of personality, genetic imperfections, and retarded moral development are all used by psychologists to account for crime in individualistic terms, political, sociological, and institutional variables over which individuals have virtually no control are given little currency in traditional psychological analyses. Of course, the fact that forensic and correctional psychologists continue to ignore these macro variables makes it much easier for the criminal law to do so as well. Debates over the validity of various contending theories of crime serve to mask the more basic message: the source of crime resides in the makeup of the individuals who commit it.

Moral-Development Theory: The New Phrenology?

A clear contemporary example of the individualizing effects of psychology on criminal justice can be found in recent theorizing about stages of moral development. Kohlberg (1969, 1976) and others have formalized some interesting psychological propositions about the way in which children and adults develop a moral or ethical world view. Kohlberg suggests that the process in some ways parallels the Piagetian stage theory of cognitive development. In particular, he posits a sequence of six possible stages of moral functioning, each characterized by a distinct framework of ethical thinking. The stages are proposed as universals; the core operations of any stage, it is argued, should be identifiable independent of cultural context and immediate situational constraint.

Not surprisingly, moral-development theory has been used to explain crime and delinquency. Criminals break the law, the Kohlbergians have contended, because they suffer from what is, in essence, an arrested level of moral development. The lower stage of morality at which certain people function accounts for their propensities toward crime. Indeed, entire correctional programs of therapy and rehabilitation have been premised on the notion that what convicted criminals really need is to have their moral development advanced a stage or two (see, for example, Hickey and Scharf 1980).

I have focused on Kohlberg's theory precisely because it is the least extreme example in a recent wave of individualistic theories of crime. Kohlberg's theory, for example, has none of the harsh and punitive qualities that characterize other so-called theories of moral defect (for example, Yochelson and Samenow 1976). It has none of the brutal pessimism embodied in theories that locate propensities toward crime in the genes of criminals (for example, Mednick 1977). Indeed, it has a decidedly liberal bent. The Kohlbergians concede that a deprived set of life experiences account for arrested levels of moral development, and they even acknowledge the contribution of institutional milieus to levels of moral functioning (see Kohlberg 1969).

Fundamentally, however, moral-development theory is entirely consistent with past attempts to psychologize the causes of crime. It places the locus of criminal behavior ultimately within those who perform it, and its therapeutic implications restrict the focus of criminal-justice remedies to the individual criminal. It seeks to encapsulate a complex interaction of personal motives and situational constraints into simplistic stages that then serve as an index of moral functioning—much as the early phrenologists typed all their patients on the basis of skull size and shape. Albeit with different instruments and with a different metric, Kohlbergian criminologists measure their lawbreaker subjects and account for crime in terms of the personal, psychological dimensions of criminals. Although the moral-development theorists have little of the psychodiagnostic extremism that characterizes many present-day forensic psychologists, who see all criminals as sociopaths, the logic of their enterprise is fundamentally compatible. Only the dimensions of the disorder—still underlying and personal—have been changed.

Moral-development theorists tend to reify stages of moral development and talk about them as though they were causal entities. People become "stage 2s" and "3s," and one's stage designation is used to explain all manner of complex social behavior. More important, however, they translate differences in moral decision making into ostensible variations in cognitive capacity. That is, stage 2s are simply incapable of *understanding* the concepts and discourse regularly employed by their higher-level brethren. In analogizing the development of a moral framework to the evolution of cognitive categories, moral-development theory implies that fundamental intellectual differences separate criminals from the law-abiding. By implication, then, crime becomes more a category of nature than simply a social or legal construction. Like most psychological perspectives on crime, moral-development theory emphasizes natural and personal dysfunction. Crime, as the product of defective levels or stages of moral functioning, is neutralized as an index of political or socioeconomic dysfunction in a society.

Moral-development theory treats morality as a platonic form, something that can be judged and graded independent of social context. Psychologists have often taken their own value-laden matrixes, or those of their culture, and applied them as though they were neutral and objective yardsticks with which to parse the material world. The closer a behavioral event or expressed opinion comes to their own norms or values, then the more adaptive, or healthy, or good it is considered.

The consequences of using arbitrary divisions along a culture- and class-bound continuum to grade people on their propensities for crime are manifold. This approach ignores the fact that criminal laws—by which crimes and hence criminals are defined—are the product of a highly imperfect and intrinsically sociopolitical process; that they are drafted and administered by persons who have little knowledge of or interest in the life circumstances of those to whom the laws are most often applied; and that the legal process represents the interests (and the world views) of some persons far better than those of others. Moreover, it ignores the possibility that radically different social conditions may produce a moral perspective that is neither higher nor lower than that of the well-educated upper-middle class—just different. The idea that crime can be reduced simply by teaching one class to think like another is both naive and unjust.

Explaining Crime: The Challenge of Situational Analysis

Consider the plight of an unemployed black factory worker in Detroit. Recent changes in affirmative-action policies and a depressed, worsening economy have resulted in massive layoffs, especially for minority residents of the inner city. Despite his unemployed status, he and many others still face high rents—made higher by a housing shortage and record interest rates—and rising prices for food and clothing. These countless mounting economic pressures mean that he will not be able to meet his family's material needs, not to mention his own personal needs for efficacy and self-respect. He drinks heavily and his family relationships soon begin to deteriorate. After he moves into an apartment by himself, an old friend makes what seems like an attractive proposition. About six months later, the two of them are arrested for a string of convenience-store robberies they have committed in a nearby Detroit suburb.

Or take a young Vietnam veteran who learned about violence, drugs, and drug trafficking while stationed just outside Saigon. Unlike some of his friends who were in college at the time, he was drafted just one year out of high school and forced to interrupt a promising apprenticeship with a plumbing contractor. He returned to the United States three years later, haunted by memories of the war and perplexed by the hostile and ungrateful reception he received, even from people he thought would understand. He senses a distance between himself and his old friends, and an inner coldness that is, perhaps, the legacy of spending too much time too close to the horrors of that war. Lacking his former direction and purpose, he drifts from job to job, tries junior college for a while, and ends up in a big drug-dealing operation near Seattle. In this lucrative business, people who are not afraid of high risks or the threat of violence are valued and successful. One night, however, the threats materialize, two people are critically wounded in a shootout, and he is charged and convicted of assault with a deadly weapon.

Finally, consider a young Chicano prisoner in a large southwestern state penitentiary, serving time on a burglary conviction. He is still angry about the long prison sentence that he is convinced he received because he refused to plea bargain. After his conviction in a jury trial, the judge sentenced him to several years in the penitentiary despite his relatively clean prior record. Although he is street-wise and sophisticated, nothing in his past life has prepared him for the world he confronts in prison. The state prison system is desperately overcrowded, and he is housed in a dormitory bulging with twice the number of men it was designed to hold. His youthful appearance makes him a likely target for homosexual attacks, and living in a dormitory makes him especially vulnerable. One night, three men make their way to his bed, a violent struggle ensues, and one man lies dead. He is charged with murder and taken to disciplinary isolation, where he remains for seven months pending trial.

Stage 2s? Sociopaths? Extraverts high in psychoticism who do not condition easily? Perhaps—but these men are also subject to the press of powerful situational forces over which they have virtually no control. Often the force of the situation accounts for far more criminal behavior than any personal characteristics of the lawbreaker. No psychological analysis that fails to consider the nature of the immediate situation can adequately explain crime in contexts like these.

Under many circumstances, in fact, crime can be interpreted as a product of a desperate struggle to maintain a subjectively valid, meaningful existence within a prevailing social context or situation. This struggle may be misguided, or it may be heroic. Sometimes the social consequences of crime are trivial or unimportant; often they are tragic. Despite these variations, there is simply no convincing evidence that crimes are committed for reasons that are fundamentally different from those that underlie non-criminal behavior. Individual personality and dispositional variables account for very little of the variance in most forms of behavior (see for example, Mischel 1968), and there is no reason to expect them to be any more useful in explaining crime. Indeed, given the powerful and extreme nature of the situations under which most crime occurs, one would expect traditional dispositional variables to play an even more marginal role.

Thus I suggest that what distinguishes most criminals from the law-abiding is not their deranged psyches, pathological personality traits, or stunted moral development, as many psychologists have argued. Rather what accounts for most crimes is the systematic exposure of some persons to criminogenic social conditions like poverty and racism. People become criminals as much because of where they are as what they are.

Critics of the situational analysis of crime are likely to identify this apparent anomaly: since not *everyone* in the same situations behaves identically, they argue, the situations could not be causally responsible for the behavior in question. The first response to this critical challenge is that often what appear to be variations in behavior within the same situation can be accounted for in terms of variations in the situations itself. Important psychological features of a social context or setting are not necessarily distributed evenly throughout the situation. In addition, people may interpret the same situation differently. Under certain circumstances, cognitive interpretations of situations carry as much psychological force as any objective features of the environment. I.W. Thomas (1928) observed some time ago that "[i]f men define situations as real, they are real in their consequence" (p. 572).

Finally, it is possible to acknowledge the existence of individual differences and still to attribute major, even primary, causal significance to social context and situations. An analogy may help to clarify this fact. Psychopharmacology commonly identifies a range of individual psychological reactions or responses to various drugs. Physical variables like body weight, along with a host of other variables such as preexisting expectations, habits, and so on, help to determine particular individual reactions. Some people fail to respond at all to certain dosages of certain drugs, and some dosages are so potent that virtually everyone reacts with a high degree of consistency. The fact that there is individual variation in response in no way undermines the causal significance of the chemical agent. The same logic applies to situational determinants of behavior. The fact that people react differently to the same situation does *not* mean that the situation is not causing the behavior. External pressures may affect people differently, just as internal chemical agents do; but they affect them nonetheless. There also exist some situations so powerful, some dosages so high, that virtually everyone responds in largely the same way.

In this context it is also important to note that criminals are often distinguished from the law-abiding not by something instrinsic in their personality or character (as I have already argued), and not even by something intrinsic to the actions they perform. Rather, criminality must also be viewed as an ascribed status whose ascription sometimes turns as much on the actions of others as on the behavior of the individual himself. That is, it represents the outcome of selective decision making by criminal-justice personnel who are more sensitive to—and regard as more dangerous—the transgressions of some persons than those of others. Note that lawbreaking of some sort occurs with high frequency at literally every level of our society. Attempts to explain crime by studying the individual characteristics or personalities of captive populations like prisoners fail to account for the criminality of virtually everyone else who—because of who they are and the particular form their criminality takes—are not arrested, prosecuted, and incarcerated—and will never be.

Personality or dispositional analyses fare no better when they restrict themselves to the extreme forms of criminality like violent crime. It is clear that under certain circumstances virtually everyone is capable of violence. In wartime, for example, persons with no discernible personality disorders or psychopathology engage in extreme, often savage, violence. Ironically, under war conditions, persons who *refuse* to engage in violent behavior are regarded as criminals. No exclusively personality-centered or dispositional theory of crime can account for these facts. It is clear that social context and situation play a major role not only in shaping the behavior of lawbreakers, but also in influencing the very decisions that determine who and what is labeled criminal.

Institutional Socialization: The Irony of Corrections

One situational variable in particular plays an especially important role in explaining crime. Exposure to criminogenic conditions like poverty and racism not only increases the probability that someone will engage in behaviors that are defined as criminal, but also makes it more likely that such behavior will be recognized and labeled as such. Labeling theory suggests that the mere act of officially designating and treating individuals as delinquents or criminals may intensify their commitment to criminality. Other research shows that these official labels drastically narrow one's legitimate opportunities for subsequent economic survival and thus worsen the nature of the situations one is likely to encounter (see, for example, Schwartz and Skolnick 1962). The most criminogenic situation that official lawbreakers encounter, however, may be one of the criminal-justice system's own devising: imprisonment.

Prison is an intriniscally dispositional institution. Founded on the premises of nineteenth-century individualistic psychology, it is the concrete and steel legacy of a now outmoded model of human behavior (see Haney, in press). In theory, at least, persons are imprisoned to have their personalities changed, their moralities upgraded, or just to be taught a lesson. Whatever the specific goal, however, individual-level change is the ultimate purpose and represents the criminal-justice system's complete response to the social problem of crime. In the name of corrections, however, many prisons force essentially criminal adjustments on prisoners. Many of these "forcing houses for the changing of persons" (Goffman 1961) constitute inherently pathological situations that create and maintain crime.

Prisons are hostile, dangerous places. They pose substantial threats to both the psychological and the physical well-being of inmates (see Haney and Zimbardo 1977). Prisons are plagued with the highest crime rates in society, and prisoners suffer mortality and illness rates that far exceed those of comparable free populations (see, for example, Jones 1976). For some prisoners, psychological survival depends on the ability to withdraw, to take refuge in whatever emotional distance one can create from surrounding events. Others adjust by adopting a predatory stance, learning to view people as so-called marks to be used or exploited. Still others adapt by conceding virtually everything to the institution, becoming highly dependent on prison structure and routine for personal order and stability. In any event, successful adjustment to imprisonment can mean intensifying and cementing a commitment to a life-style and set of values that prove highly dysfunctional in the world outside prison. For many, the experience of imprisonment is, quite literally, criminogenic: it constitutes a socialization *into*, rather than away from, criminality.

Too often, psychological individualism has acted to blunt the significance that is attached to institutional socialization and its pathological consequences. Correctional staff members, as captives of a dispositional world view, are indirectly trained and functionally required to disregard and dismiss the impact of the prison environment on the behavior of prisoners. Instead, they are encouraged to perceive behavioral deviance —in the form of apparent psychological deterioration or intensified commitments to so-called criminality—as outward expressions of inner deviance and defect. Such behavioral adjustments, often forced on prisoners by a powerfully harsh and unremitting environment, are regularly translated into dispositional terms and interpreted as confirmation of the original legal and psychological diagnosis.

Conclusion

Contemporary social research provides much evidence for the importance of situational variables in understanding complex social behavior, including behavior in correctional settings (see, for example, Haney, Banks, and Zimbardo 1973). Wider recognition of this fact should lead to a greater appreciation not only of the role that social conditions play in generating crime, but also of the role that imprisonment itself plays in the perpetuation of criminal behavior. Continued adherence to a nineteenth-century dispositional model of behavior and a related criminal-justice policy that relies exclusively on individual confinement appears socially irrational. Dispositional theories, however, continue to take the pressure off our political and economic systems. When issues are seen as the product of pathological people, we are less concerned about changing situations. Even apparent irrationality can be explained.

References

Goffman, E. *Asylums: Essays on the social situation of mental patients and other inmates.* New York: Doubleday, 1961.

Haney, C. Criminal justice and the nineteenth century paradigm: The triumph of psychological individualism in "the formative era." *Law and Human Behavior*, in press.

Haney, C.; Banks, C.; and Zimbardo, P. Interpersonal dynamics in a simulated prison. *International Journal of Criminology and Penology*, 1973, *1*, 69-97.

Haney, C., and Zimbardo, P. The socialization into criminality: On becoming a prisoner and a guard. In J. Tapp and F. Levine, eds., *Law, justice, and the individual in society: Psychological and legal issues.* New York: Holt, Rinehart and Winston, 1977.

Hickey, J., and Scharf, P. *Toward a just correctional system.* San Francisco: Jossey-Bass, 1980.

Jones, D. *The health risks of imprisonment.* Lexington, Mass.: Lexington Books, D.C. Heath and Company, 1976.

Kohlberg, L. Stage and sequence: The cognitive-developmental approach to socialization. In D. Goslin, ed., *Handbook of socialization theory and research.* Chicago: Rand McNally, 1969.

_____. Moral stages and moralization: The cognitive-developmental approach. In T. Lickona, ed. *Moral development and behavior: Theory, research, and social issues.* New York: Holt, Rinehart and Winston, 1976.

Mednick, S., and Christiansen, K. *Biosocial bases of criminal behavior.* New York: Gardner, 1977.

Mischel, W. *Personality and assessment.* New York: Wiley, 1968.

Piliavin, I., and Briar, S. Police encounters with juveniles. *American Journal of Sociology*, 1964, *70*, 206-214.

Ross, L. The intuitive psychologist and his shortcomings: Distortions in the attribution process. In L. Berkowitz, ed., *Advances in experimental social psychology*, vol. 10. New York: Academic Press, 1977.

Schwartz, R., and Skolnick, J. A study of legal stigma. *Social Problems*, 1962, *10*, 133-138.

Sudnow, D. Normal crimes: Sociological features of the penal code in a public defender's office. *Social Problems*, 1965, *12*.

Thomas, I.W., and Thomas D. *The child in America*. New York: Knopf, 1928.

Yochelson, S., and Samenow, S. *The criminal personality*, vol. I. *A profile for change*. New York: Jason Aronson, 1976.

6

A Psychoanalytic Perspective on the Diagnosis and Development of Juvenile Delinquents

Robert J. Marshall

Besides the autistic and schizophrenic child, the juvenile delinquent is most resistant to understanding and treatment. Gold and Petronio (1980), after reviewing the myriad approaches to delinquents, conclude, "Nevertheless, we know very little about what really works, and we suspect, from what careful research has been done, that very few methods have worked at all" (p. 518). Reminded of the skepticism of Freud in his treatment of the narcissistic (schizophrenic) disorders, and considering the unrewarding work with antisocial youth, we might have to formulate more accurately the diagnosis and etiology of delinquency before we can mount effective treatment programs. Only from a secure theoretical base can clinicians develop treatment strategies that attempt to meet delinquents' profound and persistent resistances to change. Programs designed to treat delinquents may have been limited by the fact that the theory of treatment had not been spelled out in any detail. This chapter endeavors to define delinquency and then provide a developmental schema for the *modal delinquent* that relies heavily on psychoanalytic theory and infant-child studies. In applying this psychoanalytic magnifying glass, we will clarify some aspects of the problem but necessarily peripheralize and neglect other parts of the field. This chapter does not purport to be a representative psychoanalytic view of the field. Rather, it is a report of a practicing psychoanalyst who has tried to synthesize his knowledge of the literature with his clinical experience. This chapter seeks to define *modal delinquency* as a type of delinquency that is characterized by certain developmental experiences that organize the character structure and result in delinquent behavior.

Definitions and Diagnoses of Delinquency

Prior to any discussion of the delinquent, the task of definition must be addressed. Also, we should note the conceptual possibility that, just as there exist schizophrenia*s*, there also exist juvenile delinquent*s*. It seems likely that a conceptual-logical error occurs when we assume that juvenile delinquency (the behavior) is a unitary concept. The task of definition is here limited to developing a classification that aids in determining etiology, from which should flow the theory of treatment. Understanding the etiology, which would include development of ego functions, defenses, affects, object relations, and so on, the therapist can more readily anticipate resistances, transferences, evoked countertransferences, and the like, and therefore operate in a more secure conceptual framework.

Legal-Behavioral Definitions

Definitions based only on legal and behavioral criteria are insufficient, if not misleading. This type of definition is ambiguous because factors such as age and definitions of crime vary according to areas of legal jurisdiction. Many studies simply define their delinquent sample as being incarcerated, being held for court, or on probation.

Possible interpretations are pointed up by Carr (1950):

1. The legal delinquent: all those who have violated the law. This traditional view of delinquency is accepted by Cloward and Ohlin (1960), among others. Since it is estimated that at least half of the population qualifies by this definition, however, it is clear that this criterion has little merit.
2. The delinquent who is detected and caught.
3. The delinquent brought to the attention of the police.
4. The delinquent brought to court.
5. The delinquent who is adjudicated.

Any of these definitions is a function of the nature and attitudes of law-enforcement and court personnel. Clark and Wenninger (1962) note that delinquency rates vary according to social class, ethnic group, and sex. Wax (1972) argues that the urban juvenile, typically black, of low socioeconomic status, and with limited resources to defend himself legally, is at the highest risk of being reported and adjudicated.

Clark and Wenninger (1962) tend to verify the variation in delinquency rates according to social class, ethnic group, and sex. Becker (1963) and Kai Erikson (1962) prefer to define deviance (delinquency) as behavior that society responds to as deviant. Williams and Gold (1972) see merit in distinguishing between adjudicated delinquency and self-reported delinquency, whereas Gould (1969) argues for three distinct operational concepts of delinquency: delinquency acts, official delinquency, and self-perceived delinquency.

These studies, which define delinquency in terms of overt behavior and gross social variables, appear to be congruent with the orientation of behavior and social therapists in that antecedent conditions (etiology) and organismic (psychodynamic and personality) variables are of minor importance. The focus on overt behavior to the neglect of antecedent and dynamic variables may prove meaningless, for there is much evidence that so-called delinquent behavior may be the final common pathway for various background and personality factors.

From Social-Moral to Psychiatric Definitions and Diagnoses

Adelaide Johnson (1959) cites a six-thousand-year-old inscription of an Egyptian priest, who declaimed "our earth is degenerate . . . children no longer obey their parents." Schimel (1974) dates the earliest recorded code of laws pertaining to children back to Babylon's Hammurabi in 2270 B.C.: "if a son strikes his father, one shall cut off his hands." The standards for judging delinquency remained arbitrary for centuries. De Mause (1974a,b) and Sanders (1970) provide historical perspectives on societal attitudes toward juvenile offenders. They point out the lack of differentiation between adult and child and the particular savagery of treatment of the child who seemed to step past societal norms.

By 1920, however, the medical model was well established, implying that criminals, especially children, were sick and hence not entirely responsible for their actions. Treatment and rehabilitation rather than punishment were prescribed. In 1924 the American Orthopsychiatric Association (AOA) was founded, with William Healy (Healy and Bronner 1948) as its first president. A high priority for the AOA was the identification and study of juvenile delinquency. Slowly but surely, especially through the impact of psychoanalysis and ego psychology, the unitary concept of delinquency—with its emphasis on the delinquent act, heredity, negative emotional valence, and poor prognosis—eroded. In its place there grew an appreciation for the individual's familial background, development, environment, intrapsychic processes, affects, ego functioning, and interpersonal and object relations.

The 1920s and 1930s were dominated by psychoanalytic workers, particularly Hug-Hellmuth, Melanie Klein, and Anna Freud. Although Sigmund Freud explicitly turned away from his study of environmental factors on the child to focus on intrapsychic development, psychoanalysts devoted considerable attention to external factors such as the family as a whole, as demonstrated by Flugel (1921). Wilhelm Reich (1925, 1949) provided new insights into the nature of the impulsive character; Alexander and Staub (1956) in 1931 elaborated on Freud's "theory of delinquency out of a sense of guilt." Lippman (1926) provided one of the first expositions of a psychoanalytic study and treatment of a thief.

Perhaps the most significant and far-reaching work was conducted by Aichhorn (1936, 1949, 1964). Aichhorn has influenced the theory and treatment of delinquents for fifty years, although the full impact of his work did not hit the United States until 1936, when *Wayward Youth* was translated. Aichhorn introduced the concept of *latent delinquency* as opposed to behavioral delinquency. He noted that certain character trends were evident before any overt symptoms of delinquency appeared. This simple formulation represented a major conceptual breakthrough. Aichhorn also distinguished between delinquents whose acts were based on neurotic conflicts and those who suffered from developmental failures in ego and superego structures.

Eissler (1949), in amplifying Aichhorn's work, decried the use of a behavioral deviance model and sought to promote a motivational model that did not rely on external criteria and focused instead on a patient's configuration of behavior, thoughts, and feelings that infringe on societal values.

Glover's far-reaching work (1944) in relating psychoanalysis to jurisprudence divided delinquency into neurotic and characterological types. Kate Friedlander (1947, 1949) identified three types as antisocial, organic and psychotic. Van Ophuijsen (1945) introduced the concept of *Primary Behavior Disorder.* The word *primary* indicates that the deviant behavior is not a result of or secondary to constitutional factors, but is a direct result of experiences. Included were habit disorders such as thumb sucking and bed wetting, and conduct disorders such as disobedience, destructiveness, and disorderliness. Marked by little anxiety, the children were assumed to have had a reasonably secure infancy but were treated negatively as autonomy and self-assertiveness grew. Based on The Adult Profile established by Freud, Nagera, and Freud (1965), Michaels and Stiver (1965) have developed a Diagnostic Profile of the Impulsive Psychopathic Character. Although the latter has promise as a theory-derived holistic description of a delinquency type, some of its categories, such as libido distribution, seem difficult to quantify.

David Levy (1932) distinguished between the *milieu delinquent,* who is created by the environment, and the *neurotic delinquent,* who creates delinquency in the environment. Adelaide Johnson (1949) described one type as functioning out of *superego lacunae,* and a *sociologic* type, whose behavior was determined by the values of peers, family, and neighborhood. Karpman (1953, 1959) whose reports typified the work of the early 1950s on delinquency, distinguished eight types. Synthesizing psychoanalytic, social, and developmental factors, Hauser focused on the etiological factors of primary narcissism. Red (1945) differentiated four types: (1) the basically healthy youth whose delinquency is a natural defense against wrong handling, wrong setting, or traumatic experiences; (2) the basically nondelinquent

youth who reacts to an acute adolescent growth crisis; (3) the neurotic delinquent; and (4) the genuine delinquent who suffers from disturbances in the
impulse systems, ego, superego, and ego ideal.

Pati (1961) outlined the following categories in 100 cases: primary
behavior disorder—22; neurotic delinquents—20; ego-immaturity patterns—12; schizoid and preschizophrenic—18; sexual delinquents—12;
mental deficiency, organic, or epileptic—16 (see Russell 1969, 1975).

One promising approach to the theory of treatment of the delinquent has
been offered by the Modern Psychoanalytic School. The staff of the Jewish
Board of Guardians, faced with treatment-resistant children and their
families, evolved unique and effective approaches, some of which appear in
works by Spotnitz (1976) and Strean (1970), and are updated by Marshall
(1979). Considering the impact of the Modern Psychoanalytic School; the
work of M. Mahler; and the contributions of Kohut, Masterson, and the
Kernbergs, one can discern a major quantitative, if not qualitative, change in
the conceptualization of delinquency, with emphasis shifting to preoedipal
phenomena and the evolution of the ego, self, and object relations.

Clinical-Statistical Diagnoses

Perhaps the most elegant way to define delinquency is to use a model that
requires a description of three interacting variables: (1) antecedent environmental conditions, (2) intrapsychic states, and (3) consequent
behavior. This so-called E-I-B model, proposed by Moles, Lippitt, and
Withey (1959), has been used to great advantage by several researchers.
Jenkins (1967), and Jenkins and Hewitt (1944), using psychoanalytic concepts, the foregoing model, and a statistical treatment of their data, have
outlined three types of delinquents: the overinhibited, the underinhibited,
and the pseudosocial. Each has its own developmental background. These
formulations suggest therapeutic approaches. Quay (1966), reviewing his
previous factor-analytic studies, finds three factors that hold up across
samples of male delinquents: (1) a neurotic disturbed delinquent
characterized by guilt anxiety, depression, and withdrawal; (2) a subcultural
socialized delinquent characterized by immaturity and identification with a
delinquent subgroup; and (3) an unsocialized psychopath marked by com-
pulsiveness, assaultiveness, rebelliousness, amorality, and lack of concern
for others. The value of this differentiation is shown in a study by Hetherington, Stowire, and Redberg (1971), who, using Quay's typology, found
significantly different parental characteristics and interactions between the
families of the different subgroups.

The Gluecks (1970) statistically filtered 200 E-I-B variables through 500
institutionalized delinquents and 500 nondelinquents who were followed up

after about seventeen years. The factors of "discipline by mother," "supervision by mother," and "cohesiveness of family" differentiated the delinquents from the nondelinquents. Rose (1967), Briggs and Wirt (1965), and Stein et al. (1971), among others, though lacking in conceptual, clinical, or methodological sophistication, do suggest a more comprehensive approach to the definition of delinquency for the future.

Female Delinquency

The development of the female as distinguished from the male delinquent has received relatively little attention. Blos (1957) has supplied one of the more relevant psychoanalytic papers. He finds that female, compared to male delinquency, stands in close proximity to the perversions: "That the girls' repertoire for delinquent acts is more limited than the boys'; that the girls' acts are less destructive, that kleptomanic stealing, vagrancy, provocative, impudent behavior or public or sexual waywardness are primary" (p. 232). From an etiological point of view, Blos sees these differences as a function of the difficulty in shifting from a female to a male object and the girl's inability to maintain the repression of her pregenital-preoedipal strivings toward the mother. Blos distinguishes two types of female delinquents: one regresses to the preoedipal mother and recreates the mother-child relationship with her out-of-wedlock child; the other maintains an illusory oedipal situation and is vengeful toward the mother, especially in her sexual activities. Blos (1961) amplifies the development of these two constellations; compares them with the developmental processes in boys; and adds a third category—namely, the girl who acts out in the service of the ego. This is the girl who, in her emotional disengagement with her family, seeks to restore a sense of continuity with her family by recreating the past that is out of awareness.

Other psychodynamic studies include Rosenthal (1979), who illustrates two types of delinquency in lower- to middle-class girls; Farley and Farley (1972), who discuss stimulation seeking based on an arousal deficit; Robey (1969), who describes the runaway girl; Hershkovitz (1969), who paints a panoramic outline of sexuality promiscuity; Pollak and Friedman (1969), who discuss family dynamics; and Konopka (1966), who cites the loneliness of her 181 delinquents.

Diagnostic and Statistical Manual of Mental Disorders

As John Johnson mentioned in chapter 4, it is of some interest that the *Diagnostic and Statistical Manual of Mental Disorders,* 3rd edition (DSM-

III) (1980), like DSM-II, does not use the term *delinquency*. Instead, DSM-II uses the term *conduct disorder* and relies heavily on behavioral criteria to define *delinquency*. DSM-III cites several predisposing factors derived from clinical and clinical-statistical studies that are observable and measurable, such as early institutional living, illegitimacy, large family size, and absent father. If DSM-III is a reflection of the current psychiatric formulation of *delinquency*, we do not seem to be far beyond an empirical, behavioral-descriptive stage of understanding.

Summary

Diagnosis of antisocial children and juvenile delinquents is still in a fairly primitive state, especially with respect to the determination of etiology, treatment, and prognosis. Legal definitions are clearly insufficient, if not misleading. Clinical definitions have been of some use to clinicians; but variables such as inner feeling states, intrapsychic processes, defensive patterns, motivations, and early childhood experiences have been difficult to define operationally. DSM-III diagnoses remain highly behavioral, with scant recognition of antecedent conditions and psychodynamics. It appears that factor-analytic studies—which can incorporate environmental, organismic, and behavioral variables in a theoretical framework from which testable hypotheses can be generated—are those that will best clarify the diagnostic picture.

A Working Definition and Typology of Delinquency

From a review of the literature and clinical experience, four types of delinquency emerge. Behaviorally they appear to be similar, but they have distinguishing characteristics in etiology, dynamics, and prognosis.

1. *Normal, social, or gang delinquency:* Although these youths may manifest many antisocial qualities, the delinquent behavior ceases when they are removed from the context of their delinquent peers. This type is similar to *conduct disorder, socialized* (may be aggressive or nonaggressive).

2. *Neurotic delinquency:* These youths manifest many antisocial behaviors, but the behavior is a function of phallic and oedipal conflicts, and they respond fairly well to psychotherapy and to environmental and familial change. This type is similar to *conduct disorder, socialized, nonaggressive.*

3. *Psychopathic or modal delinquency:* This will be the focus of our study. Manifesting a wide array of antisocial behaviors, these youths

may also demonstrate some borderline neurotic or gang symptoms. They are probably the most commonly seen in clinics—always referred by courts, schools, and family—and usually are moderately resistant to therapeutic intervention. They cut across all the subtypes of conduct disorder of DSM-III but are least like the *undersocialized, aggressive* subtype.

4. *Psychotic delinquency:* These youths engage in antisocial activities but manifest borderline to clearly psychotic symptoms. Extremely resistant to any treatment efforts, they usually develop into chronic psychotic or antisocial personalities who may be institutionalized for long periods of time. This type is akin to *conduct disorder, unsocialized, aggressive,* and is described well by Lewis and Shanak (1978).

The four types of delinquency can be ordered along continua of variables such as differentiation-individuation of self; maturity of ego; object relations; types of defenses; preoedipal-oedipal functioning; nature of superego; severity and chronicity of antisocial behavior; and other measures of maturity. In order to explore these variables, the developmental map of the modal delinquent is offered in terms of defenses against painful affects, the mother and mother-child interaction, the separation-individuation process, superego lacunae, projective identification, the emotional communication system, language and motor development, and the role of the father.

Defenses against Painful Affect

Many investigations lead to the hypothesis that the major developmental trauma or disruption occurred during the separation-individuation phase. Many clinicians, not fooled by the superficial coolness of some delinquents, discuss the latter's firm defenses against underlying painful feelings of dependence, powerlessness, anxiety, panic, and depression. Bender (1961) found her series of psychopathic children well protected against guilt and anxiety. Kaufman and Heims (1958), in exploring the body image of the delinquent, found that antisocial acts serve to protect against the experience of depression. Burks and Harrison (1962) emphasize the need to avoid recognition of helplessness and powerlessness. Allchin (1962) sees the delinquent as avoiding feelings of weakness and dependency and the loss of a feeling of reality and identity by springing into action, which reassures him of his actual being and control. Quoting R.D. Laing in an attempt to illustrate the phenomenology of the delinquent under stress, Allchin cites a patient's experience: "It's a most terrifying feeling to realize that the doctor can't see the real you, that he can't understand what you feel and that he's just going ahead with his ideas . . . I had to make an uproar to see if the doctor would respond to me and not just to his own ideas" (p. 40). Chwast

(1967), in reviewing his experience as a court psychologist and in 1977 as a consultant, finds considerable depression in his cases. Girls tended to be more depressed than boys; the older the delinquent, the greater the degree of depression. Harrower (1955) states that "delinquent acting out might be parsimoniously explicable as a means of filling a sense of emptiness the youngster might feel." She also entertains the idea that delinquency may ward off encroaching schizophrenic withdrawal. Anthony (1968), in correlating violence with a psychomotor test, summarizes his study: "a record which includes conviction for violence appears in this sample of young offenders to be positively associated with depression as measured by psychomotor speed. . . ." Frankenstein (1970) feels that the delinquent fends off anxiety stemming from fear of ego loss.

The etiology of the anxiety—whether from loss of ego or object—may be an important factor in determining whether the delinquency takes on a borderline or an antisocial character. Similarly, the defense against the experience of guilt, as cited by Bilmes (1967), may be a later oedipal problem and hence more akin to a neurotic phenomena. Offer, Marohn, and Ostrov (1972), in comparing intensely studied delinquents and normal adolescents, found that one marked difference was in the ability to "cope with the effects of anxiety, depression, shame, guilt and anger ($p < .001$)." Woddis (1957) provides fifteen cases in which depression was evident prior to the committing of a crime. Whiskin (1974) focuses on the treatment of depression in youthful offenders.

Bromberg (1961), in exploring the delinquent more deeply and intensely, discovered the anxiety, guilt, and defenses that are found in neurosis. Greenacre (1945) cannot conceive of a person existing without anxiety. She feels that the delinquent experiences the mother's guilt and shame but defends against it. Bonnard (1961), in relating truancy and pilfering with bereavement in adolescents, finds that under fear of ego disintegration the child commits an act that externalizes the fear into a predictable cause-and-effect sequence.

Slavson (1947) believes that "the psychogenic psychopath has a great deal of anxiety which he had repressed so deeply and so early that it remains dormant in ordinary situations" (p. 416). Kaufman and Makkay (1956), in their investigations of 140 children, declare that "some form of actual or emotional desertion underlay all our cases, giving rise to an infantile type of depression" (p. 316).

A common defense against the helplessness-anxiety syndrome is a reversal into feelings of omnipotence. Blos (1961) states this clearly as he discusses the emergence of feelings of omnipotence as an attempt to control the hostile world and to prove that the environment has no power over the youth: "This position masks strong dependency needs and walls off an awareness of the feeling of helplessness. These are primitive security operations which express a very primitive need, namely, to get and to have, to be given and to be done to as wanted; to be in control of the object; in short, to be omnipotent" (p. 135). It may be that the unrealistic planning, the lack of a sense of future, the great powers of rationalization, the apparent fearlessness, and the "I don't care" attitude in the face of impending danger are all derivative of the youth's position of omnipotence, which in turn is a derivative of his grave vulnerability.

Many clinicians cite the emptiness of the delinquent, implying that there is an affective void. Although this is a viable controversy (see Stolorow and Lachman 1980), my experience with the modal delinquent is that the seeming emptiness and nothingness is a defense against the experience of chaotic and painful affect. These affects are clearly expressed in the transference as the defenses are peeled away, especially if ego and milieu supportive measures are not taken.

A Portrait of The Mother and Mother-Child Interaction

Why is the delinquent unable to allow himself to experience and express the range of negative affects? The hypothesis offered here is that the child is too early exposed to stimuli against which he has no protection. Moreover, if the child has expressed the affect, the parent did not respond appropriately. Manifestations of negative affects were ignored, punished, scorned, or responded to in kind. The cause of the pain was not dispelled. Brody and Axelrod (1970) use Freud's notion of a protective shield or stimulus barrier that allows the child to function without a chronic experience of panic. Each child may maintain a certain level of tolerance for pain, but at a certain point emergency measures develop. One major source of pain is unpredictability, inconsistency, and neglect by the mother. Schwarz (1968) declares that if a break occurs in the mother-child relationship between the tenth and thirtieth month of development, the child fails to integrate feelings of love and hate, is unable to tolerate normal frustrations and restrictions, and does not grow out of a parasitic position. She goes on to say that acting out is an attempt to restore the lost object and feelings of security. Thus it is extremely important to reach the child before he or she has given up hope and before the secondary gains of antisocial acts have made him or her independent of love objects.

Aichhorn (1964), describes two basic causes of delinquency: (1) "the need for love satisfied too little or too much; being shut out of the community or overly involved with it"; and (2) the impoverished superego: "the nucleus of the superego will not develop if children are deprived of needed love. This happens when parents pay little attention to their children, neglect them or are indifferent to them." The children then take over the superego of the parents.

Bennett (1960) has used objective measures in differentiating between delinquents and neurotics. A relevant finding is that delinquents suffer more frequent interruptions in mother-child relationships before age seven, with more significant breaks occurring in the second year.

It is important to emphasize that inconsistency in itself is not sufficient to foster delinquency, as Sandler et al. (1957) point out in their analysis of three children of inconsistent mothers. The inconsistency may be evidence that the mother operates out of her own needs rather than as a nurturing agent for the child.

Bowlby (1969, 1973) synthesizes the data on attachment and separation and spells out the consequences of separation from the mother. He concludes: "thus, many of the most intense of all human emotions arise during the formation, the maintenance, the disruption, and the renewal of affectional bonds." He indicates three stages in the disruption of attachment bonds—protest, despair, and detachment—and clearly outlines the stress, pain, and behavioral correlates of each stage. A series of other workers such as Naess (1962) have continued to find a correlation between delinquency and early mother-child separation. The amount of ambivalence, rejection, and neglect leads one to suspect that many of the mothers communicated to their children their wish to get rid of or to murder them. Contrary to the social edict that mothers must only love their babies, my clinical experience is that most mothers are burdened by strong hostile and murderous feelings toward their children. The mothers of modal delinquents seemed to have a greater share of these feelings and to exercise less control over their expression. Winnicott (1958) and Rheingold (1967) amplify this topic.

Jenkins (1966, 1967) finds considerable inconsistency and neglect by parents of delinquent children. Glueck (1970) finds delinquents' parents to be lax and inconsistent, swinging from strictness to neglect with no apparent good reason. Peck and Havighurst (1960), in their study of "amoral children," find that "the most striking feature of these families is that without exception, they are markedly inconsistent . . . they are highly mistrustful and disapproving of their children." We can assume that the inconsistency and rejection with which the mother develops, maintains, and breaks the emotional bonds with her child have great impact on the development of defenses against all affect. Although the inconsistent, rejecting mother has been emphasized, implicit in this concept may be large elements of overprotectiveness, seductiveness, and overstimulation. For example, a mother who has been made anxious by her own mother, who subjected her to her mood swings and incessant attacks, may foster a child whom she cannot let alone. The overstimulation of the child produces behavior that helps the mother maintain the equilibrium of distress that was established with her own mother.

The Separation-Individuation Process

Mahler, Pine, and Bergman (1975), in their landmark studies of the separation-individuation of normal children, provide important data. Their central concept is the emotional rather than the physical presence of the mother. They distinguish four subphases: (1) differentiation and the development of the body image; (2) practicing, which includes walking; (3) rapprochement, a subphase in which the toddler becomes aware of his separateness, but at the same time, "seems to have an increased need, a wish for mother to share with him every one of his new skills and experiences, as well as a great need for the object's love." As the child realizes the separation, sadness ensues. Mahler, however, feels that the great amount of ego strength required for the experience of this affect may not be available, and that hyperactivity and restlessness may be a defense against the painful awareness of sadness. Earlier, Deutsch (1937) established that indifference occurs in a child whose ego is insufficiently developed to handle mourning. The fourth stage is consolidation of individuality and the beginnings of emotional-object constancy where verbal communication and reality testing accelerate.

Masterson (1980) has consistently employed Mahler's concepts in his treatment programs for borderline and acting-out adolescents. Parens (1979) used Mahler's developmental framework to study the epigenesis of aggression in twelve infants. In a scholarly and empirically balanced report, Parens notes the manner in which ambivalent feelings are handled in the practicing and rapprochement subphases. "The resulting balance of love and hate feelings toward the love-object significantly influenced how the child fared in object relations in following years" (p. 12).

Fleiss (1972) prefers to talk of the *asymbiotic* relationship characterized by the unpredictability and impulsivity of the partly engulfing and partly rejecting mother.

The Identification Process and Identification with the Aggressor

Instead of experiencing and integrating the negative feelings, the child incorporates those parts of the pain-producing person and acts as his perception of that person does. According to Anna Freud (1966): "A child introjects some characteristic of an anxiety object and so assimilates an anxiety experience which he has just undergone. . . . By impersonating the aggressor, assuming his attributes or imitating his aggression, the child transforms himself from the person threatening into the person who makes the threat" (p. 113).

The Superego Lacunae and
Projective Identification

An important facet of the delinquent's development has been spelled out in a series of papers by Szurek (1949), Johnson (1959), and their students who have studied a wide range of delinquency and pathology. Based on an incomplete differentiation from the mother, the child who is in close touch with the mother's unconscious acts out the defended-against impulses of the mother. The mother not only has the pleasure of seeing her impulses acted out, but is also able to rationalize punishing the child for the tabooed acts that she has unconsciously promulgated.

Johnson and Szurek have anticipated many of the concepts and processes inherent in projective identification, especially as used by Marshall (1982), Langs (1981), and Ogden (1979). Briefly, the concept of projective identification as described by Ogden is a three-part process: "a group of fantasies and accompanying object relations having to do with the ridding of the self of unwanted aspects of the self, the depositing of those unwanted 'parts' into another person, and finally with the 'recovery' of a modified version of what was extruded" (p. 357).

Many mothers of delinquents who have not successfully traversed their own separation-individuation stage evolve a symbiotic relationship (narcissistic transference) with their progeny. The mothers try to reinstate with their children the relationship they had with their own mothers. The mothers tend to project into their children those impulses, needs, and affects that have been split off and not integrated in their personalities. Sometimes the mother of a delinquent will not only say, "I'm going to give my son (daughter) everything my mother didn't give me," but will later reveal, "When he (she) was born I just knew that he (she) would care for me as I wanted my mother to care for me." In effect, the mothers want to use their children to complete their development.

Although there appear to be truly negligent and inconsistent mothers, there is a metaprinciple that determines the parent-child interaction with any mother. The goodness and health of the child are functions of the degree to which the mother is aware of the child's own physical and psychological needs and satisfies them at an optimal level. With the delinquent, we hypothesize that there is a highly interactive process between mother and child, wherein the mother unconsciously induces in her child emotions, conflicts, objects, and impulses that the child has great difficulty in integrating. The child who must accomplish his own work of integration and then faces the mother's emotional demands is overwhelmed. The child who becomes schizophrenic or borderline tends to sacrifice himself and take up the emotional work of the mother. The delinquent child, however, appears to respond with a resounding "No!" with which he attempts to stave off inroads into an already overburdened psyche.

Jurkovic and Prentice's (1974) study suggests the angry force of delinquents' mothers' intrusiveness. They found that the interactions of mothers with their delinquent sons were characterized by dominance, hostility, and a lack of warmth.

The Emotional Communication
of the Delinquent

Some apparent paradoxes in delinquents' behavior can be interpreted in light of the previous discussions, particularly the issues relating to the inability to experience painful affects.

The reported apathy and boredom and consequent sensation seeking seem to be related to the strict warding off of affect that comes into conflict with the attempt to feel something. Paradoxically, the delinquent must toy with danger and tempt death to feel alive. Through drugs and alcohol abuse, criminal activity, daredevil acts, poor health habits, and promiscuous sex, the delinquent defends against his terror of death. He turns from being passive to being active.

Another paradox is that the delinquent is overtly a staunch advocate of freedom and no controls, but acts in a manner that leads to a restriction of his liberty and institution of stringent controls. This paradox can be seen as an attempt to ward off all feelings of dependence and helplessness while, in fact, having his dependence needs satisfied and his helpless feelings rationlized.

The delinquent tends to communicate by actions rather than by words. In order to understand the language of a delinquent, one must examine the feelings the delinquent's acts evoke. Perhaps one reason that delinquents are so difficult to work with is that they induce feelings in others that are difficult to handle. Workers typically feel distressed, furious, disappointed, hopeful, then hopeless and helpless—which may be the very feelings the delinquent himself is trying *not* to experience. Through the mechanism of projective identification, the preverbal delinquent can communicate about his own emotional history and makeup.

In the scenarios that delinquents construct, there is a shift in roles as the delinquent engages in behavior that is calculated to demonstrate emotionally how he was treated by his parents. Lateness, unreliability, broken promises, and so on are seen as an identification with the aggressor, wherein the child attempts to master the original trauma by becoming the active perpetrator rather than the passive recipient. The active acting out of the trauma is no random impulsive event, however. Rather, it is seen as a reflection of ego functioning, defensive position, and level of object relations—plus an attempt to communicate to the observer the nature of the original crime and a covert request for help in resolving the problem. For example, the delinquent who doesn't care reflects the lack of care he has experienced. The persistent frustrating behavior of this type of delinquent eventually leads the examiner, therapist, or child-care worker to experience the feelings of the uncaring mother. If these feelings are acted on, the original trauma or crime will be reenacted.

What happens when one begins to peel back denial, projection rationalization, and other defenses against negative affect? A clue might be found in the descriptions provided by some analysts of the upset induced in resident therapists as they negotiate the first-line defenses of their delinquent patients. The answer lies in the countertransference reactions of the therapists and milieu staff. Often, well-trained therapists are reduced to ineffective bumbling by the delinquent. Clearer and more public is the evidence presented by institution staff who succumb to psychosomatic ailments, drugs, and—interestingly—delinquent and hedonistic behavior that suggests an identification (as a defense) with their charges. Other induced reactions are rejection and destructive behavior, which is based more on the induced reactions of the parents.

The Development of Language

Consider the possible relation between the development of speech at this stage and the common finding that delinquents are not as verbal as others and that they have lower verbal scores on the Wechsler tests, both relative to their performance scores and relative to controls. Raush and Sweet (1961), in studying well-adjusted and hyperaggressive children, assume that words function as actions designed to get someone to meet needs and that speech normally shifts from being solely a mode of action to being a verbalization of thought or trial action. In the hyperaggressive child, they find, words remain close to impulses and actions and fail to develop into communications of thought and feelings. My clinical experience in treating delinquents suggests that the traumatizing experiences have been walled off from conscious awareness and are not available at a verbal level, but are communicated in behavior. The behavior usually evokes emotions in the therapist. These findings, if properly decoded, can yield a rich understanding of the delinquents' early defended-against feelings. In order to study and treat the delinquent, one may discriminately use the induced feelings as emotional communications in lieu of verbal language. Though open to subjectivity and distortion, these emotional communication channels can be valuable if the involved investigator can subject his or her responses to supervisory control. The theory and techniques of the emotional communication between delinquent and therapist are spelled out by Marshall (1978, 1982).

The Role of the Father

Another significant variable in the development of the modal delinquent pertains to identification with the father. In terms of choice of symptoms (neurosis, psychosis, or delinquency), the father's availability for role modeling and integrity appear to be crucial.

From self-report studies such as Brigham and Ricketts (1967), delinquents on the whole see their fathers' behavior as less acceptable than their mothers'. Andry (1957, 1960), in a questionnaire given to eighty delinquents and eighty controls, and then to the parents of thirty children in each group, found that the inadequacies of the fathers' roles, rather than of the mothers', differentiated the delinquents from the nondelinquents.

Bandura and Walters (1958, 1959), in the landmark studies of twenty-six antisocial, aggressive boys and their families, conclude that there was a severe break between the delinquents and their fathers, such that identification and internalization of values were incomplete. Other work, such as Kardiner and Ovesey's (1951) analysis of black families, demonstrates the correlation between delinquency and the lack of a suitable male model of identification. The fathers, who were physically and/or emotionally absent, overtly or covertly encouraged the antisocial behavior of their sons.

In contrasting thirty adolescent delinquents with controls, Fodor (1973) found that the fathers of the delinquents were seen as being less nurturant and giving less praise than the control fathers.

The child may identify with either parent, but usually with the parent of the same sex, given any success in the separation-individuation process. In one instance, both mother and son were entranced with the father's escapades of stealing and breaking various laws. The father saw himself either as not breaking the law or as above the law while in fact sporting a "Support Your Local Police" bumper sticker. One could see a point-for-point correlation between behavior of father and son. Father would play sick, absent himself from work, and go fishing; son would be truant from school. Father would appropriate material from his office; son would steal from lockers at school. Father would break speed limits; son would provoke police and antagonize older boys with his antics on his bike. Father would brutalize the mother; son would brutalize and bully his peers as well as his mother.

In these families it seems that the marital relationship is not congenial largely because of the physical and/or emotional unavailability of the father. The son or daughter then acts out the rage of the frustrated mother. Frequently, when hearing the mother talk, one cannot tell whether she is complaining about the derelictions of her son or those of her husband, which reflects her lack of differentiation between the two. In situations like this it is clear that the mother may have a stake in being married to a neglectful and quasi-psychopathic man, for we often see a woman who has divorced and married a similar man.

The Oedipal Problem and the Development
of the Superego

Traditionally, psychoanalytic theorists have relied heavily on the concept of the superego in their discussions of the delinquent. The importance of the development of the superego cannot be underestimated, particularly as it relates to the resolution of the Oedipus complex. Because of the emphasis on earlier developmental events, however, the development of the superego will not be discussed further here. Several excellent reviews have been provided: Spitz (1958), Schmideberg (1955), Sandler (1960), Schafer (1960), and Beres (1958).

The modal-delinquent children seem to have particular difficulty with the oedipal situation, largely because they have not successfully traversed the separation-individuation stage. Moreover, in those boys whose fathers are not available, there is a minimum of castration threat, limited control, and no model for identification. In the absence of a father, the mother continues to rely on her offspring, thus strengthening the symbiosis. With the delinquent child who has an intact family, there seems to be either a cold, nonrelationship with the mother and father, or a confusing amount of inconsistency. For example, a teenager prone to delinquency was grounded because he owed a fair amount of money; yet he knew that his parents abusively put off their debtors in order to maintain a favorable flow of interest from their investments.

This is by no means a complete developmental picture of the modal delinquent. The effects of puberty, latency, peer influence, and the recrudescence of infantile conflicts in adolescence are deleted. The processes of identification and acting out are only noted. This picture focuses on early developmental events and phenomena that have relevance for a concept of delinquency and a theory of psychotherapy with the delinquent. The relevant events and phenomena are:

1. Defenses against negative and painful effects.
2. The inconsistency and rejection of the mother during the separation-individuation phase, which lead to the aforementioned defenses. The inconsistency and rejection are related to the narcissism of the mother, who cannot respond to the child's needs.
3. An immature, vulnerable ego and a quasi-symbiotic relationship with the mother, which negates her projective identification.
4. A physically or emotionally absent or delinquent father, who does not fulfill his wife's needs, provides an inadequate model of identification for the male, and diminishes appropriate superego development.

Implications for Psychotherapy

Treatment considerations should flow from the theory of development. Assuming that one of the primary defects of the delinquent is his inability to experience the affects associated with giving up the symbiosis with the mother—hence his inability to establish object relations—the first therapeutic task is to help the patient establish a symbiotic relationship with the therapist. In this relationship the child again can emotionally fuse with the therapist. This relationship is termed the *narcissistic transference.* Therapists often assume that the narcissistic transference can be evolved by providing a warm and accepting atmosphere for the patient. This may be a necessary but not sufficient condition, and it is often fraught with countertransference implications (Marshall 1982). What is necessary is that the therapist help the patient recreate the old relationship with the mother, but with the promise of a more mature resolution. The therapist, therefore, must thoroughly and quickly study the patient, his history, and the transference-countertransference field to determine those characteristics of the patient and his mother that are emotionally meaningful to the patient. For example, since most delinquents are distrustful and know they cannot be trusted, any deliberate attempt on the part of the therapist to appear trusting and trustworthy will meet with increased suspicion and aversion on the part of the youth. Therefore, it behooves the therapist to support any of the patient's feelings about mistrusting the therapist.

A typical interchange may be:

T: "Why won't you talk to me?"
P: "I don't trust you."
T: "I don't blame you." Or, "What about me gives you that impression?" Or, "If I were in your shoes, I wouldn't trust me either." Or, "I'm glad to see that you don't go around trusting strangers."

An interchange like this does several things: (1) the mistrustful patient has his feelings acknowledged and validated, and hence may feel acceptance from the therapist; (2) the patient who knows that he himself cannot be trusted begins to believe emotionally that the therapist is similar to himself; (3) the patient, who had a mother whom he could not trust, begins to see the therapist as the mother.

A 12-year-old boy, adopted as an infant, was raised by an angry and emotionally neglectful mother who had been intermittently hospitalized for depression. The father, though strict and rigid, maintained warmer ties with his son. Referred because of increasingly disruptive behavior in school and defiance at home, Tim initially related to me in an idealizing manner, as if I were his long-lost parent(s). Soon, however, he began to demonstrate with me the stubbornness, cockiness, contempt, and angry demands for freedom that had got him into difficulty in school and home. Content of sessions revolved around his attempts to influence me to obtain more independence from his parents, and from me, by virtue of reduced sessions or termination. I was able to evoke from him intense complaints about my not caring for him, not wanting him to grow up, and wanting only to control him and use him to earn money. None of these claims were challenged. In fact, from time to time I would ask him, "Why should I care for you?" "Why shouldn't I try to control you?" "Why shouldn't I earn money off you?" As his transferential reactions intensified, I could easily discern his playing out with me the role of the angry, neglected child trying to free himself from the bonds of his emotionally needy mother and controlling father. At the same time,, it seemed that he was trying to work through his feelings about being abandoned by his biological parents. Although I did nothing to dissuade him from his transference feelings, I did maintain a steady interest and regard for his feelings, which was a new experience for him. As he gave up his angry complaints and fell into sullen, depressed silence, I began to interpret some of his reactions to me. His essential response was the following essay.

Sidney the Garbage Can

> I am a garbage can and nobody cares what happens to me, all people do is fill me with trash. Nobody even stops to take out the time to clean me or to even give me a bath. They just leave me their to smell like a skunk and sometimes even worse. In the winter time when it rains and snows they don't even put me in the garage they let me freeze to death.
>
> One day a miracle happened. I was going to move to Florida but wherever I go they will still probably treat me like the garbage itself. They will probably leave me out in the rain but at least I'm glad there's no snow. But then, one day it happened. A hurricane, a terrible, fierce one and wouldn't you know they didn't put me in the garage. I was going up in the air it seems I would never land and for my sake I hoped not. But all was not lost I fell in a pool ah! now I really enjoyed it. It was the pool of a wealthy millionare. He took good care of me. I also had a good time with a shiny gold garbage can and her name was Maryann. We got married and lived in luxury for the rest of our lives.

This production suddenly showed what was beneath Tim's angry tirades and accelerating delinquent behavior. He is the empty, worthless, stinking, neglected container to be used for symbiotic needs and projective identifications. Rather than experience these feelings, he angrily projected them onto others. It is likely, too, that these feelings were part of the mother's split-off emotional life. Under the impact of therapy, he felt he was still being treated like garbage, but not as coldly. My ability to withstand his explosions, and his probable relief that I did not throw him out or damage him, led him to believe that he was in a secure environment that probably reflected his wishes about his original parents. His increased ego strength and differentiated self also allowed him to become interested in girls. He was in fact quietly interested in a girl named Mary Ann.

The relative ease with which this case was handled was made possible largely by setting up the appropriate paradigm, which was dictated by the case material interlocking with the developmental theory. The transference resistance was predictable; more important, the objective counter-transference of wanting to control, use, and abandon this boy was made clear early on and used to advantage.

References

Aichhorn, A. *Delinquency and child guidance: Selected papers*. New York: International Universities Press, 1964.

————. Some remarks on the psychic structure and social care of a certain type of juvenile delinquent. *Psychoanalytic Study of the Child*, vol. III-IV. New York: International Universities Press, 1949.

————. *Wayward Youth*. New York: Viking Press, 1936.

Alexander, F., and Staub, H. *The criminal, the judge and the public*, rev. ed. Glencoe, Ill.: Free Press, 1956.

Allchin, W.H. Some positive aspects of delinquent behavior. *British Journal of Criminology*, 1962, *3*, 38-46.

Andry, R.G. Faulty paternal and maternal-child relationships, affection and delinquency. *British Journal of Delinquency*, 1957, *8*, 34-48.

————. *Delinquency and parental pathology*. London: Methuen, 1960.

Anthony, H.S. The association of violence and depression in a sample of young offenders. *British Journal of Criminology*, 1968, *8*, 346-365.

Bandura, A., and Walters, R.H. Dependency conflicts in aggressive delinquents. *Journal of Social Issues*, 1958, *14*, 52-65.

————. *Adolescent aggression*. New York: Ronald Press, 1959.

Becker, H.S. *Outsiders: Studies in the sociology of deviancy*. New York: Free Press of Glencoe, 1963.

Bender, L. Psychopathic personality disorders in childhood and adolescence. *Archives of Criminal Psychodynamics*, 1961, *4*, 412-415.

Bennett, I. *Delinquent and neurotic children*. London: Tavistock, 1960.

Beres, D. Vicissitudes of superego functions and superego precursors in childhood. In *Psychoanalytic study of the child*, vol. 13. New York: International Universities Press, 1958.

Bilmes, M. Shames and delinquency. *Contemporary Psychoanalysis*, 1967, *3*, 113-133.

Blos, P. Preoedipal factors in the etiology of female delinquency. In *Psychoanalytic study of the child*, vol. 12. New York: International Universities Press, 1957.

_____ . Delinquency in adolescents. In S. Lorand and H. Schneer, eds., *Adolescents: Psychoanalytic approach to problems and theory*. New York: Hoeber, 1961.

Bonnard, A. Truancy and pilfering associates with bereavement in adolescents. In S. Lorand and H. Schneer, eds., *Psychoanalytic approach to problems and therapy*. New York: Hoeber, 1961.

Bowlby, J. *Attachment and loss, vol. I: Attachment*. New York: Basic Books, 1969.

_____ . *Attachment and loss, vol. II: Separation*. New York: Basic Books, 1973.

Briggs, P.F., and Wirt, R.D. *Prediction*. In H.C. Quay, ed., *Juvenile delinquency: Research and theory*. Princeton, N.J.: Van Nostrand, 1965.

Brigham, J., and Ricketts, C. Reports on maternal and paternal behaviors of solitary and social delinquents. *Journal of Consulting Psychology*, 1967, *31*, 420-422.

Brody, S., and Axelrod, S. *Anxiety and ego formation in infancy*. New York: International Universities Press, 1970.

Bromberg, W. The psychopathic personality concept reevaluated. *Archives of Criminal Psychodynamics*, 1961, *4*, 435-442.

Burks, H.L., and Harrison, S.L. Aggressive behavior as a means of avoiding depression. *American Journal of Orthopsychiatry*, 1962, *32*, 416-421.

Carr, L.J. *Delinquency Control*, rev. ed. New York: Harper and Row, 1950.

Chwast, J. Psychotherapy of disadvantaged acting-out adolescents. *American Journal of Psychotherapy*, 1977, *31*, 216-226.

Clark, J., and Wenninger, E. Socioeconomic class and area as correlates of illegal behavior among juveniles. *American Sociological Review*, 1962, *27*, 826-834.

Cloward, R.A., and Ohlin, L.E. *Delinquency and opportunity: A theory of delinquent gangs*. Glencoe, Ill.: Free Press, 1960.

De Mause, L. The evolution of childhood. *History of Childhood Quarterly*, 1974a, *1*, 503-575.

_____ . *The history of childhood*. New York: Psychohistory Press, 1974b.

Deutsch, H. Absence of grief. *Psychoanalytic Quarterly*, 1937, *6*, 12-25.

Diagnostic and statistical manual of mental disorders, 3rd ed. Washington, D.C.: American Psychiatric Association, 1980.

Eissler, K.R. Some problems of delinquency. In K.R. Eissler, ed., *Searchlights on delinquency*. New York: International Universities Press, 1949.

Erikson, K. Notes on the sociology of deviance. *Social Problems*, 1962, *9*, 307-314.

Farley, F.H., and Farley, S.V. Stimulus-seeking motivation and delinquent behavior among institutionalized delinquent girls. *Journal of Consulting and Clinical Psychology*, 1972, *39*, 94-97.

Fleiss, R. *Ego and body ego*. New York: International Universities Press, 1972.

Flugel, J.C. *The psychoanalytic study of the family*. London: Hogarth, 1921.

Foder, E.M. Moral development and parent behavior of antecedents in adolescent psychopaths. *Journal of Genetic Psychology*, 1973, *122*, 37-43.

Frankenstein, C. *Varieties of juvenile delinquency*. New York: Garden and Breach, 1970.

Freud, A. The ego and the mechanisms of defense. In *The writings of Anna Freud*, vol. II. New York: International Universities Press, 1966.

Freud, A.; Nagera, H.; and Freud, E. *Psychoanalytic Study of the Child*, vol. 20. New York: International Universities Press, 1965.

Friedlander, K. *The psychoanalytic approach to juvenile delinquency*. New York: International Universities Press, 1947.

_____. Latent delinquency and ego development. In K.R. Eissler, ed., *Searchlights on delinquency*. New York: International Universities Press, 1949.

Glover, E. The diagnosis and treatment of delinquency, being a clinical report of the work of the institute during 5 years 1937-1941. London: ISTD pamphlet, 1944.

Glueck, S., and Glueck, E. *Toward a typology of juvenile offenders*. New York: Grune and Stratton, 1970.

Gold, M., and Petronio, R.J. Delinquent behavior in adolescence. In J. Adelson, ed., *Handbook of adolescent psychology*. New York: John Wiley and Sons, 1980.

Gould, L.D. Who defines delinquency: A comparison of self-reported and officially-reported indices of delinquency for three racial groups. *Social Problems*, 1969, *16*, 325-336.

Greenacre, P. Conscience and the psychopath. *American Journal of Orthopsychiatry*, 1945, *15*, 494-509.

Harrower, M. Who comes to court? *American Journal of Orthopsychiatry*, 1955, *25*, 15-21.

Healy, W., and Bronner, A.F. The child guidance clinic: Birth and growth of an idea. In L.G. Lowry and V. Sloane, eds., *Orthopsychiatry, 1923-1948, retrospect and prospect*. New York: American Orthopsychiatric Association, 1948.

Hershkowitz, H.H. A psychodynamic view of sexual promiscuity. In O. Pollack and A.S. Friedman, eds., *Family dynamics and female sexual delinquency*. Palo Alto, Calif.: Science and Behavior Books, 1969.

Hetherington, E.M.; Stowire, R.; and Redberg, E. Patterns of family interactions in juvenile delinquency. *Journal of Abnormal Psychology*, 1971, *78*, 160-176.

Hug-Hellmuth, H. Von. On the technique of child analysis. *International Journal of Psychoanalysis*, 1921, *2*.

Jenkins, R.L. Psychiatric syndromes in children and their relation to family background. *American Journal of Orthopsychiatry*, 1966, *36*, 450-457.

_____ . The varieties of adolescents' behavioral problems and family dynamics. *American Journal of Psychiatry*, 1967, *124*, 1440-1445.

Jenkins, R.L., and Hewitt, L.E. Types of personality structures encountered in child guidance clinics. *American Journal of Orthopsychiatry*, 1944, *14*, 84-94.

Johnson, A.M. Sanctions for super-ego lacunae. In K.R. Eissler, ed., *Searchlights on delinquency*. New York: International Universities Press, 1949.

_____ . Juvenile delinquency. In S. Arieti, ed., *American handbook of psychiatry*. New York: Basic Books, 1959.

Jurkovic, G.J., and Prentice, N.M. Dimensions of moral interaction and moral judgment in delinquent and nondelinquent families. *Journal of Consulting and Clinical Psychology*, 1974, *42*, 256-262.

Kardiner, A., and Ovesey, L. *The mark of oppression*. Cleveland, Ohio: World Publishing Company, 1951.

Karpman, B. Psychodynamics of child delinquency: Further contributions. Round table. *American Journal of Orthopsychiatry*, 1953, *25*, 238-282.

_____ . *Symposia on child and juvenile delinquency*. Washington, D.C.: Psychodynamics Monograph Series, 1959.

Kaufman, I., and Heims, L. The body image of the juvenile delinquent. *American Journal of Orthopsychiatry*, 1958, *28*, 146-159.

Kaufman, I., and Makkay, E.S. Treatment of the adolescent delinquent in case studies. In G.E. Gardiner, ed. *Childhood emotional disabilities*, vol. II. New York: American Orthopsychiatric Association, 1956.

Konopka, G. *The adolescent girl in conflict*. Englewood Cliffs, N.J.: Prentice-Hall, 1966.

Langs, R. *Resistances and interventions: The nature of therapeutic work*. New York: Jason Aronson, 1981.

Levy, D.M. On the problem of delinquency. *American Journal of Orthopsychiatry*, 1932, *2*, 197-207.

Lewis, D.O., and Shanak, S.S. Delinquency and the schizophrenic spectrum of disorders. *Journal of the Academy of Child Psychiatry*, 1978, *17*, 263-276.

Lippman, W.O. A psychoanalytic study of a thief. *Archives of Criminal Psychodynamics*, 1926, *2*, 782-815.

Mahler, M.S.; Pine, F.; and Bergman, A. *The psychological birth of the human infant*. New York: Basic Books, 1975.

Marshall, R.J. The psychotherapy of antisocial youth. In J. Noshpitz, ed., *The basic handbook of child psychiatry*. New York: Basic Books, 1979.

_____ . *Resistant interactions: Child, family and psychotherapist*. New York: Human Sciences Press, 1982.

Masterson, J.F. *From borderline adolescent to functioning adult: The test of time*. New York: Brunner/Mazel, 1980.

Michaels, J.J., and Stiver, I.P. The impulsive psychopathic character according to the diagnostic profiles. In *Psychoanalytic study of the child*, vol. 20. New York: International Universities Press, 1965.

Moles, O., Jr.; Lippitt, R; and Withey, S.B. *A selective review of research and theory on delinquency*. Ann Arbor: University of Michigan Institute for Social Research, 1959.

Naess, S. Mother-child separation and delinquency: Further evidence. *British Journal of Criminology*, 1962, *2*, 361-374.

Offer, D.; Marohn, R.C.; and Ostrov, E. Delinquent and normal adolescents. *Comprehensive Psychiatry*, 1972, *13*, 347-355.

Ogden, T.H. On projective identification. *International Journal of Psychoanalysis*, 1979, *60*, 357-373.

Parens, H. *The development of aggression in early childhood*. New York: Jason Aronson, 1979.

Pati, P.K. Psychopathological patterns in delinquency. *Journal of Social Theory*, 1961, *7*, 98-103.

Peck, R.F., and Havighurst, R.J. *The psychology of character development*. New York: Wiley, 1960.

Pollak, O., and Friedman, A.S., eds. *Family dynamics and female sexual delinquency*. Palo Alto, Calif.: Science and Behavior Books, 1969.

Quay, H.B. Personality patterns in pre-adolescent delinquent boys. *Educational Psychological Measurement*, 1966, *26*, 99-110.

Raush, H.L., and Sweet, B. The preadolescent ego: Some observations of normal children. *Psychiatry*, 1961, *14*, 122-132.

Redl, F. The psychology of gang formation and the treatment of juvenile delinquents. In *Psychoanalytic study of the child*, vol. 1. New York: International Universities Press, 1945.

Reich, W. *Der triebhafte character internationaler psychoanalytiseher*. Verlag 1925. Also in *Character analysis*. 3rd ed. New York: Orgone Institute Press, 1949.

Rheingold, J.C. *The mother, anxiety, and death*. Boston: Little, Brown, 1967.

Robey, A. The runaway girl. In O. Pollak and A.S. Friedman, eds., *Family dynamics and female sexual delinquency*. Palo Alto, Calif.: Science and Behavior Books, 1969.

Rose, G. Early identification of delinquents. *British Journal of Criminology*, 1967, *8*, 6-35.

Rosenthal, P.A. Delinquency in adolescent girls: developmental aspects. In S.C. Feinstein and P.L. Giovacchini, eds., *Adolescent Psychiatry.* Chicago, Ill.: University of Chicago Press, 1979.

Russell, D.H. Diagnosing offender patients. *International Journal of Offender Therapy,* 1969, *12,* 147-152.

_____ . *Juvenile delinquency: Psychiatric annals,* vol. 10. New York: Insight Communications, 1975.

Sanders, W.B. *Juvenile offenders for a thousand years.* Durham: University of North Carolina Press, 1970.

Sandler, A.; Daunton, E.; and Schnurmann, A. Inconsistency in the mother as a factor in character development: A comparative study of three cases. In *Psychoanalytic study of the child,* vol. 12. New York: International Universities Press, 1957.

Sandler, J. On the concept of superego. In *Psychoanalytic study of the child,* vol. 15. New York: International Universities Press, 1960.

Schafer, R. The loving and beloved superego in Freud's structural theory. In *Psychoanalytic study of the child,* vol. 15. New York: International Universities Press, 1960.

Schimel, J.L. Problems of delinquents and their treatment. In Silvano Arieti, ed., *American handbook of psychiatry.* 2nd ed. New York: Basic Books, 1974.

Schmideberg, M. Maturation and integration of the superego in the treatment of delinquents. *Archives of Criminal Psychodynamics,* 1955, *1,* 101-110.

Schwarz, H. Contribution to symposium on acting out. *International Journal of Psychoanalysis,* 1968, *49,* 179-181.

Slavson, S.R. An elementaristic approach to the understanding and treatment of delinquency. *The Nervous Child,* 1947, *6,* 413-423.

Spitz, R.A. On the genesis of superego components. In *Psychoanalytic study of the child,* vol. 13. New York: International Universities Press, 1958.

Spotnitz, H. *The psychotherapy of preoedipal conditions.* New York: Aronson, 1976.

Stein, K.B.; Sarbin, T.R.; and Kulik, J.A. Further validation of antisocial personality types. *Journal of Consulting and Clinical Psychology,* 1971, *36,* 177-182.

Stolorow, R.D., and Lachmann, F.M. *Psychoanalysis of developmental arrests: Theory and treatment.* New York: International Universities Press, 1980.

Strean, H.S., ed. *New approaches in child guidance.* Metuchen, N.J.: Scarecrow Press, 1970.

Szurek, S.A. Some impressions from clinical experience with delinquents. In K.R. Eissler, ed., *Searchlights on delinquency.* New York: International Universities Press, 1949.

Van Ophuijsen, J.H.W. Primary conduct disorders. In N.D.C. Lewis and
    B.L. Pacella, eds., *Modern trends in child psychiatry*. New York: Inter-
    national Universities Press, 1945.
Wax, D.E. Social class, race and juvenile delinquency: A review of the lit-
    erature. *Child Psychiatry and Human Development,* 1972, *3,* 36-49.
Whiskin, F.E. Treating depressed offenders in the court clinic. *International
    Journal of Offender Therapy and Comparative Criminology*, 1974, *18,*
    136-152.
Williams, J.R., and Gold, M. From delinquent behavior to official delin-
    quency. *Social Problems,* 1972, *20,* 209-229.
Winnicott, D.W. *Collected papers.* London: Tavistock Publications, 1958.
Woddis, G.M. Depression and crime. *British Journal of Delinquency,* 1957,
    8, 85-94.

7

The Interpersonal Maturity of Delinquents and Nondelinquents

Philip W. Harris

The Interpersonal Maturity Classification System (I-level) was originally designed as a way of differentiating among offenders in order to clarify the different meanings offense behavior has for individuals (Sullivan, Grant, and Grant 1957). Its major application, however, has been as a method for assessing treatment needs within delinquent populations (Warren 1976). Although much is known about the ways delinquents differ from each other developmentally, much less is known about the ways in which I-level and its components differentiate delinquents from nondelinquents. This chapter will address some of the major criticisms of I-level and discuss some recent findings on I-level's relationship to delinquency.

One major criticism of I-level is the lack of normative data for the general population (Beker and Heyman 1972, p. 23). Information on the applicability of the I-level categories to the general population is necessary if one is to assess the significance of I-level characteristics for increasing our understanding of delinquent youths. Also criticized has been the lack of information on the relationship between delinquent behavior and I-level's developmental continuum, including the psychological characteristics that make up the typology (Beker and Heyman 1972, pp. 23, 49; Gibbons 1970, p. 26). Data on these relationships will be discussed, as will the relationship of I-level to self-reported delinquency (Gibbons 1970, p. 27).

This chapter will focus on normative data for the I-level system and on the relationship of I-level to delinquency. The aim will be to improve our ability to assess the usefulness and limitations of I-level, as well as to increase our knowledge of differences between delinquents and nondelinquents.

I-Level and Delinquency

The original statement of the I-level theory predicted "that those who are immature are more likely to find themselves in difficulty and to be apprehended for delinquency than are others" (Sullivan, Grant, and Grant 1957, p. 376). This statement seems to imply a relationship between I-level and delinquency; further in the article, however, one notes that (1) the stages identified as those at which delinquency becomes less likely are I-levels 5-7; and (2) the emphasis for I-levels 2-4 is on the different meanings delinquency can have for individuals at these levels (adolescents at I-level 1 are most likely to be found in mental-health institutions). Since most adolescents have been classified at I-levels 3 and 4, a relationship between I-level and delinquency is unlikely; but variation in the *reasons* for delinquency should relate to personality development.

Little empirical information is available on the relationship between delinquency and I-level, and none on self-reported delinquency. Jesness has provided frequency distributions of the I-level subtypes for delinquent and nondelinquent samples based on Jesness Inventory scores (Jesness 1974) (see table 7-1). From the Jesness data in table 7-1, one would expect a relationship between I-level and delinquency. Jesness's delinquents are considerably less mature than the other samples in the table, however. This is an artifact of the instrument used to measure I-level. Also, the Jesness Inventory forces all subjects into one of the nine delinquent subtypes and thus may give a distorted picture of the nondelinquent population.

Investigations of the role of personality have focused primarily on personality traits or on instruments that measure these traits. Schuessler and Cressey (1960) and Waldo and Dinitz (1967) indicate an increase in the number of studies able to identify and measure personality differences.

Table 7-1
Distributions of I-Levels and Subtypes among Delinquent, Nondelinquent, and General-Population Samples
(in percentages)

I-Level	This Study	CYA[a]	Jesness Nondelinquents[b]	CTP[c]
2	1	6	4	1
3	38	45	20	21
4	61	49	77	78
Subtype				
Aa } Ap }	1	2 4	0 } 4 }	1
cfm	24	16	6	12
cfc } Mp }	16	12 17	7 } 7 }	9
Na	26	21	35	27
Nx	30	21	38	46
Ci	3	4	1	3
Se	0	3	3	2
Number of cases	(196)[d]	387	104	161

[a]California Youth Authority (1973). Based on Inventory Probabilities (Jesness 1974, p. 55)
[b]Jesness (1974), p. 55.
[c]Community Treatment Project (Palmer and Werner 1973, p. 9).
[d]Weighted cases (*n* = 60). For subtypes, only those classifiable within the I-level subtypes are included. The weighted *n* for I-level is 560 (*n* = 133).

Schuessler and Cressey found that 42 percent of the studies reviewed successfully differentiated offenders from nonoffenders; Waldo and Dinitz
report that 81 percent found significant differences. A more recent review
has also found that a substantial majority of the studies reviewed found
offender-nonoffender differences (Tennenbaum 1977).

Within this body of literature are indications that I-level should be
related to delinquency. Findings by Conger and Miller on behavioral
maturity (1966), by Hindelang on the Responsibilty Scale of the CPI (1972),
and by Baker and Spielberg on the Immaturity Scale of the Jesness Inventory (1970) all suggest that maturity is related to delinquency. As conceptualized within I-level theory, however, maturity relates more to perceptual
complexity than to being considerate of others, self-controlled, or even-
tempered. Mature behavior falls more within the realm of the I-level subtypes. On the other hand, looking at the entire range of I-levels, we would
expect to find persons at higher levels of maturity to be more aware of
others, expectations, and roles, and thus more socially mature. Since most
adolescents are at I-levels 3 and 4, however, the subtypes are likely to explain more of the variation in mature behavior than are the I-levels.

The literature on personality also provides the basis for expectations of
how the I-level subtypes might be related to delinquent behavior. Delinquents have been found to be less abstract in their thinking than nondelinquents (Porteous 1973; Randolph 1973); less accepting of authority (Conger
and Miller 1966; Stein, Gough, and Sarbin 1966); less compliant (Stein,
Gough, and Sarbin 1966; Hindelang 1972); less attached to their parents
(Sumpter 1972; Venezia 1968); deficient in role-taking ability (Rotenberg
1974; Kurtines and Hogan 1972); less future oriented (Stein and Sarbin
1968; Landau 1975); less trusting (Allen and Sandhu 1967; Austrin and
Boever 1977); less socially mature (Hindelang 1972; Baker and Spielberg
1970); more anxious (Conger and Miller 1966; Dorn 1968; Eysenck 1971);
and more impulsive (Eysenck 1971; Gough 1971; Gibbens 1958). Based on
these findings, one would expect those subtypes for whom these dimensions
are most characteristic to be more delinquent than the other subtypes. The
subtypes in question are the Manipulator (Mp); the Cultural Conformist
(Cfc); and the Neurotic, acting-out (Na) subtypes.

The I-Level Classification System

The I-level theory of ego development was first presented in 1957 by
Sullivan, Grant, and Grant. Several years later the typology, further
elaborated by Marguerite Q. Warren and her associates at the California
Youth Authority, became the major framework for the well-known Community Treatment Project (Palmer 1974). The 1966 I-level manual defines

the I-level subtypes and recommends treatment modalities, treatment settings, and worker styles for the subtypes of I-levels 2, 3, and 4 (Warren et al. 1966). The typology has been refined by Palmer for the I_2 subtypes, the I_3 Immature Conformist, and the nonneurotic subtypes (1971a, b). In addition, the 1966 manual was updated in the mid-1970s and published as an audiovisual training package (Howard et al. 1974). An in-depth description of I-level stages is presented in chapter 2.

Validity

Palmer has compiled a bibliography of studies dealing with the reliability and validity of the I-level system (1973). I-level theory posits that the personalities of all individuals develop in the sequence defined by the stages of integration, although few develop beyond I-level 5. There has been no direct test of this developmental sequence, and few data are available on populations other than delinquent adolescents. The studies reported by Palmer (1973) and Jesness (1974) bear on construct validity. I-level theory also resembles other developmental theories such as Moral Development (Kohlberg 1966), Conceptual Level (Hunt 1971) and Ego Development (Loevinger 1966, 1976).

Werner (1975) reported findings on the construct validity of I-level. The standard of validity selected was the California Personality Inventory (CPI) developed by H.G. Gough. Werner hypothesized that the CPI scales should relate to I-level in particular ways. On the basis of a sample of 934 delinquent males, he first developed a set of CPI score patterns by means of cluster analysis, then from the score patterns developed six person-types. These person-types were ordered along a developmental continuum, which, as expected, was significantly related to I-level ($p<.001$); but the relationship between the two developmental models was quite small ($\phi = .23$).

Other tests of validity have been reported by Jesness (1974). He found, for instance, that I-level was strongly related to Loevinger's ego-development system ($r = .47$). Even when age, race, and verbal IQ were controlled, a substantial relationship was found ($r = .33$).

Smith (1974) has reported findings based on the scales of the Eysenck Personality Inventory (EPI) on a sample of British borstal boys that support the classifications of the I-level system. The subtypes and I-levels differed little with respect to sociability, but differed in expected ways on the Impulsivity, Neuroticism, and Psychoticism scales. For example, the Aa subtype was found to be most impulsive, the Cfm subtype least impulsive.

The developmental component of I-level is related to both age and intelligence but clearly measures more than these two variables. I-level is related to such characteristics as internalization of standards, status needs, tolerance, independence, and flexibility (Werner 1975). I-level classifications are indicative of such ego-development dimensions as social skills, respect, interdependence, self-awareness, and cognitive complexity (Jesness 1974). The I-level and subtype classifications differ in expected ways with respect to impulsivity, psychoticism, and neuroticism (Smith 1974).

Design

Details on the methodology of the study to be discussed are available elsewhere (Harris 1979). The sample consisted of 133 white, male adolescents between the ages of 13 and 16, approximately 10 percent of the population of such youths in the city where the sample was drawn. The population was first stratified on the basis of police-recorded delinquency and a socioeconomic breakdown of census tracts, and random subsamples were drawn. The subsamples were then weighted back to the populations for purposes of analysis.

In addition to police and school-record data, interviews were conducted with sample members. The interview method was that developed for the I-level classification system. From the interview an I-level classification was made, and a set of sixty-one rating scales were scored for each subject. Added to the I-level interview were questions about delinquent activity in order to obtain data on self-reported delinquency. All interviews were second rated to assess reliability of the classifications and rating scales.

I-Level Norms

Many data are available on the distribution of I-levels and subtypes within delinquent populations. The more typical distributions resemble that found for the Community Treatment Project (CTP), an example of which is found in table 7-1. The distribution of cases on I-level and subtype for this study is very close to that found for the CTP. (The distributions provided by Jesness are based on inventory scores, whereas the others are based on the interview method of classification.) It must be recalled in comparing the CTP data to those from this study that the age range for the CTP went up to 18. On the basis of these data we would expect any population of adolescent males to be classified in such a way that two-thirds to three-quarters are at I-level 4 and that one-fifth to one-third are at I-level 3. Furthermore, of the I-level subtypes, the Nx and Na are the most common, followed by the Cfm.

All the youths in the sample were successfully classified according to integration level (I-level). Only 35 percent fit any of the nine delinquent subtypes, however. The remaining 65 percent remained unclassified by subtype

(26 percent unclassified at I_3 and 39 percent at I_4). These unclassified youths, who will be labeled I_3 undifferentiated (I_3U) and I_4 undifferentiated (I_4U), will be dealt with in terms of how they differ from other youths at the same I-level. Three other pieces of normative data need mentioning here: I-level's relationship to age, socioeconomic status (SES), and intelligence (IQ).

In this study, age was found to be related to I-level as expected (r = .45, tau = .38). Table 7-2 presents the relationship between age and I-level in tabular form. According to these data, not until age 14 can one reasonably predict that a youth had developed to I-level 4; less than half of the 13-year-olds were classified at I-level 4, whereas three-quarters of the 14-year-olds were classified at this level. This relationship is higher than that reported by others (Palmer and Werner 1972: r = .34 − .37; Zaidel 1970: r = .23); previous findings were based on samples of delinquents, however, and included a wider age range.

As can be seen from table 7-2, the I-level subtypes also differed with respect to age within their respective I-levels. Within I_3, the I_3 undifferentiated subgroup was somewhat younger than the other I_3 subgroups; within I_4, the I_4 undifferentiated subgroup tended to be older. The relationship found between age and I-level, then, is largely due to the strength of the

Table 7-2
The Distribution of I-Level and Subtype on Selected Demographic Variables
(in percentages)

I-Level			Subtype				
	I_3	I_4	Cfm	Cfc/mp	I_3U	Na	Nx	I_4U
Age								
13.0-13.7	42	18	31	13	54	0	24	21
13.8-14.4	42	20	52	68	33	43	40	9
14.5-15.2	11	21	13	13	10	35	0	18
15.3-15.9	5	41	4	6	3	22	36	52
SES[a]								
Lower	14	10	22	31	7	4	7	11
Lower middle	20	23	11	38	20	24	31	22
Upper middle	49	32	34	0	66	37	36	29
Upper	17	35	33	31	7	35	26	38
IQ[b]								
Low	16	4	55	0	3	19	3	1
Low average	22	29	10	13	20	31	15	21
High average	48	37	35	53	35	22	62	19
High	14	30	0	14	42	28	20	59
Weighted *n*	205	346	46	32	127	51	58	222

[a]Based on census tract data.
[b]Lorge Thorndike, total IQ.

relationship between age and I-level among the undifferentiated subgroups. Among those youths fitting the I-level subtypes, the relationship between I-level and age is much weaker, supporting the contention that the I-level subtypes represent ways in which development becomes blocked.

Palmer has reported relationships between I-level and SES of $r = .23$ and $r = .25$ (Palmer and Werner 1972). In this study I-level was found not to be significantly related to SES, although a somewhat greater proportion of youths classified at I_4 were from upper-SES areas ($r = .19$, tau $= .10$). With respect to the subtypes, however, certain differences can be noted from table 7-2. Within I_4, SES and subtype are unrelated; but within I_3, two-thirds of the youths classified as Cfc/Mp were from lower- or lower-middle-SES areas, whereas two-thirds of the I_3U subgroup resided in upper-middle-SES areas. These differences indicate that certain response patterns reflected by the subtypes, such as the attachment of the Cfc to a delinquent peer group, are also associated with SES.

With respect to intelligence, one would expect I-level and IQ to overlap since both connote perceptual complexity, social awareness, and the ability to conceptualize. Others have reported relationships between I-level and IQ of .36 (Jesness 1974), .24 (Palmer and Werner 1972), .37 (Palmer and Werner 1972), and .59 (Zaidel 1970). For the present sample I-level was found to be related to IQ as measured by the Lorge-Thorndike, as follows: verbal: $r = .32$, nonverbal: $r = .21$, total: $r = .27$. These correlations indicate that I-level and IQ are far from synonymous. In addition, table 7-2 shows that the subtypes also vary on IQ. (The mean Lorge-Thorndike total score was 102, with a standard deviation of 15. IQ categories in table 7-2 are based on standard deviations above and below the mean.) More than half of those classified as Cfm were in the low-IQ group, whereas very few subjects in any of the other subtypes were in this IQ group. Furthermore, those youths classified as undifferentiated (I_3U and I_4U) more often had high IQ scores than did youths classified in the I-level subtypes. It would appear that youths who fit the I-level subtypes are somewhat less intelligent than those who do not, and that the characteristics of the immature-conformist (Cfm) subtype are associated with a low IQ (either intelligence or performance on the Lorge-Thorndike).

In summary, age and IQ, but not SES, are related to I-level, with age being more strongly related. Among a delinquent population, however, it appears likely that SES is also related to I-level but that age is less strongly associated. With respect to the subtypes, the Cfm subtype's characteristics appear to be associated with relatively low IQ scores; and the characteristics of the Cfc/Mp subgroups are associated with living in a low-SES area. Most important, however, the I-level delinquent subtypes appear to fit only a minority (approximately one-third) of the general adolescent population.

Characteristics of I-Level and Subtype

Tables 7-3 and 7-4 summarize the descriptions of I-levels 2-5 and the nine subtypes, as presented in the I-level video training program. The descriptions are presented in terms of how the I-levels or subtypes vary along specific dimensions. Unlike the early descriptions of the typology, the subtype dimensions cut across I-levels rather than having one set of dimensions for differentiating among the I_3 subtypes and another for differentiating among the I_4 subtypes.

Table 7-3 identifies seven dimensions that have been found to be useful for describing differences among I-levels 2-5. The first six categories describe different ways in which individuals view the world. Increasing development brings an increase in perceptual complexity and in the complexity one imposes on relationships and situations. Reasons for delinquency also vary with developmental stage. Impulsivity is likely to play a major role in delinquent behavior for youths at I-level 2, but not for youths at I-level 5. On the other hand, youths at I-level 2, who are not aware of roles, will not engage in delinquent behavior as a result of role conflicts, as might an individual at the I_5 level. In comparing youths at I_3 with those at I_4, differences in the reasons for delinquency are less extreme. For I_3, delinquency seems to center around self-protection, either through associations with others or through maintaining a protective barrier between oneself and others. At I-level 4, delinquency is affected as much by internal conflicts and value judgments as by the need to be accepted by those one admires.

The subtypes are described in terms of their differences on ten dimensions (see table 7-4). These dimensions relate to the ways individuals respond to persons and situations. The nine subtypes differ in terms of self-esteem, handling of crisis situations, responses to authority, sensitivity to various situations, and others' perceptions of them. They also differ in the reasons for their delinquency and the ways they respond to their own delinquency. For instance, the Cfm may become involved in delinquency in order to avoid rejection by peers and may later be unhappy about the anger of his parents or other adults. The Na, however, may commit a delinquent act in order to relieve pressures he is feeling that stem from internal conflicts, and may later blame someone else for his delinquent behavior.

The majority of the youths interviewed for this study did not fit the subtype descriptions found in table 7-4; these youths were labeled I_3U and I_4U. Tables 7-5 and 7-6 summarize the ways in which these youths differed from their I-level counterparts. The youths classified as I_3U were very similar to the I_3 Cfm subtype in that they expressed positive feelings about parents, teachers, and school; they were generally seen as conforming to rules. They differed from the Cfm youths in several ways, however. As can be seen from table 7-5, the I_3U subgroup was less fearful and more independent than

Table 7-3
Characteristics of I-Levels 2, 3, 4, and 5

| | I-Level | | | |
	I_2	I_3	I_4	I_5
Life theme	Maintaining position of comfort	Dealing with new situations and relationships	Meeting or not meeting up to superego ideal	Process of growth
Primary concerns	Whether or not needs are getting met	Structure or ground rules; sources of power	Understanding self and others; emancipation and being seen as unique	Relevance; becoming; role conflict
Inferences about self and others	None; people are unpredictable	Aware of impact on others; can label feelings; sees others in terms of stereotyped roles	Aware of feelings and motives; judges self and others according to rigid standards; constantly compares self to others	Sees others as complex composites of feelings, motives, roles; looks for "why"; uncomfortable with role ambiguity; expects damage
Significant others	Givers and deniers	Those with power with whom he must apply his formula	Those he wants or does not want to be like	Depends on situation, context, or available information
Adolescence	Inappropriately demanding, impulsive, unattached	Self-serving; dependent on structure; dependent on stereotyped rules or formulas	As we expect adolescent to be; has own values; judgmental; concerned about identity	Tolerant; growth-oriented; comfortable with ambiguity
Self-description	None	Behavioral	Strong belief statements; own uniqueness; "I've arrived"	Depends on situation; not overstated
Reasons for delinquency	Inability to predict; fear or anger; immediacy of needs	Conformity for acceptance or for strength by association; defiance or antagonism; self-serving	Meeting or responding negatively to superego ideal; Internal or situational conflict	Support of others; role conflict; internal or situational conflict

Source: Summarized from transcript of the I-level audiovisual program. G. Howard, J. McHale, and M.Q. Warren, "A Video-tape Training Model for I-Level Classification," Center for Training in Differential Treatment, Human Learning Systems, and NIMH, in cooperation with the California Youth Authority, 1974.

Table 7-4
Characteristics of the I_3 and I_4 Subtypes

Dimension	Subtype		
	Cfm	*Cfc*	*Mp*
Self-perception	Incapable of competing or staying out of trouble on own; preyed on by demands of others; needs help	Competent; one of the group; in control; physically strong; fearless	Adequate; independent; totally in control of self; slick; knows all the answers; more capable than others
Reasons for delinquency	Way to obtain approval or to avoid rejection	To maintain group membership: to prove competence; a natural activity in a high-crime area	Revenge; fear of closeness; to remove person seen as blocking gratification
Feelings regarding delinquency	Uncomfortable with delinquent label; wants to be seen as good; apprehensive about getting caught	Sees delinquency as commonplace; way of having fun; way to prove strength or fearlessness	Less likely to feel remorse; similar to Cfc
Nature of and reaction to crisis	Conflicting demands by opposing and equally powerful persons or unclear expectations—flight	Being put in situation where weakness might be exposed, especially to peers—hostile front	Loss of control in situation with people who have power—desperate attempt to gain control or severe depression
Reaction style	Hesitant; passive; compliant; anticipates rejection; apologetic	Insolent with adults or indolent; antagonistic toward authority	Active, physically and verbally; competes for control; aggressive
Acceptance of emotionality	Accepts emotions but when asked gives response he thinks is expected	Does not think of self as emotional; denies effect of emotions; displays of affection or hurt are unacceptable	Denies particular emotion or utility of emotions
Specific concerns	Avoiding pain or seeking approval; meeting expectations of those with power	Consistency; being seen as strong; maintaining status in group	Being in control; not being seen as inept; refining formulas for handling power situations
Reasons for anxiety	Rejection by powerful person or unclear structure	Being forced to relate to adult, thus jeopardizing peer-group status	Loss of control
Openness to information	Most open; willing to try	Avoids new experiences	Least open
How perceived by others	Passive, eagerly compliant, timid, dependent	Dependent on delinquent peers, passively antagonistic, hard-nosed	Psychopath, inconsistent, provocative, unfeeling, charming

Dimension	Na	Nx	Ci	Se
Self-perception	Above average; untroubled; underlying negative self-image	Nervous; worried; troubled; underlying negative self-image	Competent; average; capable of making own decisions	Varies; absence of long-term negative self-image
Reasons for delinquency	Validate negative self-image; avoid real reasons for bad feelings; keep others at a distance	Validate negative self-image; avoid real reasons for bad feelings; break relationship	Expression of values	Reaction to stress
Feelings regarding delinquency	Externalizes blame	Feels responsible, guilty	Justified; bad if own values were violated	Varied; usually feels bad; surprised and bewildered
Nature of and reaction to crisis	Threat of disclosure of "bad me"—denial of threat, destruction of relationship; frightening others	Threat of disclosure of "bad me"—excuses for anxiety or getting others to give up on him	Violation of strongly-held values (honesty, loyalty)—withdrawal	Inability to cope with important situation—acting out or further growth
Reaction style	Physically active or reactive; tests relationships behaviorally	Verbally active; depressed; swings from lethargy to manic level of activity	Stable, calm	Stable, varied
Acceptance of emotionality	Denies emotions; cannot enjoy good feelings or accept pain or hurt in others; can handle other feelings	Cannot enjoy good feelings; seizes on negative feelings and knows they trigger negative behavior	Open, except with regard to feelings that reflect on competence	Spontaneously accepts emotions
Specific concerns	Personal adequacy; being controlled by others	Inconsistency between stated intentions and actual performance	Value conflict; trust; respect; justice in a broad context	The how and why of his delinquency
Reasons for anxiety	Internalization of discrepant, alternating messages concerning his worth and values he should have	Internalization of discrepant, simultaneous messages concerning his worth and values; repression difficult	Situational	Situational
Openness to information	Closed regarding information relating to the neurosis; open to other information, but drives information-givers away	Open to some information; distorts information he seems to be asking for; gives false impression of wanting insight	Relatively open except when his values are challenged	Relatively open
How perceived by others	Emotionally volatile; angry; clown; agitator; big mouth; manipulator	Anxious; neurotic; wants to change; insightful; complainer	Mature; competent; sophisticated; angry with the system; a leader	Average; normal; naive; unsophisticated

Source: G. Howard, J. McHale, and M.Q. Warren, "A Video-tape Training Model for I-Level Classification," Center for Training in Differential Treatment, Human Learning Systems, and NIMH, in cooperation with the California Youth Authority, 1974.

Table 7-5

Traits Differentiating between the I₃U and I₃ Cfm Subgroups

Trait	Kendall's Tau	Characterizes I₃U	Cfm	Percentage with Trait I₃U (n = 127)	Cfm (n = 46)[a]
Accessible to new experiences	.53	+		42	0
Desires internal change	.39		+	3	30
Feels guilt about own inadequacies	.35		+	7	32
Future plans are realistic	.32	+		92	55
Trusts adults	.31		+	44	82
Independent	.28	+		42	6
Accepts authority	.26		+	48	80
Plans to go to college	.22	+		77	48
Perceives family as congenial	.19		+	17	40

[a]The analysis was based on weighted *n*s. Unweighted *n*s for these subgroups were 21 (I₃U) and 16 (Cfm).

the Cfm subgroup, and more capable of making realistic plans for the future. The Cfm youths, on the other hand, were considerably more conforming with adult authority and more likely to express low self-esteem.

Among the I₄ youths, the I₄U subgroups shared almost no characteristics with the Na and Nx subgroups. Like the Nx subgroup, half the I₄U subjects felt that they received a great deal of parental supervision; like the Na subgroup, about one-quarter were seen as conforming to a specific peer group.

Differences between the I₄U subgroup and the combined I₄N subgroup are shown in table 7-6. In contrast to the I₄U subject, those classified as I₄N demonstrated more anxiety and feelings of inadequacy, traits commonly associated with neurosis. Those characteristics that most distinguish the I₄U subjects from those classified as I₄N center around a positive self-image, self-confidence, positive relationships with adults, and high aspirations (planning to go to college). The I₄U subgroup, then, emerges as a much more stable, prosocial subgroup than those youths classified as I₄ neurotic.

I-Level and Delinquency

One major question that has been asked about I-level is the relationship of its developmental continuum to delinquency. Data presented by Jesness would indicate a negative relationship between I-level and official delinquency (Jesness 1974, p. 55), one in which nondelinquents, relative to delinquents, are more likely to be at I-level 4 than at I-level 3. The Jesness data, however, are based on inventory scores and on unrelated samples of delinquents and nondelinquents. In the study being reported here, classifications

Table 7-6
Traits Differentiating between the I_4U and I_4N Subgroups

Trait	Kendall's Tau	Characterizes I_4U	Characterizes I_4N	Percentage with Trait I_4U (n = 227)	Percentage with Trait I_4N (n = 109)[a]
Satisfied with self beneath the surface	.68	+		74	1
Motivated to resolve difficulties	.60	+		73	12
Manipulative	.55		+	0	38[b]
Anxious (long-term)	.53		+	19	79
Self-perceptions are realistic	.53	+		96	41
Accepts authority	.51	+		93	41
Accessible to new experiences	.44	+		77	28
Feels close to natural father	.43	+		76	43
Very trusting of adults	.42	+		56	12
Positive attitude toward schools	.41	+		76	36
Plans to go to college	.38	+		91	50
Compliant	.34	+		81	46
Describes self as having problems	.32		+	36	71
Accepting of own feelings	.31	+		71	26
Feels guilt about own inadequacies	.29		+	34	61
Positive attitude toward teachers	.29	+		87	53
Worried about family problems	.28		+	32	61
Positive attitude toward peers	.26	+		94	57
Judges self severely	.26	+		65	33

[a]The unweighted *n*s for these subgroups were 43 (I_4U) and 33 (I_4N).
[b]Highly characteristic of Na but not Nx.

of subjects by I-level were found to be largely unrelated to delinquency; only in a conditional sense was I-level found to be associated with delinquency.

Table 7-7 shows that almost equal proportions of youths classified at I-level 3 and I-level 4 were reported in police records as having been involved in minor or serious delinquency. (Minor and serious police-reported delinquency were defined in terms of both seriousness, misdemeanor versus felony, and frequency.) On the other hand, for self-reported delinquency there appears to be a positive relationship with I-level. This relationship, however, is not enough to be statistically significant.

It was suspected that since age was related to both delinquency and I-level, the relationship between I-level and delinquency among the older youths in the sample might differ from that for the younger age group. For self-reported delinquency, controlling age had no effect on the relationship between I-level and delinquency. Table 7-7, however, shows that among the 14.5-16 age group, 45 percent of those boys classified at I_3 were officially delinquent (32 percent serious); but only 18 percent of those classified at I_4 were officially delinquent. This would indicate that as the immaturity of the I_3 becomes less age appropriate, there is an increase in the likelihood of involvement with the juvenile-justice system, a finding that in

Table 7-7
Delinquency and I-Level
(in percentages)

	Age Group and I-Level			
	13-16		14.5-16	
Police-Reported Delinquency	I_3	I_4	I_3	I_4
None	79	81	55	82
Minor	12	13	13	8
Serious	09	06	32	10
	100	100	100	100
	(202)[a]	(351)	(31)	(218)

	13-18		14.5-16	
Self-Reported Delinquency	I_3	I_4	I_3	I_4
None	80	65	63	54
Minor	15	23	27	29
Serious	5	12	10	17
	100	100	100	100
	(187)	(343)	(30)	(198)

[a]Weighted number of cases.

part supports the statement of Sullivan, Grant, and Grant (1957) on immaturity and delinquency.

Subtype and Delinquency

Although only a limited relationship was found between I-level and delinquency, the relationship between subtype and delinquency is quite strong. Table 7-8 shows that for official delinquency, youths classified as Cfc/Mp and Na most often had official records of delinquency, followed by the Cfm subgroup. The two undifferentiated subgroups least often had records of delinquent behavior. As stated earlier, the characteristics associated with the Cfc/Mp and Na subtypes were also often associated with delinquency. This led to an expectation that the Cfc/Mp and Na subgroups would be the most delinquent. In addition, the characteristics associated with the undifferentiated subgroup indicated that delinquency was unlikely. Both expectations are supported by these findings.

The findings for self-reported delinquency, however, differ from those for official delinquency. As can be seen from table 7-8, the Cfc/Mp and Na subgroups continued to be the most delinquent, again followed by the Cfm subgroup. The I_4U subgroup, however, was found to be as involved in delinquency as the Nx subgroup. Only the I_3U subgroup emerged as nondelinquent; and, based on the official delinquency data, some of them were not truthful about their delinquent behavior.

Table 7-8
Delinquency and I-Level Subtype
(in percentages)

Police-Reported Delinquency	I-Level Subtype					
	Cfm	Cfc/mp	I_3U	Na	Nx	I_4U
None	65	53	88	44	76	90
Minor	17	19	11	44	12	8
Serious	17	28	1	12	12	2
Total	100	100	100	100	100	100
	(46)[a]	(32)	(105)	(50)	(57)	(223)
Self-Reported Delinquency	Cfm	Cfc/mp	I_3U	Na	Nx	I_4U
None	42	37	100	45	63	60
Minor	53	53	0	26	27	30
Serious	5	30	0	29	10	10
Total	100	100	100	100	100	100
	(42)[a]	(30)	(93)	(44)	(52)	(218)

[a]Weighted number of cases.

In summary, the subtypes clearly differed in their involvement in delinquency. The I_3 Cfc/Mp subtype and the Na subtype reflect characteristics associated with delinquent behavior, and youths fitting these subtypes are more likely to be involved in delinquent behavior than are other youths. The characteristics of the I_3U subgroup are associated with nondelinquency; but the I_4U subgroup, despite its prosocial characteristics, is as likely to be involved in delinquent behavior as the Nx subgroup. The I_4U subgroup is, however, less likely to have an official record delinquency.

Characteristics Related to Delinquency

Despite the relationships found between the categories of the I-level system and delinquency, this typology does not account for a large amount of variation in delinquency. Many variables associated with delinquency were not included in the analysis. In addition, the spuriousness of the relationships found has not been investigated. The point here is that the patterns of personality traits identified by the I-level system not only differentiate among delinquent youths, but also reflect differing degrees of delinquent involvement.

Several variables, most of them sociological, were found to be related to delinquency for the total sample and for every I-level category. Table 7-9 lists the interview ratings generally related to delinquency. For the official delinquency measure it was found that both the delinquency one reports of ones' friends and one's belief that future delinquency is at least a possibility

Table 7-9
Interview Ratings Related to Delinquency across I-Levels and Subtypes

Police-Reported Delinquency	Self-Reported Delinquency
Delinquency of friends (+)	Delinquency of Friends (+)
Predicts future delinquency (+)	Expresses delinquent values (+)
	Predicts future delinquency (+)
	Realism of self-descriptions (−)
	Acceptance of authority (−)
	Compliance (−)

Note: Tau < .25.

are associated with having an offical record of delinquency. These variables were also associated with the self-report measure. Four other ratings were also related to self-reported delinquency across I-level categories: (1) Expresses delinquent values, (2) Realism of self description, (3) Acceptance of authority, and (4) Compliance. The last two are clearly related to I-level subtype; but even after accounting for subtype, they remain related to self-reported delinquency.

Conclusion

Personality characteristics do not occur in isolation but in patterns; patterns that can be categorized for the purpose of making decisions such as personnel selection and assigment of persons to treatment programs. Research on personality and delinquency has typically focused on particular personality traits or on various instruments designed to measure particular traits. This chapter has focused on the usefulness of studying personality and delinquency from the perspective of patterns of personality characteristics, patterns identified by the I-level classification system.

Another major focus of this chapter has been the I-level classification system itself. Questions addressed have been I-level's relationship to delinquency and how I-level is related to such variables as age, socioeconomic status, and IQ. Among those youths who can be classified into one of the I-level subtypes, the distribution of cases on subtype is about the same in the general population as in delinquent populations. Only one-third of the general population of white male adolescents fits the subtype descriptions, however. The remaining two-thirds more often have personality characteristics that are usually seen as healthy and are less involved in delinquent behavior than are those fitting the I-level subtypes.

Although the validity of the I-level developmental continuum requires further testing, no difficulty was encountered in classifying all the sample members by integration level, and interrater reliability exceeded 85 percent. In addition, I-level was found to be related to age and IQ as expected, age being the more strongly related. SES was found to be unrelated. When relationships were investigated between the I-level subtypes and the demographic variables of age, SES, and IQ, it was found that the relationship between I-level and age was strongest among the youths who did not fit the I-level subtypes and very weak among those who did. This finding supports the contention that several of the I-level subtypes, especially those at I-level 3, represent ways in which personality development becomes blocked.

The statement by Sullivan, Grant, and Grant (1957) on the relationship between I-level and delinquency has been questioned by several writers. Whether or not this relationship was thought by the authors of this theory to be continuous across all seven I-levels is questionable. Certainly beginning with I-level 5, one would expect to find a decrease in delinquent involvement.

Although I-level was found not to be related to either police-reported or self-reported delinquency measures for the total sample, for the older half of the sample, a much greater proportion of youths classified at I_3 than at I_4 had official records of delinquency. This in part supports the statement by Sullivan, Grant, and Grant on immaturity and delinquency, but adds the element of age. Thus, as the immaturity of the I_3 level becomes less appropriate because of expectations related to age, coming to the attention of legal authorities becomes more likely.

The subtypes of the I-level system take into account variation in a majority of the personality characteristics previously found to be related to delinquency—characteristics such as anxiety, impulsivity, compliance, acceptance of authority, abstract thinking, role-taking ability, and trust. By focusing on types of persons, however, one can investigate more fully the dynamic nature of personality and its role in delinquent behavior.

Three subtypes of the I-level system emerged as highly delinquent compared with the other subtypes: the Cfc, Mp, and Na subtypes. These subtypes are most associated with the characteristics mentioned earlier that have been found to be related to delinquency. When we look beyond these characteristics, however, we see strikingly different reasons for delinquency among these three subtypes: the Cfc is typically trying to conform to the expectations of a peer subculture, the Mp is typically seeking revenge or to remove a person who is viewed as blocking his gratification, and the Na is most often reacting to internal conflict. I-level may be most valuable with respect to developing causal hypotheses. Instead of leading us to a single explanatory model or to multiple causal factors, it leads us to multiple explanatory models, some of which explain more delinquency than others. For a discussion of this issue, see Warren and Hindelang (1979).

References

Allen, D.E., and Sandhu, H.S. Alienation, hedonism, and life-vision of delinquents. *Journal of Criminal Law, Criminology and Police Science*, 1967, *58*, 325-329.

Austrin, H.R., and Boever, D.M. Interpersonal trust and severity of delinquent behavior. *Psychological Reports*, 1977, *40*, 1075-1078.

Baker, J.W., and Spielberg, M.J. A descriptive personality study of delinquency-prone adolescents. *Journal of Research in Crime and Delinquency*, 1970, *7*, 11-23.

Beker, J., and Heyman, D.S. A critical appraisal of the California differential treatment typology of adolescent offenders. *Criminology*, 1972, *10*, 23-50.

Bloch, D. The delinquent integration. *Psychiatry*, 1952, *15*, 297-303.

Conger, J.J., and Miller, W.C. *Personality, social class and delinquency.* New York: John Wiley and Sons, 1966.

Dorn, D.S. Self-concept, alienation and anxiety in a contraculture and a subculture: A research report. *Journal of Criminal Law, Criminology and Police Science*, 1968, *59*, 531-535.

Erickson, E.H. *Childhood and society.* New York: Norton, 1950.

Eysenck, S.B.G., and Eysenck, H.J. Crime and personality: Item analysis of questionnaire responses. *British Journal of Criminology*, 1971, *11*, 49-62.

Gibbens, T. The Porteous maze and delinquency. *British Journal of Educational Psychology*, 1958, 209-216.

Gibbons, D.C. Differential treatment of delinquents and interpersonal maturity level theory: A critique. *Social Service Review*, 1970, *41*, 26-27.

Gough, H.G. The assessment of wayward impulse by means of the personnel reaction blank. *Personnel Psychology*, 1971, *29*, 669-677.

Harris, P.W. The interpersonal maturity of delinquents and nondelinquents. Ph.D. diss., State University of New York at Albany, 1979.

Hindelang, M.J. The relationship of self-reported delinquency to scales of the CPI and MMPI. *Journal of Criminal Law, Criminology and Police Science*, 1972, *63*, 75-81.

Howard, G.; McHale, J.; and Warren, M.Q. A video-tape training model for I-Level classification. Center for Training in Differential Treatment, Human Learning Systems, and NIMH, in cooperation with the California Youth Authority, 1974.

Hunt, D.E. *Matching models in education.* Toronto: Ontario Institute for Studies in Education, 1971.

Jesness, C.F. *Sequential I-level manual.* Sacramento, Calif.: American Justice Institute, 1974.

Kohlberg, L. Moral education in the schools: A developmental view. *School Review*, 1966, *74*, 1-30.

Kurtines, W., and Hogan, R. Sources of conformity in unsocialized college students. *Journal of Abnormal Psychology*, 1972, *80*, 49-51.

Landau, S.F. Future time perspective of delinquents and nondelinquents: The effect of institutionalization. *Criminal Justice and Behavior*, 1975, *2*, 22-36.

Loevinger, J. The meaning and measurement of ego development. *American Psychologist*, 1966, *21*, 195-206.

_____ . *Ego development*. San Francisco: Jossey-Bass, 1976.

Palmer, T.B. *Patterns of adjustment among delinquent adolescent conformists*. Sacramento: California Youth Authority, 1971a.

_____ . *Non-neurotic, higher maturity delinquent adolescents*. Sacramento: California Youth Authority, 1971b.

_____ . A bibliography of research relating to validity and reliability of the Interpersonal Maturity Level Classification System. Sacramento: California Youth Authority, 1973.

_____ . The Youth Authority's Community Treatment Project. *Federal Probation Quarterly*, March 1974, 3-14.

Palmer, T.B., and Werner, E. *A review of I-level reliability and accuracy in the Community Treatment Project*. Sacramento: California Youth Authority, 1972.

_____ . The Phase III experiment: Progress to date. Research Report no. 13 of the Community Treatment Project, California Youth Authority, 1973.

Porteus, M.A. High school personality questionnaire: Results from a sample of delinquent boys. *Community School Gazette*, 1973, *67*, 424-426.

Randolph, K.D. Dialectical correlates of juvenile delinquency. Ph.D. diss., Texas Tech University, 1973.

Rotenberg, M. Conceptual and methodological notes on affective and cognitive role taking (sympathy and empathy): An illustrated example of delinquent and non-delinquent boys. *Journal of Genetic Psychology*, 1974, *125*, 177-185.

Schuessler, K.F., and Cressey, D.B. Personality characteristics of criminals. *American Journal of Sociology*, 1950, *55*, 476-484.

Smith, D.E. Relationship between the Eysenck and Jesness personality inventories. *British Journal of Criminology*, 1974, *4*, 376-384.

Stein, K.B.; Gough, H.G.; and Sarbin, T.R. The dimensionality of the CPI socialization scale and an empirically derived typology among delinquent and nondelinquent boys. *Multivariate Behavior Research*, 1966, *1*, 197-208.

Stein, K.B., and Sarbin, T.R. Future time perspective: Its relation to the socialization process and the delinquent role. *Journal of Consulting and Clinical Psychology*, 1968, *32*, 257-268.

Sullivan, C.E.; Grant, M.Q.; and Grant, J.D. The development of interpersonal maturity: Applications to delinquency. *Psychiatry*, 1957, *20*, 373-385.

Sullivan, H.S. *Conceptions of modern psychiatry*. New York: Norton, 1940.

Sumpter, G.R. The youthful offender: A descriptive analysis. *Canadian Journal of Criminology and Corrections*, 1972, *14*, 282-296.

Tennenbaum, D.J. Personality and criminality: Summary and implications of literature. *Journal of Criminal Justice*, 1977, *5*, 225-235.

Venezia, P.S. Delinquency as a function of intrafamily relationships. *Journal of Research in Crime and Delinquency*, 1968, *5*, 148-173.

Waldo, G.P., and Dinitz, S. Personality attributes of the criminal: An analysis of research studies, 1950-65. *Journal of Research in Crime and Delinquency*, 1967, *4*, 185-202.

Warren, M.Q. Intervention with juvenile delinquents. In M.K. Rosenheim, ed., *Pursuing justice for the child*. Chicago: University of Chicago Press, 1976.

Warren, M.Q., and CTP staff. *Interpersonal maturity level classification: Juvenile diagnosis and treatment of low, middle and high maturity delinquents*. Sacramento: California Youth Authority, 1966.

Warren, M.Q., and Hindelang, M.J. Current explanations of offender behavior. In Hans Toch, ed., *Psychology of crime and criminal justice*. New York: Holt, Rinehart and Winston, 1979.

Werner, E. Relationships among interpersonal maturity, personality configurations, intelligence and ethnic status. *British Journal of Criminology*, 1975, *15*, 51-68.

Zaidel, S.R.F. Affect awareness, intelligence, and the interpersonal maturity classification. Ph.D. diss., University of California, Los Angeles, 1970.

8

Causal Models of the Development of Law Abidance and Its Relationship to Psychosocial Factors and Drug Use

G.J. Huba and
P.M. Bentler

Of many psychological and social variables studied in conjunction with so-called deviant behaviors such as drug use, theft, property crime, gang confrontations, and early sexuality and autonomy, the most important causal variable emerging from a variety of latent-variable structural-equation models in our five-year longitudinal study of adolescence has been rebelliousness or low levels of traditional law abidance (Huba and Bentler, in press a, chaps. 23, 26, 27, 39, 43, 45; in press b). Levels of generalized rebelliousness (or low law abidance) have important implications for the developmental trajectory of the adolescent. Low levels of law abidance are causal antecedents of such undesirable activities as theft and drug use (Ginsberg and Greenley 1978; Jessor and Jessor 1977; Kandel 1978). Since these activities may be heavily punished by our society, an individual's level may have important long-term implications for the success of overall life adjustment.

Here we use accumulated data from the five-year University of California, Los Angeles (UCLA) Study of Adolescent Growth (Huba and Bentler, 1982a,b; in press a,b) to test models for the development of traditional law abidance or, conversely, rebelliousness. Longitudinal data are analyzed with latent variable causal modeling techniques (see Bentler 1980; Jöreskog 1978) to derive systematically and test models to explain the unfolding trajectory of generalized rebellious tendencies and their important psychosocial causes and consequences.

This chapter also illustrates how a single personality characteristic may be intensively studied with latent-variable causal models. Latent-variable causal models are confirmatory multivariate-analysis methods for testing

This research was partially supported by Grant no. DA01070 from the National Institute on Drug Abuse. The authors wish to thank Ngoc Suong Luong and Julie Honig for manuscript-preparation assistance. The first two parts of the results presented here (tables 8-1 through 8-11) derive from Huba and Bentler, *Antecedents and Consequences of Adolescent Drug Use: A Psychosocial Study of Development Using a Causal Modeling Approach* (New York: Plenum, in press).

certain hypotheses about the type of causal structure responsible for generating correlations among measured indicators. Statistical theory is invoked to estimate parameters, test for overall goodness of fit, and determine whether individual parameters are necessary. These methods, largely credited to Jöreskog (1970, 1978) and others, can be used to test any number of possible models. Here we study particularly interesting and specialized ones developed for a set of longitudinal personality data relevant to the theme of this book.

There is sufficient knowledge of the construct of *law abidance* (or its converse, rebelliousness) to warrant developing causal models of its natural course. Many behaviors of concern to social scientists are illegal or are milder precursors of highly illicit acts. Consistently deviant behaviors co-occur, suggesting that a general personality factor may be responsible for the initiation and maintenance of the behaviors (see Becker 1963; Hogan et al. 1970; Huba and Bentler, in press a, chaps. 20, 39; in press b; Jessor and Jessor 1977; Kaplan 1978, 1980; Segal, Huba, and Singer 1980a,b). Careful tests of the causal role of law abidance in overall personality functioning have not yet been made, however.

Causal Models for Theory Testing

Different patterns of interrelationships among major constructs in the personality, intimate support, drug use, behavioral pressure, and deviance domains (see Huba and Bentler 1982a) are studied in this chapter with latent-variable causal models. Causal modeling represents a set of statistical techniques for investigating sample data in light of hypothesized population models about the influence of certain variables on others (Blalock 1964). A model represents a simultaneous series of statements about the regressions of particular variables on various other causal or explanatory variables. In such a framework, the regressions are often at the level of the unmeasured latent variables or factor constructs, and the constructs themselves are interrelated by factor-analytic assumptions to observed, manifest variables. It is desirable to make such regressions at the level of latent variables where measurement error is explicitly estimated, so that it cannot bias estimates of the size and sign of causal influences (Huba and Bentler 1982b). The goals of causal modeling include both the testing of a proposed model against data and the development of models that adequately account for the data in hand. This chapter addresses both goals by asking whether certain hypothesized causal linkages are indeed necessary for our longitudinal data. When certain conditions of nesting are satisfied, it is also possible to compare and contrast alternative theoretical models proposed to account for the same relationships. Various more explicit theoretical tests are conducted elsewhere (Huba and Bentler, in press a,b).

Although causal models should be evaluated by many criteria, including meaningfulness, they can be tested statistically using well-known principles for adequacy in explaining observed data. A statistical assessment of the goodness of fit of a model is afforded by a large-sample chi-square test: The hypothesis that the sample variance-covariance matrix is drawn from a population having the hypothesized causal structure is evaluated against the alternative null hypothesis that the variables are simply correlated. If chi square is large relative to its degrees of freedom, the proposed causal structure must be rejected as the observed sample data would be extremely unlikely if the hypothesized model were true in the population. Although the chi-square statistic provides a formal statistical means of assessing goodness of fit for models when the assumptions are met, in very large samples of observations, trivial departures of the observed data from the hypothesized model can lead to the statistical rejection of the formulation. Therefore, we supplement our decision-making procedures with normed and non-normed fit indexes (Bentler and Bonett 1980). The normed-fit coefficient ranges from zero (indicating poor model fit) to unity (indicating perfect model fit) but is not corrected for the size of the model, whereas the non-normed coefficient is corrected for the size of the model. Of course, there are always alternative parameters for certain portions of complex mathematical models, but many of these variants are trivial in their differences from one another (Huba and Bentler, 1982a,b).

This chapter makes certain scientific assumptions about constructs and then uses appropriate statistical methods for the assumptions. First, we are interested in relating error-free constructs from our different systems to one another, rather than interrelating error-prone indicators. Consequently, we use methods explicitly employing multiple indicators of law abidance and other dimensions. We study how the construct variance common to alternative, fallible measured indicators points toward models of how different constructs are interrelated. Thus the models try explicitly to eliminate contaminating sources of error variance that serve to bias amounts of inferred relationship between constructs. Longitudinal data are employed to control various inferential confounds. Unfortunately, the methodology used here is expensive, requiring substantial computer resources. The potential advantages of this methodology far exceed the costs involved, however. No equally good alternative methods have yet been found to test such theories with nonexperimental data.

Introduction to the UCLA Study of Adolescent Growth

The UCLA Study of Adolescent Growth is a five-year, cohort-sequential study that has collected four waves of data at annual or biannual intervals.

Three grade cohorts (seventh, eighth, ninth) were used. Beginning in 1976, data were collected in project years I, II, IV, and V. A comprehensive treatment of the many different facets of the UCLA study, including the sampling plan and participants, is given by Huba and Bentler (in press a, chaps. 6, 7).

Initially, self-reports were collected from 1,634 young adolescents on aspects of personality, peer cultures, drug-use patterns, future drug use, and general school adjustment. Similar information was collected at the three retests. In the last wave we also obtained information about the patterns of deviant or criminal behavior engaged in by the adolescents. Summaries of the UCLA study have appeared in several places (Huba and Bentler 1982a, in press a).

Multiple Indicators of the
Law-Abidance Construct

A key to understanding the empirical analyses of this chapter is the notion of multiple indicators of a latent variable. Conceptually, we are studying a latent variable or factor of *law abidance*. By definition, a factor or latent variable cannot be directly observed or measured. It is possible, however, to observe the factor's effects on manifest variables or indicators that can be measured (as quantified by factor loadings). For example, intelligence is a construct or latent variable or factor that presumably strongly influences a test response, such as performance on the Wechsler Adult Intelligence Scale (WAIS). We can infer that WAIS scores are an indicator of intelligence, though not necessarily the only or best indicator. Although we cannot measure a factor directly, we can assess the effects of the latent construct on measured variables; thus we can study it with causal models. In order to study the construct, however, we must study indicators of the construct. Furthermore, in those instances where we have multiple indicators of several constructs, we can use some constructs to predict others. These regressions at the latent-variable level explicitly remove contaminating effects of measurement error. Such multiple indicator models are, of course, also extremely desirable from the viewpoint of theory, since we prefer a science to hinge not on test-specific results, but rather on constructs (Huba and Hamilton, 1976).

Operationally, we measure the construct of law abidance with three observed scales: law abidance, liberalism, and religious commitment. (We labeled the factor in terms of the scale that loads most highly on it. In this context the scale of law abidance is *not* synonymous with our factor of law abidance; rather, the scale is an error-prone indicator of the error-free factor we cannot measure. From the context of our discussion, it should be clear whether we are referring to the scale or the construct.) The three indicators were chosen both on the basis of replicated factor-analytic evidence (Huba and Bentler, in press a, chaps. 11, 20) and on the basis of theory in the area. Each scale is relatively short and contains four items. The law-abidance scale has contrasting items: returning incorrect change versus being willing to keep it; using false identification versus being afraid to do so; shoplifting certain items versus not knowing how or wanting to; and honest type versus not quite so honest. The liberalism scale contains contrasting items: see cops as law enforcers versus see cops as pigs; support women's liberation versus don't feel women need or want it; think police should carry guns versus think cops shouldn't carry guns; and approve of many protests versus approve of few protests. The religious commitment scale contrasts: am not religious versus am a religious person; believe in religion or the Bible versus believe in science; feel that prayers are answered versus feel that praying is a waste; and think religion is outdated versus think religion is not outdated. Reliabilities for law abidance and religious commitment were high in all years of the study, whereas those for liberalism were lower (Huba and Bentler, in press a, chap. 6).

In all the models, the three indicators are caused by a general factor of law abidance. Theoretically it seems to be relatively straightforward to assume that the individual high on the *construct* of law abidance will score high on the *scale* of law abidance, which measures traditional respect for the law; low on the scale of liberalism or high in the tendency to respect traditional social institutions; and high in the tendency to religious commitment or in respect for traditional religious institutions. That is, the theoretical construct of law abidance is a generalized tendency to respect the rules of law-setting institutions in society. This general construct is measured by the three scales, each of which addresses a specific aspect of the construct.

Mean Trends in Manifest and Latent Variables of Law Abidance over Adolescence

Respondents for these initial analyses were 768 individuals, who provided data at all four waves: the number in each of the six analysis-of-variance cells formed by sex and cohort is given in table 8-1a. Huba and Bentler (in press a, chap. 6) give analyses showing how the subsample compares to the full sample on a variety of characteristics: the selection effects are small.

We should comment on the inclusion of the oldest cohort in these analyses. At the final data collection, this cohort had graduated from high school and was contacted through the mail. In most other analyses in our work (Huba and Bentler, in press a), we did *not* include this cohort because of possibly confounded sources of variance due to maturation and mode of questionnaire administration. Here, however, we included the cohort because: (1) the personality scales should be least susceptible to distortion due to data collection through mailout questionnaires; and (2) there are explicit examinations of the data here for linear trends of a maturational nature that can help us to detect outlier effects. In general, there are no apparent discontinuities in the trends for the personality scales of these individuals.

For the three indicators—law abidance, liberalism, and religious commitment—we first calculated a three-factor analysis of variance using sex, cohort, and year of testing; year of testing was a repeated-measure factor. The analyses conducted use the design that Baltes, Cornelius, and Nesselroade (1979) call the sequential-longitudinal one. In addition to the usual analysis-of-variance tests for main effects and interactions in the full factorial design, we also tested whether two specific a priori contrasts associated with hypotheses of linear development were significant, using Winer's (1971) method for nonorthogonal designs.

How do the mean levels of law abidance, liberalism, and religious commitment change over the five years? Table 8-1 summarizes the mean scores obtained by each of the six classification groups (seventh grade males, eighth grade males, ninth grade males, seventh grade females, eighth grade females, ninth grade females) across four years of assessment (1975-1979).

In the analyses of variance, we partition the variance in the scores into portions attributable to sex; cohort (grade); the interaction of sex and cohort; year of testing; the interaction of sex and year of testing; the interaction of cohort and year of testing; and the triple interaction of sex, cohort, and year of testing. The sex, cohort, and sex-by-cohort sources of variation are between subject; the remaining sources are within subject. The result is an F ratio, which, if large for its degrees of freedom, indicates that the source contributed significantly to the observed mean differences. Here we used *univariate* analyses of variance since we next make a multivariate assessment of effects on factor means.

The significant F ratios are as follows: There is a significant sex effect (with 1 and 762 degrees of freedom), irrespective of cohort or year of testing, on the scales of law abidance ($F = 9.85$, $p < .01$); liberalism ($F = 8.68$, $p < .01$); and religious commitment ($F = 14.41$, $p < .001$). Of course, the F ratios do not contain information about the direction of the difference in mean scores (whether males are lower than females, or vice versa); such directionality information must be inferred from table 8-1a, where it can be seen that males rate themselves as generally less law abiding and lower in religious commitment, but also as less liberal. There were no significant cohort effects, and none of the cohort-by-sex interactions was significant. Law abidance ($F = 5.81$; d.f. $= 3,2286$; $p < .001$) and liberalism ($F = 2.14$, d.f. $= 3,2286$, $p < .10$) have at least marginally significant effects

Table 8-1
Mean Scores on Personality Scales
a. Means by sex, cohort, and year

Scale	Year	Cohort					
		7th Male	*8th Male*	*9th Male*	*7th Female*	*8th Female*	*9th Female*
Law abidance	1975	13.3	11.9	11.3	13.4	13.0	12.2
	1976	12.5	12.1	12.4	12.6	12.3	12.5
	1978	12.5	12.1	12.5	13.2	13.4	13.4
	1979	12.1	12.0	12.6	13.3	13.4	14.1
Liberalism	1975	9.2	9.8	9.5	10.0	10.4	10.1
	1976	9.7	9.6	10.1	10.6	10.3	10.0
	1978	9.7	9.6	10.2	10.4	10.2	10.1
	1979	9.5	9.9	9.7	10.4	9.8	9.7
Religious commitment	1975	15.6	14.9	12.5	15.6	15.5	15.3
	1976	15.5	14.5	13.4	15.5	15.4	14.9
	1978	15.1	14.2	13.6	15.7	15.7	14.9
	1979	15.4	14.5	13.8	16.1	15.9	14.9
Number of participants		113	85	47	222	182	119

b. Means collapsed to show grade trends by sex

Scale	Sex	Grade						
		7	*8*	*9*	*10*	*11*	*12*	*13*
Law abidance	Male	13.3	12.2	11.8	12.4	12.1	12.2	12.6
	Female	13.4	12.8	12.3	13.0	13.4	13.4	14.1
Liberalism	Male	9.2	9.7	9.5	9.8	9.5	10.0	9.7
	Female	10.0	10.5	10.2	10.2	10.3	9.9	9.7
Religious commitment	Male	15.6	15.3	13.8	14.6	14.9	14.2	13.8
	Female	15.6	15.5	15.3	15.4	15.9	15.5	14.9

for the year of testing. Law abidance (F= 5.20; d.f. = 3,2286; $p < .01$) and liberalism ($F = 5.53$; d.f. = 3,2286; $p < .001$) also have significant sex-by-year effects. Law abidance ($F = 6.61$; d.f. = 6,2286; $p < .001$) and liberalism ($F = 2.41$; d.f. = 6,2286; $p < .05$) have significant year-by-cohort effects; but only religious commitment ($F = 3.00$; d.f. = 6,2286; $p < .01$) has a significant year-by-sex-by-cohort interaction effect.

It is interesting to examine the mean differences as attributed to age. The average unweighted grade level for the individuals in the four years of assessment, respectively, are 8, 9, 11, and 12: year of testing is confounded with average grade level. There is a statistically significant year effect for the law-abidance scale. Examining the mean scores for the individuals given in table 8-1a and collapsing these means over the six groups, we might conclude from the trends that over the years of testing the respondents say they are more law abiding.

Although statistical significance is an important criterion in deciding what contributes to mean differences, with large samples it is necessary to moderate such conclusions with an assessment of importance. Such an approach is analogous to looking at the size of a statistically significant correlation coefficient. Huba and Bentler (in press a, table 47.4) used two alternative coefficients for importance and concluded that the significant effects discussed here accounted for about 2 percent of the unique variance in the scales; significant differences are of small importance.

Of the trends for each of the individual personality scales assessing the construct of law abidance, the most important is that of increasing age, ideally invariant over measurement year or cohort and sex. It is well known for cohort-sequential designs (see Baltes, Cornelius, and Nesselroade 1979), however, that developmental trends for scale do not represent a simple main effect. Table 8-1b shows the mean scores for the developmental trends after the data have been collapsed across the different cohorts and years: on none of the scales do the means seem to change strongly and systematically as the individuals get older.

An a priori contrast in the analysis of variance can determine whether there is significant linear developmental tendency. A related question is whether or not there is an interaction between the sex of the respondent and linear developmental tendency, using a series of contrast weights described by Huba and Bentler (in press a, table 47.6). There was an interaction between the patterns of linear development and the sex of the respondent for the scales of law abidance, liberalism, and religious commitment. The significant F ratios for these tests were 9.90, 13.09, and 7.30, respectively (d.f. = 1,2286). Of course, the various F tests only summarize whether the pattern of the means is a statistically systematic one; they do not show the actual direction of the slopes for the males and the females. Those tendencies must be inferred from the means already presented in table 8-1b. Thus, although there is a statistically significant linear development by sex inter-action for all three scales, we might infer from visual inspection that in fact these significant sources of variation are fairly small. We also made a test for linear developmental tendency within each of the scales. Only law abidance ($F = 6.47$; d.f. $= 1,2286$; $p < .05$) had a significant trend. Thus we conclude that the trends in the three indicators of the law-abidance construct are relatively small, and that the tendencies are generally similar across adolescence for the different cohorts. No strong developmental-change patterns are found.

So far we have solved for the effects of the different design variables on the three observed indicators. Such tests assume that the individual scales may be conceptualized as error-free measures of the underlying construct. Since this is seldom the case, we now test whether the mean levels on the law-abidance construct presumed to underlie responses on the observed scales of law abidance, liberalism, and religious commitment are affected by different design factors. These analyses are taken from chapter 47 of Huba and Bentler (in press a), and are sufficiently complex that we will refer the reader there for a fuller explanation and extended results.

Basically, the latent-variable analyses test whether the mean levels on the unobserved factor change as a function of various effects. Such tests de-pend on global assumptions made for the causal models, however; thus we should specify these. First, we assumed that there is a latent variable of law abidance at each measurement time and that this factor had invariant load-ings at each time for its three indicators: law abidance, liberalism, and religious commitment. This means that we assumed that the law-abidance factor had exactly the same factor loadings for the observed indicators on each occasion for each group. Second, we assumed that each observed vari-able had measurement error and that errors of measurement for the same observed scale were correlated over all measurement occasions. Third, we assumed that the different factors were related as follows: law abidance II was a function of law abidance I; law abidance IV was a function of law abidance I and law abidance II; and law abidance V was a function of law abidance I, law abidance II, and law abidance IV. Fourth, we assumed the paths among the factors were invariant over the group. Finally, we assumed that the error variances and covariances in the three male groups were equal to one another (with respect to elements) and that the error variances and covariances in the three female groups were equal.[1]

The model was first estimated with all factor means allowed to be freely estimated (that for seventh-grade males in year I was zero in order to identify the solution). (Such a constraint is a regular one and is hidden within typical analyses of variance.) The model for these data fit moderately well ($\chi^2 = 613.85$, d.f. $= 442$) and the fit is sufficient to have faith in the parameter estimates. Of most interest are the factor means presented in table 8-2a along with the standard errors for the estimates. Examining the different

Table 8-2
Mean Scores on the Factor of Law Abidance
a. Means by sex, cohort, and year

	Cohort					
Year	7th Male	8th Male	9th Male	7th Female	8th Female	9th Female
1975	.00[a]	−.48 (.19)	−.72 (.24)	−.03 (.14)	−.22 (.16)	−.40 (.18)
1976	−.28 (.10)	.01 (.14)	.23 (.17)	−.30 (.08)	−.19 (.08)	.04 (.11)
1978	−.12 (.10)	−.14 (.12)	−.09 (.15)	.08 (.08)	.20 (.09)	.12 (.10)
1979	−.10 (.09)	−.07 (.10)	.07 (.15)	.01 (.07)	.01 (.08)	.22 (.08)
Number of participants	113	85	47	222	182	119

b. Means collapsed to show grade trends by sex

	Grade						
Sex	7	8	9	10	11	12	13
Male	.00[a]	−.30 (.09)	−.21 (.12)	−.05 (.08)	−.10 (.07)	−.06 (.08)	.07 (.13)
Female	.00 (.11)	−.25 (.07)	−.22 (.08)	.04 (.06)	.11 (.05)	.09 (.06)	.24 (.08)

Note: Standard errors in parentheses.
[a]Parameter fixed at indicated values.

estimated factor means by visual inspection, it appears that although there may be some differences between the groups, there is no strong suggestion of an overriding trend that simply fits the data.

It is desirable to fit a more restricted model to the means to explain their variation while simplifying the conceptual pattern. From our manifest variable results, it seemed necessary to consider a model that included an interaction of developmental pattern and sex. Such a model can be specified for the factor means of table 8-2a by making the constraints equating, within each sex separately, the means for the cells where the individuals were in the same grade. This model, which solves for developmental means separately for males and females, fits the data with a chi-square value of 630.91 on 432 degrees of freedom. When we compare the chi-square value for the constrained developmental model to that of the model wherein all factor means are free, we find that the difference chi-square of 17.6 (d.f. = 10) is non-significant, which means that one can solve for the developmental trend without any loss in the fit of the overall model. Nonetheless, as the reader will infer from table 8-2b, although developmental trend can be fit into the factor means, it is not a simply interpreted linear one for males, although it appears that females exhibit increasingly higher levels of the trait of law abidance as they get older.

As a subhypothesis, we might ask whether the developmental trend in the factor means is the same for males and females. This model is a specialized case of the pattern illustrated in table 8-2b, wherein the further constraint is made on the means that the corresponding cells for the males and the females have numerically identical factor mean. This model fit the data with a chi-square value of 646.11 with 439 degrees of freedom, significantly worse than that for the model, which separately fit the developmental means for males and females ($\chi^2 = 16.11$, d.f. = 7, $p < .05$). Thus we tend to accept the representation of table 8-2b as the best one for these factor means.

The latent-variable analyses tell us how the means on a latent personality construct are influenced by different sources of variance attributable to development more directly than do analyses of variance based on fallible indicators, since measurement-error variance is controlled and multiple indicators are handled simultaneously. Further applications to this and other personality traits are given elsewhere (Huba and Bentler, in press a, chap. 47).

**Analyses of Law Abidance Causes and
Consequences: Five-Year, Four-Wave
Causal Models**

How does the construct of law abidance covary with other psychosocial constructs over time? Even more important, how does law abidance relate to other constructs as a plausible cause or consequence? These analyses answer those questions by examining portions of the data spanning all four assessment waves (five years) of the study. Specifically, we will be using the multiple-construct, multiple-wave longitudinal data to ask questions of causal priority (Kenny 1979; Rogosa 1979). For example, is peer-culture involvement a precursor of low levels of law abidance, or do individuals low in law-abidance tendencies tend to become heavily immersed in peer cultures? Alternatively, are low levels of law abidance and peer-culture involvement jointly caused by some other factor? Or do the two sets of factors tend to influence each other reciprocally? We ask such questions for law abidance and the psychosocial constructs of peer-culture involvement, time spent with friends, drug-use behavioral pressure from peers, adult drug-use exposure, alcohol use, cannabis use, and hard-drug use. The factors studied in conjunction with law abidance were theoretically hypothesized by Huba and Bentler (in press a) and empirically confirmed earlier through a series of factor-analytic studies (Huba and Bentler, in press a, chaps. 10, 12, 13, 20) within the longitudinal study.

For the present correlational analyses we used data collected from the two youngest grade cohorts in all years of the study. In the first year the individuals were in either the seventh or eighth grade, whereas in the final year they were in the eleventh or the twelfth grade. Of these 601 individuals, 229 (33.6 percent) were male, and 459 (66.4 percent) were female; 372 (54.1 percent were in the youngest cohort, and 316 (45.9 percent) were in the middle cohort. These individuals did not appear initially to be different from the total sample (see Huba and Bentler, in press a, chaps. 6, 7).

Data-Analysis Design

The prototypic analysis design employed in the eight analyses of this type is shown in figure 8-1. Although it is termed prototypic, individual analyses differ from it slightly in one respect or another. It is considerably easier, however, to grasp the general framework for all analyses presented here than to examine each individually without seeing how the analyses are designed to be as parallel as possible.

As shown in figure 8-1, two different latent constructs are measured at each of four assessment times corresponding to years I, II, IV, and V. Whenever possible, three indicators at each assessment wave are used for the latent constructs; furthermore, as possible we use identical indicators with identical response scales. Ideally, we assume that identical indicators have been assessed, since in that case an extra restriction is made. Otherwise, appropriate modifications are made. Note that in figure 8-1 we denoted certain paths (factor loadings) from latent variables to observed indicators with

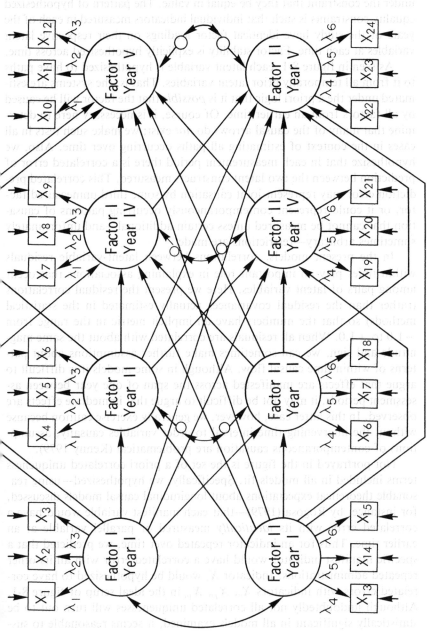

Figure 8-1. Prototype for Four-Wave, Two-Construct Time-Lagged Causal Modeling Tests

identically subscripted parameters, symbolizing that the models are estimated under the constraint that they be equal in value. The pattern of hypothesized equality constraints is such that individual indicators measured in each of the years of the study have identical factor loadings on their respective latent variables at each time. Factor stability is explicitly hypothesized across time.

As seen in figure 8-1, each latent variable is hypothesized to have paths to it from all temporally prior latent variables. That is, the systems are estimated under the a priori logic that it is *possible* that the factor will be caused by all factors from an earlier time. Of course, it is necessary here to determine that many of the causal arrows do *not* exist; we make such tests in all cases in the context of estimating all paths occurring over time. Also, we hypothesize that in each measurement period there is a correlated error of prediction between the two latent constructs measured. This correlated prediction error may represent joint causation by some third unmeasured factor, or it could represent contemporaneously occurring patterns of causation that cannot be measured unless certain additional—and unfortunately sometimes arbitrary—restrictions are made.

In the present models, correlations between latent-variable residuals within times play an important role in explaining associations that occur among pairs of latent variables. Here we present the residual correlations (rather than the residual covariances actually estimated in the statistical methods) so that the numbers have an implicit metric in the range from -1.0 to $+1.0$. When all residuals are correlated with about the same magnitude and sign, we can sometimes make further assumptions about patterns of within-time causal flow. Although in some models it is difficult to argue that effects are manifested across the span of one year between assessment periods, it may not be difficult to argue that immediate effects are observed. In this latter case, however, we generally exercise caution because without the intervening time interval to order variables causally, assumptions of contemporaneous causation are problematical (Kenny 1979).

Not portrayed in the figure is the set of a priori correlated uniqueness terms included in all models fit. Specifically, we hypothesized—using reasonable theoretical expectations about longitudinal causal models discussed, for instance, by Rogosa (1979)—that each manifest variable would have a correlated error with its *identically* measured or parallel variable at an earlier time. Thus for an indicator repeated over time, we predicted that a specific manifest indicator would have a correlated error with all its other repeated administrations: Indicator X_1 would be hypothesized to have correlated errors with indicators X_7, X_{13}, X_{19} in the ideal setup of figure 8-1. Although undoubtedly not all correlated uniquenesses will turn out to be statistically significant in all models examined, it seems reasonable to suspect that there is always *some* effect from repeatedly administering an indicator; if such covariance sources are not included within the models, they may bias the important causal coefficients.

Within the factor constraints imposed by the number of indicators actually available, we used the foregoing design. When there were not identical indicators available at all waves, we relaxed the relevant equality constraints; sometimes when there were not exactly three indicators, we deleted an indicator or two from the models, with a corresponding shift in the number of correlated uniquenesses estimated. In all cases we used a covariance matrix in LISREL-IV (Jöreskog and Sörbom 1978) to estimate parameters using maximum-likelihood methods, and obtained estimates, standard errors, and an overall chi-square goodness-of-fit statistic. Normed and nonnormed fit indexes show how well the observed covariance is explained.

We selected eight constructs to study with law abidance. The first was drug-behavioral pressure assessed with items of the number of friends perceived to use: (1) beer or wine, (2) marijuana, and (3) pills. Each item was answered with a five-point anchored response scale in each year. The second construct was peer-culture involvement. In the first, second, and fifth years, the construct was assessed with items of how often the individual and friends: (1) partied, (2) listened to records, and (3) drove around. In the fourth year of the study the construct was assessed with the single item of how many friends the individual drove around with often. Responses were made on an anchored five-point scale. The third psychosocial construct was friends' poor school performance. In the first, second, and fifth years this construct was assessed with items pertaining to the number of friends who: (1) cut class, (2) might quit school, and (3) cheated on an exam. In the fourth year the item pertaining to quitting school was not included. Drug availability was assessed with items of how many friends give the individual: (1) beer or wine, (2) marijuana, and (3) pills. The responses were made on an anchored five-point scale. Perceived adult drug use was assessed in all years using indicators of how many adults were perceived to use: (1) beer or wine, (2) marijuana, and (3) pills, with responses made on a five-point anchored scale.

Alcohol use was assessed in each year. In the first year there were indicators of frequency of beer, wine, and liquor use; in the second year there was a single indicator of frequency of alcohol use; in the fourth year there were indicators of frequency of beer, wine, and liquor; in the fifth year there were indicators of frequency of beer, wine, and liquor as well as an index of alcohol-use quantity. Cannabis use was assessed in all four years. In the first year there were frequency-of-marijuana- and -hashish-use indicators; in the second year there was a single frequency-of-cannabis-use indicator; in the fourth year there were frequency-of-marijuana and -hashish indicators; in the fifth year there were frequency-of-marijuana and -hashish indicators as well as a quantity-of-cannabis-use indicator. Hard-drug use was also measured in all four years. In the first year there were indicators of frequency of amphetamines, tranquilizers, and hallucinogenics; in the second year there was a single hard-drug-use indicator; in the fourth year there were indicators for frequency of amphetamines, minor tranquilizers, and LSD; in the fifth year there were indicators for frequency of amphetamines, minor tranquilizers, and LSD. For all drug-use indicators, responses were coded on five-point anchored scales in the first and second years and on seven-point scales in the fourth and fifth years. Since drug-use indicators varied slightly from year to year, none of the associated factor loadings were held equal across years.

The constructs were chosen for analyses here since our more extended work (Huba and Bentler, in press a) found that these factors were consistently related to law abidance. Item selections are based on extensively exploratory and confirmatory factor analyses (Huba and Bentler, in press a, chaps. 11, 12, 13, 20). The measurement structure for drug use has been described elsewhere (Huba, Wingard, and Bentler 1981; Huba and Bentler 1982b).

Law Abidance and Drug-Behavioral Pressure

The first question asked was how the construct of law abidance influenced the construct of drug-behavioral pressure—pressure to use drugs—over time. Both constructs were assessed under the ideal design shown in figure 8-1 (one of the few times our design was perfect): chi-square was 315.23, the degrees of freedom were 200, the normed-fit coefficient Δ was .954, and the non-normed fit index P was .976. Although the statistical-fit index is high enough for the degrees of freedom that we might be forced to reject the model for these data, this value is actually quite small for the sample size and large model fit. The large values of the fit indexes reinforce this conclusion and confirm that even though the fit of the model might be improved by further model modifications, the current parameter estimates are good ones. Estimates for the structural regressions or paths among factors are shown in table 8-3 and portrayed diagrammatically in figure 8-2. It appears that we can infer that any influences on the construct are such that tendencies toward lowered levels of law abidance predispose the individual toward peer-culture situations in which he or she will be exposed to models who exert generalized pressure toward drug use. This result is evinced by the fact that drug-behavioral pressure II is a function of low law abidance I, and drug-behavioral pressure IV is a function of low law abidance II. In contrast, none of the across-time paths from drug-behavioral pressure to low law abidance are statistically significant. Influences from low law abidance to drug-behavioral pressure probably also occur within time, as evidenced by the sizable negative residual correlations in all waves.

Correlations among latent variables are also in table 8-3. These correlations are analogous to usual product-moment ones; but rather than being correlations among variables, the coefficients show the amount of association

Structural Regression Coefficients and Latent-Variable Correlations for Four-Wave, Five-Year Causal Model Linking Law Abidance and Drug-Behavioral Pressure

		Independent Latent Variable						
Dependent Latent Variable	I	II	III	IV	V	VI	VII	VIII

a. Unstandardized coefficients

Dependent Latent Variable	I	II	III	IV	V	VI	VII	VIII
I. Law abidance I	—	a	a	a	a	a	a	a
II. Drug-behavioral pressure I		—	a	a	a	a	a	a
III. Law abidance II	.91 (.13)		—	a	a	a	a	a
IV. Drug-behavioral pressure II	.40 (.09)	.42 (.08)		—	a	a	a	a
V. Law abidance IV	.10 (.17)	.09 (.09)	.56 (.12)	.14 (.08)	—	a	a	a
VI. Drug-behavioral pressure IV	-.02 (.14)	-.07 (.08)	-.31 (.11)	.34 (.07)		—	a	a
VII. Law abidance V	.14 (.16)	-.05 (.08)	-.22 (.15)	.02 (.07)	.98 (.20)	-.05 (.12)	—	a
VIII. Drug-behavioral pressure V	-.21 (.13)	-.07 (.08)	.04 (.11)	.07 (.07)	-.20 (.15)	.62 (.10)		—

b. Standardized coefficients

Dependent Latent Variable	I	II	III	IV	V	VI	VII	VIII
I. Law abidance I	—	a	a	a	a	a	a	a
II. Drug-behavioral pressure I		—	a	a	a	a	a	a
III. Law abidance II	.77		—	a	a	a	a	a
IV. Drug-behavioral pressure II	.35	.37		—	a	a	a	a
V. Law abidance IV	.10	.08	.63	.15	—	a	a	a
VI. Drug-behavioral pressure IV	-.02	-.07	-.35	.36		—	a	a
VII. Law abidance V	.13	.05	-.24	.02	.94	-.05	—	a
VIII. Drug-behavioral pressure V	-.18	-.06	.04	.06	-.18	.56		—

c. Latent-variable intercorrelations and residual intercorrelations[b]

Dependent Latent Variable	I	II	III	IV	V	VI	VII	VIII
I. Law abidance I	1.00							
II. Drug-behavioral pressure I	-.62	1.00						
III. Law abidance II	.77	-.48	1.00					
IV. Drug-behavioral pressure II	-.58	.58	-.65	1.00				
V. Law abidance IV	.62	-.36	.76	-.57	1.00	-.62		
VI. Drug-behavioral pressure IV	-.45	.32	-.57	.56	-.77	1.00		
VII. Law abidance V	.50	-.26	.57	-.43	.85	-.67	1.00	-.58
VIII. Drug-behavioral pressure V	-.51	.31	-.57	.52	-.70	.77	-.78	1.00

Note: Standard error given in parentheses.

[a]Parameter fixed at value of zero.

[b]Residual correlations given above diagonal.

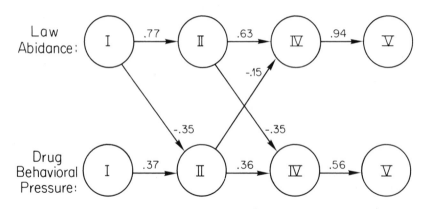

Figure 8-2. Relationship of Law Abidance to Drug-Behavioral Pressure over Five Years

of the factors. All retest-type correlations, even across several years, are sizable and positive. In contrast, the between-construct correlations are all negative.

Law Abidance and Peer-Culture Involvement

Another construct studied was peer-culture involvement. Are individuals low in law abidance more likely to be heavily involved with their peers? Both constructs were estimated with the across-time stability constraints on their loadings. The resulting model fit the data reasonably well (χ^2 = 242.14, d.f. = 165, $p < .001$, Δ = .949, P = .976). Parameter estimates are shown in table 8-4 for the structural regressions; standardized significant paths are presented diagrammatically in figure 8-3.

The relationships suggested in figure 8-3 seem quite clear: when there are across-time relationships between law abidance and peer-culture involvement, low levels in law abidance presage heightened levels in peer-culture involvement. Tendencies toward rebelliousness seem to cause the individual to become more involved with the peer culture. Converse tendencies do not operate, at least across the causal lags shown. There are significant negative residual correlations at all lags, suggesting further causation within time periods.

**Law Abidance and Friends' Poor
School Performance**

Next we asked whether having low law abidance would cause the individual to associate with adolescents who had poor adjustment within the educational

Structural Regression Coefficients and Latent Variable ... Correlations for Four Waves, ... Law Abidance and Peer-Culture Involvement

Dependent Latent Variable	Independent Latent Variable							
	I	II	III	IV	V	VI	VII	VIII
a. Unstandardized coefficients								
I. Law abidance I	—	a	a	a	a	a	a	a
II. Peer-culture involvement I	a	—	a	a	a	a	a	a
III. Law abidance II	.82 (.11)	-.13 (.09)	—	a	a	a	a	a
IV. Peer-culture involvement II	-.28 (.08)	.51 (.08)	a	—	a	a	a	a
V. Law abidance IV	.13 (.15)	.10 (.10)	.67 (.14)	.05 (.12)	a	a	a	a
VI. Peer-culture involvement IV	.02 (.12)	.09 (.09)	-.02 (.11)	.39 (.12)	a	—	a	a
VII. Law abidance V	.12 (.15)	-.03 (.09)	-.24 (.18)	.04 (.12)	1.02 (.15)	-.04 (.06)	—	a
VIII. Peer-culture involvement V	.04 (.14)	.11 (.11)	.25 (.17)	.37 (.14)	-.46 (.15)	.19 (.06)	a	—
b. Standardized coefficients								
I. Law abidance I	—	a	a	a	a	a	a	a
II. Peer-culture involvement I	a	—	a	a	a	a	a	a
III. Law abidance II	.71	-.12	—	a	a	a	a	a
IV. Peer-culture involvement II	-.29	.51	a	—	a	a	a	a
V. Law abidance IV	.13	.10	.74	.05	a	a	a	a
VI. Peer-culture involvement IV	.02	.08	-.02	.35	a	—	a	a
VII. Law abidance V	.10	-.03	-.25	.04	.96	-.04	—	a
VIII. Peer-culture involvement V	.05	.10	.27	.35	-.46	.20	a	—
c. Latent-variable intercorrelations and residual intercorrelations[b]								
I. Law abidance I	1.00	-.52						
II. Peer-culture involvement I	-.52	1.00						
III. Law abidance II	.77	-.48	1.00	-.40				
IV. Peer-culture involvement II	-.56	.66	-.65	1.00				
V. Law abidance IV	.62	-.29	.76	-.44	1.00	-.38		
VI. Peer-culture involvement IV	-.23	.32	-.27	.41	-.40	1.00		
VII. Law abidance V	.51	-.23	.56	-.31	.84	-.37	1.00	-.30
VIII. Peer-culture involvement V	-.33	.38	-.38	.50	-.49	.47	-.54	1.00

Note: Standard error given in parentheses.

[a] Parameter fixed at value of zero.

[b] Residual correlations given above diagonal.

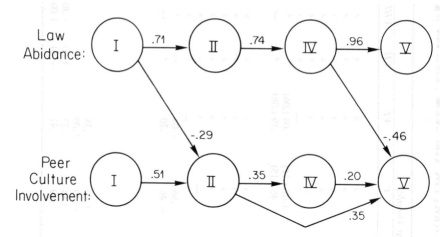

Figure 8-3. Relationship of Law Abidance to Peer-Culture Involvement over Five Years

system. Law abidance was studied across four years with the usual constraints. The indicator sets for friends' poor school performance were almost of the ideal case depicted earlier in figure 8-1: the only difference was that one of the variables was not measured in the fourth study year, and thus the year IV latent variable had only two manifest indicators. The model fit the data well ($\chi^2 = 259.68$, d.f. $= 180, p < .001$, $\Delta = .945$, $P = .975$). Parameter estimates are given in table 8-5, and statistically significant standardized paths are shown in figure 8-4.

As may be seen, in the initial waves of the study there is a tendency for low law-abidance tendencies to be followed by the development of friendships with individuals who are doing poorly in school. The only other significant across-construct path runs from first-year friends' poor school performance to fourth-year law abidance, suggesting that there is some tendency for individuals who initially have many friends to have great difficulty complying with school regulations to become more traditional or law abiding. Such a relationship is opposite in sign to the correlation of the factors and is one we might term a *suppressor* relationship. In general, the interpretation of such coefficients is tenuous. Therefore, we do not place great importance on this significant path. Also, the context of this finding is that these individuals can still be contacted after three years; thus the counterintuitive effect may be the result of restricting the analyses to those who have stayed in school and accordingly become more traditional. There are significant negative residuals indicating possible strong common or contemporaneous causation patterns within times.

Structural Regression Coefficients and Latent-Variable Correlations for Four-Wave, Five-Year Causal Model Linking Law Abidance and Friends' Poor School Performance

a. Unstandardized coefficients

Dependent Latent Variable	I	II	III	IV	V	VI	VII	VIII
I. Law abidance I	—	a	a	a	a	a	a	a
II. Friends' poor school performance I	a	—	a	a	a	a	a	a
III. Law abidance II	.93 (.12)	.05 (.10)	—	a	a	a	a	a
IV. Friends' poor school performance II	-.40 (.09)	.15 (.08)	a	—	a	a	a	a
V. Law abidance IV	.20 (.17)	.20 (.09)	.56 (.15)	-.10 (.15)	—	a	a	a
VI. Friends' poor school performance IV	-.05 (.13)	-.02 (.08)	-.16 (.12)	.20 (.15)	a	—	a	a
VII. Law abidance V	.19 (.17)	.11 (.09)	-.30 (.19)	-.12 (.15)	1.09 (.23)	.13 (.18)	—	a
VIII. Friends' poor school performance V	-.11 (.11)	.07 (.08)	-.02 (.12)	.04 (.13)	-.08 (.14)	.55 (.14)	a	—

b. Standardized coefficients

Dependent Latent Variable	I	II	III	IV	V	VI	VII	VIII
I. Law abidance I	—	a	a	a	a	a	a	a
II. Friends' poor school performance I	a	—	a	a	a	a	a	a
III. Law abidance II	.79	.04	—	a	a	a	a	a
IV. Friends' poor school performance II	-.49	.18	a	—	a	a	a	a
V. Law abidance IV	.19	.19	.63	-.08	—	a	a	a
VI. Friends' poor school performance IV	-.06	-.02	-.25	.21	a	—	a	a
VII. Law abidance V	.17	.10	-.32	-.09	1.02	.09	—	a
VIII. Friends' poor school performance V	-.14	.09	-.04	.04	-.11	.56	a	—

c. Latent-variable intercorrelations and residual intercorrelations[b]

Dependent Latent Variable	I	II	III	IV	V	VI	VII	VIII
I. Law abidance I	1.00							
II. Friends' poor school performance I	-.56	1.00						
III. Law abidance II	.77	-.40	1.00					
IV. Friends' poor school performance II	-.60	.46	-.72	1.00				
V. Law abidance IV	.62	-.21	.76	-.52	1.00	-.63		
VI. Friends' poor school performance IV	-.37	.21	-.44	.42	-.69	1.00		
VII. Law abidance V	.52	-.11	.57	-.44	.85	-.55	1.00	
VIII. Friends' poor school performance V	-.42	.17	-.47	.41	-.62	.70	-.74	1.00

Note: Standard error given in parentheses.

[a] Parameter fixed at value of zero.

[b] Residual correlations given above diagonal.

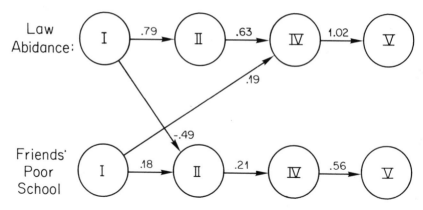

Figure 8-4. Relationship of Law Abidance to Friends' Poor School Performance over Five Years

Law Abidance and Drug Availability

The next analysis determines the unfolding relationship between law abidance and drug availability. For this model the chi-square was 367.67 with 200 degrees of freedom, the normed-fit coefficient (Δ) was .948, and the non-normed-fit coefficient (P) was .966. Parameter estimates for the structural regressions are shown in table 8-6 and portrayed diagrammatically in figure 8-5. It is possible to infer that the pattern of significant causal flow is from law abidance to perceived drug availability. Across time the correlations between low law-abidance tendencies and drug availability are sizable. Individuals low in law abidance or high in rebelliousness will tend to develop sources for drugs. Again, low levels of law abidance lead to an immersion in nontraditional cultures.

Law Abidance and Adult Drug Use

Law abidance and perceived adult drug use were examined over time. The design was virtually identical to the prototype, differing only in that the third adult-drug-use indicator in the first and second years was not identical to that of the final years. Chi-square was 250.93 (d.f. = 199; Δ = .959; P = .988). Estimates are shown in table 8-7 and given diagrammatically in figure 8-6. The pattern of significant causal flow is from law abidance to adult drug use. Again, also note the high level of the factor correlations, even across several years.

Structural Regression Coefficients and Latent-Variable Correlations for Four-Wave, Five-Year Causal Model Linking Law Abidance and Drug Availability

Dependent Latent Variable	Independent Latent Variable							
	I	II	III	IV	V	VI	VII	VIII
a. Unstandardized coefficients								
I. Law abidance I	—	a	a	a	a	a	a	a
II. Drug availability I	a	—	a	a	a	a	a	a
III. Law abidance II	.92 (.13)	.03 (.10)	—	a	a	a	a	a
IV. Drug availability II	−.43 (.09)	.43 (.08)	a	—	a	a	a	a
V. Law abidance IV	.11 (.17)	.07 (.09)	.56 (.13)	−.11 (.09)	—	a	a	a
VI. Drug availability IV	−.17 (.14)	−.03 (.08)	−.29 (.11)	.29 (.08)	a	—	a	a
VII. Law abidance V	.15 (.17)	.00 (.08)	−.18 (.16)	.12 (.08)	.99 (.22)	−.03 (.15)	—	a
VIII. Drug availability V	.01 (.12)	−.05 (.07)	.00 (.11)	.08 (.07)	−.24 (.15)	.69 (.11)	a	—
b. Standardized coefficients								
I. Law abidance I	—	a	a	a	a	a	a	a
II. Drug availability I	a	—	a	a	a	a	a	a
III. Law abidance II	.78	.00	—	a	a	a	a	a
IV. Drug availability II	−.38	.38	a	—	a	a	a	a
V. Law abidance IV	.10	.07	.63	−.11	—	a	a	a
VI. Drug availability IV	−.16	−.03	−.32	.31	a	—	a	a
VII. Law abidance V	.13	.00	−.19	.12	.95	−.03	—	a
VIII. Drug availability V	.00	−.05	.00	.08	−.22	.65	a	—
c. Latent-variable intercorrelations and residual intercorrelations[b]								
I. Law abidance I	1.00							
II. Drug availability I	−.60	1.00						
III. Law abidance II	.76	−.44	1.00					
IV. Drug availability II	−.60	.60	−.68	1.00				
V. Law abidance IV	.61	−.34	.76	−.57	1.00			
VI. Drug availability IV	−.57	.39	−.64	.60	−.82	1.00		
VII. Law abidance V	.51	−.26	.56	−.38	.84	−.68	1.00	
VIII. Drug availability V	−.48	.33	−.55	.47	−.72	.80	−.82	1.00

Note: Standard error given in parentheses.

[a] Parameter fixed at value of zero.

[b] Residual correlations given above diagonal.

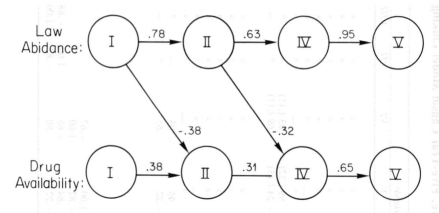

Figure 8-5. Relationship of Law Abidance to Drug Availability over Five Years

Law Abidance and Alcohol Use

In the model testing the relationship of law abidance and alcohol use over time, the loadings of the corresponding three law-abidance indicators across each time were constrained to be equal to one another, whereas the alcohol-use indicators were not. An error variance could not be estimated for the

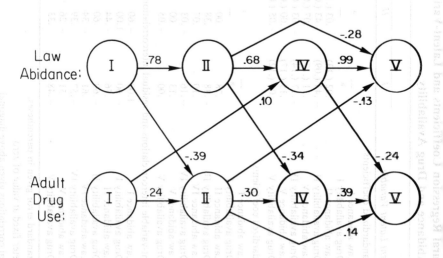

Figure 8-6. Relationship of Law Abidance to Adult Drug Use over Five Years

Structural Regression Coefficients and Latent-Variable Correlations for Four-Wave, Five-Year Causal Model Linking Law Abidance and Adult Drug Use

Dependent Latent Variable	Independent Latent Variable							
	I	II	III	IV	V	VI	VII	VIII
a. Unstandardized coefficients								
I. Law abidance I	—	[a]	[a]	[a]	[a]	[a]	[a]	[a]
II. Adult drug use I	[a]	—	[a]	[a]	[a]	[a]	[a]	[a]
III. Law abidance II	.91 (.10)	.04 (.07)	—	[a]	[a]	[a]	[a]	[a]
IV. Adult drug use II	-.33 (.06)	.20 (.06)	.61 (.12)	—	[a]	[a]	[a]	[a]
V. Law abidance IV	.10 (.16)	.10 (.06)	-.30 (.10)	-.06 (.08)	—	[a]	[a]	[a]
VI. Adult drug use IV	-.01 (.12)	.05 (.06)	-.26 (.15)	.37 (.08)	1.05 (.15)	—	[a]	[a]
VII. Law abidance V	.05 (.16)	-.03 (.06)	.04 (.10)	-.17 (.08)	-.21 (.10)	.05 (.08)	—	[a]
VIII. Adult drug use V	-.11 (.11)	.03 (.05)	[a]	.15 (.06)	[a]	.35 (.06)	[a]	—
b. Standardized coefficients								
I. Law abidance I	—	[a]	[a]	[a]	[a]	[a]	[a]	[a]
II. Adult drug use I	[a]	—	[a]	[a]	[a]	[a]	[a]	[a]
III. Law abidance II	.78	.03	—	[a]	[a]	[a]	[a]	[a]
IV. Adult drug use II	-.39	.24	.68	—	[a]	[a]	[a]	[a]
V. Law abidance IV	.10	.10	-.34	.05	—	[a]	[a]	[a]
VI. Adult drug use IV	-.01	.05	-.28	.30	.99	—	[a]	[a]
VII. Law abidance V	.05	-.03	.05	-.13	-.24	.04	—	[a]
VIII. Adult drug use V	-.12	.02	[a]	.14	[a]	.39	[a]	—
c. Latent-variable intercorrelations and residual intercorrelations[b]								
I. Law abidance I	1.00	-.49						
II. Adult drug use I	-.48	1.00						
III. Law abidance II	.77	-.34	1.00	-.17				
IV. Adult drug use II	-.51	.43	-.47	1.00				
V. Law abidance IV	.60	-.21	.75	-.38	1.00	-.43		
VI. Adult drug use IV	-.43	.29	-.49	.48	-.61	1.00		
VII. Law abidance V	.49	-.20	.55	-.39	.84	-.51	1.00	-.20
VIII. Adult drug us V	-.48	.29	-.49	.46	-.57	.64	-.56	1.00

Note: Standard error given in parentheses.

[a] Parameter fixed at value of zero.

[b] Residual correlations given above diagonal.

single second-year alcohol-use indicator. The model assessed for the data fit reasonably well (χ^2 = 232.17, d.f. = 182, p = .007, Δ = .966, P = .989). Parameter estimates for the structural regression coefficients and factor intercorrelations are given in table 8-8, and the statistically significant standardized paths are shown in figure 8-7.

Three times we find that law-abidance tendencies seem to lead or precede alcohol-use tendencies. There is one very small effect of alcohol use on law abidance—a long-term small tendency for heightened levels of alcohol use to lead to lowered levels of law abidance. Overall, however, the predominant pattern of causal flow is from law abidance to alcohol use, with low levels in the former leading to higher levels of the latter. It may also be observed in table 8-8 that there are large residual correlations at all times, suggesting further large degrees of contemporaneous causation.

Law Abidance and Cannabis Use

The model assessing the causal effects of the constructs of law abidance and cannabis use on one another parallels that used for the alcohol-use tests previously. Again, the error variance for the second-year variable of marijuana use could not be estimated because there was only one indicator of cannabis use in year II. The model fit the data well (χ^2 = 113.64, d.f. = 125, p = .76, Δ = .980, P = 1.003). Parameter estimates are given for the structural

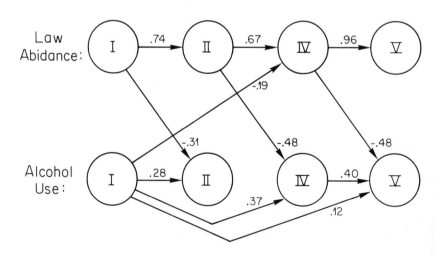

Figure 8-7. Relationship of Law Abidance to Alcohol Use over Five Years

...ctural Regression Coefficients and Latent Variable Correlations for Four-Wave, Structural Causal Model Linking **Law Abidance and Alcohol Use**

a. Unstandardized coefficients

Dependent Latent Variable	Independent Latent Variable							
	I	II	III	IV	V	VI	VII	VIII
I. Law abidance I	—	[a]	[a]	[a]	[a]	[a]	[a]	[a]
II. Alcohol use I	[a]	—	[a]	[a]	[a]	[a]	[a]	[a]
III. Law abidance II	.86 (.12)	-.04 (.10)	—	[a]	[a]	[a]	[a]	[a]
IV. Alcohol use II	-.37 (.09)	.33 (.08)	[a]	—	[a]	[a]	[a]	[a]
V. Law abidance IV	-.05 (.16)	-.20 (.08)	.59 (.11)	-.03 (.05)	[a]	[a]	[a]	[a]
VI. Alcohol use IV	.22 (.16)	.20 (.08)	-.53 (.11)	.06 (.05)	[a]	—	[a]	[a]
VII. Law abidance V	.13 (.16)	.02 (.08)	-.19 (.15)	.06 (.05)	1.03 (.23)	.00 (.12)	—	[a]
VIII. Alcohol use V	-.01 (.18)	.21 (.11)	.25 (.17)	-.01 (.06)	-.78 (.30)	.52 (.14)	[a]	—

b. Standardized coefficients

Dependent Latent Variable	Independent Latent Variable							
	I	II	III	IV	V	VI	VII	VIII
I. Law abidance I	—	[a]	[a]	[a]	[a]	[a]	[a]	[a]
II. Alcohol use I	[a]	—	[a]	[a]	[a]	[a]	[a]	[a]
III. Law abidance II	.74	-.03	—	[a]	[a]	[a]	[a]	[a]
IV. Alcohol use II	-.31	.28	[a]	—	[a]	[a]	[a]	[a]
V. Law abidance IV	-.04	-.19	.67	-.03	[a]	[a]	[a]	[a]
VI. Alcohol use IV	.17	.37	-.48	.06	[a]	—	[a]	[a]
VII. Law abidance V	.12	.02	-.20	.07	.96	.00	—	[a]
VIII. Alcohol use V	.00	.12	.17	.00	-.48	.40	[a]	—

c. Latent-variable intercorrelations and residual intercorrelations[b]

	I	II	III	IV	V	VI	VII	VIII
I. Law abidance I	1.00	-.63						
II. Alcohol Use I	-.63	1.00						
III. Law abidance II	.76	-.49	1.00	-.30				
IV. Alcohol use II	-.49	.48	-.54	1.00				
V. Law abidance IV	.60	-.51	.75	-.46	1.00	-.68		
VI. Alcohol use IV	-.44	.52	-.56	.40	-.80	1.00		
VII. Law abidance V	.50	-.41	.56	-.32	.84	-.67	1.00	-.48
VIII. Alcohol use V	-.42	.49	-.47	.35	-.74	.76	-.78	1.00

Note: Standard error given in parentheses.

[a] Parameter fixed at value of zero.

[b] Residual correlations given above diagonal.

regression equations in table 8-9 and portrayed in figure 8-8. It seems clear that low tendencies toward law abidance tend to precede tendencies to use cannabis. The large negative residual correlations also suggest concurrent causation. The direction of causal relationship substantiates important theoretical conclusions of Ginsberg and Greenley (1978), and Segal, Huba, and Singer (1980a,b), among others.

Law Abidance and Hard-Drug Use

The model tested for the relationship of law abidance and hard-drug use over time was similar to those tested previously. There was no error variance estimated for the single second-year hard-drug indicator. The model fit the data about as well as the other models in this section (χ^2 = 175.78, d.f. = 161, p = .20, Δ = .964, P = .995). Parameter estimates for the structural regression equations are shown in table 8-10, and standardized significant paths are presented in figure 8-9. Again, the overall pattern supports the contention that heightened levels of hard-drug use follow from lowered levels of law abidance. The moderate-sized negative residual correlations suggest that contemporaneous causation may also exist.

Alternate Parameterization of Law Abidance and Alcohol

As noted earlier, there are indications from several of the individual analyses that models with patterns of contemporaneous causation may also be appro-

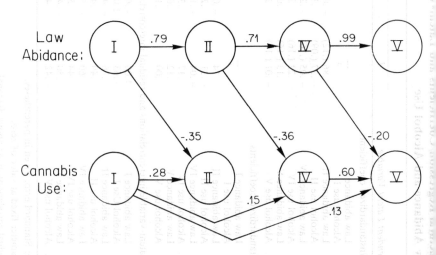

Figure 8-8. Relationship of Law Abidance to Cannabis Use over Five Years

Law Abidance and Cannabis Use

Causal Model Linking ... Five-Year ...

Dependent Latent Variable	Independent Latent Variable							
	I	II	III	IV	V	VI	VII	VIII
a. Unstandardized coefficients								
I. Law abidance I	—	[a]	[a]	[a]	[a]	[a]	[a]	[a]
II. Cannabis use I	[a]	—	[a]	[a]	[a]	[a]	[a]	[a]
III. Law abidance II	.93 (.11)	.06 (.08)	—	[a]	[a]	[a]	[a]	[a]
IV. Cannabis use II	.42 (.08)	.33 (.07)	[a]	—	[a]	[a]	[a]	[a]
V. Law abidance IV	.05 (.16)	-.04 (.07)	.63 (.12)	.00 (.05)	—	[a]	[a]	[a]
VI. Cannabis use IV	-.18 (.15)	.19 (.09)	-.39 (.12)	.06 (.06)	[a]	—	[a]	[a]
VII. Law abidance V	.13 (.16)	-.03 (.07)	-.25 (.17)	.03 (.05)	1.05 (.21)	.02 (.11)	—	[a]
VIII. Cannabis use V	.02 (.15)	.22 (.09)	.00 (.14)	.00 (.06)	-.32 (.19)	.83 (.12)	[a]	—
b. Standardized coefficients								
I. Law abidance I	—	[a]	[a]	[a]	[a]	[a]	[a]	[a]
II. Cannabis use I	[a]	—	[a]	[a]	[a]	[a]	[a]	[a]
III. Law abidance II	.79	.05	—	[a]	[a]	[a]	[a]	[a]
IV. Cannabis use II	-.35	.28	[a]	—	[a]	[a]	[a]	[a]
V. Law abidance IV	.05	-.04	.71	.00	—	[a]	[a]	[a]
VI. Cannabis use IV	-.14	.15	-.36	.06	[a]	—	[a]	[a]
VII. Law abidance V	.12	-.03	-.27	.03	.99	.02	—	[a]
VIII. Cannabis use V	-.01	.13	.00	.00	-.20	.60	[a]	—
c. Latent-variable intercorrelations and residual intercorrelations[b]								
I. Law abidance I	1.00	-.50						
II. Cannabis use I	-.51	1.00						
III. Law abidance II	.76	-.35	1.00					
IV. Cannabis use II	-.49	.46	-.53	1.00				
V. Law abidance IV	.60	-.31	.75	-.41	1.00	-.65		
VI. Cannabis use IV	-.52	.38	-.56	.39	-.77	1.00		
VII. Law abidance V	.51	-.28	.56	-.31	.85	-.66	1.00	-.46
VIII. Cannabis use V	-.49	.41	-.52	.37	-.69	.80	-.73	1.00

Note: Standard error given in parentheses.

[a] Parameter fixed at value of zero.

[b] Residual correlations given above diagonal.

Table 8-10
Structural Regression Coefficients and Latent-Variable Correlations for Four-Wave, Five-Year Causal Model Linking Law Abidance and Hard-Drug Use

a. Unstandardized coefficients

Dependent Latent Variable	Independent Latent Variable							
	I	II	III	IV	V	VI	VII	VIII
I. Law abidance I	—	[a]	[a]	[a]	[a]	[a]	[a]	[a]
II. Hard-drug use I	[a]	—	[a]	[a]	[a]	[a]	[a]	[a]
III. Law abidance II	.90 (.09)	.01 (.06)	—	[a]	[a]	[a]	[a]	[a]
IV. Hard-drug use II	-.03 (.06)	.10 (.05)	[a]	—	[a]	[a]	[a]	[a]
V. Law abidance IV	.06 (.15)	.05 (.05)	.64 (.12)	.08 (.05)	—	[a]	[a]	[a]
VI. Hard-drug use IV	-.04 (.14)	.15 (.06)	-.32 (.12)	-.06 (.05)	[a]	—	[a]	[a]
VII. Law abidance V	.12 (.15)	-.03 (.05)	-.25 (.16)	-.03 (.05)	1.07 (.16)	.07 (.07)	—	[a]
VIII. Hard-drug use V	-.28 (.19)	-.09 (.09)	.27 (.20)	.13 (.07)	-.49 (.21)	1.09 (.14)	[a]	—

b. Standardized coefficients

Dependent Latent Variable	Independent Latent Variable							
	I	II	III	IV	V	VI	VII	VIII
I. Law abidance I	—	[a]	[a]	[a]	[a]	[a]	[a]	[a]
II. Hard-drug use I	[a]	—	[a]	[a]	[a]	[a]	[a]	[a]
III. Law abidance II	.78	.01	—	[a]	[a]	[a]	[a]	[a]
IV. Hard-drug use II	-.03	.10	[a]	—	[a]	[a]	[a]	[a]
V. Law abidance IV	.06	.05	.72	.08	—	[a]	[a]	[a]
VI. Hard-drug use IV	-.03	.14	-.34	-.06	[a]	—	[a]	[a]
VII. Law abidance V	.11	.00	-.27	-.03	1.01	.07	—	[a]
VIII. Hard-drug use V	-.16	-.05	.18	.07	-.28	.67	[a]	—

c. Latent-variable intercorrelations and residual intercorrelations[b]

Dependent Latent Variable	I	II	III	IV	V	VI	VII	VIII
I. Law abidance I	1.00							
II. Hard-drug use I	-.21	1.00						
III. Law abidance II	.78	-.15	1.00					
IV. Hard-drug use II	-.05	.10	-.11	1.00				
V. Law abidance IV	.60	-.07	.75	-.13	1.00			
VI. Hard-drug use IV	-.32	.19	-.38	.00	-.54	1.00		
VII. Law abidance V	.50	-.07	.56	.00	.84	-.42	1.00	
VIII. Hard-drug use V	-.40	.11	-.41	.05	-.60	.79	-.61	1.00

Note: Standard error given in parentheses.

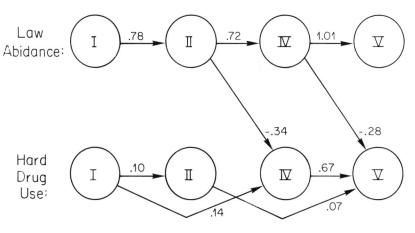

Figure 8-9. Relationship of Law Abidance to Hard-Drug Use over Five Years

priate for some of the specific pairs of latent variables. We infer this latter state when we find consistent patterns of residual correlation at the measurement times. There are often mathematical variants of a specific model parameterization that will generate the same estimated population covariance matrix (and hence the same fit indexes and chi-square value). Several such variants for the global-model design are used in this chapter, so we felt it necessary to explore the implications of using alternative ones.

In the selected example, we address the case wherein we argued that a consistent pattern of within-time residual correlations, coupled with a clear directionality in the causal direction *across* time, could be argued to mean that there was additional *within*-time causality not fully accounted for by the across-time paths. Here we use the example of table 8-8 for law abidance and alcohol use, and reparameterized the alternative model in the following way. First, at each of time periods II, IV, and V, we eliminated the residual correlation term and specified in its place that law abidance at that time would cause alcohol use at that time. This is a mathematically equivalent parameterization that reproduces exactly the same covariance matrix as the setup we used earlier and hence the same chi-square value of 232.17 with 182 degrees of freedom. For this alternative model, the structural regression coefficients are given in table 8-11. As a result of allowing the within-time causation, there are different patterns of across-time causation to some degree. Nonetheless, we can still draw the same conclusion from the overall pattern of causal coefficients: the causal influence flows from law abidance to alcohol use.

This section examined dynamic relationships of law abidance and a variety of psychosocial constructs, including peer-culture involvement,

Table 8-11
Structural Regression Coefficients and Latent-Variable Correlations for Four-Wave, Five-Year Causal Model Linking Law Abidance and Alcohol Use

			Independent Latent Variable					
Dependent Latent Variable	I	II	III	IV	V	VI	VII	VIII
a. Unstandardized coefficients								
I. Law abidance I		a	a	a	a	a	a	a
II. Alcohol use I			a	a	a	a	a	a
III. Law abidance II	.81 (.11)	-.03 (.08)		a	a	a	a	a
IV. Alcohol use II	.86 (.12)	.26 (.07)			a	a	a	a
V. Law abidance IV	-.04 (.13)	-.15 (.06)	.59 (.11)	-.41 (.10)	-.03 (.05)	a	a	a
VI. Alcohol use IV	-.05 (.16)	.29 (.11)	.10 (.23)		.04 (.06)		a	a
VII. Law abidance V	.24 (.25)	.02 (.07)	.19 (.15)	.06 (.04)	1.38 (.34)	.00 (.09)		a
VIII. Alcohol use V	.13 (.16)	.21 (.20)	.11 (.19)	.05 (.06)	1.03 (.23)	.44 (.13)	-.93 (.24)	
					.07 (.39)			
b. Standardized coefficients								
I. Law abidance I		a	a	a	a	a	a	a
II. Alcohol use I	.63		a	a	a	a	a	a
III. Law abidance II	.74	-.03		a	a	a	a	a
IV. Alcohol use II	-.03	.27			a	a	a	a
V. Law abidance IV	-.04	-.19	.67	-.39	.03	a	a	a
VI. Alcohol use IV	.14	.20	.06		.03		a	a
VII. Law abidance V	.12	.02	.20	.07	.81	.00		a
VIII. Alcohol use V	.06	.14		.03	.96	.41	-.54	
					.04			
c. Latent-variable intercorrelations and residual intercorrelations[b]								
I. Law abidance I	1.00							
II. Alcohol use I	-.63	1.00						
III. Law abidance II	.76	-.49	1.00					
IV. Alcohol use II	-.49	.48	-.54	1.00				
V. Law abidance IV	.60	-.51	.75	-.46	1.00			
VI. Alcohol use IV	-.44	.52	-.56	.40	-.80	1.00		
VII. Law abidance V	.50	-.41	.56	-.32	.84	-.67	1.00	
VIII. Alcohol use V	-.42	.49	-.47	.35	-.74	.76	-.78	1.00

Note. Standard error given in parentheses.

lrug-behavioral pressure, drug availability, alcohol use, cannabis use, and ıard-drug use. Whatever patterns of causation existed were in the direction rom law abidance to the social and behavioral constructs.

Large Models of Law Abidance and Other Psychosocial Factors over Five Years

This section presents two large causal models assessing how law abidance ınd other psychosocial factors influence one another over time. Many psy-chosocial factors are studied simultaneously, and we can use information ;ained from the analyses previously conducted in order to accurately pa-ameterize these more complicated models. It might be noted that the nodels are large and expensive by the standards of causal modeling in that .bout forty variables are handled simultaneously, with several hundred)arameters estimated.

Although the smaller models are informative in telling us about the :ausal sequences among pairs of factors, they do not take into account that nany of the different constructs studied in conjunction with law abidance ıre themselves correlated. In fact, the effects of law abidance appearing to)e direct might actually be mediated through another factor not present in he smaller analysis; and some effects may be masked through the lack of ıppropriate controls of common causes. A more complex and fully pecified causal model must be the end goal of any modeling effort: the inal models, however, often cannot be estimated without gaining further nformation through many different preliminary models.

In order to keep these models within manageable bounds, we restrict ıur attention to data from years I, IV, and V; simultaneously, we limit our najor attention to interrelationships of law abidance, peer-culture involve-nent, and drug-behavioral pressure. These design choices are discussed in ietail elsewhere (Huba and Bentler, in press a). We do, however, introduce hree related factors in the first and fourth years that may serve to explain the nterrelationships. Two different large models are used to try to obtain the nformation that might come from a somewhat larger model that in-orporated all the measures from the two models simultaneously: had the ariables all been handled simultaneously, the costs for the analyses would ıave gone up by a factor of at least ten. An extensive methodological ex-.mination of strategies for using interlocking models has shown that split-ing up the larger model into two manageable models is satisfactory and not nisleading (Huba and Bentler, in press a, chaps. 51, 19).

The design and analysis strategy used here is an offshoot of that used uccessfully in the monograph detailing the modeling of the entire longi-udinal study (Huba and Bentler, in press a, chap. 44). This model was designed to interlock as a piece of Huba's more general mathematical model of adolescent development (Huba and Bentler, in press a, preface). In the model tested here we have psychosocial factors of law abidance, drug-behavioral pressure, and peer-culture involvement, each assessed in years I, IV, and V. The factors were selected for extensive study since peer-culture involvement was demonstrated to be an important facet of a general domain of peer-culture influences in our earlier structural modeling (Huba and Bentler, in press a, chap. 12), whereas drug-behavioral pressure is a good proxy for the more general, second-order factor underlying the domain of self-perceived behavioral pressure to use drugs (Huba and Bentler, in press a, chap. 13). Additionally, there were predictor psychosocial factors of adult drug use, time spent with friends, and friends' poor school performance in the first year. All other first-year psychosocial factors were allowed to be caused by law abidance, based on the results of the cross-lag, five-year models just presented. Furthermore, each of the five factors (residuals) was allowed to be freely intercorrelated with all other first-year psychosocial factors except law abidance. Then all the constructs were hypothesized to be caused by each of the constructs occurring at an earlier time. This meant that the three fourth-year psychosocial constructs were hypothesized to be caused by the six first-year factors, whereas the three fifth-year psychosocial factors were influenced by the three fourth-year psychosocial factors and the six first-year constructs. Within such a design we interpret the direct effects of the psychosocial factors on other, later-occurring psychosocial factors to be their influence freed from other, earlier predictable levels of that type of psychosocial functioning. In the fourth and fifth years of the investigation we hypothesized that both drug-behavioral pressure and peer-culture involvement would be a function of the contemporaneously measured law-abidance construct, and that the two would have correlated errors of prediction. For each of the constructs we employed the appropriate indicators described for the factor earlier in this chapter. The factor of time spent with friends in the first year was assessed with the three indicators of how often the student gets together with friends, hangs around with friends, and tells friends (negative things?) about parents. In the fourth year the construct was measured with the single indicator of the number of friends one hangs around with a lot.

Finally, we permitted correlated errors of measurement among repeated assessments of the same construct. For each computer run we again calculated the parameters using maximum likelihood with LISREL-IV; fit coefficients were also calculated, with effect partitions obtained from PATHDI (Huba and Palisoc, submitted).

This model fit the data well considering the large sample, many variables, and few theoretically defined correlated errors ($\chi^2 = 863.19$, d.f. = 41, $p < .001$, $\Delta = .890$, $P = .929$). The fit was sufficiently good so that we have confidence in the individual parameter estimates. The measurement portion of the structural model performed expectedly, and factor loadings were significant beyond even the most stringent of conventional criteria ($p < .001$); therefore, we do not show their actual numerical values. Table 8-12 shows the structural regression coefficients among constructs, and figure 8-10 diagrams significant paths. Also shown are the standard errors for the weights, as well as the standardized weights (direct effects), indirect effects, and total effects. We will return to the meaning of indirect and total effects momentarily; first we will discuss the size of the paths in their raw form (signified in table 8-12 as B) and standardized form (called direct effects in table 8-12). The standardized residual variances for the final dependent psychosocial constructs from their predictor constructs were as follows; law abidance V, .265; behavioral pressure V, .235; and peer-culture involvement V, .491. The residual variance in the factors is small.

The significant direct effects are as follows: behavioral pressure I is, as hypothesized, a negative function of law abidance I, as are peer-culture involvement I, adult drug use I, time spent with friends I, and friends' poor school performance I. Looking next at the fourth-year constructs, law abidance IV is a positive function of law abidance I and time spent with friends I, although this latter effect is a suppressor, in the opposite direction from the latent-variable correlation (see table 8-13). Behavioral pressure in the fourth year is a negative function of fourth-year law abidance and a positive function of first-year adult drug use.[2] The fourth-year law-abidance variable almost entirely explains the reliability of the behavioral-pressure latent variable from the first to the fourth year in that the direct path from first- to fourth-year behavioral pressure is essentially zero with this explanatory effect included. Peer-culture involvement IV is a positive function of first-year peer-culture involvement as well as a negative function of fourth-year law abidance and a positive function of first-year adult drug use. Fifth-year law abidance is a function of fourth-year law abidance: the effects of the other latent variables on the fifth-year levels of this construct are all mediated through the fourth-year levels on the construct. That is, none of the other first- or fourth-year psychosocial constructs has a direct effect on fifth-year law abidance other than the fourth-year construct. Fifth-year law abidance has a negative effect on the levels of fifth-year behavioral pressure; there is a suppressor (positive) direct effect from fourth-year law abidance; and behavioral pressure is stable from years IV to V. Peer-culture involvement V is a direct function of the same variable at times I and IV, and a negative function of law abidance V and friends' poor school performance V.

Additional information for interpreting the model is the set of correlations among latent variables. Table 8-13 shows these values (a function of the data, model parameterization, and estimates). As may be seen, the correlations are

Table 8-12

Summary of Direct, Indirect, and Total Effects in Model of Effects of First-Year Psychosocial Functioning on Law Abidance

Dependent Latent Variable	Independent Latent Variable	B	Direct Effect	Indirect Effect	Total Effect
II. Drug-behavioral pressure I	I. Law abidance I	-.86 (.11)	-.65	.00	-.65
III. Peer-culture involvement I	I. Law abidance I	-.57 (.09)	-.50	.00	-.50
IV. Law abidance IV	II. Law abidance I	.73 (.13)	.71	-.06	.64
IV. Law abidance IV	II. Drug-behavioral pressure I	-.10 (.10)	-.12	.00	-.12
IV. Law abidance IV	III. Peer-culture involvement I	-.07 (.11)	-.08	.00	-.08
IV. Law abidance IV	X. Adult drug use I	.05 (.10)	.05	.00	.05
IV. Law abidance IV	XI. Time spent with friends I	.21 (.10)	.24	.00	.24
IV. Law abidance IV	XII. Friends' poor school performance I	.08 (.07)	.09	.00	.09
V. Drug-behavioral pressure IV	II. Law abidance I	.22 (.20)	.16	-.61	-.45
V. Drug-behavioral pressure IV	II. Drug-behavioral pressure I	.09 (.12)	.09	.10	.19
V. Drug-behavioral pressure IV	III. Peer-culture involvement I	-.11 (.13)	.09	.06	.03
V. Drug-behavioral pressure IV	IV. Law abidance IV	-1.05 (.17)	-.80	.00	-.80
V. Drug-behavioral pressure IV	X. Adult drug use I	.26 (.12)	.20	-.04	.16
V. Drug-behavioral pressure IV	XI. Time spent with friends I	.05 (.13)	.04	-.19	-.15
V. Drug-behavioral pressure IV	XII. Friends' poor school performance I	.02 (.08)	.02	-.07	-.06
VI. Peer-culture involvement IV	I. Law abidance I	.18 (.13)	.16	-.39	-.23
VI. Peer-culture	II. Drug-behavioral	.05 (.08)	.05	.05	.10

VI. Peer-culture involvement IV	X. Adult drug use I	.16 (.09)	.15	−.02	.13
VI. Peer-culture involvement IV	XI. Time spent with friends I	−.04 (.09)	−.05	−.09	−.14
VI. Peer-culture involvement IV	XII. Friends' poor school performance I	−.01 (.06)	−.01	−.04	−.04
VI. Peer-culture involvement IV	I. Law abidance I	.02 (.14)	.02	.52	.54
VII. Law abidance V	II. Drug-behavioral pressure I	−.01 (.07)	−.01	−.10	−.11
VII. Law abidance V	III. Peer-culture involvement I	.01 (.09)	.01	−.07	−.06
VII. Law abidance V	IV. Law abidance IV	.88 (.17)	.84	.00	.84
VII. Law abidance V	V. Drug behavioral pressure IV	.01 (.09)	.02	.00	.02
VII. Law abidance V	VI. Peer culture involvement IV	−.03 (.04)	−.03	.00	−.03
VII. Law abidance V	X. Adult drug use I	−.05 (.08)	−.04	.04	.00
VII. Law abidance V	XI. Time spent with friends I	.13 (.08)	.14	.20	.34
VII. Law abidance V	XII. Friends' poor school performance I	−.08 (.05)	−.08	.08	−.01
VIII. Drug behavioral pressure V	I. Law abidance I	−.18 (.18)	−.12	−.38	−.50
VIII. Drug behavioral pressure V	II. Drug behavioral pressure I	.02 (.10)	.01	.13	.14
VIII. Drug behavioral pressure V	III. Peer culture involvement I	−.01 (.12)	−.01	−.02	−.03
VIII. Drug behavioral pressure V	IV. Law abidance IV	.54 (.30)	.36	−.99	−.63
VIII. Drug behavioral pressure V	V. Drug behavioral pressure IV	.63 (.11)	.57	−.01	.56
VIII. Drug behavioral pressure V	VI. Peer culture involvement IV	−.11 (.06)	−.08	.02	−.06
VIII. Drug behavioral pressure V	VII. Law abidance V	−.94 (.21)	−.69	.00	−.69
VIII. Drug behavioral pressure V	X. Adult drug use I	.11 (.11)	.08	.10	.18

Table 8-12 (continued)

Dependent Latent Variable	Independent Latent Variable	B	Direct Effect	Indirect Effect	Total Effect
VIII. Drug behavioral pressure V	XI. Time spent with friends I	.07 (.11)	.05	−.22	−.17
VIII. Drug behavioral pressure V	XII. Friends' poor school performance I	−.12 (.08)	−.09	.01	−.08
IX. Peer culture involvement V	I. Law abidance I	.04 (.17)	.04	−.34	−.31
IX. Peer culture involvement V	II. Drug behavioral pressure I	−.06 (.10)	−.07	.06	−.01
IX. Peer culture involvement V	III. Peer culture involvement I	.35 (.13)	.34	.10	.44
IX. Peer culture involvement V	IV. Law abidance IV	−.13 (.27)	−.12	−.34	−.46
IX. Peer culture involvement V	V. Drug behavioral pressure IV	−.15 (.11)	−.17	−.01	−.18
IX. Peer culture involvement V	VI. Peer culture involvement IV	.28 (.06)	.26	.01	.28
IX. Peer culture Involvement V	VII. Law abidance V	−.49 (.17)	−.45	.00	−.45
IX. Peer culture involvement V	X. Adult drug use I	.10 (.12)	.09	.00	.09
IX. Peer culture involvement V	XI. Time spent with friends I	−.06 (.12)	−.06	−.19	−.25
IX. Peer culture involvement V	XII. Friends' poor school performance I	−.16 (.08)	−.15	−.01	−.16
X. Adult drug use I	I. Law abidance I	−.29 (.08)	−.28	.00	−.28
XI. Time spent with Friends I	I. Law abidance I	−.62 (.09)	−.52	.00	−.52
XII. Friends' poor school performance I	I. Law abidance I	−.52 (.08)	−.46	.00	−.46

Note: Standard errors in parentheses.

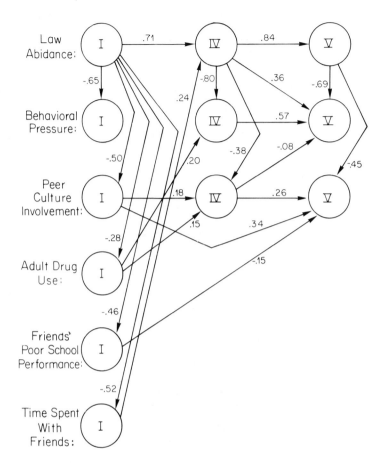

Figure 8-10. Relationship of First-Year Psychosocial Factors to the
Developing Sequence of Law Abidance, Drug-Behavioral
Pressure, and Peer-Culture Involvement over Five Years

rather high, even across periods of three years, indicating that the development of the law-abidance and social constructs is reasonably predictable
across adolescence. Gross discontinuities do not occur.

So far we have been concerned only with direct effects or causal influences that go directly from one latent variable to another. When we consider the values in table 8-13, however, we can see that often there are correlations among latent variables not connected by direct paths. How can
this be so? Correlations between latent variables arise from sources that
might be called causal or spurious. Spurious correlations occur because

Table 8-13

Latent-Variable Intercorrelations in the Year I Effects on Law-Abidance Model

Latent Variable	I	II	III	IV	V	VI	VII	VIII	IX	X	XI	XII
I. Law abidance I	1.00											
II. Drug-behavioral pressure I	-.65	1.00										
III. Peer-culture involvement I	-.50	.52	1.00									
IV. Law abidance IV	.64	-.39	-.30	1.00								
V. Drug-behavioral pressure IV	-.44	.33	.26	-.75	1.00							
VI. Peer-culture involvement IV	-.23	.19	.30	-.37	.51	1.00						
VII. Law abidance V	.54	-.30	-.24	.85	-.64	-.34	1.00					
VIII. Drug-behavioral pressure V	-.50	.33	.27	-.70	.76	.35	-.78	1.00				
IX. Peer-culture involvement V	-.31	.14	.42	-.49	.37	.46	-.55	.56	1.00			
X. Adult drug use I	-.28	.23	.58	-.17	.27	.28	-.19	.30	.36	1.00		
XI. Time spent with friends I	-.53	.70	.54	-.20	.17	.10	-.09	.16	.05	.15	1.00	
XII. Friends' poor school performance I	-.46	.63	.41	-.21	.19	.11	-.21	.17	.02	.14	.53	1.00

causal and noncausal factors are correlated, whereas causal correlations occur because one construct causes another directly (as indicated in table 8-12 and figure 8-10) *or* because there is indirect causation through another construct. For instance, although first-year law abidance does not have a direct effect on fifth-year law abidance, law abidance I does directly affect law abidance IV, which in turn directly affects law abidance V. Thus, law abidance I has an indirect effect on law abidance V that is mediated through law abidance IV. Other possible indirect effects can also be traced through the model by seeing how the causes of particular latent variables are themselves generated by one or more factors (Alwin and Hauser 1975; Fox 1980; Kenny 1979). Table 8-12 also presents a tabular summary of the total tracing process and shows how latent variables influence one another directly and indirectly. The influences on many of the latent variables are often indirect. For instance, note the large indirect effect of fourth-year law abidance on fifth-year behavioral pressure. Similarly, law abidance IV has a large indirect effect on fifth-year peer-culture involvement.

Relatively large indirect effects are the negative influences of law abidance I on behavioral pressure IV; the negative influence of law abidance I on peer-culture involvement IV; the positive influence of law abidance I on law abidance V; the negative influence of law abidance I on behavioral pressure V; the negative influence of law abidance IV on behavioral pressure V; the negative influence of law abidance I on peer-culture involvement V; and the negative influence of law abidance IV on peer-culture involvement V. There are no readily applied formulas for standard errors of indirect and total effects. Thus these values should be treated as summary indexes implied by the overall pattern of significant direct effects, rather than as numerical quantities that can unequivocally be tested for their significance.

In the second related model we examined the same three constructs of law abidance, peer-culture involvement, and behavioral pressure in the first, fourth, and fifth years—this time, using measures of the three predictor constructs of adult drug use, time spent with friends, and friends' poor school performance from the fourth year. In the fourth year, adult drug use is measured with three indicators, although time spent with friends was measured with a single indicator, and friends' poor school performance was measured with only two indicators. Because there was a single indicator of time spent with friends in the fourth year, we were not able to estimate the error variance for that variable.

Within the first year we allowed peer-culture involvement I and behavioral pressure I to be caused by first-year law abidance and to have a correlated prediction error. In the fourth year we permitted peer-culture involvement IV, behavioral pressure IV, adult drug use IV, time spent with friends IV, and friends' poor school performance IV all to be a function of law abidance IV, and for each of the five dependent factors to have correlated errors of prediction. Additionally, we permitted all six fourth-year constructs (including law abidance IV) to be caused by all three first-year constructs. In the fifth year we allowed peer-culture involvement V and behavioral pressure V to be caused by law abidance V and to have a correlated prediction error. All fifth-year factors were caused by all first- and fourth-year factors. The model was estimated under the assumption that individual variables would have correlated longitudinal errors of measurement. Again the parameters were estimated using the method of maximum likelihood in the LISREL-IV computer program, and normed and non-normed fit coefficients as well as an effects partition were calculated.

This model fit the data well (χ^2 = 752.65, d.f. = 359, $p <$ .001, Δ = .907, P = .933), and we again judged the fit sufficiently good that we could have confidence in the results. Table 8-14 shows the structural regression weights among the factors, and figure 8-11 shows the statistically significant paths. The standardized residual variances from prediction for the final dependent constructs are: law abidance V, .273; behavioral pressure V, .235; and peer-culture involvement V, .503.

The statistically significant paths were as follows. First-year peer-culture involvement and behavioral pressure were both negative functions of first-year law abidance as hypothesized. Fourth-year law abidance was a function only of first-year law abidance in a statistically significant manner. Fourth-year behavioral pressure, adult drug use, friends' poor school performance, peer-culture involvement, and time spent with friends, as well as law abidance V were all functions of fourth-year law abidance as hypothesized. Note that fourth-year behavioral pressure is not a function of first-year behavioral pressure, and that the cause by law abidance continuing from the first year explains the stability in the measure. Adult drug use in the fourth year is also a function of first-year behavioral pressure as we knew from earlier analyses (Huba and Bentler, in press a, chap. 26). Peer-culture involvement IV is also a function of first-year peer-culture involvement. Fourth-year time spent with friends IV is also a function of first-year peer-culture involvement and has a suppressor effect from first-year law abidance. When we consider the fifth-year latent variables, law abidance V has its predicted effects on behavioral pressure V and peer-culture involvement V. Law abidance V is a function only of fourth-year law abidance. Fifth-year behavioral pressure has a suppressor effect from fourth-year law abidance and a positive effect from fourth-year behavioral pressure, as well as the negative effect from law abidance V just noted. Peer-culture involvement V receives a negative suppressor effect from first-year behavioral pressure as well as a positive effect from peer-culture involvement I and IV, and a minor negative suppressor effect from fourth-year time spent with friends.

Table 8-15 shows the correlations among the latent variables implied by the model. Finally, we should again note that the partition of effects into

on Law Abidance

Dependent Latent Variable		Independent Latent Variable				
		Independent Latent Variable	B	Direct Effect	Indirect Effect	Total Effect
II.	Drug-behavioral pressure IV	I. Law abidance I	−.79 (.10)	−.62	.00	−.62
III.	Peer-culture involvement IV	I. Law abidance I	−.57 (.09)	−.50	.00	−.50
IV.	Law abidance IV	I. Law abidance I	.69 (.12)	.67	−.03	.64
IV.	Law abidance IV	II. Drug-behavioral pressure I	.03 (.07)	.04	.00	.04
IV.	Law abidance IV	III. Peer-culture involvement I	.02 (.07)	.02	.00	.02
V.	Drug behavioral pressure IV	I. Law abidance I	.17 (.18)	.13	−.57	−.45
V.	Drug behavioral pressure IV	II. Drug behavioral pressure I	.09 (.08)	.09	−.03	.06
V.	Drug behavioral pressure IV	III. Peer culture involvement I	.05 (.08)	.04	−.01	.03
V.	Drug behavioral pressure IV	IV. Law abidance IV	−1.00 (.15)	−.78	.00	−.78
VI.	Peer culture involvement IV	I. Law abidance I	.16 (.12)	.15	−.37	−.23
VI.	Peer culture involvement IV	II. Drug behavioral pressure I	−.01 (.06)	−.01	−.02	−.03
VI.	Peer culture involvement IV	III. Peer culture involvement I	.25 (.06)	.26	−.01	.26
VI.	Peer culture involvement IV	IV. Law abidance IV	−.43 (.10)	−.39	.00	−.39
VII.	Law abidance V	I. Law abidance I	.01 (.14)	.01	.53	.54
VII.	Law abidance V	II. Drug behavioral pressure I	.03 (.06)	.04	.03	.07
VII.	Law abidance V	III. Peer culture involvement I	−.01 (.06)	−.01	.02	.02
VII.	Law abidance V	IV. Law abidance IV	.89 (.15)	.84	.01	.85

Table 8-14 *(continued)*

Dependent Latent Variable		*Independent Latent Variable*		*Independent Latent Variable*			
				B	*Direct Effect*	*Indirect Effect*	*Total Effect*
VII.	Law abidance V	V.	Drug behavioral pressure IV	−.14 (.18)	−.17	.00	−.17
VII.	Law abidance V	VI.	Peer culture involvement IV	−.06 (.04)	−.06	.00	−.06
VII.	Law abidance V	X.	Adult drug use IV	−.02 (.05)	−.02	.00	−.02
VII.	Law abidance V	XI.	Time spent with friends IV	.03 (.05)	.02	.00	.02
VII.	Law abidance V	XII.	Friends' poor school performance IV	.17 (.15)	.21	.00	.21
VIII.	Drug behavioral pressure V	I.	Law abidance I	−.18 (.16)	−.12	−.37	−.50
VIII.	Drug behavioral pressure V	II.	Drug behavioral pressure I	−.02 (.08)	−.02	.02	.00
VIII.	Drug behavioral pressure V	III.	Peer-culture involvement I	.05 (.08)	.04	−.01	.03
VIII.	Drug-behavioral pressure V	IV.	Law abidance IV	.50 (.27)	.35	−.97	−.62
VIII.	Drug behavioral pressure V	V.	Drug-behavioral pressure IV	.85 (.26)	.77	.11	.88
VIII.	Drug behavioral pressure V	VI.	Peer culture involvement IV	−.13 (.06)	−.10	.04	−.06
VIII.	Drug behavioral pressure V	VII.	Law abidance V	−.83 (.19)	−.62	.00	−.62
VIII.	Drug behavioral pressure V	X.	Adult drug use IV	.06 (.08)	.05	.01	.07
VIII.	Drug behavioral pressure V	XI.	Time spent with friends IV	−.11 (.06)	.08	−.02	.07
VIII.	Drug behavioral pressure V	XII.	Friends' poor school performance IV	−.25 (.21)	−.23	−.13	−.36
IX.	Peer culture involvement V	I.	Law abidance I	.07 (.16)	.06	−.37	−.31
IX.	Peer culture	II.	Drug behavioral	−.15 (.08)	−.17	−.05	−.21

IX.	Peer culture involvement V	V.	Drug behavioral pressure IV	.13 (.25)	.14	.07	.21
IX.	Peer culture involvement V	VI.	Peer culture involvement IV	.25 (.06)	.23	.02	.25
IX.	Peer culture involvement V	VII.	Law abidance V	-.47 (.17)	-.43	.00	-.43
IX.	Peer culture involvement V	X.	Adult drug use IV	-.05 (.08)	-.06	.01	-.05
IX.	Peer culture involvement V	XI.	Time spent with friends IV	-.14 (.07)	-.13	.01	.12
IX.	Peer culture involvement V	XII.	Friends' poor school performance IV	-.23 (.21)	-.26	-.09	-.35
X.	Adult drug use IV	I.	Law abidance I	.06 (.14)	.05	-.44	-.40
X.	Adult drug use IV	II.	Drug behavioral pressure I	.15 (.07)	.16	-.02	.14
X.	Adult drug use IV	III.	Peer culture involvement I	.10 (.07)	.09	-.01	.08
X.	Adult drug use IV	IV.	Law abidance IV	-.54 (.12)	-.46	.00	-.46
XI.	Time spent with friends IV	I.	Law abidance I	.29 (.13)	.27	-.33	-.06
XI.	Time spent with friends IV	II.	Drug behavioral pressure I	.00 (.06)	.00	-.01	-.01
XI.	Time spent with friends IV	III.	Peer culture involvement I	.24 (.06)	.26	-.01	.25
XI.	Time spent with friends IV	IV.	Law abidance IV	-.33 (.09)	-.32	.00	-.32
XII.	Friends' poor school performance IV	I.	Law abidance I	.20 (.20)	.15	-.54	-.39
XII.	Friends' poor school performance IV	II.	Drug-behavioral pressure I	.06 (.09)	.06	-.03	.03
XII.	Friends' poor school performance IV	III.	Peer-culture involvement I	.15 (.10)	.13	-.01	.12
XII.	Friends' poor school performance IV	IV.	Law abidance IV	-.90 (.20)	-.69	.00	-.69

Note: Standard errors in parentheses.

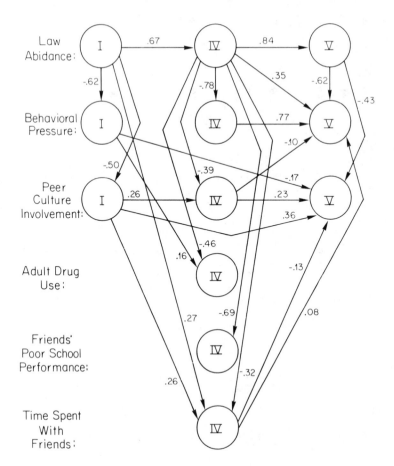

Figure 8-11. Relationship of Fourth-Year Psychosocial Factors to the Developing Sequence of Law Abidance, Drug-Behavioral Pressure, and Peer-Culture Involvement over Five Years

total and indirect sources within the current model specification and parameter estimates is presented in table 8-14. There are some large indirect effects, including the negative influence of first-year law abidance on behavioral pressure IV, the negative influence of law abidance I on peer-culture involvement IV, the positive influence of law abidance I on law abidance V, the negative influence of law abidance I on behavioral pressure V, the negative influence of law abidance IV on behavioral pressure V, the negative influence of law abidance I on peer-culture involvement V, the negative influence of law abidance IV on peer-culture involvement V, the

Table 8-15
Latent-Variable Intercorrelations in the Year IV Effects on Law-Abidance Model

Latent Variable	I	II	III	IV	V	VI	VII	VIII	IX	X	XI	XII
I. Law abidance I	1.00											
II. Drug-behavioral pressure I	-.62	1.00										
III. Peer-culture involvement I	-.50	.51	1.00									
IV. Law abidance IV	.64	-.37	-.30	1.00								
V. Drug-behavioral pressure IV	-.45	.32	.25	-.74	1.00							
VI. Peer-culture involvement IV	-.23	.18	.30	-.37	.50	1.00						
VII. Law abidance V	.54	-.29	-.24	.85	-.63	-.34	1.00					
VIII. Drug-behavioral pressure V	-.50	.32	.27	-.69	.77	.34	-.77	1.00				
IX. Peer-culture involvement V	-.31	.14	.42	-.49	.38	.46	-.55	.56	1.00			
X. Adult drug use IV	-.40	.35	.29	-.52	.68	.33	-.46	.58	.26	1.00		
XI. Time spent with friends IV	-.07	.08	.22	-.23	.27	.45	-.16	.21	.32	.16	1.00	
XII. Friends' poor school performance IV	-.39	.29	.29	-.65	.89	.50	-.51	.61	.31	.58	.36	1.00

negative influence of law abidance I on adult drug use IV, the negative influence of law abidance I on time spent with friends IV, and the negative influence of law abidance I on friends' poor school performance IV.

Discussion

This chapter has examined issues in the development of law-abidance tendencies throughout adolescence. Such tendencies are generally stable, as shown in our manifest-variable and latent-variable analyses of variance.

In a series of five-year, four-wave pairwise longitudinal causal models linking law abidance with a number of psychosocial and behavioral latent variables, we found that the general personality tendency toward low law abidance seemed to precede causally either the adoption of drug-taking behaviors or the development of peer and adult intimate support systems espousing mildly deviant behaviors. The analyses are summarized simply by saying that rebellious adolescents become progressively more immersed in subcultures that support rebellious behaviors. These relatively stable personality tendencies are most definitely important causal agents for the types of intimate support systems the individual becomes part of during adolescence. Furthermore, the personality tendencies toward low levels of law abidance are important causal agents for alcohol, cannabis, and hard-drug use, which are rebellious behaviors in this age span.

The most important models of this chapter are those that simultaneously examine the influences of many different factors on the changes in levels of rebelliousness. The reason for building toward a large model examining the influences of the different social-support dimensions on law abidance and its influences on them is simple: the single best ecology within which to obtain the most accurate estimates of the causal influences is the total relevant ecology. Obviously, computer-run size and cost considerations will never totally permit the largest necessary model to be tested for a real psychological phenomenon, but it is desirable to build the largest models possible (Huba and Bentler 1982a).

In our large models of the relationships of law abidance and the social latent variables, we found that there were consistent effects of the personality tendency of law abidance on the social factors both within and across time. There are strong tendencies for low law abiders to be individuals who are most heavily involved with their peers and who become friendly with peers and adults who use and support the use of a variety of drugs. These results were not unexpected on the basis of the smaller, four-wave models discussed in the chapter, but the fact that we could find them in the more complete ecology is strong evidence for robustness of the finding. Furthermore, in larger models we more completely partition the variance of the system into the components that actually control. In the larger models we also failed to find that the social factors had causal influences on the individual's levels of law abidance. Presumably this means that by the time we first measured the trait in early adolescence, the levels had become crystallized and not generally susceptible to change by social agents. This latter finding seems to be in direct opposition to extant metatheories of adolescence, arguing that it is a time of violent upheaval in which the values and personality characteristics of the individual are reshaped by peer socializing influences. Rather we find that the individual's overall trajectory of socialization into receiving social control from traditional institutions is apparently well established before the beginning of adolescence.

Going beyond these specific findings, this chapter illustrates ways that latent-variable causal models can be used to permit tests of hypotheses in personality research that had previously been considered almost impossible outside the laboratory. Not only do the latent-variable causal models permit the test of different formulations about how the variables relate over time in a way that can, in the presence of sufficient other inferential controls for competing hypotheses, help us to infer causality; but the tests are made in the context of statistical methods that specifically control the potentially contaminating influences of measurement error. Measurement error is unavoidable in personality and social-psychological questionnaires and surveys. Systematically testing existing theories and models using these new methods is one of the most crucial tasks for personality researchers during the next decade.

Notes

1. Various restrictions in this model were relaxed and tested to ascertain that it was the best general model for the data. For instance, relaxing the assumption of equal error variances and covariances for the three cohorts within sex, we found a significant decrement in badness of fit but also observed that several error variances became negative. Constraining the error variances and covariances of all six groups to be equal led to significantly worse fit.

2. In this chapter we adopt the following convention and all diagrams used to summarize causal models. First, we only diagram the structural-equations portion of the model or those parameters that link constructs. We do not diagram the measurement-model portions of the causal models since in all cases those portions performed as expected. Second, when we diagram the paths among the constructs, we present only those paths that are statistically significant as defined by a critical ratio of 1.65. The value chosen is the .10 two-tailed significance level (or a .05 one-tailed one); the somewhat

liberal value was chosen to ensure that paths that *may* be significant are presented visually for pattern inspection. Third, prediction errors, their correlations, and latent-variable correlations are not portrayed in diagrams: only causal paths are shown.

References

Alwin, D.F., and Hauser, R.M. The decomposition of effects in path analysis. *American Sociological Review*, 1975, *40*, 37-47.

Baltes, P.B.; Cornelius, S.W.; and Nesselroade, J.R. Cohort effects in developmental psychology. In J.R. Nesselroade and P.B. Baltes, eds., *Longitudinal research in the study of behavior and development*. New York: Academic Press, 1979.

Becker, H.S. *Outsiders: Studies in the sociology of deviance*. New York: Free Press, 1963.

Bentler, P.M. Multivariate analysis with latent variables: Causal modeling. *Annual Review of Psychology*, 1980, *31*, 419-456.

Bentler, P.M., and Bonett, D.G. Significance tests and goodness of fit in the analysis of covariance structures. *Psychological Bulletin*, 1980, *88*, 588-606.

Blalock, H.M. *Causal inferences in nonexperimental research*. Chapel Hill: University of North Carolina Press, 1964.

Fox, J. Effect analysis in structural equation models. *Sociological Methods and Research*, 1980, *9*, 3-28.

Ginsberg, I.J., and Greenley, J.R. Competing theories of marijuana use: A longitudinal study. *Journal of Health and Social Behavior*, 1978, *19*, 22-34.

Hogan, R.; Mankin, D.; Conway, J.; and Fox, S. Personality correlates of undergraduate marijuana use. *Journal of Consulting and Clinical Psychology*, 1970, *35*, 58-67.

Huba, G.J., and Bentler, P.M. A developmental theory of drug use: Derivation and assessment of a causal modeling approach. In P.B. Baltes and O.G. Brim, Jr., eds., *Life-span development and behavior*. New York: Academic Press, 1982a.

Huba, G.J., and Bentler, P.M. On the usefulness of latent variable causal modeling in testing theories of naturally-occurring events (including adolescent drug use). *Journal of Personality and Social Psychology*, 1982b, *43*, 640-647.

Huba, G.J., and Bentler, P.M. *Antecedents and consequences of adolescent drug use: A longitudinal study of psychosocial development using a causal modeling approach*. New York: Plenum, in press, a.

_____. Causal models of personality, peer culture characteristics, drug use, and criminal behaviors over a five-year span. In S. Mednick, ed., *Proceedings of the Life History Research Society Meetings*, in press, b.

Huba, G.J., and Hamilton, D.L. On the generality of trait relationships: Some analyses based on Fiske's paper. *Psychological Bulletin*, 1976, *83*, 868-876.

Huba, G.J., and Palisoc, A.L. Computerized path diagrams: A sample line printer approach. Submitted for publication.

Huba, G.J.; Wingard, J.A.; and Bentler, P.M. Comparison of two latent variable theories for adolescent drug use. *Journal of Personality and Social Psychology*, 1981, *40*, 180-193.

Jessor, R., and Jessor, S.L. *Problem behavior and psychosocial development*. New York: Academic Press, 1977.

Jöreskog, K.G. A general method for analysis of covariance structures. *Bioetrika*, 1970, *57*, 239-251.

Jöreskog, K.G. Structural analysis of covariance and correlation matrices. *Psychometrika*, 1978, *43*, 443-478.

Jöreskog, K.G., and Sörbom, D. *LISREL-IV: Analyses of linear structural relationships by the method of maximum likelihood*. Chicago: National Educational Resources, 1978.

Kandel, D.B. Convergence in prospective longitudinal surveys of drug use in normal populations. In D.B. Kandel, ed., *Longitudinal research on drug use: Empirical findings and methodological issues*. Washington, D.C.: Hemisphere, 1978.

Kaplan, H.B. Self-attitudes and multiple modes of deviance. In D.J. Lettieri, ed., *Drugs and suicide: When other coping strategies fail*. Beverly Hills, Calif.: Sage, 1978.

Kaplan, H.B. *Deviant behavior in defense of self*. New York: Academic Press, 1980.

Kenny, D.A. *Correlation and causality*. New York: Wiley-Interscience, 1979.

Rogosa, D. Causal models in longitudinal research: Rationale, formulation, and interpretation. In J.R. Nesselroade and P.B. Baltes, eds., *Longitudinal research in the study of behavior and development*. New York: Academic Press, 1979.

Segal, B.; Huba, G.J.; and Singer, J.L. *Drugs, daydreaming and personality: A study of college youth*. Hillsdale, N.J.: Lawrence Erlbaum Associates, 1980a.

Segal, B.; Huba, G.J.; and Singer, J.L. The prediction of college drug and alcohol use from personality and daydreaming tendencies. *International Journal of the Addictions*, 1980b, *15*, 849-867.

Winer, B.J. *Statistical principles in experimental design*, 2nd ed. New York: McGraw-Hill, 1971.

9

Personality, Environment, and Criminal Behavior: An Evolutionary Perspective

Douglas T. Kenrick,
Arthur Dantchik, and
Steven MacFarlane

Cesare Lombroso, a nineteenth-century researcher concerned with the genesis of criminal behavior, is regarded by some experts as the father of modern criminology (Bartol 1980; Shafer 1976). He proposed an evolutionary theory of criminal behavior that owed as much to Gall's phrenology as to the writings of Charles Darwin, a contemporary of Lombroso. Lombroso's theory, suggesting that the born criminal was atavistic—a throwback to an earlier ancestral type—sounds anachronistic to the modern reader. Lombroso's so-called *Homo delinquens* could be distinguished by physical anomalies—an asymmetric skull, prominent jaws and eyebrows, high cheekbones, a flat nose, fat lips—and by a tendency to engage in cruel and impulsive behavior adapted to an earlier stage of prehistory. He could also be distinguished by insensitivity to pain, sharp vision, laziness, and absence of shame, among other characteristics (Toch 1979).

In recent years, criminology has been dominated by a view quite at odds with Lombroso's. The most prevalent theories have been sociological ones, which seek the causes of criminal behavior not within the individual but within the larger social context of which he is a part (Warren and Hindelang 1979). Sociologists see criminal and delinquent tendencies as resulting from the influence of subcultures wherein criminal behavior is normative (Cohen 1955; Miller 1958) or due to "strain" caused by a lack of acceptable means for members of underprivileged groups to obtain socially desired ends (Cloward and Ohlin 1960), or to a lack of sufficient social control (Hirschi 1969).

Two developments—one in contemporary social science and one in criminology—prompt us to reconsider the spirit, if not the conclusions, of Lombroso's criminal anthropology. One is a renewed and controversial attempt to apply evolutionary theory to humans, kindled largely by the 1975 publication of E.O. Wilson's *Sociobiology*. Wilson's final chapter suggested that much of human behavior could be analyzed with the types of evolutionary models recently developed to understand various forms of animal behavior. The second is the emergence of a body of evidence suggesting that there are individual differences in susceptibility to those environmental forces that set the stage for criminal behavior. This biosocial approach to criminal behavior is exemplified in the work of Eysenck (see chapter 3). Of particular importance here, however, is the evidence suggesting that at least some of the variance in individual differences is attributable to physiological dissimilarities between normals and certain groups at high risk for criminal behavior. Closely related to this point is the merging behavior-genetic evidence suggesting some degree of heritability to criminal behavior.

It is important to note that a sociobiological analysis is not committed to rigid genetic determinism, but is instead interactionist, considering not only genetic constraints but also how the organism's genetic potential is molded by and adapted to ecological forces.

It follows, therefore, that adopting a sociobiological model does not imply a commitment to reactionary social programs aimed at culling out pathological genes while ignoring environmental problems. The present analysis instead has much in common with the liberal biases of the sociological viewpoint, for at least two reasons. First, we suggest that Lombroso was unfair in selecting one subgroup as atavistically adapted to an earlier period of human history. All of us are throwbacks in our possession of response characteristics that evolved for a niche quite unlike that in which we now find ourselves. Much of what would be labeled criminal behavior today was essential to survival for our hominid ancestors (including *Homo sapiens*) for all but a very short recent stretch of time during which cultural evolution could be said to have rapidly outpaced biological evolution. Second, those individual differences that predispose some persons more readily to run afoul of the law are seen here not as constitutional weaknesses, but as characteristics that evolved because they were adaptive to our ancestors (and may indeed remain adaptive under some conditions today). In line with the first point, however, we believe the search for environmental or ecological factors that trigger those formerly adaptive behavioral mechanisms is at least as fruitful as a search for the physiological and genetic substrata that underlie individual differences in those mechanisms. An ecological approach need not assume a tabula rasa organism, however. On the contrary, a familiarity with the ethological and anthropological literature bearing on the evolution of our species may help us understand and organize those ecological factors already uncovered, as well as suggesting further hypotheses and possible intervention strategies.

The remainder of the chapter comprises four sections. First, we will present some basic sociobiological assumptions that are relevant to our discussion. Second, we will review recent anthropological views of the structure and ecology of hominid evolution. Third, we will address selectively several individual differences related to criminal behavior, considering the possible adaptiveness of those characteristics given the hominid social structure that existed for most of human history. In this section we will also briefly review genetic and physiological evidence relating to individual differences in criminal behavior. Finally, we will consider selected ecological conditions that have been shown to relate to antisocial behavior, and to integrate these factors into the current evolutionary framework.

Some Relevant Sociobiological Principles

The basic premise of sociobiological theorizing is an assumption that social behaviors evolve in much the same way as physical features. Those patterns that are relatively more functional in meeting the demands of the environment will result in better chances for survival of their possessor and his or her offspring. Clear examples of the genetic transmission of functional social arrangements can be seen in the *hymenoptera* (social insects such as ants and bees) who have evolved complex patterns of social stratification, cooperation, and communication (Wilson 1975). The simple rule is that organisms will act so as to improve their *genetic fitness* (usually defined as the number of offspring who are themselves raised to mating age). This principle is basically tautological—organisms that act in a less functional fashion than their competitors will be less well represented in future generations.

Strategies

To suggest that organisms act generally so as to increase their genetic fitness does not mean that every social action is the most sensible one available. Organisms tend to adopt strategies that, on the average, maximize the ratio of benefits to costs. In calculating this ratio, benefits to the organism's kin are also considered (Hamilton 1964). Thus an act that benefits a sibling more than twice what it costs an individual A can evolve, since a sibling shares (on average) half the genes of individual A. Even self-sacrificial altruism can thereby be selected for (Hamilton 1964), although such self-sacrifice is ultimately selfish (Dawkins 1976) in promoting the survival of more copies of one's genes than would otherwise be the case.

Sociobiologists have made much use of game-theory analyses (like the familiar prisoner's dilemma) in their reasoning about adaptive strategies (for example, Maynard-Smith 1972; Trivers 1971, 1972). For instance, Maynard-Smith (1972), in discussing the development of "evolutionary stable strategies," argues that in a population of peaceful cooperators—or "doves," to use Dawkin's (1976) term—who shy away from aggressive competition, a "hawkish" genetic tendency toward aggressive behavior will result in a relative fitness advantage in its possessor, since doves will back down from any fight over resources. Since an interaction between two hawks can result in serious injury, however, the dove strategy will be relatively advantageous when the ratio of hawks becomes too high. Given only these two strategies, what will emerge is a relatively stable ratio of hawks to doves that balances the advantages and disadvantages to each. This will be the case even though all organisms might have done best if everyone was a dove. A population completely composed of doves is not stable, since it favors any tendency toward hawkishness.

Cheating

Maximizing outcomes for one's own genes (in oneself and one's kin) is crucial to evolutionary success, and organisms will be selected for expending the least energy in the pursuit of resources. This sometimes results in cheating behaviors that offend the moral sensibilities of the human observer. For instance, several species of birds, such as cowbirds and cuckoos, engage in nest parasitism that involves laying their eggs in the nest of a member of another species (Wallace 1979). In some cases the parasite young hatch before those of the host and proceed to push the remaining eggs out of the nest so as not to have to share the host parents' attentions. Another example is the saber-toothed blenny (*Aspidontus taeniatus*), which has evolved to look almost exactly like a cleaner wrasse (*Labroides dimidiatus*). Since cleaner wrasse perform a function for larger fish, they are permitted in close proximity. The blenny, however, disguised as a cleaner wrasse, swims up to an unsuspecting larger fish, then suddenly tears a chunk out of its flesh and darts away (Eibl-Eibesfeldt 1975). In enacting such strategies, there is nothing sacred about one's own species. If a strategy favors one subgroup of a species (those closely related to the cheater) time will favor that strategy over a more philanthropic pattern.

A Capsule Summary of Human Evolution

In this section we will briefly review research and theory to suggest that contemporary humanity evolved in such a way that the following characteristics are likely to have been predisposed via natural selection: (1) strong dominance hierarchies, (2) antisocial behavior toward unrelated individuals, and (3) sexual division of labor such that (1) and (2) will be more characteristic of males. These conclusions are based on a review of recent theories resting largely on data from naturalistic studies of group-living primates, archaeological findings of early human groups and our hominid ancestors, and anthropological studies of human hunter-gatherer groups.

Two crucial trends emerge from the fossil evidence on the ecology of our hominid ancestors. First, the development of our bipedal gait seems to have accompanied a move out of the forests (to which most primates are adapted) and onto the open grasslands where large game as well as large predators are more abundant (Lancaster 1975; Pfheiffer 1972). A related development is that early hominids became more carnivorous than most primates and also became one of the predators on the large game of the savannah. These developments had some important implications for hominid social structure. Although typical group-living primates fend largely for themselves in providing for food, hominids became group hunters, whose cooperation and use of artificial weapons enabled them to bring down large game and share their capture with the other group members (Baer and McEachron 1982). Pfeiffer (1972) has noted that savannah primates have strong dominance hierarchies, and Baer and McEachron (1982) have recently argued that the need for such dominance hierarchies would have become crucial with the development of fatal weapons that make intragroup aggression exceedingly costly. Although a certain amount of aggressive interaction occurs at the formation of a dominance hierarchy, once each member has established his or her position vis-à-vis the other group members, the need for further hostility is diminished (Bernstein 1969; Southwick 1969). In groups with well-established dominance hierarchies, intragroup aggression is usually quite low unless the status quo is disrupted by introduction of a strange member into the group (Bernstein 1969; Bernstein, Gordon, and Rose 1974; Dittes 1977).

Outgroup Aggression

Baer and McEachron (1982) have noted that primate groups tend to be highly xenophobic, a tendency that makes for some danger in individual migration as well as sometimes brutal clashes between groups. For instance, Southwick (1969) has observed groups of rhesus monkeys living near abandoned temples where they are regularly fed. Under these conditions density has increased, and intergroup clashes are common and particularly violent, with many adults showing numerous severe scars obtained in earlier battles.

Baer and McEachron (1982) argue that these xenophobic tendencies would have become, if anything, more pronounced in early hominids because of the development of fatal weapons and the increase in intragroup genetic relatedness that presumably would have followed the need for cooperation among males within such a group. Consistent with their argument are the findings suggesting that *Australopithecus* and *Homo erectus* engaged in high rates of homicide (around 50 percent). Even today some modern hunter-gatherer cultures, such as the Yanomamo (Chagnon 1977) and the Mundurucu (Murphy 1957) appear to consider their enemies simply as very dangerous game, and to use the adaptations developed for group hunting against their own neighbors. Further, the Yanomamo patterns suggest how tendencies toward such antisocial behavior against members of unrelated groups can perpetuate themselves through an increase in genetic fitness in their possessors. The most successful warriors have more wives (and more offspring) than their less fierce compatriots (Wilson 1978). Thus those individuals who are aggressive, physically strong, and lacking in fear will be more likely to contribute their genes to future generations. Although this relationship seems to hold under conditions faced by groups like the Yanomamo, Washburn and Lancaster (1973) argue that "almost every human society has regarded killing members of certain other human societies as desirable" (p. 64), and has showered advantages on successful warriors (Wilson 1978).

Division of Labor

The hunter-gatherer adaptation was also accompanied by a division of labor more pronounced than that of earlier primates. Although both males and females subsist on self-provided diets in most other primate species, group hunting became the sole province of males in hominid groups, probably largely because caring for an infant and hunting large game are mutually exclusive. These sex differences may have been exacerbated when high intelligence evolved to favor long periods of offspring dependency. Further, increased pelvis size in females, an adaptation suited to the large brain size of hominid offspring, interferes slightly with running ability (Pfeiffer 1972), thereby further hampering success in hunting.

Even prior to hominid evolution, males were more aggressive and dominant than females. In many primate species all the adult males are higher in the dominance order than any females (Wilson 1975). Also, dominance rank is related to a male's reproductive success in most primate species (Wilson 1975) while it is generally less important for females. This state of affairs is likely due to the fact that females contribute more resources to the offspring than do males (in mammals, the female carries the fetus, may die in childbirth, and nurses the offspring for some period of time). Since females can have only a small number of offspring, whereas the male could conceivably have many with little investment, the female is in a position to be more selective in her choice of mates. This leads to male competition to prove their relative fitness via intrasex competition.

In making the transition to group hunting, the male's preadaptation for agonistic behavior was retained. In directing that adaptation toward aggressive interchanges with other hominid groups, the male-female differentiation was also retained. In hunter-gatherer groups, outgroup aggression is the province of the male.

Recent History

It is reasonable to accept our argument so far and yet to wonder about the relevance of these principles for modern humanity. Most people are no longer hunter-gatherers living in small groups on the savannahs, but are instead residents of large urban or suburban population centers. Technological and cultural evolution might seem to have made genetic evolution irrelevant to a discussion of modern human behavior. It is important to note, however, that although our modern ecological surrounds may differ greatly from those in which our ancestors dwelled, the modern human organism is virtually identical to that of our hunter-gatherer ancestors. For one thing, all humans were hunter-gatherers until very recently. Agriculture did not emerge until approximately ten thousand years ago (Washburn and Lancaster 1973). As Washburn and Lancaster point out, agriculture has existed for only the last 1 percent of human history, and for most of that time was practiced by only a small minority of the population. Even if this were sufficient time to produce changes in our genetic tendencies (and Washburn and Lancaster argue it is not) the agricultural life-style specifically did not select against those traits we have focused on, but instead may have exacerbated their selective advantage. As the urban anthropologist Basham (1978) points out, the move into earlier agricultural cities was likely to have exaggerated dominance hierarchies and the rewards for male warriorlike behavior. This was due to a number of factors, including increases in the value of the spoils of war and the consequent need for protection of cities. Basham notes that residents of the fertile river valleys were continually under threat from seminomadic groups in the hinterlands. Any text on the history of so-called civilization tells a story of warlike behavior in which the principal contestants have been male warriors who have generally regarded their adversaries as somewhat less than completely human. Thus none of the three major developments suggested earlier—strong dominance hierarchies, outgroup aggression, or a division of labor exacerbating those tendencies in males—would seem to have been in the least diminished with the change from a hunter-gatherer life-style. Also, until very recently, social organization tended to revolve around extended kinship groups for most of humanity. The move into large cities has occurred only in the last two centuries, and before the last half-century the vast majority of the world's populace lived outside of cities (Basham 1978). Although a very small minority of the world's population lived in preindustrial cities, Basham notes that the nuclear family as a unit of social organization emerged only after the industrial revolution. In preindustrial cities, extended kinship groups are still the norm.

Individual Differences

Implicit in our argument is an assumption that at least some of the variance in tendencies toward criminal behavior is heritable. This does not imply DNA programming for specific acts, but perhaps the inheritance of (1) learning dispositions; (2) varying thresholds for motivational states such as anxiety, anger, and so on; or (3) morphological features such as body build or physical attractiveness that elicited differing patterns of environmental reinforcement. None of these predispositions is presumed to determine criminal behavior in a unicausal fashion; rather, they are assumed to interact with environmental events. Following a brief review of the behavior-genetic evidence on the heritability of criminality, we will give two examples of traits that could be seen to affect criminal behavior within a sociobiological framework.[1]

Behavior Genetics

If one wishes to argue that predispositions to criminal behaviors are genetically transmitted, it is useful to examine the research on heritability of criminal tendencies. In studying genetic links to antisocial behaviors, two primary research methodologies have been used: twin studies and adoption studies. The bulk of data from such studies suggests that some of the variance in criminal behavior is accounted for by biological-inheritance factors.

Investigators have looked at the differences in concordance rates of criminal behavior between monozygotic (MZ) and dizygotic (DZ) twin pairs. If MZ concordance rates are significantly higher than DZ rates, this tends to support a genetic role in criminal behaviors because MZ pairs are genetically closer to each other than are DZ pairs. Indeed, much of the early research (Lange 1929; Stumpfl 1936; Legras 1932; Kranz 1936) on twins demonstrated higher concordance rates in criminality for MZ pairs. Furthermore, Kranz (1936) has shown that MZ concordant twins are much more similar than DZ pairs with respect to type of crime committed, age at onset of criminal career, and frequency of crimes. He also identified high concordance rates of alcoholism in MZ twins and discordance in DZ twins, leading him to conclude that in those who were predisposed to criminal behavior, alcohol acted as a releasing mechanism. Although Kranz considered environmental explanations, he maintained that MZ and DZ pairs were reared under similar enough conditions to accept the role of genetics when accounting for concordance-rate differences. In line with these findings, Yoshimasu (1965) constructed life curves for criminal pairs and found that MZ twins exhibited curves much more similar than those of DZ twins.

Some of the aforementioned studies have been criticized on methodological grounds. Christiansen (1977) has pointed out that there are often questions of determination of zygosity, classification of concordance, and sampling procedures. A more recent investigation by Dalgard and Kringlen

(1976) used the Norwegian Twin Register to obtain an unbiased sample, employed blood- and serum-type tests to judge zygosity when possible, and used two different criteria for concordance. Although MZ pairs in this study had higher concordance rates than DZ pairs, the effect was not statistically significant. Forde (1978), however, has criticized Dalgard and Kringlen for not considering such relevant measures as number of offenses, seriousness, persistence, and rate of offending. Christiansen (1977) also controlled for biased sampling procedures by drawing a sample from the Danish Twin Register. He found much higher rates of concordance for MZ same-sex pairs than DZ equivalents. In addition, male MZ concordance rates were higher than female MZ concordance rates, a finding that is consistent with the sex differences in criminal behavior, to be discussed in the next section.

Twin-pair studies yield suggestive results concerning the role of genetic factors in criminality, but they are not themselves conclusive. Much stronger data come from adoption studies that contrast the rates of criminality between adoptees of biological parents who themselves were either criminal or noncriminal. To the extent that adoptee subjects can be matched with respect to characteristics such as age, sex, length of time in foster care, and socioeconomic status of adoptive parents, then any observed differences in rates of criminality can likely be attributed to the effects of heredity.

Hutchings and Mednick (1977), in a study of 1,145 adoptees and matched nonadopted controls, have reported results that support a genetic role in criminality. Using multiple-regression techniques, they found that criminality of the biological father was an important determinant of adoptee criminality and had an effect independent of other predictors in the regression equations. Other studies have shown a genetic link between biologic parent and antisocial behavior in adoptees (Crowe 1974; Cadoret 1978; Hutchings and Mednick 1974).

In this section we have not considered exactly what tendencies affecting criminal behavior might be inherited. The following sections suggest two candidates—aggressiveness and psychopathy.

Aggressiveness

Although aggressive behavior can have high costs associated with it, since it is likely to elicit defensive retaliation, the rewards of an aggressive strategy may outweigh those costs under certain circumstances. The individual who exhibits a readiness to stand and fight for some necessary resource has a survival advantage, particularly when the resource is scarce. Certain morphological features (such as relatively large or strong body build, or sharp teeth) will of course be associated with the success of such a strategy.[2] In addition to allowing for more direct control of resources, aggressiveness is one important component of an individual's relative dominance; as we have already discussed, a number of rewards accrue to dominant individuals.

We will now focus on the evidence relating to the sex difference in aggression. From our earlier discussion of hominid evolution, it would be expected that males would be more aggressive, given their greater involvement in dominance contests, hunting, and outgroup competition. Two types of evidence bear directly on this issue: (1) the hormone testosterone (found in much greater concentrations in males than females) has been found to be related to aggression, and (2) direct epidemiological data suggest an overwhelming sex difference in criminal behavior, with the incidence much higher for males.

Testosterone. Beeman (1947) controlled the initiation and cessation of aggressive behavior in mice by manipulating testosterone level. When mice that usually fight intraspecifically were castrated before puberty, they did not fight on reaching maturation. Members of the control group, who were not castrated, showed typical fighting behavior. When Beeman implanted testosterone pellets subcutaneously in the castrated mice, they fought as much as the control animals. When these pellets were removed, however, the mice ceased fighting. More recently Watson and Moss (1971) found that red grouse cocks, when implanted with androgens, became more aggressive, increased territorial boundaries, and mated with more than one hen. In this instance high levels of androgens would clearly be adaptive for any particular grouse. Increased territory yields increased access to resources, and the concomitant rise in aggression will better enable the grouse to successfully defend his new area. Increased matings will obviously increase the chances that offspring and parental genes will survive.

The relationship between testosterone and aggression has also been observed in primates. It has been shown (Rose, Holaday, and Bernstein 1971), that high testosterone levels of male rhesus monkeys living in groups are correlated with frequency of aggressive behavior and rank in the dominance hierarchy. This same researcher later showed (Rose, Gordon, and Bernstein 1972) that testosterone levels and dominance behavior could be manipulated as a function of the social environment. Adult males who were exposed to receptive females showed increases in testosterone levels and noncontact aggressive behaviors. On the other hand, they showed a dramatic decrease in testosterone and an increase in submissive behaviors when introduced into an established order of rhesus macaques.

Sex Difference. According to the 1970 Federal Bureau of Investigation crime statistics, women accounted for 14.4 percent of arrests for all crimes. Of crimes involving aggressive acts, women accounted for 19.4 percent of murder-manslaughter arrests, 12.6 percent of aggravated-assault arrests, and only 6.1 percent of robberies. Broom and Selznick (1957) have pointed out that males have committed many more crimes for all periods and in all places in which statistics have been recorded. Interestingly, studies of young male criminals (Kreuz and Rose 1972) have revealed that prisoners who committed the more aggressive and violent crimes of armed robbery, assault, attempted murder, murder, and escape from prison during adolescence had the highest levels of testosterone.

Psychopathy

Psychopathy is another characteristic that is much more likely to be found among males than among females (Bartol 1980) and that can be seen to have benefits as well as costs associated with it. In fact, it is customary in discussing psychopathy to note that not all individuals with such tendencies are apprehended criminals. Some may be successful politicians or businessmen (see Davison and Neale 1982). Note that the behavioral traits that Cleckley (1976) observed to be associated with psychopathy include considerable social charm, absence of anxiety, lack of remorse, untruthfulness, and an incapacity for real love and attachment. A psychopath may marry more than one woman without informing each of the other's existence, and may gracefully talk his way out of repeated trouble for his antisocial behavior by feigning sincere regret, only to repeat the same behaviors again.

It is clear how the tendency for such a trait could have evolved. The psychopath adopts a cheater strategy analogous to those of the blenny and the cuckoo, investing little to obtain resources while running some risk of detection. An individual who is capable of convincing more than one monogamously inclined female to mate with him, and of eliciting cooperation from other people in exchange for minimal reciprocation, has some selection advantage. Additionally, the psychopath's relative insensitivity to physical punishment and his calm poise could, when combined with a moderate degree of aggressiveness, allow him to advance to positions of dominance, from which he can more freely exploit his subordinates. It is important to note the limitations on the advantages of such a tendency. Given a strong value to the detection of cheating, and social groupings in which prolonged and repeated contacts occur (Trivers 1971), more than subtle inclinations toward psychopathy would have been selected against.

Ecological Factors

Whatever tendencies to exploit other individuals in a criminal manner exist in the human species as a whole or in certain human subgroups, they are not enacted continuously or randomly, but in response to particular environmental circumstances. The use of exploitive or aggressive strategies is presumed to reflect the differential payoff matrixes for different exigencies. We will discuss two factors (density and resource scarcity) that have been found to increase the use of exploitive strategies across numerous species, and two (genetic relatedness and dominance hierarchies) that have been found to decrease the use of such strategies.

Competition for Resources

Competition for resources will result when there is a demand for a particular resource by two or more organisms. Competitive interactions take place between species that inhabit the same niche, especially between members of the same species. Intraspecific competition is quite common and often fierce since members of the same species have the same needs for survival. Southwick (1969) found that when food was scarce, a strange rhesus monkey introduced into a new group was most often attacked by those most directly in competition with it. In addition, cases of highly aggressive acts between competitors, including murder and cannibalism, have been well documented in lions (Schaller 1972), langurs (Sugiyama 1967), hyenas (Kruuk 1972), and the social insects (Wilson 1971). Contrary to what Lorenz had proposed in *On Aggression* (1963), it appears that man is not the only species that kills conspecifics.

The victor in a competitive interaction gains control over the resource. This can serve to enhance its genetic fitness—survival value—in two ways. The resource itself, if it is something like food, water, or shelter, will better enable the organism to survive in the face of scarcity and thereby result in greater opportunity for that organism to mate. In addition, the victor has achieved dominance relative to the loser; and, as has been shown by DeFries and McClearn (1970, 1972), dominant males reproduce much more successfully than subordinate males. This is also the case in modern hunter-gatherer tribes. Neel (1970) studied three South American polygamous tribes: the Makiritare of Southern Venezuela, the Xavante of the Brazilian Mato Grasso, and the Yanomamo of Southern Venezuela and Northern Brazil. He found that in four villages a highly disproportionate number of grandchildren could be traced to a few of the headmen, who are the most dominant members of the tribe. Thus there appears to exist a parallel relationship between dominance and reproductive success in animals and humans.

The modern hunter-gatherer tribes provide an unusual link to our past history since they are similar in breeding structure to the conditions under which humans evolved (Neel 1970). Their cultural evolution is indeed responsive to "the necessities imposed by the environment in which society finds itself" (Wilson 1978, p. 114). Although many of their practices may seem abhorrent, they are functionally similar to those of infrahuman animals as well as of modern humans. This is not to imply that all organisms respond in the same way to scarcity of resources, but that those that are able to respond to environmental stress thereby increase their genetic fitness. Perhaps the best chronicled hunter-gatherer tribe is the Yanomamo, whose customs have been recorded by the ethnographer Napoleon Chagnon (1977). The Yanomamo warriors compete fiercely for women, which represents a limiting factor in their environment. Wallace (1979) argues that when there is a limiting factor, fitness can be increased only by contributing one's own genes relative to unrelated others in the population. Yanomamo women that are captured are raped and then given to deserving warriors. Curiously, one reason that females are a valuable commodity is that the Yanomamo practice female infanticide as a means of population control. The tribe needs fewer females to produce offspring than males to become hunters. The advantage to capturing females stems from the fact that, given their protein-scarce environment and their competitive neighbors, the costs of *raising* a high ratio of females outweigh the advantages. Infanticide is also directed against infants whose older siblings are not ready for weaning, deformed infants, and those from extramarital affairs (Chagnon 1977; Neel 1969). These are effective means for exercising control over growth and overutilization of resources.

The Mundurucu of Brazil inhabit territory that is scarce in game, and hence essential protein is a limiting factor in their environment. They hunt in groups, traversing territories that often lead to competitive interactions with other hunting tribes. The Mundurucu treat other tribesmen as game and kill them, returning to their villages with decapitated heads as trophies (Wilson 1978). Killing competitors gives the Mandurucu hunters increased territory and access to game.

If these illustrations seem alien to us, it might be helpful to remember our own recent violent history. Wars have been fought and people subjugated in much the same manner and for many of the same reasons as those of our less cultured predecessors. The millions exterminated in concentration camps; in Hiroshima and Nagasaki; in Southeast Asia, the Middle East, and Latin America, along with the current threat of nuclear decimation, belie our civilized and humanitarian self-perceptions. The major difference is that today the definition of *resources* is broader.

There have been several correlational studies examining the relationship between criminal behavior and economic conditions. An often cited study by Hovland and Sears (1940) reported highly significant negative correlations between cotton prices and the number of lynchings.[3] This is consistent with data obtained by Raper (1933) who found a correlation of $-.53$ for the years 1900-1930 between lynchings and the per-acre value of cotton. Thomas (1927) looked at the correlations among a variety of social behaviors and the business cycle. She found that when economic conditions were relatively poor, property crimes involving violence went up dramatically ($r = -.44$). These results indicate that when resources are scarce—that is, when harsh economic conditions exist—criminal behaviors increase. Predictions based on the application of sociobiological parameters to this situation yield results that are consistent with empirical evidence. Competition for resources should cause people to engage in behaviors to increase their genetic fitness relative to others. If an effective strategy in achieving this end involves engaging in criminal activities, then an increase in certain indexes of crime should become apparent as resources become scarce.

Density

Density is a factor that has been shown to affect social behaviors in both animals and humans. As density increases, the space per organism decreases. Therefore, the frequency of encounters between organisms increases, as does the chance for agonistic interactions. Increased density also leads to greater competition for available resources, which in turn elicits aggressive behaviors. Calhoun (1962) has demonstrated the deleterious effects of high density on a population of Norway rats. He found that crowded conditions resulted in deviant sexual behaviors, cannibalism, and infanticide. Southwick (1969) showed that crowding among rhesus monkeys also yielded aggressive behaviors, and Leyhausen (1965) found a similar pattern of behavior in cats.

The relationship between density and human behavior is less well defined. Some researchers have reported significant positive correlations between density and crime rates (Galle, McCarthy, and Zimmern 1973; Galle, Gove and McPherson 1972), only to have these effects reduced on reanalysis (Freedman, Heshka, and Levy 1975). Other studies in which socioeconomic variables were controlled, however, found significant positive relationships between density and crime rates. Stichor, Decker, and O'Brien (1979) report high correlations between robbery, with and without injury, and density ($r = .42$ and $r = .52$, respectively). Booth, Welch, and Johnson (1976) surveyed 656 U.S. cities with populations greater than 25,000 and 100,000. After partialing out the effects of social characteristics, density (as measured by dwelling units per square mile, and within-household density) consistently accounted for some portion of the variance in rates of criminal behavior. Schmitt (1957) also controlled for social variables and found a high positive correlation between density and crime in Honolulu.

The fact that the relationship between density and criminal behavior is not always strong does not necessarily mean that the tenets of evolutionary theory and population biology do not apply to human social behaviors. Density is certainly not the only variable to be considered in explaining criminal behavior. Density probably interacts with other factors in influencing criminal behavior, and other factors probably influence criminal behaviors independent of density. The fact remains, however, that density consistently accounts for some part of the variance.

A stronger predictor of criminal behavior is city size. Sadalla (1978) has noted from comparisons of sites of ancient and modern settlements that population density has remained relatively stable, while only the size of cities has increased. From a review of a number of studies that examine the relationship between urbanization and crime, Quinney (1979) concludes that crime rates are higher in urban than in rural areas and that they increase with city size. Quinney (1979) and Wilks (1967) find strong relationships between property crimes, violent crimes, and urban settings. Similar patterns of criminal activity have been reported for a number of European cities (Clinard 1968; Wolfgang 1970).

The pattern of criminal behavior in modern societies closely conforms to sociobiological predictors. Crime is greatest in city centers, in low-wealth areas (Shaw and Mackay 1931), and in larger cities than in smaller ones or rural settings; that is, crime is higher where competition for resources is more marked. In addition, large cities are associated with the breakdown of dominance hierarchies and the degree of genetic relatedness. From a sociobiological standpoint, these factors would also be expected to increase criminal behavior. We will now proceed to a discussion of these factors.

As we have previously indicated, probably the single most important motivational force contributing to aggression and criminal behavior stems from a need on the part of the individual to obtain the necessary resources required to survive and reproduce. Given that available resources are often scarce, one would naturally expect a certain degree of competition among organisms whose resource requirements overlap, and a greater degree of overlap should result in increased competition. As indicated earlier, the greatest natural competitor to any organism is another member of the same species, since conspecifics show the greatest degree of overlap in resource requirements. In light of these conditions, it is perhaps as important to ask why organisms of the same species sometimes refrain from aggressive competitiveness as it is to ask why they engage in aggressive behaviors. Thus our attention will now be directed toward an examination of two mechanisms, genetic relatedness and dominance hierarchies.

Genetic Relatedness

A basic postulate of sociobiology states that the greater the degree of genetic relatedness two individuals share, the less likely each will be to engage in aggressive competition for resources with the other. In general, high genetic interrelatedness serves to reduce competition between conspecifics by increasing the costs and reducing the benefits associated with such pursuits. Genetic relatedness, as a mechanism for reducing competition for resources, acts in two ways. First, it reduces the amount of fitness an individual stands to lose when he or she fails to gain control of a resource, since that resource is more likely to be won or retained by a genetic relative. Thus, in addition to showing less perseverance in competition for a resource with a genetic relative, an individual would also be less likely to initiate an aggressive conflict for control over a resource held by a genetically related conspecific. Second, genetic relatedness serves to reduce aggression by increasing the cost of physical combat, since in a battle of genetic relatives, an injury to either lowers the inclusive fitness of both.

We have proposed that earlier hominids lived in small groups of highly related individuals. Primate and social carnivore groups are similarly composed of a small number of highly related individuals (Packer 1979; Fiennes 1976; Kruuk 1972). If genetic relatedness actually does serve to reduce aggression, one would expect intragroup strife among related primates and social carnivores to be minimal, whereas extreme xenophobic tendencies should predominate in encounters with the nonrelated members characteristic of other troops or packs. Consistent with this prediction, a large body of studies (reviewed in McEachron and Baer 1982) reveal that, for primates and social carnivores alike, intragroup aggression is relatively rare, whereas intergroup contact usually results in aggressive encounters or serious fighting.

The importance of genetic relatedness as a variable in determining social behavior is dramatically illustrated in Sugiyama's (1967) observations of the hanuman langurs of India. For these primates, when a male takes over a troop by driving off or killing his predecessor, he quickly sets to the task of killing the infants of his newly acquired troop. Even more astounding, however, is the fact that the conquering male will continue to kill future-born infants (sired by his predecessor) up until that point at which his own offspring begin to be born. In considering human behavior, one sees surprising parallels to the langur's behavior. Killing the offspring of one's enemy has been a recurrent strategy throughout human history (Barash 1977). Moving to modern U.S. society, the finding that nonbiological fathers abuse their children far more, proportionally speaking, than do natural fathers (Gil 1970; Lenington 1981) further supports the importance of genetic relatedness in the determination of social behavior.

Crime statistics revealing that a large majority of homicides are committed by someone with whom the victim was familiar (such as a spouse or relative) may seem to contradict the sociobiological contention that genetic relatedness serves to reduce aggression. One needs to keep in mind, however, that such individuals are more likely to come in contact with one another than with unrelated individuals. It is crucial to examine the relative rates of homicide directed against nonrelated versus genetically related individuals who come into frequent contact. From the present perspective, we would expect that given similar amounts of contact, homicide rates would be lower among individuals who are genetically related. In fact, a closer analysis of homicide data indicates that the perpetrator is much less likely to be genetically related than nonrelated, such that close friends or spouses commit homicides much more frequently than do blood relatives. For instance, in a well-known study analyzing 550 homicides committed in Philadelphia from 1948 to 1952, Wolfgang (1957) found that 46.4 percent involved either close friends or spouses (28.2 percent and 18.2 percent, respectively), while only 6.5 percent involved *all* relatives other than a spouse.

Dominance Hierarchies

A second mechanism that serves to control aggression within a species is a well-established and stable dominance hierarchy (Wilson 1975). The existence of a dominance hierarchy reduces the need for agonistic interactions because it allows individuals to predict the outcome of such encounters from past experiences. A number of studies have found that aggressive interactions are high while dominance hierarchies are being formed or with the introduction of a new group member to an established hierarchy. For instance, Southwick (1969) has observed that, with the introduction of a new member to a troop of rhesus monkeys, aggression directed against the newcomer is invariably quick to follow and is most likely to come from troop members who are either at or near that individual's eventual place in the dominance hierarchy. Along these same lines, Bernstein (1970) has reported that when a group of previously unacquainted rhesus monkeys are put together, fighting is frequent at first, yet diminishes within a day or two with the emergence of a fairly clear dominance hierarchy.

Although we are unaware of any direct data on this issue, we can offer three predictions within the domain of criminal behavior. We would expect that violence in prison populations is highest (1) when a new individual is first introduced, (2) when a new unit is being opened, and (3) between individuals roughly equivalent in the dominance order.

Considering the present line of reasoning, cities have an additional strike against them. Since individuals are likely to come into contact with many others with whom they are unacquainted and with whom they have not established relative dominance ranking, that potential inhibitor of aggression is unable to operate effectively.

Conclusion

We have suggested that an understanding of principles emerging from current evolutionary theory can be fruitful in understanding criminal behavior. In addition to suggesting how certain individual differences that were functional to our ancestors could predispose one toward exploitive strategies, the current perspective suggests particular ecological factors that would be expected to increase the incidence of criminal behavior. Research was reviewed that is consistent with predictions emerging from this biosocial interactionist position.

The ultimate utility of the present viewpoint must be decided with respect to the standard criteria for evaluation of scientific theories. We believe that the viewpoint we have presented here fares well with regard to parsimony, comprehensiveness, and heuristic potential. That is, with a small number of principles one can organize much of the existent data from varying theoretical viewpoints, and a wealth of testable hypotheses could flow from this approach. It will of course be useful to apply the strong-inference approach (Platt 1962) to the testing of such hypotheses, pitting them against the predictions of alternative viewpoints. An excellent example of such an approach can be found in Lenington's (as yet untested) predictions about child abuse, which allow for discrimination between sociobiological and sociocultural explanations. Of crucial importance at the present time is a consideration of how cultural factors interact with organismic variables, and some interesting theoretical efforts along these lines have been made by a number of writers (see Lumsden and Wilson 1981).

In addition to the traditional value considerations normally applied to a theory by philosophers of science (such as comprehensiveness and parsimony), it is appropriate to consider the social implications of adopting an evolutionary viewpoint. The present perspective, unlike a noninteractive genetic-determinist view, would not place as much emphasis on individual-based medical-model interventions designed to, say, reduce testosterone levels in aggressive criminals or raise the autonomic arousal levels of psychopaths. Although we agree that such individual differences play a role in the etiology of criminal behavior, they may have already done most of their work once an individual comes to be in trouble with the law. That is, such predispositions play their role developmentally, in producing different learning experiences and responses to socialization—not in eliciting some automatic criminal fixed action pattern. Although awareness of such individual differences may have utility in assigning differential treatment strategies, we think large-scale preventive interventions aimed at the major ecological factors could be at least as fruitful in the long run.

In direct contradiction to some of the critics of sociobiological theory, we believe the present perspective mandates anything but a laissez-faire social-Darwinist approach. Given that the human organism is biased toward xenophobic exploitation of outgroup members, and that this bias is intensified by resource scarcity and increasing group size, we believe that large-scale cultural-intervention programs are needed to prevent further increases in crime rates. Of primary importance are measures designed to alleviate resource scarcity and to turn back population increases.

In sum, we do not feel that an evolutionary-based theory necessarily supports conservative ideology or neglect of the environment in dealing with criminal behavior, but agree with E.O. Wilson (1976) that "Whatever direction we choose to take in the future, social progress can only be enhanced, not impeded, by the deeper investigation of the genetic constraints of human nature. . . ." (p. 190)

Acknowledgments

The authors wish to thank John Alcock, Peter R. Killeen, John W. Reich, Melanie R. Trost, and Stephen G. West for comments on an earlier draft of this manuscript.

Notes

1. Although it was fashionable for some time following Mischel's 1968 work to disregard traits as nonexistent constructions of the perceiver, recent empirical developments (Kenrick and Stringfield 1980; Kenrick and Braver 1982) and reviews of the relevant literature (Hogan, DeSoto, and Solano 1977) have supported the viability of the trait construct.

2. Along these lines, it should be noted that mesomorphic body build has been found to occur much more frequently than would be expected by chance in criminal and delinquent populations (Cortes and Gatt 1972; Glueck and Glueck 1956). To suggest that such muscular individuals become involved in aggressive behaviors because they were more likely to be reinforced for doing so in social contexts does not disfavor a biological view, but is precisely in line with the interactionist view taken here. Genes do not act in a vacuum, but genetic tendencies are perpetuated when they result in behaviors that are functional, given the ecological realities of the ancestors of the gene carrier.

3. Mintz (1946) reanalyzed Hovland and Sears's (1940) data and reduced the correlations between total lynchings and the Ayres index of economic activity from $-.62$ to $-.34$.

References

Baer, D., and McEachron, D.L. A review of selected sociobiological principles: Application to hominid evolution I. The development of group social structure. *Journal of Social Biological Structures*, 1982, *5*, 69-90.

Barash, D.P. *Sociobiology and behavior*. New York: Elsevier, 1977.

Bartol, C.R. *Criminal Behavior*. Englewood Cliffs, N.J.: Prentice-Hall, 1980.

Basham, R. *Urban anthropology*. Palo Alto, Calif.: Mayfield, 1978.

Beeman, E.A. The effect of male hormone on aggressive behavior in mice. *Physiological Zoology*, 1947, *20*, 393-405.

Bernstein, I.S. The integration of rhesus monkeys introduced to a group. *Folia Primatologica, 2*, 1964, 50-64.

——— . Introductory techniques in the formation of pigtail monkey troops. *Folia Primatologica*, 1969, *10*, 1-19.

——— . Primate status hierarchies. In L.A. Rosenblum, ed., *Primate behavior*. New York: Academic Press, 1970.

Bernstein, I.S.; Gordon, T.P.; and Rose, R.M. Factors influencing the expression of aggression during introductions to rhesus monkey groups. In R.L. Holloway, ed., *Primate aggression, territoriality, and xenophobia*. New York: Academic Press, 1974.

Booth, A.; Welch, S.; and Johnson, D.R. Crowding and urban crime rates. *Urban Affairs Quarterly*, 1976, *11*, 291-307.

Broom, L., and Selznick, P. *Sociology: A text with adopted readings*. New York: Harper and Row, 1957.

Cadoret, R.J. Psychopathology in adopted-away offspring of biological parents with antisocial behavior. *Archives of General Psychiatry*, 1978, *35*, 2, 176-184.

Calhoun, J.B. Population density and social pathology. *Scientific American*, 1962, *206*, 139-148.

Caplan, A.L. *The sociobiology debate*. New York: Harper and Row, 1978.

Chagnon, N.A. *Yanomamo: The fierce people*. New York: Holt, Rinehart and Winston, 1977.

Christiansen, K.O. A preliminary study of criminality among twins. In S.A. Mednick and K.O. Christiansen, eds., *Biosocial Bases of Criminal Behavior*. New York: Gardner Press, 1977.

Clark, R. *Crime in America*. New York: Simon and Schuster, 1970.

Cleckley, H. *The mask of sanity*, 5th ed. St. Louis: Mosby, 1976.

Clinard, M.B. *Sociology of deviant behavior*. New York: Holt, Rinehart and Winston, 1968.

Cloward, R., and Ohlin, L.E. *Delinquency and opportunity: A theory of delinquent gangs*. Glencoe, Ill.: Free Press, 1960.

Cohen, A. *Delinquent boys*. Glencoe, Ill.: Free Press, 1955.

Cortes, J.B., and Gatt, F.M. *Delinquency and crime: A biopsychosocial approach.* New York: Seminar Press, 1972.

Crowe, R.R. An adoption study of antisocial personality. *Archives of General Psychiatry*, 1974, *31*, 785-791.

Dalgard, O.S., and Kringlen, E. Norwegian Twin Study of Criminality. *British Journal of Criminology*, 1976, *16*, 213-232.

Davison, G.C., and Neale, J.M. *Abnormal psychology*, 3rd ed. New York: John Wiley and Son, 1982.

Dawkins, R. *The selfish gene.* Oxford: Oxford University Press, 1976.

DeFries, J.C., and McClearn, G.E. Social dominance and Darwinian fitness in the laboratory mouse. *American Naturalist*, 1970, *104*, 408-411.

———. Behavioral genetics and the fine structure of mouse populations: A study in microevolution. In T. Dobzhansky, M.K. Hecht, and W.C. Steere, eds., *Evolutionary Biology*, vol. 5. New York: Appleton-Century-Crofts, 1972.

Dittes, W.P.J. The sociology of population density and age-sex distribution in the toque monkey. *Behaviour*, 1977, *63*, 281.

Eibl-Eibesfeldt, I. *Ethology: The biology of behavior.* New York: Holt, Rinehart and Winston, 1975.

Fiennes, R. *The order of wolves.* New York: Bobbs-Merrill, 1976.

Fischer, C.S. *The urban experience.* New York: Harcourt, Brace, Jovanovich, 1976, 95-96.

Forde, R.A. Twin studies, inheritance, and criminality: A criticism of Dalgard and Kringlen. *British Journal of Criminology*, 1978, *18*, 71-74.

Freedman, J. *Crowding and behavior.* New York: Viking, 1975.

Freedman, J.L.; Heshka, S.; and Levy, A. Population density and pathology: Is there a relationship? *Journal of Experimental Social Psychology*, 1975, *11*, 539-552.

Galle, O.R.; Gove, W.R.; and McPherson, J.M. Population density and pathology: What are the relations for men. *Science*, 1972, *176*, 23-30.

Galle, O.R.; McCarthy, J.; and Zimmern, W. Population density, social structure, and interpersonal violence: An intermetropolitan test of competing models. Paper presented at the American Psychological Association Meetings, Montreal, 1973.

Gil, D.G. *Violence against children: Physical child abuse in the U.S.* Cambridge, Mass.: Harvard University Press, 1970.

Glueck, S., and Glueck, E. *Physique and delinquency.* New York: Harper and Row, 1956.

Hamilton, W.D. The genetical evolution of social behavior. *Journal of Theoretical Biology*, 1964, *7*, 1-52.

Hirschi, T. *Causes of delinquency.* Berkeley: University of California Press, 1969.

Hogan, R., Desoto, C.B., and Solano, C. Traits, tests, and personality research. *American Psychologist*, 1977, *32*, 255-264.

Hovland, C.J., and Sears, R.R. Minor studies in aggression: VI correlation of lynchings with economic indices. *Journal of Psychology*, 1945, *9*, 301-310.

Hutchings, B., and Mednick, S.A. Registered criminality in adoptive and biological adoptees. In S.A. Mednick et al., eds., *Genetics, environment, and psychopathology*. Amsterdam: North Holland/American Elsevier, 1974.

———. Criminality in adoptees and their adoptive and biological parents: A pilot study. In S.A. Mednick and K.O. Christensen, eds., *Biosocial bases of criminal behavior*. New York: Gardner Press, 1977.

Kenrick, D.T., and Braver, S.L. Personality: Idiographic and nomothetic: A rejoinder. *Psychological Review*, 1982, *89*, 182-186.

Kenrick, D.T., and Stringfield, D.O. Personality traits and the eye of the beholder: Crossing some traditional philosophical boundaries in the search for consistency in all of the people. *Psychological Review*, 1980, *87*, 88-104.

Kranz, H. *Lebensschicksale Kriminellen Zwillinge*. Berlin: Julius Springer, 1936.

Kreuz, L.E., and Rose, R.M. Assessment of aggressive behavior and plasma testosterone in a young criminal population. *Psychosomatic Medicine*, 1972, *34*, 321-332.

Kruuk, M. *The spotted hyena*. Chicago: University of Chicago Press, 1972.

Lancaster, J.B. *Primate behavior and the emergence of human culture*. New York: Holt, Rinehart and Winston, 1975.

Lange, J. *Verbrechen als Schisksal*. Liepzig: George Thieme, 1929. English edition, London: Unwin Brothers, 1931.

Legras, A.M. *Psychese en criminaliteit bij Twellingen*. Utrecht: Kemink en Zoon N.V., 1932.

Lenington, S. Child abuse: The limits of sociobiology. *Ethology and Sociobiology*. 1981, *2*, 17-29.

Leyhausen, P. The communal organization of solitary mammals. *Symposia of the Zoological Society of London*, 1965, *14*, 244-263.

Lorenz, K.Z. *On aggression*. New York: Harcourt, Brace and World, 1963.

Lumsden, C.J., and Wilson, E.D. *Genes, mind, and culture: The coevolutionary process*. Cambridge, Mass.: Harvard University Press, 1981.

Maslow, A.M. *Motivation and personality*. New York: Harper and Row, 1954.

Maynard-Smith, J. *On evolution*. Edinburgh: Edinburgh University Press, 1972.

McEachron, D.L., and Baer, D. A review of selected sociobiological principles: Application to hominid evolution II. The effects of intergroup conflict. *Journal of Social Biological Structures*, 1982, *5*, 121-139.

Miller, W. Lower class culture as a generating milieu of gang delinquency. *Journal of Social Issues*, 1958, *14*, 5-19.

Mintz, A. A re-examination of correlations between lynchings and economic indices. *Journal of Abnormal and Social Psychology*, 1946, *41*, 154-160.

Mischel, W. *Personality and assessment*. New York: John Wiley and Sons, 1968.

Murphy, R.F. Intergroup hostility and social cohesion. *American Anthropologist*, 1957, *59*, 1018-1035.

Neel, J.V. Some aspects of differential fertility in two American Indian Tribes. *Proceedings*, VII International Congress of Anthropological and Ethnological Sciences, vol. 1. Tokyo: Science Council of Japan, 1969.

_____ . Lessons from a "primitive" people: Do recent data concerning South American Indians have relevance to problems of highly civilized communities? *Science*, 1970, *170*, 815-822.

Packer, C. Inter-troop transfer and inbreeding avoidance in Papio Anubis. *Animal Behavior*, 1979, *27*, 1-36.

Pfeiffer, J.E. *The emergence of man*. New York: Harper and Row, 1972.

Platt, J.R. Strong inference. *Science*, 1962.

Quinney, R. *Criminology*. Boston: Little, Brown, 1979, 225.

Raper, A.G. *The tragedy of lynching*. Chapel Hill: University of North Carolina Press, 1933.

Rose, R.M.; Gordon, T.P.; and Bernstein, I.S. Plasma testosterone levels in the male rhesus: Influences of sexual and social stimuli. *Science*, 1972, *178*, 643-645.

Rose, R.M.; Holaday, I.W.; and Bernstein, I.S. Plasma testosterone, dominance rank and aggressive behavior in male rhesus monkeys. *Nature*, 1971, *231*, 366-368.

Sadalla, E.K. Population size, structural differentiation, and human behavior. *Environment and Behavior*, 10, 2, 1978.

Schaller, G.B. *The serengeti lion: A study of predator-prey relations*. Chicago: University of Chicago Press, 1972.

Schmitt, R.C. Density, delinquency, and crime in Honolulu. *Sociology and Social Research*, 1957, *41*, 274-276.

Shafer, S. *Introduction to criminology*. Reston, Va.: Reston Publishing Company, 1976.

Shaw, C.R., and Mackay, H.D. Social factors in juvenile delinquency. *National Commission on Law Observance and Enforcement: Report on the Causes of Crime*, vol. II. Washington, D.C.: U.S. Government Printing Office, 1931.

Southwick, C.H. Aggressive behavior of rhesus monkeys in natural and captive groups. In S. Garattini and E. Sigg, eds., *Aggressive behavior*. Amsterdam: Excerpta Medica, 1969.

Stichor, D.; Decker, D.L.; and O'Brien, R.M. Population density and criminal victimization: Some unexpelled findings in central cities. *Criminology*, 1979, *17*, 184-193.

Stumpfl, F. Die ursprunge des verbrechens. Dargestllt am levenslauf von zwillingen. Leipzig: Georg Thieme, 1936.

Sugiyama, Y. Social organization of hanuman langurs. In S. Altmann, ed., *Social communication among primates*. Chicago: University of Chicago Press, 1967.

Thomas, D.S. *Crime and the business cycle*. New York: Knopf, 1927.

Toch, H., ed. *Psychology of crime and criminal justice*. New York: Holt, Rinehart and Winston, 1979.

Tokuda, A., and Jensen, G.D. Determinants of dominance hierarchies in a captive group of pigtail monkeys (Macaca nemestrina). *Primates*, 1969, *10*, 227-236.

Trivers, R.L. The evolution of reciprocal altruism. *Quarterly Review of Biology*, 1971, *46*, 35-57.

———. Parental investment and sexual selection. In B. Campbell, ed., *Sexual selection and the descent of man*. Chicago: Aldine, 1972.

Wallace, R.A. *The ecology and evolution of animal behavior*, 2nd ed. Santa Monica, Calif.: Goodyear, 1979.

Warren, M.Q., and Hindelang, M.J. Current explanations of offender behavior. In H. Toch, ed., *Psychology of crime and criminal justice*. New York: Holt, Rinehart and Winston, 1979.

Washburn, S.L., and Lancaster, C.S. The evolution of hunting. In C.L. Brave and J. Metress, eds., *Man in evolutionary perspective*. New York: John Wiley and Sons, 1973.

Watson, A., and Moss, R. Spacing as affected by territorial behavior, habitat, and nutrition in red grouse (Lagopus I. Scoticus). In A.H. Esser, ed., *Behavior and environment: The use of space by animals and men*. New York: Plenum Press, 1971.

Wilks, J.A. Ecological correlates of crime and delinquency in the Presidents' Commission on Law Enforcement and Administration of Justice. *Crime and its impact: An assessment*. Washington, D.C.: U.S Government Printing Office, 1967, 138-156.

Williams, G.C. Natural selection, the costs of reproduction and a refinement of Lack's principle. *American Naturalist*, 1966, *100*, 687-690.

Wilson, E.O. *The insect societies*. Cambridge, Mass.: Belknap Press, Harvard University Press, 1971.

———. *Sociobiology: The new synthesis*. Cambridge, Mass.: Harvard University Press, 1975.

———. Academic vigilantism and the political significance of sociobiology. *Bioscience*, 1976, *26*, 187-190.

———. *On human nature*. Cambridge, Mass.: Harvard University Press, 1978.

Wolfgang, M.E. Victim-precipitated criminal homicide. *Journal of Criminal Law, Criminology, and Police Science*, 1957, *48*, 1-11.
_____ . Urban crime. In J.Q. Wilson, ed., *The metropolitan enigma.* Garden City, N.Y.: Doubleday Anchor, 1970.
Yoshimasu, S. Criminal life curves of monozygotic twin-pairs. *Acta Criminologiae et Medicinae Legalis.* Japanica, 1965.

10 Violence in Every Soul?

Stanton E. Samenow

In the 1960s the United States was swept by violent student demonstrations; the burning, looting, and destruction of cities; and the assassination of three national leaders, including a president. In the 1970s there was a wave of kidnappings, skyjackings, and other forms of terrorism. By the early 1980s, except for the economy, crime was reported to be the issue most on the minds of Americans. National alarm over violent crime had resulted in a plethora of crime-prevention programs, increased security measures, reexamination of laws and national policy, and reflection on the nature of American society.

Twenty-two years ago, at age 55, Dr. Samuel Yochelson left his private practice of psychiatry in Buffalo and joined the staff of Saint Elizabeths Hospital in Washington, D.C., as a researcher with the dual aim of understanding psychological and sociological factors that give rise to crime and developing procedures to alter criminal behavior. In 1961 he began to study men who had been declared not guilty of a crime by reason of insanity. During the course of this project, the sample was broadened to include criminals who never were patients in the hospital but were referred to Yochelson by the courts or community agencies. I joined him early in 1970. The criminals we studied included men from poor families and from affluent ones, from broken homes and from stable two-parent homes, blacks and whites, grade-school dropouts and college graduates, and criminals from a variety of religious backgrounds.

Our investigation began as a study in causation. Despite Yochelson's eclectic techniques, his conceptual framework was largely psychoanalytic. He promised all participants privileged communication and informed them that because he was not part of the hospital's forensic division, he would play no role in administrative decisions about their privileges or release. In the early days, he not only spent more than thirty hours gathering histories from participants in the study, but he also began treating them individually and in groups. Yochelson spent literally hundreds of hours with these men, probing their early experiences, fantasies, psychosexual development, and conflicts. The patients were generally cooperative and rapidly developed insight. A puzzling phenomenon occurred, however. After a while, as this copious material seemed to dry up, the men asked for less intensive therapy and asserted that they understood themselves and were ready for release. At the same time, Yochelson started to learn that his patients, for all their in-

243

sights, really had not changed. He found that they were violating hospital rules, stealing from hospital supplies, using drugs and alcohol, and committing a variety of other offenses. His long-term effort at intensive treatment had produced criminals with insight rather than without insight. Therapy had become a criminal enterprise; the criminal used insights from therapy to excuse further violations. If he did not have enough excuses for crime before exposure to psychiatry, he certainly had more than enough afterward.

Nevertheless, after spending hundreds of hours with these men, Yochelson had learned a great deal despite his failure to produce change. He found that his patients, rather than being victims of their environment or of intrapsychic conflicts resulting from early trauma, had made a series of choices early in life. In most cases they had chosen a different path from that of siblings or peers. (Even among deprived and unstable families of the slums, most members had not become criminals.) The criminals as youngsters had rejected their families, their schools, and other responsible forces in their lives long before being rejected by them. They viewed people who lived responsibly as "square," by which they meant stupid. They sought excitement by doing the forbidden. No single factor or combination of factors that emerged in studying them could account for why they had chosen a criminal path. Yochelson's persistence in looking for causes resulted in no satisfactory explanations and, to his surprise, impeded the process of change.

Once Yochelson stopped searching for causation, new vistas opened up. No longer did he place much credence in criminals' self-serving stories about their pasts. Furthermore, he was not interested in their feelings, which they used to justify anything. As Yochelson adopted a firmer approach, closing off the alleys into which his patients tried to divert him, more material emerged. They described how they had sought admission to a psychiatric hospital to beat a serious charge. Their objective had been to convince the examining doctor and the court that they were mentally ill and, once in the hospital, to persuade the staff that they had recovered sufficiently to be released. Most were successful in these endeavors. Not one criminal in our study was mentally ill, unless one drastically distorts the definition of mental illness. The criminal is in control of his behavior, deliberate in his choices, and very much in contact with reality.

Having eliminated sociological and psychological excuses, Yochelson turned to an examination of thinking patterns. He expected to find a very different profile among people who had committed different types of crimes; he thought that the personality of the street criminal would differ from that of the so-called white-collar criminal. Among participants in our study, a broad range of crime was represented, so we had an opportunity to study offenders of different types. As Yochelson carefully examined the *thinking patterns* of criminals, he was surprised to find very few differences between the different types of offenders. In dealing with a rapist, he discovered that although rape had been the only crime for which the offender had been caught, he had also committed property crimes, other sex crimes, and crimes of violence. Yochelson found that the thinking patterns of the rapist were the same as those of the embezzler and the mugger.

It was true that criminals in the study had different tastes and preferences in crime and different modes of operation. Criminals who characteristically used force looked down on the con men as being weak. The con men were contemptuous of those who used muscle, regarding them as crude. All had been liars from an early age, however. All considered themselves unique and superior to others. All had sought power and control through doing the forbidden. If they achieved a legitimate station of power, they did so by exploiting others and then misused the power. All were totally unfamiliar with how to make responsible decisions. They prejudged situations, failed to fact-find, and did not consider the effect of their actions on others. We found fifty-two thinking patterns that all criminals shared. They were not born with these but, from a very early age, developed them to fulfill their chosen objectives.

Violence is the focus in this chapter, though not that of the seventeen-year study. Criminals arrested for nonviolent crimes in many instances had been violent. They had destroyed property and been in fights, and some had committed serious assaults, but they had never been apprehended. Others had no history of violence, mainly because they were afraid of being hurt. Violence was habitually present in their thinking as a means for dealing with any adversary, however. A person cannot be arrested for his thinking—perhaps a good thing for us all. We found, however, that thoughts about violence in people with long histories of nonviolent crimes provide a fertile ground for future violent crime. Often both youngsters and adults referred to me for evaluation after committing a violent act were never before regarded by others as particularly violent.

I define criminality not in terms of crimes committed but rather by the presence of certain thinking patterns. The thinking patterns that Yochelson found to characterize criminals also *to a degree* characterize people who are basically responsible. The key phrase is *to a degree*. Each pattern lies along a continuum characterizing on the one end the person who is responsible and on the other the extreme criminals with whom we have been dealing. There are degrees of irresponsibility in between. Anger is one example. It is considered a universal human emotion. We become angry when we are frustrated and fearful and occasionally vent our anger at our spouses, children, colleagues at work, or others. The question is: What does it take to make us angry? What do we expect of ourselves? What do we expect from other people and from life in general? The criminals in our study experienced anger with such frequency and intensity that they inflicted extensive damage on others. Whether he shows it or not, the criminal is nearly always angry.

How does the criminal view himself? No matter how many serious crimes he has committed, every criminal believes he is a good person. He will acknowledge that he broke the law and, if he is in jail, may say that he is a criminal because society has said he is. His view of himself is, however, that he is a decent person at heart. He likes babies, old people, and animals. He may write poetry, paint, play an instrument, love Bach, and have other laudable interests and talents. He may go to church and believe in God. He may embrace humanitarian causes and give money to a beggar or help an old lady across the street, even en route to a crime. He does not view the world with malice. He just assumes that people are his pawns. He does not consider himself obligated to others; rather, others are indebted to him. He believes he is superior and need not be accountable to anyone. He shrouds himself in secrecy and does whatever he regards as necessary to preserve a self-created image of a powerful, totally self-determining human being. If he is interfered with, he considers himself the victim and decries the injustice. He is intolerant of adversity or any threat to his view of himself.

Although each criminal regards himself as an extraordinary person and looks down on others who live what he considers a mundane and boring existence, he also is fear-ridden. He suffers from neurotic fears, few of which can be traced to an early trauma—fears of heights, water, insects, closed spaces, and the dark. The criminal's fear of illness and pain keeps him away from the doctor until a condition is so debilitating that he is virtually forced to seek professional medical help. Another class of fear is the occupational hazard of crime—injury, death, or arrest.

But the greatest fear is different from any of these. The criminal is hypersensitive. Anything that does not reinforce his unrealistically inflated image of himself is a personal affront. The fear of being totally deflated pervades his life, and he is threatened with being massively put down by any event over which he lacks control. This might be something as innocuous as a bus being late. Anything that fails to provide him with a buildup is a put-down. Even when no personal affront is intended, the criminal responds as though it were a total indictment of himself as a person. Every day his fundamental belief that the world will do his bidding is challenged. If someone disagrees with him over a point in a conversation, he is put down. If his boss rejects a request, he is put down. If his wife or girlfriend refuses him anything, he is put down. Any time a possibility does not become a reality, the criminal is put down.

Although the criminal regards himself as powerful, unique, and superior, he is, as a result of his fearfulness, very vulnerable. Fear can reduce him to a state in which he regards himself as totally worthless. Believing that others share this view, he then considers himself without a future. Yochelson termed this the *zero state* because the criminal's view of himself and of the world is totally bleak. The mere threat of a putdown raises the specter of the zero state. This differs from the neurotic's feelings of inferiority in which an individual regards himself as deficient in particular aspects of his personality. The zero state is an all-encompassing phenomenon.

What is germane to the topic of violence is how the criminal deals with fear. He is intolerant of it and rarely admits that he is afraid. It is a putdown in itself to do that. He may show that he is afraid by avoiding particular situations, and he will say that he is afraid if it is to his advantage to do so. As a youngster, he will say he is afraid in order to avoid something he does not want to do. If he is interviewed by a psychiatrist, he will exaggerate his fears in order to show that he has a mental illness. His usual stance, however, is to convey that he is invincible even when he is intensely afraid. To demonstrate his toughness, for example, he responds to severe punishment as a personal challenge. The criminal does succeed in eliminating fear quickly, at least long enough to do what he wants. He knows that he may get caught, injured, or killed while committing a crime. As he perfects his scheme, however, uncertainty is reduced, and he is no longer afraid. Yochelson termed his control over fear the *cutoff* because it is so sharp and precise.

The criminal's reaction to fear is automatic. In any situation, he cuts it off and acts to gain the upper hand. When put down, he angrily tries to reassert control. He does not show anger if it is expedient to conceal it, but it is present. Of course, fear also gives rise to anger in the responsible person; but the criminal is more vulnerable. Because of his unrealistic view of himself, he is more easily threatened and angered. Anger to achieve control is a way of life. Even as a youngster, the criminal lashes out at people to get his way. The responsible person usually does not react to life's many frustrations and disappointments as though his entire existence is being threatened. The criminal does, and he attempts to reassert the worth of his entire being. If in his view everything is at stake, there is a strong possibility of violence. Thousands of times in his thinking, the criminal has destroyed people who stand in his way.

Eleven-year-old Tom reported the following thoughts as he experienced conflict at home. On one occasion, he balled up his fist and shook it at his mother, with the thought of beating her up. He was deterred by his father's intervention. Tom reported that he was making a paddle in woodshop that he would like to kill his father with by beating him on the side of the head. After a temper tantrum for which he was restricted to his room, Tom stated that he did not know why he had not killed his mother by now because he had thought so many times about doing it: "I wish I had knocked her clear through the wall." He reported thoughts of knocking his parents heads around the room. When angry, he smashed possessions, including his own model airplane and camera.

Tom's habitual way of dealing with the world was to retaliate whenever he was put down. In his thinking, he had killed his parents countless times. In action, up to the age of 11, his violence was limited to property destruction. An assault was just waiting to happen.

The criminal reacts to life's problems in a manner that is different from the responsible person. All of us have our frustrations, fears, disappointments, and resulting anger. The responsible person's objectives are different from the criminal's, as is the way he strives to achieve them. Most people desire a modicum of power but do not injure and exploit others to acquire it. When they obtain power, they try to exercise it constructively. When they are thwarted, they respond differently from the criminal. Their entire estimation of themselves does not plunge to zero, nor do they perceive life as totally meaningless. They learn from failure and strive to overcome adversity. They become angry occasionally, but anger is not a way of life. When the responsible person is angry, his thinking is illogical and he alienates other people. His objective, however, is not to reestablish a position in the world in which he is the number one individual. He may fantasize violent retaliation but is unlikely to express this in his actions. There is violence in every soul in the sense that there is larceny in every soul or lust in every heart. A person may think fleetingly of having an extramarital affair or of cheating on his income tax. The thought is dismissed as quickly as it occurs, however, because it is too risky or is in opposition to the responsible person's values. Unlike the criminal, the responsible person puts himself in the place of others and tries not to injure them. Again, it is a matter of degree. For the hard-core criminals with whom I have worked, violence is pervasive in thought if not in action. Even the slick con man who has strong fears of physical injury thinks frequently about violence. Given the proper circumstances, it is not surprising when these thoughts are translated into action.

I have described some of the cognitive components of violence for which the concept of a *continuum* of thinking patterns is indispensable. Is there a way to change thinking patterns that result in violent behavior and in other crimes?

Yochelson was not satisfied simply to study criminals and describe their thinking. He wanted to develop procedures to help people change their thinking so that career criminals could become responsible citizens. He found that the dimensions of this task are far greater than he had believed at first. The inner man must change. To accomplish this requires eliminating criminal thinking patterns and simultaneously learning and putting into practice new thinking patterns.

When I first meet a criminal, he usually has few options available to him. He has been apprehended for a crime and thus has failed, at least at that time, as a criminal. In my interviewing, I do not ask him a great deal about himself. Instead, I tell him who he is. I control the interview and make a series of statements about how he has lived and how his mind works. During several meetings, I hold up a mirror to the criminal and describe him, without using his language, courting his favors, or being at all abusive. From the beginning I attempt to build self-disgust rather than enhance his self-esteem. (The criminal has had times during which he has been fed up with his life, but these phases have never lasted.) As I present my view of him, I also inform him of what I have to offer—a demanding program that will afford him the opportunity to change to a life he has heretofore held in contempt. I do not accept any of his excuses about why he is the way he is or any of his justifications for what he has done. Choice and will are fundamental concepts in this approach. The criminal has made choices throughout his life. He is now in a position to make a new series of choices. To validate those choices, he must pay the price of living without criminal excitement and must struggle with altogether new problems. Enduring the consequences of the choice to become responsible may best be termed *will*. It is similar in concept to the price the dieter pays as he watches others devour foods he craves and denies himself what he wants. *Will* is comparable to *will power*. Although a criminal may be sincere about wanting to change, he will doubt this decision many times as he learns what his new life entails. Yochelson developed a procedure of phenomenological reporting in which the criminal presents to a group of people like himself his thinking of the previous day without interpretation or editing. These are the raw data of experience. Group members listen to one another's reports, not so much to criticize as to learn and apply what emerges to their own lives. Criminals are eager to be critics but are less willing to apply corrective measures to themselves. It is necessary to introduce corrective concepts and teach criminals a sophisticated set of deterrents to criminal thinking and action.

Of course, talk is cheap; the criminal can feed me what he thinks I want to hear, just as he has done with others. In dealing with him on an intensive basis, however, I can eventually gauge the effectiveness of his participation. I also maintain contact with outside sources, such as wives, girlfriends, and employers. I do not focus on crime alone. Rather, my emphasis is on the errors of thinking that invariably result in crimes. Thus the murderer is subjected to the same procedures as the check forger. Because all criminals share the same thinking patterns, the particular crimes they have committed are irrelevant to the change process. All participants have to learn a new way of life. As they are exposed to corrective concepts, most of which are second nature to responsible youngsters, they respond that the material is foreign. They know nothing about long-range planning, unless it is scheming a big score. They do not know what trust is, except to trust someone not to inform on them. Their concept of injury to others is limited to hitting someone on the head. They have no concept of a love relationship. Thus I function more as an educator than as a therapist. Of course, this program is not embraced by all criminals. Many elect not to participate; they do not want to adhere to the rigors of this program. The others have chosen to change rather than commit suicide or continue a life of crime. Working at Saint Elizabeths Hospital and in the community, the late Dr. Yochelson and I have been effective in helping some hard-core criminals make far-reaching changes. Nearly all these men have committed violent acts or have demonstrated considerable potential for violence.

In conclusion, I want to consider what might be done to prevent crime, both violent and nonviolent. I am familiar with the thinking patterns of the persistent offender, and I believe it should be feasible to identify people who develop these thinking patterns early in life and help them before they become career criminals. Future work is needed in early identification and prevention, much as children with learning disabilities are diagnosed and treated early in their school careers. The type of project I propose will require precautionary measures so that youngsters are not labeled and thereby stigmatized for life. Labels conceal more than they reveal. I hope that in the future, people who share my interest can help educators, parents, and children by counseling them so that much of the heartbreak and injury that lies ahead can be averted.

11

An Empirical Assessment of the Value of Utilizing Personality Data in Restitution Outcome Prediction

Kathleen M. Heide

Until recently research ignored personality characteristics of offenders ordered to make restitution.[1] A review of evaluation studies and descriptive accounts of existing restitution programs revealed that virtually no attention was given to identifying the personality or psychological characteristics of offenders who complete restitution obligations satisfactorily.[2]

The decision of program evaluators and planners to limit the identification of offender variables associated with successful completion of restitution to the analysis of demographic and social variables and prior-record data is understandable in light of the assumptions typically made by advocates of restitution. Proponents of restitution and criminal-justice agents responsible for its imposition and enforcement have seemed to assume that most adults will acknowledge responsibility for the consequences of their behavior and will understand the concept of repaying the victim.

These assumptions, however, appear questionable in view of the tenets of several theories of personality development. A number of theories of human development have posited that an individual is able to assume personal accountability for his behavior and to recognize different behavioral ways of dealing with certain situations only when he has reached a certain stage along a continuum of personality growth.

To respond to the need to study the perceptions of offenders and to explore further whether personality characteristics are correlated with successful completion of restitution, convicted offenders and preprosecution participants in restitution programs in three sites in New Mexico were classified by one theory of ego development and by specific personality dimensions.[3] This research, part of a larger study of restitution conducted by the National Evaluation of Adult Restitution Programs (NEARP),[4] was undertaken because it seemed naive to continue to assume that all offenders are equally capable of understanding the restitution concept and of completing restitution successfully when one of the few facts agreed on in the correctional literature is that offenders are not all alike.[5]

NEARP Substudy of Personality Dimensions

This substudy of NEARP classified offenders by interpersonal-maturity level and by behavioral subtype, and by structural and content dimensions of personality, to achieve two broad aims. First, the study was designed to assess whether I-level and specific personality dimensions were related to various indicators of restitution outcome. Second, and more important, the study was designed to determine whether the use of personality data—alone or in combination with demographic, social, and prior-record characteristics of offenders; current offense data; and restitution-related variables—made an appreciable difference in our ability to predict which offenders would succeed in a restitution program. Following the discussion of the rationale for investigating the relationship of different types of personality dimensions to restitution outcome, the findings of the substudy are summarized briefly in preparation for assessing the value of utilizing personality data in restitution outcome prediction.

The Interpersonal Level of Maturity Classification System devised by C. Sullivan, M.Q. Grant, and J.D. Grant is a theoretically derived system that classifies people into one of seven categories according to the complexity of their socioperceptual framework. The assumption is made that all individuals, from infancy through old age, strive to make sense of the external world and over time develop a "relatively consistent set of expectations and attitudes" which becomes for them, "a kind of interpreting and working philosophy of life."[6] The theory is essentially an ego-development theory in which movement across an invariant stage sequence is determined by the resolution of a crucial interpersonal problem at each of the stages. Resolution requires that individuals become increasingly more involved with other persons and social institutions to make greater perceptual discriminations regarding their relationships to themselves and the external environment. All persons do not advance to equal points along the developmental continuum, and few individuals if any reach the ideal of social maturity associated with level 7. Research has established that the range of maturity levels found in an adult offender population is from integration level 2 (I_2) to integration level 5 (I_5).[7]

The examination of the characteristics associated with integration levels 2-5 suggests that individuals do not see things in the same way and do not react similarly across levels of personality development. From I-level theory one would predict that the requirement to pay restitution would not be equally meaningful to all offenders. For the restitution concept to make sense to the offender, it would seem necessary for the offender to perceive the nature of his relationship to the victim, to have some awareness of the victim's needs, and to appreciate the notion of paying back the victim for damages caused by the offender. I-level theory suggests a way to identify offenders who would appear likely to succeed in paying restitution or performing community service and those who would appear likely to fail.

The basis of the notion of restitution is that most adults will acknowledge responsibility for the consequences of their behavior.[8] Individuals for whom personal accountability and responsibility are generally meaningful dimensions are classified as I_4 or higher in the I-level schema. Thus I-level theory would predict that high-maturity offenders—those classified as I_4 or higher—would be more successful in completing their restitutive obligations successfully than would low-maturity offenders (I_3 and lower).

Prediction of success and failure in completing restitutive obligations was not restricted to level of socioperceptual development in the NEARP study. In working with offender populations, Warren found that juvenile delinquents and adult criminals had characteristic ways of behaving in and coping with the external world. These behavioral styles were related to the offender's level of integration or I-level but not exclusively defined by it because there were two or more behavioral styles empirically associated with each theoretically defined level.[9]

From these behavioral descriptions it was possible to predict the subtypes, as well as the I-level groups, that would seem more likely to be successful in a restitution program. Subtypes for whom criminal behavior had some private meaning and was part of a neurotic pattern of coping would appear unlikely to complete restitution obligations. In contrast, subtypes for whom criminal behavior was a means to obtaining pecuniary ends or to demonstrating loyalty to peers, or an atypical emotional response to a crisis situation, would seem more likely to satisfy the restitution demands imposed on them than would offenders whose typical behavioral response to events was self-defeating.

In the process of assessing I-level and behavioral subtype, the relationship between specific personality characteristics and the offender's completion of the restitution sanction was also explored. Inherent in interpersonal-maturity theory are two types of personality characteristics, which can be studied independently of I-level: one type is concerned with structural dimensions and the other is oriented to content dimensions. *Structural dimensions* of personality describe qualitatively different patterns of perception and focus on the ways in which the individual reasons and processes information with respect to himself, others, and his environment. In contrast, *content dimensions* essentially reflect *what* the individual thinks rather than *how* he thinks. In addition, content dimensions may reflect differences in the types of behavioral responses made by individuals whose style of perceiving things may in fact be quite similar. For example, I-level classification is made on the basis of structural aspects of the developing organism. Persons classified at level 3 have a somewhat restricted view of themselves. They focus on self-descriptions at the concrete levels of appearance and behavior. They do not tend to compare themselves with others and do not describe themselves as changing over time or from circumstance to circumstance. These dimensions of complexity of perception, degree of abstraction and qualification, and relationship to change and variation are structural dimensions of personality. In contrast, content dimensions of personality include high and low self-esteem, perception of self as cool and controlling versus easily excitable and victimlike, and self-perception as high or low in delinquency orientation.[10] The structural and content dimensions investigated in this study are diagrammed in figure 11-1.

Structural dimensions that appeared valuable to explore in the context of restitution research included complexity of the offender's thought processes, extent of perceptual differentiations made by the offender, internal or external orientation of thought patterns, internalization of a value system, and accessibility of the offender to change. Complexity may be used to illustrate the reasons that structural dimensions of personality might be hypothesized to relate to successful completion of restitution.

Complexity may be defined as the degree to which offenders are able to perceive and to integrate the relationships between two or more events. Offenders whose perceptual style is complex would seem more likely to succeed in making restitution than those whose way of perceiving is less complex. Understanding the restitution concept would seem to require that the offender integrate the perception of the relationship of self to the victim with the perception of the relationship of the payment of restitution to his behavior in the criminal incident.

The content dimensions examined in this study of the relationship of personality variables to restitution outcome focused on both the offender's perceptions and his typical response patterns. The offender's perceptions were solicited with respect to criminal-justice-related events and other areas of interest. Criminal-justice-related events included the criminal event, processing through the criminal-justice system, sentence or disposition, and supervision. Other content areas of interest included the offender's self-definitions and his perceptions of his family, friends, and relationship to school or work.

The offender's self-concept, his perceptions of others, and his attitudes toward his work and school involvements might not seem on the surface to be related to his performance on restitution. The offender's perceptions in those areas were explored despite their low face validity, however, in light of prior research findings of the correlates of delinquent involvement. Hirschi found, for example, that attachment to teachers, parents, and friends and commitment to school were negatively correlated with delinquency.[11] From control theory, one would predict that perceptions in some

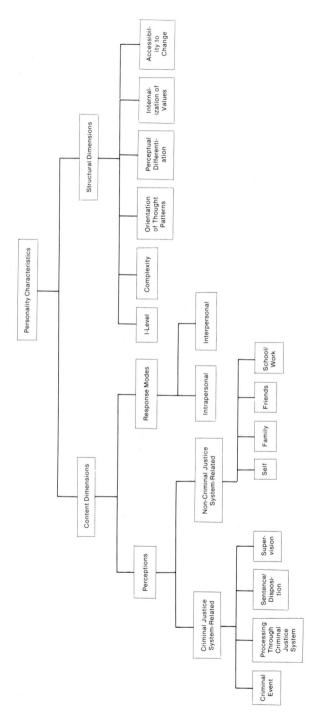

Figure 11-1. Diagram of Personality Components

of these areas might be related more strongly to successful completion of restitution than would perceptions of variables in areas more closely related to the imposition of restitution.

The typical response modes of offenders investigated in this study included both intrapersonal and interpersonal behaviors. A behavioral pattern was considered an *intrapersonal* response mode if the behavior seemed self-contained—that is, if it did not typically require the presence of others to be expressed or if it was not generally emitted in response to others. In contrast, a behavior was designed as *interpersonal* if it typically occurred as a response to others' behavior, tended to be manifested when others were present, or required the existence of others to be expressed. Characteristic response patterns, whether intrapersonal or interpersonal, would appear likely to affect the offender's ability or willingness to complete restitution obligations.

Restitution outcome measures employed in the NEARP study of the relationship of I-level and behavioral subtype, and of structural and content dimensions to fulfillment of restitution outcome, were extensive. They were designed to reflect the payment of financial restitution, fulfillment of community-service obligations, and adherence to payment schedules among convicted and diverted offenders. In addition to measures directly related to restitution payment, other outcome measures consisted of compliance with non-restitution-related conditions of participation in the restitution program and subsequent violations. The use of multiple criterion measures revealed that offenders who satisfactorily completed the restitution conditions measured by one criterion measure were not necessarily the same offenders who succeeded on other performance measures investigated in this study.

Bivariate analysis revealed further that interpersonal-maturity level and specific personality dimensions were significantly related to various measures of restitution outcome among convicted and preprosecution offenders. When the effects of I-level and behavioral subtype were controlled, additional personality variables were found to be related to indicators of restitution outcome among one or both values of the control variable.[12]

The detection of relationships between a large number of personality variables and various indicators of restitution performance suggested the need to conduct a frank assessment of the gains made by using personality data, alone or in combination with demographic, social, prior-record, current-offense, and restitution-related data. Personality data are more difficult to collect than these other kinds of data. Collection of personality data can be expected to increase the cost of processing offenders through the criminal-justice system at least in the short run, because of the use of staff time and other programmatic resources. In addition to increased system costs, the collection of personality data would seem to increase the intrusiveness of the offender's experience with the criminal-justice system.[13]

The offender would be required to provide more information to restitution staff, some of which would seem to be of a more personal nature than the demographic and social kinds of data typically collected. This chapter is designed to provide a preliminary assessment of whether personality data make an appreciable difference in our ability to predict which offenders will succeed in a restitution program and under what types of conditions.

Method

Sample

The subjects used to assess the value of using personality data to predict restitution outcome were participants in a postconviction restitution program in the Second Judicial District of Albuquerque, New Mexico. This restitution program, one of three operated by the New Mexico Restitution Program (NMRP), functioned within the Probation and Parole Department of the District Court. The court has jurisdiction in felony and misdemeanor cases occurring in Bernalillo County, the most densely populated in New Mexico.

Three criteria dictated the selection of participants in the conviction program: imposition of financial restitution, participation in the I-level interview, and availability of follow-up data. Sixty-seven offenders who were ordered by the court to pay financial restitution to the victims of their crimes were given I-level interviews by NMRP staff during the fourteen-month period from March 1979 to May 1980. Although follow-up data were available for sixty of the sixty-seven cases interviewed, in eleven of these cases no determination of restitution payment could be made because of the nature of the restitution order.[14] The comparative assessment of the predictive power of personality variables and that of offender and restitution-related characteristics is limited to the forty-nine cases for whom follow-up data sufficient to provide some indication of payment of restitution obligations were available at the time of the follow-up.

Procedures

Measurement of Restitution Outcome. The assessment of success or failure with respect to restitution outcome was not a straightforward procedure. The amount of time that an offender was monitored was often not extensive enough to see if he completed payment in the manner prescribed.[15] An assessment of restitution outcome was made possible for forty-nine cases by the creation of a composite variable that provided a measure of restitution performance for offenders who were expected to pay restitution monies during the available monitoring frame.

In brief, extensive analysis of outcome data among these forty-nine offenders led to the use of CONFAIL, a variable that combined two measures of outcome. The first performance measure, PERCENT PAID OF EXPECTED, measured the percentage the offender paid of the restitution monies he was expected to pay during the available monitoring frame.[16] Offenders who paid less than 75 percent of the restitution monies expected during the available monitoring frame were considered failures by CONFAIL; those who paid at least 75 percent of the monies expected were defined as successes by this criterion measure. The second performance measure, CONSECUTIVE MISSES, recorded the number of consecutively missed payments by offenders who were scheduled to make payments during the available monitoring frame. Offenders who missed two or more consecutively scheduled payments during the available monitoring frame were identified as failures by CONSECUTIVE MISSES.

The cross-tabulation of PERCENT PAID OF EXPECTED with CONSECUTIVE MISSES revealed that the two variables were strongly related to each other and were essentially designating the same cases as failures (τ B = .71, p < .01; Gamma = .95). The new variable CONFAIL added the four cases who missed consecutive payments, but who paid 75 percent or more of the restitution monies expected, to the nineteen cases who paid less than 75 percent of the restitution monies expected. Thus, as diagrammed in table 11-1, CONFAIL designated twenty-three cases as failures with respect to restitution outcome.

Assessment of Personality Dimensions. The semistructured nature of the I-level interview provided an unusually rich way to gather data on the offender's perceptions of the world and on his behavioral responses to events. In addition to revealing the socioperceptual framework of the offender, the open-ended questions in the I-level interview were designed to provide information on content and structural dimensions of the offender's personality.

The data amassed during these interviews made ratings on over 300 content and structural dimensions of personality possible. After the exclusion of items that were found to be unreliable or to have an unacceptable percentage of missing data in relation to the sample sizes available in this study, 122 personality variables remained for subsequent analysis.

Analysis

The presentation of data relevant to the comparative assessment of the predictive power of personality and nonpersonality variables proceeds in

Table 11-1

Percentage Paid of Expected by Consecutive Misses, Conviction Sample

Percentage Paid of Expected	Consecutive Misses			Row Total
	Yes	No	Not Applicable	
Less than 75%	14[a]	2	3	16
	87.5[b]	12.5	.0	37.2
	77.8[c]	8.0	.0	
	32.6[d]	4.7	.0	
75% and above	4	23	3	27
	14.8	85.2	.0	62.8
	22.2	92.0	.0	
	9.3	53.5	.0	
Column total	18	25	6	43
	41.9	58.1	.0	100.0

Note: Kendall's tau B = .71, $p < .001$; gamma = .95. These cases, though expected to pay restitution monies during the available monitoring frame, were not required to pay restitution in scheduled monthly amounts. Three of the six cases were required to pay the restitution monies due in a lump sum within sixty days and the remainder were allowed to pay by the expiration of their probationary period. The monitoring frames available for these lump-sum and pay-by cases, as those for the schedule cases, were sufficient to assess compliance with restitution obligations.
[a]Number of cases.
[b]Row percentage.
[c]Column percentage.
[d]Total percentage.

four phases. In the first phase, record data are used to describe the sample in terms of demographic, social, prior-record, current-offense, and restitution-related variables. In the second phase, the number of personality variables found to be significantly related to CONFAIL using bivariate analysis is summarized briefly and the relationships of the most strongly related personality variables are discussed. In the third phase, the relationship of *offender* (demographic, social, prior-record, and current-offense) and restitution-related variables to the measure of restitution outcome selected for this analysis is explored using bivariate techniques. In the final phase, the spuriousness of the initial relations of the most strongly related personality variables and restitution outcome is addressed by controlling for the effect of the record variables found to be significantly related to CONFAIL.

Characteristics of the Sample

Offender characteristics and restitution-related data are summarized in tables 11-2 and 11-3. Because of the sample size, each variable was dichotomized in accordance with the distribution of data. The number of

Table 11-2
Frequency and Percentage Distribution of Offenders by Demographic,
Social, Prior-Record, and Current-Offense Variables

	Number	Percentage
Age		
22 or younger	23	48
23 or older	25	52
Sex		
Male	39	80
Female	10	20
Ethnicity		
Non-Hispanic	19	41
Hispanic	27	59
Marital status		
Married	16	33
Not married	33	67
Education		
Less than 12 years	16	33
12 and above	33	67
Work status		
Not full-time	20	43
Full-time	26	57
Prior record		
Yes	26	53
No	23	47
Prior conviction		
Yes	17	35
No	32	65
Current offense type		
Burglary-theft	22	45
Other	27	55
Current sentence type		
Restitution ± Probation	37	76
Restitution + Probation + Other	12	24

cases on which percentages were based varies as a result of the incompleteness of some of the presentence reports.

Inspection of table 11-2 reveals that almost half the adult offenders in this sample were 22 years of age or younger, and 80 percent of them were male. Because of the composition of the New Mexican population, the sample was dichotomized into Hispanic and non-Hispanic categories. As table 11-2 reveals, almost three-fifths of the offenders in this sample were Hispanic. At the time of the study two-thirds of the offenders were not married and had at least a twelfth-grade education. More than half the participants were working full-time when they were ordered to pay restitution.

Table 11-3
Frequency and Percentage Distribution of Offenders
by Restitution-Related Variables

	Number	Percentage
Amount of financial restitution ordered		
Less than $250	18	37
$250 and above	31	63
Amount of restitution expected		
Less than $250	25	51
$250 and above	24	49
Amount per payment period (sch. cases only)		
Less than $40	23	53
More than $40	20	47
Victim type		
Personal victim involved	13	27
Personal victim not involved	35	73
Restitution program structure		
Low	20	36
High	35	64

Although more than half of these offenders had a record of prior arrests, only slightly more than one-third had a record of prior convictions.

Almost half of the offenders ordered to make restitution in this study were convicted of a burglary or theft-related offense. Less than one-quarter of these offenders were ordered to participate in other treatment programs or sentenced to jail, in addition to making financial restitution and being placed on probation.

As depicted in table 11-3, nearly three-quarters of the criminal incidents involved organizational victims only. Although almost two-thirds of the offenders were *ordered* to pay restitution in amounts of $250 and above, less than half were *expected* to pay restitution amounts exceeding $249 during the available monitoring frame. Less than half of the forty-three offenders ordered to pay restitution in monthly installments were scheduled to pay more than $40 per payment period.

Almost two-thirds of the offenders in this substudy were exposed to supervision styles characterized as high with respect to program structure. An offender was considered to have been exposed to high program structure if his probation officer expressed a clear preference for delineation of program rules and expectations, and for their enforcement to the extent possible throughout the period of supervision, for all clients in his case load or for the particular offender. An offender was considered to have been exposed to low program structure if his probation officer was receptive to new ideas and very willing to change his style of supervision to meet the needs of all his clients or of the particular offender under his supervision.

Personality Variables Related to Restitution Outcome

Table 11-4 reports the personality variables found to be related to successful completion of restitution below the .05 level of significance. Bivariate analysis revealed that 20 of the 122 content and structural dimensions examined in this study were significantly related to CONFAIL.[17] Perusal of the table reveals that 12 of these relationships could be categorized as at least moderately strong (tau B $\geq$ .30), and five could be considered to be strong (tau B $\geq$ .40).

The comparative assessment of the gains made using personality data, alone and in combination with offender characteristics and restitution-related variables, proceeded using the five most strongly related personality variables. The relationships detected between these five variables and CONFAIL can be summarized briefly. As one would predict from I-level theory, convicted offenders who paid less than 75 percent of the restitution monies expected of them and/or who missed at least two consecutively scheduled payments were more likely to have been classified earlier as low-maturity subjects. Their perceptions of themselves were typically unrealistic and biased regarding their strengths and weaknesses. Offenders later identified as failures by CONFAIL generally perceived themselves as weak and not in control of their lives. Their behavior not unexpectedly indicated that they had a high need for external structure: as a group, these offenders seemed concerned with identifying power and seemed to function most comfortably when environmental demands were clearly drawn and when others' expectations of them were specified. The data suggested further that CONFAIL failures had little or no need for recognition and acceptance as autonomous human beings.

Comparative Assessment of the Predictive Power
of Personality and Nonpersonality Variables in
Predicting Restitution Outcome

The Relationship of Offender and Restitution-Related Variables to CONFAIL. The relationship of ten offender and five restitution-related variables to restitution outcome was assessed among convicted offenders in this study. Perusal of table 11-5 reveals that one restitution-related variable was found to be significantly related to CONFAIL, and that two offender variables showed tendencies toward relationships with this criterion. Bivariate

Table 11-4
Content and Structural Dimension Items Found to be Significantly Related to CONFAIL

Content Dimensions	Tau B (p)	Gamma
Non-criminal-justice-related perceptions:		
Self		
Unrealistic and biased perception of self	.40 (.00)	.69
Desire to get ahead and make something of self was not salient	.36 (.01)	.64
Source of difficulties or problems was not self	.33 (.01)	.61
Self as sort of person who gets strong feelings about things	− .28 (.03)	− .54
Desire to be a better person was not salient	.27 (.03)	.50
Self as inadequate, incapable, dependent, and irresponsible	.25 (.04)	.49
Life-style was more characteristic of lower class than of middle class	− .24 (.047)	− .46
Intrapersonal-response modes		
Dissatisfaction with self on surface	.36 (.01)	.71
Dissatisfaction with self beneath surface	.29 (.02)	.56
Interpersonal-response modes		
Presentation of self as not strong and in control	.47 (.00)	.77
Behavior was indicative of a high need for external structure	− .47 (.00)	− .77
Behavior indicated little or no need for recognition and acceptance as autonomous	.43 (.00)	.72
Inability to delay response to immediate stimuli	.39 (.00)	.67

Structural Dimensions

		Tau B (p)	Gamma
I-level			
Trichotomized	Tau C =	.28 (.03)	.44
Dichotomized		.42 (.00)	.80
Complexity			
Overall assessment of offender's thought processes as not complex		.34 (.01)	.62
Knowledge of criminal-justice processing as not complex		.34 (.01)	.64
Perceptual differentiation			
Little or no differentiation between categories of friends		.27 (.04)	.50
Accessibility to change			
Inability to perceive self as changing over time		.31 (.02)	.60
Little or no ability to assume new modes of behavior and to find new solutions when the old ones were no longer successful		.27 (.03)	.50

Note: Personality variables have been restated when necessary to accord with designation as a failure by the criterion measure. Thus, the reader need only attend to the magnitude of the association and need not be concerned with directionality.

Table 11-5
Offender and Restitution-Related Variables, by CONFAIL

Offender and Restitution-Related Variables	CONFAIL	
	Tau B	Gamma
Demographic-social		
Age	−.21 (.07)	−.41
Sex	a	
Ethnicity	a	
Marital status	a	
Education	a	
Full-time work	.21 (.08)	.41
Prior record		
Prior arrests	a	
Prior convictions	a	
Current offense		
Sentence	a	
Offense	a	
Restitution-related		
Victim type	a	
Amount FR ordered	a	
Amount FR expected	a	
Scheduled payment amount	a	
Restitution-program structure	− .25 (.04)	− .50

Note: The number of cases on which this assessment was made depended on the availability of data for offender and restitution-related variables reported in tables 11-2 and 11-3.
aProbability exceeded .0999.

analysis revealed that the variable measuring restitution-program structure was weakly related to CONFAIL. Offenders who were exposed to a more structured approach while paying restitution on probation were significantly more likely to fail to pay less than 75 percent of the restitution monies expected and/or to miss consecutively scheduled payments. The two tendencies toward weak relationships detected involved age and work status. Convicted offenders who were at least 23 years of age and who were not working full-time tended to be identified as failures by CONFAIL more than offenders who were younger than them and working full time.

Personality Correlates of CONFAIL within Categories of RESTITUTION PROGRAM STRUCTURE. The relationships of the five personality variables found to be strongly related to CONFAIL were examined within dichotomous categories of the one nonpersonality variable found to be related to this criterion measure to achieve two aims. The analysis tested for the spurious nature of the initial findings by examining these relations within categories of RESTITUTION PROGRAM STRUCTURE. If the relationships of personality variables found to be strongly correlated to CONFAIL persisted when the effect of this restitution-related variable was controlled, the conclusion that the initial relationships detected between personality variables and CONFAIL were genuine would appear warranted. In addition, the analysis looked for interaction effects by examining the initial relations detected within categories of RESTITUTION PROGRAM STRUCTURE.

Table 11-6 presents the zero-order associations and first-order partials for the five personality variables found to be strongly related to CONFAIL, after controlling for the effect of RESTITUTION PROGRAM STRUCTURE. Examination of table 11-6 reveals the nonspurious nature of the initial relations. Although none of the initial relations disappeared completely, interaction effects between the personality variables and values of the control variable were suggested in four of the five initial relations examined. The one personality variable that remained equally strong among both values of RESTITUTION PROGRAM STRUCTURE in affecting designation as a failure by CONFAIL was high need for external structure. Offenders whose behavior reflected a high need for structure were significantly more likely than those whose behavior indicated a low need to fail to pay 75 percent of the restitution monies expected and/or to miss consecutively scheduled payments whether they were exposed to a low or high degree of structure while on probation. Apparently even the more highly structured supervision styles in this study were not structured sufficiently to aid offenders with a high need for external control to meet restitution obligations. Although the differences between the groups were not large, it is interesting to note that, contrary to what would be expected, the relationship between high need for structure and designation as a failure by CONFAIL was slightly stronger among convicted offenders in the high-program-structure group than in the low-program-structure group.

Logically, one would have predicted that those offenders whose behavior suggested a high need for external control would have been more likely to complete restitution obligations if they were exposed to probation officers who set rules and regulations for these offenders to follow and made program demands explicit for them. The reason that these high-need offenders who were exposed to high program structure were no more likely to succeed than those who were exposed to low program structure might have been related to the construction of this personality variable. The further possibility exists that offenders whose behavior suggested a high need for external structure might have varied with respect to their receptivity to structural demands imposed on them by their probation officers. If this were the case, receptivity to the imposition of structural demands by the probation officer might be the more important predictor variable.

Table 11-6
Content and Structural-Dimensions Items Found to be Strongly Related to CONFAIL, before and after Controlling for the Effect of Restitution-Program Structure

Personality Variables[a]	CONFAIL		
		Restitution-Program Structure: Tau B (p) Gamma	
	Zero-Order	Low	High
Content			
Non-criminal-justice-related:			
Self			
Unrealistic perception of self	.40 (.00) G = .69	[b]	.55 (.00) G = 85
Interpersonal			
Self as not strong	.47 (.00) G = .77	[b]	.72 (.00) G = .96
High need for external structure	−.47 (.00) G = −.77	−.45 (.03) G = −.78	−.50 (.01) G = −.80
Little need for recognition as autonomous	.43 (.00) G = .72	.35 (.07) G = .67	.57 (.00) G = .87
Structural			
I-level			
Low maturity	.42 (.00) G = .80	[b]	.54 (.00) G = .89

Note: The zero-order relationship between restitution-program structure and CONFAIL was −.25 (.04), gamma = −.50.

[a]For the reader's convenience, the personality variables have been restated when necessary to accord with designation as a failure by the criterion measure. Thus the reader need only attend to the magnitude of the associations and need not be concerned with directionality.

[b]Probability exceeded .0999.

It is equally plausible to suggest that receptivity to constraints imposed by the probation officer was not the determining factor in affecting outcome. Offenders whose behavior expressed a high need for external structure might not have varied in their receptivity to structural demands made by their probation officers. They may have differed from one another, however, in the extent to which they were exposed to other people or situations that made conflicting demands on them. It does not seem unreasonable to suggest that the demands made by the probation officer in a restitution field setting might have paled in comparison to others made by different people in various situations, particularly when these offenders spent most of their time away from their probation agents.

The strong interaction effects detected among the other four personality variables related to CONFAIL and RESTITUTION PROGRAM STRUCTURE reveal the importance of these personality variables to offenders exposed to high program structure while on probation. The absence of a relationship between these four personality variables and restitution performance among offenders exposed to supervision styles characterized as low with respect to program structure should not be interpreted as suggesting that these personality dimensions were unimportant for offenders under conditions of low program structure. Since far fewer cases were exposed to supervision styles rated as low with respect to RESTITUTION PROGRAM STRUCTURE than as high with respect to this variable, conclusions about the effect of these personality variables on restitution performance for offenders exposed to low program structure would appear ill advised from these data.

Each of the interaction effects detected among offenders exposed to high program structure was in the direction that would be predicted from logic and/or I-level theory. Convicted offenders in the high-program-structure group who perceived themselves in unrealistic ways and who presented themselves as not strong or in control of their lives were significantly more likely to be identified as failures by CONFAIL than were offenders whose self-perceptions were realistic and whose behavior was indicative of control over events in their lives.

The variable indicating the offender's need for acceptance and recognition as autonomous, though showing a tendency toward a moderate relationship with CONFAIL among offenders in the low RESTITUTION PROGRAM STRUCTURE group, emerged as strongly related to this criterion among offenders in the high RESTITUTION PROGRAM STRUCTURE group. Convicted offenders with little or no need for recognition and acceptance as autonomous were significantly more likely to fail in a high-structure program than were offenders whose behavior reflected a need to be recognized and accepted as autonomous.

The last interaction effect to be examined, that between I-level classification and program structure, in affecting restitution outcome is of particular importance. From I-level theory one would predict that low-maturity offenders would be less likely to satisfy restitution obligations than high-maturity offenders under conditions characterized by low program structure—that is, when restitution demands were loose and penalties for noncompliance were not stated.

Table 11-7 presents CONFAIL by I-level classification, controlling for the effect of program structure. Examination of the left-hand side of the table reveals that there was no relationship between I-level and CONFAIL among convicted offenders exposed to supervision styles rated as low with respect to program structure. This finding is not particularly surprising

Table 11-7
CONFAIL by I-Level Classification, Controlling for the Effect
of Restitution-Program Structure

		Restitution-Program Structure			
		Low		High	
CONFAIL		I-Level Maturity		I-Level Maturity	
Failure		Low	High	Low	High
Yes		1[a]	4	9	6
		20.0[b]	80.0	60.0	40.0
		50.0[c]	25.0	90.0	33.3
		5.6[d]	22.0	32.1	21.4
		1	12	1	12
		7.7	9.3	7.7	92.3
		50.0	75.0	10.0	66.7
		5.6	66.7	3.6	42.9
Total	N	2	16	10	18
	%	11.1	88.9	35.7	64.3
		Tau B = .18 (p = .23)		Tau B = .54 (p < .01)	
		G = .50		G = .89	

[a]Number of cases.
[b]Row percentage.
[c]Column percentage.
[d]Total percentage.

in light of the distribution of low- and high-maturity offenders on RESTITUTION PROGRAM STRUCTURE. Since only two low-maturity offenders were exposed to probation styles low with respect to structure, any conclusions about the relationship between I-level classification and CONFAIL among those exposed to low program structure would seem inappropriate from these data.

Perusal of the right-hand side of table 11-7 clearly reveals that nine of the ten low-maturity offenders subjected to supervision styles rated as high on RESTITUTION PROGRAM STRUCTURE were identified as failures by CONFAIL in contrast to six of the eighteen higher-maturity offenders. Low-maturity offenders exposed to high program structure were significantly more likely than high-maturity offenders to fail to pay 75 percent of the restitution monies expected and/or to miss consecutively scheduled payments.

The interaction effects detected suggested that supervision styles characterized as high in program structure were not sufficient to overcome the negative effects of unrealistic self-perceptions and of behavioral styles that evinced little or no need for recognition as autonomous on restitution performance. Even the more highly structured supervision styles did not ensure that low-maturity offenders would be as likely to complete restitutive demands as high maturity offenders under similar programmatic conditions.

Specification of the Relationship between RESTITUTION PROGRAM STRUCTURE and CONFAIL. In addition to testing for the spurious nature of the initial findings relating personality dimensions to CONFAIL, the initial relations of RESTITUTION PROGRAM STRUCTURE and CONFAIL were examined within categories of the most strongly correlated personality variables. The tests for specification were undertaken to clarify the initial relationship detected between supervision style and restitution outcome and to determine if identification of suitable and unsuitable restitution candidates would be enhanced by the inclusion of personality dimensions into the analysis.

Examination of table 11-8 reveals that without exception there was no relationship between type of program structure and CONFAIL among categories of offenders who were rated as possessing the value of the personality dimension hypothesized to be correlated with completion of restitution successfully. As would be predicted by I-level theory, high-maturity offenders were likely to fulfill restitutive demands under conditions of varying program structure. Convicted offenders whose self-perceptions appeared unbiased and those whose presentations of themselves suggested strength and control were as likely to pay restitution under conditions of low program structure as under high program structure. Substudy participants whose behavior suggested a low need for external structure and a high need for autonomy did not perform significantly differently with respect to paying restitution whether exposed to supervision styles characterized as high or low with respect to program structure.

In contrast, perusal of table 11-8 reveals strong interaction effects between restitution-program structure and self-presentation as weak and not in control in affecting CONFAIL. The tests for specification of the initially weak relationship between STRUCTURE and CONFAIL also suggested moderately strong and strong interaction effects between this restitution-related variable and two of the other strongly correlated personality variables—self-perception as unrealistic and low-maturity classification—in affecting CONFAIL. Convicted offenders who presented themselves as weak and not in control of events in their lives were significantly more likely to fail to pay 75 percent of the restitution monies expected and/or to miss consecutively scheduled payments when they were exposed to supervision styles high in structure rather than low. Low-maturity offenders and those whose self-perceptions were unrealistic and unbiased tended to be identified as failures more by CONFAIL when their programmatic experience was characterized by a high degree of structure rather than by a low degree of structure.

The number of cases exposed to low program structure in each of the subgroups for which a significant relationship was found or for which tendencies were discerned suggest that these findings should be treated as tenuous. Five of the nineteen offenders who perceived themselves

Table 11-8
Restitution-Program Structure by CONFAIL, before and after Controlling for the Effects of Personality Variables Found to be Strongly Related to this Criterion, Conviction Sample Only

Criterion Variable, CONFAIL:
Personality Variables Strongly Related to CONFAIL

Restitution-Program Structure: Zero Order	Tau B (p) G	Tau B (p) G Self-Perception		Tau B (p) G Self-Presentation		Tau B (p) G Need/Structure		Tau B (p) G Need/Autonomy		Tau B (p) G I-Level	
		Biased	*Unbiased*	*Weak*	*Strong*	*Low*	*High*	*Low*	*High*	*Low*	*High*
	-.25 (.04) G = -.50	-.37 (.06) G = -.69	a	-.40 (.03) G = -.75	a	a	a	a	a	-.40 (.09) G = -.80	a

[a]Probability exceeded .0999.

unrealistically and five of the twenty-two offenders who presented themselves as weak and not in control were exposed to supervision styles assessed as low in structure. Only two of the twelve low-maturity offenders were exposed to supervision styles assessed as low in structure.

Thus the data suggest that these personality correlates might have been predictive, to some extent, of the way that probation officers would respond to these offenders rather than predictive of the negative effects of high program structure on these offender groups. Probation officers might have imposed more structure on offenders with these personality characteristics in the vain hope that the added demands and constraints might have enabled them to fulfill restitutive obligations. Thus the data should be read as tentatively suggesting that exposure to high program structure did not seem to aid offenders with biased perceptions of themselves and with little control over events in their lives to succeed in paying restitution. Because of the small number of cases exposed to low program structure, conclusions that offenders with these self-perceptions and presentations of themselves would do better with less structured programmatic experiences are not warranted.

The tendency toward a strong relationship between low-maturity classification and designation as a failure by CONFAIL among the level-3 offenders who were exposed to high program structure would not have been predicted. From I-level theory one would predict that level-3 offenders would be more apt to succeed in a restitution program if they were exposed to a high degree of programmatic structure than to a low degree. Although the distribution of the data and the number of low-maturity offenders exposed to low program structure suggest caution in generalizing from these findings, the fact that nine of the ten offenders exposed to supervision styles rated as high in structure were identified as failures by CONFAIL strongly suggests that supervision styles of this type are not sufficient to ensure that low-maturity offenders will succeed in a restitution program.

The disappearance of the initial relation between program structure and CONFAIL within categories of two of the most strongly correlated personality variables—need for structure and need for autonomy—at first appeared puzzling. Contrary to logic, convicted offenders who expressed a high need for structure were no more likely to pay 75 percent of the restitution monies expected and/or to make all payments when exposed to high program structure than to low program structure. Convicted offenders who expressed a low need for recognition and acceptance as autonomous were as likely to be designated as failures by CONFAIL when they had been exposed to supervision styles characterized as high in structure as to those assessed as low in structure.

Inspection of the distribution of cases on these two personality dimensions and RESTITUTION PROGRAM STRUCTURE, however, suggested that these particular needs might have been related to the type of supervision that specific groups of offenders were more likely to receive. For example, thirteen of the eighteen convicted offenders who expressed a low need for external structure were exposed to supervision styles characterized as low with respect to structure, whereas sixteen of the twenty-eight who expressed a high need for external structure were exposed to supervision styles characterized as high with respect to structure. Twelve of the eighteen convicted offenders whose behavior indicated a low need for recognition as autonomous were exposed to high program structure. In contrast, seventeen of the twenty-eight whose behavior reflected a high need for recognition and acceptance as autonomous experienced supervision conditions assessed as low with respect to structure. Thus the data suggest that these personality correlates might have been more predictive of the way that probation officers would respond to particular offenders than predictive of the relationships of program structure to CONFAIL among different personality subgroups.

Summary

This chapter summarized the relationship between content and structural dimensions of personality and one measure of restitution outcome: paying less than 75 percent of the restitution monies expected during the available monitoring payment and/or missing two or more consecutively scheduled payments. The analysis made a preliminary attempt to assess the value of the use of personality data in predicting outcome by comparing the magnitudes of the associations of the personality variables strongly correlated to restitution outcome with the associations of demographic-social, prior-record, current-case, and restitution-related variables. Tests for the spuriousness of the initial relations of the personality variables and restitution outcome were made to assess the genuineness of the initial relationships. Interaction effects noted during the examination of the relationships between personality variables and restitution outcome, after the effect of restitution-program structure was controlled, provided a first step in the identification of the types of offenders most likely to succeed in restitution programs.

The comparison of the magnitudes of the associations of the personality variables found to be most strongly related to restitution outcome with that of the one nonpersonality variable found to be significantly related to CONFAIL revealed that the strengths of the relationships of the predictor variables and the criterion measure were stronger among personality variables. This comparison suggested, at least preliminarily, that personality data were more effective in predicting restitution outcome than were the demographic, social, prior-record, current-offense and restitution-related variables examined in this study.

Tests for the spuriousness of the initial relationships between the most strongly correlated personality variables and CONFAIL, by the one record variable found to be significantly related to the same outcome measure, provided further support for this conclusion. When the effects of RESTITUTION PROGRAM STRUCTURE were controlled, the genuineness of the initial relations between the most strongly correlated personality variables and restitution outcome was demonstrated. The interaction effects that were detected among offenders exposed to supervision styles rated as high on structure were in the direction that would have been predicted. In addition, the interactions detected and the increases in the strength of the relationship between RESTITUTION PROGRAM STRUCTURE and CONFAIL among certain offender groups when personality data were entered into the analysis suggested that the inclusion of personality data could make a difference in identifying good- and poor-risk restitution candidates under varying conditions. Thus the comparison of the magnitudes of the associations between the different types of predictor variables, the persistence of the initial relations involving personality variables, and the tests for specification of the initial relation involving program structure in concert provided additional evidence of the predictive value of the most strongly correlated personality variables to restitution outcome.

To the extent the results found among convicted offenders in New Mexico can be generalized to other populations, these data suggest that if restitution program staff had to choose between the use of personality data or record data in identifying the candidates most likely to succeed on a restitution program in a conviction setting, they would do better to rely on personality data.

Both the test of the spuriousness of the initial personality relations and the tests for specification of the initial relation of program structure to CONFAIL suggested that identification of the most suitable candidates for restitution programs might be made more effective by the use of both types of data. These data suggest that the assessment of personality dimensions might enable practitioners to identify offenders with a better chance of succeeding in certain types of programs.

Introduction of program structure into the analysis of the relation between I-level and CONFAIL, for example, provided support for the value of using ego-development theory in a restitution field setting. The data clearly revealed that, even within groups exposed to highly structured supervision experiences, high-maturity offenders were more likely to succeed than low-maturity offenders. This finding suggests that supervision styles characterized as high in structure may not be sufficient to ensure that low-maturity offenders will succeed in a restitution program. The engineering of more highly structured programmatic experiences than those available in this study seems necessary to assess whether low-maturity offenders are capable of succeeding in restitution programs under any kinds of conditions.

Identification of the conditions under which low-maturity offenders could be expected to succeed in meeting restitution obligations merits attention for more than pragmatic considerations. Ethical issues are also raised by data that suggest that low-maturity offenders are incapable of fulfilling restitution obligations under the current conditions. On the one hand, denying low-maturity offenders the opportunity to make restitution may be challenged as a violation of their right to equal protection of the law. On the other hand, ordering them to fulfill restitutive demands with the knowledge that they probably will be unable to satisfy these obligations may be seen as setting them up for another experience with failure.

In the process of identifying the programmatic conditions under which certain groups of offenders could be helped to succeed in fulfilling restitution obligations, issues related to the external validity of this study's findings could be assessed. The extent to which the findings revealed in this study, with respect to the relationships of both personality variables *and* record variables to restitution outcome, are generalizable to offender populations outside the state of New Mexico needs to be addressed. The composition of the New Mexico population, for example, is known to differ from that of other states, particularly with respect to the percentage of Hispanics and to the distribution of income levels.[18]

Notes

1. *Restitution* is used throughout this chapter in the broad sense of reparation. Thus the concept is intended to include both financial restitution and community-service obligations. Financial restitution involves the payment of monies by an offender to the victim of the offense for losses, damages, or injuries incurred as a result of the criminal incident. Community service involves the rendering of service by an offender to a designated third party, such as a local charity organization or government agency, rather than to a victim directly involved in the crime, as compensation for any harm caused by the offender's behavior. In some cases in which the latter sanction is used, the crime is considered victimless unless the state or community is defined as the victim.

2. Kathleen M. Heide, "Classification of Offenders Ordered to Make Restitution by I-level and by Specific Personality dimensions," Paper delivered at the Fourth National Symposium on Restitution, Minneapolis, Minnesota, September 1980 (Rockville, Md.: National Criminal Justice Reference Service, 1981).

3. Kathleen M. Heide, "Classification of Offenders Ordered to Make Restitution by Interpersonal Maturity Level and by Specific Personality Dimensions," Ph.D. diss., State University of New York at Albany, 1982.

4. This research effort was a substudy of the "National Evaluation of Adult Restitution Programs," supported by Grant no. 76-NI-99-0127 and awarded to the Criminal Justice Research Center, Albany, New York, by the National Institute of Law Enforcement and Criminal Justice, Law Enforcement Assistance Administration (LEAA), U.S. Department of Justice. The evaluation was codirected for the Criminal Justice Research Center by Marguerite Q. Warren and Alan T. Harland, and monitored for LEAA by Phyllis Jo Baunach. Points of view or opinions stated in this chapter are those of the author alone and do not necessarily reflect the official position or policies of the U.S. Department of Justice.

5. Marguerite Q. Warren, "Classification of Offenders as an Aid to Effective Management and Effective Treatment," *Journal of Criminal Law, Criminology and Police Science* 62(1971):239.

6. Clyde Sullivan, Marguerite Q. Grant, and J. Douglas Grant, "The Development of Interpersonal Maturity: Applications to Delinquency," *Psychiatry* 20(1957):373-385.

7. Ibid.; Warren, "Classification of Offenders," p. 239.

8. See Steven Chesney, "The Assessment of Restitution in the Minnesota Probation Services," Summary Report: Minnesota Department of Corrections, pp. 19-22. In a survey undertaken to assess attitudes toward the use of restitution, Chesney reported that 85 percent of the judges and 89 percent of the probation officers interviewed stated that restitution would help to *strengthen* the sense of responsibility in some offenders. These judges and probation officers obviously assumed that the notion of accountability for one's behavior was already a meaningful concept that needed to be strengthened rather than instilled.

9. Warren, "Classification of Offenders," pp. 248-249.

10. Marguerite Q. Warren, "Interpersonal Maturity Level Classification: Juvenile. Diagnosis and Treatment of Low, Middle, and High Maturity Delinquents," California Youth Authority, 1966.

11. Travis Hirschi, *Causes of Delinquency* (Berkeley: University of California Press, 1969).

12. For a detailed review and discussion of the findings, see Heide, "Classification of Offenders by Interpersonal Maturity Level and by Specific Personality Dimensions," chaps. 4 and 5.

13. These projected consequences may be undesirable from the standpoint of the purposes and objectives of some restitution programs. A program designed to benefit the offender may define reduced recidivism and reduced intrusiveness of the offender's experience with the criminal-justice system as the objectives that it should pursue. A program that focuses on

benefiting the criminal-justice system may see the reduction of operating costs as its primary objective. For a more extensive discussion of program purposes and objectives, see National Evaluation of Adult Restitution Programs, "Research Report 5: A Guide to Restitution Programming" (Albany, N.Y.: Criminal Justice Research Center, 1979).

14. The eleven cases were allowed to pay at any time up to the expiration of their probationary period. Since the available monitoring frame was shorter than their probationary periods, no assessment of restitution outcome could be made for these cases.

15. Extensive analysis of outcome data among participants of the conviction sample suggested the use of three measures of restitution performance: a fail-to-pay-restitution composite; a characterization of payment habits; and violations of the conditions of probation. Since the analysis in this chapter concentrates on the fail-to-pay-restitution composite, only its development is discussed.

16. In twenty of the forty-nine cases, the number of months of monitoring available was sufficient to determine if the offender had paid the complete restitution amount within the time frame required by the court. In the remaining cases, existence of a monthly schedule of restitution payments made it possible to calculate the amount that each offender should have paid within the available monitoring frame if he adhered to the schedule of payments imposed on him.

17. The predictor variables were considered to show a tendency toward a relationship with the criterion measure if the probability of the association occurring by chance was at least 5, but less than 10, chances in 100. In addition to the 20 significant relationships detected between personality variables and CONFAIL, 8 tendencies toward significance were also suggested between 8 personality variables and this criterion measure. Only 6 of the 122 relationships examined would have been expected to be significant by chance, given the .05 level of significance selected.

18. The Hispanic population makes up approximately 40 percent of the New Mexican population.

References

Chesney, Steven. The assessment of restitution in the Minnesota Probation Services. Summary report, Minnesota Department of Corrections, 1976.

Heide, Kathleen M. Classification of offenders ordered to make restitution by I-level and by specific personality dimensions. Paper delivered at the Fourth National Symposium on Restitution, Minneapolis, Minnesota, September 1980 (Rockville, Md.: National Criminal Justice Reference Service, 1981).

_____ . Classification of offenders ordered to make restitution by interpersonal maturity level and by specific personality dimensions. Ph.D. diss., State University of New York at Albany, 1982.

National Evaluation of Adult Restitution Programs. Research report 5: A guide to restitution programming. Albany, N.Y.: Criminal Justice Research Center, 1979.

Sullivan, Clyde; Grant, Marguerite Q.; Grant, J. Douglas. The development of interpersonal maturity: Applications to delinquency. *Psychiatry,* 1957, *20,* 373-385.

Warren, Marguerite Q. Interpersonal maturity level classification: Juvenile. Diagnosis and treatment of low, middle, and high maturity delinquents. California Youth Authority, 1966.

_____ . Classification of offenders as an aid to efficient management and effective treatment. *Journal of Criminal Law, Criminology and Police Science,* 1971, *62,* 239-258.

Part II
Moral Development

12 Moral-Development Theory and Practice for Youthful and Adult Offenders

William S. Jennings,
Robert Kilkenny, and
Lawrence Kohlberg

This chapter attempts to provide a comprehensive review of theory, empirical findings, and treatment interventions that relate the role of moral development to delinquency. We begin with an outline of the cognitive-developmental approach to moral development. We assume that growth toward moral maturity involves a series of qualitative changes in how each person understands the sociomoral world. We will present the theory about how these structures or ways of understanding become increasingly complex, inclusive of other people, and adequate to the demands. We will also examine the nature of the relationship between these differences in moral action.

A series of thirteen studies are reviewed that look at the relationships between juvenile delinquency and moral reasoning. Other sociological and psychological theories of the causes of delinquency are discussed with a view toward integrating the best insights of each. Finally, we propose an approach to treatment intervention that reflects what we have learned first hand from theory, research, and practice in this area. We call this the Just Community approach to corrections. Our experiences in applying theory to practice are recounted in an analysis of three delinquency-treatment programs. Included here is a section on specific recommendations for running such programs based on our experience.

Moral-Development Theory

The refinement of moral-development theory based on Piaget's (1932) pioneering insights and Kohlberg's (1958) elaborations has continued to evolve in the last two decades. The development of the scoring system has paralleled a refinement of the stage descriptions.

Stage Development

According to Kohlberg (1976) and Colby and Kohlberg (1981) moral-judgment development focuses on the qualitative form of the moral reasoning and on developmental changes in that reasoning. It attempts to describe general organizational or structural features of moral judgment that can be shown to develop in a regular sequence of stages. The concept of structure implies that a consistent logic or form of reasoning can be abstracted from the content of an individual's responses to a variety of situations. Thus moral development may be defined in terms of the qualitative reorganization of the individual's pattern of thought rather than the learning of new content. Each new reorganization integrates within a broader perspective the insights that were achieved at lower stages. The developing child becomes better able to understand and integrate diverse points of view on a moral-conflict situation and to take more of the relevant situational factors into account. In this sense each stage presupposes the understanding gained at previous stages, and each provides a more adequate way of making and justifying moral judgments. The order in which the stages develop is the same in each individual not because the stages are innate, but because the underlying logic of the sequence is such that each stage subsumes the logical structures of its predecessor.

There are three major levels of moral-judgment development. The first is the *preconventional* level, characteristic of children under age 9-11 and of many adolescent and adult offenders. At this level the moral rules and values of society are understood as "do's" and "don'ts" associated with punishment. [A preconventional person is one for whom rules and social expectations are something external to the self.]

The *conventional level* is the level of the average adolescent and adult in our society and others. He or she understands, accepts, and attempts to uphold the values and rules of society. For a conventional person the self is identified with or has internalized the rules and expectations of others, especially those of authorities.

The *postconventional level* is the level at which customs and social rules are critically examined in terms of universal human rights and duties and universal moral principles. It is characteristic of a minority of adults after age 20. A postconventional person has differentiated his or her self from the rules and expectations of others and defines his values in terms of self-chosen principles.

Within each of the three moral levels there are two stages of moral reasoning. Each is a more advanced and organized form of the general perspective of each major level. There is also a unique social perspective characteristic of each stage. This is a single unifying structure to generate the major structural features of each stage. [Whereas the stage of judgment is characterized by the reasons for prescriptive (ought) judgments, a person's social perspective is characterized by where the person stands in society when he makes an ought judgment.] For example, at the conventional level such reasons as a concern for social approval; a concern about loyalty to persons, group, and authority; and a concern about the welfare of others and society all derive from the social perspective of the individual in a shared relationship with others. Table 12-1 defines the six moral stages in terms of (1) what is right, (2) the reason for upholding the right, and (3) the social perspective behind each stage.

Our analysis of longitudinal data in recent years has revealed that each stage can be broken down further according to the moral orientation of the person's reasoning. Some people orient to (1) the rules and roles of the social moral order or (2) the good and bad welfare consequences. Some orient to (3) relations of equality or reciprocity or (4) the virtue or goodness of a person. The first two orientations are more descriptive and predictive and constitute our type A substage at each stage. This is an orientation to the given rules of the authority. The person at the B substage chooses the action that is more just from the point of the principled stage at each level. It is more autonomous, universalistic, prescriptive, and oriented to the intrinsically moral. As we discuss later, substage B reasoning predicts to more just action in real-life situations (Colby et al., in press).

The Kohlberg longitudinal data show that movement is always from substage A to B. Once B is attained, the person tends to remain at substage B in future development. Those whose reasoning never demonstrates substage B tend to maintain substage A throughout their development.

Stage Justification

Kohlberg (1969) has hypothesized that the developmental levels and stages constitute stages in the strict Piagetian sense. They are universal, they are hierarchical integrations of previous stages, and they constitute structural wholes.

The results of previous studies of moral judgment have not completely supported this strong stage claim. It has not been clear whether the anomalies represent a failure of fit of the strict stage model to moral-judgment development, confusions in the conceptual definitions of the stages, or problems in the validity of the measure.

To address the validity of the stage models, Colby and Kohlberg (1981) have reanalyzed the Kohlberg 1956-1968 data as well as subsequent data collected from the same longitudinal subjects in 1968-1976. This analysis involved the application of the new Standard Issue Scoring System (to be discussed later in this section). Here we briefly summarize the results as they support the Piagetian stage model.

Although many possible stages of moral development may be conceptualized, only one set of stages can be manifested as a longitudinal invariant sequence. We claim that anyone who interviews children about moral

Table 12-1
The Six Moral Stages

Level and Stage	Content of Stage		Social Perspective of Stage
	What Is Right	*Reasons for Doing Right*	
Level I—Preconventional Stage 1—Heteronomous morality	To avoid breaking rules backed by punishment, obedience for its own sake, and avoiding physical damage to persons and property.	Avoidance of punishment and the superior power of authorities.	*Egocentric point of view.* Doesn't consider the interests of others or recognize that they differ from the actor's; doesn't relate two points of view. Actions are considered physically rather than in terms of psychological interests of others. Confusion of authority's perspective with one's own.
Stage 2—Individualism, Instrumental purpose, and exchange	Following rules only when it is to someone's immediate interest; acting to meet one's own interests and needs and letting others do the same. Right is also what's fair, what's an equal exchange, a deal, an agreement.	To serve one's own needs or interests in a world where you have to recognize that other people have their interests, too.	*Concrete individualistic perspective.* Aware that everybody has his own interest to pursue and these conflict, so that right is relative (in the concrete individualistic sense).
Level II—Conventional Stage 3—Mutual interpersonal expectations, relationships, and interpersonal conformity	Living up to what is expected by people close to you or what people generally expect of people in your role as son, brother, friend, etc. "Being good" is important and means having good motives, showing concern about others. It also means keeping mutual relationships, such as trust, loyalty, respect, and gratitude.	The need to be a good person in your own eyes and those of others. Your caring for others. Belief in the Golden Rule. Desire to maintain rules and authority that support stereotypical good behavior.	*Perspective of the individual in relationships with other individuals.* Aware of shared feelings, agreements, and expectations which take primacy over individual interests. Relates points of view through the concrete Golden Rule, putting yourself in the other guy's shoes. Does not yet consider generalized system perspective.

Stage	What is right	Reasons for doing right	Social perspective of stage
Stage 4—Social system and conscience	Fulfilling the actual duties to which you have agreed. Laws are to be upheld except in extreme cases where they conflict with other fixed social duties. Right is also contributing to society, the group, or institution.	To keep the institution going as a whole, to avoid the breakdown in the system "if everyone did it," or the imperative of conscience to meet one's defined obligations (easily confused with stage 3 belief in rules and authority; see text).	*Differentiates societal point of view from interpersonal agreement or motives.* Takes the point of view of the system that defines roles and rules. Considers individual relations in terms of place in the system.
Level III—Post-conventional, or Principled Stage 5—Social contract or utility and individual rights	Being aware that people hold a variety of values and opinions, that most values and rules are relative to your group. These relative rules should usually be upheld, however, in the interest of impartiality and because they are the social contract. Some nonrelative values and rights like *life* and *liberty*, however, must be upheld in any society and regardless of majority opinion.	A sense of obligation to law because of one's social contract to make and abide by laws for the welfare of all and for the protection of all people's rights. A feeling of contractual commitment, freely entered upon, to family, friendship, trust, and work obligations. Concern that laws and duties be based on rational calculation of overall utility, "the greatest good for the greatest number."	*Prior-to-society perspective.* Perspective of a rational individual aware of values and right prior to social attachments and contracts. Integrates perspectives by formal mechanisms of agreement, contract, objective impartiality, and due process. Considers moral and legal points of view; recognizes that they sometimes conflict and finds it difficult to integrate them.
Stage 6—Universal ethical principles	Following self-chosen ethical principles. Particular laws or social agreements are usually valid because they rest on such principles. When laws violate these principles, one acts in accordance with the principle. Principles are universal principles of justice: the equality of human rights and respect for the dignity of human beings as individual persons.	The belief as a rational person in the validity of universal moral principles, and a sense of personal commitment to them.	*Perspective of a moral point of view* from which social arrangements derive. Perspective is that of any rational individual recognizing the nature of morality or the fact that persons are ends in themselves and must be treated as such.

Reprinted with permission from *Moral Development and Behavior: Theory, Research, and Social Issues,* edited by Thomas Lickona. Copyright 1976 by Holt, Rinehart and Winston, CBS Educational and Professional Publishing.

dilemmas and follows them longitudinally in time will come to the three levels or moral judgment and no others.

Kohlberg (1976) argues that the ideas of universal structure used to define the stages are those of real subjects from cultures around the world, not ideas from a psychological theory. It is the logical connections among ideas that define a given stage. The logical analysis of the connections in a child's thinking is itself theoretically neutral.

In addition to being universal, the stage concept implies that under normal environmental conditions developmental change will always be upward in direction. The fact that a later stage includes and presupposes the prior stage is, again, a matter of logical analysis, not psychological theory. Reanalysis of the data using test-retest results supported the notion of upward change with any deviation attributable to measurement error.

In addition to predicting that a subject will never move downward in the developmental sequence, cognitive-developmental theory holds that each stage is a prerequisite for those that follow. This is, the concept of invariant stage sequence implies that no stage will be omitted as development proceeds. In no case on any form of the interview did a subject reach a stage in the sequence without having gone through each preceding stage. For the most part, changes across our four-year longitudinal intervals were less than a full stage.

Finally, the stage concept implies that an individual's thinking will be at a single dominant stage across varying content, although use of the stage adjacent to the dominant stage may also be expected. This claim that a given person's ideas *cohere* in a stagelike way is a matter of logical analysis of internal connections between the various ideas held by the stage. In this respect the great majority of interviews were scored at only one moral-judgment stage or at most two adjacent stages. The *structured-wholeness* assumption was also supported by the high degree of alternative form and test-retest reliability, the high Cronbach's alpha, and the results of factor analyses of issue scores. One indication of degree of internal consistency in moral judgment is provided by distributions for each subject of proportions of reasoning scored at each of the five stages. Our analysis of these distributions showed that most interviews received all their scores either at a single stage or at two adjacent stages. The mean percentage of reasoning at the individual's modal stage was 68 percent from Form A; 72 percent for Form B; 69 percent for Form C; and 67 percent for Forms A, B, and C combined. The mean percentage of reasoning at the subject's two most frequently used stages (always adjacent) was 98 percent for Form A; 97 percent for Form B; 99 percent for Form C; and 97 percent from Forms A, B, and C combined.

Moral-Judgment Assessment

Before discussing the evolution of the Kohlberg scoring methodology, we discuss two other methods based on the Piagetian model. Like the Kohlberg scoring methods, they are used to assess moral-stage development in numerous correctional studies.

Rest (1979) developed the Defining Issues Test (DIT) to eliminate numerous problems he found with the Kohlberg issue-scoring method. He wanted to develop a paper-and-pencil method scorable by computer, thus avoiding the inferential leap a scorer has to make from the interview to the scoring manual. The DIT is thus a questionnaire that presents six moral dilemmas, each followed by numerous statements about the dilemma. The statements conform to stage-related structure and content, and the person's task is to rate the importance of each statement on a scale from *no* importance to *great* importance. When all statements on all six dilemmas receive a rating of importance, the computer can determine one's moral stage. Overall, Rest (1979, pp. 153-158) reports a correlation in the seventies with Kohlberg's issue-scoring method.

With the use of DIT data, Rest disagrees with our claim that development proceeds through a stepwise sequence of internally consistent stages. He holds instead that individuals simultaneously use reasoning of many types and that an adequate description of an individual's moral judgment must include a quantitative account of the proportion of each type rather than a global stage designation for the individual. He interprets our finding of internal consistency as a methodological artifact and points to his own results with the Defining Issues Test as consistent with a more complex model of development.

One interpretation of the discrepancy between Rest's results and our own derives from the fact that the DIT is measuring comprehension and preference of moral judgments made by others, whereas the Standard Issue Scoring System is measuring an individual's spontaneous production of moral judgments in response to very open-ended questions. We suggest that the development of moral judgment as a whole (including comprehension and preference as well as spontaneous production) may be too broad a scope for what Rest calls the "simple stage model." Development of moral-judgment comprehension and preference may not follow a stagelike pattern, but spontaneous production may do so when assessment conditions pull for the subject's competence.

Another consideration is methodological. When subjects endorse an item on the DIT, it is not clear how they understand the item. The Standard Issue Moral Judgment Interview involves probing for elaboration and clarification and pooling all responses to the dilemmas that refer to a single idea (as defined by norm and element). This system naturally leads to greater internal consistency than assigning a score for each unelaborated statement that the scorer judges to have some validity. We do not interpret our finding as an artifact. It is true that according to Standard Issue Scoring rules, an interview cannot receive more than one stage (or stage transition) score for a single dilemma/issue/norm element intersection. Scores at all five stages may be assigned to a single issue, dilemma, or interview, however, if interview/manual matches at those stages occur. In fact, such variance does not occur in our data, even though the nine dilemmas were scored independently and by three different raters. We agree with Rest that moral-judgment comprehension and preference are important aspects of moral development that are separable from spontaneous moral-judgment production and that a full developmental account of an individual's moral judgment requires scores on all those aspects as well as many others. We feel, however, that a careful look at our methods and data should convince the reader of the validity of the Piagetian stage model for describing the development of spontaneous moral judgment, at least within the limits of our instrument and sample.

We believe Rest's method is useful for exploratory examination of the correlates of moral maturity, but not for testing theoretical propositions derived from the cognitive-developmental theory of moral stages. Choice of various methods, then, must weigh facility of data gathering and analysis against relatively error-free tests of structural theory.

Gibbs (Gibbs and Widaman 1982) has developed a second scoring system, the Sociomoral Reflection Measure (SRM), designed to serve as a group-administerable counterpart to the Moral Judgment Interview. It is also based on Kohlberg's stage theory of moral-judgment development. Overall SRM protocol ratings are derived from subject scores on eight sociomoral norms, such as affiliation. The SRM yields two primary types of overall protocol rating: (1) modal stage, which is simply the stage most frequently used by the subject in his or her protocol responses (stage 1, 2, 3, 4); and (2) the Sociomoral Reflection Maturity Score (SRMS), a psychometrically more differentiated rating that extends from 100 to 400.

Previous studies have established high test-retest, parallel-form, interrater, and internal-consistency reliability for the SRM; high concurrent validity of the SRM with the MJI; and high correlations with age and educational level. Where a qualitative stage score of spontaneous reasoning is desired, the Gibbs measure is a compromise between Rest's objective method and the Kohlberg structural method. The correlation between the Gibbs test and the Kohlberg interview is in the fifties. The percentage of agreement within one-third of a stage is 79 percent.

The Kohlberg scoring method has evolved through three procedures: aspect scoring, intuitive issue scoring, and standardized issue scoring. Numerous anomalies occurred using the two earlier methods, which resulted in a reanalysis of Kohlberg's longitudinal data and a subsequent refinement of the scoring methodology (Kohlberg and Kramer 1969; Colby and Kohlberg 1981). The earlier scoring methods were employed in some moral-judgment and delinquency studies, reviewed here, perhaps detracting from a strict comparability of methodology.

With *Aspect Scoring* (Kohlberg 1958) the moral stages were defined in terms of twenty-five aspects, grouped in turn under the following major sets: rules, conscience, welfare of others, self's welfare, sense of duty, role taking, punitive justice, positive justice, and motives. Each higher stage had a more internalized and autonomous idea of moral rules, a greater concern about the welfare of others, a broader conception of fairness, and so on.

Scoring by aspect was done with two methods: sentence scoring and story rating. Sentence scoring used a manual listing prototypical sentences on each aspect in each moral dilemma. Every statement of a subject was scored by aspect and stage: these statements were then converted into percentages, generating a profile of stage usage for each subject. The second method, story rating, involved assigning the subject's total story response to a stage in terms of that stage's overall definition on each aspect. Stage mixtures were handled by intuitively weighting a dominant and a minor stage of response. This method, however, turned out to contain too much extraneous content to yield a measure or classification meeting the invariant-sequence postulate of stage theory. Our aspect scoring was based not on structure, but on certain statistical or probabilistic associations between structure and content.

The *intuitive scoring system* evolved as a more structural scoring system. The first step was to standardize or analyze types of content used at every stage. These types of content, called *issues* or *values*, represent what the individual is valuing, judging, or appealing to rather than his mode of reasoning about that issue. To analyze stage differences, we must first make sure that each stage is reasoning about or from the same values. We had attempted to do this with the aspects; but they were a mixture of formal or structural characteristics of judgment (for example, motives versus consequences and sense of duty) and direct issues or value content (for example, law and rules). Accordingly, we developed the following list of issues, values, or moral institutions found in every society and culture:

1. Laws and rules
2. Conscience
3. Personal roles of affection
4. Authority
5. Civil rights
6. Contract, trust, and justice in exchange
7. Punishment and justice
8. The value of life
9. Property rights and values
10. Truth
11. Sex and sexual love

These new content issues each embody several different moral aspects. For example, thinking about the issue of contract and trust involves formal aspects of altruism, duty, rules, role taking, fairness, and so on.

Our classification of contents in terms of issues also gave rise to a new unit to be rated. This unit is all the ideas a person uses concerning an issue in a story. The old system had rated each idea separately (sentence scoring) or else rated the story as a whole (story rating). The sentence unit had proved too small for structural classification, however, whereas the story unit had proved too large for analytic, as opposed to ideal, typological scoring. Having decided on issues, we then defined stage thinking on each issue and intuitively assigned the person a stage for all his ideas on each issue.

Intuitive issue scoring is reliable (90 percent interrater agreement) in the hands of thoroughly trained or experienced scorers. Reliable intuitive scoring, however, cannot be learned without personal teaching and supervised experience. It also is too intuitive to provide satisfactory test-construction characteristics of item difficulty, item independence, written versus oral interviews, and so on.

We have now developed a manual entitled *Measurement of Moral Judgment: A Manual and Its Results* (Colby et al. in press). This manual is based on a standardized interview that probes only two issues on each of three stories. The standard form, form A, contains three stories covering six issues. It presents criterion concepts defining each stage on each issue for each story. A *criterion concept* is the reasoning pattern that is most distinctive of a given stage. Theoretically, such reasoning follows from the structural definition of the stage. Empirically, the criterion concept is actually used by a substantial number of subjects at that stage (as defined by their global score) and not at other stages.

In our opinion, this standardized scoring system goes as far toward standardization as is possible while maintaining theoretical validity. We define *validity* as true measurement of development—that is, of longitudinal invariant sequence.

A more common notion of test validation is prediction from a test to some criterion external to the test of which the test is presumed to be an indicator, such as moral behavior. From the point of view of cognitive-developmental theory, the relationship of the development of judgment to action is something to be studied and theoretically conceptualized; the issue is not one of validating a judgment test by a quantitative correlation with behavior. We now turn to a more detailed discussion of the relation of judgment and action.

Moral Judgment and Moral Action

Because this is primarily a theory of moral reasoning, one may ask what light it sheds on moral action. There would, of course, be little point to such research were it not for an implicit assumption that there is a relationship between moral judgment and action. Before one can claim to explain even a portion of the causes of juvenile delinquency by using measures of moral judgment, it is important to review briefly the empirical evidence linking judgment with action.

In a comprehensive review of this subject, Blasi (1980) states that there are two prevalent assumptions underlying most research on moral action. The most common approach assumes that the individual possesses a myriad of habits, traits, and tendencies, with strengths varying according to the circumstances. The interaction of these factors, along with inhibitions, objectively determines the behavioral outcome. The goal of research with such a model is to come as close as possible to assigning the correct weights to each of the interacting tendencies. This approach bridges a variety of theories that otherwise have little in common. Such disparate theories as psychoanalysis, learning theory, and sociobiology together assume that moral actions are best understood in light of the interplay of motivational forces with one's perception of a particular situation. Their guiding notions of superego, reinforcement, and survival, respectively, lead to differing interpretations of the origin, nature, and strength of these motivations. Therefore, each theory might point to different salient characteristics of a given situation (danger to self, previous positive experience, and so on) to account for a person's actions. By emphasizing the affective and instinctual motivations for moral action, such theories assume moral behavior to be largely irrational. Instead, it is the almost mathematical interplay of various motivations with perceived circumstances that objectively determines the behavioral outcome.

The role of cognitive processes in these theories is to mediate the complex interplay of motivations, determine the options available, and determine the behavior that most nearly meets the individual's primary goal (species survival, superego demands, likelihood for reward, and so on). Other variations hold that the cognitive processes described as moral reasoning exist but play no functional role in determining moral behavior. A common view among learning theorists, for example, is that cognition determines verbal moral statements, whereas actual moral behavior is due entirely to social learning. Still another view postulates that moral reasoning serves merely as rationalization to allow us to do what we are otherwise inclined to do anyway, or to justify our behavior after the act itself.

In the cognitive-developmental approach, however, these accounts ignore the single most important goal of cognitive processes—to *make meaning and discern truth*. This special dimension of human thinking enables people to transcend the instinctual imperatives of survival and the learned conventions of a particular society in order for each to create his or her own notions of the right and the good. The widely varying content of individual moral values within and between cultures is apparent, so there is undoubtedly a strong interplay between self and environment that affects how each of us sees the moral world. The concept of each person as an autonomous moral philosopher recreating universal moral principles remains an ideal. Any theory of moral action, however, must not be oblivious to this essential human characteristic.

Central to our position is the assumption that moral reasoning mediates moral action. Since common sense tells us that moral action is often not in keeping with reasoning for a particular situation, the question becomes one of how and to what extent they are related.

A fundamental premise of the cognitive-developmental position is that for an act to be considered moral, the intention and reasoning behind that act must be moral in an objective, philosophic sense. There is, of course, an age-old debate in moral philosophy over the objective criteria for judging something moral. Kohlberg's own preferences are elucidated at length elsewhere (Kohlberg 1971). There is, however, a broad consensus among formalist moral philosophers ranging from Kant to Rawls that certain formal features apply to valid moral principles and the resulting rules and laws. These features include: universalizability (they apply to everyone, everywhere in all similar situations); prescriptivity (they state what should actually be done); reversibility (they are equally fair from the point of view of moral questions). It is not enough to act in accordance with these moral criteria; the actor must also be motivated by the moral concerns that underlie the criteria. For example, if a person dives into a river to save a drowning man because he believes it is his duty to save another's life, most people (and philosophers) will agree that it is a moral act. If the same action were taken because the rescuer is hoping to receive a reward or get his picture on the evening news, however, then we would consider the act less than fully moral. In this view, for an act to be moral, it must be based on a will to act that is moral. The difference lies in the actor's reasoning and motivation, not in the results, which in both cases cause a life to be saved. The act itself may be praiseworthy in both cases for its outcome. The reward seeker, however, would seem to be an unreliable moral agent in that the drowning person's fate rests on the rescuer's perception of personal gain, rather than the more dependable moral principle of helping all others in distress—conditioned only on some degree of prudence in deference to self-preservation. In this model, moral judgment is a necessary but not sufficient condition for moral action. In a philosophically ideal view, moral judgment is necessary and sufficient for moral action.

If moral judgment is necessary, what other conditions are required for sufficiency? This question is the least explored and most problematic for moral psychology. It is also the most crucial for anyone contemplating applying theory in practice. In the case of juvenile delinquency, one might ask what benefit will result in attempting to improve moral reasoning if it is not sufficient for moral action. There is no simple or certain answer. We will, however, offer some empirical and theoretical arguments that attempting to improve moral judgment is a reasonable place to begin trying to improve moral behavior.

One justification for the cognitive-developmental approach in this area is that it appears to have broader explanatory power than such widely applied alternatives as behaviorism and social-learning theories. The behavioristic approach, long a favorite in corrections systems, would seem to offer remarkable promise. By means of operant conditioning, one can hope to shape virtually any behavior, moral conduct included. Indeed, B.F. Skinner claimed that he could teach a pigeon to bowl—and then proceeded to do so! Reducing the temptation for a 16-year-old car thief to practice his craft would sound simple by comparison. History has shown, however, that the behaviorist approach to corrections has not fulfilled its promise. One of the glaring weaknesses has been its inability to cause lasting change once the conditions for reinforcement are removed—after release, for example. Ironically, the cause of the weakness is also the reason it is still so widely used in correctional programs; it is very amenable to managing behaviors (as opposed to truly changing them) when the person's total environment can be modified to support the experimental design, and when the power of reinforcement lies exclusively in the hands of the correctional authorities. It is easy to understand why in such settings the more pressing goal is generally to control behavior on an immediate, ad hoc basis. Effecting behavioral change after incarceration often seems an abstract goal to line personnel. There is also the problem of generalizing conditioned learning. The kind of behaviors one might learn in a correctional setting are often not even similar to those required in real-life moral decision-making situations. One's conditioning not to steal the institution's silverware would be unlikely to generalize to not stealing someone's family silver in an affluent suburb. Skinner's bowling pigeon wouldn't even be an intermediate bocci player.

Social-learning theory is vulnerable to similar critiques. In fact, many social-learning experiments proudly demonstrate the reversibility of learned behavior—that is, that learning extinguishes without reinforcement. We can infer that a learned change in a given antisocial behavior can be unlearned when the delinquent reenters his former environment, as is often the case. Moreover, social-learning theories do not even contend that a large part of learning is transformed or generalized to other situations. They do not hold, for example, that socially reinforced learning creates consistent personality traits that we might look for in moral decision making—such as resistance to temptation, prosocial disposition, or strength of conscience.

The application of behavioral and social-learning paradigms to moral action has obvious appeal for some situations. From our theoretical perspective, however, there are several deficiencies. First, although all social-science theories are by nature reductionist, it is an extemely narrow conceptual frame that views moral judgment as irrelevant to subsequent moral action. Second, it defines as moral those behaviors and values that various authorities choose to reinforce by means of operant conditioning and social-learning mechanisms. This form of moral relativism does not even require the utilitarian insistence on maximizing the good. It therefore lacks an objective means for evaluating the inherent moral worthiness of behaviors and values; it is enough that they are socially sanctioned. Third, their own research shows that reinforced learning is not readily generalized to other, more complex situations; that it abates over time without additional reinforcement; and that it does not lead to consistent integrated personality traits that might predispose one to act, if not fully morally, at least benevolently. These approaches do offer insights into how some conforming behaviors may be taught by reinforcement, and cultural values transmitted through social learning. This exclusive emphasis on external or environmental stimuli, however, overlooks the importance of the individual's understanding of the moral world and the resulting meaning and motivation behind a particular action.

By contrast, the cognitive-developmental view assumes that a dialectic exists not only between moral judgment and action, but between all cognition and experience. This interaction between the person and his or her environment, between subject and object, forms the essence of the Piagetian model of learning and development. The point here is that thought and action are intertwined; looking at either one alone, one misses the innate interdependence of the psychological processes leading to moral action. The stimulus-response (S-R) model assumes a relatively passive learner responding reflexively to environmental stimuli. The Piagetian model, on the other hand, stresses *reflectivity* over reflexivity. Thus stimuli are reinforcing only to the extent that they become meaningful to the individual.

In the case of juvenile delinquents, one often finds a structural understanding that it is a dog-eat-dog world in which one must assume that the other guy will use you to his advantage if he thinks he can get away with it. This can lead to association with like-minded peers and to antisocial acts that become self-reinforcing. One's thoughts and actions and the reaction one gets from others are in harmony. In such cases the judgment-action loop can become a vicious cycle. The challenge in intervening here has to go beyond merely modifying a given behavioral manifestation of this way of seeing human relationships. Rather, the goal should be to change the very structural understanding of the moral world that makes the antisocial behaviors a logical and consistent way of coping with the individual's understanding of his own social reality. Here it is less the stimulus or precipitating event that is salient than the way the individual construes his environment and his place in it. This implies the need to alter environments that arrest moral development by making preconventional thinking and even antisocial behavior adaptive.

Our emphasis on moral judgment reflects this belief in the active role of the individual in making personal meaning of events. It goes back to the point about the different moral nature of the reasons to save a drowning person; that is, the moral meaning of an act itself lies in the intention and reasoning of the actor, not in the act alone. The cognitive-developmentalist seeks to alter structures of social and moral cognition that can make delinquent acts at best easier to rationalize and at worst inescapable. We hold, like Piaget, that the development of all forms of cognition is fueled by action, and that this mutually transforming process leads invariantly to more complex and adequate ways of perceiving the moral world. If action leads to more moral reasoning, however, does this reasoning result in more moral action? It is, of course, not a one-to-one relationship. Moral action is mediated in too complex a way for any simplistic notion that mature moral reasoning is the sole antecedent to moral action. Both common sense and a number of studies suggest that other psychological variables play a role. Some of these are attention span, ego strength, degree of impunity, strength of conscience, guilt feelings, perceived responsibility, empathic arousal, nature of the relationship to the person in need, understanding of the moral question, and alternative actions. We can, however, cite empirical evidence that a monotonic pattern exists in which the higher the stage of moral reasoning, the more likely one is to resist temptation, to conform one's actions to one's beliefs, and to act at a philosophically higher moral level.

One can conceptualize the reasoning process leading up to moral action as having two components: (1) a deontic judgment of rightness and (2) a judgment of responsibility. Philosophers like Frankena (1963) use *deontic* to describe judgments of what is morally right or obligatory. In addition to such classical judgments we have the more practical ones of responsibility, which Frankena refers to as *aretaic* judgments of the morally good, bad, responsible, or blameworthy. According to Galen (1981), deontic judgments constitute a first-order appraisal of what is right, whereas responsibility judgments determine the extent to which we feel compelled willfully to act on our first-order deontic judgment. Responsibility judgments not only tell us why a deontic judgment is right in a given situation, but also become important as we examine the judgment-action studies and the ongoing work to include responsibility judgments as substages with the Kohlberg scoring system.

First we will examine a study by McNamee (1978) that measures the relationship of moral stage to the consistency of acting according to deontic choice. McNamee brought naive student subjects into a situation in which they could choose whether or not to become involved in assisting what appeared to be a fellow student with a drug problem. Moral behavior was evaluated first according to whether or not each subject offered help, and second by the extent of the assistance actually provided—offering the drug user information about other sources of assistance, or offering personal help such as taking him home.

McNamee found a monotonic pattern in helping behavior. Each higher stage was more likely to help at least by referral, and only the postconventionals were willing actually to provide the help personally. Conversely, the discrepancy between deontic judgment about helping and subsequent action decreases with each higher stage of development. The only exception to this pattern in McNamee's study is found at stage 2, where, uniquely, the majority of subjects did not even verbally endorse helping the victim.

The increase with stage in deontic moral endorsement of helping is consistent with moral stage structures becoming more inclusive of the rights and welfare of others. The increase in consistency with advancing stages reflects the affective and characterological or ego press for integrity between moral judgment and action. Each stage creates new, broader, clearer, and more compelling notions of moral obligation that increase the motivation for moral action. We hypothesize that each stage also develops characteristic justifications for not acting according to one's deontic choices. We refer to these as *quasi-obligations* because they do not reflect universal moral principles, but instead reflect the types of rationalizations consistent with the sociomoral structures of each stage. Concern for approval by conforming to the perceived expectations of the experimenter is a quasi-obligation, a psychological preference rather than a moral obligation. Since quasi-obligations are logically superseded by universal moral principles and therefore untenable in postconventional reasoning, we would expect stage 6 subjects to both choose and act to help the victim. Of the five subjects originally scored stage 6 by McNamee (using the pre-1975 scoring system), 100 percent thought they should help at least by referral and act accordingly. Sixty percent of that group also gave personal assistance. Although this corresponds perfectly to the theory, the post-1975 scoring system collapsed stage 6 into stage 5; and they are presented here as merged.

This perfect judgment-action concordance was not true in McNamee's original stage 5 subjects. Although stage 5 is a principled moral level, it is not by definition fully equilibrated. We would therefore predict that dilemmas at this stage can generate disagreements and confusion over which principle to apply. Almost without exception, deontological and utilitarian principles do prescribe helping the victim in some form. One can, however, construct a stage 5 utilitarian argument that the subject's obligation is to the contract made with the experimenter, and that breaking contracts in one situation devalues the underlying societal dependence on fulfilling contracts between individuals. This is not a fully adequate argument, as it can lead to using the victim cruelly as a means to some abstract utilitarian end—"the greatest good for the greatest number." It does underscore our preference for the more adequate and universalizable stage 6 tenet of the categorical imperative "always treat individuals as an end in themselves, never as a means." This is, however, a rare construction of stage 5 principles; and from the results in table 12-1, it seems to be empirically unlikely also.

Quasi-obligations as justification for not helping the drugged student go no higher than stage 4. At this stage the most commonly found quasi-obligation related to the experimenter's greater role authority. Quasi-obligations reflect the structural distinctions between stages, which are apparent alone in what each stage perceives as the crucial dimensions of a particular dilemma. With each advancing moral stage these concerns become more differentiated and hierarchically integrated. Whereas the dilemma for stage 3 is how best to secure the experimenter's approval, the stage 5 person's only problem is the extent of the personal help he feels obliged to offer the suffering student. The conventional thinker is so preoccupied with meeting the quasi-obligation of conforming to what he perceives as an expectation of the experimenter that it is difficult for him to see the victim as having an equal—let alone overriding—claim on their response. The postconventional thinker, however, has already ordered his principles so that conventional conformity to mere role expectations or contract fulfillment is predetermined as subordinate to the superseding principle of protecting the welfare of others in need. Therefore, we see that at each higher stage the percentage of those who both endorse and actively help the victim increases, as does the extent of the personal involvement.

The McNamee data suggest some other important components of how adequately to define moral action. We have seen that postconventional reasoning leads to a high degree of agreement about the right moral course of action. We also see that it is the deontic determination of one's *responsibility* to help that increases with stage and is highly associated with actually providing aid. If, by means of the highly intellectualized moral method of deontic moral philosophy, we can presume to show what the most moral action is, then how do we determine the least moral? For example, is it the stage 2 subject, who offers no help because from his world view it's not his responsibility, especially when a trained psychologist is not even helping? Or is it one of the 10 percent at stage 5 who thought they should help but did not? The stage 2 person is at least acting consistently with his moral belief; the stage 5 person is that most scorned of all actors, the moral hypocrite. One can see from this example the intuitive appeal of moral relativism, where one's moral fitness is judged not by the content (and certainly not by the structure) of his moral choice, but by its integrity and consistency.

Our point here is not simply to demonstrate our role-taking ability for the position of the moral relativists. Consistency in the service of immoral ends is no virtue. Deontic moral principles do lead to prescriptions for action that are more universal, inclusive, reversible, and just. Rather, we want to demonstrate that to the extent that a perception of responsibility obliges one to act accordingly, then responsibility must be given a special place in both explaining the judgment-action relationship, and in evaluating the moral worth of behaviors. The need for this is clear from certain anomalies in the McNamee data. For instance, in what ways are the 11 percent of the stage 2 subjects who thought they should—and indeed did—offer help to the victim morally different from the 17 percent of the stage 5s who did not even think they should offer help, or from the 10 percent of stage 5s who thought they should help but did not? Beyond those stage 2 persons being more morally commendable and apparently more reliable as moral agents, there may be other important differences.

Although moral-stage theory can demonstrate that those stage 2 thinkers are less mature in the moral complexity of their thought, the theory must also take account of the full moral worth—even the superiority—of their actions. This need becomes even more compelling when we go beyond the results of experimental situations to the many people in everyday life who, though conventional in their moral thinking, perform moral actions the inherent worth of which is not to be denied.

The question remains how best to define moral worth in light of, and in spite of, moral action. We want to avoid the relativistic quagmire of defining as morally right any act as long as it is in unison with "what is right for him." It is also apparent that in a practical sense, principled moral judgment is not always sufficient for corresponding moral action. It seems that a judgment of moral responsibility can bridge the judgment-action chasm. That is, a principled thinker will be more likely to act if forced to move beyond abstract deontological choice by a perception of personal responsibility. The postconventional thinker cannot rely on quasi-obligations to help rationalize away the duty to act on moral choice. Likewise, the conventional or even preconventional person may be motivated to perform the same moral act if his perception of personal responsibility is stronger than any tendency to employ quasi-obligations. It may be, therefore, that nonpostconventional persons may intuit in their hearts or consciences the same morally obligating responsibility to act as their more philosophically principled stage 5 counterparts. Thus persons at this substage B responsibility orientation may be making the same morally right choices and acting on them as consistently as those guided by more fully principled moral stages.

Important differences do still exist between levels of moral thought. The data do show that one is significantly more likely to make the deontically right choice and act on it at a postconventional level, whether substage B or not. Also, in the more subtle moral dilemmas—as those in real life tend to be—principled thinking can be crucial to ordering principles and weighing conflicting deontic and affective claims on one's moral action. The role of substage then helps to explain differing moral orientations and action tendencies. In terms of intervention theory, it may lead to ways of stimulating greater within-stage equilibration by means of movement across substages. This form of Piagetian decalage, or broadening of competence within and across domains, may also aid in fully preparing the individual for movement to the next higher stage.

Reference to the McNamee study serves to outline the need to assess a person's understanding of his responsibility to act in moral situations. After reanalyzing several other studies in light of the constructs discussed here, such as Haan, Smith, and Block's (1968) study of the 1964 Berkeley Free Speech Movement (FSM), and Milgram's (1974) study of obedience to authority, we found even more support for our theory of the relation of moral judgment to moral action. This theory can be summarized as follows:

1. The influence of moral judgment on moral action is a one-track process. Moral-stage structures interpret morally relevant features of a situation. Structures influence behavior through two judgments, one deontic (a judgment of right) and one responsibility (a judgment of commitment to follow-through).

2. Moral action may be considered right in two senses. In the weaker sense right action is any action consistent with the actor's own deontic decision of what is right. We have also called this type of right action *responsible action*. In the stronger sense morally right action is that which would be chosen by stage 5 moral principles and which is, in fact, carried out with at least an intuitive sense of those principles in mind.

3. In moral situations where there is deontic agreement by persons at the conventional stages and above, we expect to find a monotonic relationship between moral stage and moral action due to increasing judgment of responsibility at each higher stage. This relationship was demonstrated in the McNamee experiment.

4. In moral situations that are controversial at conventional stages but on which stage 5 subjects agree, we expect to find a monotonic relationship between moral stage and action due to both the increasing likelihood of subjects at each higher stage making the stage 5 deontic choice and to the increasing judgment of responsibility at each higher stage.

5. Where lower-stage subjects perform the moral action (defined in the stronger sense), we expect those subjects to reason at the B substage. Reasoning at substage B is more universal, generalizable, and internally consistent than is reasoning at substage A. Persons who reason at the B substage of any moral stage can be considered to intuit the same principles that are clearly articulated only at stage 5. This phenomenon was demonstrated in both the FSM and the Milgram studies.

In our view, the most important future direction for research in this area is to identify and describe the function and development of judgments of responsibility.

Moral Judgment and Delinquency Studies

One of the few things that can be said with certainty about the relationship of moral judgment to delinquency is that the interaction is too complexly mediated to justify any causal claims. The overwhelming weight of the evidence is that moral judgment is, at least, a significant correlate of some types of delinquency. The varying methods of the studies we report, however, reflect the many questions that remain about such basic issues as (1) what the operational definition of delinquency should be—behavioral, psychological, or both; (2) what constitutes an adequate control group; (3) what are the salient variables to be controlled for; (4) which measures of moral judgment are most sensitive to differentiating delinquents from nondelinquents; and (5) whether some types or quantities of delinquent behaviors are most likely to be present at different stages of moral development. Given these limitations, we will review thirteen studies that, despite these different approaches, reveal a pattern in which delinquents consistently demonstrate less mature moral reasoning than do matched nondelinquent controls (see table 12-2).

Theoretical and Methodological Problems

One problem in understanding the relation of moral judgment to delinquency is that we assume that delinquency, by definition, has a moral dimension. That is reasonable if what one means by *delinquency* is anti-social behavior causing harm to the person or property of others. Studies in this area, however, often use such general criteria in selecting subjects as their having been adjudicated delinquent or being institutionalized. Either situation can result from so-called status offenses such as truancy, unmanageability, or suspected drug use. These offenses generally reflect the child's status as a juvenile; that is, they would not be illegal if committed by an adult. The moral component of such offenses can be remote at best. In addition, the legal systems of different states and countries are so various that criteria like adjudication and institutionalization can represent responses to widely varying behaviors. Delinquency, then, refers to a heterogenous group of behaviors, some with more moral relevance than others. It is important for researchers to distinguish between types of delinquent behaviors and to analyze moral reasoning in light of the moral nature of the offenses committed.

A similar problem applies to the selection of control subjects or normals. The very notion of *normality* or nondeviance in adolescence, in an increasingly relativistic culture, is problematic. Most researchers attempt to control for such variables as age, race, SES, and intelligence. There is evidence in the sociological literature, however, that offenses like truancy, vandalism, and drug use are so endemic to the matched social environments from which controls are drawn that one can question whether the major difference between delinquents and controls is that the former got caught (Johnson 1979). One way to lessen this possibility is to use indexes of nondelinquents such as reports from school personnel, self-reports, parent reports, and school or other public records. This becomes important the more closely matched controls are for community environment and social class. Only four of the studies presented here explained these or similar attempts to avoid including undetected delinquents in their control groups (Campagna and Harter 1975; Jurkovic and Prentice 1974, 1977; and McColgan 1975). Indeed, McColgan went to extraordinary lengths by mathching on fourteen variables. His referral process for selection of subjects was equally rigorous.

Selection Characteristics

Implicit in the studies reviewed here is the assumption that a relationship exists between delinquency as a behavioral trait and a form of moral reasoning that is consistent with such behavior. The preponderance of preconventional reasoning reported in delinquents is consistent with a world view characterized by egocentric perspective taking, instrumental relationships, opportunism, moral relativism, and a weak adherence to and identification with conventional moral norms—that is, what we refer to as preconventional morality. At the same time, some studies show a sizable minority of delinquents who reason at conventional levels. Thus the question arises: How do delinquents who are conventional in moral reasoning differ psychologically or behaviorally from their preconventional counterparts? Part of the approach required to address these questions is offered in three of the studies to be reviewed that go beyond the behavioral indexes of delinquency to more specific psychological variables (Campagna and Harter 1975; Fodor 1973; and Jurkovic and Prentice 1977). They hypothesize that delinquency is not merely a unitary construct, and introduce into their designs ratings to separate subjects into sociopathic, neurotic, and subcultural categories to determine if they can differentiate preconventional from conventional delinquents. In addition, we offer an analysis of drug-related offenses (Hickey 1972; Kohlberg and Freundlich 1973) in relation to moral reasoning in a similar attempt.

Table 12-2
Studies Relating Moral Judgment and Delinquency

Sample Number	Study	Subject	SES	Delinquency Criteria	Basis for Matching	Measure of Moral Judgment	Relation Tested	Statistical Outcome ± or 0	Relation of Delinquent M.J. to Nondel. M.J.	Delinquent MMS in Predicted Direction, Lower
1	Kohlberg (1958) (Indiana)	10 M. Del. Age 15.9; 12 M. Non-Del. Age 15.9	Common Man[a]	Awaiting trial, institutionalization offenses: repetitive car theft, burglary, robbery by assault.	Age, IQ,[b] SES	Kohlberg MJI, aspect scoring, not blind	Delinquency and M.J. $p < .01$	+	Del. Lower M.J. X̄MMS Del. 224 X̄MMS Nondel. 293	Yes
2	Hickey (1972)	20 M. Del. Age 19.3; 14 M. Non-Del. Age 19.9	Common Man	Incarcerated offenses: Felonious burglary and assault, first offenders and repeaters.	Age, IQ, SES	Kohlberg MJI, intuitive scoring, blind	Del. & M.J. $t = 2.62$, $p < .05$	+	Del. Lower M.J. X̄MMS Del. 260 X̄MMS Nondel. 319	Yes
3	Kohlberg and Freundlich (1973) (Scotland)	13 M. Del. Age 15.5; 13 M. Non-Del. Age 14.9	Lower Class	Salvation Army hostel, on probation.	Age, IQ, SES	Kohlberg MJI, aspect scoring, not blind	Del. & M.J. $p < .10$	0	Del. Lower M.J. X̄MMS Del. 219 X̄MMS Nondel. 286	Yes
4	Critchley (1961) (England)	15 M. Del. Age 15.0; 20 M. Cont. Age 15.0	Common Man		Age, IQ, SES	Kohlberg MJI, aspect scoring	Del. & M.J. $p < .05$	+	Del. Lower M.J. X̄MMS Del. 206 X̄MMS Nondel. 282	Yes
5	Hudgins and Prentice (1973)	10 M. Del. Age 14-16; 10 M. Non-Del. Age 14-16	Lower Class	Auto-theft conviction (several times). Local juvenile court clients.	Age, IQ, race, SES, geographic area	Kohlberg MJI, intuitive scoring	Del. & M.J. $t = 2.93$ $p < .01$	+	Del. Lower M.J. X̄MMS Del. 208 X̄MMS Nondel. 252	Yes
6	Campagna and Harter (1975)	21 M. Sociopath Age 10-13; 23 M. Normals Age 10-13	Working Class	Sociopath, institutionalization. Selection by Robins's criteria.	Age, IQ, SES, geo. area	Kohlberg MJI, intuitive scoring, blind	Socio. & M.J. $f = 58.79$ $p < .001$	+	Socio. Lower M.J. X̄MMS Socio. 165 X̄MMS Normal 229	Yes
7	Jurkovic and Prentice (1977)	36 M. Del. Age X̄15.7 (12 psychopathics, 12 neurotic, 12 subcultural) 12 Non-Del. Age X̄15.7	Lower Class	Quay's classification system for the 3 groups.	Age, IQ, SES, length of inst. soc. env.	Kohlberg MJI, intuitive scoring, blind	1. Psychopaths vs. neurotics & M.J. $p < .10$; 2. Psychopaths vs. Sub. cul. cw. & M.J. $p < .005$; 3. Psychopaths vs. Non. Del. & M.J. $p < .005$ Diff. among other groups	0 ... +	Del. Lower M.J. Combined Del. MMS 216 Normals MMS 260	Yes

	Study	Sample	Social class	Subjects	Variables controlled	Measure	Statistics	Result	Findings	Common man
8	Jurkovic and Prentice (1974)	8 M. Del. Age 15, 8 M. Non. Del. Age 15	Lower class	Local juvenile courts On probation Adjudicated generally several times—auto theft, burglary	Age, IQ, race, SES, geographic area	Kohlberg MJI, intuitive scoring, blind	Del. & M.J. $f = .65$ $p < .20$	0	Del. Lower M.J. $\bar{X}$MMS Del. 261 $\bar{X}$MMS Nondel. 284	Yes
9	Fodor (1973)	30 M. Psychopaths Age $\bar{X}$16.1 30 M. Non. Del. Psy. Age $\bar{X}$16.2		Institutionalization, psychopath: counselors' judgment according to Cleckley's criteria	Age, IQ, race	Kohlberg MJI, intuitive scoring, blind	Psycho & MJ Stage 1 & 2 vs. 3 & 4. $X^2 = 5.94$ $p < .02$	+	Del. Lower M.J	Yes
10	McColgan (1975)	26 M. Pre. Del. Age $\bar{X}$14.7 26 M. Non. Del. Age $\bar{X}$14.9		Teacher identification as aggressive, inadequate impulse control, poor self-image, mood changeable, poor interactions with peers, poor work habits.	Age, IQ, SES, race, sex, interviewer, geo. area, school grades, number of parents and others	(Rest) DIT, scoring, blind	Pre-Del. & M.J. on DIT $p < .001$	+	Pre. Del. Lower than M.J. p index for Predel. 16.9 p index for Nondel. 23.7	Yes
11	Gibbs (1981)	30 M. Del. Age $\bar{X}$16.6 30 F. Del. $\bar{X}$16.6 14 M. Non. Del. $\bar{X}$16.6 14 F. Non. Del. $\bar{X}$16.6	Lower and Lower-middle class	Males—medium security Institution females	Age, race, SES.	Sociomoral reflection measure (SRM), scored blind (Gibbs)	Delinquency & M.J. on socio-moral score Stages 1 & 2 vs. 3 & 4	+	Delinquents Lower $\bar{X}$SMS Del. 264 $\bar{X}$SMS Nondel. 291	Yes
12	Fodor (1972)	40 M. Del. Age 14-17 40 M. Non. Del. Age 14-17		Court referred, petty larceny to attempted homicide	Age, race, mother's education	Kohlberg MJI, intuitive scoring, blind	Delinquency & M.J. $+ = 5.43$ $p < .001$	+	Del. Lower M.J. $\bar{X}$MMS Del. 162 $\bar{X}$MMS Nondel. 196	Yes
13	Hains and Miller (1980)	Del. Age: 21 M. 10-11 (N = 14) 21 F. 12-13 (N = 14) 14-16 (N = 14) Non. Del. Age: 27 M. 10-12 (N = 18) 27 F. 12-13 (N = 18) 14-16 (N = 18)	Middle Class	72 del. subjects had status offenses 33 misdemeanors 51 felonies	Types of offenses	(Rest) DIT, scoring blind	Del. & M.J. on DIT $f = 5.93$ $p < .05$	+	Del. Lower M.J.	Yes

[a] Common man refers to Warner's level of upper-lower class with some members of the lower-middle class.
[b] IQ scores were available only for five subjects of the delinquent (del.) group.

Another criterion for the selection of studies was the compatibility of the moral-judgment measure with the cognitive developmental approach. We therefore report studies using Kohlberg's Moral Judgment Instrument (MJI) as well as Rest's (1979) Defining Issues Test (DIT) and Gibbs's (1981) Sociomoral Reflection Measure (SRM). The MJI measure has itself gone through stages of development, so the studies using it here have applied sentence, global or intuitive, and standard-issue scoring methods. For a discussion of correlation between scoring-system methods, see Colby et al., in press.

Studies Using the MJI Instruments

The first five samples were reported elsewhere (Kohlberg and Freundlich 1973). The moral-maturity scores (MMS) of the control group were significantly higher than those of the delinquent group for each of these five samples, with a monotonic pattern with significantly fewer delinquents than controls at each higher moral stage. Analyses of variance were performed separately for each of these samples. The F values for each comparison had a probability of less than .05, except for the Hudgins and Prentice (1973) sample ($p < .10$). Also, the Jurkovic and Prentice (1977) data revealed a significant difference between the psychopathic delinquents and controls ($p < .005$) and between psychopaths and subculturals ($p < .005$), and psychopaths tended to reason at less mature levels than neurotics ($p < .10$). Neurotics, however, did not differ significantly from either the subculturals or the controls; and the latter two did not vary from each other. Finally, the earlier Jurkovic and Prentice (1974) study did not find significance between delinquents and controls ($p < .20$) in moral judgment. The n of 8 for each group, however, was so small as to make a finding of significance very unlikely.

The actual percentage of usage of preconventional versus conventional reasoning on the MJI is shown in table 12-3 for those eight studies reporting it.

Race Differences

Nine samples included both black and white offenders. In no sample were there significant differences between the moral-maturity scores of black subjects and white subjects.

Sex Differences

Only two samples included females. Neither of these samples found significant differences in moral maturity between males and females.

Table 12-3
Mean Moral Maturity Scores and Dominant Levels (Preconventional and Conventional) of Delinquent and Control Samples

Sample	Mean MMS	Percentage of Subject's Modality	
		Preconventional	Conventional
(Kohlberg 1958) Indiana			
Delinquents	224	80	20
Controls	293	25	75
(Hickey 1972)			
Delinquents	260	53	47
Controls	319	7	93
(Kohlberg 1958) Scotland			
Delinquents	219	92	8
Controls	286	58	42
(Critchley 1961) England			
Delinquents	206	87	13
Controls	282	15	85
(Hudgins and Prentice 1973)			
Delinquents	208	80	20
Controls	252	30	70
(Campagna and Harter 1975)			
Delinquents	165	n.a.[a]	n.a.
Controls	229	n.a.	n.a.
(Jurkovic and Prentice 1977)			
Psychopathic delinquent	188	87	13
Neurotic delinquent	221	69	31
Subcultural delinquent	239	55	45
Combined delinquent	216	71	29
Controls	260	43	57
(Jurkovic and Prentice 1974)			
Delinquent	261	n.a.	n.a.
Controls	284	n.a.	n.a.

[a]n.a. = not available.

Moral Orientation and Drug Use

Our results indicate that whereas a large majority of delinquents are preconventional in moral orientation, a sizable proportion are at the conventional (stage 3) level of judgment. The proportion of conventional-stage delinquents is particularly large in the Connecticut reformatory group. In part the greater proportion of higher-stage individuals in this sample is probably due to their older average age, 18 as opposed to 15. In part, however, it might be due to the fact that a large proportion of the Connecticut sample were incarcerated for drug-related offenses. We reasoned that conventional-stage moral reasoning was an insulator against delinquent behavior. Where situational or intrapsychic pressures and needs were strong, conventional adolescents might become delinquent. Such pressures would not be required as factors for delinquent behavior in adolescents at the preconventional moral stages.

To examine this question, the Connecticut reformatory sample was classified as to whether they had a hard-drug habit supported by their illegal activities (usually theft). This classification was based on both records and personal discussions in the course of a moral discussion and research program discussed elsewhere.

Half of the forty inmates were classified as drug users. The moral stage of 70 percent of the drug users was conventional (stage 3), compared with only 35 percent of the non-drug users. Drug addiction, then, seems to play a greater role in the delinquency of conventional as opposed to preconventional adolescents.

Recidivism

Further light on the relation of moral judgment to delinquent behavior comes from the prediction of follow-up data on recidivism. A follow-up study of the Connecticut reformatory sample was conducted after their release. The period of time elapsed from release ranged from one year to eighteen months. This study offers some preliminary data on the prediction of recidivism from moral stage. Thirty-three of the forty subjects were involved in this analysis. Subjects were classified as recidivist if they had been reincarcerated or were awaiting trial for reincarceration. Of the fifteen preconventional-stage inmates followed up, only one-third were not recidivists. Of the eighteen conventional subjects, 60 percent were not recidivists. This difference in recidivism was marginally significant ($p < .10$).

Classification as recidivist versus nonrecidivist in an eighteen-month period is a relatively noisy, uncertain index. Another classification was made of nonrecidivist subjects who were not in the hands of the law. Such subjects were classified as to whether they seemed to have a stable nondelinquent postrelease adjustment or not. Of the preconventional subjects, only two (13 percent) had made a stable adjustment. Of the conventional subjects eight (44 percent) had made a stable adjustment. This difference was statistically significant ($p < .05$). Judging by this limited sample, conventionals had three times the probability of making a stable adjustment as did the preconventionals.

In summary, although the data are very preliminary, they do suggest that a conventional moral orientation predicts to postrelease adjustment. This suggests that the lower stage of delinquents, as compared with nondelinquents, is not a mere passive correlate of the differential life experiences of the two groups, but is an active agent in the avoidance of offenses by conventional-stage adolescents.

Studies Using the DIT and SRM Instruments

Three studies used measures other than the MJI to assess moral reasoning. McColgan (1975) conducted an ambitious study of twenty-nine institutionalized delinquents (average age 16 years) and a nondelinquent control group roughly comparable on age, race, sex, and IQ. Using the Defining Issues Test (DIT), he found that the percentage of principled thinking in Rest's measure (*p* index) was significantly lower (18.8 percent) for delinquents than for controls (28.7 percent). In addition, he studied a group of twenty-six predelinquents (mean age 14.1 years) with a like number of controls matched across fourteen dimensions: age, IQ, SES, race, sex, test instruments, interviewer, environmental conditions for all interviews, time of testing, scoring system, residential locale, school, school grades, and family with one parent. This remarkable degree of matching reflects McColgan's concern that the tendency to define delinquency in terms of institutionalization is much too vague. The *p* index on the DIT for the predelinquents was 16.9 percent versus 23.7 percent for the controls, which proved to be significant at the .001 level. The MJI, however, did not discern a significant difference between the two groups.

In a 1980 study using the DIT, Hains and Miller assessed the moral reasoning of forty-two delinquents and fifty-four nondelinquents at three age levels: 10-11 years (younger), 12-13 years (intermediate-aged), and 14-15-16 years (oldest). Both experimentals and controls contained an equal number of males and females. In each age group there were fourteen delinquents and eighteen nondelinquents. Twenty-six delinquents and sixteen nondelinquents had to be eliminated from the sample because their performance did not pass a consistency criterion suggested by the coding manual. All subjects were middle class—very unusual in delinquency studies. Delinquency status (types of offenses) was controlled for; but IQ and sex were not, with no mention made of race.

The findings indicated a significant main effect for delinquency: $F(1,90) = 5.93$, $p < .05$, with delinquents scoring lower. Also, a significant effect for age was observed: $F(2,90) = 3.50$, $p < .05$, reflecting higher D scores (moral reasoning) with greater age, suggesting a developmental trend for both delinquents and nondelinquents. The two oldest delinquent groups, however, were "about the same or lower than those of the youngest non-delinquents," further indicating a retardation in the rate of moral development for delinquents.

Data from Gibbs's (1981) moral discussion intervention study are relevant here. Thirty male and thirty female incarcerated delinquents aged 14-18 (average age 16.6) were matched for age, race, and SES. All subjects were administered the Sociomoral Reflection Measure (SRM). This instrument is designed as a group-administered, paper-and-pencil counterpart of the Kohlberg MJI. Test results showed that the delinquent subjects' mean sociomoral score was 264, with no significant difference between males and females. The nondelinquent controls obtained a mean SRM score of 291. This study demonstrates the predicted trend of delinquents scoring lower on sociomoral measures than controls. Further, it is one of the few studies with a high percentage of female delinquents. Its finding that female controls and experimentals did not differ significantly from one another in sociomoral maturity is of interest.

Studies of Psychopathic Delinquents

Three studies examined the relationship of psychopathy or sociopathy to moral reasoning. Although debate exists on the meaning of these different classifications, they are here used interchangeably. Campagna and Harter (1975) conducted a study ($n = 44$, boys) of the relationship between being diagnosed as sociopathic using Robins's (1966) diagnostic criteria, and stage of moral reasoning. They found that the moral reasoning of the sociopathic ($n = 21$) children was significantly less mature ($\overline{X} = 165$) than that of mental-age-matched normal children ($n = 23$) ($\overline{X} = 229$) at two mental-age levels (10-13) ($F = 58.79$, $p < .001$). These results held true even when the superior verbal abilities of the normals were controlled.

Fodor (1973) tested the hypothesis that psychopathic delinquents are less advanced in moral reasoning than are nonpsychopathic delinquents. A control group was not included. Each group contained thirty boys aged 14-17, matched for age, race, and verbal intelligence. Cleckley's (1964) psychopathic personality characteristics were used as the criteria for inclusion in the psychopathic group. All but three in each group were institutionalized delinquents. Level of moral reasoning was assessed using the MJI and scored blind using the intuitive-issue scoring method. No moral maturity scores were reported, however. Fodor's findings are as follows:

	Stages 1 and 2	*Stages 3 and 4*
($n = 30$) Psychopathic delinquent	24	6
($n = 30$) Nonpsychopathic delinquent	15	15
Total	39	21

The greater number of psychopathic delinquents represented as preconventional was found to be significant (X^2 = 5.94 with 1 df, p < .02).

Fodor's finding suggests that immature moral reasoning may have greater explanatory power for delinquent acts committed by psychopaths. Also, that psychopathic personality characteristics in combination with retarded moral development might be used to screen for early adolescents at greater risk for delinquency. But even when the two groups are combined we see again the nearly 2 to 1 (39 to 21) use of preconventional moral reasoning among delinquents.

Jurkovic and Prentice (1977) studied three groups of twelve institutionalized delinquents, each of whom was either: (1) unsocialized-psychopathic, (2) neurotic-disturbed, or (3) socialized-subcultural. A control group of twelve nondelinquents was matched for age, SES, and ethnicity. The nondelinquent group, however, was significantly higher in verbal ability (p < .025) on the WISC or WAIS than the delinquent groups. Their Kohlberg MJI scores were coded blind. Even controlling for differences in verbal ability, the groups differed significantly from one another, $F(3,34)$ = 4.30, p < .025. Psychopaths tended to reason at less mature levels than neurotics, $F(1,43)$ = 3.02, p < .10; and significantly less than subculturals, $F(1,43)$ = 9.08, p < .005; and controls, $F(1,43)$ = 10.01, p < .005. Neurotics, however, did not differ significantly from either subculturals or controls; and the latter two groups did not differ from each other. This evidence supports that of Fodor (1973) in that psychopathic delinquents once again were found to reason at significantly lower levels of moral judgment than did nonpsychopaths. Although the differences between controls and neurotics and subculturals were not significant, the results were in the predicted direction. The fact that any significance was found with an n of only twelve per group is itself significant. The results do add to the monotonic pattern of delinquents of whatever psychological subtype to reason at lower moral stages, and to tend toward preconventional moral reasoning—here, 71 percent for delinquents and 42 percent for controls.

Future research designs that look at various psychological and behavioral types of delinquency in relation to moral reasoning should contribute to our understanding of the differential effect of moral judgment on action.

Moral Reasoning of Mothers and Delinquent Sons

Two studies examined the interaction of mothers' moral reasoning on their son's delinquency. Hudgins and Prentice, in a 1973 study (reported earlier) of ten delinquent and ten nondelinquent male adolescents aged 14.5-16.1, matched for age, intelligence, social class, and ethnicity, also examined the moral reasoning of each boy's mother. They found a significant difference in moral stage between adolescents in both groups and their mothers, with their mothers using a higher stage ($p < .001$). This supports both the idea that moral judgment advances with age and that it continues past adolescence. The difference between the mean MMS for the mothers of the delinquents ($\overline{X} = 300$) versus that of the control mothers ($\overline{X} = 370$) was significant ($F = 12.22$, df = $1/16$, $p < .01$). The significantly lower moral reasoning of the delinquents' mothers emphasizes the possible role of parents' moral stage in influencing the rate of moral growth in their children.

Jurkovic and Prentice (1974) expanded this approach to include other aspects of the mother's interaction with her son derived from Hetherington and Martin (1972). These were: conflict, maternal dominance, maternal hostility, maternal encouragement, and maternal warmth. The MJI was administered to each of the eight delinquents and their mothers, as well as the same number of controls' mothers and sons who were matched for education, number of siblings, verbal intelligence, and SES. The average age of the adolescents was 15.0; the mothers of the delinquents were 5.5 years younger (40.4) than were the controls' mothers (45.9).

The findings did not indicate a significant relationship between the moral-maturity score (MMS) of the delinquent ($\overline{X} = 261$, SD = 67) and the nondelinquent adolescents ($\overline{X} = 284$, SD = 42), $F = .65$, df = $1/14$, $p < .20$. Likewise, the MMS of the delinquents' mothers ($\overline{X} = 334$, SD = 50) did not vary significantly from those of the nondelinquents' mothers ($\overline{X} = 360$, SD = 35), $F = 1.41$, df = $1/14$, $p < .20$). In addition, the level of moral maturity of the combined scores of the delinquent sons and mothers ($\overline{X} = 298$) and that of the control mothers and sons ($\overline{X} = 322$) did not reach significance ($F = 1.39$, df = $1/14$, $p < .20$). The fact that these results are not statistically significant (though in the predicted direction) is, as the authors themselves concluded, quite possibly due to the very small n.

The mother-son interaction measures did yield significant results, however. From a series of one-tailed t tests, the delinquent dyads were shown to be significantly higher on maternal dominance ($p < .025$), hostility ($p < .025$), and conflict ($p < .05$). Nondelinquent pairs were significantly higher on warmth ($p < .05$), but only a trend toward encouragement ($p < .10$) could be found. The scores on the complexity ratings were not significantly different for the two groups, consistent with the lack of statistical differentiation on the MJI.

The positive findings in this study point to the need to examine other psychological correlates of delinquency. The design had a number of failings, notably the inadequate sample size; but the fact that significance was obtained on the family-interaction dimensions despite the small n only reinforces the apparent salience of those variables in understanding the delinquent's psychological environment. Further research would be of interest in determining whether these aspects of the moral atmosphere of the family are contributing elements to low moral reasoning and/or delinquency.

The lack of positive findings in the delinquency-moral judgment relationship may well be due to small sample size and is outweighed by the contribution of the other findings and directions for future research using larger samples and possibly including fathers, other family members, and female delinquents. Also, one can speculate that these and other family-interaction variables may serve as mediators in moral judgment and behavior to the extent that attachment, role-taking, and empathy have been shown to contribute to moral action, and could account partially for both differences in moral maturity and moral versus immoral actions in persons at the same moral stage.

Summary

The overwhelming weight of the empirical data reviewed here supports the notion that juvenile delinquents' moral judgment is at a less advanced level than that of nondelinquent controls matched on a variety of variables. We do not believe that this demonstrates that immature moral reasoning is the root cause of juvenile delinquency. Rather, these studies lend support to the more modest claim that moral reasoning of increased maturity has an insulating effect against delinquency. Advanced stages of moral judgment cause one's moral orientation to be more integrated, stable, and consistent. Higher reasoning makes one a more reliable moral agent and thus better able to withstand some incentives to illegal conduct postulated by a variety of sociological and psychological theories of the etiology of delinquency. The preconventional thinker is not more delinquent by nature, but simply feels less obligated to conform to any conventions, whether of the larger society or of a subcultural group.

Although there is a strong pattern of preconventional reasoning in juvenile delinquents, it remains to be fully explained in what way stage 3 and 4 delinquents are unusual other than being a relatively small minority of the total delinquent population. The studies examining different psychological classifications bear further investigation, as does the examination of other family-interaction variables. The attempts to discern relationships between delinquency and moral reasoning with parenting styles and bonds of affection between parent and child promise useful insights into both delinquency causation and the differing rates of moral development.

Theoretical Approaches to the Causes of Delinquency

The structural-developmental approach to delinquency causation emphasizes the dialectical nature of the growth of moral reasoning and moral action. Here the interaction between person and environment leads to ways of understanding the moral world that become increasingly complex in response to the emerging cognitive abilities and social demands on the child. This paradigm reflects the pioneering work of Jean Piaget (1965) in exploring the nature of cognitive and moral structures. These structures must evolve in order to remain adequate and adaptive to the child's needs. With the passage of time, these structures can become maladaptive if for some reason the individual's growth in this area does not keep pace with the growing demands of his or her environment. Juvenile delinquency, then, can result from one's acting from the same self-centered, hedonistic world view that has been adequate to the more constrained and dependent world of the child.

The major self-constraining factor in preconventional children is the morality of prudence—avoiding the risk of incurring the consequences of misbehavior. The more savvy and independent adolescent at this level, however, is more likely to view conventional norms of conduct as an obstacle to getting what he wants, or at best not much more than a fair trade to protect him from what he assumes to be the equally self-centered designs of others. From his slowed or arrested stage of moral development, rules may be viewed as heteronomously imposed by the adults he feels in competition with for power. His more advanced peers are engaged in a process of discovering the legitimacy and fairness behind many rules, and are therefore internalizing and abiding by them more consistently and for reasons other than mere prudence. Meanwhile, the morally preconventional adolescent may well be undergoing age-appropriate development in other psychological areas, so that his personality needs for identity, self-esteem, peer approval, independence, and so forth continue to press, but without the fairness-oriented constraint or positive guidance afforded by conventional moral reasoning.

This approach to delinquency causation is at once intrapsychic and social psychological. Because of the latter we are keenly interested in the environmental conditions that enhance or retard the individual's rate of moral growth. The contribution of other fields that study the effect of these larger social structures on the individual is important. Sociology in particular has a broad literature on the societal variables that may be relevant to the rate and content of moral reasoning and behavior. We will examine the sociological contributions to delinquency causation in light of our own approach.

The field of criminology in general, and juvenile delinquency in particular, has largely been the domain of sociology. Only recently has psychology entered the fray by postulating theories of causation related to personality variables, behavioral learning theories, and stages of qualitatively distinct reasoning structures. Sociological theories of delinquency focus on such macrosocial structures as economics, education, and government. Most psychology, on the other hand, tends to address such individual aspects of personality as intelligence, learning styles, self-esteem, and forms of cognition. Sociology, then, is more interested in predicting which segments of the overall population are more likely to be delinquent and why, rather than which individuals.

Although most psychological accounts of delinquency do look for interactions between the individual and his or her environment for possible causal elements, the societal role is generally used as a means of understanding individual rather than group differences. The analysis and critique of social structures by psychology is therefore often only perfunctory and descriptive in nature, leading to the common criticism that psychology is the servant of the established order—that it emphasizes the adjustment of the individual to society instead of encouraging transformations in society. It would, however, be a false dichotomy to frame the debate over the etiology of delinquency as existing between the psychology of the individual and sociology. Many other fields could, with some justification, lay claim to a portion of the causal explanation of delinquency, such as psychobiology and sociobiology. The fact is, however, that by far the greatest amount of empirical examination of delinquency has been undertaken by sociologists. Thus any psychological theory attempting to explain even a part of deviant behavior must address itself to the prevailing sociological explanations.

There are conflicting levels of empirical support for the three major sociological theories: strain, subcultural, and control (Johnson 1979). Each has a certain explanatory power and intuitive appeal. None is all-encompassing; each probably has certain strengths in explaining the role of different personality variables, social situations, and types of delinquency. Any theory of sociology or psychology, however, that attempts to isolate a limited set of types of causes for types of delinquency is bound to be unsatisfactory. Delinquency is an arbitrary classification of action, not a genotypal or causal category.

Given these reservations, we find the basic tenets of social-control theory to be the most compatible with both a developmental-psychological approach to delinquency causation and the empirical findings on the relationship of moral reasoning to delinquency. A major problem with the strain and subcultural explanations is that although their assumed etiology rests on the special stresses encountered by the lower classes, they do not account satisfactorily for why the majority of its members do not become delinquent. Since most members of a lower social class are likely to be exposed to its particular vicissitudes, we must look for individual differences to explain why only a fraction succumb to delinquent life-styles. The advantage of control theory, then, is that it takes a social-psychological perspective incorporating the best features of sociological and psychological appraoches.

By focusing almost exclusively on the exigencies of lower-class life, strain and subcultural theories fail to explain middle-class delinquency, which remains a relatively unexamined phenomenon. By emphasizing the absence or breakdown of bonds between the individual and society, control theory would seem better able to account both for the factors that contribute to different psychological types of delinquency (neurotic, psychopathic, and so on), and for the different rates of incidence depending on social class. Also, the implications for treatment are at once more clear and more promising. The process of prevention and treatment does not await a radical transformation of society.

Female Delinquency

Another factor in our preference for control theory is greater ability to explain sex differences in both incidence and types of delinquency. Female delinquency is a relatively ignored subject within the criminology literature. That important differences in incidence and type exist, with males higher in all categories, seems clear (Trojanowicz and Morash 1982; Hindelang 1981; Warren 1979; Feyerherm 1977, 1981). Also apparent is that female crime is on the rise (Hindelang et al. 1975; Simon 1975; Hindelang 1976) though generally not at rates greater than those for males (Warren 1979). Since this is a subject being given increasing attention, it is worth evaluating the three theories for their applicability to the causes of female delinquency.

As Warren (1979) points out, for strain theory to account for the lower delinquency rate among females we would have to assume that the discrepancy between aspirations and expectations is lower than for males. There is little reason to believe that women aspire to material rewards any less than men do. Yet we have ample evidence that females' earning power and realistic expectations for material success are reduced. The result should be greater strain and thus greater incidence of delinquency. Not only is this unsupported by the evidence, but the opposite is true.

Subcultural deviance theory implies that delinquency is largely an act of conformity to subcultural norms. To the extent that these norms reflect membership in a particular social class and/or exposure to life in a delinquency prone environment, and since we can expect that women will comprise half the members of that class or community, we should find that women are responsible for half the crime. This is, in fact, not the case.

The concepts of delinquency causation within social control theory are more amenable to what we do know about delinquency in female adolescents.

There is empirical evidence that the strength of the bond to society is stronger among females. Girls are more conforming in their opinions about conventional norms ranging from their respect for the police to their quantity of communication with parents (Hirschi 1969; Wilson, Hirschi, and Elder 1965). In addition, the types of crimes committed by females are less socially destructive and more likely to be self-destructive. Feyerherm (1977) reported on a study of offense types self-reported by more than five hundred each of male and female high school students. He found that as compared with boys, girls reported for each category a relatively small percentage of the total crimes committed.

Though female juvenile delinquency appears to be rising, petty offenses like shoplifting account for much of the increase. The increase in their involvement in violent crimes like assault are less dramatic when arrests for being bystanders to assaults are included (Steffensmeir et al. 1980). Girls are much less likely to commit crimes of violence in general (Feyerherm 1981). Moral judgment theory has not found any consistent differences in the moral reasoning stages of male and female adolescents; thus, we cannot offer an explanation in terms of deontic moral reasoning as to why young women commit fewer crimes and of a less morally troublesome nature. It does, however, seem that social control theory's findings that girls are more securely bonded to social conventions by means of attachment, involvement, and so forth, may offer some interesting insights into this question.

Conventional Delinquency

Just as we have discussed the need to account for why most members of the lower classes are not delinquent, and why some members of the middle and upper classes are, so too we should explain why most preconventional thinkers are not delinquent, yet some conventional and even postconventional thinkers are.

It seems likely that moral reasoning is more directly related to positive or prosocial moral action than to immoral or even morally neutral acts. That is, a mature structure of moral judgment and emotion seems required to explain consistent and reasoned prosocial action at personal-hedonistic expense. It is not required to explain an absence of delinquent behavior that incurs potential punishment and reduction of positive social status. Also, to the extent that some immoral or delinquent acts are impulsive or psychotic, the role of any kind of reasoning would seem to be minimal in such cases. We can know that mature moral judgment is not required to explain resistance to delinquent behavior because, of course, most preconventionals do not engage in such actions, and because even delinquents who are preconventional are able to resist many if not most such temptations.

In our discussion of moral judgment and action, we reported findings that show that the higher the individual's moral stage, the more likely he or she was to resist situational forces and to act in accordance with what his moral reasoning judged to be the right thing to do. Thus, although preconventional moral reasoning is not a cause of delinquency, conventional reasoning is an important condition for resisting delinquent behavior when personal need or situational forces provide strong incentives for delinquent action. In contrast to strain and subcultural theories, the social-control position stresses the irrational and situational aspects of deviant acts (Johnson 1979). Control theories "focus attention on the dynamics of the interactional processes by which people move toward and beyond the brink of deviant behavior . . . (a) deliberate and autonomous decision to commit an act of crime, followed by an appropriate sequence of responses leading to the act, is an uncommon occurrence" (Schrag 1971, p. 109).

Our concept of the role of moral reasoning in delinquents emphasizes the part played by the situational forces such that reasoning structures are not entirely free to exercise abstract, deontic judgments. Therefore, the lower the stage of moral reasoning, the easier it is to ignore or rationalize away one's highest moral reasoning and act in a hedonistic manner. The McNamee (1978) study discussed previously showed that this was due to higher stages having more prescriptive and obliging imperatives that made inaction or immoral action more clearly in violation of what one's reasoning suggested. Even with the press of situational forces, a preconventional thinker may discern the appropriate moral action but not feel compelled to act accordingly. He can more easily rationalize a self-serving action by means of quasi-obligations.

Then again, why does neither immature moral judgment nor weak social bonds alone necessarily lead to deviant behavior? In the case of a preconventional thinker, a strong social bond may serve to make the moral orientation more stable and resistant to situational forces than it might otherwise be. Also, it can infuse deontic reasoning with a predisposition of benevolence in which the child thinks he would like to act in a way that would make his parents proud. An intimate bond with adults can facilitate role taking of these older and presumably conventional thinkers. Conversely, a person with a weak social bond might be insulated against delinquency by having a more equilibriated moral stage—substage B, for example. Here the person's behavior is controlled by a deeper understanding and valuing of responsibility or personal integrity. Thus he may willfully avoid delinquent temptation and act instead on the prescriptions of his or her full moral competence. The theoretical symmetry between social-control and moral-stage theories is complementary. Each can work to protect the individual against pressures toward delinquent behavior, whereby a strength in one may compensate for a deficit in the other.

We now raise the seeming paradox of *morally conventional delinquents*.

Although most juvenile delinquents are not conventional thinkers, some conventional thinkers are juvenile delinquents. The most basic reason is that moral reasoning is not a necessary and sufficient cause of delinquency; at most it is necessary, but not sufficient. We say it is at most necessary because not all delinquent acts involve moral reasoning (impulsive, psychotic, and so on) and because not all delinquent acts are immoral. It is not sufficient because there are undoubtedly many other intervening personality variables, such as resistance to temptation or empathic arousal. These variables may intervene before, with, or after moral reasoning; or they may either seriously diminish the role of moral reasoning in action or displace it altogether. There are, however, situations in which it is necessary *and* sufficient—when we make a moral judgment and act on it simply because we believe it is the right thing to do. Conventional structures control delinquent acts only insofar as moral reasoning is salient in a particular individual's decision-making process.

In our review of the moral-reasoning and delinquency studies, we reported on the relatively large number of stage 3 thinkers among the older (age 18-20) incarcerated delinquents. This same group of primarily stage 3 inmates had a very high incidence of having a hard-drug habit that they supported by their illegal activities—most often theft. Seventy percent of the total sample of drug users ($n = 40$) were stage 3, versus 35 percent for the non-drug users. This raises a general question of the moral culpability of crimes committed to fulfill a physical addiction. Also, one can wonder how much moral reasoning is even involved in such crimes. Then there is the question of whether drug addiction or abuse is itself a moral offense (when crimes are not committed to support it). The same question is pertinent for those labeled delinquent as a result of status offenses (which are heavily represented in delinquency studies), and who therefore may have acted unconventionally, but not immorally in any philosophic sense. The point is that there may be a sizable number of stage 3 delinquents whose offense does not necessarily involve a question of moral reasoning or action. Those in these categories of offenses might be better understood as *deviants* from conventional norms, rather than delinquents. The Hickey (1972) data support this notion and indicate a need for future studies to examine moral stage in relation to the types of offenses committed. Additional evidence for this can be found in two studies in England reported by Thornton and Reid (1982).

We have pointed out the relative inadequacies of strain and subcultural models of delinquency causation. We have also implied an even stronger assumption that the causes of delinquency are so complexly mediated that any single theory of causation is reductionist. The insights of the strain and subcultural models have considerably intuitive appeal and not inconsiderable empirical support.

The contribution of strain theory to this question of conventional delinquency lies in its suggestion that the predictability of any individual becoming delinquent is in the degree of strain between expectation and aspiration. From this we might assume that to the moderate extent moral reasoning is related to social class (Colby and Kohlberg 1981), then delinquent behavior by low-SES stage 3 persons would be facilitated by the conflict between their possibly heightened competence to perceive the discrepancies in their social position leading to the strain, and their stage 3 tendency to want to conform themselves to conventional norms as a means of becoming full members of adult society. The stage 3 notions of fairness, trust and cooperation would be sorely disillusioned and frustrated, leading perhaps to extreme anger, or what Cohen (1955) calls a "reaction formation" against conventional norms.

Although debate exists among sociologists about the validity of the general explanation of delinquency by subcultural theorists, even critics conclude that delinquent associates and delinquent values are related to delinquency (Johnson 1979). The support in the sociological literature for the link between becoming delinquent and having delinquent associates is extensive (Hirschi 1969; Hindelang 1973; Liska 1973; Erickson and Empey 1965; Schoenberg 1975; Conger 1976; Akers et al. 1979; Poole and Regoli 1979; Giordano 1978).

Moral-development theory views the adolescent peer group as important for the role-taking opportunities it affords. The differing perspectives the adolescent encounters lead to cognitive conflict when his structures seem less adequate than those he hears from a person one stage above his own reasoning. This is a mechanism for sociomoral growth that relies on groups of individuals reasoning at different stages. We know from our review of studies that the delinquent group will be heavily weighted with preconventional thinkers, thus reducing the role-taking and growth-inducing opportunities available to the delinquent adolescent. The presence of some stage 3 delinquent group members may afford some limited opportunities for role-taking growth for preconventional delinquents, but less than preconventional nondelinquents would likely experience in their peer group. We would assume, therefore, that preconventional delinquents would move toward conventional thinking, but at a significantly slower pace than that of their nondelinquent counterparts. There is evidence of this trend in the prison-intervention studies discussed later in this chapter.

We would also expect that delinquents' reasoning at conventional stages would be at an even greater disadvantage in continued stage growth because there are few if any opportunities for role-taking from higher-stage delinquent peers. In addition, the delinquent subgroup or prison life would tend to make lower stages more adaptive to the environment, which is often in structural equilibrium with lower forms of moral reasoning. The prediction for older delinquents, then, would be a gradual leveling off at the conventional stages at an age significantly higher and at stages significantly lower than for the general population.

We disagree with the morally relativistic position held by some subcultural theorists who have argued that "the process of becoming a delinquent gang member is the same as becoming a boy scout" (Cohen 1955). This tendency to romanticize subcultural life does not square with their other emphasis on the powerful delinquency inducement of the debilitating stress of impoverishment in all its forms. This is not to say that delinquent gangs are anomic and totally instrumental in their treatment of members. On the contrary, certain of the impulses for friendship and identity formation that characterize adolescence are certainly present in the minds if not always the mores of gang members. Whether it is "reaction formation," or "strain," or "focal concerns" that draw kids into gangs, however, the group moral atmosphere for growth cannot be higher than that of its individual members. As our data show, delinquents suffer an additional disadvantage beyond their economic and other deprivations—an impaired rate of moral growth. Thus the occasional tendency to wax euphoric about the essential moral equivalence of delinquency is misconceived.

From a developmental-psychological perspective, delinquent values can inhibit psychological growth. Membership in a delinquent subculture can impose pressures to conform that rob the adolescent of the opportunity to move out from under the heteronomy of externally imposed moral constraints known in childhood, toward the autonomy of making one's own moral choices by exercising emerging intellectual strengths not present in childhood. There is evidence that social bonds of friendship and affection are stunted by delinquent subcultures (Hewitt 1970), and certainly the anomic but coercive ethos of some gangs does little to stimulate empathy or any of the other hypothesized factors leading to moral action. The naive romanticism of the relativist position is succinctly undercut by Hirschi's analysis:

> The interpersonal relations among delinquents are not of the same quality of warmth or intensity as those among nondelinquents; failure in one group decreases the likelihood that one will find intimate personal relations in some other group; delinquents do not possess the skills requisite to the argument that they are somehow the finest product of their own culture. [1969, p. 229]

The issue is not whether group norms and norm-guided behavior exist in delinquent groups; they do exist. Nor is the question whether the content of some of these norms is the same as those in conventional society, such as group loyalty; they can be the same. The important factor here is the *moral orientation* by group members to these norms. Sociologists like Durkheim (1961) have attempted to characterize the moral component of orientations to social norms in terms of attributes first clearly seen in what we term stage 4 moral orientation. Attitudinally, such a moral orientation includes intrinsic respect and loyalty to the group and its rules, a concern for maintenance of the solidarity of the collective and for the welfare of its members for intrinsic rather than extrinsic reasons. On the cognitive side, it involves taking the perspective of a general member of society, G.H. Mead's "generalized other," as distinct from one's own egocentric role-perspective.

Our findings indicate that adolescent delinquent groups do not enlist such moral attitudes. Because delinquent groups lack such a moral orientation, they do not have the stability or cohesion of groups that do enlist a moral orientation. This lack of such a stage 4 moral orientation to the group is reflected not only in the instabilities of delinquent groups, but also in the fact that the content of their norms does not demand an appeal to anything more moral than preconventional concerns about gratifications. This is evident in the usually sociological description of delinquent norms as stressing trouble, immediate gratification, toughness, and so forth.

Our data indicate that delinquent groups tend to enlist preconventional adolescents, who view the norms of the group in preconventional ways. Although this is a psychological fact, we may still ask the sociological question, Why do criminal groups not enlist individuals with more moral orientations, or why do they not generate a moral orientation in their members, as do other groups? The answer is a refinement of the commonsense answer that immoral groups do not attract moral people or generate moral attitudes. Such a refinement implies clarifying the distinction between deviant groups and immoral ones. Groups that engage in deviant or illegal activities but that justify these acts in the name of moral concerns are different from criminal groups that systematically violate the rights of others. Similarly, nondeviant groups like the army and the police that engage in so-called legitimate violence differ morally from criminal groups in that the rationale for conventional violence is that it is necessary for the welfare of the larger society. Those toward whom violence is practiced are defined as outside of society or as not having generalized conventional group employing violence rights. Actions are not legitimated that in general deny a consideration of rights of those outside the group. It can hardly be doubted that both deviant noncriminal groups and conventional groups engaging in violence recruit considerable proportions of members with preconventional moral orientations. They also recruit members with conventional or even principled moral orientations, however, who in most circumstances represent the leadership of these groups.

Summary

The three major sociological theories of the causes of delinquency each offer valuable insights compatible with moral-stage theory. We have discussed ways in which the hypothesized contributions of macrosocial structures like class can interact with psychological moral structures of the individual and either induce or reduce delinquent behavior. The social-psychological bridge between these disciplines offered by control theory compliments the explanatory power of moral-stage as well as strain and subcultural theories. It suggests mediating variables in the moral judgment-action process that merit further investigation. The social-control position also points to ways in which social bonding may partially explain the relatively unexamined nature of conventional delinquency.

Just Community Intervention Theory

The difference in the moral reasoning of offenders and nonoffenders led us to think about what is absent in offenders' development and what might overcome any such developmental lags. A first step was to examine the practical implications of the more formal developmental theory. Kohlberg (1976) summarizes the common assumptions among cognitive-developmental theories of morality as follows:

1. Moral development has a basic cognitive-structural or moral-judgmental component.
2. The basic motivation for morality is a generalized motivation toward acceptance, competence, self-esteem, or self-realization, rather than to meet biological needs and to reduce anxiety or fear.
3. Major aspects of moral development are culturally universal because all cultures have common sources of social interaction, role taking, and social conflict, all of which require moral integration.
4. Basic moral norms and principles are structures arising through experiences of social interaction, rather than through internalization of rules that exist as external structures; moral stages are not defined by internalized rules, but by structures of interaction between the self and others.
5. Environmental influences in moral development are defined by the general quality and extent of cognitive and social stimulation throughout the child's development, rather than by specific experiences with parents or by experiences of discipline, punishment, and reward.

Since our first intervention in the early 1970s, we have tried to meld these characteristics into the Just Community approach to moral development. Four major implications of our intervention theory will be described.

In many traditional human-services programs, *development* implies an increase in appropriate behavior, attitude, or information. A client is considered to have matured if he stops stealing, stops lying, or obeys program rules. In our approach, however, development is defined primarily by changes in the underlying processes one uses to interact in the world. This process change may include changes in behavior or increases in information; but most important, it involves an improvement in the way a person organizes his world when he solves problems—his *world view.*

In the following example, response *a* compared with response *a'* indicates change in a person's moral view or problem-solving process, but not in overt behavior. The person's thinking has changed from considering only his rights to considering the rights of others also. The same is true for *b* compared with *b'*. The cognitive-developmental interventionist considers these as developmental changes. On the other hand, response *a* compared with *b* and *a'* compared with *b'* indicate changes in behavior but not in problem-solving process. The traditional interventionist might view these as developmental changes, but the cognitive-developmentalist would not. The structural, process change is a necessary condition for change.

Reasons for Lying	*Reasons for Not Lying*
a. I lied because it got me what I needed and it kept me out of trouble. It's nobody's business anyway.	*b.* I didn't lie around here because I got into trouble when I lied. I couldn't go out at night, and I wanted to get out of here at night. You gotta look out for yourself.
a'. I lied because I wanted to get a job. My family needed the money and I'm not going to let them starve. You have to think of other people too, besides yourself. I can't tell the boss I don't have an education or no experience or my brother and sister won't eat.	*b'.* I stopped lying because it just wasn't fair to people. It hurts them and they wouldn't trust me anymore. You have to think about hurting others too, you know.

Although an emphasis on a person's moral thinking structure is a first implication, a second implication is the quality of the social interaction necessary for normal development of this underlying structure. This quality of interaction between the self and others involves a continual equilibration process described by Piaget (1963) as the organism's adaptation to the environment. It is by adapting to things that thought organizes itself, and it is by organizing itself that thought structures things (Piaget 1963).

The equilibration occurs when the outside stimulation from an environment is similar enough to a person's present organization to allow understanding and absorption. Here the person is able to bend the reality event to fit his present structure. The equilibration also includes outside stimulation dissimilar enough to ensure optimal pressure or conflict to encourage a person to adjust to new (slightly different) realities in the environment.

This quality of interaction is important partly because it describes a process that ensures that clients experience good feelings about their actions and problem-solving abilities as they also improve their thinking and behavior in permanent ways. The process maintains integrity and continuity at the same time that it incorporates newly discovered realities.

To facilitate this process, staff must understand a resident's present stage of development and must provide enough stimulation to ensure that he applies stage-appropriate thinking to problems. This process further requires that staff provide new information from the environment to create optimal conflict to ensure the growth of the thought process.

In addition to a focus on structural thinking and the equilibration process, a third implication of cognitive-developmental theory is that program goals are not futuristic, but are the present reconstruction of experience where the means and the goals are one and the same thing. A program's means must have a necessary connection to what they are means for (the goals). Preaching, personally attacking, restricting a resident, or avoiding conflict and problem solving as a means for enhancing self-control and responsible behavior have no logical connection to the end of improving a person's level of responsibility. Ensuring that a resident uses *his* present level of social thinking and acting about social responsibility does have such a connection. It allows a resident's current state of responsibility to be active and present so that it can be examined, criticized, and updated with new information, leading to a new, more integrated and consistent state of responsibility. In this way, means and ends are united.

The equilibration process is the interaction of a person's structure with the slightly more inclusive structure of others; it unites means and goals. Equilibration occurs when people experience some excitement about their interests, when they value their own ideas and behaviors, as they simultaneously experience the unfairness or harm their thinking and actions might cause others.

The absence of this unit represses natural development in traditional programs, not because goals and means are absent, but because their logical connection is clouded. Often residents do not see any connection between their desires and the means staff employ. Residents have one set of goals; staff (often each staff member) have others. There is an absence of matching of the residents' means-goals capabilities and expectations with staff planning for each resident. Thus what occurs is not a goal-means unity, but rather an array of ambiguous goals and means bouncing off each other in continual tension. If the goal is to facilitate the development of respect for other people's rights and of just action toward others, then the means must be a demonstration of respect and just action.

So far we have argued that applied cognitive-development theory requires a developmental focus on a person's thought structure, a process of interaction and equilibration between the form of a person's structure and an environment containing slightly more inclusive structural forces, and a necessary and logical connection between a program's goals and means. We are now directed to the most encompassing implication: that a democratic living atmosphere defined by certain developmental conditions is crucial to natural development. Such developmental conditions must conform to the rules of deontic moral principles of justice. In this sense they are prescriptive, because they describe what actually should be done to resolve interpersonal conflicts in a nonrelative manner. They are reversible because they are equally fair from all points of view. They are generalizable in that they apply to all content areas in moral-conflict situations.

We will discuss five such developmental conditions that are presented, in similar forms, elsewhere (Kohlberg et al. 1974; Wasserman 1976; Jennings 1979). The five conditions are (1) moral discussion, (2) discussion in the fairness form, (3) role-taking opportunities, (4) stage-adjacent reasoning, and (5) mutual decision making.

1. *Moral discussion* involves two or more people in talk about issues of conflict or decision. It requires sufficient time for discussion and the participation of all parties. The issues for discussion must be relevant to the discussants, not important only to staff or administrators. Having parents who encourage such discussion on moral issues is one of the clearest determinants of moral-stage advance (Holstein 1968). Socioeconomic status is also correlated with moral development in various cultures (Colby and Kohlberg 1981). This is because middle-class children have more opportunities to take the point of view of the more distant, impersonal, and influential roles in society's basic institutions (law, economy, government, economics) than do lower-class children. In general, the greater an individual child's participation in a social group or institution, the more opportunities he has to take the social perspectives of others. Thus, although extensive participation in any particular group is not essential to moral development, participation in some group is.

2. The *fairness form* refers to a focus on why the discussants think something is good or bad, why a proposal is fair or not, and why something is fair or unfair to the people involved. This form of discussion contrasts with arbitrary decision making; one-on-one dialogues; mere storytelling (arguing about facts, events, times, and so on); and opinion giving. Kohlberg's stages of moral judgment are formal descriptions of the fairness form. They describe the development of a person's perception of what is fair between

himself and others. Discussion in the fairness form allows people to discuss a problem using their own various structural stages of moral judgment.

Numerous experiments have demonstrated the effectiveness of such fairness moral discussion when compared to groups employing other forms of discussion (Blatt 1971; Colby et al. 1977; Hickey 1972; Berkowitz 1977).

3. *Role-taking:* According to Kohlberg (1969, p. 339; 1976) moral development is fundamentally a process of the restructuring of modes of role taking. Role taking is what differentiates social experience from mere interaction. Social experience involves taking the attitude of others, becoming aware of their thoughts and feelings, and putting oneself in their place. When the emotional side of role taking is stressed, it is typically termed *empathy* (or *sympathy*). The term *role taking*, coined by G.H. Mead (1934), is preferable, however, because (1) it emphasizes the cognitive as well as the affective side; (2) it emphasizes an organized structural relationship between self and others; (3) it emphasizes that the process involves understanding and relating to all the roles in the society of which one is a part; and (4) it emphasizes that role taking goes on in *all* social interactions and communication situations, not merely in ones that arouse emotions of sympathy or empathy.

The first prerequisite for role taking is participation in a group or institution in which interaction and communication are emphasized and active role taking is encouraged. The more the individual is held responsible for the decisions of the group and made aware of the group's response to his own behavior, the more he must take the role of other group members.

We have examined the environments at opposite extremes in role-taking opportunities. The American orphanage had children at the lowest levels, stages 1 and 2, even through adolescence (Thrower, 1980). Of all environments studied, an Israeli kibbutz had children at the highest level, with adolescents mainly at stage 4 and with a considerable percentage at stage 5 (Bar-Yam, Reimer, and Kohlberg 1972). Both environments involved low levels of interaction with parents, but were dramatically different in other ways. The U.S. orphanges not only lacked parental interaction, but also involved very little communication and role taking between adults and children. Relations among the children themselves were fragmentary, with very little communication and no stimulation or supervision of peer interaction by the staff. That the deprivation of role-taking opportunities caused a retardation in role taking as well as in moral judgment was suggested by the fact that the orphanage adolescents failed a role-taking task passed by almost all children of their chronological and mental age. In contrast, children in the kibbutz engaged in intense peer interaction supervised by a group leader who was concerned with bringing the young people into the kibbutz community as active and dedicated participants. Discussing, reasoning, communicating feelings, and making group decisions were central, everyday activities.

Robert Selman (1976a, 1980) has attempted to clarify the role-taking (social-perspective-taking) component of moral judgment as an important condition in natural development. He defines *role taking* as the way a person takes another person's perspective and relates that perspective to his own, and further, how a person understands the relation between his own perspective and that of others. As a person comes to have a truer picture of the other person in relation to himself, his perspective-taking (role-taking) ability matures.

In several studies, Selman and his colleagues have demonstrated significant role-taking advances with human-services clients when moral discussions in the fairness form were employed in experimental groups (Selman and Jacquette 1976; Jacquette and Parkhurst 1977).

4. *Stage-adjacent reasoning* refers to reasoning elicited during discussions in the fairness form that is one stage or a part of a stage above that of participants. Stage-adjacent reasoning exposes a person to fairness structures not too unlike his own, thereby maintaining interest by the use of different but recognizable reasoning and context. Yet the person also is exposed to foreign concepts of fairness one step above his own, thereby challenging him to grow to a higher stage because of the realization that these notions are more complex and adequate to solving problems. The fact that the stage-adjacent reasoning is close enough to be both vaguely understood and intellectually stimulating makes it the optimal match for cognitive equilibration. This facilitates movement to the next level of development and behavior. Reflective reorganization arises from the sensed contradictions in one's current stage structure. The moral reasoning of significant others is viewed as discrepant in content or structure from one's own reasoning.

To test this notion, Elliot Turiel (1966) demonstrated systematically that exposing students to reasoning one stage above their own would stimulate moral-stage development, whereas exposure to moral reasoning two stages above or one stage below a student's was not significantly effective. One criticism of Turiel's study was that the experimenter served as the facilitator. To test the effect of exposure to one-stage-higher reasoning without the experimenter, Berkowitz, Gibbs, and Broughton (in press) instructed twenty-four male and twenty-four female undergraduates to reach consensual solutions to a series of one nonmoral and four moral dilemmas. Discussion partners were prearranged to be at either the same stage, a minor stage apart, or a major or full stage apart.

Their results showed that lower-stage members of the minor-stage disparity dyads increased significantly more in moral stage (measured by Kohlberg's instrument) than did any of the other groups, although small but consistent minor-stage increases were observed for the lower-stage partners in the full-stage disparity condition. The higher-stage partners in the disparity groups did not change. The general patterns of these results were consistent with Turiel's; that is, lower-stage subjects grew significantly in their moral reasoning by interacting with higher-stage partners.

It is also plausible that participation in institutions that have the potential of being seen as at a higher stage than the person's own is a basic determinant of moral development.

5. *Mutual decision making:* As a direct condition for moral growth, everyone involved in issues must have equal responsibility in their resolution (Kohlberg, Wasserman, and Richardson 1975).

In numerous Just Community school and human-services programs, we have consistently found significant advances in development for persons experiencing decision-making power when compared with persons experiencing little or no power (Reimer 1977; Jennings 1979; Higgins, Power, and Kohlberg 1981; Bar-Yam, Reimer and Kohlberg 1972; Hickey and Scharf 1980).

Mutual decision making means that everyone involved in an issue not only discusses it, uses the fairness form, experiences role-taking opportunities, and is exposed to adjacent reasoning, but also literally has a voice in and vote on the final decisions. Only then can a sense of mutual responsibility develop.

In addition to these direct conditions of a developmental atmosphere, three indirect but related conditions are necessary for moral development (Kohlberg, Wasserman, and Richardson 1975)—democracy, fairness, and a sense of community. *Democracy*, as an indirect condition, refers to the degree of responsibility people experience for a program's rules and decisions. *Fairness* refers to the degree to which people perceive rules and decisions as fair. *Sense of community* refers to the degree to which the residents perceive that the group helps them and that they are helpful to the group. These conditions are measured by our moral-atmosphere interview, whereas the direct conditions are measured by an analysis of community-meeting transcripts as well as a moral-atmosphere interview (Jennings 1979).

The most obvious characteristic of the cognitive-developmental approach is its use of some type of stage concept, of some notion of age-linked sequential reorganizations in the development of moral attitudes. For intervention theory, this implies an effort to facilitate the natural development of a persons' structural understanding of the moral world by encouraging him to create his own notions of the right and the good through social interaction with others. This social interaction requires an environment with definite developmental conditions. In the next section we briefly discuss our effort to implement these conditions in three experimental Just Community programs.

The Just Community Programs

Our Just Community pilot programs emerged as an effort to better understand the nature of developmental-intervention theory and practice. They were also efforts to be more effective than traditional rehabilitative programs. In this respect, our implementation efforts were influenced by the reviews of program effectiveness that emerged in the early 1970s. Overall, these findings support our notions of what is important in delinquency rehabilitation.

From our cognitive-developmental perspective, many of these programs failed because they operated with an arbitrary and relative psychology and philosophy. Often program goals and means were arbitrary. Goals and means might change from day to day or from staff to staff. Further, many programs did not involve residents in regular and intense experiences aimed at compensating for developmental deficiencies, such as decision making, responsibility to others, and reasoning and communication to resolve stress. Instead of such experiences, custodial settings focused on security and obedience; therapeutic programs analyzed the client's supposedly inadequate experiences and behaviors; behavioristic programs stressed repetition or imitation of adult behaviors; and humanistic programs focused on respecting clients' rights. There was little opportunity for clients to experience other people's perspectives so that they could criticize and improve their own. Clients seldom developed the ability to integrate the conflicting roles of various people. Instead of stimulating positive social interaction, growth, and inclusiveness, this situation encouraged physical and psychological isolation.

Traditional programs failed in part because they did not allow clients to apply their present behaviors and attitudes (the ones they think are right) in interactions. These programs often encouraged residents to demonstrate adult behavior and thinking that seemed artificial, arbitrary, and incomprehensible to the clients. Clients were encouraged to see themselves as being behaviorally or emotionally ill and in need of a cure. They were discouraged from applying the attitudes and behavior that, for better or worse, are the foundation—because they exist—for development.

Considering this review of past interventions, along with our intervention theory, our first program was a modest attempt by Joseph Hickey (1972) to apply the moral-discussion approach with prisoners at a Connecticut reformatory. His overall aim was to determine the effectiveness on moral reasoning about hypothetical dilemmas and the practical feasibility of using a Just Community approach in a prison environment. The reaction of prison staff and residents to discussing moral issues with a democratic process was uncertain. Discussions using hypothetical dilemmas seemed the place to start since (1) these had been successful with student and Sunday-school populations, and (2) they were less threatening to residents, staff, and administrators (in contrast to real-life prison dilemmas).

Hickey's subjects were thirty-six residents from a medium security prison, ranging in age from 16 to 22 years. They were heterogeneous on the dimensions of types of crime, number of offenses, social class, and race. Subjects were interviewed using the Kohlberg moral-judgment measure, roughly matched by preliminary moral-maturity scores, and divided into experimental and control groups.

Hickey divided the thirty-six residents into two groups, with each group involved in moral discussion, using prison moral dilemmas adapted from the Kohlberg dilemmas. The experimental group met in a private room three times a month. Here, Hickey facilitated the group to ensure that all the residents who so desired could participate in the discussions, that as much role taking as possible occurred, and that the discussion focused on fairness. After thirty-six discussion sessions, Hickey found a significant increase in the residents' reasoning abilities. After twelve weeks there was an increase of seventeen points in moral maturity for nineteen experimental subjects. For eight experimental subjects the discussions lasted for one year. For these subjects there was an increase of thirty-nine moral maturity points. There was no significant stage change for the seventeen control subjects who continued in the regular prison routine. These positive results using hypothetical-dilemma discussions have also been demonstrated with adolescent offenders (Fleetwood and Parish 1976; and Gibbs 1981).

The Hickey study paved the way for more extensive Just Community programs by demonstrating the effectiveness of moral discussion in prison. These hypothetical discussions usually led to discussion of real-life dilemmas of general interest to prisoners, suggesting the possibility for application to the larger prison environment. This research also suggested that prison administrators and staff can be supportive of the moral-discussion approach. Equally important, this study established a precedent in a Connecticut prison that led directly to the establishment of the womens' Just Community Unit at Niantic, Connecticut.

The Connecticut Project

In 1971 there was a near riot at the Niantic Connecticut State Farm for Women. Since Joe Hickey worked for the Connecticut Correctional System and was also associated with Professor Kohlberg at Harvard, this situation presented an opportunity to establish a Just Community program with real-life dilemmas. Here we briefly discuss the Connecticut projects, which are described in detail elsewhere (Kohlberg et al. 1974; Scharf and Hickey 1976; and Hickey and Scharf 1980).

After the riot, feelings between staff and residents were generally hostile. In spite of these antagonisms, residents, staff, and administrators all expressed a willingness at least to explore the possibility of cooperating to create a democratic program focusing on the real dilemmas before them.

Suddenly, it was possible to implement the developmental conditions in a total program. The staff participated in weekly training sessions to develop their facilitation skills. Moral issues from cleaning responsibilities to homosexuality were allowed for discussion and resolution. The residents' issues were as important as the staff's. They were discussed and resolved in daily planning meetings, weekly community meetings, emergency meetings, ten-week rule-review marathon meetings, and weekly personal-issue small-group meetings. The staff ensured that the group discussions were about fairness and that outside people were brought in to provide role-taking opportunities. The interaction of peer reasoning dominated the meetings. Using democratic process, the residents and staff members each had one vote. After a number of months of conflict and confusion, staff and residents arrived at a common definition of a program and a rules contract acceptable to most of the staff and residents. Community members controlled discipline within a single cottage through community meetings, and the residents received many new privileges. Residents indicated a willingness to make some accommodation with the staff and also agreed to try to settle grievances and conflicts through a framework of cottage community meetings.

The community meeting was the program's core. Here conflicts were resolved, and a constitution of rules and procedures was developed. This constitution was the common structural document that provided everyone with a unified way of acting. It contained all the rules, meeting schedules, and discipline procedures. This common creation of the rules and procedures generated feelings of trust and responsibility among community members.

The Half Way House

The difficulty of reintegration into the community while living within a prison became an issue for the Niantic Women's unit community meeting. A community Half-Way House Just Community program was developed by the womens' unit staff and residents (Hickey and Scharf 1980). They created the first set of rules for the half-way house and decided which residents would go to the program. The aim was to provide a more realistic living environment and the possibility of a more democratic work environment. Once it began, a democratic atmosphere began to grow. Much energy was expended working through the difficulties of (1) adjusting to the program's location in a high crime area, (2) developing a community atmosphere when most residents worked unpredictable hours, (3) integrating the program rules with street rules, (4) involving concerned administrators in the program, (5) obtaining and training staff for the difficulties of a community program and (6) trying to keep a low public image. The half-way house closed after a year of operation. The major difficulties were never overcome.

The Mens' Unit

While the Just Community Women's Unit and the half-way house were operating, an effort to establish a Just Community program for men was undertaken (Hickey and Scharf 1980). This program was established on the grounds of the women's prison in Niantic, Connecticut. An attempt was made to establish a program similar to the women's unit. However, the men were more politically active and focused their attention on such issues as a prisoner's right to be in one institution or another, freedom of speech, and so forth. While these are important issues, the program staff and consultants had little power to facilitate discussion and resolution of these issues. The men's group failed to resolve issues about living together at Niantic, and they failed to establish a relationship with the Niantic staff or with each other. They did not first establish a sense of community within the program itself as a base of operations for more political action. The unit was finally closed after one year.

Hickey and Scharf (1980) report several categories of results from the Niantic Women's Unit project—moral judgment change, moral atmosphere perceptions and behavioral change. When moral judgment change was compared between seventeen Just Community residents and residents in control group programs, a significant positive difference was found. The Just Community residents advanced thirty-nine moral maturity points compared to essentially no change for women in a traditional program and for men in a traditional prison environment. A variety of significant moral atmosphere differences were also found. Seventy-five percent of the Just Community residents perceived the program as fair. These residents saw themselves as author and enforcer of the rules. They used the program as a context for mutual aid and problem solving. The residents in the men's unit also found the program fairer than the prison they came from. The majority of residents in control programs (custody, behavior-modification and transactional analysis) saw their programs as arbitrary, brutal and generally unfair. As a rough effort to examine behavioral change, recidivism was studied for the women's unit residents. Preliminary data indicates a 15 percent recidivism rate as compared to a 35 percent recidivism rate for the rest of the institution.

The Niantic program demonstrated that difficult real life dilemmas could be handled in a correctional program. It also showed that administrators and staff can support and participate in such a program. The program also demonstrated areas that require more integration. Some of these include direct administrative involvement, staff development and political and public support.

The Florida Intervention

In 1975 Jennings had the opportunity to establish and direct a Just Community program with adolescents committed to the state of Florida's Department of Youth Services (Jennings 1979). When he became director in 1975, the Florida model was a strong behavior-modification program. The aim was to transform this authoritarian program to a Just Community model along the lines developed at Niantic.

The program had ten residents (ages 12-16) living in an unlocked residential home and attending alternative programs within public schools. Staff included a director, a social worker, and five-day staff. One day staff slept overnight.

The heart of the program was the weekly community meeting. In its first weeks the community meeting was used primarily to make and change rules and develop a constitution. Later, meetings were used to discuss issues of rule enforcement, as well as interpersonal issues and conflicts. Emergency meetings were held when needed, as in the case of a fight between residents. Marathon meetings were held every two months to review and modify the rules and constitution.

Applying the Just Community approach was possible in part because the highest-level administrator supported the approach and participated actively. Her presence made it possible to discuss and resolve all types of moral issues, including administrative rules and constraints on the program. Trust between staff and residents and mutual responsibility for rules developed quickly, since all involved parties participated in the community meetings.

Moral-judgment data from the Florida program were compared with data from a transactional-analysis program and a secure behavior-modification program. Moral-atmosphere data were compared with those two programs and also with the moral-atmosphere perceptions of the Just Community residents before the program became a Just Community. (Then, it was a behavior-modification program.)

From pretest to posttest on Kohlberg's Moral Judgment Interview, the Just Community residents had an average gain of thirty-five moral-maturity points. Each Just Community subject gained at least half of a stage. For behavior-modification residents there was a gain of fifteen moral-maturity points. There was no gain for transactional-analysis residents.

This one-third moral-maturity change in the Just Community group is equivalent to the amount of change found in good moral discussion for Just Community educational interactions with junior-high and high-school students (Lockwood 1978; Power 1979). It is larger than that found in moral discussion or Just Community interventions with older offenders (Hickey 1972; Scharf 1973). Because of the small number (4) of transactional-analysis residents, the result of no gain is of uncertain meaning. The behavior-modification residents changed slightly. The fifteen-point difference from pretest to posttest was not statistically significant. This change was expected, however, since the program's residents participated in a community school program for two hours each day.

An overall test of the differences between the mean change scores showed the three groups to differ significantly ($F = 8.86$, $p < .005$). A post-hoc test among group means revealed the Just Community mean change to be greater than the behavior-modification mean change ($p < .05$), and also greater than the transactional-analysis mean change ($p < .05$).

Moral-atmosphere data were collected from residents in all four programs. Before Jennings became director of the Just Community program, he administered moral-atmosphere interviews to the then behavior-modification residents. After six months of the Just Community program, he again administered moral-atmosphere interviews to the same residents. He therefore obtained data from the same residents experiencing very different environments. Atmosphere data were also collected from secure behavior-modification residents and transactional-analysis residents.

The moral-atmosphere interviews were categorized on the following four dimensions: (1) effects of the program on the residents; (2) the fairness of the program as perceived by the residents; (3) the existence of discussion in the fairness form (discussing why things are good, bad, or fair) as a way of solving problems; and (4) the amount of decision-making power the residents experienced.

Once the resident's responses were placed in the categories, all responses were analyzed and given a score. Two scorers were used to establish interjudge reliability, yielding agreement of 95 percent. The responses were scored on a four-point Guttman scale, ranging from extreme negative to extreme positive.

The first scoring level was denying the existence of the category content (-1). For example, if a resident said, "We don't discuss nothing around here," this response was scored -1, indicating that he believed discussion of issues was not part of the program. The next scoring level was 0, indicating an ambiguous or contradictory set of responses. For example, if a resident said, "I don't get to discuss nothing, but there is one staff I discuss things with once in a while," it was scored 0, indicating ambiguous or contradictory statements about the category. The next level was $+1$, indicating the resident saw the category as a definite or positive part of the program.

For example, "We discuss things around here," would be scored + 1. The final category was scored + 2, indicating a higher quality or intense existence of the category. In the case of discussion, an intense degree of the category meant the existence of discussion in the fairness form—that is, talking about reasons for behavior. For example, "We discuss everything around here. We talk about why we do things," would be scored + 2.

To exemplify the moral-atmosphere results, the results for decision-making power and for effects of the program are presented in table 12-4. For decision-making power, the modal perception of the Just Community residents was that they had power to influence both the program and their own personal lives (+ 2). The modal perception of the transactional-analysis residents was ambiguous; in some ways they had power, in some not. The modal perception of residents in the two behavior-modification programs was (− 1) that they had no power. The distribution of resident perceptions on decision-making power is presented in table 12-4.

An example of the + 2 perception of the Just Community residents on decision-making power is:

> The community as a whole makes all the rules. It helps you govern your own life. We discuss issues at the community meeting and anybody we have to bring up for discipline we bring up here. We have a constitution. We talk about why someone broke a rule.

An example of the + 1 perceptions of a transactional-analysis resident is:

> Certain rules you can change but some you can't do nothing about. On restrictions they say what you can and can't say.

An example of the modal − 1 perceptions of a behavior-modification resident is:

> We say things but we never get a response. The director makes the rules.

What effect did the residents perceive the programs to have on their lives? If the Just Community program led to greater moral change by an objective measure, the Kohlberg Moral Judgment Interview, did these changes correspond to subjective self-perceptions of residents about change in the programs? An analysis of their responses revealed the modal response for the Just Community residents to be + 2—that the program had changed their actions toward other persons in morally relevant ways. The modal response for transactional-analysis residents was + 1—that it had improved self-understanding. It should be made clear that these were not two alter-

Table 12-4
Percentage of Residents in Each Program Responding to the Categories
of Decision-Making Power

Resident Responses	Just Community	Open Behavior Modification	Secure Behavior Modification	Transactional Analysis
I have power in the program and in my personal life (+2)	57	0	0	0
I have power in the program (+1)	43	0	0	28
I have power over some things but not others (0)	0	14	14	43
I have no power (−1)	0	85	71	0
Never mentioned power	0	0	14	28

native responses, since the categories formed a rough cumulative Guttman scale. Thus a resident who perceived himself as changing morally (+2) usually also saw himself as having increased self-insight or the ability to verbalize problems and conflicts (+1). Finally, the modal response for residents in both behavior-modifications programs was −1—no effects or bad effects. The percentage of all residents' self-perceptions about change based on the four-point scale is presented in table 12-5.

Table 12-5
Percentage of Residents in Each Program Responding to Categories of Self-Perceived Program Effects

Level	Just Communtiy	Open Behavior Modification	Secure Behavior Modification	Transactional Analysis
Moral effects (I treat people better) +2	72	—	14	—
Personal effects (I can talk better) +1	28	—	—	72
Ambiguous effects (I don't know) 0	—	29	14	—
No effects or bad effects (It made me worse) −1	—	57	42	14
No comment	—	14	28	14

Two examples of the modal (+ 2) responses from the Just Community residents are:

> Before I'd fight. Now I talk it out or bring it to the group. This place has taught me to respect the feelings of others.
>
> To handle my temper and respect people, sit down and talk. I'm friendlier, before I didn't give a shit about anybody.

Two examples of the modal (+ 1) responses of the transactional-analysis residents are:

> The transaction analysis helped me figure out where my attitude came from.
>
> I talk to people now, I learned to communicate better.

Two examples of the modal (− 1) response of the behavior-modification programs are:

> The program didn't do nothing. It just made me madder.
>
> I didn't like nothing about the program, it made me want to get out of here. But I learned something in school.

Whereas the + 2 responses of the Just Community residents and the + 1 responses of the transactional-analysis program may be viewed merely as testimonials to the ideology of each program, such testimonials may be viewed as necessary if not sufficient indicators of desired change. Their absence in the behavior-modification program may be interpreted, at the minimum, as indicating that these programs do not have an ideology that the residents can accept and verbalize.

The Massachusetts Intervention

In 1979 Jennings (Jennings, Higgins, and Power 1980) had the opportunity to develop another Just Community program for older adolescents who were diagnosed as being a danger to themselves or others and were committed to either the Department of Mental Health or the Department of Youth Services. This was our first opportunity to employ the Just Community model with severely assaultive clients and clients diagnosed as mentally ill. All clients had histories of court involvement, hospitalization, and other institutionalization. The state considered them to be in need of a secure setting because less restrictive alternatives had failed.

The main program was a locked ward on the grounds of a state hospital.

A second unit was a halfway house in a cottage on the hospital grounds. The locked program housed twelve clients and the halfway house had four clients. The funding was very generous. There were thirty-two total staff, including a director, assistant director, thirteen counselors, four certified teachers, a family counselor, a consulting psychiatrist, two nurses, and a full-time psychologist.

Both units had a daily schedule of activities, chores, and meetings established by staff and residents. The total program was dominated by thinking about the fairness and unfairness of interactions between people and by working out mutual solutions to problems.

Through this process, a comprehensive program evolved that included, among other things, a sophisticated staff manual, a sophisticated staff-client constitution, an elaborate client-staff orientation process, and a professional individual client service plan process. The program's evolution is evident in the fact that the collected staff effectively hired and discharged staff and that the community group of staff and residents played a primary role in client discharge.

In terms of preliminary evaluation, positive moral-judgment change was evident for the Just Community residents. There was an increase of between fifteen and forty MMS points or about one-quarter to one-half stage change for the three residents interviewed over a five-month period.

The major evaluative focus was on behavioral change. In addition to obtaining significant self-reported change, as in the Florida program, independent evaluators came in to perform interviews with the clients and parents. They also analyzed the daily staff log and the staff individual progress notes on each client. This analysis showed dramatic decreases in suicide attempts, running, assaultive behavior, and destruction of property. It also showed changes in behavior on weekend passes.

Conclusion

The three pilot interventions were successful in terms of moral-judgment change and moral-atmosphere improvement. We are not certain about recidivism, although we have found change in client behavior within the programs as recorded in staff logs and as reported by client and parent perceptions. Politically, however, they are difficult programs. When funding ended, the programs continued because the staff and clients felt better about the Just Community atmosphere. Neither the Connecticut, Florida, nor Massachusetts program continued once there was a change in management, however. There is a latent tension between the typical bureaucratic model and democratic operation of staff and clients.

Just Community Practice

Our experience with the Just Community programs helped us to clarify the practical nature of daily operations. Common daily operations evolved, which ensured the existence of the developmental conditions and which correlated with positive changes in moral reasoning, moral atmosphere, and moral behavior. Here we briefly present some of these operational processes.

Starting a Just Community Program

In a given situation, there may or may not be a Just Community program already in place. Whatever the situation, in the Just Community approach, the program's administrators, staff, and clients create the rules and procedures. If a program is already in place, they decide which rules and procedures should remain and which are unfair and should be changed. This process continues throughout the program's history.

Other key aspects of starting a Just Community program include client involvement in program entry and orientation. New clients play a central role in first deciding whether even to enter the program. Programs that follow this procedure, agree with our finding that fewer runaways occur, that rules are easier to enforce, and that greater trust between staff and residents exists. With regard to orientation, old clients often are involved in the orientation of new clients. Part of their job is to present the program and its rules as something they, the clients, actively create with the staff, maintain with the staff, and work on to change with the staff.

Program Foundation

Program foundation refers to the framework of ideas, meetings, and documents that the program participants have created and that provide the foundation for consistent, unifying daily operations. One common concern is that a Just Community program lacks order and standards because the clients are given power or because the program stresses continual change. This is not the case. Rather, such conditions result in a common set of procedures for participants to follow, consistency in rule enforcement, an effective problem-solving apparatus, and an environment in which tension and conflict are mutually resolved.

Providing this foundation involves an operational philosophy and psychology that staff discuss, approve, and follow. How the clients develop in thought and behavior and why what staff members are doing is ethical are central concerns that are written into a statement of program psychology and philosophy. The theoretical framework is discussed regularly and, when advisable, changed by administrators and staff together. This is often called *staff training*. At times, clients are included in this process if the program evolves to that point, as it did in the Connecticut and Massachusetts programs. In Connecticut the theory was discussed with the clients, and in Massachusetts there was a client representative at the staff-training sessions.

Written agreements are the central mechanism of a Just Community program. When administrators and staff or staff and clients arrive at consensus and make specific decisions, these are written down immediately for everyone to follow. These documents bind people together so that everyone is responsible to the rules and procedures that everyone created. Staff are then seen as consistent and legitimate in enforcing the rules. It becomes everyone's job to enforce them or else work to change them.

A staff manual is created by administrators and staff together. It includes job descriptions, hiring and firing guidelines, meeting schedules and procedures, staff conduct, staff disciplinary procedures, and whatever else is important to administrators and staff members. In our programs it was created at the beginning of a program and revised as often as necessary. It becomes the major orientation document for new staff.

A program *constitution* of daily rules and procedures is created by all involved administrators, staff, and clients. In our programs the major categories of constitutional rules and procedures were the following:

Decision-making procedures
Cleanup, food, health
Disciplines
Groups
New residents
Physical, verbal and property abuse
School
Bedtime, wake-up, overnight
Daily operations (music, phone calls, off-limit areas, and so on)
Nonnegotiable rules
Outside time, jobs
Running away
Program advancement and release

When created by everyone, these rules become the heart of the program. They are referred to regularly when problems occur and provide a common direction for everyone in terms of daily operations, rule enforcement, and personal advancement.

Another root component involves regular *meetings* for administrators and staff and for staff and clients. Regular meetings between staff and the appropriate community or state agencies may also be necessary. Meetings must occur at frequent enough intervals to resolve adequately the urgent concerns of everyone. At first, the meetings may occur frequently; but they may become less frequent as the quality of the developmental conditions is improved within the meetings. The program's participants decide exactly what meetings occur and when.

Several major staff-client meetings have evolved in all our Just Community programs. They include a weekly *community meeting* wherein administrators, staff, clients, and consultants meet to make all types of major and minor decisions. In all our programs this evolved as the most important decision-making forum. This is where the program constitutions were hammered out. Daily *house meetings* are also necessary to plan the day and evening. Usually there is one after breakfast and another after supper. *Emergency meetings* are crucial so that any community member can resolve an urgent issue. Usually some method for determining an emergency is established, such as a rule whereby two residents and two staff members agree that an emergency does indeed exist. Our Just Community programs also had a *marathon meeting* approximately every ten weeks to review the program's total set of rules and procedures (the constitution). Sometimes this was done gradually at the community meetings. Finally, some programs may have *small-group meetings* where very personal issues are discussed and resolved.

Another basic aspect of the Just Community program is a *service plan* for each client. This is the individual's written plan that everyone agrees to, follows, and changes regularly. Important characteristics of the meetings to develop the service plan include: (1) the existence of the developmental conditions; (2) the presence of all the key people involved with the client; (3) moral discussion and decision making concerning what the client's life should look like now, in the program; (4) moral discussion and decision making concerning what the next phase of the client's program will look like; and (5) moral discussion and decision making about how she or he can progress to the next phase. Each phase of the client's plan includes the activities he participates in; whatever privileges he has; and how he is going to work on his specific issues, such as not fighting, attending class or group, or beginning to talk about problems. The service plan is reviewed and revised at regular intervals until the client and group think it is fair.

Group Process

Group process in a Just Community program is characterized by the developmental conditions. Ensuring that these group conditions exist is the responsibility of the staff, although clients may also intuitively implement them.

The major content issues for the groups are the issues urgent to all participants (administrators, staff, and clients). Too often only the administrator's or the director's issues dominate the staff meetings, and only the staff's issues dominate the community meetings. The issues are issues of social content urgent to the people involved. If an issue is not important to some group members, they should feel confident that their urgent issues will be brought up and resolved later in the meeting, or at a future meeting.

Probably the most crucial and difficult condition to achieve of a Just Community group is having discussions in the form of fairness. Such Just Community discussions focus on what is right or fair about what happened and what should now happen. Talking about feelings and other internal experiences is incorporated at some point into discussing and resolving real social issues. Feelings and other internal experiences are relevant insofar as they improve social life.

The Just Community group also regularly exposes the participants to the roles, feelings, needs, and tensions of the people involved in the problems—the people affected by one's actions. We have done this by (1) making sure all the people involved in problems are also involved in the discussion and resolution of those problems; (2) having residents and their peers articulate how their actions affect others not present; (3) ensuring that staff and residents present the points of view and reasoning of other involved people; and (4) bringing in specific outside people who are affected by the resident's actions.

The reasoning that goes on in groups must also be comprehensible to the participants if the groups are to be of interest to them or are to effect client development. This stage-adjacent thinking is absent in many human-services programs because staff dominate groups by using reasoning that is too many stages morally and cognitively removed from the clients, or by not using reasoning at all. When staff ensure stage-adjacent reasoning, they allow the resident's present stage of reasoning and particular behavior patterns to be valid for him, while at the same time exposing the resident to a level of reasoning and behavior pattern one stage above his own. This ensures that the resident will feel confident about his particular reasoning ability, no matter how immature it might be, while being exposed to thinking and behavior that reflects more inclusive sociomoral ideas.

After these conditions have been operating in the group, the staff and clients ensure that the group comes to *democratic* resolutions. This allows the residents to move forward with their lives by actually using and learning from their discussions. The resident then has a self-chosen responsibility to others and feels obligated by the moral norms and specific decisions of the group.

Some general group-process guidelines reflecting the existence of the developmental conditions are as follows.

1. *Procedural aspects of group process:*
   a. Having a chairperson ensures that someone organizes an agenda, that things are kept moving, and that leadership skills are developed. Alternate the chairperson if the group decides. All our Just Community programs have had chairpersons. Initially a staff chairperson is necessary for the community meeting because of the insecurity and instability about starting a democratic program. Once conditions are stable, it is desirable to have a resident chairperson.
   b. Have an agenda. Decide as a group which are the most important issues, and discuss and resolve those first. Usually all the issues will not be covered in the allotted time. We often presented a list of issues and then asked the group for more issues. The first issues resolved were those causing the most tension in the program.
   c. Have a legal eagle. She or he is someone who brings the present rules and procedures to the meeting for referral concerning any conflicts, such as rule infraction. New rules can also be added.
   d. Have a sergeant-at-arms. This person ensures that the community rules about group conduct are enforced. The community group decides the limits of this person's power.
   e. Make sure that any new rules are put into written form immediately. This ensures an ongoing common foundation.
   f. Use the straw vote when appropriate. Often discussions get bogged down. Asking for a straw vote (one that does not count) uncovers who is for or against the issue and usually stimulates people to begin confronting and reasoning with each other.
2. *Process aspects of developmental group discussion:*
   a. When the group strays, bring them back to the issue and resolve it. Do this in a nonjudgmental way. For example: "That's another issue. Should we consider it later and finish the first issue now?" A supportive and nonjudgmental tone is important.
   b. Hear the residents' issues first, and bring them to some positive resolution for the residents.
   c. If someone wants to disrupt the group (for example, make a phone call or go to the bathroom), let the group decide. Take the person seriously even if he is being obnoxious or breaking a rule. The group of his peers will usually make their judgments loud and clear.
   d. Ensure that all the people involved in a crisis situation are at the group meeting.
   e. Facilitate the group participants to reason about what they think is good, fair, bad, or unfair about the issue at hand.
   f. At first, make terse, specific issues—"John probably stole the money"—into general issues—"Let's talk about stealing in the

program." Make some stronger rules around the issue. Get specific, if things move in that direction.

g. Stop one-on-one dialogue so that the entire group is included.

h. Make sure the point of view of people not present at the meeting is considered.

i. Avoid preaching, defensiveness, and storytelling.

j. Know what the next best step is for the staff or resident, and support it when it occurs. For example, just talking or proposing a solution, or even just joining the group, may be the most positive step possible for a person at that time.

k. End the group on a high note—for example, when people are feeling positive or laughing.

Individual Counseling

Whether or not counseling is formal and structured, personal counseling should occur in these programs. For a Just Community program, the counseling takes the form of the developmental conditions applied on an individual or group basis; this has been called the constructive-developmental approach. This counseling approach differs from the traditional approach in human service programs in several critical ways. First, the client is not viewed as sick or as having problems, but rather as experiencing stress resulting from a person's destabilization from one formerly comfortable world view, no longer appropriate to his age and environment, to a new and somewhat frightening way of seeing himself in the world. It may be what some call an identity crisis (Erickson 1963), resulting in depression or acting out. The counselor's role is to join the client at this place in development to help him examine and use his present structure for making new meaning, and for acting in new ways.

Second, the counselor's role is to ensure that the developmental conditions are applied within the counseling situation. Thus the counselor helps the client in decision-making around the client's life directions. He helps him to clarify critical issues, reason them through in terms of fairness, examine how his actions affect others and implement concrete resolutions that are developmentally appropriate.

Staff Responsibilities

During the daily interaction of staff and residents, staff face numerous problems that are unique, difficult, and sometimes traumatic. A major staff responsibility is to ensure that residents do the routine tasks of getting up in the morning, going to bed at night, cleaning, and attending activities such as school or work. In the Just Community program, residents themselves help to define these tasks and take the major responsibility for carrying them out. This is done at the regular meetings. When a resident fails at a task, he is breaking a rule that he had responsibility in making. He also knows the consequences because he was involved in determining them. In addition, he faces the rebuke of his peers, who also have a stake in the rules.

Such discipline is another major staff issue. Traditionally, the line staff have the major responsibility for discipline and often take abuse from residents who object to specific disciplines, as well as from other staff or administrators. In our Just Community programs, discipline became less arbitrary and more a function in which everyone participated, thereby decreasing the pressure on any one staff member. Residents in this atmosphere felt an ownership of the discipline process and thus a responsibility for seeing that rules and sanctions were carried out. According to Just Community residents' statements, they followed the discipline decisions because they felt an obligation to their peers and staff, rather than to an adult authority of the system. They took disciplines seriously because they understood the underlying reasons (which included their own reasons).

Staff also have the responsibility of maintaining a program that is both secure and humane. At first glance, a program like the Just Community program, which suggests that residents have a great deal of power, would seem to be a threat to security. In fact, problems that are considered security issues (such as running away or violence) are diminished. Violence decreased as residents developed the ability to talk things out with other people or the groups, and as the residents experienced a sense of responsibility to the community. Initially the whole group was involved in resolving violent conflicts. As the residents developed their own discussion skills, however, they solved potential violent conflicts by talking things out on a one-to-one basis as well as in groups. The implication for correctional practice is that the dreaded factor of violence can be decreased, not by implementing punishment, but by the socially acceptable method of discussing and resolving the fairness and unfairness of the factors involved in potentially violent situations.

Running away from the Just Community programs was controlled by the residents themselves. Because running was an important issue to the program, some of the most intense discussion and decision making concerned this issue. The entire community developed methods of eliminating running and of dealing with it when it did occur. The reason for not running away evolved as one's own obligation to peers and staff. Further, this discussion process provided the program with a built-in method of predicting the potential for running. Residents were able to use regular meetings to discuss and resolve conditions and situations that made them tense. Security no longer was determined by bars and locks, but rather by the relationships between staff and residents.

This brief discussion has attempted to provide the flavor of the line staff's role as facilitator in a Just Community program. The daily operations evolve through the process of mutual discussion and decision making. The right answers come from the people involved, employing universal conditions that ensure a more adequate social life for the individual and for the group.

Conclusions

This chapter has reviewed a number of theoretical assumptions and findings as they relate moral-stage theory to juvenile delinquency and criminal behavior. We have tried to describe what we see as the present strengths and weaknesses of the explanatory power of moral reasoning in causing and treating delinquency, while making suggestions for future study.

An important contribution of developmental psychology has been its attempt to explain deviance and psychopathology in terms of normal developmental processes. This is a departure from the traditional illness model, whereby abnormal development is viewed as having its own, presumably different, ontogenic path. We earlier discussed the universal conditions of development common to stage theories. The implication is that deviance can best be understood in terms of that from which it deviates—normal development. Therefore, intervention should address the structural understanding or world view of the individual, wherever he or she is in the developmental process. The aim is to encourage normal development by creating those conditions that surround the natural development of gradual accommodation to one's changing environment and abilities.

Piaget, however, warned against applying developmental theory to interfere in normal psychological growth. Indeed, he referred to such concerns as "the American question." He said that whenever he spoke in the United States and had finished explaining the human intellectual-growth process as a balance between assimilation and accommodation, someone would invariably ask, in effect, "That's all very well and good, Professor, but how can we speed up that process?" When development is proceeding normally, it would seem unnecessary and possibly ill advised to try to accelerate it. A sounder approach with normal populations is simply to create environments designed to ensure that everybody has access to such stimulation. In this way we attempt to broaden and integrate developmental conditions so that the individual can achieve at a rate appropriate to his or her needs and abilities.

The case of arrested or otherwise impaired development is different. Here there is a greater justification for intervention and acceleration. Environmental demands grow more complex with increasing age, whether or not the individual's developmental abilities keep pace. When development is arrested or lags seriously, failure to adapt psychologically to these changes may lead to increasingly inadequate ways of responding to one's environment. The data presented here, showing the tendency for delinquents to reason at less mature levels of moral development, provide one compelling example. What we know about conditions of development can then be employed, with the more easily justifiable goal of increasing the rate of psychological development.

Moral-stage theory holds that certain cognitive and social perspective-taking structures are prerequisites for each stage of moral reasoning. These represent the necessary but not sufficient conditions for growth in moral judgment. Therefore, an individual can have a higher level of cognitive or social reasoning than moral reasoning—never the other way around. Where this is the case, the goal would be to develop the moral structures that correspond to the person's highest present social and cognitive competence. An important additional implication for delinquent intervention is that other aspects of stage development (cognitive, social, ego) must be stimulated in order to provide the basis for further moral-stage advance, once equilibration across domains has been achieved. This has special significance for the role of education in delinquency prevention or treatment. Educators should be aware of the possibilities of, and need for, schools to address directly these areas of psychological development, as a means both of better teaching course content and of laying the foundation for continued psychological development. The various measures of developmental stages can be used as a means of diagnosing the individual needs of students and evaluating the educational or program effectiveness in remediating deficits in these areas.

In our discussion of the relation of moral judgment to moral action, we concluded that there is a significant, though not direct, relationship. Higher moral stages appear to act as an insulator against immoral action by making it more difficult to rationalize conformity to authority that conflicts with what one thinks is right, or to act hedonistically. We postulate that this more responsible autonomy with each higher stage would make one less susceptible to the negative peer pressure that often accompanies delinquent behavior. We also saw that at each stage a predisposition to perceive responsibility for others can predict greater concurrence between action and what one believes to be right.

Our understanding of the judgment-action link as it relates to delinquency will advance with future research into the nature of substage of moral reasoning. Also needed is further investigation of the other psychological variables in moral action and the means to remediate those that contribute to delinquent acts. Finally, there is a pressing need to better define *moral action* and such manifestations in delinquents as recidivism and positive life adjustment.

Our review of the relevant studies on delinquency and stage of moral reasoning showed a definite monotonic pattern, in which delinquents were consistently more likely to reason at levels lower than matched nondelinquents, and generally at a preconventional level. This held true even for psychological subtypes of delinquents (psychopathic, neurotic, subcultural), although statistically significant differences in small samples are more readily observed with psychopaths.

Future research should use larger samples, control for more variables, and use delinquency-inclusion criteria related to antisocial behavior rather than mere institutionalization or status offense. Also, more research on female juvenile offenders should be undertaken with a view toward explaining the lower frequency and less violent nature of their offenses. The causes of delinquency are not fully clear, although each of the major theories on the topic offers insights. The portion of delinquent behavior that is explained by immature moral reasoning is most theoretically and empirically compatible with social-control theory. It would be useful to examine whether the strengths of social bond can also compensate for preconventional moral reasoning, or strengthen resistance to delinquency at conventional levels. Studies should examine the nature of particular situational pressures that surround delinquent acts, and relate the strength of resistance to these pressures with the stage of moral reasoning and strength of social bond.

The Just Community intervention is theoretically guided in its design to create conditions that maximize developmental growth. These include an optional match between the client's world view and the moral atmosphere of the program. Practically speaking, this implies that rules and authority relationships within the program be perceived as fair, yet intellectually and emotionally challenging to the client. This optional match between client and program reflects the stage-adjacent stimulus for development, in which the program rules are understood by the client but are slightly more inclusive of other perspectives, causing the client both to stretch cognitively and to see the greater adequacy and fairness of that world view as issues are actually adjudicated by the group. This is a difficult task to build into each program's design, both because several stages may be represented within the client and staff population, and because the actual moral structure should represent social and democratic ideals that are postconventional in their structural conception of what is just. An effort must therefore be made to see that rules and social expectations can be interpreted and understood by several stage structures. The goal is to create an environment that is at once simple enough to be comprehensible and complex enough to aid development by means of moral discussions, role-taking opportunities, stage, adjacent reasoning, and genuine responsibility for creating and maintaining the moral atmosphere of the community.

References

Akers, R.L.; Krohn, M.D.; Lanza-Kaduce, L.; and Radosevich, M. Social learning and deviant behavior: A specific test of a general theory. *American Sociological Review,* 1979, *44,* 636-655.

Bandura, A., and Walters, R.H. *Adolescent aggression.* New York: Ronald Press, 1959.

Bar-Yam, M.; Reimer, J.; and Kohlberg, L. The development of moral reasoning in the kibbutz: Unpublished manuscript, 1972.

Berkowitz, M.W. Heterogeneous vs. homogeneous dyadic moral discussions: A test of the cognitive-developmental model of moral reasoning development. Ph.D. diss., Wayne State University, 1977.

Berkowitz, M.W.; Gibbs, J.; and Broughton, J. The relationship of moral judgment stage disparity to developmental effects of peer dialogue: *Merrill-Palmer Quarterly,* in press.

Blasi, A. Bridging moral cognition and moral action: A critical review of the literature. *Psychological Bulletin,* 1980, *88,* 1-45.

Blatt, M. The effects of classroom discussion on the development of moral judgment. Unpublished diss. abstract, University of Chicago, 1971.

Blatt, M., and Kohlberg, L. The effects of classroom moral discussion upon children's level of moral judgment. *Journal of Moral Education,* 1975, *4,* 129-161.

Campagna, A.F., and Harter, S. Moral judgment in sociopathic and normal children. *Journal of Personality and Social Psychology,* 1975, *31,* 199-205.

Cleckley, H. *The mask of sanity.* St. Louis: Mosby, 1964.

Cloward, R.A., and Ohlin, L.E. *Delinquency and opportunity.* New York: Free Press, 1960.

Coates, R. A working paper on community based corrections: Concept historical development, impact and potential dangers. Unpublished paper, Center for Criminal Justice, Harvard University, 1974.

Coates, B.; Miller, A.D.; and Ohlin, L.E. *Diversity in a youth correctional system: Handling delinquents in Massachusetts.* Cambridge, Mass.: Ballinger, 1978.

Cohen, A.K. *Delinquent boys.* Glencoe: Free Press, 1955.

Colby, A., and Kohlberg, L. Invariant sequence and internal consistency in moral judgment stages. Paper presented at Florida International University Conference, December 1981.

Colby, A.; Kohlberg, L.; Fenton, E.; Speicher-Dubin, B.; and Lieberman, M. Secondary school moral discussion programs led by social studies teachers. *Journal of Moral Education,* 1977, *6,* 90-111.

Colby, A.; Kohlberg, L.; Gibbs, J.; Candee, D.; Speicher-Dubin, B.; Hewer, A.; Kauffman, K.; and Power, C. *Measurement of moral judg-*

ment: A manual and its results. New York: Cambridge University Press, in press.

Conger, R.D. Social control and social learning models of delinquent behavior: A synthesis. Criminology, 1976, 14, 17-40.

Dixon, M.C., and Wright, W.E. Juvenile delinquency prevention programs: An evaluation of policy related research on the effectiveness of prevention programs. Unpublished paper, Peabody College for Teachers, Nashville, 1975.

Durkheim, E. Moral education: A study in the theory and application of the sociology of education, trans. E.K. Wilson and H.S. Schnarer. New York: Free Press, 1961. (Originally published 1925.)

Erickson, E.H. Insight and responsibility. New York: Norton, 1963.

Erickson, M.L., and Empey, L.T. Class position, peers, and delinquency. Sociology and Social Research, 1965, 49, 268-282.

Feld, B.C. Neutralizing inmate violence: Juvenile offenders in institutions. Cambridge, Mass.: Ballinger, 1978.

Feyerherm, W. The interrelationships of various indicators. Ph.D. diss. School of Criminal Justice, State University of New York, Albany, 1977.

_____ . Gender differences in delinquency: Quantity and quality. In L. Bowker, ed., Women and crime in America. New York: Macmillan, 1981.

Fleetwood, R., and Parish, T. Relationships between moral development test scores of juvenile delinquents and their inclusion in a moral dilemma discussion group. Psychological Reports, 1976, 39, 1075-1080.

Fodor, E.M. Delinquency and susceptibility to social influence among adolescents as a function of level of moral development. Journal of Social Psychology, 1972, 86, 257-260.

_____ . Moral development and parent behavior antecedents in adolescent psychopaths. Journal of Genetic Psychology, 1973, 122, 37-43.

Gibbs, J. Facilitation of sociomoral development in delinquents. Unpublished preliminary research project, Ohio State University, Columbus, 1981.

Gibbs, J., and Widaman, K.F. Social intelligence: Measuring the development of sociomoral reflection. Englewood Cliffs, N.J.: Prentice-Hall, 1982.

Giordano, P.C. Girls, guys and gangs: The changing social context of female delinquency. Journal of Criminal Law and Criminology, 1978, 69, 126-132.

Glueck, S., and Glueck, E. Unraveling juvenile delinquency. Cambridge, Mass.: Harvard University Press, 1950.

Gold, M. Undetected delinquent behavior. Journal of Research in Crime and Delinquency, 1966, 3, 27-46.

Haan, N.; Smith, M.B.; and Block, J. Moral reasoning of young adults: Political-social behavior, family background, and personality correlates. *Journal of Personality and Social Psychology,* 1968, *10,* 183-201.

Hains, A.A., and Miller, D.J. Moral and cognitive development in delinquent and nondelinquent children and adolescents. *Journal of Genetic Psychology,* 1980, *137,* 21-35.

Hartshorne, H., and May, M.A. *Studies in the nature of character,* vol. 1: *Studies of deceit.* New York: Macmillan, 1928.

Hartshorne, H.; May, M.A.; and Maller, J.B. *Studies in the nature of character,* vol. 2: *Studies in self control.* New York: Macmillan, 1929.

Hartshorne, H.; May, M.A.; and Shuttleworth, F.K. *Studies in the nature of character,* vol. 3: *Studies in the organization of character.* New York: Macmillan, 1930.

Hetherington, E.M., and Martin, B. Family interaction and psychopathology in children, In H.C. Quay and S.J. Werry, eds., *Psychopathological disorders of childhood.* New York: Wiley, 1972.

Hewitt, J.P. *Social stratification and deviant behavior.* New York: Random House, 1970.

Hickey, J.E. The effects of guided moral discussion upon youthful offenders' level of moral judgment. Ph.D. diss., Boston: Boston University School of Education, 1972.

Hickey, J., and Scharf, P. *Toward a just correctional system.* San Francisco: Jossey-Bass, 1980.

Higgins, A.; Power, C.; and Kohlberg, L. Student judgments of responsibility and the moral atmosphere of high schools: A comparative study. Paper presented at Florida International University Conference, December 1981.

Hindelang, M.J. Causes of delinquency: A partial replication and extension. *Social Problems,* 1973, *20,* 471-487.

_____ . Variations in sex-race-age specific incidence rates of offending. *American Sociological Review,* 1981, *46,* 461-474.

Hindelang, M.J.; Dunn, C.; Aumick, A.; and Sutton, L.P. *Sourcebook of criminal justice statistics.* Washington, D.C.: Law Enforcement Assistance Administration, 1975, 1976.

Hirschi, T. *Causes of delinquency.* Berkeley: University of California Press, 1969.

Holstein, C.B. Parental determinants of the development of moral judgment. Ph.D. diss., Berkeley: University of California, 1968.

Hudgins, W., and Prentice, N.M. Moral judgment in delinquent and nondelinquent adolescents and their mothers. *Journal of Abnormal Psychology,* 1973, *82,* 145-152.

Jaquette, D., and Parkhurst, V. Class meetings and peer socio-therapy: An interpersonal problem-solving approach for remedial social development. Unpublished paper, Harvard University, 1977.

Jennings, W. The juvenile delinquent as a moral philosopher: The effects of rehabilitation programs on the moral reasoning and behavior of male youthful offenders. Ph.D. diss., Harvard University, 1979.

Jennings, W.; Higgins, A.; and Power, C. Preliminary program evaluation for a regional adolescent program: Resident behavior and thinking, program atmosphere, and parent perceptions. Unpublished paper, Center for Moral and Personality Development, Harvard University, 1980.

Johnson, R.E. *Juvenile delinquency and its origins.* Cambridge: Cambridge University Press, 1979.

Jurkovic, G.J., and Prentice, N.M. Dimensions of moral interaction and moral judgment in delinquent and nondelinquent families. *Journal of Consulting and Clinical Psychology,* 1974, *42,* 256-262.

_____ . Relation of moral and cognitive development to dimensions of juvenile delinquency. *Journal of Abnormal Pscyhology,* 1977, *86,* 414-420.

Kohlberg, L. The development of modes of moral thinking and choice in the years ten to sixteen. Ph.D. diss., University of Chicago, 1958.

_____ . Moral development and identification. In H. Stevenson, ed., Child psychology. *62nd yearbook of the National Society for the Study of Education.* Chicago: University of Chicago Press, 1963.

_____ . Development of moral character and ideology. In M.L. Hoffman, ed., *Review of child development research,* vol. 1. New York: Russell Sage Foundation, 1964.

_____ . Stage and sequence: The cognitive-developmental approach to socialization. In D. Goslin, ed., *Handbook of socialization theory and research.* New York: Rand McNally, 1969.

_____ . The moral atmosphere of the school. In N. Overley, ed., *The unstudied curriculum: Its impact on children.* Washington, D.C.: Monograph of the Association for Supervision and Curriculum Development, 1970.

_____ . From is to ought: How to commit the naturalistic fallacy and get away with it in the study of moral development. In T. Mischel, ed., *Cognitive development and epistemology.* New York and London: Academic Press, 1971.

_____ . Continuities in childhood and adult moral development revisited. In P. Balter and K.W. Schaie, eds., *Life-Span Developmental Psychology: Personality and Socialization.* New York: Academic Press, 1973.

_____ . Moral stages and moralization: The cognitive-developmental approach. In T. Lickona, ed., *Moral development and behavior: Theory, research and social issues.* New York: Holt, Rinehart and Winston, 1976.

Kohlberg, L., and Freundlich, D. Moral reasoning and delinquency. Unpublished paper, Harvard University Laboratory of Human Development, 1973.

Kohlberg, L., and Kramer, R. Continuities and discontinuities in childhood and adult moral development. *Human Development,* 1969, *12,* 93-120.

Kohlberg, L.; Kauffman, K.; Hickey, J.; and Scharf, P. *Correctional manual, parts I and II.* Cambridge, Mass.: Moral Education Research Foundation, 1974.

Kohlberg, L.; Wasserman, E.; and Richardson, N. The just community school: The theory and the Cambridge cluster school experiment. In L. Kohlberg, ed., *Collected papers.* Cambridge, Mass.: Harvard University Graduate School of Education, 1975.

Kramer, R. Moral development in young adulthood. Unpublished dissertation, University of Chicago, 1968.

Liska, A.E. Delinquency involvement and delinquent peers. *Sociology and Social Research,* October 1973, *58,* 23-36.

Lockwood, A.L. The effects of values clarification and moral development curriculum on school age subjects: A critical review of recent research. *Review of Educational Research,* 1978, *48,* 241-259.

Lundman, R.J.; McFarland, P.T.; and Scarpitti, F.R. A description and assessment of projects reported in the professional literature. *Delinquency Prevention,* 1976, *22,* 297-308.

Martison, R. What works? Questions and answers about prison reform. *The Public Interest,* Spring 1974, 22-52.

Matza, D. *Delinquency and drift.* New York: Wiley, 1964.

_____. *Becoming deviant.* Englewood Cliffs, N.J.: Prentice-Hall, 1969.

McColgan, E. Social cognition in delinquents, predelinquents and non-delinquents. Ph.d. Diss., University of Minnesota, 1975.

McCord, J., and McCord, W. The effects of parental role model on criminality. In R.S. Covan, ed., *Readings in juvenile delinquency.* Philadelphia: Lippincott, 1964.

McCord, W., and McCord, J. *Psychology and delinquency.* New York: Grune and Stratton, 1956.

McEwen, C.A. *Designing correctional organizations for youth: Dilemmas of subcultural development.* Cambridge, Mass.: Ballinger, 1978.

Mead, G.H. *Mind, self and society.* Chicago: University of Chicago Press, 1934.

Milgram, S. *Obedience to authority: An experimental view.* New York: Harper and Row, 1974.

Miller, A.D.; Ohlin, L.E.; and Coates, R.B. *A theory of social reform: Correctional change processes in two states.* Cambridge, Mass.: Ballinger, 1977.

Miller, W.B. Lower class culture as a generating milieu of gang delinquency. *Journal of Social Issues*, 1958, *14*, 5-19.

Ohlin, L.E.; Coates, R.B.; and Miller, A.D. *Reforming juvenile corrections: The Massachusetts experience*. Cambridge, Mass.: Ballinger, 1978.

Piaget, J. *The origins of intelligence in children*. New York: Norton, 1963. (Originally published in 1952.)

————. *The moral judgment of the child*. New York: Free Press of Glencoe, 1965. (Originally published London: Routledge and Kegan Paul, 1932.)

Pittel, S.M., and Mendelsohn, G.A. Measurement of moral values: A review and critique. *Psychological Bulletin*, 1969, *66*, 22-35.

Poole, E.C., and Regoli, R.M. Parental support, delinquent friends, and delinquency: A test of interaction effects. *Journal of Criminal Law and Criminology*, 1979, *70*, 188-193.

Power, C. The development of the moral atmosphere of a just community high school program. Ph.D. diss., Harvard University, 1979.

Power, C., and Reimer, J. Moral atmosphere: An educational bridge between moral judgment and action. In W. Damon, ed., *Moral development*, New directions for Child Development, no. 2. San Francisco: Jossey-Bass, 1978.

Reimer, J. A study in the moral development of kibbutz adolescents. Ph.D. diss., Harvard University, 1977.

Rest, J. *Development in judging moral issues*. Minneapolis: University of Minnesota Press, 1979.

Rest, J.; Turiel, E.; and Kohlberg, L. Relations between level of moral judgment and preference and comprehension of the moral judgment of others. *Journal of Personality*, 1969, *37*, 225-252.

Robins, L. *Deviant children grown up*. Baltimore, Md.: Williams and Wilkins, 1966.

Ruma, E.H., and Mosher, D.L. Relationship between moral judgment and guilt in delinquent boys. *Journal of Abnormal Psychology*, 1967, *72*, 122-127.

Scharf, P. Moral atmosphere and intervention in the prison. Ph.D. diss., Harvard University, 1973.

Scharf, P., and Hickey, J. The prison and the inmate's conception of legal justice: An experiment in democratic education. *Criminal Justice and Behavior*, 1976, *3*, 107-122.

Schoenberg, R.J. A structural model of delinquency. Ph.D. diss., University of Washington, 1975.

Schrag, C. *Crime and justice: American style*. Washington, D.C.: U.S. Government Printing Office, 1971.

Selman, R. Social-cognitive understanding: A guide to educational and clinical practice. In T. Lickona, ed., *Moral development and behavior*. New York: Holt, Rinehart and Winston, 1976a.

_____ . Toward a structural analysis of developing interpersonal relations concepts: Research with normal and disturbed preadolescent boys. In A. Pick, ed., *Annual Minnesota symposium on child psychology,* vol. 10. Minneapolis: University of Minnesota press, 1976b.

_____ . *The growth of interpersonal understanding: Developmental and clinical analyses.* New York: Academic Press, 1980.

Selman, R., and Jaquette, D. To understand and to help: Implications of development research for the education of children with interpersonal problems. *Contemporary Education,* 1976, *22,* 105-117.

_____ . Stability and oscillation in interpersonal awareness: a clinical-developmental approach. In C.B. Keasey, ed., *Nebraska symposium on motivation,* vol. 25. Lincoln: University of Nebraska Press, 1978.

Shaw, C., and McKay, H.D. *Juvenile delinquency in urban areas.* Chicago: University of Chicago Press, 1942.

Simon, R.J. *Women and crime.* Lexington, Mass.: Lexington Books, D.C. Heath and Company, 1975.

Steffensmeir, D.J., and Steffensmeir, R.H. Trends in female delinquency: An examination of arrest, juvenile court, self-report, and field data. *Criminology,* 1980, *18,* 62-85.

Sutherland, E.M. *Principles of criminology.* Philadelphia: Lippincott, 1947.

_____ . *White collar crime.* New York: Dryden, 1949.

Thornton, D., and Reid, R.L. Moral reasoning and type of criminal offense. *British Journal of Social Psychology,* 1982, *21,* 231-238.

Trojanowicz, R., and Morash, M. *Juvenile delinquency: Concepts and control.* Englewood Cliffs, N.J.: Prentice-Hall, 1982.

Turiel, E. An experiment test of the sequentiality of developmental stages in the child's moral judgment. *Journal of Personality and Social Psychology,* 1966, *3,* 611-618.

Warren, M. The female offender in psychology of crime and criminal justice. In H. Toch, ed., *The Psychology of Crime and Criminal Justice.* New York: Holt, Rinehart and Winston, 1979, 444-469.

Wasserman, E. Implementing Kohlberg's "just community program" in an alternative high school. *Social Education,* 1976, April, 203-207.

Wilson, A.B.; Hirschi, T.; and Elder, G. *Richmond Youth Project,* Technical report no. 1. Berkeley: Survey Research Center, University of California, 1965.

Additional References

Bar-Yam, M.; Kohlberg, L.; and Naame, A. Moral reasoning of students in different cultural, social, and educational settings. *American Journal of Education,* 1980, *88,* 345-362.

Colby, A.; Kohlberg, L.; Gibbs, J.; and Lieberman, M. A longitudinal study of moral development. *Monographs of the Society for Research in Child Development,* in press.

Frankena, W.K. *Ethics.* Englewood Cliffs, N.J.: Prentice-Hall, 1963.

Galen, D. The theories of Kohlberg and Lonergon. Ph.D. diss., Ontario Institute for the Study of Education, 1981.

Kohlberg, L. Continuities in childhood and adult moral development revisited. In P. Baltes and K.W. Schaie, eds., *Life span developmental psychology: Personality and socialization.* New York: Academic Press, 1973.

Kohlberg, L., and Candee E. Relationship of moral judgment and moral action. Paper presented at Florida International University Conference, 1981.

Kohlberg, L., and Kramer, R. Continuities and discontinuities in children and adult moral development. *Human Development,* 1969, *12,* 93-120.

McNamee, S. Moral behavior, moral development and motivation. *Journal of Moral Education,* 1978, *177,* 27-32.

Thrower-Tim, J. Group care of children and the development of moral judgment. *Child Welfare,* 1980, *59,* 323-333.

13 The Psychopath and Moral Development

Joan McCord

Perry Smith slaughtered Herbert, Bonnie, Nancy, and Kenyon Clutter, having robbed them of about forty dollars. Gary Gilmore went on a killing spree that ended when he shot a night clerk at a motel. Jack Abbott, recently released on parole to begin a new career as a writer, fatally stabbed a young waiter because of an imagined insult. All these men had long histories of crime, beginning as juveniles. Each was aggressive and impulsive. Each, according to reasonable criteria, could be considered a psychopath. Whether they are and what can be learned about psychopaths depends partly on what definition of *psychopathy* is chosen.

Psychopathy can be defined as a discrete category or as a point on a continuum; further, it can be defined in terms of personality or in terms of behavior. In practice, three of the four possible combinations of these dimensions have been used. For the purpose of exposition, these will be called the *categorical*, the *dimensional*, and the *behavioral*. The categorical approach presumes that some people are psychopathic and others are not. The dimensional approach considers psychopathy as an extreme value of a continuum. Both the categorical and the dimensional approaches define psychopathy in terms of personality characteristics. The behavioral approach, on the other hand, defines psychopathy simply in terms of the presence of a pattern of antisocial, irresponsible behavior. Psychopaths are taken to be whichever sorts of people perform such actions.

The earliest definitions were categorical. Philippe Pinel apparently originated the clinical concept of psychopathy in 1801, when he coined the term *manie sans délire* as diagnosis for uncontrolled rage coupled with normal intellectual functioning. James Prichard interjected the concept into British criminology through his *Treatise on Insanity and Other Disorders Affecting the Mind*, published in 1835. Prichard considered mania without mental defects as "moral insanity."

Ascribing moral insanity to the "born criminal," Cesare Lombroso believed the disease was a variant of epilepsy. Gina Lombroso-Ferrero (1911) described her father as the first to recognize the importance of "irresistible atavistic impulse" in explaining the crimes of those whom others had diagnosed as morally insane. "They differed from ordinary people," she wrote of psychopaths, "because they hated the very persons who to normal beings are the nearest and dearest . . . and because their inhuman deeds seemed to cause them no remorse" (p. 52). Lombroso believed that moral insanity could be diagnosed in childhood and that the disorder could be transmitted through neurotic—as well as through criminal or psychotic—parents.

Despite the apparent precision with which the psychopath had been isolated by Pinel, Prichard, Lombroso, and others, a clear description of the category remained elusive. Seeing "psychic immaturity" as the underlying characteristic, D.K. Henderson (1939) suggested that impulsive aggression is but one of several manifestations of "psychopathic states." Hoping to decrease the heterogeneity of the classification, Benjamin Karpman (1941) distinguished *idiopathic* psychopaths, marked by congenital aggressiveness, from *symptomatic* psychopaths who might better be considered neurotic. Hervey Cleckley (1941) captured the clinical picture of the psychopath through a list of symptoms that included poor judgment, irresponsibility, and lack of remorse or shame. Cleckley, like Henderson, recognized that psychopaths could be both charming and successful. William McCord and Joan McCord (1956) suggested that an accurate definition of a psychopath would portray an impulsive, aggressive, emotionally isolated person whose exaggerated craving for excitement is restrained neither by social norms nor by conscience.

The categorical approach to refining the concept of psychopathy assumes that psychopaths are recognizable. Those who approach psychopathy from a dimensional perspective deny the recognizability, the distinctiveness, of psychopaths. Hans and Sybil Eysenck, for example, have criticized the idea that psychopaths represent a distinct class of individuals. According to Eysenck and Eysenck (1978), diagnostic categories are "points of multidimensional space" (p. 198). The Eysencks identified neuroticism, extraversion, and psychoticism as central dimensions and argued that psychopaths are those individuals who are relatively high on all three.

Critical evaluations of the Eysenck theory (for example, Blackburn 1975; Farrington, Biron, and LeBlanc 1982; Hare 1968; Trasler 1978) raise doubts whether the three dimensions adequately identify the factors relevant to psychopathic behavior. Some suggest alternative dimensions. Herbert Quay (1965, 1977), for example, focused on impulsivity and intolerance for boredom in attempting to define psychopathy. Mordechai Rotenberg (1978) identified sociophysiological insensitivities as the relevant dimension. Others have claimed that no addition of personality dimensions will result in a successful definition, suggesting that a good definition requires an appeal to behavior.

The behavioral approach, perhaps best exemplified by the work of Lee Robins, avoids the controversy about which character traits are most essential to psychopathy. Robins (1978) noted that people behaviorally identified as psychopaths often claim to feel anxious or sorry or to love someone, particularly their mothers. If psychopaths lack anxiety and the capacity to feel love or guilt, such claims by psychopaths must be false. Robins identified psychopaths as nonpsychotic, nonretarded adults who have failed to conform to a variety of social norms. Contrary to expectation from theories that contrast psychopaths with neurotics, Robins found that psychopaths (whom she called "sociopaths") were more likely than nonpsychopathic controls to report such symptoms of anxiety as chest pains or palpitations.

Not surprisingly, each approach has had its detractors. Disagreement about the properties of psychopaths has sometimes been taken as showing that psychopathy is not a categorical variable. This argument, however, could demolish even such a clearly categorical variable as pregnancy. A woman either is or is not pregnant. Physicians nevertheless disagree about the metabolism of pregnant women, about changes in temperature due to pregnancy, about effects of various environmental conditions on pregnancy and occasionally about whether a given woman is pregnant.

Dimensional definitions of psychopathy have been supported on the grounds that aggression, capacity to love, scope of conscience, impulsiveness, and willingness to violate norms appear to be continuous variables. This argument is misguided, however. Continuous measures do not necessarily imply continuous states. An adequate definition of psychopathy might include requirements for some minimum amount of aggression, impulsiveness, willingness to violate norms, and so forth. Beyond that minimum, the amount might be irrelevant. The case would be similar to that of gender. An individual who produces even a small amount of spermatozoa is a male, although different males produce different amounts. The existence of hermaphrodites does not force a dimensional definition of gender; nor should the existence of puzzling cases with respect to psychopathy be seen as forcing a dimensional definition.

Behavioral definitions of psychopathy circumvent some problems of validity. If a psychopath is defined as a person who repeatedly violates norms, then the misbehavior guarantees psychopathy. Yet, as Barbara Wooton (1978) points out, such a definition renders psychopathy merely a convenient reference to a behavior pattern, not a possible cause of that behavior. Behavior provides the evidence for diagnosis; and although the evidence may be considered an operational definition, the operational definition should not be confused with the conceptual definition.

The properties used to define psychopathy impose restrictions on what conclusions should be drawn from research on psychopaths. A definition of psychopathy that includes, for example, the presence of a history of impulsive antisocial behavior during childhood precludes the discovery that hyperactivity presages psychopathy. A definition of psychopathy that includes guiltlessness precludes the discovery that psychopaths cover their feelings of remorse. In the first case, an individual could not be classified as psychopathic unless the classification as hyperactive during childhood would also have been appropriate. In the second case an individual who was found to feel remorse would be reclassified as nonpsychopathic (perhaps as *pseudopsychopathic* or as a secondary psychopath). Failure to distinguish between properties related to a concept by definition and those that are related empirically has contributed to confusion about psychopathy.

A categorical definition for psychopathy has several advantages. First, a categorical definition provides a decision rule for identifying people similar to those whose peculiarities mark them as *unlike* other criminals. Defining *psychopathy* so that it points only to those who are more extreme on some dimensions (such as extraversion or aggression) assumes the difference is only one of degree.

Second, a categorical definition appropriately permits absolute (as opposed to comparative) judgments. Personality characteristics are properties of individuals; and as a personality diagnosis, psychopathy designates a dispositional property or dispositional properties of individuals. Appeal to relative standing should not be required.

Third, if psychopaths differ qualitatively from nonpsychopaths, that difference cannot be detected unless psychopaths are identified as a separable category. On the other hand, if psychopaths do not differ qualitatively from nonpsychopaths, the use of a categorical definition can contribute to the discovery of the similarity. A parallel problem, perhaps easier to perceive, occurs with consideration of alcoholism. If alcoholics are merely people who drink more than others, then a study of drinkers can be used to understand the movitation of alcoholics. Alcoholics and nonalcoholics may have different reasons for drinking, however. To learn whether they do, a categorical definition of alcoholics must be used. The motivation of alcoholics identified by criteria other than the amount they drink can then be compared with the motivation of nonalcoholic drinkers.

Fourth, a categorical definition promotes understanding of psychopathy. Inspection of instances can show whether particular theories are true of psychopaths. If impulsiveness has many causes, for example, then the correlation between impulsiveness and desire for stimulation could be low despite the fact that a search for stimulation might explain *psychopathic* impulsiveness.

In their review of research on psychopathy, Robert Hare and David Cox (1978) showed that global judgments of psychopathy can be reliable if based on explicit criteria. They cautioned against use of single scales to identify psychopaths among prison populations.

Bernard Rimé and his associates (1978) carried out an unusual study of psychopathy that incorporated measures of both reliability and validity. They designed a scale for rating eighteen items that were drawn from the clinical descriptions of psychopaths given by Cleckley (1941) and McCord and McCord (1964). Two counselors independently rated seventy-three boys who were living in a group home. Interjudge reliability was .68 ($p < .001$). The distribution was bimodal, and the researchers used the scores to identify as psychopaths the twenty-five boys who received the highest scores. They identified the twenty-five who received the lowest scores as nonpsychopaths. Differences in age and IQ were small and not statistically significant. Clinical descriptions led Rimé et al. to believe psychopaths would have under-developed social skills and fail to notice interaction cues, as predicted by Hare (1970). Raters blind to the classification rated videotapes and sound record-ings of the boys describing their leisure activities. Compared with the non-psychopaths, psychopaths more constantly looked into the interviewer's eyes, gestured with their hands, and leaned forward. The nonpsychopaths smiled more frequently. Judges also estimated emotions of the boys. These estimates indicated that sadness, disgust, surprise, and fear were more highly correlated among psychopaths than among nonpsychopaths. The authors suggested that the absence of differentiation among emotions represents the emotional im-maturity one would expect to find among psychopaths if they lack empathy and are unable to form close attachments. Two years after completion of the study, to evaluate validity of the categories, the counselors were asked whether each of the boys from the study had been a discipline problem or had difficulties with the police over antisocial behavior. Although the counselors were unaware of the designations, their answers showed that those who had been considered psychopaths were more likely to have been disciplinary prob-lems in the home ($p < .001$) and to have had trouble with the police ($p < .005$).

Evidence that psychopaths are not necessarily detected criminals adds to the grounds for treating psychopathy as a description of personality. Cathy Widom (1977) advertised for "charming, aggressive, carefree people who are impulsively irresponsible but are good at handling people and at looking after number one" (p. 675). Widom identified psychopaths from the respondents by selecting those who had submitted autobiographical ac-counts revealing impulsive, aggressive, antisocial behavior plus absence of anxiety and guilt. Her study showed, among other things, that psychopaths who have not been convicted for crimes resemble incarcerated psychopaths in terms of their drug use, affectional ties, and personality-test scores.

The description of people as aggressive, impulsive, egocentric, and ir-responsible appears to identify a type of person for whom predictions of an-tisocial behavior tend to be accurate. Therefore, it seems reasonable to treat psychopathy as a legitimate personality description, one for which a categorical definition is suitable.

Around 1950, psychologists stressed the absence of guilt. They often cast this in a Freudian context of superego deficit. Theories about stages of moral development (for example, Erikson 1950; Kohlberg 1963; Piaget 1948) provided another basis for considering the psychopath as immature. Empirical evidence has not been kind to these theories (Hoffman 1980), and the idea that moral judgments can rest on maturational processes is fundamentally wrong. Conceivably, some particular types of moral judgments may be agreed upon by mature people; yet no amount of alchemy can turn this agreement into a prescription for how people *ought* to make their judgments.

Recent studies of psychopaths have brought attention to two other characteristics that bear on their moral development: their relative immunity to the deterrent effects of punishment and their attraction to new experiences.

Several studies have produced evidence to suggest that, compared with nonpsychopaths, psychopaths are less likely to exhibit fear in response to stimuli that provoke anxiety in normal people. David Lykken (1957), for example, compared the avoidance learning of imprisoned psychopaths with that of high-school and university students. He found that psychopaths more often chose alternatives that resulted in their being given shocks. Hare (1978) compared prisoners rated as psychopaths with those classified as nonpsychopathic. The former showed smaller skin conductance responses to loud (120 db) tones. Reviews of studies on electrodermal responsiveness of psychopaths by Sarnoff Mednick and Jan Volavka (1980), by Hare (1978), by David Siddle (1977), and by Anthony Mawson and Carol Mawson (1977) highlight different interpretations of the evidence.

Mednick and his co-workers (Loeb and Mednick 1977; Mednick 1977; Mednick et al. 1977; Mednick and Volavka 1980) emphasized the slow electrodermal recovery rate found among psychopaths and criminals. These authors argued that moral learning depends on fear and its reduction, an idea derived from the two-factor theory of learning generally attributed to O. Hobert Mowrer (1960). According to this theory, people learn to be moral by going through a process that involves being punished for misbehavior, learning to fear punishment, learning to inhibit behavior in response to fear. The reduction of fear presumably reinforces inhibition. Mednick et al. believed that psychopaths fail to receive reinforcement for inhibition since they fail to experience the fear reduction found among nonpsychopaths. Their own studies lend some support to the position that failure to learn how to conform to social norms may be related to slow autonomic processes. One study measured electrodermal recovery among criminals and noncriminals, cross-classified by their fathers' criminality. Criminals whose fathers had not been criminals evidenced slow recovery rates; noncriminals whose fathers had been criminals evidenced fast electrodermal recovery rates (Mednick et al. 1977). Another study yielded evidence that slow electrodermal recovery rates are predictive of criminal convictions. Among the 311 subjects included in a study that measured such rates in 1962, the 36 convicted for violations of the Danish penal code since 1962 had lower recovery rates than the remainder

Furthermore, "Those nine who have been clinically diagnosed psychopathic have even slower recovery" (Mednick 1977, p. 4). The theory specified by Mednick emphasized hyperactivity of the autonomic nervous system among psychopaths. In addition to these electrodermal studies, Mednick cited two other studies to show that psychopaths might be autonomically hyperactive. M.E.J. Wadsworth (1976, 1979) measured pulse rates of 11-year olds prior to an anticipated medical examination. Retraced for criminal records at age 20, those whose homes had been broken when they were less than 5, regardless of their criminal records, and those from unbroken homes, *if subsequently delinquent*, had had lower pulse rates than the boys from unbroken homes who did not become criminals. Daisy Shalling (1978) reported on studies of twenty-four men awaiting trial. Tested two weeks, one week, and immediately before court appearance, the urine of those who were least delinquent showed a significant increase in catecholamines on the last test; the most delinquent men showed no change in catecholamine level.

Hare (1978) considered several interpretations of the low autonomic arousal seemingly common to psychopaths under conditions that increase anxiety among nonpsychopaths. Noting that psychopaths tend to find experiments boring, Hare acknowledged the possibility that their lack of interest might produce low levels of skin conductance. In support of this interpretation, Hare pointed to a study by Frank Schmauk (1970). Schmauk had used a 3 x 3 design in which primary psychopaths, neurotic psychopaths, and nonpsychopaths were assigned to one of three conditions for response to errors while learning a maze: receiving shock, losing a quarter, or being told disapprovingly that they were wrong. The psychopaths showed less anticipatory galvanic skin response in the shock and disapproval conditions, but the difference in the tangible-punishment condition was not statistically significant. The primary psychopaths reported feeling less anxious than the other groups and were less aware of the contingencies when shock or social disapproval was used to teach them. Yet the primary psychopaths learned as well as the other groups when tangible punishments were used. With tangible punishments, moreover, primary psychopaths reported as much anxiety as did the other groups. In order to eliminate possible effects of drowsiness on autonomic activity, Hare and his colleagues experimented on prisoners, telling them when to expect either strong electric shock or a loud noise. Even in these studies, psychopathic inmates gave smaller anticipatory skin responses than did nonpsychopathic inmates. Their cardiovascular responses, however, presented a different picture: warned of impending aversive noise, psychopaths showed anticipatory heart-rate increase *larger* than those of nonpsychopaths. Hare believed that the system-specific differences suggested that psychopaths have unusually efficient physiological coping capabilities. These reduce the impact of noxious stimuli, a process that would be adaptive except for occasions when fear might serve a useful purpose. Hare doubted that electrodermal recovery represents fear reduction, but recognized the need for evidence regarding his own interpretation.

Believing that abnormal autonomic functioning accompanies poverty of affect, absence of guilt, and inability to learn from experience, Siddle (1977) attributed the abnormalities to deficient orienting responses. Orienting responses appear to be related to both stimulus reception and learning, and attentional deficiency could account for a psychopath's abnormal responses to the environment.

Although many studies report evidence of low cortical arousal among psychopaths, contradictory evidence is abundant. In reviewing the evidence, Karl Syndulko (1978) concluded that studies of contingent negative reinforcement have failed to show that psychopaths have deficient cortical arousal. Concurring, David Siddle and Gordon Trasler (1981) cited many inconsistencies in the evidence regarding any hyporesponsivity among psychopaths.

Inconsistencies in the results of research would disappear, Mawson and Mawson (1977) suggested, if one posited abnormal oscillation as the underlying differential feature. With high arousal conditions, psychopaths appear to respond more dramatically than others; with low arousal, they seem to respond more passively. The Mawsons hypothesized that a biochemical imbalance in psychopaths disturbs neurotransmitter functioning. The disturbance might create intense activity during noradrenaline and dopamine arousal, while also creating intense inhibition during acetylcholine and serotonin activation.

Whereas the relative immunity to deterrent effects of punishments among psychopaths has characteristically been attributed only to the autonomic nervous system, their attraction to new experiences has been attributed to both the autonomic and the central nervous systems.

Marvin Zuckerman and his colleagues (1972) designed measures of "sensation seeking." They found, as expected from the work of Quay (1965), that one of the scales measuring sensation seeking, "disinhibition," was related to the Minnesota Multiphasic Personality Inventory (MMPI) measure of psychopathy.

Both Quay (1977) and Zuckerman (1978) linked the "pathological need" for sensory input of psychopaths to their putatively low levels of emotional arousal. Quay argued that psychopaths learn better when exposed to varied stimuli and that their behavior requires strong punishment since they are relatively insensitive to anticipation of pain. Zuckerman postulated that the low emotional reactivity of psychopaths increases their attraction to emotionally arousing situations. "The low emotional arousability of the psychopath makes it easy for him to handle high intensities of emotional arousal, particularly anger, which would be intolerable for others" (p. 172).

Zuckerman (1978) also cited evidence indicating that psychopaths are *hyperarousable* when the central nervous system is considered. People who have high scores for disinhibition tended to increase their responsiveness to increasing intensities of a stimulus measured by electroencephalogram (EEG). People who have high scores for disinhibition also tended to have biochemical correlates of facilitated neural transmission: low plasma monoamine-oxidase (a metabolizing enzyme for brain catecholamines), and high levels of androgens and estrogens (hormones that seem to reduce monoamine-ozidase).

As Ronald Blackburn (1978) noted, the evidence shows that psychopaths have a strong desire for adventure and thrills; yet the psychophysiological evidence purporting to explain that desire is less than compelling.

Three adoption studies favor the hypothesis that constitutional factors contribute to psychopathy. Using enduring consistently impulsive behavior, aggression, and absence of neurosis or psychosis as criteria, Fini Schulsinger (1972, 1977) identified fifty-seven adopted psychopaths. He matched each of these to a nonpsychopathic adoptee of the same sex, age, socioeconomic status, length of institutionalization, length of stay with the biological family, and number of environmental shifts. A search in mental hospitals for records of all adult relatives disclosed the names of 129. Although the adoptive relatives of the psychopaths were only slightly more likely to have records for mental illness, a greater difference appeared with comparison of their biological relatives: 58 of the 305 relatives of psychopaths (19 percent), compared with 37 of 285 relatives of controls (13 percent) had records for mental illness. Unfortunately, Schulsinger did not control the number of relatives traced for each subject. Since members of the same family can overrepresent a poor environment as well as a bad gene pool, the comparison is seriously marred. Nevertheless, the evidence is suggestive.

Raymond Crowe (1975) studied fifty-two adopted children of forty-one incarcerated women, matching each to an adoptee of the same sex, race, approximate birth date, and approximate age at the time of adoption. When retraced, the twenty-seven pairs of sons and twenty-five pairs of daughters were between 15 and 46 years old. A search through arrest and hospital records uncovered eleven children of criminals and four controls who had manifested antisocial behavior. Six had been diagnosed as antisocial personality; all were children of the criminals. Barry Hutchings and Sarnoff Mednick (1975, 1977) used three approaches to check effects of heredity on criminality. In one, they matched 1,145 male adoptees to male nonadoptees of similar age, social class, and residence. They traced criminal records in 1971, when the subjects were aged 30-44. Compared with control fathers, only a slightly higher proportion of the adoptive fathers had criminal records. For both groups, those whose biological fathers had criminal records were more likely to have criminal records themselves. In a second approach, 143 criminal adoptees and 143 noncriminal adoptees were matched for the adopting father's occupational status and their own age. Stepwise multiple regression identified the criminality of biological fathers as having a stronger effect than criminality of the adoptive father or the psychiatric diagnosis for the biological mother. In the third approach, criminal records were compared for four groups of adoptees: those whose biological fathers had criminal records and whose adoptive fathers had criminal records; those having only biological fathers with criminal records; those having only adoptive fathers with criminal records; and those with neither father having a criminal record. A trend in the evidence favored hereditary effect, although the differences were not statistically reliable. Neither the Crowe nor the Hutchins and Mednick studies showed an hereditary link for psychopathy in particular, although their criminal groups probably included more psychopaths than did their noncriminal groups.

In sum, the search for biological causes of the psychopath's behavior has produced clues. Yet these clues fall short of solving the mystery. Much the same can be said of the search for social causes.

Both parental rejection and inconsistent punitiveness have been implicated in the etiology of psychopathy. Case studies typically show that the psychopaths were rejected as children (Gough 1948; Jenkins 1966; McCord and McCord 1964; Partridge 1928). Yet the data have been retrospective; and the behavior of a psychopath might well have caused, rather than resulted from, parental rejection. To learn how childhood is related to psychopathy, Robins (1966) traced 525 former patients from a child-guidance clinic and 100 matched normal controls. Based on interview protocols and adult records, two psychiatrists identified 80 men and 14 women as psychopaths. A relatively high proportion of the offspring of parents who had been "too lenient or uninterested" and of those who had been removed from their parents' home by parental request became psychopaths. Lack of parental interest and overt parental rejection, however, added little information predictive of psychopathy beyond what was available from knowledge of the child's antisocial behavior. David Farrington (1978) also reported relevant evidence from a longitudinal study of London males first studied in 1961, when they were eight. Farrington and Donald West (1980) followed the boys, collecting information about and from them, for fourteen years. On the basis of criminal records collected in 1975, the boys were divided into delinquents and nondelinquents. The delinquents were subdivided into those who had been charged with violent offenses and those charged only with nonviolent offenses. The families of violent and non violent delinquents tended to be similar to each other and different from those of nondelinquents. The two groups of delinquents differed, however in that the violent criminals were more likely to have cold, harsh parent ($p < .01$). Unfortunately, although parental harshness appears to hav preceded criminality, the evidence does not show whether the boys who were treated harshly had otherwise instigated the parental rejection.

Studies of psychopaths have shown that, compared with non-psychopaths, psychopaths are less likely to notice verbal or physical punishments (Schmauk 1970; Spielberger, King, and O'Hagan 1978). Yet psychopaths are responsive to tangible rewards and punishments. Schmauk (1970) found that imprisoned psychopaths responded as did non-psychopathic hospital and farm workers to loss of money as a punishment. Psychopaths reported more anxiety for the tangible punishment (though less for verbal and physical punishments), and their anticipatory galvanic skin responses showed corresponding autonomic arousal. Widom (1976) used a prisoners' dilemma game to compare male nurses with psychopathic patients in maximum security. Players could earn money. Contrary to a prediction that psychopaths would be less tolerant of repetition, the psychopaths made more repetitive choices than the controls. The psychopaths also predicted their partners' behavior as accurately as did nonpsychopaths. Furthermore, the psychopaths chose the cooperative alternative as frequently as did the nonpsychopaths. These findings are more consistent with environmental than biological theories.

The easy rage of psychopaths seems to run counter to a view of psychopathy as a product of hyporeactive autonomic arousal. If Mawson and Mawson (1977) are correct, however, then psychopaths might inherit the biochemical imbalance to which they attribute much psychopathic behavior. A baby easily enraged would make the tasks of rearing a child more difficult. Parents of such a child might well resort to inconsistent discipline and retaliatory aggression. Poor parenting techniques would do little to discourage further aggressive behavior, and the continued aggressive behavior of the child might well trigger further parental rejection and retaliation.

Psychopaths, accustomed to rejection and physical pain, could be expected to show the desensitization found among children exposed to television (Cline, Croft, and Courrier 1973). More important, the habituation to physical pain and rejection may trigger what Richard Solomon (1980) called "opponent processes." Opponent processes explain why people voluntarily, and without extrinsic rewards, do what appears to be painful. Solomon postulated the existence of a motivational system tied to primary motivational states by something akin to inversion. Positive reinforcers acquire aversive characteristics, and aversive reinforcers acquire positive properties. Repetition seems to trigger the opponent processes. Solomon and his co-workers have tested deductions from his theory and have been able to map the strength and duration of opponent processes under varying conditions.

Explanations of psychopathy that rely on a putative inability to feel pain or recognize social cues overlook the responsiveness to tangible punishments and ability to manipulate others typical of psychopaths. Explanations of psychopathy that emphasize hedonistic behavior ignore the risks that psychopaths often knowingly take. Opponent processes might give a correct account of the psychopath's attention to risky activities as well as of the psychopath's immunity to the deterrent effects of the physical and social punishments.

Several studies have demonstrated continuity of antisocial aggressive behavior (Farrington 1982; Kirkegaard-Sorensen and Mednick 1977; Robins 1966; Satterfield 1978). In the process of wondering whether psychopathy should be considered a syndrome with early onset or a chain reaction, Robins (1978) pointed to the evidence that "parents beat them, and police chase them . . ." (p. 269). Their history suggests that psychopaths have had exposure that would lead them to develop opponent processes.

Whether wicked and deserving punishment or mentally ill and not morally responsible, psychopaths wreak havoc on those whose lives they touch. Yet Perry Smith, Gary Gilmore, and Jack Abbott never really had a fair chance to lead decent lives. Perhaps for that reason, discussions of psychopathy often turn to philosophical questions. Some have assumed that discovery of the causes would settle the question of moral responsibility. Eysenck (1977), for example, argued that heredity and environment determine conduct, and that since a criminal is responsible for neither, moral responsibility is meaningless. This argument cuts too broadly, for the behavior of everyone is determined by heredity and environment. Yet we, at least, are free to consider the extent to which we *ought* to hold a psychopath responsible for his actions.

References

Blackburn, R. An empirical classification of psychopathic personality. *British Journal of Psychiatry*, 1975, *127*, 456-460.

_____ . Psychopathy, arousal, and the need for stimulation. In R.D. Hare and D. Schalling, eds., *Psychopathic behaviour*. Chichester: Wiley, 1978.

Cleckley, H. *The mask of sanity*. St. Louis, Mo.: Mosby, 1941 (5th ed., 1976).

Cline, V.B.; Croft, R.G.,; and Courrier, S. Desensitization of children to television violence. *Journal of Personality and Social Psychology*, 1973, *27*, 360-365.

Crowe, R.R. An adoptive study of psychopathy: Preliminary results from arrest records and psychiatric hospital records. In R.R. Fieve, D Rosenthal, and H. Brill, eds., *Genetic research in psychiatry* Baltimore: Johns Hopkins University Press, 1975.

Erikson, E.H. *Childhood and society.* New York: Norton, 1950.

Eysenck, H.J. *Crime and personality.* London: Routledge and Kegan Paul, 1977 (first published in 1964).

Eysenck, H.J., and Eysenck, S.B.G. Psychopathy, personality, and genetics. In R.D. Hare and D. Schalling, eds., *Psychopathic behaviour.* Chichester: Wiley, 1978.

Farrington, D.P. The family backgrounds of aggressive youths. In L.A. Hersov and M. Berger, eds., *Aggression and antisocial behaviour in childhood and adolescence.* Oxford: Pergamon, 1978.

_____ . Stepping stones to adult criminal careers. Paper presented at Conference on Development of Antisocial and Prosocial Behavior, Voss, Norway, July 1982.

Farrington, D.P.; Biron, L.; and LeBlanc, M. Personality and delinquency in London and Montreal. In J. Gunn and D.P. Farrington, eds., *Abnormal offenders, delinquency, and the criminal justice system.* Chichester: Wiley, 1982.

Farrington, D.P., and West, D.J. The Cambridge Study in Delinquent Development (United Kingdom). In S.A. Mednick and A.E. Baert, eds., *Prospective longitudinal research: An empirical basis for primary prevention.* Oxford: Oxford University Press, 1980.

Gough, H.G. A sociological theory of psychopathy. *American Journal of Sociology,* 1948, *53,* 359–366.

Hare, R.D. Psychopathy, autonomic functioning, and the orienting response. *Journal of Abnormal Psychology,* Monograph Supplement, 1968, *73,* no. 3 (pt. 2).

_____ . *Psychopathy: Theory and research,* New York: Wiley, 1970.

_____ . Electrodermal and cardiovascular correlates of psychopathy. In R.D. Hare and D. Schalling, eds., *Psychopathic behaviour.* Chichester: Wiley, 1978.

Hare, R.D., and Cox, D.N. Clinical and empirical conceptions of psychopathy, and the selection of subjects for research. In R.D. Hare and D. Schalling, eds., *Psychopathic Behaviour.* Chichester: Wiley, 1978.

Henderson, D.K. *Psychopathic states.* New York: Norton, 1939.

Hoffman, M.L. Moral development in adolescence. In J. Adelson, ed., *Handbook of adolescent psychology.* New York: Wiley, 1980.

Hutchings, B., and Mednick, S.A. Registered criminality in the adoptive and biological parents of registered male criminal adoptees. In R.R. Fieve, D. Rosenthal, and H. Brill, eds., *Genetic research in psychiatry.* Baltimore: Johns Hopkins University Press, 1975.

_____ . Criminality in adoptees and their adoptive and biological parents: A pilot study. In S.A. Mednick and K.O. Christiansen, eds., *Biosocial basis of criminal behavior.* New York: Gardner Press, 1977.

Jenkins, R.L. Psychiatric syndromes in children and their relation to family background. *American Journal of Orthopsychiatry*, 1966, *36*, 450-456.

Karpman, B. On the need of separating psychopathy into two distinct clinical types: the symptomatic and the idiopathic. *Journal of Criminal Psychopathology*, 1941, *3*, 112-137.

Kirkegaard-Sorensen, L., and Mednick, S.A. A prospective study of predictors of criminality: 4. School behavior. In S.A. Mednick and J.O. Christiansen, eds., *Biosocial basis of criminal behavior*. New York: Gardner, 1977.

Kohlberg, L. Moral development and identification. In H.W. Stevenson, ed., *Child psychology*. Chicago: National Society for the Study of Education, 1963.

Loeb, J., and Mednick, S.A. A prospective study of predictors of criminality: 3. Electrodermal response patterns. In S.A. Mednick and K.O. Cristiansen, eds., *Biosocial basis of criminal behavior*. New York: Gardner, 1977.

Lombroso-Ferrero, G. *Criminal man*. Boston: G.P. Putnam, 1911.

Lykken, D.T. A study of anxiety in the sociopathic personality. *Journal of Abnormal and Social Psychology*, 1957, *55*, 6-10.

Mawson, A.R., and Mawson, C.D. Psychopathy and arousal: A new interpretation of the psychophysiological literature. *Biological Psychiatry*, 1977, *12*, 49-74.

McCord, W., and McCord, J. *Psychopathy and delinquency*. New York: Grune and Stratton, 1956.

———. *The psychopath*. Princeton, N.J.: Van Nostrand, 1964.

Mednick, S.A. A biosocial theory of the learning of law-abiding behavior. In S.A. Mednick and K.O. Christiansen, eds., *Biosocial basis of criminal behavior*. New York: Gardner, 1977.

Mednick, S.A.; Kirkegaard-Sorensen, L.; Hutchings, B.; Knop, J.; Rosenberg, R.; and Schulsinger, F. An example of biosocial research: The interplay of socioenvironmental and individual factors in the etiology of behavior. In S.A. Mednick and K.O. Christiansen, eds., *Biosocial basis of criminal behavior*. New York: Gardner, 1977.

Mednick, S.A., and Volavka, J. Biology and crime. In N. Morris and M. Tonry, eds., *Crime and justice*, vol. 2. Chicago: University of Chicago Press, 1980.

Mowrer, O.H. *Learning theory and behavior*. New York: Wiley, 1960.

Partridge, G.E. A study of 50 cases of psychopathic personality. *American Journal of Psychiatry*, 1928, *7*, 953-973.

Piaget, J. *The moral judgment of the child*. Glencoe, Ill.: Free Press, 1948.

Quay, H.C. Psychopathic personality as pathological stimulation seeking *American Journal of Psychiatry*, 1965, *122*, 180-183.

_____. Psychopathic behavior: Reflections on its nature, origins, and treatment. In F. Weizmann and I. Uzgiris, eds., *The structuring of experience*. New York: Plenum, 1977.

Rimé, B.; Bouvy, H.; Leborgue, B.; and Rouillon, F. Psychopathy and nonverbal behavior in an interpersonal situation. *Journal of Abnormal Psychology*, 1978, *87*, 636-643.

Robins, L.N. *Deviant children grow up*. Baltimore: Williams and Wilkins, 1966.

_____. Aetiological implications in studies of childhood histories relating to antisocial personality. In R.D. Hare and D. Schalling, eds., *Psychopathic behaviour*. Chichester: Wiley, 1978.

Rotenberg, M. Psychopathy and differential insensitivity. In R.D. Hare and D. Schalling, eds., *Psychopathic behaviour*. Chichester: Wiley, 1978.

Satterfield, J.H. The hyperactive child syndrome: A precursor of adult psychopathy? In R.D. Hare and D. Schalling, eds., *Psychopathic Behaviour*. Chichester: Wiley, 1978.

Schalling, D. Psychopathy-related personality variables and the psychophysiology of socialization. In R.D. Hare and D. Schalling, eds., *Psychopathic behaviour*. Chichester: Wiley, 1978.

Schmauk, F.J. Punishment, arousal, and avoidance learning in sociopathy. *Journal of Abnormal Psychology*, 1970, *76*, 325-335.

Schulsinger, F. Psychopathy: Heredity and environment. *International Journal of Mental Health*, 1972, *1*, 190-206.

_____. Psychopathy: Heredity and environment. In S.A. Mednick and K.O. Christiansen, eds., *Biosocial basis of criminal behavior*. New York: Gardner Press, 1977.

Siddle, D.A.T. Electrodermal activity and psychopathy. In S.A. Mednick and K.O. Christiansen, eds., *Biosocial basis of criminal behavior*. New York: Gardner Press, 1977.

Siddle, D.A.T. and Trasler, G.B. The psychophysiology of psychopathic behaviour. In M.J. Christie and P.G. Mellett, eds., *Foundations of Psychosomatics*. Chichester: Wiley, 1981.

Solomon, R.L. The opponent-process theory of acquired motivation: The costs of pleasure and the benefits of pain. *American Psychologist*, 1980, *35*, 691-712.

Spielberger, C.D.; Kling, J.K.; and O'Hagan, S.E.J. Dimensions of psychopathic personality: Antisocial behaviour and anxiety. In R.D. Hare and D. Schalling, eds., *Psychopathic behaviour*. Chichester: Wiley, 1978.

Syndulko, K. Electrocortical investigations of sociopathy. In R.D. Hare and D. Schalling, eds., *Psychopathic behaviour*. Chichester: Wiley, 1978.

Trasler, G. Relations between psychopathy and persistent criminality— methodological and theoretical issues. In R.D. Hare and D. Schalling, eds., *Psychopathic behaviour*. Chichester: Wiley, 1978.

Wadsworth, M.E.J. Delinquency, pulse rates and early emotional deprivation. *British Journal of Criminology*, 1976, *16*, 245-256.

_____. *Roots of delinquency*. New York: Barnes and Noble, 1979.

Widom, C.S. Interpersonal conflict and cooperation in psychopaths. *Journal of Abnormal Psychology*, 1976, *85*, 330-334.

_____. A methodology for studying noninstitutionalized psychopaths. *Journal of Consulting and Clinical Psychology*, 1977, *45*, 674-683.

Wooton, B. *Crime and penal policy*. London: Allan and Unwin, 1978.

Zuckerman, M. Sensation seeking and psychopathy. In R.D. Hare and D. Schalling, eds., *Psychopathic Behaviour*. Chichester: Wiley, 1978.

Zuckerman, M.; Bone, R.; Neary, R.; Mangelsdorff, D.; and B. Brustman, What is the sensation seeker? Personality trait and experience correlates of the sensation-seeking scales. *Journal of Consulting and Clinical Psychology*, 1972, *39*, 308-321.

14

The Adolescent View of Crime and Justice

Joseph Adelson and
Judith Gallatin

> A man was caught stealing supplies from his neighbors. He was known to be a lazy fellow and most people who knew him didn't trust him. Some people believed that he ought to be put into jail, but there were others who weren't so sure. They said that just because jail was the usual way of dealing with criminals didn't make it the best way. Perhaps, since the people on the island were starting a new system, they might think of new and better ways to deal with people who got into trouble. What do you think would be the best way to deal with this man?

This was one of many questions we posed to a large number of adolescents in the hope of learning how they think and talk about crime and punishment. It is worthwhile to examine some sample responses to this item, since—as we will soon see—the answers given are representative of more extensive domains of thought.

1. A great many youngsters simply reject the ambiguous prospect of "new and better ways." They see jail or some variant thereof as the only solution. If jail does not work the first time, then it should be tried again, perhaps with a longer sentence. Some suggest blood-curdling solutions—life imprisonment or capital punishment. One youngster talks darkly of cutting off a thief's arm. Yet on the whole the responses are flat and unimaginative. We coded these answers *punitive*.

2. A second group also emphasizes jail but places that solution in a corrective context. The thief should be talked to or reasoned with; if that fails, harsher means are called for—imprisonment or perhaps fines. These alternatives are, however, offered grudgingly—*faute de mieux*, and more in sorrow than anger. We coded these responses *conditionally punitive*.

3. A third group of youngsters chooses the other path alluded to in the question. They agree that imprisonment is not the solution to persistent crminality and that one must attempt rehabilitation. Their specific proposals vary: for some, psychiatry is the answer; for others, getting the person a good job. Here is one of the more articulate responses: "But there should be people, you know, like parole officers . . . that can work with these people and help them, because I think he must have some kind of psychological problem and need the help of a psychiatrist or something." Most responses of this sort are less focused, suggesting moral reasoning and moral suasion. Some propose no particular solution, but merely affirm a strong but unsupported belief that one can be found. We termed this category *rehabilitation*.

Table 14-1 shows the distribution of these responses by age through the adolescent period. The findings are clear: at the onset of adolescence, among sixth graders (ages 11-12), the vast proportion of responses are in the punitive categories. By the end of high school a majority of youngsters favor rehabilitation or some approach other than prison.

The findings in this chapter derive largely from our study of urban youngsters, but it is worth mentioning that this research itself represented a replication and extension of an earlier cross-national study, using a slight variant of the interview schedule. On the whole, we have found few developmental differences among the various populations we have studied—no differences associated with gender, and only trivial ones associated with race. Even the national differences are not strong and can be accounted for largely by differences in the political cultures. There are, however, strong and sometimes astonishing changes associated with age.

Punishment and Coercion

It is safe to say that the younger an adolescent is, the more likely he is to favor punishment or other coercive measures as a solution to crime—indeed, to social disorder in general. Our data provide abundant evidence. Generally, where punishment (or some variation) is a plausible response, one finds it far more frequently in the early adolescent years. For example, when we asked about the best reason for imprisoning those who commit crimes, we found that the simple asseveration of punishment declined sharply over time—that is, such responses as "You've got to punish them or put them in jail," or "People who commit crimes have to be punished" (table 14-2). In contrast, ideas of protecting the public and of promoting rehabilitation increase over time (table 14-3).

To take another example, our youngsters were asked, "If you had the power to take whatever actions you thought were necessary, what would you do to reduce or eliminate crime?" Once again, punitive responses decline

Table 14-1
Dealing with the Lazy Thief

	Age			
	12	*14*	*16*	*18*
Punitive	52	45	34	18
Conditionally punitive	33	32	23	17
Rehabilitation	11	18	39	55
Miscellaneous	4	5	5	9
N	114	106	106	99

Note: Ages: $X^2 = 83.02$ (12), $p < .001$.

Table 14-2
Reasons for Imprisonment: Punishment
(percent)

	Age			
	12	*14*	*16*	*18*
Punishment	23	12	11	8

with age (see table 14-4), whereas both the appeal to reason ("educate the parents so that they will influence the children") and other measures of rehabilitation increase (table 14-5). When we ask what can be done about juvenile delinquents, we find the same pattern (table 14-6).

In short, younger children take a harder line toward crime and the criminal than they will later in adolescence. That hardness—whether we term it punitive, coercive, authoritarian, or whatever—is by no means limited to crime. It makes up part of a more general perspective on both human behavior and the social order. In all the studies we have done, we find that whatever the topic, younger children tend to think in terms of superordination, power, absolute morality, and rigid regulation. They see the purpose of government, for example, as keeping people in line, keeping them from doing bad things. Social problems are to be solved by setting rigid rules and enforcing them strictly. Other ideas of governance, decision making, or sustaining social harmony do not come easily to the youngster. We offer a few examples from previous work to suggest the general disposition of the young adolescent mind, in the hope of making it clear that the punitiveness of the child vis-à-vis crime is part of a far more extensive mind set.

In our cross-national study, Adelson and Beall (1970) found the distribution of responses shown in table 14-7 regarding the purpose of government as restrictive (keeping people in line) or as beneficial (providing services). In the same study, an authoritarianism index, made up of the responses to several questions, showed the distribution found in table 14-8.

Table 14-3
Reasons for Imprisonment: Protection and Rehabilitation
(percent)

	Age			
	12	*14*	*16*	*18*
Protection of public	6	8	17	32
Rehabilitation	3	13	13	18

Table 14-4
Reducing Crime: Punishment
(percent)

		Age		
	12	*14*	*16*	*18*
Punishment	44	39	33	20

These findings—and a great many others—will of course bring to mind Piaget's writings on moral development, particularly his observations on "heteronomous morality" or "moral realism." In the early period of the child's moral thinking, we see such phenomena as moral absolutism, a belief in rules as unchangeable, and a belief in arbitrary punishment. In general, the child, prior to adolescence, transfers to the social order and to phenomena within it a moral outlook that itself reflects the authoritied relationships the child is accustomed to—parent over child, teacher over student.

Two questions come to mind immediately. First, to what degree can these findings be generalized? Do these data reflect a more extensive pattern wherein the adolescent moves from the punitive, or authoritarian, to more liberal or humane or perhaps sophisticated approaches to criminal behavior? Second, assuming that some such movement can be found more generally, how do we understand it? To what is it related? To anticipate some of the argument of this chapter, we will hold that adolescent thinking on crime and justice undergoes some marked and distinctive changes but that these are not to be understood sui generis, but rather as reflecting parallel changes in the adolescent's overall mode of thought about psychology and society.

Having begun in the middle, so to speak, we will now return to the beginning and say something about the studies that generated the findings reported here. Most of our data will be drawn from a study of about 450 American youngsters, from grades six, eight, ten, and twelve—spanning the age range from 11 to 18—residing in two communities in the industrial capital Midwest. These youngsters were evenly divided by gender and by

Table 14-5
Reducing Crime: Reasoning and Rehabilitation
(percent)

		Age		
	12	*14*	*16*	*18*
Reasoning	11	18	28	25
Rehabilitation	2	2	7	19

Table 14-6
Responses to Juvenile Delinquents

	Age			
	12	14	16	18
Punitive	41	29	24	16
Family intervention	5	23	25	18
Rehabilitation, kindness	3	12	20	36

race (half are black, half white). Our research instrument was an open-ended interview schedule that began with the premise that a thousand people leave their country to go to a Pacific island. Once there, they confront the problems of establishing a new society. Using this framework, we were able to raise numerous issues having to do with the choices the new community must make—about modes of governing, establishing equity, developing an appropriate system of law, and so on. Most of the actual items were fairly concrete, written so as to be accessible to the younger children in the sample; the item on the lazy thief is an example. The interview contains about a hundred items, not including probes, and on the average takes about an hour to complete.

The Motivation of the Criminal

Inherent in any theory of crime is a larger theory of the sources of human action. Is the person stirred by something within himself—some drive or conflict—or is action initiated by forces outside the self—group contagion, the influence of others, or perhaps larger social and economic forces? To what degree is behavior influenced by the past, by personal history, and to what degree impelled by the needs or circumstances of the moment or by some calculation about the future? Throughout our study we were especially interested in civic behavior—behavior in the public realm: Why are

Table 14-7
Purpose of Government

	Age			
	11	13	15	18
Restriction alone	27	10	8	1
Restriction and benefit	23	35	27	17
Benefit	35	48	64	69

Table 14-8
Authoritarianism Index

	Age			
	11	*13*	*15*	*18*
High scorers (%)	85	67	51	17

some people virtuous and others wicked? Can the wicked man be reformed? If so, how? What are the qualities or the social circumstances leading to political leadership, or to public prestige? We think we can begin to answer a few of these questions. We have learned that what is important is not any particularized theory of human goodness and evil—that the child's theories, here as elsewhere, reflect larger cognitive changes. On the whole the adolescent's views on criminal motivation reflect his changing thinking about human psychology.

We asked why some people are law abiding, whereas others always seem to get into trouble (table 14-9). At the beginning of adolescence, most children seem unable to cope with a problem. Their responses resemble a simplified repetition of the question itself: "The one that is law-abiding, he's the one that don't get into too much trouble. The other one is the one that

Table 14-9
What Is the Difference between Law-Abiding People and Those Who Get into Trouble?

	Age			
	12	*14*	*16*	*18*
Training, family influence, social class: "It's the way they were brought up," "They are poor and live in slums," "They don't have a good education"	21	36	52	67
Impulse or externalization: "Some don't have much to do so they get bored and get into trouble," "They might drink or something," "Everyone breaks the laws"	19	20	21	15
Economic necessity or dissatisfaction: "They don't have things they want"	3	9	3	1
Disagreement versus agreement with laws: includes feelings against the government	7	3	6	5
Simplistic repetition: "The one who obeys the laws doesn't get into trouble, and the ones who don't obey them get into trouble"	50	33	18	13
N	157	222	102	102

Note: Ages: $X^2 = 74.06$ (12), $p < .001$.

gets into all kinds of trouble and always do wrong." Or, "The person that goes by the law doesn't get into as much trouble, and the person that doesn't go by the law gets in more trouble." Explanations, such as they are, do not go much beyond the stark asseveration of virtue and vice, "Because one is better than the other," or the plaintive query, "One is nice and one is bad?" At times we have judgments based on religious convictions: "God made him like that," or, "He might have the devil in him."

That simplicity of discourse is characteristic of the youngest adolescents whenever they are called on to comment on almost any aspect of human behavior. As we put it on another occasion (Adelson 1971):

> The youngster enters adolescence with a remarkably thin repertoire of motivational and psychological categories available to him. He is like a naive behaviorist: he does not look beneath action to its internal springs. There is little sense of inner complication. Men act as they do because they are what they are.

As we see in table 14-9, half of the sixth graders can do little more than repeat the question; even at the eighth-grade level, one-third of the youngsters are so limited. The table also tells us that with increasing age we have a marked shift to environmental explanations—the kind of family one has had and the moral influences one has been exposed to, at home or in the community at large. Among our older subjects some of these responses are remarkably elaborate, involving long dispositions on the relations of crime, character, family, and society; but even the most succinct answers from 18-year-olds capture the essence. For example: "I think there's probably lots of things that influence their actions. Probably the way they were brought up or the area in which they lived." Or, somewhat more loquaciously: "It depends on the way they are raised. If they are raised in a household which teaches you to be kind and love your neighbor as yourself, then you won't need laws. You'll have your own kind of law. This is a law in itself. And the rest are raised in households where they are taught to get what they can by force."

This shift reflects what almost all of our work has revealed—the movement from a concrete and personalized understanding of human events to one that is sociocentric in that it looks to either the social system as a whole ("society"), or its segments (the family, the school) as the central source of personal conduct. That change is at times so dramatic that we may lose sight of equally important movements in adolescent thinking. Consider the following response to the "law-abiding" item: "I think it's the family background, the way you've been brought up. If you've been brought up under a family with very strict rules why then you might rebel and go against those rules, but on the other hand you might stick to them."

That second sentence shows a mental operation that appears rarely in our interviews, and never before late adolescence—the youngster avoiding strict linearity between a given cause and its effects. The bad or neglectful family or the slum background lead to criminal behavior, whereas the virtuous family or the middle-class community lead to law-abiding conduct. That is the usual way of stating the proposition in middle and late adolescence; but some of our older respondents can imagine more complex or ambiguous relationships, as in the example, wherein the strict family is seen as inducing opposite outcomes: compliance on the one hand, rebellion on the other.

In another instance, the youngster (also 18) posits an interaction effect. Of those who get into trouble, he says: "Well, his upbringing has a certain amount to do with it, and the type of people that he associates with. When a group gets together they are more likely to do things they wouldn't when they are alone." Hence, the situation—group intoxication—reinforces what is already there by way of upbringing. Yet he goes on, "It seems as though a lot of people who have had a good upbringing have turned bad through association or through some process which is unknown at this time."

That last phrase is important. The older—and among these, ordinarily, the more intelligent—seem to be aware of the limits of current knowledge and of the multiplicity of potential causes for a given outcome. They resist dogma and are relatively serene about uncertainty. One girl's first response to the question is: "I think that seems to me asking to try and explain what makes human beings different." The questioner agrees. She then says that she doesn't know—and goes on to adduce a larger number of possibilities: "other people, background, family, religion."

That easy fluency is also characteristic of many of the older and brighter adolescents. In one case an interviewee spoke for a full five minutes on this issue; a summary should be of interest in suggesting the range of ideas available to an intelligent 18-year-old. She first mentions economic necessity, especially as a motive for theft; then says that some rebel against parental "repression," which is often displaced to society; then says that some are "adventurous" in temperament and thus drawn to high-risk activities; then adduces "a more subtle type of upbringing problem, [those] who are not taught the spirit of cooperation"; then says that some are not sufficiently thoughtful—meaning reflective rather than considerate; and finally mentions those who are conscientious objectors against certain laws. (She is a Quaker whose parents were tax resisters, and were so well before the Vietnam War.)

Clearly, we come a long way in six years, from the 12-year-olds' "some are nice and some are bad," to the outpouring of ideas we see here, or the intricate argumentation we find in some other interviews. That growth in the capacity to understand and talk about human behavior is to be seen in all areas we studied—in politics, economics, social policy—and is one of the most important cognitive acquisitions of the adolescent years.

The Future of Crime

Before beginning our research, we had heard much about the idealism of the adolescent young, their utopianism, their tendency toward chiliastic expectations of the secular future. For that reason we were much concerned to trace the growth of adolescent idealism and to get some sense of its origins and its course. When does it begin? How extensive is it? What is it connected to, both demographically and with respect to other facets of the child's emerging social and political attitudes? It soon became evident that these questions did not admit of the easy answers we hoped for. To quote again from an earlier paper:

> The pursuit of adolescent idealism has proven to be like other celebrated quests—such as the searches for the Abominable Snowman and the Loch Ness Monster, for example. Rumors are heard that it exists, sightings are made, footsteps are found. Finally a scientific expedition equipped with the latest technology is sent out, and it returns to report that no reliable evidence can be found. Still, the rumors persist, as do reports of sightings, findings, and death-bed testimony [Adelson 1975]

We hunted idealism in a number of contexts, largely political and social; but we were especially interested in how the child viewed the prospects for a society entirely free of crime. That has been a fairly standard aim in most utopian constructions, whether religious or economic in inspiration; and we fully expected that possibility to loom large in the consciousness of our youngsters, especially as they grew older and were less tied to the concrete, to the here and now, and better able to imagine the hypothetical. We could not have been more mistaken. Here are some typical 18-year-olds on the question of whether it would ever be possible to eliminate crime from the island:

> No, I don't think so, because you've got people who can't live with laws or they can't cope with being governed by laws.

> Crime can never be ended. I think that will always continue. It might be remedied a little bit, but not to a great extent. [How come?] Because people are—they just don't want to follow rules. There's always a few that go against them.

> No, I don't think it's possible because even if a person is completely aware of himself and why he does things, a person cannot maintain emotional control of himself all of the time. There's always going to be some human error no matter what you do, and so maybe you could eliminate premeditated crime and not the accidental things that come from emotional outbursts.

These are typical responses at the age; one also finds some unusual twists, as in this young woman who offers a Manichean view of the matter:

No. [Why not?] Well you have people, you're bound to have some type of conflicts or a temptation someplace and you're going to run into crime, I don't care where you are. And I don't feel this earth would be right without crime of some kind. I don't feel you could be happy, you have to have good and evil both together.

Another youngster, a political radical, puts it this way:

Crime is another way of expressing discontent for existing institutions . . . so in this sense you can never eliminate crime. It's a way of voicing the opinion of a minority.

We get a much more mixed picture among younger adolescents. Although a great many are skeptical about the elimination of crime, there are almost as many who believe it can be done. Here are some 11- and 12-year-olds:

Yes. [Probe] Yah. [How?] In the old times they didn't have too much crime because they whipped them or something like that.

Yes. [How?] Well, have everybody on the whole island come and pick the people out that you've been sending to prison and put them in one state and sort of like build a prison in that state then and keep them there until they've learned their lesson. And then let them out for maybe a week or so—that's suspension—let them out for about a week and if he does it again we'll keep him in prison all his life.

In table 14-10 we see the shift over time to the belief that crime cannot be eliminated. In all likelihood, the figures at the 16- and 18-year-old level are underestimates in that many of those who said they thought it possible did so with a strong sense of its unlikelihood; that is, they were announcing themselves as open-minded. Anything is possible, after all, they seem to be saying. This as-if tonality contrasts with the certainty with which most middle and late adolescents say that crime will persist either because of the imperfection of man or because of social processes.

Table 14-10
Do You Think It Would Be Possible to Eliminate Crime Altogether from the Island?

	Age			
	12	14	16	18
No. Crime cannot be eliminated from the island.	48	66	72	75
Yes. Crime can be eliminated.	44	30	19	22
Conditional answers. It all depends.	8	5	9	3
N	117	111	110	103

Note: Ages: $X^2 = 26.69$ (6), $p<.001$.

Hence it is clear that adolescents are not idealistic on this issue, the hypothetical elimination of crime. The younger ones, more of whom say they think it can be done, say so not because they are utopian but because they tend to believe in the omnipotence of authority and the effectiveness of Draconian punishments. The older adolescents reject utopian outcomes in general. (They believe, for example, that the poor will always be with us.) But how shall we interpret this? If we understand idealism as involving a naive innocence, then clearly we are mistaken to so characterize adolescents. The more adolescent they become, the more innocent—thus (in this sense) the less idealistic.

There is, however, another connotation of idealism that has to do with social optimism as opposed to pessimism, cynicism, and despair. In this sense we can disern no distinctive patterning by age. When we look through the findings on a large number of variables, we discover, first, that strongly pessimistic responses tend to be unusual (except when one asks about utopian prospects), and that there is no consistent relation to age. Social pessimism is uncommon, and it neither grows nor lessens markedly during the course of adolescence.

We find no strong measure of optimism, if by that we mean a fervent belief in the inevitability of social or personal progress. To be sure, many of our youngsters believe in psychiatric technique and will advise you that the reform of miscreants will be accomplished by the universal provision of psychotherapy for wrongdoers. That doctrine is not, however, held strongly or deeply by most of the youngsters espousing it. They are merely voicing the prevailing beliefs of the more "progressive" elements of the culture, diluted and trickled down to the high-school level. No doubt we will be hearing in a few years, from equivalent youngsters, the somewhat less sanguine views on crime and rehabilitation drawn from James Q. Wilson or Ernest Van den Haag, also diluted and trickled down to the high-school level.

With respect to social policy—whether in the areas of crime or economics or politics—the adolescent seems to become neither idealistic nor despairing. The prevailing attitude is best captured by a term such as *social realism*. The outlook is pragmatic, functional. Reform ought to aim at the achievable, taking into account the complexity and imperfection of both human nature and society. During adolescence the youngster gradually absorbs the skepticism and caution about the human prospect that we take for granted among adults. To the degree that he seems naive or overoptimistic about weighty matters, he generally reflects a body of similar opinion found in the society at large—as in the widely held optimism about the rehabilitation of criminals. One is reminded of what ought to be obvious—that adolescence is fundamentally a period in which one becomes adult. Youngsters accomplish this in part by achieving adult modes of thinking, in part by internalizing and then voicing the common opinions of the culture.

References

Adelson, J. The political imagination of the young adolescent. *Daedalus,* 1970, *100*, 1013-1050.

Adelson, J. The development of ideology in adolescence. In S. Dragstin and G.H. Elder, eds. *Adolescence in the life cycle.* Washington, D.C.: Hemisphere Press, 1975.

Adelson, J. and Beall, L. Adolescent perspectives in law and government. *Law and Society Review,* 1970, *4*, 495-504.

15 An Explanation of Juvenile Delinquency: The Integration of Moral-Reasoning Theory and Sociological Knowledge

Merry Morash

This chapter focuses on the potential for integrating three alternative but related models of moral reasoning with key sociological propositions to explain delinquency. The chapter also compares the adequacy of the three models as explanations of well-established patterns of delinquency in our society. The models that are compared include: (1) Kohlberg's stages of moral reasoning, (2) Gilligan's revision of Kohlberg's stages, and (3) Haan's model of moral structures. Because there is considerable contemporary debate and revisionary activity relevant to models of moral reasoning, and because no model has unquestionable empirical support, a comparison of the three psychological models is appropriate at this time.

The first of the three, Kohlberg's model of moral reasoning, has been a major stimulus to research on the link between individuals' moral structures and their behavior, including delinquent behavior (see chapter 12). Kohlberg (1958) posited that there are three sequential stages in moral reasoning—preconventional, conventional, and postconventional—each characterized by increased capabilities for abstract reasoning about the social contract between individual and society.

Both Gilligan (1982) and Haan (1977, 1978) developed models of moral reasoning by revising the Kohlberg model.[1] Working separately, each added a dimension to moral reasoning that grows parallel to abstract reasoning and that involves an orientation towards the needs and feelings of other people. Gilligan called the second dimension *contextual thinking*, and Haan called it *interpersonal morality*. This chapter refers to both contextual thinking and interpersonal morality as *other-oriented reasoning*, and to Kohlberg's conceptualization of moral reasoning as *abstract reasoning*. Although Gilligan and Haan did not apply their models to explanations of delinquency, their revisions to the Kohlberg model are substantial and, along with the Kohlberg model, can profitably be considered in relation to delinquency.

By considering the relationship of psychological models of moral reasoning to sociological propositions and to patterns of delinquency, it is

385

possible to take a potentially fruitful but relatively undeveloped approach in theoretical work on the etiology of delinquency: the integration of psychological theory with sociological frameworks. For many years the utility of this approach has been a recurring theme in discussions of the requirements for advancing criminology. Vold (1958, p. 155) for example, wrote that the inadequacy of empirical support for all types of criminological theory required an "eclectic syncretism" of theories from different academic disciplines. Yinger (1965) subsequently proposed that criminological theory would benefit from the specification of individual characteristics (such as personality structures or cognitive abilities) that result in lawbreaking in certain social situations. Yinger's recommendation recently was reiterated in Inkeles's (1970) discussion of the relevance of psychology to sociology in general, and in Gibbons's (1979, pp. 212-216) discussion of the relevance of psychology to criminology in particular. Both Inkeles and Gibbons stressed the need not only to specify the qualities of the individual that are conducive to delinquent behavior in particular social situations, but also to link these qualities to patterns and rates of delinquency.

In accordance with the recommendations for cross-disciplinary integration of knowledge, the psychological models of moral reasoning will be considered here in light of their potential for integration with key sociological propositions linking family dynamics, peer-group membership, and the status of adolescents with delinquency. Furthermore, the psychological models will be considered as explanations for the sporadic involvement of most adolescents in delinquent activity, and the concentration of delinquent behavior among males in mid- to late adolescence.

Key Sociological Explanations of Delinquency

Sociological and psychological factors can be combined in at least two ways to explain delinquency. First, in certain social situations the level of moral reasoning can interact with the social situation to produce delinquent behavior. This logic for integrating theories is illustrated by the well-known finding that good boys in a high-delinquency area resisted social influences toward delinquency by virtue of their personal characteristics, particularly their self-esteem (Scarpitti et al. 1960). Second, social factors can produce the level of moral reasoning that subsequently results in delinquency. The effect of social factors on the rate and perhaps direction of moral development would be demonstrated through studies of socialization. If there is an effect, the patterns in socialization that lead to retarded development also would be precursors of delinquent behavior.

Given the ongoing controversy over the sociological influences of delinquency, only a few consistently supported sociological propositions will be considered as relevant to the specification of social factors that directly influence delinquent behavior, or that influence the rate of moral development and thereby indirectly influence delinquent behavior. As concluded from thorough reviews of the literature (Trojanowicz and Morash 1983, chap. 3; Gibbons 1979), there is an accumulation of evidence that:

1. Association with delinquent peers is a strong influence on delinquent behavior (Akers et al. 1979; Poole and Regoli 1979; Hirschi 1969; Giordano 1978).
2. Family conflict and parental rejection promote delinquency (Glueck and Glueck 1968; Rodman and Grams 1967).
3. Pattern of discipline used by parents can influence delinquency (McCord and Zola 1959; Bartol 1980, p. 121).

In addition to these three propositions, there is a general recognition among many sociologists that the status of most adolescents in contemporary society contributes to delinquency. Specifically, adolescents are excluded from the labor force and segregated into same-aged groups. Thus their role relationships—that is, their meaningful interactions with people in a variety of roles—are severely restricted (Friday and Hage 1976). In particular, adolescents often are restricted from roles in which they can assume major responsibilities for themselves or other people; and, especially for boys, their roles in leisure-time, peer-group activities are heavily emphasized. It is possible that such restrictions provide a pressure toward delinquency by blocking opportunities for attaining material possessions (Greenberg 1977) or that the restrictions impede moral development in such a way as to contribute to delinquency.

Patterns of Delinquency

A large proportion of adolescents are involved in some delinquent activity, and they usually do not specialize in any one form of delinquency (such as status offenses of truancy or running away, property offenses, or offenses against other people) (Wolfgang, Figlio, and Sellin 1972; Gold 1970). A very small proportion of adolescents are chronic offenders, and an even smaller proportion—estimated at less than 2 percent of all offenders—are violent *and* chronic delinquents (Dinitz and Conrad 1980). Because most delinquency is not part of a repeated and regular pattern of lawbreaking, an adequate moral-reasoning explanation of delinquency must either concentrate on youths who are frequent delinquents or allow for situational influences or transitory individual factors to account for widespread but sporadic delinquency (Gibbons 1971).

A second well-established pattern in delinquency is the peak in delinquent activity after the age of 16, but before adulthood. Arrest rates for property offenses rise at the beginning of adolescence and fall off sometime between age 16 and 20, the exact age varying with the data source (Glaser 1978, p. 163). Surveys of victims have shown that the incidence of offenses against the person and property are highest for both black and white males at ages 18-20 (Hindelang 1981). Similarly, recidivism studies have shown that people are rearrested less often once they become adults (Wolfgang, Figlio, and Sellin 1972; Glueck and Glueck 1937). Moreover, self-report studies, which require youths to admit their delinquency for a specified time period, have revealed that recruitment to delinquency becomes less common once individuals reach adulthood (Greenberg 1977). To be adequate, moral reasoning models must allow for an explanation of these age-related patterns in delinquency.

The final pattern in delinquency that would benefit from a psychological explanation is the well-established differences in the amount and type of illegal activity by boys and girls. Numerous studies have established that with the exception of status offenses and drug and alcohol use, girls have markedly lower levels of all types of delinquency than do boys; see review of research in Trojanowicz and Morash (1983, chap. 2) and Hindelang (1981). Furthermore, girls are particularly unlikely to engage in very serious offenses, including violence against other people (Feyerherm 1981). Recent increases in girls' delinquency do not contradict the findings that girls are less delinquent than are boys; the increases have been concentrated in the area of petty shoplifting; and official records showing increased arrests of girls for assaults are heavily weighted by arrests for the relatively minor offenses of being bystanders to an assault (Steffensmeir and Steffensmeir 1980). To the extent that girls hold a different status in adolescence than do boys and/or are socialized differently, they may progress at different rates through the stages of moral development. An adequate model of moral reasoning would explain developmental or other differences between boys and girls, and thereby explain differences in their delinquent behavior.

The rest of this chapter will analyze the Kohlberg model of moral reasoning and those of Gilligan and Haan as psychological approaches (1) to explain individual's delinquency, (2) to be integrated with key sociological propositions to explain delinquency, and (3) to explain consistently demonstrated patterns in delinquency including concentrations of delinquency in age and sex subgroups.[2] Because Kohlberg's theory has received the most attention and is the seminal model, it will be considered first.

The Kohlberg Model Applied to Delinquency

In his initial work on moral development, Kohlberg (1958) pinpointed th ages 10-13 as the time of movement from the preconventional to conventiona thinking, and he attributed delinquency to an arrest in development at these ages. The ages 10-13 coincide with the onset of increased delinquency among adolescents in our society; and thus Kohlberg's developmental theory holds some promise as an explanation for delinquency.

After having spent several years expanding his work on delinquency, Kohlberg (1978, p. 216) recently hypothesized that preconventional moral judgment is not a direct cause of delinquency. Instead, conventional moral judgment is the major factor in avoiding delinquency when personal or situational forces provide incentives to break the law. Kohlberg's recent explanation of delinquency parallels the reasoning that personal predisposition —here moral structure—acts to insulate the individual against personality and situational pressures toward delinquency. On the surface this formulation would seem to invite the incorporation of specific individual and situational pressures into an integrated sociological and psychological explanation of delinquency.

As further empirical support that moral structure is an insulation against delinquency, Kohlberg (1978) presented data on forty-three youths institutionalized for repeated delinquency and thirty-nine others who were considered to be nondelinquent controls. Because of the small sample sizes and inconsistent findings between samples from three different institutions, Kohlberg recognized his conclusions as speculative. They do show, however, that, particularly for youths in mid-adolescence, the institutionalized youths as a whole were more likely to be at the preconventional level of reasoning than were the controls.

Unfortunately, Kohlberg's finding of an association between institutionalization and preconventional reasoning lacks a straightforward interpretation. Because institutionalization was shown in the same study to support a regression in reasoning, it may be that the lower reasoning of incarcerated youths was a result, not a determinant, of incarceration. Moreover, the age of the youths, their types of offenses, and the specific institutions in which they were placed were not introduced as statistical controls. These variations may confound the relationship between reasoning and institutionalization. In fact, Kohlberg's results suggested that age and/or type of offense did render the relationship of reasoning to institutionalization spurious.

Even if Kohlberg's findings do accurately reflect that preconventional youths are most prone to delinquency, there is considerable room for refinement in his explanation, for he did not adequately specify the social and individual pressures towards delinquency. Kohlberg (1978) only speculated that drug addiction, a personal pressure for which a measure was available, accounted for theft by even conventional-level youths. The causal effect of drug addiction on theft has been considered questionable at best in the criminological literature (Inciardi 1980); furthermore, Kohlberg's (1978) demonstration that insulation by conventional reasoning does not work for addicts contradicts the notion that moral reasoning can insulate youths from pressures toward delinquency, unless drug addiction is not considered a type of immoral behavior. The one other social factor to which Kohlberg made reference as a pressure toward delinquency was subcultural influences, which have consistently been shown to lack empirical evidence as a major determinant of delinquency (Gibbons 1979, p. 107; Kornhauser 1978). Thus, although Kohlberg's 1978 statement opened the door for considering moral structure as an insulation from pressures to be delinquent, it did not adequately specify the factors against which insulation is needed, and it did not demonstrate the effectiveness of the insulation.

Besides the recent research by Kohlberg, several other studies purported to show a relationship between reasoning and delinquency, but have questionable conclusions. One shortcoming of this prior research was the use of official classification as delinquent to indicate illegal behavior (Kohlberg 1958, 1978; Fodor 1972). Since delinquent behavior is not necessarily related to official classification as delinquent, these studies may measure the decision making of court and police personnel rather than adolescent behavior. It is even possible that youths who reason at a low level are more often arrested and incarcerated than are other equally delinquent youths. Another problem detracts from the studies by Fodor (1973) and Jurkovic and Prentice (1977), who concluded that moral reasoning was related to sociopathology. Because the indicators of sociopathology (Cleckley 1964; Quay and Parsons 1967) included items that reflected limited ability in moral reasoning, the findings may be an artifact of the measurement approach; that is, they may be tautological.

Other studies (Morash 1981; Emler, Winton, and Heather 1977; Hudgins and Prentice 1973; Jurkovic and Prentice 1974; Miller, Sumoff, and Stephens 1974) showed moral reasoning to be unrelated to delinquency. Two of these (Morash 1981; Emler, Winton, and Heather 1977) did use a self-report measure of delinquency; thus they raised particularly serious questions about the relationship of reasoning to delinquency.

The Kohlberg Model and Sociological
Explanations of Delinquency

Along with the research that has directly questioned the association o[f] reasoning with delinquency, the empirical research on the relationship o[f] both family atmosphere and patterns of family discipline to delinquen[t] behavior raises some specific dilemmas in applying the Kohlberg model t[o] delinquency. Kohlberg (1969, p. 363) stressed the importance of inductiv[e] reasoning as a stimulus for moral development, and he has insisted that oth[er] aspects of family life are of minimal or no importance in the development of moral reasoning. Punishment that relied on inductive reasoning could be a stimulus, although the punishment was not a necessary accompaniment to the inductive reasoning. In their research on delinquency, McCord and Zola (1959) specifically found that the form of punishment—and thus the presence of inductive reasoning—was not predictive of delinquency, but that the consistency of all forms of punishment was predictive. As already noted, research has also shown parental tension and lack of affection for the child to be related to delinquency. If these family conditions and patterns of punishment are related to delinquency but, according to Kohlberg's theory, unrelated to moral development, then it is inconsistent to argue that delinquency is related to moral development.

Empirical research on the peer group and delinquency raises additional questions about the Kohlberg explanation of delinquent behavior. Kohlberg has described the peer group primarily as it functions to provide role-taking opportunities for adolescents. He also noted (1978) that just as preconventional youths do not regard standard societal norms as morally obligatory, so they do not consider deviant subcultural norms to be obligatory. Kohlberg's first view of the peer group identified a positive effect on development, and his second view suggested that deviant subcultural norms of a peer group have a limited negative effect on behavior because they are not considered as binding by preconventional youths. Neither of these two views of adolescent peer groups provides a basis for explaining the consistent findings that interaction with delinquent peers is strongly predictive of delinquent behavior for both boys and girls (Akers et al. 1979; Poole and Regoli 1979; Giordano 1978).

In the context of a developmental theory, it would be fruitful to depart from Kohlberg's propositions and explore two ways in which the peer group can promote delinquency. First, if peers are considered to be a social pressure, then they may influence youths to act in a delinquent way that is inconsistent with the youths' own conventional moral reasoning. Disregard of one's own reasoning is most likely for youths at a mixed stage in development. Consistent with this hypothesis that peer pressure affects the consistency of action and reasoning, Ward and Wilson (1980) found that female undergraduates at conventional and postconventional levels, and who were exposed to group pressure, tended to state moral judgments that were lower than their assessed stages. Because Ward and Wilson found peer pressure to influence conventional-level individuals, their findings provide a particularly strong basis for hypothesizing that peers can influence most adolescents, who are at the conventional level, to exhibit delinquent behavior.

A second way in which peers can promote delinquency is by offering alternatives to legally prescribed definitions of right and wrong behavior. In this vein, Akers et al. (1979) demonstrated that during peer interactions, social learning of perceptions that were favorable to drug use was strongly related to drug use. Particularly for an offense like drug use, which is condoned by many people in our society, social learning that certain illegal behaviors are of questionable relevance to maintaining a social contract can result in illegal behavior by conventional-level or even postconventional youths. In support of this view, research (Tsujimoto and Nardi 1978) has revealed that Kohlberg's stages are better predictors of judgments about stealing than about drug or alcohol use. As additional though indirect support, Minor (1981) reported that "neuralizations" to redefine drug use as consistent with societal norms were related to subsequent drug use but were much more weakly related to aggressive behavior. Thus it is likely that social learning from peers that trivial acts are not really wrong results in considerable but relatively minor lawbreaking by conventional-level youths.

One area that holds considerable potential for explaining the high levels of delinquency in the United States, and that is related to the influence of peer groups, has not been explored in Kohlberg's framework. This is the degree to which our society provides role-taking opportunities to adolescents. It has been confirmed that adolescents who participate in a variety of activities, or who attend progressive schools and therefore have greater role-taking opportunities, achieve higher levels of development than do other youths (Clinchy, Lief, and Young 1977; Keasey 1971). Kohlberg has attributed the limited moral development in some primitive societies to a lack of such role-taking opportunities. It is useful, though of course speculative, to apply this same reasoning to an examination of American adolescence. At the same age that Kohlberg's model requires development from the preconventional to the conventional levels—that is, early adolescence—youths in our society are increasingly segregated from adults. Minority and lower-class youths in particular are cut off from employment opportunities and from meaningful educational and leisure-time programs. Peers suffering from a similar lack of opportunities for role taking may not be able to stimulate moral development among one another. Further research is needed to identify the social-structural conditions that provide so minimal a level of this type of opportunity that movement beyond even a preconventional level is unlikely during adolescence. A general lack of role-taking opportunity—particularly for boys, who rely on extrafamilial activities very heavily during adolescence—may account for those youths who are regularly delinquent because of a combination of fixation in the preconventional level and prevailing individual and social pressures toward delinquency. Not only might the status of adolescents retard development, but their status as consumers without a legitimate income might create the pressures toward delinquency (Greenberg 1977).

The Kohlberg Model and Patterns of Delinquency

Although the effects of personal and situational factors and of the restricted roles available to adolescents in our society can be considered as tentative explanations for the sporadic nature of much delinquency, there remain questions about the well-documented patterns of delinquency. An alternative explanation for the sporadic involvement of most youths in trivial delinquency is the inability of commonly used scales to obtain a measure of the transitional points between levels of moral reasoning. In many studies not even a majority of subjects' responses are at their predominant level of reasoning (Morash 1981; Kohlberg 1969; Flavell and Wohlwill 1969). As a solution to the measurement problem, Rest (1976, p. 208) proposed to "rephrase the assessment question from 'What stage is a subject?' to 'What are the probabilities of occurrence of each stage type for a subject?' " The methodological adjustment would be to use the proportion of responses at each level of reasoning to predict behavior. Attention to mixed stages during adolescence would seem to be particularly important because adolescence is the time for movement from the preconventional level as well as for the emergence of some postconventional thought.

A second pattern in delinquency that requires an explanation is the lower involvement of girls in illegal behavior in general, and in particular their much lower levels of violence. According to the Kohlberg theory, a greater proportion of boys than girls would be fixated at the preconventional stage and would be subjected to greater pressures toward delinquency. In support of the idea that boys experience greater pressures toward delinquency, there is evidence that boys are more concerned with status goals that are difficult to attain, whereas girls are concerned with more easily attainable relational goals (Morris 1964). In contradiction to the idea that boys are more often fixated at a preconventional level, however, some research has shown that adolescent boys and girls are equally advanced in moral reasoning (Cauble 1975), or that girls are *less* advanced (Turiel 1973; Gilligan et al. 1971). Thus the primary determinant that Kohlberg identified as the cause of delinquency—that is, preconventional reasoning—is not more common among boys than among girls, and does not help us to explain boys' greater delinquency.

The application of Kohlberg's ideas to a consideration of sex-role stereotypes and moral development raises additional problems in explaining the gender distribution of delinquency. Kohlberg (1966) wrote that young children see conformity to their sex-role stereotype as moral, and they imitate stereotyped behavior. Adolescent girls who do not conform to sex-stereotypic behavior, then, would be expected to be morally undeveloped and therefore delinquent. On the contrary, research has shown that girls with nonstereotypic attitudes are *least* delinquent (James and Thornton 1980).

Recent empirical research (Cullen, Golden, and Cullen 1979) also has revealed that stereotypic masculine traits were related to delinquency. This would suggest that for boys, the entry into the conventional stage involves conformity to sex-stereotypic attitudes that are consistent with delinquent behavior. The implied association of conventional reasoning with boys' delinquency is at odds with the hypothesis that conventional reasoning is an insulation from delinquency.

The possibility that girls experience some developmental achievement that is realized at a later time by boys and that accounts for girls' lower delinquency has not been considered by most people who have used Kohlberg's model. The construct that is a likely candidate as the girls' special achievement involves affective empathy—the capacity to share the feelings of another person. Hoffman (1977) (see also Rosenberg and Simmons 1975; Eisenberg-Berg and Mussen 1978; Romer 1975) has summarized several studies showing affective empathy to be more developed among adolescent girls than boys; Hoffman (1975) also has proposed that the greater pressure on boys to succeed may conflict with concern for other people. Hoffman (1977) has provided his own empirical evidence of girls' greater capacity for empathy during adolescence. Holstein (1976) also found that the moral reasoning of girls reflected more empathy and compassion than the reasoning of boys. Because empathy and a recognition of oneself as a cause of another person's distress is often translated into guilt (Hoffman 1975), and because both empathy and guilt are highly related to prosocial behavior, Hoffman (1977, p. 720) concluded that girls "may have a more highly developed affective base for prosocial behavior than do males." By this logic, girls would have a more highly developed affective motivation to avoid delinquent behavior that hurts other individuals—although, consistent with empirical research, they would not be expected to differ in levels of involvement in victimless offenses, such as the status offenses and drug and alcohol use.

The inclusion of affective empathy as an aspect of moral development or as a motivation for applying high levels of reasoning would strengthen Kohlberg's model. It would be consistent with the findings of experimental research attributing females' prosocial behavior and their refusal to hurt other people to their empathic development (Hoffman 1975; Kilham and Mann 1974). Despite empirical demonstrations of the relevance of empathy to behavior, Kohlberg has explicitly omitted affective empathy from his scheme. He (1969, p. 423) has, however, described a rather negatively valued concern for others as typical of stage 3 reasoning: "Most adults of stage 3 are women with a 'good-girl' orientation and an emphasis on love and romantic relationships involving idealization of the other, identification or sharing between selves and unselfish or sacrificial concern for the love object." This reference to the concern for others at the early conventional level is close enough to the concept of empathy that women, who characteristically exhibit a great deal of empathy, tend to be classified at stage 3 even as adults (Fishkin, Keniston, and MacKinnon 1973; Haan, Block, and Smith 1968; Haan, Langer, and Kohlberg 1976; Holstein 1976). The characteristic as described by Kohlberg, however, bears little resemblance to the mature and positively valued concern for others that is typically meant by the term *affective empathy.*

There is a second way in which the inclusion of affective empathy as an aspect of moral development would provide an explanation of patterns in delinquency. The higher development of empathy in girls would account for their particularly low rates of serious and other violent delinquency that would injure other people; but it would allow for the moderate involvement of girls in shoplifting, with its indirect effects on others, and for the high involvement of girls in drug use, which primarily affects the offender.

Whereas the inclusion of affective empathy as an aspect in the development of moral reasoning would serve to strengthen the Kohlberg model, its exclusion creates problems in explaining delinquency. As already noted, the presence of empathy is empirically related to moral behavior. Empirical research (Kalle and Suls 1978) also has demonstrated a lack of relationship between the highest, postconventional levels of moral reasoning and empathy. This is not surprising, since by definition individuals who are concerned with others are relegated to stage 3. If empathy is related to moral behavior and is unrelated to moral reasoning, then the hypothesized relationship between moral reasoning and moral behavior is precluded.

Although it is somewhat tangential to the application of Kohlberg's model to delinquent behavior, the irony in his approach as applied to women is worth mentioning. It is a strange twist of reasoning that adolescent girls, who on the whole are less delinquent than adolescent boys, are not considered to have achieved any special, highly valued developmental positions by virtue of their greater empathy; while at the same time older adolescent and adult women, who are less criminal as a group than men, are considered to lag in moral development because of their expression of an orientation toward others. The strong tendencies for social scientists to consider the stereotypical male characteristics as most desirable seem to have blinded us from recognizing the positive aspects of females' characteristics and the related desirable socialization.

Alternative Models of Morality
Applied to Delinquency

As might be expected from the foregoing analysis of the application of Kohlberg's model of moral development to delinquency, one of the most striking consistencies in revision is the emphasis on adding an affective concern for other people to the dimension of abstract reasoning. This consistency is reflected in the models of Gilligan and Haan that will be reviewed, as well as in the work of many other theorists (Bloom 1977; Gibbs 1979; McGeorge 1974; Hoffman 1976).

An additional consistency in revisions to Kohlberg's model is the emphasis on moving away from a predominantly bivariate explanation to link reasoning with behavior, and toward complex explanations that consider many aspects of personality and/or the social situation as intervening variables. The multivariate explanations of delinquency require verification through research that considers the relationship of reasoning to delinquency in a wide variety of situations, and among people with varying personal characteristics. This type of research is rare in studies of moral development, although it is clearly suggested by the alternative models.

Gilligan and Contextual Reasoning

Gilligan's (1982) revision of the Kohlberg model was developed from studies of adults who confronted a variety of moral dilemmas. Some of the subjects were women contemplating an abortion, some were college students, and the remainder were adults at different stages in the life cycle. From these data, Gilligan concluded that women tended to speak about morality "in a different voice." The essential feature of this other voice was termed *contextual relativism,* which is the consideration of personal and special obligations to other people. Unlike the concern with other people at Kohlberg stage 3 reasoning, contextual relativisim was found to be compatible with fully developed logical systems to justify moral choice (Murphy and Gilligan 1980, p. 90). Contextual relativism involves a recognition and sharing of the feelings of other people and thus incorporates some aspects of affective empathy.

A particularly important contribution of Gilligan's work is the recognition that women tend to use contextual relativism more than men do. It is noteworthy that Gilligan presents this as a tendency rather than an absolute division between men and women.

Gilligan has relied heavily on Chodorow's (1978) refinement of Freudian theory to explain those gender differences that are found in very young children and eventually produce women's unique capabilities in moral reasoning. Chodorow reasoned that because women in our society carry primary responsibility for child rearing, early in life girls are encouraged to define themselves through a close connection to their mothers. Boys, in contrast, must define themselves through their differences from and therefore lack of connection with their mothers. As a result, girls experience empathy as a fundamental part of their personalities, whereas boys are less directed toward others. This other-directedness eventually results in girls' earlier and/or greater development of an "ethic of care" that "rests on the premise of nonviolence—that no one should be hurt" (Gilligan 1982, p. 174). Boys, of course, also can develop the ethic of care; but this may require the life experiences that occur at the end of adolescence, when work and intimate relationships stimulate males in our society to take responsibility and care for others. The tendency for boys to develop an ethic of care at a later time than girls do may explain their higher rates of delinquency during adolescence, particularly delinquency that harms other people.

The Gilligan model may also provide an explanation for the relationships of family atmosphere and discipline to delinquency. The accepting and less conflictual atmosphere, as well as the consistent discipline, associated with low delinquency would be very important in fostering other-oriented reasoning. Thus it may be that the family affects delinquency not through promoting abstract reasoning, which many other social institutions can promote, but through stimulating concern, responsibility, and care for others. The family is usually a more singular influence in these areas than in challenging youths to use progressively more developed abstract reasoning.

Gilligan's model is highly consistent with research linking empathy to an avoidance of actions, including delinquency, that hurt other people. It is also consistent with research that has attributed girls' delinquency primarily to a breakdown in their relations in the family. Konopka (1966), for example, described the sense of loneliness experienced by most delinquent girls. Her case studies of delinquent girls who experience negative relationships with their parents are very similar to Gilligan's (1982, p. 110) description of one woman's stage 1 reasoning about the "interpersonal context" as "indicating her preoccupation with her own needs and her struggle to ensure her own survival in a world perceived as exploitive and threatening, a world in which she experiences herself as uncared for and alone." Several studies have confirmed the greater importance of family relations in explaining girls' rather than boys' delinquency (Morris 1964; Gold and Petronio 1980, p. 508). This is consistent with the idea that girls' typical concern for others, which has developed in their families, will lead them to avoid delinquent activity; when they are not positively involved with their families because of rejection or other tensions, however, there is a tendency toward delinquency.

By identifying the "ethic of responsibility" as an accompaniment to the "ethic of fairness" stressed in Kohlberg's model of moral reasoning, Gilligan raised another possible explanation for boys' greater delinquency, particularly their violence against other people. Abstract reasoning about the fairness of certain actions may be more amenable to reinterpretation than is a concern for other people. In other words, it is more difficult to neutralize affective empathy and concern for other people than to redefine an abstract conceptualization of fairness. As a result, the earlier development of girls in the ethic of responsibility may serve as a stronger insulation against delinquency than an ethic of fairness.

Gilligan has offered her model of moral reasoning as tentative, and as requiring further testing to establish that the ethic of responsibility develops in sequential stages. Despite the exploratory nature of her research, Gilligan's model has provided a particularly important correction to the Kohlberg conceptualization of moral reasoning. The corrected model holds promise for explaining the gender-related differences in delinquency, although the establishment of a link between contextual reasoning and behavior remains to be accomplished in future research.

Haan and Interpersonal Morality

Like Gilligan, Haan has proposed that there are "two moralities" and that one of these, interpersonal morality, is omitted from the Kohlberg model. Like the concept of contextual reasoning, Haan's concept of inter-personal morality involves a consideration of other people's feelings and expectations. These similarities are surprising given the disparate research methods used by Gilligan and Haan. In contrast to Gilligan, who used interviews with subjects after they had made their moral choices, Haan (1978) relied on direct observations of behavior to indicate both reasoning and other individual characteristics. In research on adolescents, for example, Haan (1978) measured moral reasoning by recording the spontaneous verbalizations of the subjects as they interacted with friends to resolve moral dilemmas.

Despite similarities in the conclusions of Haan and Gilligan, they have fundamentally different conceptions of the individual. Haan proposed structures and particularly ego processes that are interdependent on and in constant flux with the environment to which they must adapt. Gilligan, on the other hand, more nearly conformed her view to Kohlberg's emphasis on a relatively stable moral structure that is not markedly affected by other aspects of the personality or by the immediate situation.

In another departure from the models of both Kohlberg and Gilligan, Haan (1978) concluded that interpersonal morality is the more fundamental and that the Kohlberg concept of abstract reasoning is of little importance. To illustrate the more fundamental nature of interpersonal morality, Haan argued that in making moral decisions and taking related actions, people are primarily concerned not with applying abstract rules but with their interactions with other people. These interactions, or *dialogue* in Haan's term, involve "grasping one's own and another's peculiarities and one's own implicit and nonformal obligations to him because of his mutual expectancies of you and yours of him" (Haan 1977, p. 120). Interpersonal morality grows from a stage at which a young child is undifferentiated from others to the point that a person is cognizant of his or her own position in maintaining a moral balance with other people in a social situation.

Haan did not develop her description of personality processes and the dual moral structures to predict behavior. Instead, she (1977, p. 2) asserted that "people's constructions result in their doing the same thing for different reasons and different things for the same reason." In this framework we would not expect interpersonal morality to be a strong predictor of delinquency. Nevertheless, Haan's conceptualization and related empirical findings are relevant to assessing prior attempts to link moral reasoning with delinquent behavior. In a study of adolescents who took part in a series of games which required moral decisions, Haan (1978) found that in action situations, adolescents more often resolved dilemma with interpersonal reasoning than with Kohlberg's abstract reasoning. Furthermore, neither abstract nor interpersonal reasoning as measured in a previous interview situation were much related to reasoning in the game-playing situation; abstract and interpersonal reasoning were not related to each other; and the level of reasoning, particularly abstract reasoning, was negatively affected by the unpleasantness of the game being played. In a statement that would explain the situational nature of much delinquency, Haan (1978, p. 303) concluded from her research on adolescents in their peer groups that interpersonal morality is "contextual, inductive, and interactional."

Not only do external contextual factors strongly affect moral structures (interpersonal morality and formal reasoning) according to Haan; so do other parts of the personality, which she called *ego processes*. In her view, empathy is not part of interpersonal morality, but is an ego process that her research (Haan 1978) demonstrated to contribute heavily to interpersonal morality. Though quite dissimilar from Gilligan's conceptualization of the connection of empathy with moral structure, Haan's view is, like Gilligan's, explanatory of the greater interpersonal morality or concern for others exhibited by adolescent girls than by boys. Her model suggests that given similar contextual pressures, compared with boys, girls with the greater empathy would manifest greater interpersonal morality and thus less delinquency that harms other people.

Discussion and Conclusion

Kohlberg developed his model of moral reasoning in part to resolve a problem posed some time ago by Hartshorne and May (1928), who revealed the lack of a relationship between values and behavior. The problem that Hartshorne and May identified was to explain how variations in the situation produced variations in human behavior. Rather than looking at these situational variations, Kohlberg developed a strong argument that not values, but moral reasoning about rules and laws, would explain behavior. His theoretical and empirical work made the invaluable contribution of drawing attention to the construct, moral reasoning. Now we have come almost full circle, and it is expedient to abandon the emphasis on moral reasoning as a sole determinant of behavior. Instead, the ways in which moral reasoning, together with situational and other personal variations, interact to produce behavior require exploration in theoretical and empirical work.

Besides abandoning the univariate explanation of delinquency, it is expedient to expand the content of moral reasoning to include the other-oriented reasoning that Gilligan and Haan have emphasized. Since some research (Haan 1978) has shown other-oriented and abstract reasoning to be relatively independent and differentially affected by the immediate situation, the two dimensions should be considered separately.

In addition to the aforementioned general reformulations in moral-reasoning theory as an explanation of delinquency, sociological knowledge has suggested several specific propositions that would be useful guides in future research. The key proposition is that a combination of both other-oriented reasoning and abstract reasoning act to insulate adolescents against social and personal pressures to break the law. Other-oriented reasoning, in particular, may act as an insulation from delinquency that would harm other people, although it would not be expected to be a particularly effective insulation against victimless offenses, such as drug use.

A consideration of sociological knowledge further suggests that delinquent peers are an important source of direct social pressure to break the law for even youths at the conventional level of reasoning. The influence of peers is expected to be strongest for youths at a mixed stage of development. Social learning from peers that redefines the degree to which delinquent acts are at odds with social norms also may influence youths at the conventional level or above to commit delinquent acts that are not consistent with conventional reasoning. It is further proposed that the influence of social learning from peers would be strongest for minor acts such as drug use, and weakest for serious delinquency that is more difficult to neutralize. Moreover, it would seem that social learning from peers would be more likely to result in the neutralization of formal principles relevant to abstract reasoning than in the neutraliztion of the concern for other people that is relevant to other-oriented reasoning.

In seeking the sources of developmental retardation and the resulting lack of insulation offered by both conventional abstract reasoning and conventional other-oriented reasoning, the family and the status of adolescents in our society are possible root causes. Although the family may not be necessary to promote the development of abstract reasoning, it would seem to be essential in promoting the development of other-oriented reasoning. Families that are characterized by conflict, rejection of their children, and inconsistent discipline, in particular, might contribute to a retardation in other-oriented reasoning and thus would be associated with delinquency.

In adolescence the family becomes increasingly less important as a source of stimulation in development; and the role-taking opportunities in peer groups and other institutions, such as schools and religious institutions, grow in importance. This shift is particularly strong for boys. It would seem likely that the limitations of peer groups and the failure of our society to engage youths in a variety of interactions in work and educational settings would mitigate against many individuals developing abstract and other-oriented reasoning. In keeping with our recognition that girls usually maintain more central roles in their families, they would not be as deleteriously affected by the lack of stimulus for moral development; hence they would be less delinquent. It should be possible to identify experiences that hasten moral development (such as early work responsibilities, family responsibilities, or progressive educational opportunities), as well as those that retard development (such as isolation in preconventional peer groups or negative school settings). It is true that some of these are likely to be concentrated among lower-class and minority populations; but this concentration is by no means absolute, just as the concentration of delinquency is not invariate according to social class or minority group.

Using the framework proposed so far, it is possible to explain repeated and serious delinquency, particularly against people and property. The most serious delinquency would result from social conditions, primarily those that are enduring, that impinge on youths who possess the personality factors and the preconventional reasoning conducive to serious delinquent behavior. An advantage of this explanation is that it allows for the many preconventional individuals who do not break the law regularly or at all, and it accounts for different patterns in delinquency—that is, the repeated serious delinquency and sporadic and/or less serious delinquency.

When abstract and other-oriented reasoning are considered to be insulation against social and personal pressures toward delinquency, and the family and status of adolescents are identified as influences on the rate of development in reasoning, then it is possible to explain well-established patterns in delinquent behavior. Even conventional or higher-level youths may be pressured by peers to act in a way that contradicts their own reasoning. Thus we can explain the apparent widespread delinquency of many youths who do not seem to be markedly retarded in their development. Additionally, the recognition of the influence of the limitations on experiences for adolescents in our society leads us to expect some uneven and perhaps slow development among youths without exceptional advantages. Finally, the recognition of the importance of other-oriented reasoning, with its relationship to empathy, explains the greater delinquency of boys in comparison to girls; the other-oriented reasoning that tends to be stimulated among girls would be a particularly strong insulation from pressures to commit the offenses against other people, which in fact are rarely committed by girls.

A number of issues related to the application of an integrated psychological and sociological model to explain delinquency remain to be resolved. One of the most important of these is the relative weight given to each dimension of moral reasoning. At one extreme on this issue, Kohlberg (1975, p. 672) has asserted that abstract reasoning, "while only one factor in moral behavior, is the single most important or influential factor yet discovered in moral behavior." At the other extreme, Haan (1978, p. 303) described abstract reasoning as "one particular, late-developing branch of interpersonal morality, preferred by specialized problem solvers and used in special kinds of rule-governed, interpersonal situations." Along with a lack of knowledge of the relative importance of different moral structures, there is inadequate information on whether these dimensions are related or develop unevenly.

Also at issue is the importance of moral reasoning relative to that of personal and social pressures toward delinquency, and the exact specification of the factors that are important. Social pressures would include both transitory situational factors and more stable and enduring factors, such as adolescents' exclusion from the labor force. In one of the few attempts to demonstrate empirically the combined effects of abstract reasoning and personality factors, Tsujimoto and Nardi (1978) demonstrated that both types of variables together predicted more variation in delinquent behavior than did either alone. The personality factors that were considered included the dimensions of moral character that have been identified by Hogan (1975a): knowledge of social rules, empathy, autonomy from peers, socialization to regard the rules as obligatory, and a preference for abstract system of rules versus intuitive understandings of morality. Krebs (1967) found that the personality factors, attention and IQ, had an effect on moral judgment beyond the effect of level of reasoning. Haan (1978) demonstrated that ego processes, particularly empathy, contributed to the use of interpersonal morality. Only Haan's research attempted to identify a very wide range of personality variations that might contribute to the use of various levels of reasoning. She also specified the pleasantness of the situation as an influence. On the basis of sociological theories, we have suggested that the special circumstances of adolescence and peer groups are likely social pressures toward delinquency. The identification of a wide range of salient personal and social pressures toward delinquency, and the mediation of these influences by conventional or postconventional reasoning, are still only partially accomplished.

A third issue is the specification of the role of affective empathy in producing behavior. Empathy has been alternatively considered a part of other-oriented reasoning, a stimulus for the individual to act in accord with mature levels of reasoning, and a personality characteristic (or, in Haan's terms, ego process) that results in the manifestation of a high level of reasoning. Hoffman (1979) has established stages in the development of affective empathy that parallel stages in moral reasoning. Research is needed to determine the degree to which empathy is associated with other-oriented reasoning, and to establish whether some amount of development in empathic capacity is a prerequisite for the use of high-level reasoning.

Fourth, there is a need to untangle sex-role stereotypes from levels of both other-oriented and abstract moral reasonings. Gilligan's (1982) recognition of other-oriented reasoning as more, rather than exclusively, developed among women is a defensible approach. It is not defensible, however, to define specific levels of reasoning as congruent with sex-stereotypic behavior. This type of confounding of definitions makes it impossible to separate the effects of reasoning from the effects of stereotypic sex-role identification.

In conclusion, it is appropriate to comment briefly on the implications of an integrated sociological and moral-reasoning perspective on delinquency for prevention and correctional programs. If we have learned anything from considerable debate over the efficacy of different treatment methods, it is that the treatment must be carefully matched to the needs of each youth (Palmer 1975). Given the diversity in social influences and personal pressures that may impinge on youths who come to be labeled as delinquents, treatment methods must be equally diverse. Regardless of the appeal of simplicity, it would be a mistake to consider development of moral reasoning, of either the other-oriented or the abstract variety, to be a sole solution to the problem of delinquency.[3] Much broader efforts are needed to increase role-taking opportunities for adolescents. There is also a need to rethink those socialization practices and social pressures that contribute to boys' greater delinquency. Given our inability to attribute more than a small part of delinquency to moral reasoning, it would be best to develop multivariate programs as well as multivariate research insofar as delinquency is concerned. Evaluations would profitably focus on differentiating the sole and the combined effects of actions to alleviate social pressures, to stimulate the development of empathy, to stimulate the development of other-oriented reasoning, and to stimulate the development of abstract reasoning among specific populations of youths.

Notes

1. Hogan (1974, 1975) also has developed a model of moral character that consists of the five components: (1) learning about social rules; (2) socialization to consider the rules binding; (3) empathy; (4) autonomy

from the influence of peers; and (5) reliance on intuitive moral feelings versus conventions, contracts, and formal agreements in making moral decisions. Because this model deemphasizes the effect of the moral reasoning on delinquency, it is not considered here. It might be noted, however, that in contrast to Gilligan and Haan, who considered reasoning to be a variable of interest, Hogan departed more fully from Kohlberg's approach, and considered only enduring aspects of character to be the salient predictors of behavior.

2. In this chapter, models of moral reasoning will not be considered as explanations of race or social-class concentrations of delinquency. Social-class and racial patterns of delinquency are not clearly established in the criminological literature. In general, official court and police records have shown that lower-class and minority youths are more delinquent than others (Wolfgang, Figlio, and Sellin 1972; Braithwaite 1979), and self-report studies have shown a less pronounced difference or none (Gold 1970). Surveys of victims showed that a higher proportion of victimizations can be attributed to black than to white youths (Hindelang 1981). It is not known, however, whether the concentration of victimizations by blacks is due to their lower class or to the tendency of a small number of black youths to commit a very high proportion of offenses.

3. In fact, the correctional programs that apply moral-reasoning theory usually do offer a diverse combination of treatments. Unfortunately, research has not focused on discerning the individual effects of each type of treatment.

References

Akers, R.L.; Krohn, M.D.; Lanza-Kaduce, L.; and Radosevich, M. Social learning and deviant behavior: A specific test of a general theory. *American Sociological Review,* 1979, *44,* 636-655.

Bartol, C.R. *Criminal behavior: A psychosocial approach.* Englewood Cliffs, N.J.: Prentice-Hall, 1980.

Bloom, A.H. Two dimensions of moral reasoning: Social principledness and social humanism in cross-cultural perspective. *Journal of Social Psychology,* 1977, *101,* 29-44.

Braithwaite, J. *Inequality, crime and public policy.* Boston: Routledge and Kegan Paul, 1979.

Cauble, M.A. Interrelations among Piaget's formal operations, Erickson's ego identify, and Kohlberg's principled morality. Ph.D. diss., Arizona State University, 1975.

Chodorow, N. *The reproduction of mothering.* Berkeley: University of California Press, 1978.

Cleckley, H. *The mask of sanity.* St. Louis: Mosby, 1964.

Clinchy, B.; Lief, J.; and Young, P. Epistemological and moral development in girls from a traditional and progressive high school. *Journal of Educational Psychology,* 1977, *69,* 337-343.

Cullen, F.T.; Golden, K.M.: and Cullen, J.B. Sex and delinquency: A partial test of the masculinity hypothesis. *Criminology,* 1979, *17,* 301-310.

Dinitz, S., and Conrad, J.P. The dangerous two percent. In D. Shichor and D.H. Kelly, eds., *Critical issues in juvenile delinquency.* Lexington, Mass.: Lexington Books, D.C. Heath and Company, 1980.

Eisenberg-Berg, N., and Mussen, P. Empathy and moral development in adolescence. *Developmental Psychology,* 1978, *14,* 186-196.

Emler, N.P.: Winton, M.; and Heather, N. Moral reasoning and delinquency: Some limitations of Kohlberg's theory. *Bulletin of the British Psychological Society,* 1977, *30,* 161.

Feyerherm, W. Gender differences in delinquency: Quantity and quality. In L. Bowker, ed., *Women and crime in America.* New York: Macmillan, 1981.

Fishkin, J.; Keniston, K.; and MacKinnon, C. Moral reasoning and political ideology. *Journal of Personality and Social Psychology,* 1973, *27,* 109-119.

Flavell, J.H., and Wohlwill, J. Formal and functional aspects of cognitive development. In D. Elkind and J. Flavell, eds., *Studies in cognitive development.* New York: Oxford University Press, 1969.

Fodor, E.M. Delinquency and susceptibility to social influence among adolescents as a function of moral development. *Journal of Social Psychology,* 1972, *86,* 257-260.

————. Moral development and parent behavior antecedents in adolescent psychopaths. *Journal of Genetic Psychology,* 1973, *122,* 37-43.

Friday, P.C., and Hage, J. Youth crime in postindustrial societies: An integrated perspective. *Criminology,* 1976, *14,* 347-368.

Gibbons, D.C. Some observations on the study of crime causation. *American Journal of Sociology,* 1971, *77,* 262-278.

————. *The criminological enterprise: Theories and perspectives.* Englewood Cliffs, N.J.: Prentice-Hall, 1979.

Gibbs, J.C. Kohlberg's moral stage theory: A Piagetian revision. *Human Development,* 1979, *22,* 89-112.

Gilligan, C. *In a different voice.* Cambridge, Mass.: Harvard University Press, 1982.

Gilligan, C.; Kohlberg, L.; Lerner, J.; and Belensky, M. *Moral reasoning about sexual dilemmas: Development of an interview and scoring system.* Technical report of the President's Commission on Obscenity and Pornography, vol. 1. Washington, D.C.: U.S. Government Printing Office, 1971.

Giordano, P.C. Girls, guys and gangs—the changing social context of female delinquency. *Journal of Criminal Law and Criminology,* 1978, *69,* 126-132.

Glaser, D. *Crime in our changing society.* New York: Holt, Rinehart and Winston, 1978.

Glueck, S., and Glueck, E. *Later criminal careers.* New York: Commonwealth Fund, 1937.

_____. *Delinquents and nondelinquents in perspective.* Cambridge, Mass.: Harvard University Press, 1968.

Gold, M. *Delinquent behavior in an American city.* Belmont, Calif.: Brooks/Cole, 1970

Gold, M., and Petronio, R.J. Delinquent behavior in adolescence. In J. Adelson, ed., *Handbook of adolescent psychology.* New York: Wiley-Interscience Publication, 1980.

Greenberg, D.F. Delinquency and the age structure of society. *Contemporary Crisis,* 1977, *1,* 189-223.

Haan, N. *Coping and defending: Processes of self-environment organization.* New York: Academic press, 1977.

_____. Two moralities in action contexts: Relationships to thought, ego regulation, and development. *Journal of Personality and Social Psychology,* 1978, *36,* 286-305.

Haan, N.; Block, J.; and Smith, M.B. Moral reasoning of young adults: Political-social behavior, family background, and personality correlates. *Journal of Personality and Social Psychology,* 1968, *10,* 184-201.

Haan, N.; Langer, J.; and Kohlberg L. Family moral patterns. *Child Development,* 1976, *47,* 1204-1206.

Hartshorne, H., and May, M.A. *Studies in the nature of character.* New York: MacMillan, 1928.

Hindelang, M.J. Variations in sex-race-age specific incidence rates of offending. *American Sociological Review,* 1981, *46,* 461-474.

Hirschi, T. *Causes of delinquency.* Berkeley, Calif.: University of California Press, 1969.

Hoffman, M.L. Sex differences in moral internalization and values. *Journal of Personality and Social Psychology,* 1975, *32,* 720-729.

_____. Empathy, role-taking, guilt, and development of altruistic motives. In T. Lickona, ed., *Moral development and behavior: Theory, research, and social issues.* New York: Holt, Rinehart and Winston, 1976.

_____. Sex differences in empathy and related behaviors. *Psychological Bulletin,* 1977, *84,* 712-722.

_____. Development of moral thought, feeling, and behavior. *American Psychologist,* 1979, *34,* 958-966.

Hogan, R. Moral development and the structure of personality. In D.J. Depalma and J.M. Foley, eds., *Moral development: Current theory and research.* Hillsdale, N.J.: Lawrence Erlbaum Associates, 1975a, 153-167.

———. The structure of moral character and the explanation of moral action. *Journal of Youth and Adolescence,* 1975b, *4,* 1-15.

Holstein, C. Irreversible, stepwise sequence in the development of moral judgment: A longitudinal study of males and females. *Child Development,* 1976, *47,* 51-61.

Hudgins, W., and Prentice, N.M. Moral judgment in delinquent and non-delinquent adolescents and their mothers. *Journal of Abnormal Psychology,* 1973, *82,* 145-152.

Inciardi, J.A. Youth, drugs, and street crime. In F.R. Scarpitti and S.K. Datesman, eds., *Drugs and the youth culture.* Beverly Hills, Calif.: Sage, 1980.

Inkeles, A. Sociological theory in relation to social psychological variables. In J.C. McKinney and E.A. Tiryakian, eds., *Theoretical sociology: Perspectives and development.* New York: Appleton-Century-Crofts, 1970.

James, J., and Thorton, W. Women's liberation and the female delinquent. *Journal of Research in Crime and Delinquency,* 1980, *17,* 230-244.

Jurkovic, G.J., and Prentice, N.M. Dimensions of moral interaction and moral judgment in delinquent and nondelinquent families. *Journal of Consulting and Clinical Psychology,* 1974, *42,* 256-262.

———. Relation of moral and cognitive development to dimensions of juvenile delinquency. *Journal of Abnormal Psychology,* 1977, *86,* 414-420.

Kalle, R.J., and Suls, J. Relationship between Kohlberg moral judgment stages and emotional empathy. *Bulletin of Psychonomic Society,* 1978, *11,* 191-192.

Keasey, C.B. Social participation as a factor in the moral development of preadolescents. *Developmental Psychology,* 1971, *5,* 212-220.

Kilham, W., and Mann, L. Level of destructive obedience as a function of transmitter and executant roles in the Milgram obedience paradigm. *Journal of Personality and Social Psychology,* 1974, *29,* 692-702.

Kohlberg, L. The development of modes of moral thinking and choice in years 10 to 16. Ph.D. diss., Harvard University, 1958.

———. A cognitive-developmental analysis of children's sex role concepts and attitudes. In E.E. Maccoby, ed., *The development of sex differences.* Palo Alto, Calif.: Stanford University Press, 1966.

———. Stage and sequence: The cognitive-developmental approach to socialization. In D.A. Goslin, ed., *Handbook of socialization theory and research.* Chicago: Rand-McNally, 1969.

_____. The cognitive-developmental approach to moral education. *Phi Delta Kappan,* 1975, 670-677.

_____. The cognitive-developmental approach to behavior disorders: A study of the development of moral reasoning in delinquents. In G. Serban, ed., *Cognitive defects in the development of mental illness.* New York: Brunner/Mazel, 1978.

Konopka, C. *The adolescent girl in conflict.* Englewood Cliffs, N.J.: Prentice-Hall, 1966.

Kornhauser, R.R. *Social sources of delinquency: An appraisal of analytic models.* Chicago: University of Chicago Press, 1978.

Krebs, R.L. Some relations between moral judgment, attention, and resistance to temptation. Ph.D. diss., University of Chicago, 1967.

McCord, W., and Zola, I. *Origins of crime.* New York: Columbia University Press, 1959.

McGeorge, C. Situational variation in level of moral judgment. *British Journal of Educational Psychology,* 1974, *44,* 116-122.

Miller, C.K.; Sumoff, L.; and Stephens, B. A comparison of reasoning skills and moral judgments in delinquent, retarded, and normal adolescent girls. *Journal of Psychology,* 1974, *86,* 261-268.

Minor, W.W. Techniques of neutralization: A reconceptualization and empirical examination. *Journal of Research in Crime and Delinquency,* 1981, *18,* 295-318.

Morash, M. Cognitive developmental theory: a basis for juvenile correctional reform? *Criminology,* 1981, *19,* 360-371.

Morris, R. Female delinquency and relational problems. *Social Forces,* 1964, *43,* 82-88.

Murphy, J.M., and Gilligan, C. Moral development in late adolescence and adulthood: A critique and reconstruction of Kohlberg's theory. *Human Development,* 1980, *23,* 77-104.

Palmer, T. Martinson revisited. *Journal of Research in Crime and Delinquency,* 1975, *12,* 133-152.

Poole, E.C., and Regoli, R.M. Parental support, delinquent friends, and delinquency: A test of interaction effects. *Journal of Criminal Law and Criminology,* 1979, *70,* 188-193.

Quay, H.C., and Parsons, L.B. The differential behavioral classification of the juvenile. Washington, D.C.: U.S. Bureau of Prisons, 1967.

Rest, J.R. New approaches in the assessment of moral judgment. In T. Lickona, ed., *Moral development and behavior: Theory, research and social isues.* New York: Holt, Rinehart and Winston, 1976.

Rodman, H., and Grams, P. Juvenile delinquency and the family: A review and discussion. *Task force report: Juvenile delinquency and youth crime.* Washington, D.C.: U.S. Government Printing Office, 1967.

Romer, N. The motivation to avoid success and its effects on performance in school-age males and females. *Developmental Psychology,* 1975, *11,* 689-699.

Rosenberg, F.R., and Simmons, R.G. Sex differences in self-concept in adolescence. *Sex Roles,* 1975, *1,* 147-160.

Scarpitti, F.R.; Murray, E.; Dinitz, S.; and Reckless, W. The good boy in a high delinquency area: four years later. *American Sociological Review,* 1960, *25,* 555-558.

Simpson, E.L. Moral development research: A case study of scientific cultural bias. *Human Development,* 1974, *17,* 81-106.

Steffensmeir, D.J., and Steffensmeir, R.H. Trends in female delinquency: An examination of arrest, juvenile court, self-report, and field data. *Criminology,* 1980, *18,* 62-85.

Trojanowicz, R., and Morash, M. *Juvenile delinquency: Concepts and control.* Englewood Cliffs, N.J.: Prentice-Hall, 1983.

Tsujimoto, R.N., and Nardi, P.M. A comparison of Kohlberg's and Hogan's theories of moral development. *Social Psychology,* 1978, *41,* 235-245.

Turiel, E. Stage transition in moral development. In R.M.W. Travers, ed., *Second handbook of research on teaching.* Chicago: Rand-McNally, 1973.

Vold, G.B. *Theoretical criminology.* New York: Oxford University Press, 1958.

Ward, L., and Wilson, J.P. Motivation and moral development as determinants of behavioral acquiescence and moral action. *Journal of Social Psychology,* 1980, *112,* 271-288.

Wolfgang, M.E.; Figlio, R.M.; and Sellin, T. *Delinquency in a birth cohort.* Chicago: University of Chicago Press, 1972.

Yinger, J.M. Toward a field theory of delinquency. New York: McGraw-Hill, 1965.

16 Theoretical Perspectives on Moral Development and Restitution

Patricia Van Voorhis

Theoretical and philosophical rationales for restitution devote considerable attention to the issue of the offender's receptivity to the sanction.[1] Several proponents of restitution confidently state that offenders view the restitution sanction as fair and rationally related to the harm caused to the victim.[2] Others focus on certain ameliorative effects to be derived by offenders in the course of repaying their victims, such as alleviating the distress resulting from the exploitive encounter with the victim and helping offenders to cope with feelings of guilt.[3] Further claims relate to the offender's responsibility. Advocates bill restitution as the offender's "functional responsibility,"[4] as well as a vehicle for strengthening the offender's "feelings of responsibility."[5]

Caught up in the optimism of reform, these endorsements have been widely accepted and reflected in recent profusions of restitution legislation and programming.[6] Unfortunately, there exists little evidence of how offenders perceive restitution or of the impact of offender perceptions on the successful completion of restitution. Indeed, research on offenders ordered to pay restitution is scarce, and most of the available research only superficially taps the pertinent attitudinal dimensions. Moreover, most research in this area has emerged from a theoretical vacuum. Highly relevant psychological and social-psychological theories and typologies, which could provide sorely needed theoretical frameworks for the study of offender attitudinal patterns, have been underutilized. As a result, few attempts have been made to organize and analyze the data according to the heterogeneous qualities of the populations being studied. Attitudinal measures are typically presented for the research sample as a whole, with no consideration for the impact of personality or psychological characteristics on offender assessments of restitution and restitution outcome.[7]

One source of theory and knowledge relevant to individual perceptions of justice, responsibility, and fairness appears in the literature on moral development. Most of this research is the work of Lawrence Kohlberg and his associates at the Center for Moral Development at Harvard University (see chapter 12). Kohlberg's work supplies tested theoretical structures for measuring individual perceptions of morality in developmental stages. Moral-Development Theory suggests that individuals possess different

orientations toward such moral issues as fairness, obedience to law, affiliation, and conscience.[8] Individuals positioned at some developmental stages,
for example, base moral decisions on concerns for reward and punishment,
whereas individuals at other stages orient primarily to legal mandates. Still
others, those at the high end of Kohlberg's continuum, apply universal principles of morality to their decision making.

When offender attitudes toward restitution are considered in this framework, crucial questions must be raised about the offender's method of conceptualizing fairness, rationality, distress, and responsibility. With few empirical demonstrations of the meaning of restitution to offenders and strong
suggestions that some offenders may be unable to conceptualize their responsibility to the victim, it cannot be said with certainty that restitution instills a
sense of responsibility. Skepticism must also be reserved for overenthusiastic
beliefs that restitution is perceived by offenders to be fair and is, therefore, a
viable method for reimbursing victims, reeducating offenders, and dis-
couraging repeated criminal involvements. Since Moral-Development Theory
suggests that not all offenders view restitution in a similar fashion, offender
attitudes toward restitution may differ greatly from those envisioned by
writers, planners, and other proponents of restitution.

Although the Kohlberg scheme clearly seems relevant to understanding
the diverse ways in which offenders make sense of restitution, most of the
moral-development research comes from educational settings; the theory, as
well as the diagnostic instrument, has received very little use among adult
offender populations.[9] Furthermore, since Kohlberg's research is relatively
new, most of it having taken place since 1960, contributions to the current
theoretical understanding of moral development are warranted. Thus
research on offender populations can contribute to the knowledge bases of
both moral development and restitution.

This chapter will outline areas of inquiry relevant to both moral development and restitution and will outline an agenda for research that endeavors to study moral development in an applied restitution setting.
Several of the questions posed in this chapter emerge from an interfacing of
Moral-Development Theory with appropriate theories of restitution; others
identify voids in our current understanding of moral development among
offender populations. Most of the questions put forth in this chapter were
empirically addressed in recent research conducted as a substudy of the National Evaluation of Adult Restitution Programs.[10] The findings are available elsewhere and will receive no attention in this chapter.[11]

Moral-Development Theory

Kohlberg's Theory of Moral Development shares assumptions and research
strategies common to several ego and cognitive developmental theories.[12]
The theories all postulate:

1. Development involves changes in cognitive structures or qualitative patterns of reasoning. Structures also have been referred to as stages, levels, types, and so on.
2. Development occurs through an invariant sequence of stages. The sequence of developmental stages is the same for all persons.
3. Development occurs along a continuum in which the structures become increasingly more differentiated and complex.
4. Stages are clustered wholes. The underlying logic used in forming perceptions and making choices, in other words, appears to be similar across situations. Although the subject of the actual choices may differ, the structure of the reasoning is the same.
5. Stages are hierarchical integrations. Individuals comprehend all stages below and one stage above their own stage of reasoning.

Since development can cease at any point along the continuum, it follows that individuals differ from one another in the complexity of their reasoning and the manner in which they make sense of their environment. A cross-section of the population would theoretically show a distribution of persons at all stages.

Kohlberg's Theory of Moral Development deals with a narrow component of ego and cognitive development, that of moral development.[13] The developmental stages in this system represent a hierarchical sequence of structures relating to moral reasoning or ways of thinking about justice, fairness, and right courses of action. They are discussed in depth in chapter 12.

Preliminary research suggests the usefulness of moral development theory to offender populations. In the Cheshire Reformatory and the Niantic State Farm for Women, for example, Kohlberg and several of his associates developed intervention strategies based upon moral judgment stages and assessments of the institutional environments.[14] The classification system has also been used to show the relation between stage and offender behavior. Kohlberg and Freundlich,[15] for example, found adolescents classified at the conventional level to be less likely to engage in delinquent behavior than persons classified at the preconventional level. In a study conducted with grade school children, stage 2 students engaged in more cheating behavior in school than did stage 4 students.[16]

The logic of Moral Development Theory offers one explanation for this difference. Development of moral structures eventually leads to a more universal type of reasoning. Principled thinking at the postconventional level suggests single "just" conclusions to decisions. Theoretically, individuals at these stages apply moral principles to decision making and do so across the exigencies of situations. The "right to life," for example, exists prior to concern for law and friends. Even individuals at conventional levels seem to be less situation-bound in their behavior than do those at lower stages. Thus, cheating behavior in stage 4 school children was not brought on when the teacher left the room, since the presence of an authority figure was not a salient concern among these students.[17]

Moral-Development Theory suggests that stage may interact with some of the situational factors of restitution (for example, victim type—personal or organizational—or restitution type—community service or financial) to improve or discourage the successful completion of the offender's obligation. Kohlberg has suggested, for example, that individuals at lower stages of moral judgment may recognize their social obligations to individuals but may not understand debts they may have to organizations, to communities, or to society.[18] For these persons, restitution to organizational victims or community service in victimless situations may not be as successful as monetary restitution to a personal victim. Equally important questions might be asked about other conditions of restitution, such as the amount of restitution expected, the participation of co-offenders, or the structure of the payment plan.

In a more subtle sense, moral-judgment stage also relates to attitudes and choice.[19] Candee, for example, found in a survey of 370 persons that approval of Watergate conspirators came more frequently from participants at stages 3 and 4 than from their counterparts at stage 5.[20] Moral-judgment stage has also been found to be significantly related to justifications for capital punishment,[21] justification of the military's behavior in Mylai,[22] and police officers' attitudes toward the use of deadly force.[23] In a review of several studies on attitudes and moral development, Candee concludes:

> The consistent results of these studies have been that subjects at the highest stage included in the sample (usually Stage 5) performed actions which were more consistent with the rights and welfare of other individuals, especially in situations where the environment provided either no incentive or actually punished one for doing so.[24]

Besides its practical relevance to the issues of how and for whom restitution should be used, Moral-Development Theory also poses cogent questions to restitution theory, many of which will be asked in the following analysis of the restitution literature. Since restitution theory and Moral-Development Theory rest on similar notions of deserts, fairness, rationality, and justice, Moral-Development Theory should prove to be a useful and necessary framework for examining restitution theory—a heuristic tool for sorting out some nebulous concepts and ultimately determining the extent to which they hold true—at least from the perspective of the offender.

Moral Development and Restitution: A Syntheseis of Theories

Four issues that receive repeated attention in the restitution literature are pertinent to Moral-Development Theory: (1) the effects of restitution on offender feelings of distress over the criminal incident; (2) offenders' assessment of the fairness and rationality of restitution; (3) the offender's ability to assume responsibility for reimbursing the victim; and (4) the purpose of restitution relative to traditional sentencing aims. It is apparent from the issues enumerated above that a discussion of the relevance of Moral-Development Theory to restitution must necessarily occur on several conceptual planes. To suggest that knowledge of restitution may be increased by interfacing Moral-Development Theory with restitution theory is also to assume an interdependence between certain psychological, legal, and philosophical constructs. This section will map a theory of social psychology that has identifiable moral and legal implications onto theories of restitution and jurisprudence. In the process, important questions are posed about the efficacy of some of the claims made in the restitution literature.

The value of this task is easily supported by the interactionist and the differential perspectives common to cognitive developmental theories. In the Lewinian tradition, individual behavior is a function of interactions between the individual and his environment. Although cognitive structures dictate the manner in which individuals make sense of their environment, the characteristics of the environment, in turn, are crucial to promoting growth along cognitive developmental continuums.[25] Cognitive developmental theories, particularly Moral-Development Theory, provide two valuable insights for understanding legal environments. First, the interactionist tenets of Moral-Development Theory advocate agreement between the perceptions of a people and the legal principles that govern them. Legal environments that are incompatible with the cognitive capabilities of a people create confusion, deviance, distrust, and disloyalty.[26] Second, the differential tenets of Moral-Development Theory suggest that, because cognitive capabilities are not the same for all members of society, individual assessments and perceptions of the legal environment are innately different. Failure to anticipate and plan for the differential appeal of a given sentence may invite some members of the population to perceive the sentence as unjust. Conversely, an understanding of how subgroups of the offender population perceive a sanction or treatment may provide the information needed to facilitate a better understanding and to promote growth along the developmental continuum.

From this framework emerges a general criticism applicable to several aspects of restitution. Restitution proponents, administrators responsible for imposing restitution, and jurisprudential theories providing the underlying rationales of restitution have failed to recognize the heterogeneity of the offender population. Broad generalizations are used to characterize all offenders, when in fact they may pertain to only a portion of the offender population. Moreover, the literature does not appear to have anticipated the differential appeal that specific types of restitution may hold for subgroups of the offender population. Moral-Development Theory suggests that offender assessments of restitution, their ability to assume responsibility for their victims, and the credibility of the theoretical rationales behind restitution vary by moral-development stage and interact in some instances with the conditions of restitution and the circumstances leading to the offender's involvement with the criminal-justice system.

The restitution literature pertaining to each of the four issues enumerated earlier is reviewed next, accompanied by a discussion of the relevance of each issue to Moral-Development Theory. The questions posed by Moral-Development Theory are also drawn out for each of the issues discussed, demonstrating why and how stage theory provides a useful framework for analyzing the claims made in the restitution literature.

The Effects of Restitution on Offender Feelings of Distress Resulting from the Criminal Incident

Many restitution advocates believe that restitution helps offenders confront feelings of distress (guilt, anxiety, low self-esteem, fear of retaliation, and empathy for the victim) that result from the offender's involvement in a criminal incident.[27] In some instances these benefits are expected to accrue from the victim-offender collaboration that occurs during restitution. This effort purportedly reduces the offender's sense of alienation by engaging him in the type of behavior that is likely to receive acceptance from victims and members of the community.[28] Gandy maintains that restitution in the form of community service enhances the offender's feelings of self-esteem by enabling him to play a significant role in a worthy cause.[29] Community service, according to Gandy, harnesses human desire for recognition and acceptance and therapeutically reinforces socially acceptable forms of behavior and positive attitudes.

In a more intricate framework, Equity Theory holds that similar gains can be derived by restoring the balance disturbed by the criminal incident. Equity Theory maintains that:

> When a normal person participates in a profoundly inequitable relationship (e.g., a criminal incident), he should feel at least some glimmerings of distress. Presumably people are motivated to reduce their distress by restoring equity to their relationship.[30]

The offender manifests feelings of distress in the form of guilt, anxiety, empathy, fear of retaliation, dissonance, shame, anger, and so forth. Restoring equity ideally takes the form of restitution, but can less advantageously consist of retaliation or distortions of reality such as denigrating the victim, denying responsibility, and minimizing the assessment of suffering.[31]

Utne and Hatfield are among the few writers to have acknowledged the complexity of these feelings. They suggest, for example, that distressing emotions may have "cognitive correlates."

> Of course when we say that "individuals accept a code of fairness" we do not mean that everyone internalizes exactly the same moral principles, accepts them to the same extent, and follows them without deviation.[32]

Notions such as guilt, desire for recognition, anxiety, empathy, fear of retaliation, dissonance, and shame indeed can be viewed in cognitive structural terms. In fact, all aspects of the personality (social, emotional, perceptual, intellectual, and so on) undergo developmental changes in thought patterns similar to that which moral judgment undergoes. Underlying these seemingly parallel developments is the development of underlying logical structures that act as necessary but not sufficient prerequisites for the development of other aspects of the personality. An individual does not reason at a stage 5 level of moral judgment, for example, unless he has the logical capabilities for complex reasoning or, in Piagetian terms, "formal operations." Formal reasoning, however, does not guarantee a stage 5 level of moral reasoning. Kohlberg explains this incongruity in terms of "decalage," which depicts a specific sequence to the development of personality attributes. In this sequence, logical structures develop first, followed by social or interpersonal structures (ego development); moral reasoning develops last.[33] Moral judgment, therefore, should correlate highly with other personality aspects, such as those mentioned in the restitution literature (guilt, desire for recognition, fear of retaliation, and the like). These factors are called *affective aspects* of moral reasoning. Some of them, however, are beyond being simply related to moral judgment. Guilt and fear of punishment, in fact, are the very essence of moral judgment; the presence or absence of these qualities theoretically can be ascertained from an individual's moral-judgment stage.[34]

Thus Moral-Development Theory appears to be a unique and useful framework for discussing notions of guilt, empathy, and the desire for recognition. An examination of how these notions may vary according to moral-judgment stage, however, throws into question some of the claims that restitution will deal with these feelings. Of particular importance to both theoretical and operational rationales for restitution is the strong possibility that some individuals may not experience these feelings to begin with and that others may experience them in different forms.

According to Moral-Development Theory, for example, guilt is not discernible among stage 1 and stage 2 individuals. Moreover, individuals at stage 3 and above may experience guilt in varying ways. To the stage 3 individual, guilt is likely to represent shame or concern for the disapproval of others. Guilt over the breaking of conventional rules affects stage 4 persons. Persons at stages 5 and 6 experience guilt as a reaction to violations of their own internal principles.[35] Thus programs or program components designed in part to relieve an offender's guilt over the criminal incident may have little impact on the stage 1 or 2 individual. According to Kohlberg, these individuals are motivated by fear of physical harm. Thus stage 1 and 2 individuals may consider restitution meaningful to the extent that it keeps them from experiencing harsher sanctions, prevents victim retaliation, and so on.

The restitution literature also addresses notions of *empathy*—the extent to which the offender is aware of the thoughts and feelings of the victim. Empathy is also an aspect of Moral-Development Theory. To Kohlberg, "the whole social life of the child is based upon empathy"—that is, on the awareness of other selves with thoughts and feelings like those of the self. Empathy is a primary phenomenon that grows in an organizational sense to a more consistent use as a moral concern.[36] One could conclude on the basis of theory, however, that empathy, like guilt, is not evident below the stage 3 level of moral reasoning unless the object of the empathy is characteristically very similar to the stage 2 individual and the issue is of an instrumental nature ("If I were the victim, I would want my money back"). One might surmise that only individuals positioned at conventional and postconventional levels of moral judgment have empathy for those who are different from the self, and that only postconventional individuals have empathic qualities existing exclusive of additional influences such as recognition and duty.

Another notion, *desire for recognition*, is discussed in the restitution literature as a desire that can be satisfied by recognition from the victim, from supervisors in a community-service setting, or from the offender's probation officer. Insofar as this approval (or disapproval) comes from individuals, it may affect the self-esteem of individuals diagnosed at stage 3. Stage 1 and 2 individuals, however, theoretically should find tangible consequences more meaningful than recognition from others.

Since the tenets of Equity Theory address attitudes generated during the criminal encounter and its disposition, questions about the offender's reactions to the incident and to restitution are crucial to an examination of Equity Theory in the context of restitution. For example: Are offenders distressed over their criminal behavior? Do they feel guilty about the present offense? Do they perceive the seriousness of the offense that they have committed? Do they express concern for the victim? Does the act of reparation ameliorate these feelings of distress? If, as Moral-Development Theory suggests, individuals demonstrate empathy, guilt, and the need for social approval only after reaching a certain stage of moral judgment, it is possible to hypothesize that feelings of distress resulting from the criminal encounter may not be evident among all offenders.

Offender Assessments of the Fairness and
Rationality of Restitution

A growing body of theory and knowledge about legal environments suggests that fair, participatory, and democratic environments stimulate the development of fair and just reasoning patterns.[37] It should be obvious, however, that some forms of punishment, particularly imprisonment, are the antithesis of fairness. Prison brutality and exploitation confirm the dysfunctional perceptions of inmates who have already demonstrated an inability to adhere to the cooperative norms of a democratic society. In an attempt to alter the moral environment of two prisons, Kohlberg and his associates established the Just Community program, a prison experiment that developed intervention strategies designed to give prison inmates the opportunity to assume some responsibility for the governance of their living units. In their account of the Just Community program, Hickey and Scharf move beyond their own interventions to advocate a punishment scheme in which the duration of one's prison sentence becomes contingent on repaying the victim, paying a punitive fine consistent with the gravity of the offense, providing partial financial reimbursement for institutional room and board expenses, and contributing to the support of family members on the outside.[38] The authors promote restitutions as an approach that symbolizes a more equitable criminal-justice system to victims, offenders, and society.

The restitution literature makes similar claims. According to several writers, restitution, compared with other sanctions, is a fair sentence, one that is rationally and logically related to the harm caused to the victim.[39] In fact, the very idea of repaying one's victim for the harm caused seems to be a prima facie requirement of fairness. The notion of repayment is, according to some, a natural process, one that begins to occur in childhood and becomes integrated into everyone's behavioral patterns; when misbehavior occurs, amending acts occur spontaneously.[40] From this perspective it is natural for harmdoers to want to make good to someone whom they have hurt.

Outcomes forecasted by the proponents of restitution also appear to be consistent with those suggested by the interactionist tenets of Moral-Development Theory. The extent to which offenders perceive restitution as fair purportedly encourages positive results. When offenders believe they have been treated fairly, vicious circles of bitterness likely to lead to future criminal behavior are broken.[41] Conversely, Galaway warns that the alternative results of more punitive sanctions lead offenders to perceive the unfairness of their situation, to react with bitterness to their assessment of the injustice of their environment, and to manifest these perceived injustices in the form of future criminal behavior.[42]

The broader ethical picture, once the criminal-justice system considers the victim, focuses on principles of fairness to all individuals and lends consideration to the rights of all actors involved.[43] This stance has its basis in deontological ethics and the ideas of the moral philosopher John Rawls.[44] In *A Theory of Justice*, Rawls reasons that individual rights must be considered from a "veil of ignorance"; fairness must extend to all participants regardless of other individual or collective interests.[45] Right courses of action are those that would be based on moral principle alone, absent any knowledge of one's role in the decision-making process (for example, actor or acted on) or the individual or collective benefits to be derived as a result of the action.

From the moral-development framework, Rawls's ideas exemplify principled, postconventional reasoning that is characteristic neither of the offender population nor of the larger nonoffender population. Most people do not consistently shed all vestiges of individual or collective self-interest. More realistically, individuals may not evaluate restitution solely from an ethical or moral stance.

Sources suggest that a number of programmatic factors may influence offender perceptions of the fairness and rationality of restitution. Hudson and Galaway, for example, advocate clear and explicit restitution contracts and concerted efforts by correctional personnel to inform offenders of their progress toward completing restitution.[46] A logical relationship between the amount of harm done and the amount of compensation ordered may also affect offenders' assessments of fairness, as well as their willingness to compensate their victims.[47]

How to achieve optimally the rational qualities of the restitution sanction has also been an issue in terms of program variables such as the type of restitution (for example, community service versus financial restitution) and type of victim (organizational victim versus personal victim).[48] Concern for the effectiveness of symbolic forms of restitution, such as service to the community or payment to a charity symbolically related to the offense, provides a fitting example. On the one hand, Harland warns that community service may not seem "related to the natural and logical consequences of a drug offense or an attempted burglary."[49] On the other hand, Gandy speculates that these two forms of symbolic restitution may offer the greatest potential to the offender, since "monetary payments could possibly lack the level of social investment and involvement that might be present in the other two forms."[50] Furthermore, Gandy maintains that it *is* possible, within a service context of restitution, to relate the service rationally to the offense.

The literature does not adequately delineate the concepts of fairness and rationality according to subgroups in the offender population that may make these judgments differentially. These notions are concepts of justice, however, and are therefore amenable to empirical study within the moral-development framework. Moral-Development Theory suggests that offenders factor different considerations into their assessments of the fairness and rationality of the sanction. Different cognitive structures dictate different factors to be weighed in the course of assessing restitution. Fairness to the individual who is oriented to the punitive aspect of his sentence is entirely different from fairness as assessed by one who considers the victim's rights. Moral-Development Theory suggests further that offender determinations of fairness and rationality vary by program characteristics. This would specifically characterize offenders diagnosed at stage 3 and lower for a number of reasons. One explanation is offered by the fact that moral reasoning tends to be situation-specific among individuals diagnosed at lower stages of moral development.[51] Moreover, persons at lower stages may not be able to relate to concepts of fairness to nonpersons. Thus community service, symbolic restitution, and restitution in victimless situations may not appear fair or rational to some individuals. This does not imply, however, that these forms of restitution will be difficult for all offenders to conceptualize. Individuals positioned at higher stages of moral judgment (stages 4-6) generally cite legal mandates and ethical principles that override situational considerations. Holding these convictions, individuals diagnosed at higher stages are not expected to allow conditional factors to affect their decision to pay.

Thus, in reviewing one of the claims made in the restitution literature— that offenders will consider restitution fair and rationally related to the harm done—Moral-Development Theory does not dispute this claim, but suggests that concepts of fairness and rationality need to be considered in light of the cognitive structures of offenders and the circumstances of their restitution. Therefore, the use of Moral-Development Theory refines this inquiry. In the context of stage theory, a more realistic line of questioning might be as follows: Which offenders consider restitution fair and rational? Under what conditions do certain subgroups consider restitution fair and rational?

The Offender's Ability to Assume Responsibility
for Reimbursing the Victim

With the introduction of the victim as a primary consideration in criminal courts of law, the offender's as well as the state's role in the criminal proceedings is fundamentally altered. In addition to the responsibility for attending to the matters of his own defense, such as retaining an effective counsel, obtaining as lenient a sentence as possible, and completing the requirements of the sentence in an expedient fashion, he has been handed the additional responsibility of repaying the victim. In addition, the rights meted out by the criminal courts extend beyond the due-process rights granted solely to the offender—to the victim's right to reimbursement. Moreover, the term *responsibility* refers to more than an assessment of the offender's intent at the time of the crime; it also implies the offender's responsibility to the party whom he has harmed.

This context suggests a considerably less self-centered yet more complex role for offenders. They are asked to balance the interests of all parties to the dispute, to increase their concern for the victim, and to decrease their concern for themselves in order to be fair to both parties. Incorporated into the complexity of this task is the notion of *functional responsibility*, the relative weighing of the individual roles in the incident—"the variable quantity and quality of the offender's responsibility in relation to that of his victim."[52] As Hans von Hentig has suggested, absolute responsibility may not be solely attributable to offenders, since the victims themselves share varying degrees of responsibility for the crime, ranging from the responsibility for having precipitated the offense to responsibility merely for being vulnerable.[53]

At the operational level, several authors expound on the reeducative potential of restitution, particularly in the area of instilling offender responsibility.[54] In one of the earliest suggestions of restitution for this purpose, Fry writes: "to the offender's pocket, it makes no difference whether what he has to pay is a fine, costs, or compensation. But to his understanding of the nature of justice, it may make a great deal [of difference]."[55] Schafer contrasts this to what occurs in traditional sanctions that alert the offender to the harm done to the state: "The offender's awareness of having wronged an individual victim will have become dull or disappear."[56] Given this warning, one would, of course, expect offenders who are ordered to pay restitution to acknowledge some consideration and sense of obligation for their victims.

Regardless of how responsibility is interpreted by theorists, planners, philosophers, or researchers, each stage of moral judgment has its own sense of responsibility. Moral-Development Theory suggests that responsibility in an outward and altruistic sense begins at stage 3. At lower stages, individuals are more likely to be motivated by more instrumental concerns. If individuals classified at stage 1 or 2 assume responsibility for repaying the victim, for example, it may be under external duress or in anticipation of a reward rather than through internal motivation. To the stage 3 person, however, responsibility may take the form of altruistic actions for specific others. In a restitution setting, stage 3 responsibility might incur the approval of others and be viewed from a golden-rule attitude toward the victim. In addition to wanting to reimburse their victims for altruistic reasons, stage 4 individuals may be oriented to their legal responsibility for repaying the victim. Principled reasoning at stages 5 and 6 may conceptualize responsibility in a contractual sense, as an agreement made with the victim; with the court; or, more abstractly, with society to pay for the damages caused. Individuals at principled stages of moral reasoning may also acknowledge their responsibility after weighing the rights of all parties to the dispute in a disinterested manner, absent considerations of self-interest, the personal qualities of the victim, the laws, or the agreement itself.

The Purpose of Restitution Relative to Traditional Sentencing Aims

Both operational and theoretical confusion characterize the current dialogue on the purposes of restitution. For some, restitution is a multiple-aim sanction, conforming to several traditional sentencing philosophies at once. Restitution has also been viewed as a supplement to other correctional goals. Thorvaldson, for example, defines the notion of reparation in terms of other traditional approaches to sentencing (such as "reparation as a deterrent punishment," "reparation as a rehabilitative technique," or "reparation as doing justice").[57] Still others identify a single purpose from among the traditional philosophies of sentencing.[58] Consideration is also given to the notion that reparation is a sentencing aim unto itself that does not require additional justification from other philosophical perspectives.[59]

One of the first and most fundamental issues to become lost in this confusion concerns whether or not restitution is indeed a punishment. A widely accepted definition of punishment incorporates the following five points:

1. It must involve pain or other consequences normally considered unpleasant.
2. It must be for an offense against legal rules.
3. It must be of an actual or supposed offender for his offense.
4. It must be intentionally administered by human beings other than the offender.
5. It must be imposed and administered by an authority constituted by a legal system against which the offense is committed.[60]

The first of these five points appears to present the most discord and confusion among restitution theorists. Barnett, for one, argues against the punitive notions of restitution.[61] Barnett's arguments maintain that the victim's rights are more important than the standard retributive or utilitarian aims of punishment. Punishment, in other words, has traditionally obscured the victim's right to reparation, which is the essence of justice. Against this notion, Dagger makes a case for punitive restitution by enumerating the debts that the criminal has to society in addition to those he has to the victim.[62] Dagger faults Barnett's arguments for several additional shortcomings, including Barnett's failure to acknowledge society's need to express its moral condemnation of the offender and society's need to exercise the opportunity to reform offenders and deter future criminal activity.[63]

Outside of the debate between Barnett and others, additional sources address the punishment question from a different perspective. Menninger, for example, focuses on a single rehabilitative aim for restitution and clearly proposes this notion as a substitute for punishment, particularly in the case of lesser crimes.[64] For most offenders, Menninger maintains that punishment and rehabilitation cannot coexist. Schafer, however, warns against restitution conditions that enable solvent offenders to purchase liberty and relegate less fortunate offenders to the punitive qualities of the sentence.[65] Schafer's notion of "punitive restitution" clearly conceptualizes restitution as a supplement to, rather than a substitute for, punishment.

Retribution, the oldest justification for restitution, intuitively falls within the rubric of punishment. From this perspective, restitution is a "moral concept grounded in the notion of desert and requital."[66] Restitution, according to McAnany, is a vehicle for expressing society's disapproval for wrongdoers according to their just deserts.[67] Theoretically, sentencing according to deserts and requital also returns the offender to a position of equality with nonoffenders.

Deterrent rationales for restitution are not widely recognized. To meet deterrent goals, restitution would necessarily instill fear by inflicting enough suffering to discourage actual and potential offenders from future criminal activity. Tittle, one of the few writers to propose this as a primary aim of restitution, outlines several models of restitution that are designed to serve deterrent functions in a variety of settings.[68] Thorvaldson, however, questions the logic and efficiency of considering restitution a deterrent.[69] Amounts of money high enough to constitute a deterrent in many cases have to be larger than the amount of harm caused during the crime. This practice in turn obscures the reparative qualities of the sanction.

Justifications of restitution are not limited to the identification of single or predominant rationales for its use. Several writers suggest that restitution is a flexible, multiple-aim sanction. Restitution, from this view, is lauded for its versatility in meeting the conflicting aims of the criminal-justice system and in satisfying diverse political tastes. Schafer, for example, considers restitution a "synthetic punishment," one that would seem to unite all correctional rationales into a single sentencing option.[70] Eglash presents a slightly narrower focus: "Restitution contains the best features of punishment (deterrence; justice) and of clinical treatment (recognition of psychological bases of behavior; returning good for evil)."[71] Moreover, Gandy argues that, in restitution, the philosophies of retribution and rehabilitation are conceptually related. The sanction, according to Gandy, confronts the offender with his wrongdoing and, in a rehabilitative sense, provides him with the opportunity to make amends.[72] Finally, Thorvaldson constructs one of the more complicated justifications for the sanction. After dismissing reparative, reformative, and retributive aims separately, Thorvaldson concludes that restitution is reparation performed for the sake of justice in order to teach moral values to offenders.[73]

At the operational level, this uncertainty and the resulting extreme shifts in focus have serious implications for programs and offenders. Programmatic procedures, particularly those related to the mechanics for assessing loss and determining restitution amounts, most logically follow from well-articulated intentions.[74] Among programs operating within a deserts framework, for example, it seems reasonable to assume that staff will strive to set loss amounts that the offenders deserve to pay. Loss assessments in these settings become problematic, however, when the following issues arise: (1) an imprisoned co-offender's share of the damage; (2) an overzealous victim's assessment of loss; and (3) questions of whether to assess loss at the replacement value, the depreciated value, or the original cost. Another set of questions develops when programs endeavor to operate within rehabilitative guidelines. Efforts to convey to the offender a fair and rational indication of harm may be discouraged by overzealous victims; different methods of estimating value; and additional costs (such as court, attorney, and probation costs).[75] Conversely, considerations for deterrence would most logically put these issues aside, focusing instead on the assessment most likely to discourage future criminal incidents.[76]

In order to clarify the purpose of restitution within the wider correctional picture, several research projects have endeavored to tap the viewpoints of criminal-justice officials and/or members of the community.[77] In addition, one study has examined offenders' interpretations of their sentences in terms of traditional sentencing philosophies. Thorvaldson compared the effects of three sanctions (community service, fine, and probation) on the attitudes of offenders in the respective groups.[78] A portion of the research examined offenders' receptivity to the principles that their sentences were designed to serve.

At least two studies have recognized the relevance of Moral-Development Theory to this inquiry. Thorvaldson, for example, used a quasi-experimental design in the study cited earlier and included moral development among the extraneous variables that needed to be controlled during the analysis phase of his research.[79] Another study, conducted by Gandy, cited Moral-Development Theory for theoretical rather than empirical purposes in order to illustrate the rehabilitative function of restitution. Gandy argued from the interactionist perspective for the purpose of advocating fair and participatory correctional environments.[80]

When Moral-Development Theory is used to unpack the confusion that currently plagues efforts to identify rationales for restitution, it seems likely that the efficacy of each correctional rationale will vary across subgroups of the offender population. The theory suggests, for example, that deterrent theories, operating on the principle of fear, may have meaning to stage 1 and 2 individuals, but may create bitterness in higher-staged individuals. At the same time, policies fitting into a deserts framework may prove meaningful to individuals who reason at the conventional and postconventional levels of moral judgment. For offenders classified at the postconventional level of reasoning, restitution might be most meaningful if it is viewed as a matter of fairness to the victim (exclusive of considerations of duty, punishment, and the like). At conventional levels, offenders may consider it a duty to reimburse the victim. Finally, offenders at preconventional levels of moral judgment may not relate to the idea that they are repaying because they deserve to—unless, vicariously, they have experienced a similar victimization.

Additional Questions: A Research Agenda for Two Fields

Research endeavoring to use Moral-Development Theory as a framework for studying offenders in restitution settings ought not to be limited to questions relevant to offender attitudes and interpretations of restitution. Three additional areas of inquiry also warrant attention: (1) What can be learned about offenders and about moral development in the course of studying offender populations? (2) What, in fact, is the impact of moral development on the successful completion of restitution? (3) Among offenders at specific stages of moral development, do certain circumstances or conditions of restitution improve or discourage chances of successfully discharging restitution obligations?

Answers to the first question are needed to fill a void in the existing knowledge base of moral development. The paucity of data among adult offender populations is a situation that assuredly warrants the attention of future research endeavors. The second and third questions seek practical knowledge of offenders in applied settings. The pursuit of answers to these questions should attempt to provide criminal-justice agencies with the understanding needed to identify offenders most likely to succeed on restitution and to anticipate the circumstances that will pose difficulties to certain types of offenders.

What Can Be Learned about Offenders and about Moral Development?

How does the distribution of moral-development stages among offender populations compare with the distribution of moral-development stages among nonoffender populations? Are offenders more likely than nonoffenders to be classified at lower stages of moral development? Are there postconventional individuals among offender populations? If not, it hardly makes sense to plan for them. Is the distribution of offenders across moral-development stages wide enough to make meaningful distinctions among subgroups of the offender population? What are the social and demographic correlates of moral development among offender populations? What types of criminal behaviors appear to be associated with moral development? Are offenders at lower stages of moral development more likely to commit more serious offenses than are offenders diagnosed at higher stages of moral development? Are offenders at lower stages of moral development more likely to commit repeated acts of criminal behavior than are offenders at higher stages of moral development?

To date, the answers to these questions are speculative. The moral-development field has made some advances among juvenile offender populations but furnishes few clues of what to expect from adult offenders.[81] Currently, there exists only one published report of the application of the Kohlberg classification system among adult offenders, Hickey and Scharf's account of the Just Community.[82] Funding for this treatment program, however, was not sufficient to conduct a "scientifically rigorous research effort."[83] Although research among juvenile populations has led researchers to conclude that juvenile offenders reason at lower stages of moral development than nonoffenders, these findings cannot be generalized to adult offenders.[84]

Two reports of research with nonoffender populations present correlations between moral judgment and several demographic and intellectual variables. In research designed to examine the relationship between moral judgment and several other background factors to job status, Candee et al. report significant correlations between moral judgment and IQ ($r = .52$, $p \leq .05$), education ($r = .71$, $p \leq .05$) and job status (Hollingshead Scale) ($r = .63$, $p \leq .05$).[85] In addition, a recently completed longitudinal study notes a high correlation between moral develoment and age ($r = .78$).[86] Controlling for the age variable, product-moment correlations between moral judgment and IQ ranged from .17 to .59 for separate age groups. Similar partial correlations with education ranged from .53 to .69, and with parents' socioeconomic status (SES) the measures ranged from .32 to .62. The authors explained that the correlations between moral judgment and IQ increased with age; the range of correlations obtained for adult groups age 19 and above ranged from .37 to .59. No clear pattern of fluctuations across age categories appeared for the correlations of education and SES with moral judgment.

Currently very few data exist relevant to adult offender populations. The search for comparable findings is frustrated further by recent revisions of both Moral-Development Theory and the classification system for diagnosing moral-judgment stage.[87] Redefinitions of stage categories and the advent of the Standard Form Scoring Manual throw into question any attempts to compare research findings to studies that were conducted using at least two outdated scoring mechanisms. Unfortunately, these studies include most of the moral-development research currently in print. It is apparent from the paucity of moral-development research data on offender populations that contributions to the descriptive information base in this area are sorely needed.

What Is the Impact of Moral Development on Restitution Outcome?

This would appear to be the most obvious question that researchers using the moral-development classification system in the applied restitution setting would ask. Sometimes, however, the moral-development literature qualifies the relationship of moral development to behavior. Kohlberg cautions, for example, that it is possible for individuals reasoning at a principled stage 5 to fail to live up to their ideals.[88] In addition, one might anticipate different justifications for similar modes of behavior, where both good and bad behaviors may be justified by different stage-related reasons. This observation applies primarily to individuals positioned at stages 1, 2, and 3 of moral judgment, however, because the underlying logic of Moral-Development Theory suggests that individuals at higher stages of moral reasoning will act morally more frequently than those at the lower stages. The reason for this is apparent from the nature of the qualitative differences between the stages—the nature of the differences among the three different types of relationships between the self and society's rules—as follows:

> From this point of view, a person at the *preconventional* level is one for whom rules and social expectations are something external to the self. A *conventional* person has achieved a socially normative appreciation of the rules and expectations of others, especially authorities, and identifies the self with the occupants of social or societal role relationships. The *principled* person has differentiated self from normative roles and defines values in terms of self-constructed reflective principles.[89]

Developing structures of moral judgment become increasingly more differentiated since new concepts are brought into the decision-making process that enable individuals to relate decisions to more factors than those affecting themselves alone. For example, growth to stage 4 differentiates action out of a sense of obligation to society's laws from action for interpersonal motives, which are stage 3 orientations. In this way moral reasoning becomes more universal as the structures of moral judgment develop; in the process, decisions and behaviors tend to become more consistently based on laws, contracts, and moral principles rather than on the exigencies of particular situations. Kohlberg writes:

> Although individuals at different stages may sometimes make the same ultimate decision, usually a stage will favor one side of a decision. In addition, a higher stage person is more likely to demonstrate a consistent and predictable pattern of behavior. This is because higher stage individuals (Stages 4, 5 and 6) base their moral judgments and actions on laws and/or principles that remain stable over time, whereas those at Stages 1, 2 and 3 base their decisions on a fear of punishment or on personal whim or on a desire for approval, all of which vary with circumstances.[90]

Moral-development research has found some empirical support for this position.[91] Consistent with these findings, one would hypothesize that offenders positioned at higher stages will complete restitution in more instances than will offenders positioned at lower stages. Stage 4 individuals, for example, may show greater success than lower-staged individuals. At stage 4, the legal duty outweighs issues of reward and punishment (stages 1 and 2) or of obtaining approval from the probation officer or the victim (stage 3). Individuals at stage 5 may show an even greater differentiation of these concerns by a tendency to consider the victim's right to reimbursement for his loss.

What Is the Impact of Specific Circumstances of Restitution on Restitution Outcome among Subgroups of the Offender Population?

Offenders in restitution settings typically are ordered to perform restitution under a variety of circumstances and possess differential resources for meeting their reparative obligations. Their success in meeting these obligations may depend on the circumstances that led to their involvement with the criminal-justice system, the nature of their restitution requirements, and the financial or time resources at their disposal. The following factors, for example, could affect the successful completion of restitution: (1) the magnitude of the restitution; (2) the manner in which the restitution was expected to be completed (for example, on a scheduled basis or by a payment deadline); (3) the type of victim helped to instigate the offense; (5) acquaintance with the victim; (6) seriousness of the offense; (7) magnitude of the loss; (8) whether or not a loss was inflicted;[92] (9) the involvement of co-offenders; (10) the offender's employment status (employed or unemployed); (11) the offender's income; and (12) the type of restitution (financial or community service).

Research addressing this issue ought to identify the circumstances, conditions, and resources that improve the chances of success among subgroups of the offender populations. The results may show that some circumstances are successful with all participating offenders, whereas others are successful only among certain types of offenders. Since restitution to businesses and communities, for example, may not be meaningful to individuals reasoning at stages 1, 2, and 3, restitution to personal victims may be more successful than restitution to organizational victims with these offenders. In examining hypotheses put forth by Kohlberg, restitution may not be successful with stage 1 offenders; with offenders at stages 2 and 3, restitution to personal victims may be more successful than restitution to organizational victims; and among stage 4 offenders, there may be no distinction between personal and nonpersonal victims in terms of restitution outcome.[93]

Insight into which forms of restitution are most meaningful to certain types of offenders will certainly have programmatic value for future restitution efforts. This differential theme is one that has met with success in both correctional and educational settings. Use of the I-level classification scheme to match delinquent personality types with appropriate treatments and treater personality types, for example, has shown that specific types of treatment can prevent reconviction among offenders with specific characteristics.[94] In another example, Heide found specific conditions of restitution and characteristics of program structure to affect restitution outcome among offenders at specific levels of Interpersonal Maturity.[95] Work with another cognitive developmental theory, Conceptual-Systems Theory,[96] has taken place in educational settings and has identified teaching models,[97] models of environmental structure,[98] and counselor styles appropriate to individuals positioned at various conceptual levels.[99] Among a delinquent population, Brill reported that the postrelease behavior of institutionalized delinquent boys at low conceptual levels was more favorable among boys placed in highly structured environments than among boys placed in settings having less structure.[100]

Conclusion

Use of differential strategies in correctional settings stems from a fundamental conviction that not all offenders are alike, and that no one correctional intervention is effective with all offenders.[101] Only on rare occasions, however, have programs in the criminal-justice system recognized the value of implementing variable modes of a chosen correctional modality and matching these options to the offenders most likely to be amenable to them. Use of the moral-development classification system for these purposes is even less prevalent. Moreover, in applying moral development to treatment settings, moral-development practitioners have appeared to be wedded to the interactionist tenets of their theory. Differential implications seem to have been ignored. Exposure to participatory and fair environments, such as those developed by Kohlberg and his associates in both schools and prisons, does, after all, represent an undifferentiated treatment modality.[102] Indeed, one could argue that if exposure to fair and participatory environments is the only treatment implication to be deduced from Moral-Development Theory, it hardly makes sense to classify the participants of such a program. In contrast, use of other cognitive developmental systems (such as I-level and conceptual level) has resulted from arduous research designed to identify specific program options and the types of individuals most likely to be receptive to them. This chapter has intended to push for greater consideration of the differential implications of Moral-Development Theory in the applied restitution setting. A number of the questions posed may be relevant to other applied settings as well. What, for example, can be learned about program participants from the context of Moral-Development Theory? How do participants at different stages of moral development make sense of a given treatment modality, sanction, school program, and so on? Finally, how might a program be differentially structured in order to enhance the chances of success among participants at specific stages of moral development?

Notes

1. Throughout this chapter the term *restitution* is used in the generic sense to mean "reparation" or making amends for criminal behavior. In this sense restitution encompasses both financial restitution and community service. Financial restitution requires the offender to reimburse victims for losses incurred during the criminal incident. Community service requires offenders to make amends by rendering a service to a community agency or local civic organization. Community service is sometimes ordered in response to victimless crimes, a victim's refusal to accept restitution, or an offender's inability to pay financial restitution.

2. See, for example, Steven Chesney, "The Assessment of Restitution in the Minnesota Probation Services," Minnesota Department of Corrections, 1976; and Joe Hudson and Burt Galaway, "Undoing the Wrong," *Social Work* 19 (May 1974):315-318.

3. See, for example, Stephen Schafer, *The Victim and His Criminal: A Study in Functional Responsibility* (New York: Random House, 1968); Mary K. Utne and Elaine Hatfield, "Equity Theory and Restitution Programming," in *Offender Restitution in Theory and Action*, eds. Burt Galaway and Joe Hudson (Lexington, Mass.: Lexington Books, D.C. Heath

and Company, 1977), pp. 73-87; and Ellen Berscheid and Elaine Walster, "When Does a Harm-Doer Compensate a Victim?" *Journal of Personality and Social Psychology* 6 (August 1967):435-441.

4. A number of authors have maintained that victims sometimes share a portion of the blame for crime. The term *functional responsibility* incorporates this notion by assessing responsibility in terms of both the offender's and the victim's role in the incident, or "the variable quantity and quality of the offender's responsibility in relation to that of his victim." For a more detailed discussion, see Schafer, *Victim and His Criminal.*

5. See, for example, Albert Eglash, "Creative Restitution: Some Suggestions for a Prison Rehabilitation Program," *American Journal of Corrections* 20 (December 1958):20-34; Virginia Black, "Responsibility and Management: The Primary Objective of Moral Education," *Journal of Moral Education* 7 (May 1978):166-181; and Schafer, *Victim and His Criminal.*

6. For a review of recent developments in restitution legislation and programming, see Alan T. Harland, "Restitution as a Sentencing Option: An Examination of Legal, Theoretical, and Operational Issue," Diss. prospectus, State University of New York at Albany, 1977.

7. Two recently completed substudies for the National Evaluation of Adult Restitution Programs, however, report findings relevant to this inquiry. For an empirical assessment of the impact of personality characteristics on restitution outcome, see Kathleen M. Heide, "Classification of Offenders Ordered to Make Restitution by Interpersonal Maturity Level and by Specific Personality Dimensions," Ph.D. diss., State University of New York at Albany, 1982. For an assessment of the impact of moral development on attitudes toward restitution and restitution outcome, see Patricia Van Voorhis, "The Relationship of Moral Development to Offender Assessments of Restitution and Restitution Outcome," Ph.D. diss., State University of New York at Albany, 1982. Heide's dissertation also contains a review of the literature pertaining to the impact of offender characteristics on restitution outcome. Van Voorhis's dissertation contains a review of the literature pertaining to offender attitudes toward restitution.

8. See Lawrence Kohlberg, "Stage and Sequence: The Cognitive-Developmental Approach to Socialization," in *Handbook of Socialization Theory and Research*, ed. David Goslin (Chicago: Rand McNally, 1969), pp. 347-480.

9. The only published accounts of the use of Moral-Development Theory among adult offender populations refer to the Just Community Experiment, which is discussed in greater detail later in this chapter. See also Joseph Hickey and Peter Scharf, *Toward a Just Correctional System* (San Francisco: Jossey Bass, 1980). For research among delinquent populations, see, for example, Lawrence Kohlberg and Douglas Freundlich, "Moral

Judgment in Youthful Offenders" (Harvard University: Center for Moral Education, 1973); Gregory J. Jurkovic and Norman M. Prentice, "Relation of Moral and Cognitive Development to Dimensions of Juvenile Delinquency," *Journal of Abnormal Psychology* 86 (August 1977):414-420; Eugene M. Fodor, "Delinquency and Susceptibility to Social Influence among Adolescents as a Function of Moral Development," *Journal of Social Psychology* 86 (April 1972):257-260; and Merry Ann Morash, "Cognitive Developmental Theory: A Basis for Juvenile Correctional Reform?" *Criminology* 19 (November 1981):360-371.

10. The grant for the National Evaluation of Adult Restitution Programs (Grant No. 76-NI-99-0127) was awarded to the Criminal Justice Research Center in Albany, New York, by the National Institute of Law Enforcement and Criminal Justice, Law Enforcement Assistance Administration, U.S. Department of Justice. The opinions put forth in this chapter are those of the author alone and do not necessarily represent the official position of the U.S. Department of Justice.

11. Van Voorhis, "Relationship of Moral Development to Offender Assessments of Restitution."

12. See, for example, Jean Piaget, *The Moral Judgment of the Child* (Glencoe, Ill.: Free Press, 1948); Clyde Sullivan, Marguerite Q. Grant, and J. Douglas Grant, "The Development of Interpersonal Maturity: Applications to Delinquency," *Psychiatry* 20 (1957):373-385; Kohlberg, "Stage and Sequence"; and Jane Loevinger, "The Meaning and Measurement of Ego Development," *American Psychologist* 21 (March 1966):195-217.

13. For an explanation and discussion of the relationships between moral development, ego development, and cognitive development, see Lawrence Kohlberg, Anne Colby, John Gibbs, Betsy Speicher-Dubin, and Dan Candee, "Standard Form Scoring Manual" (Harvard University: Center for Moral Education, 1978), part I, pp. 10-16; and Lawrence Kohlberg, "The Meaning and Measurement of Moral Development," Heinz Werner Memorial Lecture, April 1979.

14. Joseph Hickey and Peter Scharf, *Toward a Just Correctional System.*

15. Lawrence Kohlberg and Douglas Freundlich, "Moral Judgment in Youthful Offenders."

16. Richard Krebs and Lawrence Kohlberg, "Moral Judgment and Ego Controls as Determinants of Resistance to Cheating" (Harvard University: Center for Moral Education, 1973).

17. Ibid., pp. 30-33.

18. This hypothesis was advanced by Kohlberg in earlier discussions held during the planning phases of the National Evaluation of Adult Restitution Programs.

19. Kohlberg et al., "Standard Form Scoring Manual," part I, p. 33.

20. Dan Candee, "The Moral Psychology of Watergate," *Journal of Social Issues* 31 (February 1975):183-192.

21. Lawrence Kohlberg and Don Elsenbein, "Capital Punishment, Moral Development, and the Constitution," in *The Philosophy of Moral Development*, ed. Lawrence Kohlberg (San Francisco, Calif.: 1981), pp. 243-293.

22. Peter Scharf, *Moral Education* (Davis, Calif.: Responsible Action, 1978).

23. Peter Scharf, Rod Linninger, and Dave Marrero, "The Use of Deadly Force by Police Officers in a Democratic Society," in *Determinants of Law Enforcement Policies*, ed. Fred A. Meyer, Jr. and Ralph Baker (Lexington, Mass.: Lexington Books, D.C. Heath and Company, 1979), pp. 87-98.

24. Dan Candee, "Structure and Choice in Moral Reasoning," *Journal of Personality and Social Psychology* 34 (June 1976):1294.

25. See, for example, Piaget, *Moral Judgment of the Child*; and Lawrence Kohlberg, "Education for Justice: A Modern Statement of the Platonic View," in *Moral Education*, ed. T. Sizer (Cambridge, Mass.: Harvard University Press, 1970), pp. 57-83.

26. June L. Tapp and Felice J. Levine, "Legal Socialization: Strategies for an Ethical Legality," *Stanford Law Review* 27 (November 1973):6.

27. See, for example, Eglash, "Creative Restitution"; John T. Gandy, "Community Attitudes toward Creative Restitution and Punishment," Ph.D. diss., University of Denver, 1975; and Utne and Hatfield, "Equity Theory."

28. Burt Galaway, "Restitution as an Integrative Punishment" in *Assessing the Criminal: Restitution, Retribution, and the Legal Process*, ed. Randy E. Barnett and John Hagel III (Cambridge, Mass.: Ballinger, 1977), p. 341.

29. Gandy, "Community Attitudes," p. 43.

30. Utne and Hatfield, "Equity Theory," p. 76.

31. Gresham Sykes and David Matza, "Techniques of Neutralization: A Theory of Delinquency," *American Sociological Review* 22 (December 1957):664-670, cited in Utne and Hatfield, "Equity Theory," p. 77.

32. Utne and Hatfield, "Equity Theory," p. 76.

33. Kohlberg et al., "Standard Form Scoring Manual," part I, pp. 11-15.

34. Kohlberg, "Stage and Sequence," p. 391.

35. Ibid., p. 392.

36. Ibid., p. 393.

37. See, for example, Piaget, *Moral Judgment of the Child*; Kohlberg, "Education for Justice"; and Tapp and Levine, "Legal Socialization."

38. Hickey and Scharf, *Toward a Just Correctional System*, pp. 170-177.

39. Eglash, "Creative Restitution."

40. Barbara Dockar-Drysdale, "Some Aspects of Damage and Restitution," *British Journal of Delinquency* 4 (July 1953):4-13.

41. Randy E. Barnett, "Restitution: A New Paradigm of Criminal Justice," in *Assessing the Criminal: Restitution, Retribution, and the Legal Process*, eds. Randy E. Barnett and John Hagel III (Cambridge, Mass.: Ballinger, 1977), p. 375.

42. Galaway, "Restitution as an Integrative Punishment," p. 339.

43. Randy E. Barnett and John Hagel III, "Assessing the Criminal: Restitution, Retribution, and the Legal Process," ed. Randy E. Barnett and John Hagel III (Cambridge, Mass.: Ballinger, 1977), pp. 1-32.

44. John Rawls, *A Theory of Justice* (Cambridge, Mass.: Harvard University Press, 1971).

45. In order to reason in accordance with deontological principles, one must reason from "a veil of ignorance." This type of reasoning puts aside an awareness of all interests and influences except the moral law. One does not consider such matters as self-interest, expedience, prudence, sympathy, or love, but makes moral decisions from universally valid moral laws— "ignorant" of other (even the most noble) influences. Moreover, one cannot be cognizant of one's role but must reason as one who could be any of the actors involved in the issue under examination. Decision making attempts to maximize the fairness for all concerned.

46. Hudson and Galaway, "Undoing the Wrong," p. 317.

47. Berscheid and Walster, "When Does a Harm-Doer Compensate a Victim?"

48. Marguerite Q. Warren, "Evaluation of Recent Developments in Restitution Programming," in *Offender Restitution in Theory and Action*, ed. Burt Galaway and Joe Hudson (Lexington, Mass.: Lexington Books, D.C. Heath and Company, 1977), p. 114.

49. Alan T. Harland, "Theoretical and Programmatic Concerns in Restitution: An Integration," in *Offender Restitution in Theory and Action*, ed. Burt Galaway and Joe Hudson (Lexington, Mass.: Lexington Books, D.C. Heath and Company, 1977), p. 197.

50. Gandy, "Community Attitudes toward Creative Restitution," p. 30.

51. Lawrence Kohlberg et al., "The Just Community Approach to Corrections: A Theory," *Journal of Moral Education* 4 (1975):255.

52. Schafer, *Victim and His Criminal*, p. 38.

53. Hans von Hentig, *The Criminal and His Victim* (New Haven: Yale University Press, 1948).

54. See, for example, Margaret Fry, *Arms of Law* (London: Victor Gollanz, 1971); Schafer, *Victim and His Criminal*; Paul W. Keve, "Therapeutic Uses of Restitution," in *Offender Restitution in Theory and Action*, ed. Burt Galaway and Joe Hudson (Lexington, Mass.: Lexington

Books, D.C. Heath and Company, 1977), pp. 59-64; and Black, "Responsibility Management."

55. Fry, *Arms of Law*, p. 125.

56. Stephen Schafer, "Corrective Compensation," *Trial Magazine* 8 (December 1972):26.

57. Sveinn A. Thorvaldson, "Toward the Definition of the Reparative Aim," in *Victims, Offenders, and Alternative Sanctions*, ed. Joe Hudson and Burt Galaway (Lexington, Mass.: Lexington Books, D.C. Heath and Company, 1980), pp. 15-28.

58. See, for example, Karl Menninger, *The Crime of Punishment* (New York: Viking Press, 1968); Barnett, "Restitution"; Patrick D. McAnany, "Restitution as Ideas and Practice: The Retributive Prospect," in *Offender Restitution in Theory and Action*, ed. Burt Galaway and Joe Hudson (Lexington, Mass.: Lexington Books, D.C. Heath and Company, 1977), pp. 15-32; and Charles R. Tittle, "Restitution and Deterrence: An Evaluation of Compatibility," in *Offender Restitution in Theory and Action*, ed. Burt Galaway and Joe Hudson (Lexington, Mass.: Lexington Books, D.C. Heath and Company, 1977), pp. 33-58.

59. Thorvaldson, "Toward a Definition of Punishment," p. 17.

60. H.L.A. Hart, *The Concept of Law* (Oxford: Oxford University Press, 1961), p. 193.

61. Barnett, "New Paradigm of Criminal Justice."

62. Most members of society, according to Dagger, incur avoidance costs (such as the expense of installing security systems, paying police, and avoiding unsafe locations); insurance costs; and attitudinal costs (such as fear, insecurity and social divisiveness). See Richard Dagger, "Restitution, Punishments, and Debts to Society," in *Victims, Offenders, and Alternative Sanctions*, ed. Joe Hudson and Burt Galaway (Lexington, Mass.: Lexington Books, D.C. Heath and Company, 1980), pp. 3-13.

63. For a more detailed account of these arguments, see Dagger, "Restitution," pp. 3-13.

64. Menninger, *Crime of Punishment*, p. 68.

65. Stephen Schafer, *Compensation and Restitution to Victims of Crime* (Montclair, N.J.: Patterson Smith, 1970).

66. McAnany, "Restitution," p. 15.

67. Ibid., pp. 21-22.

68. Tittle, "Restitution and Deterrence."

69. Thorvaldson, "The Reparative Aim," pp. 19-20.

70. Stephen Schafer, "Restitution to Victims of Crime—an Old Correctional Aim Modernized," *Minnesota Law Review* 50 (December 1965):248.

71. Albert Eglash, "Creative Restitution: A Broader Meaning for an Old Term," *Journal of Criminal Law, Criminology, and Police Science* 3 (April 1978):619.

72. Gandy, "Community Attitudes toward Creative Restitution," p. 67.

73. Thorvaldson, "The Reparative Aim," p. 22.

74. Alan T. Harland, Marguerite Q. Warren, and Edward J. Brown, "A Guide to Restitution Programming" (Albany, N.Y.: Criminal Justice Research Center, 1979), pp. 4-9.

75. Ibid., pp. 20-39.

76. Tittle, "Restitution and Deterrence," p. 36.

77. See, for example, Gandy, "Community Attitudes Toward Creative Restitution" Burt Galaway and William Marsella, "An Exploratory Study of the Perceived Fairness of Restitution as a Sanction for Juvenile Offenders," Paper presented at the Second International Symposium on Victimology, Boston, September 1976; and Chesney, "Assessment of Restitution."

78. This segment of the study reports the sanction's effects on the offenders' self-esteem, feelings of integration/alienation, sense of self, sense of justice, and understanding of the rights of others. Reactions to the respective deterrent and redemptive effects of the three sentences were also ascertained. Findings may be reviewed in Sveinn Thorvaldson, "The Effects of Community Service on the Attitudes of Offenders," Ph.D. dissertation, University of Cambridge, 1978.

79. Thorvaldson surmised that the failure to do this would entertain an alternative hypothesis to explain offender interpretations of their sentence—that interpretations of the sentence were attributable not to the sentence itself but to the moral maturity of the participants. When the three groups were compared on this dimension, however, no significant differences were detected. The study did not employ the standard procedures developed by Kohlberg in order to diagnose moral development. Thorvaldson considered the alternative scheme used in his study to be a crude measure of moral development. For a more detailed account, see Thorvaldson, "Effects of Community Service," pp. 202-203.

80. Gandy, "Community Attitudes Toward Creative Restitution," pp. 81-83.

81. See note 9.

82. For an unpublished account of research using moral development among adult offenders, see Van Voorhis, "Moral Judgment and Offenders' Assessments of Restitution and Restitution Outcome." See also Milton Gearing II, "The Relationship of Megargee and Bohn's MMPI Subtypes and Other MMPI Dimensions to Kohlberg's Moral Stages in Prisoners," Paper presented at the Fifth Annual Conference of the International Differential Treatment Association. Rensselaerville, New York, April 1981.

83. Hickey and Scharf, Toward a Just Correctional System, p. 128.

84. Kohlberg and Freundlich, "Moral Judgment in Youthful Offenders."

85. Dan Candee, Richard Graham, and Lawrence Kohlberg, "Moral Development and Life Outcomes" (Harvard University: Center for Moral Education, 1978), p. 21.

86. The authors do not report significance levels for these findings, however. See Colby et al., "Longitudinal Study of Moral Judgment," p. 39.

87. The Standard Form Scoring Manual was completed in 1978. A re-analysis of Kohlberg's longitudinal data (see Colby, "Longitudinal Study of Moral Judgment") was the first study to report findings based on these theoretical and diagnostic revisions. Research that predates the Standard Manual was conducted under the Aspect Scoring System or the Issue Rating System. See Kohlberg et al., "Standard Form Scoring Manual," for a detailed review of theoretical revisions to the stage 3 and stage 4 definitions and alterations in the system.

88. Kohlberg et al., "Standard Form Scoring Manual," part I, p. 13.

89. Ibid., p. 17.

90. Kohlberg et al., "The Just Community Approach to Corrections," p. 255.

91. See the section entitled Moral-Development Theory in this chapter.

92. This circumstance would occur in programs that ordered community service or symbolic restitution for crimes that resulted in no losses to victims.

93. See note 14.

94. See, for example, Marguerite Q. Warren, "The Community Treatment Project," in *Sociology of Punishment and Correction*, ed. Leonard Savitz and Marvin Wolfgang, 2nd ed. (New York: Wiley, 1970), pp. 671-683; and Ted Palmer, "The Youth Authority's Community Treatment Project: Recent Findings and Overview" (Sacramento: California Youth Authority, 1973).

95. Heide, "Classification of Offenders."

96. O.J. Harvey, D.E. Hunt, and H.M. Schroder, *Conceptual Systems and Personality Organization* (New York: Wiley, 1961).

97. See, for example, P. Murphy and M. Brown, "Conceptual Systems and Teaching Styles," *American Educational Research Journal* 4 (November 1970):529-540; B.R. Joyce and M. Weil, *Models of Teaching* (Englewood Cliffs, N.J.: Prentice-Hall, 1972). and David E. Hunt, *Matching Models in Education: The Coordination of Teaching Methods with Student Characteristics* (Toronto: Ontario Studies in Education, 1971).

98. Hunt, *Matching Models in Education*.

99. A.D. Goldberg, "Conceptual Systems as a Predisposition Toward Therapeutic Communication," *Journal of Counseling Psychology* 21 (September 1974):364-368.

100. Ronald Brill, "Implications of the Conceptual Matching Model for Treatment of Delinquents," *Journal of Research in Crime and Delinquency* 15 (January 1978):229-246.

101. See note 90.

102. See, for example, Kohlberg, "Education for Justice"; Kohlberg et al., "The Just Community Approach to Corrections"; and Hickey and Scharf, *Toward a Just Correctional System*.

17 Cognitive Moral Development, Neutralizing Definitions, and Delinquency

Lonn Lanza-Kaduce,
Maria Radosevich,
and *Marvin D. Krohn*

Our normative orientations are consistently and strongly related to the nature and frequency of our rule departures. Two of the major theoretical perspectives used to study legal compliance (see Clark et al. 1972; Koeppen 1970)—the cognitive moral-development tradition and the differential association-reinforcement tradition—are distinguished by the approaches they take to how deviance is learned. To date, much of the theory in the sociology of deviance has concentrated on the direct learning of specific normative definitions favorable to law violation (see, for example, Sutherland 1947; Burgess and Akers 1966; Akers 1977). The developmental perspective, however, has taken a more indirect learning approach to normative socialization and deviance. The value of this perspective for understanding deviant behavior awaits further theoretical development and research.

We will examine some of the ways in which moral development may be related to both detected and undetected delinquency. In the process we explore some possible points of convergence between the indirect learning entailed in the developmental sequence and the direct learning of specific norms relevant to deviance. Rather than being mutually exclusive, the two perspectives may complement each other and provide new insights for the inchoate but important explorations into the relationship between normative orientation and behavior.

A preliminary version of this chapter was presented at the Annual Meetings of the Law and Society Association in Toronto in June 1982. We want to acknowledge the contributions made by persons at those meetings to the clarification and revision of this chapter. In particular, we would like to thank June Tapp, Ellen Cohn, and Susan White, whose comments, discussion, and paper presentations proved very helpful. In addition, we are grateful to Barb Carson, who performed an early analysis of these data. We would also like to express gratitude to Ronald L. Akers, who contributed greatly to the conceptualization of the survey instrument and made data collection possible. Our thanks also go to the staff of the Boys Town Center for the Study of Youth Development.

441

Cognitive Moral Development

The cognitive moral-development tradition, derived from the work of Piaget (1965), has been developed and refined by Kohlberg (1958, 1964, 1968, 1975) and his students (Rest 1974, 1976, n.d.). Kohlberg has asserted that the development of moral reasoning follows a universal sequence of distinct stages wherein cognitive structures provide the framework within which information is processed and organized. Cultural factors may stimulate or retard age trends of development, but they do not affect the quality or order of development.

The cognitive developmental model emphasizes the interaction between the environment and the individual's developing capacity to deal with the environment. How maturing individuals respond to and understand their experiences depends on their thinking capacity, which develops sequentially. Different stages involve qualitatively distinct modes of thinking (not necessarily different beliefs). Thus this is an indirect process of acquiring normative orientations. The ways in which people experience, categorize, and relate to objects in the environment change as they move from infancy through childhood and adolescence to adulthood. Different cognitive capacities are thereby related to age—a finding that is consistent with research reporting that the general level of knowledge and more accurate images of law are related to age, at least from childhood through the adolescent years (Hess and Tapp 1969). Older children and adults, whose cognitive capacity is further advanced, can understand and think about politics, morality, and law in a manner quite different from that of younger children. The cognitive shift is from reasoning controlled by the physical consequences of an action to that influenced by groups and authority to reasoning that is rational and autonomous (Tapp and Kohlberg 1971). The respective cognitive shifts are toward increased rationality of and consistency among the considerations used to evaluate situations of moral, political, and/or legal relevance. A discussion of the cognitive sequence is presented in great detail by Jennings, Kilkenny, and Kohlberg, in chapter 12.

Moral Development, Definitions, and Behavior

The extent to which effects of cognitive moral development are either directly related to deviant behavior or are mostly mediated by the learning of more specific normative definitions is unclear. Since there are logical and empirical reasons for positing both, the question merits our attention.

Unmediated Effects of Moral Development

It is Kohlberg's position that persons with more principled normative reasoning are better able to think through situationally specific behavioral options so that their choices are more independent of the influences of friends or the consequences. They are more likely to do what they think is right and less likely to act in accord with pleasure seeking or peer pressure. Kohlberg et al. (1974) assume that moral development is sufficiently related to behavior to advance a developmental framework for prison rehabilitation programs. In an evaluation of this Just Community approach, structural features of the Kohlbergian scheme were found to relate better to prison adjustment than did features of other treatment modalities (Lanza-Kaduce and Stratton 1980).

Turiel and Rothman (1972) have also argued that concrete, situationally specific actions, as well as attitudes, reflect the cognitive moral structure. They found that behavioral choices were most consistent with preferred advice presenting higher-order reasoning for students at stage 4. Stage 3 subjects were indecisive and would behave inconsistently with advice and reasoning they claimed to prefer.

There are other empirical grounds for expecting an inverse relationship between moral development and deviance. Harris, Mussen, and Rutherford (1976) found test cheating (as measured by peer nomination into cheat and no-cheat groups) to be common among those who were below mean levels of moral development, but rare among those above the mean. Kohlberg (1958) found that boys in custody awaiting juvenile hearings were at lower levels of development than would be expected from a sample of their age population (see also Fodor 1972). Hudgins and Prentice (1973) found that adolescents with official delinquency records had developmental levels lower than those of matched adolescents with no official records. Consequently, there are empirical gounds in addition to theoretical reasons for expecting an inverse relationship between moral development and criminal or deviant behavior.[1]

The studies just reviewed raised a new question of considerable interest: Is moral development linked (1) to deviant behavior itself or (2) to the social reaction to deviance either because of varying vulnerability to detection or differential reaction by authorities once detected?

All the studies purporting to link moral development with deviant behavior can be criticized for having committed the dualistic fallacy (see Reid 1982). Comparing individuals who have been officially labeled deviant by others with those who have not does not necessarily indicate differences in the amount of deviant behavior. Any observed differences may result from the social reaction—something that may distort the actual relationship between moral development and deviance.

The social reaction may be skewed for several reasons. First, those labeled may be more blatant, irrational, or careless in when, where, and how they deviate. There is reason to believe that an ability to think through moral matters relates to general intelligence (Rest 1974); and intelligence is once again being advanced as a correlate of official deviance (Hirschi and

Hindelang 1977). It stands to reason that less logical and consistent moral thinkers might be less rational and easier to detect in their deviance. Second, even when detected, officials and others may elect to react to so-called reasonable deviants informally but to arrest and label more unreasonable ones. See Piliavin and Briar (1964) for a classic discussion of how demeanor is related to police disposition of juveniles in field encounters. Therefore, we will begin to compare and contrast the relationship between moral development and *detected* deviance with any association found between moral reasoning and *hidden* delinquency or crime. Because of the social reaction, we expect the relationship between moral development and deviance to be stronger when we examine measures of detected rule departures.

Mediated Effects of Moral Development

As an indirect learning process, cognitive moral development does not dictate specific normative definitions hypothesized and known to be associated with crime/deviance, but the stages do represent cognitive structures that erect parameters around how people think about and orient themselves to normative questions. There is reason to believe that a relationship exists (though not an isomorphic one) between the actual content of the morality of a level and its cognitive structure. Kohlberg and Elfenbien (1975) demonstrated this by examining the pattern of relationships between attitudes toward capital punishment and moral development. Cognitive moral development has also been shown to be related to attitudes toward the law and politics (Adelson, Green, and O'Neil et al. 1969; Rest 1974); opinions and moral evaluations of the law (Haan, Smith, and Block 1968; Radosevich and Krohn 1981); and orientations toward punishment for violations of the law (Kohlberg 1964; DeJong, Morris, and Hastorf 1976; Radosevich and Krohn 1981). Therefore, this research will focus secondarily on how level of cognitive moral development may be related to more directly acquired specific definitions favorable to law violation, which in turn may facilitate involvement in illegal or deviant behavior.

We start our exploration of the interaction between general level of moral development and more specific normative orientations by examining the relationships among age, moral development, and behavior. We know that age is related to both cognitive moral development and delinquency, albeit in different ways. Age tends to be positively and linearly related to the developmental sequence, but curvilinearly related to delinquency. Indeed, one of the more intriguing empirical findings in the sociology of delinquency is that youths seem to mature out of delinquency. Many theories of delinquency leave this spontaneous recovery unexplained, but it is consistent with a developmental extension of Matza's (1964) argument that juveniles drift into and out of delinquency.

In accordance with Matza, the drift may occur in part because delinquents hold specific normative definitions that provide excuses for behavior inconsistent with societal norms, even though these neutralizing definitions are not entirely antithetical to the moral precepts of the dominant culture. The drift may also be due, in part, to the reasoning-behavior disjunction of younger people (who are more likely to be operating at lower levels of cognitive moral development). This would comport with Turiel and Rothman's findings reported earlier. Therefore, level of development should be negatively related to deviant behavior because persons at lower levels of development are (1) more likely to act inconsistently with normative dictates and (2) less independent in their moral reasoning and more likely to learn specific excuses for misconduct from their social environment.[2]

In this research we focus on the propensity to use specific definitions that neutralize the wrongness of nonconforming behavior and that may mediate the relationship between moral development and deviance. There is empirical evidence that level of cognitive moral development is related to intention-based versus consequence-based moral evaluations of behavior (Rule, Wesdale, and Meara 1974; Armsby 1971; Suls and Kalle 1979; Surber 1977; Costanzo et al. 1973; Elkind and Dabek 1977; Rule and Duker 1973). DeJong, Morris, and Hastorf (1976) and Darley, Klosson and Zanna (1978) have found that advocated sanctions for rule-breaking behavior vary according to the perceived legitimacy of and propensity to consider situational factors that mitigate the perceived wrongness of behavior.

The most detailed examination of the relationship between level of cognitive moral development and the use of mitigating circumstances as legitimate justifications or neutralizing definitions for rule violation is that reported by Radosevich and Krohn (1981). They examined the impact of four of Sykes and Matza's (1957) "techniques of neutralization" on moral evaluations of behavior and advocated sanctions for that behavior within stages of moral development. It was this neutralization theme that Matza (1964) subsequently related to the larger social environment of youth.

Sykes and Matza (1957) identified five generic types of justifications or excusing definitions for rule-breaking behavior. If these specific techniques of neutralization were learned, a relaxation in the moral condemnation of forbidden behavior would follow that would facilitate involvement in deviance. *Denial of responsibility* represents an extension of the legal distinction between intentional and unintentional acts and may mitigate the moral condemnation of behavior by claiming that the actor was not responsible for her or his actions. *Denial of injury* allows mitigation of moral condemnation on the basis of the claim that any damage resulting from an act was only minor. *Denial of victim* allows mitigation by arguing that the victim somehow deserved the damage or harm done to her or him. *Condemnation of the condemners* consists of ad hominem arguments that deflect attention from the rule-breaking behavior of the deviant to the morally questionable behavior of those judging her or him. *Appeal to higher loyalty* neutralizes moral condemnation by arguing that deviant behavior was necessary to satisfy the needs or demands of a social subgroup that take precedence over societal proscriptions.

Radosevich and Krohn (1981) found that use of the techniques of neutralization did mitigate moral condemnation of rule-breaking behavior and the sanctions advocated for that behavior. More important for our present purposes, they also reported that use of particular neutralizing definitions varied by stage of cognitive moral development. With only a few exceptions, respondents at higher stages of development were less likely to use specific neutralizations in their moral evaluations of behavior. In general, there was an inverse linear relationship between level of cognitive moral development and use of the techniques.

This is consistent with the predictions advanced earlier. We expect to find that as level of cognitive moral development increases, use of the techniques of neutralization decreases, resulting in lower levels of deviant behavior. It needs to be made explicit, however, that the techniques of neutralization are only a small subset of all possible learned definitions specifically related to deviance. Although there is some empirical support for a relationship between use of the techniques and deviant behavior (Ball 1966; Priest and McGrath 1970), research also shows that other specific normative definitions bear at least as strong a relationship to deviance (Akers et al. 1979; Lanza-Kaduce 1981). Consequently, failure to find evidence of relationships among cognitive moral development, neutralizing definitions, and deviant behavior must be interpreted cautiously. It would not mean that other learned definitions fail to mediate effects of moral development on deviance, because the scope of our effort is restricted to neutralizing definitions only.

Methodology

Sample

A questionnaire was administered to a sample drawn from a population of seventh- through twelfth-grade boys and girls enrolled in two junior high schools and one senior high school in a midsized community (population approximately 60,000). Every effort was made to obtain a representative (though not random) sample. Comparisons of demographic characteristics of our sample with those for the population of the school district indicate that our sample was representative of the sex, race, age, and social-class characteristics of adolescents enrolled in the school district. Participation in the study was voluntary and required affirmative parental permission. The 414 adolescent respondents represent 77 percent of those students in the classes from which we sampled.[3]

Measurement of the Variables

Cognitive Moral Development. To assess the level of cognitive development, Rest's (1974) short version of the Defining Issues Test (DIT) was used. The DIT is a paper-and-pencil descendant of Kohlberg's (1958, 1975) interview technique, and its reliability and validity have been established (see Rest 1974, 1976). The short form consists of three vignettes, each describing a person in a particular moral dilemma and providing twelve statements reflecting considerations that people at different stages of cognitive moral development would have in assessing the dilemma. Respondents were asked to rate the level of importance of each statement and to rank-order the four most important considerations. Seventy-four respondents who showed inconsistencies between their rankings and ratings were deleted from the analysis, leaving 340 cases to begin data analysis.

Three measures are obtained from the DIT. The *stage* score represents the exceptional use of reasoning consistent with one of the respective stages. The P score indicates the priority given to responses that represent higher-level, principled reasoning (stages 5 and 6) in considering moral dilemmas. The D score is a sophisticated measure (weighted according to a standardization sample) that reflects and balances a respondent's reliance on all levels of moral reasoning.

For our purposes we use the P score and stage score because of shortcomings or uncertainties about the D score for the short version of the DIT. Davison, Robbins, and Swanson (1977) state there are no validity and reliability data for the D score computed on less than the full version of the DIT.

However, the P and stage scores have relative strengths and weaknesses. The stage descriptions provide more theoretical direction than do P-score levels, but their weakness is methodological. Stage scores are computed by taking the statements that are ranked as the four most important considerations in evaluating the moral dilemma and assigning them weights of 4, 3, 2, or 1 for the first through the fourth ranks. The weights assigned to statements representing the different stages are then summed for each stage and transformed into a standard score based on Rest's (1974) original sample. This provides a measure of the exceptional usage of a stage in the consideration of the moral dilemma. Rest (1974), however, reports reservations about the reliability of the stage typing and notes that up to 20 percent of the sample may be lost as a result of nontypes (people whose responses fail to load on any one stage).

Also consistent with previous research, we did not obtain a sufficient number of respondents in either stage 1 or stage 6. Hence we have grouped these respondents in stage 2 and stage 5, respectively. Even then we found so few adolescents operating at stage 5 that it poses problems for interpretation of our data. Those loading in stage A (endorsing mostly antiestablishment considerations) have been deleted from the stage analyses. In addition, people relying on too many meaningless considerations are excluded from stage analysis.[4]

P scores are also derived from the ranking of the four most important considerations used to evaluate each of the moral dilemmas. P scores, however, only sum the weights of ranked considerations reflecting postconventional or principled reasoning (stages 5 and 6). P scores on the short version of the DIT can range from 0 to 27; for our respondents, P scores ranged from 0 to 18, lower than would usually be expected. The young ages of many of our respondents seems to cause the variability on the P score to be restricted. None of our respondents have high P scores except relative to others in our sample.

Moreover, since the computation of the P score ignores lower-level reasoning and attends only to postconventional moral thought, there is room for slippage and further constriction of variability. Those who endorse no principled considerations are grouped together, creating a floor effect. Since the correlation between P score and stage score for our sample is unusually low (.17), caution is warranted in interpreting our results.

However, theoretically the P score should indirectly reflect all but the lowest levels because of the cumulative, progressive nature of the developmental sequence. Since stages are generally not skipped but are gradually worked into from an immediately lower level (see Kohlberg 1964), people showing no principled reasoning should be lower on the continuum than those who use it a little, and the latter lower than those who predominantly rely on it. Unfortunately, P scores provide less theoretical direction for hypothesis construction.

Rest and his associates have tried to establish the utility of the P score using the short version. Its correlation with the P score based on all six dilemmas is .93 (Rest 1974). Reliability estimates for the P score range in the .70s and .80s, depending on the sample.

It seems prudent for us to use both the richer measure for theoretical development (the stage score) and the better established empirical measure (the P score). Consequently, we will conduct alternative analyses using both P and stage measures of moral development.

Propensity to Neutralize. Four of Sykes and Matza's (1957) techniques of neutralization provided the basis for computing our measure of propensity to neutralize: *denial of responsibility* for one's rule breaking; *denial of in-*

jury resulting from one's rule breaking; *denial of the worth of the victim* of one's bad behavior; and excusing one's behavior by *appealing to a higher loyalty,* group, or authority to justify it. Moral condemnation of behavior is expected when neutralizing conditions are absent; but when neutralizing circumstances are present, moral evaluations of the same behavior should become more positive. To measure this, we used a vignette describing an arson situation involving the transferred intent of a person whose careless conduct resulted in a nearby building catching fire. Moral evaluations were first obtained without presenting any of the conditions reflecting the techniques of neutralization. Later in the questionnaire moral evaluations were obtained for the same vignette with each of the neutralizing techniques individually added as a condition. Respondents could select from five ordinal responses ranging from very wrong to very right. Propensity to neutralize is a summation of the number of times each respondent relaxed his or her moral evaluations across the four techniques (using the original, unmitigated evaluations as the point of comparison). The scores could range from 0 (no relaxation or neutralization for any of the techniques) to 4 (neutralization across all techniques). Individuals who became more condemning given a neutralizing condition were assigned a 0 for that technique.

Unfortunately, this is only a rough indicator of the propensity to neutralize, and it is open to several methodological criticisms. First, the techniques of neutralization do not exhaust all the possible ways individuals have to relax moral dictates. Second, the arson vignette addresses only one norm content and one different from our dependent variables. We cannot be certain whether persons who neutralize their moral evaluations for this norm have a general tendency to excuse norm violations.[5] Third, the before-and-after nature of the computation poses some difficulties. Change scores compound reliability problems (see Bohrnstedt 1969). Moreover, because the original moral evaluations were strongly condemning, susequent relaxation may reflect in part a regression effect. The variability observed among respondents over the four techniques, however, militates against interpreting changes as only a regression artifact. Despite these limitations, we think the indicator is sufficient to permit exploration of the relationship among moral development, propensity to neutralize, and deviance.

Delinquency. Since one of our purposes is to see whether moral development is related to deviance itself or to the social reaction to deviance, we include two approaches to the measurement of deviance. The first taps the social reaction to misconduct. *Detected* delinquency was operationalized by asking respondents how many times they had been in trouble with the law.

To get at a form of *undetected* delinquency, respondents were asked how frequently they used marijuana. There may be a little overlap between the two measures in that some of those who report getting into trouble with the law (detected deviance) may have come to the attention of the authorities for their use of marijuana. We know, however, that the vast majority of users avoid legal detection, and so their deviance remains hidden. Therefore, our measure of undetected deviance should suffice.

Results

Unmediated Effects of Moral Development on Delinquency

To test our hypothesis that moral development would be inversely related to both detected and undetected delinquency, simple regression analyses were performed. The results were unexpected and somewhat perplexing at first. When P scores were used as the measure of moral development, we found a small positive relationship between it and marijuana use, our measure of undetected delinquency ($\beta = .13$), but no relationship with detected delinquency ($\beta < .01$). When stage scores were used to measure the developmental sequence, however, we found that level of development bore little relationship to marijuana use ($\beta = -.09$) but a moderate negative relationship with detected delinquency ($\beta = -.20$). Only the negative relationship between stage score and detected delinquency supports our hypotheses, and the positive relationship between P score and marijuana use simply contradicts our predictions. Even more disconcerting are the differences in results by measure of development. Why do P scores and stage scores relate differently to our measures of delinquency?

To obtain a better picture of what exactly was occurring, we moved to cross-tabular analysis, which provides more detail than do summary regression statistics. Cross-tabular analysis categorizes responses and permits us to visualize the comparisons across different levels of variables. For example, we can use it to isolate and contrast distant categories to supplement the regression analysis, which is more sensitive to variation within categories or between adjacent categories. Epistemologically—because moral development is conceptualized as a protracted, dynamic, and indirect socialization process rather than an immediate and direct learning experience—cross-sectional data about it necessarily entail some imprecision, which would distort the examination of general categories less than it would analysis relying on the measurement accuracy of continuous variables. Because regression analysis is designed to fit the best prediction line between covarying continuous variables, it may not alert us to important categorical differences. We turn now to a discussion of the results from the cross-tabular analyses.

Undetected Delinquency (Marijuana Use). Table 17-1 displays the cross-tabular results relating cognitive moral development to marijuana use—our measure of undetected delinquency. Turning first to the top half of the table where P score is used, we begin to see why we obtained a small positive β coefficient between P score and marijuana use in our regression analysis. The bulk of our respondents (65 percent) mostly refrain from marijuana use (used once or twice or never at all). A higher proportion of respondents with a low P score, however, report low levels of use (71 percent) than of those with high P scores ($<$ 60 percent). More respondents with high P scores reported high levels of marijuana use (at least weekly use) than those with low P scores (23 percent to 14.5 percent, respectively). The regression statistic would have been larger if P scores better differentiated moderate users (those using less than monthly but more than once or twice). Almost equal proportions of those reporting moderate use scored in the low (14.5 percent), medium (15.7 percent), and high (17.3 percent) categories of the P score. The magnitude of the regression coefficient also suffered from some curvilinearity among those in our sample having middle- or higher-range P scores. These people were less likely to fall in the medium range of use (15.7 percent and 17.3 percent) than in either of the extremes (63.5 percent and 59.6 percent for low use, and 20.9 percent and 23.1 percent for high use).

This ability of moral development to differentiate between the more extreme use categories makes some theoretical sense. Since cognitive moral development represents only general (rather than specific) normative orientations, which are indirectly (as opposed to directly) learned, it seems reasonable to expect level of development to be more accurate in distinguishing across more distant and broader categories than in predicting a linear covariance across the complete range of continuous scores.

Table 17-1
Undetected Delinquency (Marijuana Use) by Moral Development
(percent)

Moral Development	Undetected Delinquency (Marijuana-Use Level)		
	Low	*Moderate*	*High*
P score ($N = 244$)			
Low	71.1	14.5	14.5
Medium	63.5	15.7	20.9
High	59.6	17.3	23.1
Stage score[a] ($N = 157$)			
2	53.6	25.0	21.4
3	56.6	18.4	25.0
4	75.9	17.2	6.9

[a]Respondents typed as stage 5 or 6 have been deleted from the analysis because there were too few ($n = 13$) to establish trends.

Theoretically, what is more perplexing is the direction of the relationship. Why are those lowest in their moral development least likely to use? We first needed to check to see whether this had anything to do with age, which correlates with both moral development (see Rest 1974) and marijuana use (see Radosevich et al. 1980). Accordingly, we examined the relationship between P score and marijuana use after first removing the effects of age. The attentuation in the magnitude of the β weight was slight, so the small positive relationship between P score and marijuana use seems not to be spurious.

How then do we account for the positive relationship? It might well be that the developmental sequence relates differently to various types of deviant behavior. The important difference may reside in the nature of *mala in se* versus *mala prohibita* offenses. Substance-use research conducted at the same time and in the same area as the survey from which these data were obtained revealed that secondary students who use marijuana clearly believe it is morally acceptable at least under some conditions (Akers et al. 1979). Peer reactions to marijuana use are mostly nonjudgmental, as opposed to either positive or negative (Lanza-Kaduce 1981). Secondary students, not unlike their college counterparts (see Waldo and Chiricos 1972), seem to view marijuana use as merely prohibited (*mala prohibita*) rather than intrinsically wrong (*mala in se*). More principled thinkers should be relatively unaffected by *mala prohibita* declarations of wrongness, since their reasoning is relatively independent of external social influences. Since P score measures only the reliance on considerations reflecting stage 5 and 6 thinking, it is a purer measure for this particular research question than are the stage scores, which bore no relationship to marijuana use in the regression analysis. Perhaps stage scores would have shown a relationship if more stage 5 and 6 types were included in our sample.

This account does not lay the issue to rest, however. If we look at the bottom part of table 17-1, where stage scores are cross-tabulated with marijuana use, we see that the regression analysis may have suppressed a relationship. If once again we examine the extremes, we see that stage 4 persons are considerably *more* likely to refrain from marijuana use (75.9 percent) than are stage 2 individuals (53.6 percent) and *less* likely to use frequently (6.9 percent to 21.4 percent). This is the exact reverse of what the cross-tabular results for the P scores produced, but it is consistent with our original hypothesis: preconventional moralities are more prone to deviance. Can the apparent discrepancy in the direction of the observed cross-tabular relationships by measure of cognitive moral development be reconciled?

Given the low correlation between P score and stage score (.17), it is very possible that the two measures are tapping different things. This correlation is much lower than Rest (1974) reports, but it may be due to some unusual characteristics of our sample. Because we surveyed seventh and eighth grades as well as high schoolers, we have disproportionate numbers of preconventional persons, where the P score is least able to differentiate. Rest usually does not use the DIT with seventh- and eighth-grade students, so his correlations are premised on different kinds of samples. Moreover, we also have so few postconventional people that our stage analysis is restricted. Because the respective measures are truncated at opposite ends in our sample, contradictory results could be produced. This would be exacerbated by the substantial loss of cases in the stage measure due to nonstage types ($n = 78$). Whatever the reason for the disparity in results by moral-development measures, it should strike a cautionary note for future research using the DIT. Rest's (1974) warning about using the DIT with young students is well placed.

Detected Delinquency. Recall that in the regression analyses, only the stage score was moderately (and inversely) related to the number of times persons reported having been in trouble with the law ($\beta = -.20$). Table 17-2 presents the cross-tabular results for both P score and stage score measures and detected delinquency. An examination of the extreme categories for both measures confirms our regression results.

Across levels of P scores the table shows little systematic variation in the amount of detected delinquency, which comports with failure to find a relationship in the regression analysis. Respondents with low P scores and high P scores are about as likely to have avoided trouble (65.8 percent and 64.7 percent, respectively) or to have been in a lot of trouble (18.4 percent and 15.7 percent, respectively). There is little relationship between P scores and detected delinquency.

Table 17-2
Detected Delinquency (Trouble with the Law) by Moral Development
(percent)

Moral Development	Detected Delinquency (Frequency of Trouble with the Law)		
	Never	*Some*	*A Lot*
P score ($N = 241$)			
Low	65.8	15.8	18.4
Medium	61.1	21.1	17.7
High	64.7	19.6	15.7
Stage score[a] ($N = 159$)			
2	44.8	31.0	24.1
3	57.5	16.4	26.0
4	73.7	15.8	10.5

[a]Respondents typed as stage 5 or 6 have been deleted from the analysis because they were too few ($n = 8$) to establish trends.

When one examines categories of the stage scores, however, we see why there was a moderate regression coefficient. Stage 2 persons are much less likely to avoid all trouble (44.8 percent) than are stage 4 persons (73.7 percent). The hedonists of stage 2 are also more likely to get in some trouble (31.0 percent) or a lot of trouble (24.1 percent) than are their law-and-order stage 4 counterparts of whom 15.8 percent report some trouble, and 10.5 percent report a lot of trouble.

These findings regarding detected delinquency are consistent with theoretical predictions and the way the two measures of cognitive development are derived. Unless we are willing to assume that most trouble with the law arises due to *mala prohibita* offenses, *P* scores should be unrelated to detected delinquency. Because *P* scores cannot differentiate preconventionals very well, this developmental measure should be mostly unrelated to detected delinquency. On the other hand, stage scores do identify preconventionals. Thus it is no accident that the stage measure achieves some magnitude of association with delinquency.

The next logical question is whether preconventionals are simply more likely to get caught or are truly more often involved in delinquent acts. If getting into trouble with the law mostly reflects vulnerability to detection, it may be that preconventionals are simply more unreasonable and less intelligent in their conduct. In other words, intelligence that is known to be related to moral development (see Rest 1974) and to delinquency (see Hirschi and Hindelang 1977) could account for our observed relationship.

For lack of a better indicator of intelligence, we first controlled for school grades (GPA, or grade point average) and then regressed detected delinquency on stage scores. The magnitude of the partial regression coefficient between stage and detected delinquency ($-.19$) was virtually unchanged from its zero-order level. This suggests that there is something about the lower stages of moral development themselves that relates to detected deviant behavior. The relationship cannot be written off merely as a function of intelligence.

Mediated Effects of Moral Development

In order to explore how the cognitive moral structure translates into specific instances of behavior, we proposed examining the relationships among moral-development measures, propensity to neutralize, and detected and undetected delinquency. Propensity to neutralize was just one of the types of specific normative definitional processes thought to relate to deviance that might mediate the cognitive structure. Recall that Radosevich and Krohn (1981) found the stages to relate to particular techniques of neutralization (although less so for a criminal-law item than for constitutional- and civil-law vignettes). Because the particular techniques of neutralization were not specified for the kinds of delinquency we explore here, we were left with examining the general propensity to use neutralization techniques—a flawed measure from the outset.

This may be why we found very little in the way of relationships between propensity to neutralize and either measure of moral development ($\beta = .04$ for P score and $\beta = .01$ for the stage score). The βs were only slightly higher when examining the relationships between propensity to neutralize and our measures of delinquency (ranging from $-.08$ to $-.11$ for marijuana use and from $-.07$ to $-.16$ for detected delinquency). Cross-tabulations and even table elaborations controlling for various levels of moral development to see what effect neutralizing had on delinquency within developmental levels did not produce different results. Our first shot at trying to specify how the general normative structures of the developmental sequence relate to more directly acquired specific normative orientations to produce deviance was a complete misfire.

Further Discussion and Future Directions

In many ways our research is more important for the questions it raises than for the answers it provides. The unresolved issues run the gamut of theory, epistemology, and methodology. Methodologically, there is the question of whether P scores are adequate to gauge relationships expected to exist between preconventional moral development and behavior. There are also problems with the loss of cases in stage typing and using the DIT with younger than high-school-age students. Epistemologically, the theory must be better linked to measurement. Is the developmental sequence so protracted, global, and indirect that it can be most fruitfully applied only to grosser, more categorical distinctions in behaviors and outcomes? Are we left primarily with an analysis of extreme types? Theoretically, we must learn how the discontinuity between general cognitive structures and specific behaviors can be bridged. How does the development of moral-reasoning capacity relate to the direct learning of norms that in turn relate to deviance and conformity? Are there different domains of deviance for which the process of deviance generation varies (for example, *mala en se* versus *mala prohibita*)? It may be useful to close by exploring some of these questions and their implications.

The P scores seem to be inadequate to explore how lower-level moralities relate to other variables. For example, P scores measure cognitive development differently from stage scores, and it is in the description of stages 2 and 3 that there is strongest theoretical linkage to deviance. We expect preconventionals to commit more delinquency not because of an absence of principled reasoning but because of the presence of hedonism. Therefore, crimes of gain and thrill-seeking acts should be disproportionately committed by preconventionals. We cannot measure that by using P score, however. Even with the loss of cases due to nontypes, stage scores offer us more theoretical guidance and a more interpretable measure. To the extent that marijuana use is thrill-seeking and hedonistic, our cross-tabular results using stage scores make theoretical sense. This does not mean, however, that our finding that more reliance on principled and independent reasoning (relatively higher P scores) is related to more marijuana use is wrong and irreconcilable. By summating only postconventional considerations, the P score purifies a measure of postconventional morality and does permit us to speculate that endorsing more independent, principled reasoning permits violation of norms viewed to be *mala prohibita*. In principled reasoning, morality is more independent from the law and social influences and is freer to reject the legal norm.

We are suggesting that a curvilinear relationship really exists between cognitive development and marijuana use, but we were unable to uncover it because the P score was truncated at the bottom end of its measurement domain and the stage score did not yield enough respondents at its top end to establish trends there. We would speculate, however, that for *mala en se* offenses, stage 2 and 3 moralities would be disproportionately involved. The P score would not suffice to investigate these deviant acts. For more expansive samples and for most kinds of deviance, the stage score may be an adequate measure.

There was an intriguing feature of our findings addressing the fit between theory and measurement that also warrants speculation. Developmental levels were most clearly related to noncontiguous categorical differences in delinquency. The middle ranges of delinquency were less clearly associated. This suggests that the theory may require analysis techniques that recognize its global, unrefined character. Fortunately, when we are applying moral development to problems of legal compliance and deviance, this may be all that is necessary. Since almost all youths commit some delinquency, our most important task may be to account for discrete differences at the extremes of our variables rather than continuous variation overwhelmed by the many at the middle ranges. To understand legal compliance, unusual overconformity and underconformity may be the more interesting theoretical outcomes to study. There are already reasons for attending to extreme types in the study of delinquency. Elliot and Ageton (1980) found important social characteristics (such as race and social class) related to self-reported (and mostly undetected) delinquency, but largely among those who engaged in the deviance extremely often. These same correlates have long been established for official (that is, detected) delinquency. Akers et al. (1981) confirmed Ageton and Elliot's percentage differences in social correlates between delinquents at extreme ends of the delinquency continuum, but found the magnitude of the relationships to be no greater than when the full range of delinquency was analyzed.

We are suggesting here that there is an important cleavage in our data separating those in the law-and-order stage (stage 4) from those in lower stages (instrumental relativism/stage 2 and interpersonal concordance/ stage 3) that distinguishes the more extreme categories for both detected and undetected delinquency (see tables 17-1 and 17-2). Whereas only about half of stage 2 and 3 individuals seldom smoke pot or never have gotten into legal trouble, 75 percent of the law-and-order people have remained pure. Similarly, 10 percent or less of the law-and-order people deviate often or a lot, but roughly one-quarter of the stage 2 and 3 adolescents do. Therefore, these data indicate that moral development is at least as important as race or social class as a correlate of the more extreme categories of conforming or deviating behavior. This was true even after removing the effects of age and grade point average—two of the other social variables examined in extreme-types analysis (see Akers et al. 1981).

For these reasons we argue that moral development can support further theorizing about crime and delinquency. Our attempt to interpose propensity to neutralize as a more specific normative orientation that mediates the effect of moral development on delinquency failed. Our finding that stage 2 and 3 persons were least likely to conform and most likely to commit frequent delinquent acts, however, suggests other approaches to specific normative definitions that may specify how moral development affects particular deviant behaviors.

The descriptions of stages 2 and 3 bear some affinity for several features of social-learning theory (Burgess and Akers 1966; Akers 1977). The instrumental hedonism of stage 2, where rightness is determined by the physical consequences of the act, is directly analogous to differential reinforcement (particularly nonsocial reinforcement) (Burgess and Akers 1966; Akers 1977). The interpersonal concordance of stage 3, where the morality of behavior derives from expectations established by friends or families, is conceptually akin to differential association and definitions (see Sutherland 1947; Burgess and Akers 1966; Akers 1977). Other research we have conducted has demonstrated that both differential reinforcement and differential peer association are strongly related to the frequency of use and abuse of substances (Akers et al. 1979) and to the progression through the various stages of use (Lanza-Kaduce 1981). We speculate that the developmental sequence relates to and perhaps mediates the direct learning processes known to foster or retard deviant behavior. Although all processes are at work in each stage and peer behavior remains the best predictor regardless of stage, direct reinforcement and punishment for behavior should play a bigger role for preconventionals (stages 1 and 2) than for persons in stage 3 (interpersonal concordance). Perceptions of group expectations and one's own normative definitions will be more important in explaining deviant behavior among those at stage 3 than those in stage 2.

Indeed, this may account for our finding in our past research that differential peer association and definitions were more important than differential reinforcement (reactions of others and effects of drugs) in explaining most substance use among adolescents (see Akers et al. 1979; Lanza-Kaduce 1981). There are relatively more adolescents at stage 3 than at lower levels, and for adolescents the most important groups are peer groups. If these groups accept delinquency and engage in it, the individual most open to their influence will go along. A suggestive pattern emerges when we put this all together. The mean age of our sample was about 14.6; most of our sample was typed at stage 3 (see tables 17-1 and 17-2); the average onset of marijuana use (see Radosevich et al. 1980) and the most active period for delinquency generally are between ages 14 and 16 (see Thornton, James, and Doerner 1982); and peer associations are the strongest and most consistent predictors of delinquent behavior. The potential of using the developmental sequence as contextualizing or mediating more direct social-learning processes to integrate diverse findings such as these warrants further study and thought.

Cognitive moral development may also allow us to begin to make sense out of the maturation phenomenon, whereby most delinquents spontaneously recover from their waywardness as they grow older. Part of the reason could be cognitive reorganization and movement into the law-and-order stage, where we found the greatest likelihood of conforming behavior. Because people develop at different rates and because some level off at lower stages, the timing and noninevitability of recovery are consistent with the developmental framework.

Finally, implications of moral development for social control deserve our attention. If our theorizing has any merit, then deterrence doctrine, especially general deterrence, is not likely to be effective. For preconventionals, the consequences of one's own actions control moral orientations and behavior. Example setting by punishing others may be irrelevant to the cognitive structure of preconventionals. To the extent that specific deterrence personalizes negative consequences for the offender, preconventionals would be more open to this form of resocialization. This, however, assumes a relatively high likelihood of detection and sanctioning (rather than diversion) on getting caught. Neither certainty, celerity, nor severity of official sanctions is typically present; even when present, these would have to offset or extinguish behaviors that have a history of nondetection and immediate reinforcement.

Official sanctions are not salient to stage 3 (interpersonal-concordance) individuals. Peer and family expectations would be expected to override official legal pronouncements and reactions. Prevention and intervention programs that deal with youth in their naturally occurring peer groups may be the most efficacious social-policy orientation. Punishing stage 3 persons may do little more than drive them deeper into their old peer groups, which are probably already engaging in deviance, or into even more delinquent institutionalized populations. Programs (not unlike Kohlberg's Just Community) that seek to foster and encourage the transition into the law-and-order stage may also be indicated.

The social-control consideration of relevance for stage 4 (law-and-order) persons is maintaining the legitimacy and authoritativeness of the law. Indeed, there is a growing body of literature that reports that infrequent deviance is associated with moral condemnation and belief in legal norms as much as (or more than) it is to deterrence perceptions (Silberman 1976; Erickson, Gibbs, and Jensen 1977; Minor 1977; Schwartz and Orleans 1967; Salem and Bowers 1970). Stage 4 individuals seem most insulated from deviance, but probably only as long as the law provides clear, authoritative directives. What would happen to these individuals were there to be a breakdown in the legal order—something akin to legal anomie—is open to conjecture. Given the present perceived malaise in our criminal-justice system and the growing crime problem, the issue at least has some currency. The more important question, however, revolves around how the legitimacy of the law is maintained for people at this level, especially since this is the stage at which most adults operate. Indeed, the lessons from Durkheim (1933) on normative validation (see also Gibbs 1975) rather than traditional arguments about deterrence may be instructive in this regard.

For postconventional or principled moralities (stages 5 and 6), we may have to look to the law itself to find the seeds of illegality. As long as the law is internally consistent, reasonable in content and procedure, and harmonious with the independent morality of the stage 5 or 6 individual, there should be few problems with conformity. In the absence of these, however, the law would be expected to hold little sway over principled reasoners and even perhaps to contribute to civil disobedience (see Haan, Smith, and Block 1968) or disregard for the law. Perhaps as Mill (1956, p. 101) argued: "if there be among those whom it is attempted to coerce into prudence or temperance any . . . vigorous and independent characters. . . , they will infallibly rebel and do the exact opposite. . . ." Significantly, the normative orientations of postconventional thinkers might alert us to inconsistencies and shortcomings in the law (or its application). People operating at this level may be able to pierce the mystique of the dominant order, expose some unanticipated consequences of the extant normative system, and point out new directions for a more rational future.

Notes

1. Generally we expect these relationships to hold, but we would be remiss if we did not acknowledge the complexity of this theoretical problem. For some issues, higher deviance would be expected among more principled thinkers. There is reason to believe that civil disobedience may be due to *personal* conviction and conscience. For example, Haan, Smith, and Block (1968) found that, of the people participating in the Berkeley Free Speech Movement, persons at stage 6 were much more likely to engage in civil disobedience than were those at stages 3 and 4.

2. Tapp (1970) has demonstrated that older children (who are more likely to be operating at the principled level of reasoning) are more likely to accept the legitimacy of breaking a rule if there are personal moral reasons for doing so. Consistent with our desire to contextualize the direct learning of specific normative definitions within the general developmental sequence, we focus only on those specific definitions most widely shared with and provided by one's relevant social environment. We exclude from consideration excusing definitions that reflect autonomous, independent moral reasoning because these are likely to be more idiosyncratic and therefore less likely to be systematically related to deviant behavior.

3. In order to conform to the requests of the school principals, we sampled classrooms rather than individuals. We selected required or general-enrollment classes. Thus we can assume that each student had an approximately equal chance of being selected. We administered the questionnaire to two or three classes in each grade level (seven through twelve). We employed an affirmative permission procedure wherein parents had to agree to allow their child to participate before he or she could be included. Over 95 percent of the parents granted permission. The attrition resulted from the failure of students to return the forms or absenteeism on the day the questionnaire was administered.

4. Seventy-eight respondents were lost to typing problems—half loaded on antiestablishment considerations and the others nontypes or those who endorsed too many meaningless statements.

5. We are somewhat reassured about generalizing from our results for the following reasons. Parallel analyses were performed using a propensity-to-neutralize scale summated across the arson item and a constitutional-law and a civil-law vignette. The results were no different from what is reported here. We chose to report propensity to neutralize only on the arson item because it was conceptually most similar to delinquency and because

responses to the civil-law item were qualitatively different from those to the arson and due-process constitutional vignettes. That normative orientations toward civil-law concerns differ from those toward criminal or constitutional matters is consistent with past work (see Lanza-Kaduce et al. 1979).

References

Adelson, J.B.; Green, B.; and O'Neil, R. Growth of the idea of law in adolescence. *Developmental Psychology*, 1969, *1*, 327-332.

Akers, R.L. *Deviant behavior: A social learning approach*, 2nd ed. Belmont, Calif.: Wadsworth, 1977.

Akers, R.L.; Krohn, M.D.; Lanza-Kaduce, L.; and Radosevich, M. Social learning and deviant behavior: A specific test of a general theory. *American Sociological Review*, 1979, *44*, 636-655.

Akers, R.L.; Krohn, M.D.; Radosevich, M.; and Lanza-Kaduce, L. Social characteristics and self-reported delinquency: Differences in extreme types. In *Sociology of delinquency, current issues*, ed. G.F. Jensen. Beverly Hills, Calif.: Sage, 1981, 48-62.

Armsby, R.E. A reexamination of the development of moral judgment in children. *Child Development*, 1971, *42*, 1241-1248.

Ball, R.A. An empirical exploration of neutralization theory. *Criminologica*, 1966, *4*, 22-32.

Bohrnstedt, G. Observations on the measurement of change. In *Sociological Methodology 1969*, ed., E. Borgatta. San Francisco: Jossey-Bass, 1969.

Burgess, R.L., and Akers, R.L. A differential association-reinforcement theory of criminal behavior. *Social Problems*, 1966, *14*, 128-147.

Clark, J.N.; Boyum, K.O.; Krislov, S.; and Schaefer, R.C. Compliance, obedience, and revolt. In *Compliance and the law*, ed. S. Krislov, K.O. Boyum, J.N. Clark, R.C. Schaefer, and S.O. White. Beverly Hills, Calif.: Sage, 1972, 9-32.

Costanzo, P.R.; Coie, J.D.; Grument, J.F.; and Farnill, D. A reexamination of the effects of intent and consequences on children's moral judgments. *Child Development*, 1973, *44*, 154-161.

Darley, J.M.; Klosson, E.C.; and Zanna, M.P. Intentions and their contexts in the moral judgments of children and adults. *Child Development*, 1978, *49*, 66-74.

Davison, M.L.; Robbins, S.; and Swanson, D.B. DIT: A Fortran IV program for scoring the Defining Issue Test. Unpublished manuscript, University of Minnesota, 1977.

DeJong, W.; Morris, W.N.; and Hastorf, A.H. Effect of an escaped accomplice on the punishment assigned to a criminal defendent. *Journal of Personality and Social Psychology*, 1976, *33*, 192-198.

Durkheim, E. *The division of labor in society*, trans. G. Simpson. New York: Free Press, 1933.

Elkind, D., and Dabek, R.F. Personal injury and property damage in the moral judgments of children. *Child Development*, 1977, *48*, 518-522.

Elliott, D.S., and Ageton, S.S. Reconciling race and class differences in self-reported and official estimates of delinquency. *American Sociological Review*, 1980, *45*, 95-110.

Erickson, M.L.; Gibbs, J.; and Jensen, G.F. The deterrence doctrine and the perceived certainty of legal punishment. *American Sociological Review*, 1977, *42*, 305-317.

Fodor, E.M. Delinquency and susceptibility to social influence among adolescents as a function of level of moral development. *Journal of Social Psychology*, 1972, *86*, 257-260.

Gibbs, J.P. *Crime, punishment, and deterrence*. New York: Elsevier, 1975.

Haan, N.; Smith, M.B.; and Block, J.H. The moral reasoning of young adults: Political-social behavior, family background, and personality correlates. *Journal of Personality and Social Psychology*, 1968, *10*, 183-201.

Harris, S.; Mussen, P.; and Rutherford, E. Some cognitive behavioral and personality correlates of maturity of moral judgment. *Journal of Genetic Psychology*, 1976, *128*, 123-135.

Hess, R.D., and Tapp, J.L. *Authority, rules and aggression: A cross-national study of the socialization of children into compliance systems,* part I. Washington, D.C.: U.S. Department of Health, Education and Welfare, 1969.

Hirschi, T., and Hindelang, M.J. Intelligence and delinquency: A revisionist view. *American Sociological Review*, 1977, *44*, 571-587.

Hudgins, W., and Prentice, N.M. Moral judgments in delinquent and nondelinquent adolescents and their mothers. *Journal of Abnormal Psychology*, 1973, *82*, 145-152.

Koeppen, S. Children and compliance: A comparative analysis of socialization studies. *Law and Society Review*, 1970, *4*, 545-564.

Kohlberg, L. The development of modes of moral thinking and choice in years ten to sixteen. Unpublished dissertation, University of Chicago, 1958.

_____ . Development of children's orientations toward a moral order: I. Sequence in the development of moral thought. *Vita Humana*, 1964, *6*, 11-33.

_____ . The child as moral philosopher. *Psychology Today*, 1968, *2*, 24-31.

_____ . Moral stage scoring manual, parts 1-5. Unpublished manuscript, 1975 (edited 1976).

Kohlberg, L., and Elfenbein, D. Moral judgments about capital punishment: A developmental-psychological view. In *Capital Punishment in the*

United States, ed. H.A. Bedau and C.M. Pierce. New York: AMS Press, 1975, 247-295.

Kohlberg, L.; Kaufman, K.; Scharf, P.; and Hickey, J. *The just community approach to corrections: A manual.* Cambridge, Mass.: Harvard University, Moral Education Research Foundation, 1974.

Kohlberg, L., and Turiel, E. Moral development and moral education. In *Psychology and educational practice*, ed. G. Lesser. Chicago: Scott, Foresman, 1971.

Lanza-Kaduce, L. Starting and stopping substance use: A further test of social learning theory. Unpublished dissertation. University of Iowa, 1981.

Lanza-Kaduce, L.; Krohn, M.D.; Akers, R.L.; and Radosevich, M. Law and Durkheimian order: An empirical examination of the convergence of legal and social definitions of law. In *Structure, law and power*, ed., P.J. Brantingham and J.M. Kress. Beverly Hills, Calif.: Sage, 1979, 41-61.

Lanza-Kaduce, L., and Stratton, J. Paper presented at the Annual Meeting of the Midwest Sociological Society at Milwaukee, April, 1980.

Matza, D. *Delinquency and drift.* New York: Wiley, 1964.

Mill, J.S. *On liberty.* Indianapolis: Liberal Arts Press, 1956.

Minor, W.W. A deterrence-control theory of crime. In *Theory in criminology: Contemporary views*, ed. R.F. Meier. Beverly Hills, Calif.: Sage, 1977, 117-137.

Piaget, J. *The moral judgment of the child.* Glencoe, Ill.: The Free Press, 1965.

Piliavin, I., and Briar, S. Police encounters with juveniles. *American Journal of Sociology*, 1964, *70*, 206-214.

Priest, T.B., and McGrath, J.H. III. Techniques of neutralization: Young adult marijuana smokers. *Criminology*, 1970, *8*, 185-194.

Radosevich, M., and Krohn, M.D. Cognitive moral development and legal socialization. *Criminal Justice and Behavior*, 1981, *8*, 401-424.

Radosevich, M.; Lanza-Kaduce, L.; Akers, R.L.; and Krohn, M.D. The sociology of adolescent drug and drinking behavior: A review of the state of the field, part I. *Deviant Behavior*, 1979, *1*, 15-35.

_____ . The sociology of adolescent drug and drinking behavior: A review of the state of the field, part II. *Deviant Behavior*, 1980, *1*, 145-169.

Reid, S.T. *Crime and Criminology*, 3rd ed. New York: Holt, Rinehart and Winston, 1982.

Rest, J.R. The cognitive-developmental approach to morality: The state of the art. *Counseling and Values*, 1974, *18*, 64-78.

_____ . New approaches in the assessment of moral judgment. In *Moral Development and Behavior*, ed. T. Lickona. New York: Holt, Rinehart and Winston, 1976, 178-220.

_____ . A theoretical analysis of moral judgment development. Unpublished manuscript, n.d.

Rule, B.G. and P. Duker. The effect of intentions and consequences on childrens' evaluations of aggressors. *Journal of Personality and Social Psychology*, 1973, *27*, 184-189.

Rule, B.G.; Wesdale, A.R.; and Meara, M.J. Children's reactions to information about the intentions underlying an aggresive act. *Child Development*, 1974, *45*, 794-798.

Salem, R.G., and Bowers, W.J. Severity of formal sanctions as a deterrent to deviant behavior. *Law and Society Review*, 1970, *5*, 21-40.

Schwartz, R.D., and Orleans, S. On legal sanctions. *University of Chicago Law Review*, 1967, *34*, 274-300.

Silberman, M. Toward a theory of criminal deterrence. *American Sociological Review*, 1976, *41*, 442-461.

Suls, J., and Kalle, R.J. Children's moral judgments as a function of intention, damage, and actor's physical harm. *Developmental Psychology*, 1979, *15*, 93-94.

Surber, C.F. Developmental processes in social inference: Averaging of intentions and consequences in moral judgment. *Developmental Psychology*, 13 June 1977, *13*, 654-665.

Sutherland, E.H. *Principles of criminology*, 4th ed. Philadelphia: Lippincott, 1947.

Sykes, G.M., and Matza, D. Techniques of neutralization: A theory of delinquency. *American Sociological Review*, 1957, *22*, 664-670.

Tapp, J.L. A child's garden of law and order. *Psychology Today*, 1970, *4*, 29-39.

Tapp, J.L., and Kohlberg, L. Developing senses of law and legal justice. *Journal of Social Issues*, 1971, *27*, 65-91.

Thornton, W.E.; James, J.A.; and Doerner, W.G. *Delinquency and justice*. Chicago: Scott, Foresman, 1982.

Turiel, E., and Rothman, G.R. The influence of reasoning on behavioral choices at different stages of moral development. *Child Development*, 1962, *43*, 741-756.

Waldo, G.P., and Chiricos, T.G. Perceived penal sanction and self-reported criminality: A neglected approach to deterrence research. *Social Problems*, 1972, *19*, 522-540.

Part III
Future Directions

Part III
Implementations

18 My Brief Life in Crime

Joseph Adelson

As it happens, my first internship in clinical psychology was at a juvenile detention unit. It was not an assignment I valued, not at the time, since it was distinctly of low status. It was the placement you had to endure before getting to the Real McCoy, the big leagues, which were the great psychiatric hospitals or the outpatient clinics. Why this was so, why one type of internship was of high status and the other devalued, had almost nothing to do with the interest of the work or the quality of the internship experience. Rather, it had to do with both the sociology and economics of mental health practice; and this is a topic which need not concern us here. I mention it only because I think my experience was characteristic. Among the dozens— indeed hundreds—of experienced clinicians I know, only a handful have had any experience with criminal offenders, either juvenile or adult.

Among those who have, the experience seems to be limited to the more exotic segments of that population. The cases I was given to evaluate were chosen not because they were typical, but because they were not. The first Rorschach test I ever gave on my own was administered to a 15-year-old who would intersperse his decidedly peculiar responses with abusive comments to an invisible person located somewhere behind me. Shortly after that bracing initiation, I administered a TAT to a pleasant, well-mannered, middle-class boy of 14 who told stories of violent murders to nineteen of the twenty cards he was shown. (My prediction, based on this and other information, that he was a candidate to attempt a homicide sometime soon was greeted with some incredulity by most of the professional staff, but alas it turned out to be all too true.)

Only occasionally did I have any contact with run-of-the-mill juvenile offenders, and I found some of those experiences simply puzzling. I had no categories to explain why these juveniles acted as they did. I vividly remember examining a young man, just about to turn 18, whose delinquent career had begun at 13 and who had been in the courts, on probation, or in detention more or less steadily ever since. In the five-year period between 13 and 18 he had been free—that is, neither on probation nor in custody—for a total of five months. Not that he had been singled out for severe treatment; on the contrary, he had been treated, I thought, quite leniently, largely because the crimes were trivial to the point of being nearly meaningless— breaking into a service station and stealing some hubcaps, with no apparent intention of either using or reselling them.

As I read through this youngster's massive dossier, I was struck by the extraordinary repetitiousness of the pattern—a stay in reform school for a few weeks or a few months, then release, then rearrest, generally within a week or two. How could one explain this? "Aha" I thought to myself, "a compulsive criminal." My mind teemed with hypotheses—doubtless some superego pathology, let us say "a criminal out of a sense of guilt feelings," or a hidden parricidal rebellion; something along those lines. Yet when I finally met the young man, interviewed him, and tested him, these notions simply vanished. I had expected to see someone tormented by the Hounds of Hell; instead I found myself talking to a rather indolent, amiable, gullible young man, a kind of good-ol'-boy, urban variety, who simply went along with the gang. Rereading the police reports, I could see that he had never initiated a delinquency, but had gone along at the urging of some stronger personality. Incarceration held few terrors for him; on the contrary, he rather liked it, since he got on quite well with his peers, and with the authorities. He didn't have no trouble with no one, as he told me, rather piously.

These memories were brought to mind by reading many of the manuscripts assembled in this pioneering book. Not very much has changed in the more than thirty years since I took my graduate training. So far as one can tell, very few clinicians—either clinical psychologists or psychiatrists—receive much training with delinquent or criminal populations, and even fewer of them work in or for the criminal justice system. Among the few who do, even fewer are graduates of the elite departments of psychology or psychiatry. Of the hundreds of doctoral students in clinical psychology who have come through our—very elite—clinic at Michigan, only one as far as I know has worked in the realm of criminal behavior (he is represented in this book, in fact); and I can clearly recall my amazement when I first learned that Stan Samenow was writing a book on the criminal personality: "What is he doing *that* for?"

What is true of clinical work is equally true of psychological research. It is extremely underdeveloped. To persuade yourself of that, pick up any textbook of abnormal psychology, and compare the chapters on, let us say, schizophrenia with the coverage given to criminal behavior. You will find that in the former case, the author is frantically compressing, trying to squeeze all that is known into the two or three chapters traditionally given to the topic in a typical text. In the treatment of criminal personality, he is stretching, earnestly trying to find enough information for respectable coverage. Yet the two conditions are equally burdensome in social cost, and equally worthy of scientific scrutiny. Why such neglect? In part, I suspect, because crime has long been seen as essentially sociological in origin. In the scientific division of labor, it has become a territory occupied by sociology. Further, at least in this country, the overrepresentation of minority-group members in the criminal population has produced some resistance, or perhaps diffidence, toward its study among some social scientists. Yet clearly, if crime is sociological, it is also psychological; just as clearly, it is not intrinsically connected with race or ethnicity. Whatever the reasons, we find ourselves faced with a remarkably primitive grasp of the psychology of crime, especially ordinary, garden-variety crime.

We have not yet developed a compelling taxonomy of critical conduct or the criminal personality. Until we do, we are likely to find ourselves dogged by inconclusive or incoherent findings. We can see parallel examples in other domains of deviant psychology. Our understanding of depression, for example, was markedly advanced by a more certain grasp of the nosology involved. An adequate taxonomy will not necessarily mean that the condition is understood or that appropriate therapies will be forthcoming; but it will generally mean that research will be more intelligently targeted. One problem in the study of schizophrenia has been the fact that the most prominent differentiation of schizophrenic subtypes (simple, catatonic, hebephrenic, paranoid, schizoaffective) does not seem to correspond to any deeper differentiations; there has been a continuing search for more fruitful taxonomies, such as process versus acute. We are now beginning to see that the so-called borderline states—a category devised to solve some puzzling taxonomic questions—are also inadequate to encompass the variety of conditions enclosed in that rubric.

This book contains several efforts to develop an appropriate taxonomy—particularly Marguerite Q. Warren's use of a developmental schema, which seems most promising. Had her work been done while I was taking my internship, I might have recognized that the "compulsive criminal" I puzzled over was an example of her Passive-Conformist type, commonly represented in delinquent populations. Nevertheless, the taxonomic search is just beginning, and has a very long way to go. I see few signs in this book of much convergence in informed opinion on the most profitable ways to divide and organize conceptually the vast domain of the criminal.

One reason seems to be that the fundamental models are constructed from research carried out elsewhere—in experimental laboratories, college classrooms, or the nursery—and transplanted willy-nilly to the street corner and the lockup. Theoretically, there is nothing wrong with that. If the principles are deep enough, they can be applied to the widest range of human circumstances. In practice, however, it just does not work out—it is too procrustean a solution. As one reads through this book, one can hear, faintly but distinctly, the sighs and groans of concepts being stretched, mercilessly.

One senses this most acutely in the chapters on the applications of moral theory. It is difficult in any case to understand the avidity with which that theory has been pursued in our social science, except perhaps as one more derivative of the pietistic strain in U.S. culture. Be that as it may, the absence of what Lionel Trilling termed "moral realism" in U.S. liberal thinking is painfully evident in the notion that wickedness can be understood as moral defect and can be rectified by systematic moral instruction. The stage theories of the moral life, having been formed by the asking of simple questions in Arcadian contexts—such as the classroom or the playpen, cannot capture either the active or the gratuitous or the absurd elements of the criminal enterprise. I think of a one-time patient of mine, an elderly man about to be charged with a series of embezzlements going back many years. He came to see me presumably to calm his nerves, though in actuality to lay the foundations for a plea of temporary insanity, or something similar. You could not have invented a man of more conventional morality—a straight stage 4: a devoted husband and father, a pillar of the church, an ethical practitioner of his profession. But there was also at work within him a will so distended as to have become demonic, which willed the idea of limitless wealth achieved through the boldest means. Avariciousness, will, and daring—all of these raised to megalomaniacal intensity—made up the submerged part of that personality.

One would not of course want to take this man, or these dynamics, as a model for all variations of the criminal personality. Nor would one want to argue that crime does not involve anomalies and distortions of the moral sense. But it involves much more than that, and our current theories tend to separate the moral life from the total personality. Through a kind of conceptual imperialism, one limited view of moral functioning has been taken, erroneously, as the key to criminal behavior at large.

19 The Future of Crime and Personality Research: A Social Psychologist's View

Craig W. Haney

Theories of the nature of human nature are generated and accepted or rejected in a social and political context. We evaluate the plausibility of our theories not only in terms of their objective goodness of fit with the real world, but also in terms of how they feel to us and to the critical audiences to whom we present them. This is especially true for theories that are used as the scientific justification for political and social policies, such as theories about the causes of crime.

The recent resurgence of individualistic personality theories about the causes of crime coincides with the widespread popularity of a political perspective that is founded on a nineteenth-century world view. The rediscovery of the so-called criminal type is perfectly consistent with the rediscovery of nineteenth-century laissez-faire. Both these doctrines are more ideologically persuasive than they are scientifically justified. I predict that they are short-lived reversions that delay only temporarily an inevitable paradigm shift to a model of human behavior that accounts much more fully for the situational determinants of behavior.

Our social environment is vastly different from that of our psychological forefathers. Contemporary social life is bounded by massive social institutions. Our social existence is permeated by bureaucratic decision making. Nearly every aspect of our lives is touched by powerful organizations and agencies that have developed a logic and momentum of their own, one that often transcends the intentions and values of their individual members.

Psychologists, however, still have little to say about these places and their unique effects on human behavior. Too much of our psychology has changed little, in its shape and direction, from its nineteenth-century origins. But this older view of human nature is better suited to a society of ox-carts and sailing ships, a time when men were, much more simply and clearly, captains of their own destiny. The nineteenth century paradigm is slowly giving way to a more contemporary model of behavior that recognizes the impact of powerful social and institutional variables.

Continued commitment to an increasingly anachronistic view leads to a failure to account for much contemporary social behavior. Worse, in the

471

name of individualism and autonomy, we may have inadvertently contributed to the erosion and undermining of personal power and freedom. People have been given a framework with which to account for their own behavior and that of others that diverts attention from the impact of social and institutional variables, even as these variables have been increasing in strength and acquiring massive dimensions. When the nineteenth-century model of behavior is used as the basis for contemporary social and political policies, widespread unfairness and injustice result.

Nowhere is this clearer than in criminal-law and criminal-justice policy. Our legal system's noblest aspiration—equal protection of the laws—guarantees formal equality, *not* substantive equity. All individuals are to be treated *as though* they were equal, ignoring differences in opportunity and vast inequalities of circumstance. When situations and social context are ignored, differences in legally relevant behavior can be accounted for only in terms of individual shortcomings and defects. Thus individuals alone are held responsible for their inability or unwillingness to measure up. It is this fact that makes Anatole France's well-known aphorism—that the law in all its majesty draws no distinctions among men, but forbids rich and poor alike from begging in the streets and sleeping in the public parks—so compelling. Those whose circumstances render them least personally responsible are precisely the ones our legal system holds most liable. The prospect of a new psychology, however, heralds the possibility of a new concept of justice.

Some argue that the legal implications of a more situation-centered psychology are too impractical ever to implement. They argue that social and situational change is too cumbersome and politically infeasible. Yet those who urge continued allegiance to traditional solutions have no unencumbered claim to practicality. Our nation's individual-centered, prison-oriented crime policy is one of the least successful experiments in modern history. To paraphrase Kurt Lewin, "nothing is so impractical as a bad theory."

The traditional nineteenth-century paradigm is not equal to the task of explaining contemporary social behavior. Criminal-justice policies based on this dispositional view of behavior are not only unfair, they don't work. Effective social policy must be founded on theories that account for a significant portion of the variance in behavior or, if their explanatory power is modest, at least focus on variables over which we have some control. Individual trait-centered personality theories qualify on neither ground.

In this light, the challenges for crime and personality research in the next decade can be seen as fourfold. First, we must confront the malleability of personality in the face of enormously powerful social and institutional forces. Next, we must account more fully for individual deviant behavior like crime in terms of deviant and pathological situations. Third, we must help policymakers to change and control these chronically problematic situations by developing a psychology of structural change. Finally, we must work in legal contexts to fashion a more equitable social justice, one whose behavioral assumptions are more valid and whose ethical principles are more sensitive to concepts of collective and situational responsibility.

20 Future Reflections

Robert Hogan

It is extremely difficult to predict where research on personality and criminal conduct will go in the future. I can, however, speak with some confidence about what developments I would like to see take place. Four kinds of development seem important; unfortunately movement in these areas would have to be in the face of some major trends in contemporary psychology and criminology.

First, more effort needs to be put into developing an adequate conceptualization of the relationship between personality and criminal conduct. U.S. social science can be characterized as hostile to speculative inquiry at best and anti-intellectual at worst. Graduate training focuses on methodology, statistics, and issues in the current literature. Courses in the history of various topics, if offered at all, are confined to the undergraduate curriculum. Courses in philosophy of science are presented in other departments. Social theory is taken seriously by only a handful of persons who are regarded as mavericks or deviants from the professional mainstream.

A number of consequences result from this commitment to methodology and hostility to theory. To the degree that social science research in North America is conceptually based, it is based largely in theories of European origins—psychiatry and social work owe an incalculable debt to Freud, Rank, and Adler; sociology owes a comparable debt to Durkheim, Weber, and Simmel; psychology is in virtual bondage to Piaget, Pavlov, Lewin, Wundt, Broadbent, Luria, Vygotski, Asch, Kohler, Darwin, Spearman, and others. There are, to be sure, some distinctly American "theoretical" contributions, for example behaviorism and attribution theory. Closely examined, however, behaviorism becomes a methodology, a technique for communicating with subhumans, rather than a conceptual system in itself. Attribution theory, like all the other theories of the middle range that have sailed across the psychological horizon in the last forty years, will soon be replaced by another fad. Conversely, one of the great contributions, and a large part of the appeal, of Kohlberg's writings in moral development is that he has produced a full-bodied conceptual system that is rather uncharacteristic of American psychology.

A second consequence of our hostility toward conceptual inquiry is that inevitably, over time, the current conceptual basis for research will be falsified—we will, in a sense therefore, use up our intellectual capital because it is so limited. But we have an impoverished capacity to generate new capital.

475

This means, finally, that the social science enterprise is in danger of collapsing back on itself in an intellectual sense—that is, there will continue to be a great deal of data gathering and analysis, but because it will be uninformed by larger conceptual visions it will not lead to an advance in knowledge comparable to its costs.

So, to repeat, the first change I would like to see is a heightened appreciation for the virtue and necessity of conceptual analysis in the social sciences. This would be manifested in terms of professional recognition, publication outlets, and funding sources.

The second important change is somewhat related to the first. Although many sociologists would disagree, individual differences in personality and character structure *are* related to criminal conduct. Moreover, these differences can be assessed with some precision using existing psychometric devices such as the CPI. That is, criminal conduct can be *predicted* surprisingly well using current psychometric procedures. It is not enough to stop with the establishment of these empirical linkages, however. The next step is to provide a conceptual account of why the tests work as they do. A fallacy of traditional sociological models of criminality is that they confound prediction with explanation. To be able to predict certain phenomena reliably is a major goal in science, and a difficult one to attain. Nonetheless, it is important to move past prediction to explanation, so that knowledge is deepened and more powerful prediction becomes possible.

The third important development is also the most fruitful avenue for further analyzing the links between personality and criminal conduct. This is what I call item-response theory (Mills and Hogan 1978; Johnson 1981). Here the goal is to provide an adequate account of why people endorse the items they do and, more particularly, why they are willing to endorse items that are obviously socially undesirable. If we know what the dynamics of this process are for ordinary or normal people, then we will begin to understand why criminals endorse socially undesirable items—what their strategies and goals are when they use such odd self-presentational tactics.

Thus it is not enough to know *that* certain CPI items reliably discriminate criminals from noncriminals. We now need to know *why* the items discriminate.

Finally, I would like to see further development evaluating treatment programs for felons. What evidence there is on this topic suggests that rehabilitation does not work. At the same time, however, some of the best informed criminal-justice researchers think the proper test has yet to be performed. The detailed analysis of this problem has fundamental implications for understanding the relationship between personality and criminal conduct. At the same time it is a matter of great practical importance. It seems inconceivable that funding agencies have not budgeted funds for research on this specific topic.

Of these three future directions, the development of a climate of ideas and a congeniality toward conceptual analysis seems to me to be the most generic issue. With more adequate ways of conceptualizing the dynamics of criminality, a lot of empirical doors that are currently both closed and undiscovered will become at least accessible.

References

Mills, C., and Hogan, R. A role-theoretical interpretation of personality scale item responses. *Journal of Personality*, 1978, *46*, 778-785.

Johnson, J.A. The self-disclosures and self-presentation views of item response dynamics and personality scale validity. *Journal of Personality and Social Psychology*, 1981, *40*, 761-769.

Author Index

Abramson, L.Y., 18
Adelson, J., 375, 379, 381, 444
Ageton, S.S., 456-457
Aichhorn, A., 122, 128
Akers, R.L., 318, 387, 391, 392, 441, 446, 452, 456-457, 458
Alexander, F., 121
Allchin, W.H., 126
Allen, D.E., 147
Alloy, C.B., 18
Alwin, D.F., 205
Anderson, C.M., 88
Andre, Carl R., 35
Andreason, N.J.C., 86, 98
Andry, R.G., 134
Anthony, H.S., 127
Armsby, R.E., 445
Athay, M., 8
Austrin, H.R., 147
Axelrod, S., 128
Azcarate, E., 75-76

Bachtold, L.M., 89
Baehr, M.E., 89
Baer, D., 221, 232
Baker, J.W., 147
Ball, R.A., 446
Baltes, P.B., 170, 172
Bandura, A., 6, 15, 134
Banks, C., 116
Barash, D.P., 232
Barnett, R.E., 423-424
Barron, F., 82, 84, 86, 87, 89, 90, 98
Barron, R., 90
Bartol, C.R., 217, 227, 387
Barry, J.V., 73
Bar-Yam, M., 325, 327
Basham, R., 223
Beall, L., 375
Becker, H.S., 120, 166
Beeman, E.A., 226
Beker, J., 145
Bender, L., 126
Bennett, I., 129

Bentler, P.M., 165, 166, 167, 168, 169, 172, 173, 175, 176, 180, 197-198, 206, 212
Beres, D., 135
Berg, I., 76-77
Bergman, A., 130
Berkowitz, M.W., 325, 326
Bernstein, I.S., 221, 226, 233
Bilmes, M., 127
Biondi, A.M., 82, 84-85
Biron, L., 358
Blackburn, R., 358, 365
Blalock, H.M., 166
Blasi, A., 291
Blatt, M., 325
Block, J., 11, 18, 94, 96, 299, 395, 444, 459, 460
Block, J.H., 94, 96
Bloom, A.H., 396
Blos, P., 124, 127-128
Boever, D.M., 147
Bohman, M., 90, 98
Bohn, M.J., xiii
Bohrnstedt, G., 449
Bonett, D.G., 167
Bonnard, A., 127
Booth, A., 230
Bowers, W.J., 459
Bowlby, J., 129
Braithwaite, J., 403
Braver, S.L., 235
Briar, S., 108, 444
Briggs, P.F., 124
Brigham, J., 134
Brill, R., 430
Brodsky, S.L., xiii
Brody, S., 128
Bromberg, W., 127
Bronner, A.F., 121
Broom, L., 226-227
Broughton, J., 326
Brown, B.S., xiv
Brown, R., 11
Burgess, R.L., 441, 457

479

Subject Index

List of Contributors

Joseph Adelson
Psychological Clinic
University of Michigan
Ann Arbor, Michigan

Peter M. Bentler
Department of Psychology
University of California
    Los Angeles
Los Angeles, California

Arthur Dantchik
Department of Psychology
Arizona State University
Tempe, Arizona

H.J. Eysenck
Institute of Psychiatry
    and Psychology
University of London
London, United Kingdom

Judith E. Gallatin
Helppie and Gallatin
Portland, Oregon

Craig W. Haney
Department of Psychology
Stevenson College
University of California
    Santa Cruz
Santa Cruz, California

Philip W. Harris
Department of Criminal Justice
Temple University
Philadelphia, Pennsylvania

Kathleen M. Heide
Department of Criminal Justice
University of South Florida
Tampa, Florida

Robert Hogan
Department of Psychology
University of Tulsa
Tulsa, Oklahoma

George J. Huba
Department of Psychology
University of California
    Los Angeles
Los Angeles, California

William S. Jennings
Center for Moral Development
    and Education
Harvard University
Cambridge, Massachusetts

John A. Johnson
Pennsylvania State University
Dubois Campus
Dubois, Pennsylvania

Warren H. Jones
Department of Psychology
University of Tulsa
Tulsa, Oklahoma

Douglas T. Kenrick
Department of Psychology
Arizona State University
Tempe, Arizona

Robert Kilkenny
Center for Moral Development
and Education
Harvard University
Cambridge, Massachusetts

Lawrence Kohlberg
Center for Moral Development
and Education
Harvard University
Cambridge, Massachusetts

Marvin D. Krohn
Department of Sociology
University of Iowa
Iowa City, Iowa

Lonn Lanza-Kaduce
Department of Sociology
University of Florida
Gainesville, Florida

Steven MacFarlane
Department of Psychology
Arizona State University
Tempe, Arizona

Robert J. Marshall
Northern Westchester Center
for Psychotherapy
Yorktown Heights, New York

Joan McCord
Department of Sociology

Drexel University
Philadelphia, Pennsylvania

Merry Morash
School of Criminal Justice
Michigan State University
East Lansing, Michigan

Marcia J. Radosevich
Department of Sociology
Yale University
New Haven, Connecticut

Stanton E. Samenow
Center for Responsible Living
Alexandria, Virginia

Patricia Van Voorhis
Department of Criminology
Indiana State University
Terre Haute, Indiana

Marguerite Q. Warren
School of Criminal Justice
State University of New York
at Albany
Albany, New York

Marvin E. Wolfgang
Department of Criminology
Wharton School
University of Pennsylvania
Philadelphia, Pennsylvania

About the Editors

William S. Laufer received the J.D. from Northeastern University School of Law and the B.A. in social and behavioral sciences from The Johns Hopkins University. His research on criminal and asocial behavior has been published in the *Journal of Research in Crime and Delinquency, Journal of Personality and Social Psychology, Journal of Clinical Psychology, Journal of Vocational Behavior,* and *Psychological Reports.* Currently he is engaged in a comprehensive study of the role of personality and moral psychology in judicial decision making.

James M. Day received the Ed.M in counseling and consulting psychology from Harvard University and the A.B. in religious studies at Oberlin College. He completed additional graduate study at Yale University and Union Theological Seminary (New York), and is currently in the professional psychology program at the University of Pennsylvania. He is coediting a collection of essays with William Laufer on crime, values, and religion.